W9-CQL-296

Fodor's

TOKYO

4th Edition

Fodor's Travel Publications   New York, Toronto, London, Sydney, Auckland
www.fodors.com

Eugene Fodor:
The Spy Who Loved Travel

As Fodor's celebrates our 75th anniversary, we are honoring the colorful and adventurous life of Eugene Fodor, who revolutionized guidebook publishing in 1936 with his first book, *On the Continent, The Entertaining Travel Annual.*

Eugene Fodor's life seemed to leap off the pages of a great spy novel. Born in Hungary, he spoke six languages and graduated from the Sorbonne and the London School of Economics. During World War II he joined the Office of Strategic Services, the budding spy agency for the United States. He commanded the team that went behind enemy lines to liberate Prague, and recommended to Generals Eisenhower, Bradley, and Patton that Allied troops move to the capital city. After the war, Fodor worked as a spy in Austria, posing as a U.S. diplomat.

In 1949 Eugene Fodor—with the help of the CIA—established Fodor's Modern Guides. He was passionate about travel and wanted to bring his insider's knowledge of Europe to a new generation of sophisticated Americans who wanted to explore and seek out experiences beyond their borders. Among his innovations were annual updates, consulting local experts, and including cultural and historical perspectives and an emphasis on people—not just sites. As Fodor described it, "The main interest and enjoyment of foreign travel lies not only in 'the sites,' . . . but in contact with people whose customs, habits, and general outlook are different from your own."

Eugene Fodor died in 1991, but his legacy, Fodor's Travel, continues. It is now one of the world's largest and most trusted brands in travel information, covering more than 600 destinations worldwide in guidebooks, on Fodors.com, and in ebooks and iPhone apps. Technology and the accessibility of travel may be changing, but Eugene Fodor's unique storytelling skills and reporting style are behind every word of today's Fodor's guides.

Our editors and writers continue to embrace Eugene Fodor's vision of building personal relationships through travel. We invite you to join the Fodor's community at fodors.com/community and share your experiences with like-minded travelers. Tell us when we're right. Tell us when we're wrong. And share fantastic travel secrets that aren't yet in Fodor's. Together, we will continue to deepen our understanding of our world.

Happy 75th Anniversary, Fodor's! Here's to many more.

Tim Jarrell, Publisher

FODOR'S TOKYO

Editor: Stephanie E. Butler

Writers: Brett Bull, Nicholas Coldicott, Paige Ferrari, Misha Janette, Peter MacMillan, Kevin Mcgue, Robert Morel

Production Editor: Jennifer DePrima
Maps & Illustrations: David Lindroth and Mark Stroud, *cartographers;* Bob Blake, Rebecca Baer, *map editors;* William Wu, *information graphics*
Design: Fabrizio La Rocca, *creative director;* Guido Caroti, Siobhan O'Hare, *art directors;* Tina Malaney, Nora Rosansky, Chie Ushio, Jessica Walsh, Ann McBride, *designers;* Melanie Marin, *senior picture editor*
Cover Photo: (Outside Tower Records in Shibuya, Tokyo) David Clapp/Ticket/photolibrary.com
Production Manager: Steve Slawsky

COPYRIGHT

4th Edition

ISBN 978-0-307-48050-7

ISSN 1554-5881

SPECIAL SALES

This book is available at special discounts for bulk purchases for sales promotions or premiums. Special editions, including personalized covers, excerpts of existing books, and corporate imprints, can be created in large quantities for special needs. For more information, write to Special Markets/Premium Sales, 1745 Broadway, MD 6-2, New York, NY 10019, or e-mail specialmarkets@randomhouse.com.

AN IMPORTANT TIP & AN INVITATION

Although all prices, opening times, and other details in this book are based on information supplied to us at press time, changes occur all the time in the travel world, and Fodor's cannot accept responsibility for facts that become outdated or for inadvertent errors or omissions. So **always confirm information when it matters,** especially if you're making a detour to visit a specific place. Your experiences—positive and negative—matter to us. If we have missed or misstated something, **please write to us.** Share your opinion instantly through our online feedback center at fodors.com/contact-us.

PRINTED IN CHINA

10 9 8 7 6 5 4 3 2 1

CONTENTS

Fodor's Features

MAPS

ABOUT
THIS BOOK

Our Ratings

As travelers we've all discovered a place so wonderful that its worthiness is obvious. And sometimes that place is so unique that superlatives don't do it justice: you just have to be there to know. These sights, properties, and experiences get our highest rating, **Fodor's Choice**, indicated by orange stars throughout this book. Black stars highlight sights and properties we deem **Highly Recommended.** By default, there's another category: any place we include in this book is by definition worth your time, unless we say otherwise. And we will. Disagree with any of our choices? Care to nominate a place or suggest that we rate one more highly? Visit our feedback center at www.fodors.com/feedback.

Hotels

Hotels have private bath, phone, TV, and air-conditioning, and do not offer meals unless we specify that in the review. We always list facilities but not whether you'll be charged an extra fee to use them.

For expanded hotel reviews, visit **Fodors.com**

Restaurants

Unless we state otherwise, restaurants are open for lunch and dinner daily. We mention dress only when there's a specific requirement and reservations only when they're essential or not accepted—it's always best to book ahead.

Credit Cards

We assume that restaurants and hotels accept credit cards. If not, we'll note it in the review.

Budget Well

Hotel and restaurant price categories from ¢ to $$$$ are defined in the opening pages of the respective chapters. For attractions, we always give standard adult admission fees; reductions are usually available for children, students, and senior citizens.

Listings
★ Fodor's Choice
★ Highly recommended
⊠ Physical address
✛ Directions or Map coordinates
🕮 Mailing address
🖀 Telephone
🖷 Fax
⊕ On the Web
✎ E-mail
🖃 Admission fee
🕓 Open/closed times
Ⓜ Metro stations
🖿 No credit cards

Hotels & Restaurants
🏨 Hotel
🛏 Number of rooms
🛆 Facilities
🍽 Meal plans
✕ Restaurant
🖎 Reservations
🏛 Dress code
☇ Smoking

Outdoors
🏌 Golf
⛺ Camping

Other
🖔 Family-friendly
⇨ See also
⊠ Branch address
☞ Take note

Experience
Tokyo

WHAT'S WHERE

1 **Imperial Palace District.** This is the center of Tokyo, where Edo Castle once stood. Although the imperial residence is only open two days a year, you can explore the palace grounds and gardens at your leisure.

2 **Akihabara.** Akihabara is northeast of the Imperial Palace. Akihabara's famed for its electronics stores, manga shops, and cafés.

3 **Ueno.** Ueno Park, directly north of Akihabara, is home to three superb national museums, a university of fine arts, and a zoo. A stone's-throw south is Ameyoko market.

4 **Asakusa.** The sacred merges with the secular and ancient tradition with modernity in Asakusa. The area is home to Tokyo's oldest temple, Senso-ji, as well as the Asakusa Jinja shrine.

5 **Tsukiji and Shiodome.** Tsukiji is home to the famed sumo stables and what is purportedly the world's largest fish market—the Central Wholesale Market. Shiodome is a massive development zone, with plenty of fashionable shops and restaurants.

6 **Nihombashi, Ginza, and Marunouchi.** Nihombashi, east of the Imperial Palace, lays claim to the geographical and financial center of Tokyo.

Follow the money slightly south to Ginza, where you'll find Tokyo's traditional high-end stores and art galleries. Marunouchi is home to retail and office complexes.

7 **Aoyama, Harajuku, and Shibuya.** Aoyama and Harajuku, west of the Imperial Palace, are chic neighborhoods saturated with designer and chain stores, independent boutiques, and malls. To the south is Shibuya, which is an urban teen's dream packed with people, hip shops, megachain stores, and eateries.

8 **Roppongi.** Southeast of Shibuya is Roppongi, with a rich and sometimes sordid history of catering to foreign nightlife; here you'll find the massive Roppongi Hills development.

9 **Shinjuku.** Northeast of Roppongi, Shinjuku is home to the city's government and what is said to be the busiest train station in the world. The station is adjacent to the towering Takashimaya Times Square mall. When the sun sets, the bars and clubs in the red-light area of Kabuki-cho come to life.

10 **Odaiba.** Odaiba, an artificial island in Tokyo Bay, is an isolated hub for shops, restaurants, clubs, parks, and office complexes.

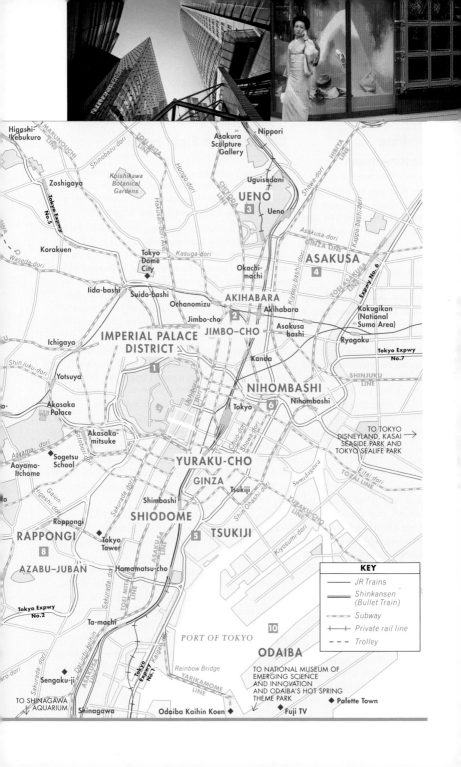

HOTEL AND RESTAURANT PRIMER

Making Reservations

The best way to book major chain hotels is through the company's Web site. The Web sites for smaller business hotels and ryokan usually lack English content online. Travel sites, such as **Rakuten** (⊕ *travel. rakuten.co.jp/en*), can assist booking these hotels. **Welcome Inns** (⊕ *www.itcj.jp*), a Japan National Tourist Organization affiliate, lists low-priced hotels in Tokyo and across the country. We highly recommend making your Tokyo hotel reservation before you arrive. Should this be impossible, head to a tourist office at the airport or major rail station for assistance.

Lodging Costs

Rates for the top foreign and domestic chains are generally in the ¥30,000–¥60,000 range (and could even go a bit higher). Business hotel rooms, with far fewer amenities, are available for under ¥20,000. A minshuku provides Japanese-style lodging and meals for roughly ¥8,000. The ryokan offers stays for between ¥10,000 and ¥30,000 that includes use of the onsen. Shoestring travelers head to hostels where night's stay costs around ¥3,000. Capsule hotels are similarly priced.

Choosing the Right Hotel

Tokyo-area accommodations range from Japanese-style inns to large Western-style hotels, in all price categories. It's essential to book in advance if you're traveling during peak travel seasons and is recommended at other times.

The *ryokan*, a traditional Japanese inn, provides the most unique experience. Japanese-style interiors include tatami flooring, paper (shoji) blinds, a low table for tea service, and pillows. Futons that are rolled out in the evening serve as beds. Stays usually include traditional Japanese morning and evening meals, often with small seafood dishes and regional specialties. Lodges usually offer the use of an *onsen* (hot-spring bath), which is typically for bathing, rather than an in-room shower.

Similar to the ryokan, but less expensive, *minshuku* are Japanese-style bed-and-breakfasts. Usually family-run, these inns feature Japanese-style rooms and meals. Baths (there are usually no in-room bathing options) are part of the shared public areas, which also include toilets.

Business hotels feature Western-style digs in basic, small rooms; these are ideal for one night and are usually close to major transportation hubs. Tokyo features high-end Western-style hotels with ritzy spas, fully equipped gyms, and some of Japan's better restaurants. Many are situated at the top of skyscrapers and provide fantastic views of the city's skyline.

The boutique hotel arrived late to Japan, but these quirky, trendy properties have taken hold. Earth tones, funky bathrooms, and curvy, chrome fixtures dominate at these hotels, which are priced just below business hotels.

Capsule hotels—generally men-only—are the most spartan accommodations around, providing a chamber that you slide your body into laterally, much like a coffin. There are no frills here, but the price is right. Common areas with televisions and lockers for valuables and luggage come standard.

Resorts in hot-spring areas, such as Hakone, near Tokyo, focus their services and amenities on the relaxation provided by onsen—either while naked or in a swimsuit.

Types of Restaurants

The Japanese love to dine out and there is something for every taste and budget. In the more popular tourist areas English menus are often available. There is nearly always someone who can speak a little English. If all else fails there are always the plastic models in the window outside to point at.

Many restaurants specialize in just one kind of food. Ramen, soba (buckwheat noodles), and *udon* (thick, white-wheat noodles) restaurants are hard to beat for value and reliability. Choose between table and counter seats. To order, just choose the toppings for the broth.

Okonomiyaki-ya are no-frills eateries serving thick savory pancakes. Expect tables to be fitted with a hot plate as most often diners do the cooking themselves using their choice of ingredients to fill the okonomiyaki.

In the evening *akachochin*—red lantern restaurants, so called because these hang outside their doors—establishments are a safe, inexpensive bet. Customers sit at a counter space in an informal, convivial environment. *Robata* specialize in grilled foods and to order customers simply point at what they want grilled. *Oden-ya,* which serve a variety of slowly simmered meats and vegetables, have a similar atmosphere. Again, to order just point to your desired morsels. *Izakaya,* publike dens, have counter and table service and have more extensive menus.

Sushi restaurants, usually reserved for special occasions, are a breed apart. Expect a subdued atmosphere with wooden surfaces. Sit at the counter to get to see the *itamae* (sushi chef) in action. Point at the fish in the glass case to order or ask for *omakase*—or chef's choice.

At tempura restaurants customers sit at the counter and enjoy the attention of their personal chef. Choose the course you desire (usually by how much you want to spend), which the chef will serve to you piece by piece.

Ryotei specialize in *kaiseki*. Expect to be greeted by kimono-clad waitresses who usher you to your private room. Leave your shoes and worries behind in the hallway, and enjoy this unforgettable experience. Those on a budget should visit at lunchtime, when many ryotei offer *kaiseki bento* at a fraction of the dinner price.

The regular bento, or Japanese box lunch of rice, fish or meat, and vegetable sides, is available everywhere from department stores to convenience stores. Sandwiches, sushi, and *onigiri* (rice balls with various fillings) are other popular to-go items.

Meals and Mealtimes

Office workers eat lunch from noon to 1, so eat later to avoid crowds. Most restaurants have lunchtime specials, which provide an opportunity for fine dining at a considerably lower price, until 2:30. Many restaurants close their doors between 3 and 5. Unless otherwise noted, the restaurants listed in this guide are open daily for lunch and dinner. For dinner at upmarket establishment ask hotel staff to make reservations—this gives the management time to locate an English menu or staff with some language skills.

Paying

These days, credit cards are widely accepted in restaurants, but this isn't a given in more informal eateries. Check that your card will be accepted before sitting down.

Menus

Many less expensive restaurants have plastic replicas of the dishes they serve, displayed in their front windows, so you can always point to what you want to eat if the language barrier is insurmountable.

TRANSPORTATION PRIMER

JR Pass

Japan Railways offers the Japan Rail Pass, an affordable way to see the country. It can be used on all JR railways, buses, and ferryboats including the Shinkansen "bullet" trains—except for Nozomi trains on the Tokaido and Sanyo lines. Hikari or Kodama trains, however, serve these same routes and are included. Passes must be purchased at an authorized JR outlet outside of Japan before your trip and are available for 7-, 14-, or 21-day periods. Activate them upon arrival at a major rail station or Narita airport. A first-class version allows access to the Shinkansen Lines' special Green Cars.

Prepaid Cards

JR East offers **Suica,** a rechargeable debit card in Tokyo. **PASMO,** another rechargeable prepaid card in Tokyo, can be used on subways and JR and non-JR trains. The one-day **Holiday Pass** works in the entire Tokyo–JR network on holidays, weekends, and the summer holiday period (July 20–August 31). Tokyo's other one-day passes include the **Tokunai Pass** for JR lines and the **Tokyo Free Kippu,** which also covers subways and buses.

Getting Around by Train

Tokyo's train and subway system is on time, has clean facilities, and provides a safe environment. But it's also quite complicated.

Shinkansen: The JR Shinkansen bullet trains travel up and down Honshu and into Kyushu. Tokyo Station is Tokyo's main hub, with lines heading north, south, and west.

Regional trains: In Tokyo, Japan Railways Yamanote Line loops around the city, while its Sobu and Chuo lines split that circle into east and west directions. Tokyu's Toyoko Line travels between Shibuya Station and Yokohama to the south. For Tokyo Disneyland take the JR Keiyo Line east. The main line of the Odakyu company and Keio Inokashira Line use Shinjuku and Shibuya, respectively, as hubs to serve Tokyo to the west.

Subways: The easiest way to explore Tokyo is via subway. There are two subway companies: Tokyo Metro and Toei. Each system has separate fares, and it's cheaper to stay with one company. The Ginza Line moves between Asakusa and Shibuya, which is also served by the north–south-running Fukutoshin Line and the east–west-bound Hanzomon Line. Like the JR Yamanote Line, the Oedo and Marunouchi lines loop around the city center. The Namboku Line begins in residential Meguro and heads through Korakuen, the station for Tokyo Dome. At the outer edges of the subway networks, private companies operate the line; be prepared to pay an additional fare.

Tokyo Monorail: Beginning at Hamamatsu-cho Station, the monorail provides the simplest access to Haneda Airport.

PURCHASING TICKETS

In Tokyo basic train and subway fares are between ¥110 and ¥310. Purchase tickets from machines that take coins or cash near the gates. Maps above each machine—usually in Japanese and English—give destinations.
■**TIP**➔ **Sometimes the station map will be only written in Japanese. In that case, buy the lowest-priced ticket and adjust the fare upon arrival.** For purchasing Shinkansen and other long-distance train tickets that require a seat reservation, go to ticket windows or counters where staff will assist you.

HOW TO USE A TICKET MACHINE

Use the map above the ticket machine to determine how much money to put on your ticket. The numbers next to each stop indicate the price from your current station.

Follow direction in English on touch screen. Find the English option at the top of the screen.

Place coins in this slot.

Your ticket will pop out here.

Slide bills into the machine here.

⚠ You'll need your ticket to enter the train's boarding area as well as to exit the station.

TOKYO
TOP ATTRACTIONS

Imperial Palace East Gardens

Open to the public, the gardens are all that remain of the former innermost circle of defense for Edo Castle, the residence of the Tokugawa shogun between 1603 and 1867. The gardens can be entered by three gates: Hirakawa-mon, Ote-mon, and Kita-hane-bashi-mon. In addition to the sculpted, rolling greenery, remaining structures include stone walls, moats, and guardhouses.

Toshogu Shrine

This beautiful complex set within a forest in Nikko, 130 km (81 mi) north of Tokyo, is the mausoleum of Ieyasu Tokugawa, who began the Tokugawa Shogunate that reigned over the nation between 1603 and 1868. Decorated with gold leaf and numerous wood carvings, the compound also includes multiple Shinto and Buddhist buildings, many of which are acknowledged by the government as Important Cultural Properties.

Kappabashi

"Kitchen town," as it's often referred to, is a collection of 170 small shops on Kappabashi Dogugai street near Asakusa. Here you can find just about everything needed to open a restaurant or bar. Cutlery, uniforms, pans, wall furnishings, cash registers, cleaning supplies, and even the plastic food models seen in front of shops are all on offer and in large quantities.

Asakusa Shrine

Constructed in 1649, the Asakusa Shrine—also referred to as Sanja Sama (Shrine of the Three Guardians)—is one of Japan's most famous places of worship. The structure survived the U.S. bombing raids of 1945. Its annual festival, which attracts hundreds of thousands and features the carting of numerous portable shrines around the compound and nearby streets, takes place each May.

Tsukiji Fish Market

If it lives in the sea, chances are that it can be found at Tsukiji, affectionately referred to as "Tokyo's kitchen." Thousands of wholesalers and buyers broker deals for crabs piled in buckets, squirming eels, bagged clams, and endless varieties of fish at this chaotic market. The biggest draw is the tuna auction, which gets underway in the wee hours of the morning and features rapid-fire bidding on hundreds of frozen carcasses weighing up to 200 kilograms (441 lbs).

Takeshita-dori in Harajuku

Popularized on a global scale by Gwen Stefani's song "Harajuku Girls," this pedestrians-only street outside JR Harajuku Station features various shops selling some of Japan's trendiest and most garish clothing to swarms of Tokyo youth. Since the target is teenagers, prices are low, at least in comparison to the upscale boutiques found in nearby Aoyama.

Harajuku is only about 500 yards long, but the shopping hordes are so dense and relentless on weekends that it can take 20 minutes to navigate from one end to the other.

Mt. Fuji

At an elevation of 12,388 feet, Mt. Fuji is the nation's highest peak. It's also one of Japan's most famous symbols and is a point of inspiration for artists and commoners alike. The dormant volcano sits between Yamanashi and Shizuoka prefectures. In nice weather, it can be viewed from Tokyo and Yokohama. For a closer peek, climb it in summer or see it from a Shinkansen bullet train traveling between Tokyo and Osaka.

TOP EXPERIENCES

Ryokan

The *ryokan,* or traditional Japanese inn, offers rooms outfitted with Japanese-style interiors, such as tatami flooring and paper (shoji) blinds. Pillows and small tables make sitting for the in-room tea service comfortable. At bedtime, futons are rolled out onto the tatami. The room rate usually includes breakfast and dinner. Hakone, near Tokyo, has a wonderful selection of these inns.

Japanese Gardens

Gardens in the traditional Japanese style appear in parks, on castle grounds, and in front of shrines and temples. Featuring stone lanterns, rocks, ponds, a pavilion, and rolling hedges, many of the principles that influence Japanese garden design come from religion. Shintoism, Taoism, and Buddhism all stress the contemplation and re-creation of nature as part of the process of achieving understanding and enlightenment. Hamarikyu Gardens in Tokyo is one of Japan's more prominent gardens.

Karaoke

Karaoke is a Japanese institution whose rabid popularity cannot be understated. Millions of locals enjoy this after-work recreation, in which they sing popular songs into a microphone as the instrumental track plays on the in-room sound system and its lyrics roll across a monitor. Rooms, referred to as karaoke boxes, can be rented by the hour and seat between 2 and 10 customers. Choose a song from the song selection book and fortify yourself for your performance with drinks and light snacks.

Seafood and Sushi

As might be expected of a nation consisting of 3,000 islands, Japan is synonymous with the fruits of the sea. Sashimi and sushi have gained popularity with restaurant goers around the world, but it's hard to imagine some other so-called delicacies catching on. The northern island of Hokkaido boasts of the quality of its *uni* (sea urchin), while Akita Prefecture is famous for *shiokara* (raw squid intestines), but if you are in Tokyo you can see just about anything living in the sea at the fish market at Tsukiji.

Tea Ceremony

The tea ceremony, or *chanoyu* (the way of tea), is a precisely choreographed program that started more than 1,000 years ago with Zen monks. The ritual begins as the server prepares a cup of tea for the first guest. This process involves a strictly determined series of movements and actions, including the cleansing of each utensil to be used. One by one, the participants slurp up their bowl of tea and then eat a sweet confectionary served with it. In Tokyo, the teahouse at Hamarikyu Gardens offers a wonderful chance to enjoy this tradition.

Kampai!

Whether you're out with friends, clients, or belting out a tune at the local karaoke bar, you're sure to have a drink at least once during your stay. Rice-based sake, pronounced *sa*-kay, is Japan's number one alcoholic beverage, with more than 2,000 different brands available. The sake bar Amanogawa, in the Keio Plaza Hotel Tokyo, provides a wonderful opportunity to sample different varieties. *Shochu* is made from grain and is served either on the rocks or mixed with juice or water. As to beer, Asahi and Kirin are the two heavyweights, constantly battling for the coveted title of Japan's leading brewer, but many beer fans rate Suntory's Malts brand and Sapporo's Yebisu brand as the tastiest brews in the land.

Maid Cafés

Though spawned in the geek town of Akihabara, the maid café can be found in many of Tokyo's major entertainment areas. These cafés allow customers to engage in a pseudo master-and-servant relationship with a young lady wearing a frilly black dress with curvy tails or a white apron with matching headpiece. Conversations often include overly polite addresses as "my lord" or "my lady" and menus are written in deliberately antiquated Japanese offering drinks, small food dishes, and even full-body massages. This is truly an experience like no other.

Basement Food Halls

Entire basement floors (*depachika*) of many Japanese department stores (*depato*) are often occupied by grocery sections featuring high-end food fare. Entire sections are dedicated to fish (including sushi), meats, cheese, and tea. At least one bakery will serve fresh baguettes. Exotic foods, like German sausages, are here as well. Specially prepared foods for those in a hurry fill large cases, with housewives scooping up mixed salads, fried dumplings, and various meat dishes.

Sumo

Sumo pits two extremely large athletes against one another in a ring (*dohyo*). A wrestler who breaches the ring's boundary or touches the ground with a body part (other than the sole of his foot) loses. Originally intended as entertainment for Shinto gods, single bouts usually last less than a minute. Tournaments, running 15 days, are held three times a year in Tokyo. Novice wrestlers (*jonokuchi*) compete in the morning and top athletes (*yokozuna*) wrestle in the late afternoon. Crowds get pretty boisterous, especially for the later matches.

EARTHQUAKE UPDATE

On March 11, 2011, a 9.0-magnitude earthquake struck an area approximately 45 mi (72 km) east of Sendai. The earthquake and resulting tsunami caused massive destruction and death along the coast of northern Honshu but had a relatively modest impact on Tokyo.

Clean-up from the disaster is ongoing at this writing. Most road and rail repair work is already underway, and much of that was expected to be completed by fall 2011. Repairs to some buildings are ongoing as well. But damage to the Fukushima Daichi nuclear power plant, which has been stabilized but not shut down, is still ongoing and may continue for some months.

IF YOU LIKE

Nightlife

Wining and dining, cocktails with class, the sultry sounds of jazz, other live performances, or clubbing and carousing—you'll find it all, and more, beneath Tokyo's neon-soaked night sky where the city's popular nightspots are open till the early-morning hours. Tipping isn't customary, but some upscale establishments may have extra service charges that range from a few hundred yen to a few thousand. Karaoke clubs and *izakaya*—traditional watering holes—are ubiquitous and provide a great way to mix with locals. All-night revelers might want to consider the likes of Shinjuku or Roppongi, but tamer entertainment is available in Ebisu or Yuraku-cho.

Mille Café Bakery and Wine Bar, Harajuku. This relaxed bar in the Harajuku high-fashion district offers a rotating selection of wines dictated by the season.

Red Shoes, Aoyama. Featuring live shows and DJ sets, it is Tokyo's premier rock bar. Don't forget your leather jacket.

Sweet Basil 139, Roppongi. Come for dinner or just a drink at this upscale club featuring a variety of musical performances, considered by many to be Tokyo's best.

Natural Wonders

Tokyo is an urban paradise for traveler and resident alike. That doesn't mean, however, that local Japanese sensibilities—steeped in centuries of cultural appreciation for nature—have been paved over. Much like inner-city cherry blossom viewing, tiny veranda gardens, and well-groomed parks, nature's more awesome wonders are well preserved, too—albeit just outside the concrete jungle. If you pine for more pristine surroundings follow the lead of the locals.

TIPS

The transit system in Tokyo is amazingly complex. Get a map that clearly defines the subways and rail lines.

The rainy season of June makes sightseeing very unpleasant. If there is a choice, it's best to avoid this time of year.

To reach Tokyo from Narita Airport requires more than an hour by train or bus. A taxi, however, is not any faster and much more expensive, around ¥25,000.

No matter what you do, Tokyo will require plenty of walking. Wearing comfortable shoes during all seasons is advisable.

Every year roughly 300,000 Tokyoites and visitors scale nearby Mt. Fuji during peak climbing season (July and August). It's an opportunity a local saying deems "foolish" to pass up (or to do more than once). Thousands take to Nikko National Park to see Kegon Falls and other natural wonders, especially when foliage begins to bloom in spring.

Mt. Fuji, in Fuji-Hakone-Izu National Park. Well within reach of the big city, beautiful, snowcapped Mt. Fuji is bound to make an impression, whether you climb to the summit or view it from afar.

Kegon Falls, Nikko National Park. You can view Japan's most famous waterfall from either the top or the bottom of the 318-foot drop and make a day of enjoying this shrine-peppered scenic park. And it's all just two hours from Tokyo.

Onsen

Japan is perched on a geothermal gold mine and *onsen* (hot springs) are everywhere. Locals consider bathing in these hot springs to be a near-ritual experience,

with unique healing properties attributed to the water. These baths are more about self-pampering than getting clean, but give yourself a thorough shower before your soak. Proper etiquette demands it.

There are indoor and outdoor pools of different sizes, with varying temperatures to choose from, but the ones outside are best if you want to admire the natural setting. Some places may also offer a sauna or professional massage. Afterward, retire to the casual dining room for a light meal or some sake, and lounge at a low table on a tatami (straw mat) floor, where napping is permitted.

Oedo Onsen Monogatari, Odaiba. This onsen at Yurikamome Telecom Center pays homage to this tradition at an Edo-period–style facility with all the trimmings; it's the city's finest.

Hakone Kowakien Yunessun Resort, Kanagawa Prefecture. Just 90 minutes by train from Tokyo, Kanagawa is famed for its abundance of onsen resorts and inns, from the budget to the lavish. The resort offers an exquisite traditional onsen, water amusement park, and bathing-suit-only grounds. Visitors can even soak in green tea and sake.

Onsen of Kusatsu, Guma Prefecture. Those with spare time and an interest in hot springs should travel three hours from Tokyo and 3,937 feet above sea level to Kusatsu. Japanese have flocked here for centuries for all manner of cures, including one from the most dreaded disease—lovesickness.

Baseball

It's fair to say that baseball is as much a national pastime in Japan as it is in the U.S. The Japanese have adopted and adapted the sport in a way that makes it a fascinating and easy-to-grasp microcosm of both their culture and their relationship to the West. The team names alone—the Yakult Swallows and the Hiroshima Carp, for example—amuse Westerners accustomed to such monikers as the Yankees and Indians, and the fans' cheers are chanted more in unison than in United States. ballparks. The season runs from April through October. Same-day baseball game tickets are hard to come by; try the respective stadiums or various ticket agencies. You can buy tickets for most events at convenience stores, such as Lawson, 7-Eleven, and Family Mart. The two main ticket agencies are **Ticket PIA** (☏ *03/5237–9999*), with various locations nationwide, mainly in department stores, and **CN Playguide** (☏ *03/5802–9999*). Depending on the stadium, the date, and the seat location, expect to pay from ¥1,500 to ¥8,000.

Tokyo Dome. Cheers for the Yomiuri Giants go up at this 45,600-seat stadium. ✉ *1–3–61 Koraku, Bunkyo-ku* ☏ *03/5800–9999* ⊕ *www.tokyo-dome.co.jp/e* Ⓜ *Marunouchi and Namboku lines, Koraku-en Station (Exit 2); Toei Oedo and Toei Mita lines, Kasuga Station (Exit A2); JR Chuo Line, Suido-bashi Station (West Exit).*

Meiji Jingu Baseball Stadium. The home turf of the Yakult Swallows, the city's second team, is in the Outer Gardens of Meiji Jingu. ✉ *13 Kasumigaoka, Shinjuku-ku* ☏ *03/3404–8999* Ⓜ *Ginza Line, Gaien-mae Station (Exit 2); JR Chuo Line, Shinanomachi Station.*

GREAT ITINERARIES

TOKYO IN 3 DAYS

Tokyo is a metropolis that confounds with its complexity: 34 million people occupy a greater metropolitan area that includes soaring towers of glass and steel, rolling expressways, numerous temples, parks, and square mile and after square mile of concrete housing blocks. Since the end of World War II, the city has constantly reinvented itself with new building developments and cultural trends. Few things have remained static other than its preeminence as Japan's economic center.

Day 1: Tsukiji and Ginza

Start *very* early (around 5 am) with a visit to the **Tokyo Central Wholesale Market** (Tokyo Chuo Oroshiuri Ichiba) in the Tsukiji district to have the finest, freshest sushi for breakfast. Take a morning stroll through **Ginza** to explore its fabled shops and depato (department stores). Then hit a chic restaurant or café for lunch (more-reasonably priced ones are found on the upper floors of most department stores). The **Sony Building** and its showroom of electronics are worth a stop, as are the art galleries. The skyscrapers of **Shiodome** are just down the street, in the direction of **Shimbashi**. Take a peek on the first floor of the **Shiodome Media Tower;** aerial photographs show Ginza as it was roughly 100 years ago—a network of canals. In the evening, head back up towards Ginza and enjoy *yakitori* (grilled chicken) at one of the many small restaurants in **Yuraku-cho.**

Day 2: Asakusa and Ueno

Spend the morning at **Senso-ji** and adjacent **Asakusa Jinja** in Asakusa. If you're looking for souvenir gifts—sacred or secular—allow time and tote space for the abundant selection local vendors at the **Nakamise Shopping Arcade** have to offer. Consider taking a tour with one of the numerous *jinrikisha* (rickshaws) lined up here. **Kappabashi** is a nearby street dedicated to outfitting restaurants and bars with dishes, cups, chopsticks, and even plastic food models. From there go to **Ueno** for an afternoon of museums, vistas, and historic sites, and take a break at **Ueno Park.** Keep in mind that in the evening the crowds in Asakusa are not as intrusive as during the day, and many of the major attractions, including the five-tier pagoda of Senso-ji, are brightly lit. It's worth it to loop back to get a different view of the area.

Day 3: Shibuya and Shinjuku

Start off at **Hachiko Square** and the famous "Scramble Crossing" intersection and hit the nearby stores. Inside the station building is the once-lost masterpiece by avant-garde artist **Taro Okamoto,** "Myth of Tomorrow." In the afternoon see the Shinto shrine, **Meiji Jingu,** and walk through the nearby Harajuku and **Omotesando** fashion districts. Spend the rest of the afternoon on the west side of **Shinjuku,** Tokyo's 21st-century model city; and savor the view from the observation deck of architect Kenzo Tange's monumental **Tokyo Metropolitan Government Office;** cap off the day visiting **Shinjuku Gyo-en National Garden.** For those seeking a bit of excitement, the red-light district of **Kabuki-cho,** just to the east of **JR Shinjuku Station,** comes alive once the sun goes down.

TOKYO IN 5 DAYS

Add these two days onto the three-day itinerary.

Day 4: Akihabara and Imperial Palace

Spend the morning browsing in **Akihabara,** Tokyo's electronics quarter, and see the nearby Shinto shrine **Kanda Myojin.** Stop at

a maid café for a glimpse of one of Japan's many subcultures; come for the spectacle but don't stay for the food. Then use the afternoon for a tour of the **Imperial Palace** and environs. The **Chidorigafuchi National Cemetery** has a wonderful park and a boat-rental facility—both great for unwinding. If the **Yomiuri Giants** are in town, catch a game at **Tokyo Dome** in the evening.

Day 5: Various Sites

Fill in the missing pieces: see the Buddhist temple, **Sengaku-ji**, in Shinagawa; the remarkable **Edo-Tokyo Hakubutsukan** in **Ryogoku**; a tea ceremony; a Kabuki play; or a sumo tournament, if one is in town. Or visit the **Kokugikan**, National Sumo Arena, in the Ryogoku district, and some of the sumo stables in the neighborhood.

If You Have More Time

With a week or more, you can make Tokyo your home base for a series of side trips (⇨ *Chapter 7, Side Trips*). After getting your fill of Tokyo, take a train out to **Yokohama**, with its scenic port and Chinatown. A bit farther away but still easily accessible by train is **Kamakura**, the 13th-century military capital of Japan. The **Great Buddha** (Daibutsu) of the **Kotoku-in** is but one of the National Treasures of art and architecture here that draw millions of visitors a year. For both Yokohama and Kamakura, an early morning start will allow you to see most of the important sights in a full day and make it back to Tokyo by late evening. As Kamakura is one of the most popular of excursions from Tokyo, avoid the worst of the crowds by making the trip on a weekday, but time it to avoid rush-hour commuting that peaks roughly at 8 am and just after 6 pm.

Still farther off, but again an easy train trip, is **Nikko**, where the founder of the

WHEN TO GO

Spring and fall are the best times to visit. *Sakura* (cherry blossoms) begin blooming in Tokyo by early April. Fall has clear blue skies, though occasional typhoons occur. June brings an intense rainy season. July and August bring high temperatures and stifling humidity. Winter's gray and chilly, with Tokyo and other areas along the coast receiving very little snow. ■TIP➔ Seasons are the same in Japan as they are in North America.

Japanese vacation during three holiday periods: the few days before and after New Year's; Golden Week in early May; and the mid-August week for Obon. Travel's not advised during these times as plane and train tickets book up fast.

Tokugawa Shogun dynasty is enshrined. **Tosho-gu** is a monument unlike any other in Japan, and the picturesque **Lake Chuzen-ji** is in a forest above the shrine. Two full days, with an overnight stay, would allow you an ideal, leisurely exploration of both. Yet another option would be a trip to **Hakone** where you can soak in a traditional onsen or venture a climb to the summit of **Fuji-san** (Mt. Fuji).

JAPANESE ETIQUETTE

Many Japanese expect foreigners to behave differently and are tolerant of faux pas, but they are pleasantly surprised when people acknowledge and observe their customs. The easiest way to ingratiate yourself with the Japanese is to take time to learn and respect Japanese ways.

General Tips

■ Bow upon meeting someone.

■ Japanese will often point at their nose (not chest) when referring to themselves.

■ Pointing at someone is considered rude. To make reference to someone or something, wave your hand up and down in his or her direction.

■ Direct expression of opinions isn't encouraged. It's more common for people to gently suggest something.

■ Avoid physical contact. A slap on the back or hand on the shoulder would be uncomfortable for a Japanese person.

■ Avoid too much eye contact when speaking. Direct eye contact is a show of spite and rudeness.

At Someone's Home

■ Most entertaining is done in restaurants and bars. Don't be offended if you're not invited to someone's home.

■ Should an invitation be extended, a small gift—perhaps a bottle of alcohol or box of sweets—should be presented.

■ At the entryway, remove your shoes and put on the provided slippers. Remove your slippers if you enter a room with tatami flooring. Before entering the bathroom, remove your house slippers and switch to those found near the bathroom doorway.

■ Stick to neutral subjects in conversation. The weather doesn't have to be your only topic, but you should take care not to be too nosy.

■ It's not customary for Japanese businessmen to bring wives along. If you're traveling with your spouse, don't assume that an invitation includes both of you. If you want to bring your spouse, ask in a way that eliminates the need for a direct refusal.

In Business Meetings

■ For business meetings, *meishi* (business cards) are highly recommended. Remember to place those you have received in front of you; don't shove them in your pocket. It's also good to have one side of your business card printed in Japanese.

■ Japanese position their employees based upon rank within the company. Don't be surprised if the proceedings seem perfunctory—many major decisions were made behind the scenes before the meeting started.

■ Stick to last names and use the honorific -san after the name, as in Tanaka-san (Mr. or Mrs. Tanaka). Also, respect the hierarchy, and as much as possible address yourself to the most senior person in the room.

■ Many Japanese businessmen still don't know how to interact with Western businesswomen. Be patient, and, if the need arises, gently remind them that, professionally, you expect to be treated as any man would be.

At Lodgings and Ryokan

■ When you arrive at a minshuku or ryokan, put on the slippers that are provided and make your way to your room. Remember to remove your slippers before entering your room; never step on the tatami (straw mats) with shoes or slippers.

■ Before entering a thermal pool, make sure you wash and rinse off entirely before getting into the water. Do not get soap in the tub. Other guests will be using the same bathwater, so it is important to observe this custom. After your bath, change into the yukata provided in your room. Don't worry about walking around in it—other guests will be doing the same.
⇨ *For more tips on ryokan behavior, see the box in Chapter 7.*

At Restaurants

■ *Oshibori* is a small hot towel provided in Japanese restaurants. This is to wipe your hands but not your face. If you must use it on your face, wipe your face first, then your hands, and never toss it on the table: fold or roll it up.

■ When eating with chopsticks, don't use the part that has entered your mouth to pick up food from communal dishes. Instead, use the end that you've been holding in your hand. Always rest chopsticks on the edge of the tray, bowl, or plate; sticking them upright in your food is reminiscent of how rice is arranged at funerals.

■ There's no taboo against slurping your noodle soup, though women are generally less boisterous about it than men.

■ Pick up the soup bowl and drink directly from it, rather than leaning over the table to sip it. Eat the fish or vegetables with your chopsticks.

■ When drinking with a friend, never serve yourself. Always pour for the other person, who will in turn pour for you. If you would rather not drink, don't refuse a refill, just sip, keeping your glass at least half full.

■ It's considered gauche to eat as you walk along a public street.

While Shopping

■ After entering a store, the staff will greet you with *irasshaimase*, which is a welcoming phrase. A simple smile is an appropriate acknowledgment. After that, polite requests to view an item or try on a piece of clothing should be followed as anywhere in the West. Bargaining is common at flea markets, but not so in conventional stores.

■ There's usually a plastic tray at the register for you to place your money or credit card. Your change and receipt however, will be placed in your hand. It should be noted that many small shops do not accept credit cards.

Giving gifts

■ Gift giving is a year-round national pastime, peaking during summer's *ochugen* and the year-end *oseibo*. Common gifts between friends, family, and associates include elegantly wrapped packages of fruit, noodles, or beer.

■ On Valentine's Day women give men chocolate, but on White Day in March the roles are reversed.

■ For weddings and funerals, cash gifts are the norm. Convenience stores carry special envelopes in which the money (always crisp, new bills) should be inserted.

SHINTO AND BUDDHISM

Although both Buddhism and Shinto permeate Japanese society and life, most Japanese are blissfully unaware of the distinction between them. A wedding is often a Shinto ceremony while a funeral is a Buddhist rite.

There's a saying in Japan that you're Shinto at birth (marked with a Shinto ceremony), Christian when you marry (if you choose a Western-style wedding), and Buddhist when you die (honored with a Buddhist funeral). The Japanese take a utilitarian view of religion and use each as suits the occasion. One prays for success in life at a shrine and for the repose of a deceased family member at a temple. There is no thought given to the whys for this—these things simply are.

Buddhism

Buddhism in Japan grew out of a Korean king's symbolic gift of a statue of Shaka— the first Buddha, Prince Gautama—to the Yamato Court in AD 538. The Soga clan adopted the foreign faith and used it as a vehicle for changing the political order of the day. After battling for control of the country, they established themselves as political rulers. It was during this period that Japan sent its first ambassadors to China and began to import Chinese culture, writing, and religion into Japan. By the 8th century, Buddhism was well established.

Three waves of development in Japanese Buddhism followed the religion's Nara period (710–794). In the Heian period (794–1185), Esoteric Buddhism was introduced primarily by two priests who studied in China: Saicho and Kukai. Saicho established a temple on Mt. Hie near Kyoto, making it the most revered mountain in Japan after Mt. Fuji. Kukai established the Shingon sect of Esoteric Buddhism on Mt. Koya, south of Nara. It is said that Kukai is still in a state of meditation and will be until the arrival of the last bodhisattva (the Buddhist messianic saint, or *bosatsu* in Japanese). Esoteric Buddhism introduced the separation of the temple into an interior for the initiated and an outer laypersons' area.

Amidism (Pure Land) was the second wave, and it flourished until the introduction of Zen in 1185. Its adherents saw the world emerging from a period of darkness during which Buddhism had been in decline, and asserted that salvation was offered only to the believers in Amida, a Nyorai (Buddha) or enlightened being. Amidism's promise of salvation and its subsequent versions of heaven and hell earned it the appellation "Devil's Christianity" from visiting Christian missionaries in the 16th century.

In the Post-Heian period (1185 to the present) the influences of Nichiren and Zen Buddhist philosophies pushed Japanese Buddhism in new directions. Nichiren (1222–82) was a monk who insisted on the primacy of the Lotus Sutra, the supposed last and greatest sutra of Shaka. Zen Buddhism was attractive to the samurai class's ideals of discipline and worldly detachment and thus spread throughout Japan in the 12th century. It was later embraced as a nonintellectual path to enlightenment by those in search of a direct experience of the sublime.

Visiting a Buddhist Temple

The first thing to do when visiting a temple is to stop at the gate (called *mon* in Japanese), put your hands together, and bow. Once inside the gate, stop to wash your hands at the stone receptacle near the entrance. Fill one of the ladles with water using your right hand and wash

your left hand first. Then refill the ladle using your left hand and wash your right hand. Some people also pour water in their right hand to rinse their mouth, but this is not necessary. After washing your hands, you can ring the temple bell.

Next, light a candle in front of the main altar of the temple and place it inside the glass cabinet. Then put your hands together and bow. You can also light three sticks of incense (lighting them together is customary) and put them in the large stone or brass stand. Follow this with a prayer and a bow. Some people may light both a candle and three sticks of incense, others may just do one or the other. Some may skip this part entirely.

Proceed to the main altar, put your hands together, bow, and pray. While you can make your own prayer here, many people pray by reciting one of the Buddhist sutras. If you'd like to have a closer look at the interior of the altar building, climb the steps and look inside. You can also throw a coin inside the wooden box on the top step as an offering, again putting your hands together and bowing. Most temples have subaltars dedicated to different Buddhist saints or deities, and you can repeat the candle, incense, and prayer rituals observed at the main altar.

After seeing the altar and subaltars spend some time walking around the temple grounds. Most temples are incredibly beautiful places. Many have gardens and sculpture worthy of a visit.

Upon leaving the temple, you should stop at the gate, turn, put your hands together, and bow to give thanks.

Shinto

Shinto—literally, "the way of the *kami* (god)"—is a form of animism or nature worship based on myth and rooted to the geography and holy places of the land. It's an ancient belief system, dating back perhaps as far as 500 BC and is indigenous to Japan, though it's name is derived from a Chinese word, *shin tao*, coined in the 8th century AD, when the Yamato dynasty ruled much of Japan and divine origins were first ascribed to the royal family. Fog-enshrouded mountains, pairs of rocks, primeval forests, and geothermal activity are all manifestations of the *kami-sama* (honorable gods). For many Japanese, the Shinto aspect of their lives is not attached to a religious framework as it would be in the West. In that sense, the name describes more a way of thinking than a religion.

Visiting a Shinto Shrine

Shrines, like temples, have gates, though they are called *torii* and are often painted bright orange. In appearance, torii look much like the mathematical symbol for pi. As with the gates of temples, one enters and exits through the torii bowing on the way in and again on the way out. However, when visiting a shrine one claps twice before bowing. This is to summon the kami. Once you have their attention, you clap twice again to pay them homage.

Inside the shrine, you wash your hands in the same manner that you wash them when you visit a temple (left hand and then right hand). You then proceed to the main altar, clap twice and bow. In a shrine, clapping twice and bowing is often repeated as there may be special trees, stones, and other holy objects situated throughout the grounds.

After you have finished visiting the shrine, you should turn around at the torii, clap twice, and bow upon leaving.

BUDGET TRAVEL TIPS

Travelers posting in the Travel Talk Forums at Fodors.com recommend the following money-saving tips.

Lodging

"A hotel's own Japanese website usually gives the best rates and choices—some guarantee they beat any other online quotation!" —Alec

"If there are four of you traveling together, youth hostels can be an attractive budget option. Rooms are often set up for four people, so no sharing with strangers! We've found them to be very clean and usually well located." —lcuy

"Big hotel chains (Western or Japanese) can be expensive, but Japan also has "business hotels" that provide small basic hotel rooms at reasonable prices." —mrwunrfl

Transportation

"We used a rail pass for our travel outside of Tokyo (super), and found a Pasmo card very convenient for the subways in Tokyo." —teacherhiker

"Not only will the JR Pass get you on the Shinkansen, but it'll also get you on JR sleeper trains. Your pass entitles you to a small enclosed space (not private though), and for a surcharge you can get a private cabin. You can save one night's accommodation by traveling overnight." —Sydney2K

"Use frequent flyer miles to get around Japan. The award levels are low, just 15K or 20K miles. Once, I flew from Tokyo to Sapporo, poked around Hokkaido a bit with JR Pass, and then flew from Sapporo to Hiroshima. Then I used my JR Pass to get back to Tokyo, after a couple of stops." —mrwunrfl

Food

"Eating takeout from department store basement food halls is a excellent way to save money. You will save even more if you wait until an hour before closing when many prepared foods are marked down 25% to 50%. Makes for nice inexpensive dinners." —mjs

"I second the suggestion about grabbing food at the "depa-chika" (food section of department stores). For people who aren't fans of Japanese food or miss a hotdog or burger, try Mos Burger's Spicy Mos. One of the best fast-food burgers I've had anywhere. The convenience stores like Lawson, 7-11 etc. sell hotdogs and croquettes for lunch on-the-go. The hotdogs are pretty good but the packaging of the free mustard and ketchup (similar to the ketchup packs at fast food vendors in the U.S.) is simply amazing. Also ramen is a great option for cheap meals! I like Jiro, but several others in the Shijuku area are good." —mdn

Shopping

"If you like beautiful fabrics or kimonos, get one from a vintage kimono shop. Japanese people do not wear vintage stuff so these can be had for a fraction of the original price. There's one in Tokyo off Omotesando." —Cilla_Tey

"While in Tokyo, head to the Ameyoko Street Market located right in front of the JR Ueno station. There you'll find a Bangkok style street market right in the middle of Tokyo. You can find everything from the freshest seafood to a can of spam, real Rolex watches to fake Gucci bags and everything else in between." —hawaiiantraveler

ISOLATION AND ENGAGEMENT
A HISTORY OF JAPAN   By Robert Morel

A century and a half after opening its shores to outsiders, Japan is still a mystery to many Westerners. Often misunderstood, Japan's history is much deeper than the stereotypes of samurai and geisha, overworked business-men, and anime. Its long tradition of retaining the old while embracing the new has captivated visitors for centuries.

Much of Japanese history has consisted of the ongoing tension between its seeming isolation from the rest of the world and a desire to be a part of it. During the Edo period, Japan was closed to foreigners for some 250 years. Yet while the country has always had a strong national identity, it has also had a rapacious appetite for all things foreign. Just 50 years after opening its borders, parts of Tokyo looked like London, and Japan had become a colonial power in Asia. Much earlier, the Japanese imported Buddhism, tea, and their first writing system from China.

In the 19th century, the country incorporated Western architecture, technology, and government. More recently, the Japanese have absorbed Western fashion, music, and pop culture. Nevertheless, the country's history lives on in local traditions, festivals, temples, cities, music, and the arts.

Senso-ji Complex in Tokyo's Asakusa neighborhood

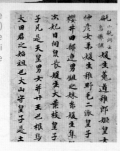

(top) Horyu-ji Inner Gate and pagoda, (bottom) Nihon Shoki, (right) Large Buddha statue at Todai-ji Temple

Ancient Japan

10,000 BC–AD 622

The first people in Japan were the hunters and fishers of the Jomon period, known for their pottery. In the following Yayoi period, hunting and fishing gave way to agriculture, as well as the introduction of rice farming and metalworking. Around AD 500 the Yamato tribe consolidated power in what is now the Kansai plain, with Yamato leaders claiming descent from the sun goddess Amaretsu and taking the title of emperor. Prince Shotoku promoted the spread of Buddhism from China and commissioned Horyu-ji Temple in Nara in 607.

- Horyu-ji Temple (Nara)
- National Museum (Tokyo)

Nara Period

710–784

As Japan's first permanent capital and urban center, Nara is often considered the birthplace of Japanese culture. Under the Emperor Shomu, who commissioned the Great Buddha at Todai-ji Temple, Buddhism rose to prominence. The first Japanese written histories, the *Kojiki* and *Nihon Shoki,* were compiled during this period, as was the *Many-oshu,* Japan's first collection of poetry. Since the country was the Eastern terminus of the Silk Road, Japan's royal family amassed an impressive collection of treasures from mainland Asia, many of which are still on display at Todai-ji Temple's Shoso-in.

- The Great Buddha at Todai-ji Temple (Nara)

Heian Period

794–1160

Partly to escape intrigues and the rising power of the Nara's Buddhist Priests, in 794 the Emperor Kammu moved the capital to Heian-kyo (now Kyoto). *Heian* translates roughly as "peace and tranquility," and during this time the Imperial court expanded its power throughout Japan. Inside the court, however, life was far from calm. This was a period of great courtly intrigue, and struggles for power between aristocrats, the powerful Fujiwara clan (the most powerful of Japan's four great noble families), and the new military class known as *bushi.* Though some emperors managed to maintain control of the court, the Heian period saw the

794–1160 The capital is moved from
Nara to Heian-kyo (now Kyoto)

1467–77 The Onin Wars initiate a
100-year period of civil war

1100   1250   1400   1550

1

IN FOCUS ISOLATION AND ENGAGEMENT: A HISTORY OF JAPAN

(right) Zen Garden at
the Ryoan-ji Temple,
(top) Noh masks,
(bottom) Kyoto Imperial
Palace's wooden
orange gates.

slow rise of the military class, leading to a series of wars that established them as the ruling class until well into the 19th century. Considered Japan's great classical period, this was a time when courtly arts flourished. The new Japanese *kana* script gave rise to a boom in literature. Compiled in 990, Sei Shonagon's *Pillow Book* gave a window into courtly life, and Shibuki Murasaki's *Tale of Genji* is often regarded as the world's first classic novel. Japanese *waka* poetry experienced a revival, breeding the new forms of poetry such as *tanka* that are still in use today.

■ The Imperial Palace (Kyoto)

1185–1335 Kamakura Period

As the Imperial Court lost control, the Genpei War (1180–1185) resulted in the defeat of clans loyal to the emperor in Kyoto and the rise of a new government in Kamakura. Yoritomo Minamoto named himself *Sei-i Tai Shogun* and established the *Kamakura bakufu*, a spartan military government. During this time, Japan repelled two Mongol invasions, thanks to timely typhoons that were later dubbed *kamikaze*, or divine wind. In this militaristic climate, Zen Buddhism, with its focus on self-reliance and discipline, exploded in popularity.

■ Eihiji Temple (Fukushima)
■ Hachimangu Shrine and the Great Buddha (Kamakura)

1336–1568 Muromachi (Ashikaga) Period

The heyday of the samurai, the Muromachi period was one of near constant civil war. Feudal lords known as *daimyo* consolidated their power in local fiefdoms. Peasant rebellions and piracy were common. Nevertheless, trade flourished. The movement of armies required *daimyo* to build roads, while improved communications gave birth to many merchant and artisan guilds. Trade with China grew, and in 1543 Portugal began trading with Japan, introducing firearms and Christianity. Noh theater and the tea ceremony were founded, and Kyoto's most famous temples were built in this period.

■ Kinkaku-ji Temple (Kyoto)
■ Ryoan-ji Temple (Kyoto)

TIMELINE | 1637 Japan is closed to the outside world except for a Dutch trading post in Nagasaki | 1720 Ban on Western literature lifed

1600   1650   1700   1750

(left) Matsumoto Castle, (top) three wise monkeys at Toshogu shrine, (bottom) woodcut of Kabuki actor by Utagawa Toyokuni

National Unification (Momoyama Period)

1568–1600

In 1568 Oda Nobunaga, a lord from Owari in central Japan, marched on Kyoto and took the title of Shogun. He controlled the surrounding territories until his death in 1582, when his successor, Toyotomi Hideyoshi, became the new Shogun. After unifying much of central and western Japan, he attempted unsuccessful invasions of Korea before his death in 1598. In 1600 Tokugawa Ieyasu, a top general, defeated Hideyoshi's successor in the battle of Sekihagara.

- Osaka Castle (Osaka)
- Matsumoto Castle (Matsumoto)

Edo (Tokugawa) Period

1600–1867

The Edo period ushered in 250 years of relative stability and central control. After becoming Shogun, Ieyasu Tokugawa moved the capital to Edo (present-day Tokyo). A system of *daimyo*, lords beholden to the Shogun, was established along with a rigid class system and legal code of conduct. Although Japan cut off trade with the outside world, cities flourished. By the mid-18th century, Edo's population had grown to more than 1 million, and urban centers like Osaka and Kyoto had become densely populated. Despite such rapid growth, urban life in the Edo period was highly organized, with districts managed by neighborhood associations that have persisted (in a modified way) to the present day. Popular entertainment and arts arose to satisfy the thriving merchant and artisan classes. Kabuki, flashy and sensational, overtook Noh theater in popularity, and Japan's famed "floating world" (*ukio*), with its theaters, drinking houses, and geishas emerged. Sumo, long a Shinto tradition, became a professional sport. Much of what both Japanese and foreigners consider "Japanese culture" dates to this period. But by 1853, the Shogun's hold on power was growing tenuous.

- Toshogu (Nikko)
- Katsura Imperial Villa (Kyoto) Muhammad Ali Mosque

| 1853 U.S. Commodore Matthew Perry reopens Japan to foreign trade | 1868 Meiji Restoration begins | 1941 Japan attacks Pearl Harbor |

1800   1850   1900   1950

1

IN FOCUS ISOLATION AND ENGAGEMENT: A HISTORY OF JAPAN

(top) Tokyo University, (left) wedding in Meiji Shrine, (bottom) A6M5 fighter plane at Yusyukan museum.

Meiji Period
1868–1912

The Tokugawa Shogunate's rigid class system and legal code proved to be its undoing. After U.S. Commodore Matthew Perry opened Japan to trade in March 1854, the following years were turbulent. In 1868, the last Shogun, Tokugawa Yoshinobu, ceded power to Emperor Meiji, and Japan began to modernize after 250 years of isolation. Adopting a weak parliamentary system from Germany, rulers moved quickly to develop national industry and universities. Victories over China and Russia also emboldened Japan.

- Tokyo University (Tokyo)
- Heian Shrine (Kyoto)
- Nara National Musuem (Nara)

Taisho Period
1912–1925

In the early 20th century, urban Japan was beginning to look a lot Europe and North America.

Fashion ranged from traditional *yukata* and kimono to zoot suits and bobbed hair. In 1923 the Great Kanto Earthquake and its resulting fires destroyed Yokohama and much of Tokyo. Although city planners saw this as an opportunity to modernize Tokyo's maze of streets, residents were quick to rebuild, ensuring that many neighborhood maps look much the same today as they did a century ago.

- Asakusa (Tokyo)
- The Shitamachi Museum (Tokyo)
- Meiji Shrine (Tokyo)

Wartime Japan
1926–1945

Although Japan was was increasingly liberal throughout the 1920s, the economic shocks of the 1930s helped the military gain greater control, resulting in crackdowns on left-leaning groups, the press, and dissidents. In 1931 Japan invaded Manchuria; in 1937 Japan captured Nanking, killing many civilians. Joining the Axis powers in 1936, Japan continued its expansion in Asia and in 1941 attacked Pearl Harbor. After the atomic bombings of Hiroshima and Nagasaki, the Emperor announced Japan's surrender on August 15, 1945.

- Hiroshima Peace Memorial Park (Hiroshima)
- Yasukuni Shrine Museum (Tokyo)

TIMELINE

| 1964 Tokyo hosts the Summer Olympic games | 1989 Emperor Hirohito dies | 2006 Shinzo Abe elected as the country's youngest prime minister |

1950   1970   1990   2010

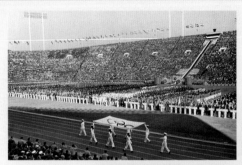

(top) 1964 Summer Olympics, Tokyo, (bottom) manga comic books, (right) Shinjuku, Tokyo

1945–1989 Postwar Japan and the Economic Miracle

The initial postwar years were hard on Japan. More than half of Japan's total urban area was in ruins, its industry in shambles, and food shortages common. Kyoto was the only major metropolitan area in the country that escaped widespread damage. Thanks to an educated, dedicated population and smart planning, however, Japan was soon on the road to recovery. A new democratic government was formed and universal suffrage extended to all adult men and women. Japan's famous "Peace Constitution" forbade the country from engaging in warfare. With cooperation from the government, old companies like Matsushita (Panasonic), Mitsubishi, and Toyota began exporting Japanese goods en masse, while upstarts like Honda pushed their way to the top. In 1964 Japan joined the Organization for Economic Cooperation and Development's group of "rich nations" and hosted the Tokyo Olympics. At the same time, anime began gaining popularity at the box office and on TV, with Osamu Tezuka's classic *Tetsuwan Atom* (*Astro Boy*) making a splash when it aired in 1963. In the 1970s and '80s Japan became as well known for its electronics as its cars, with Nintendo, Sony, and Panasonic becoming household names abroad.

■ Showa-Kan (Takayama)
■ National Stadium (Yoyogi Park)

1990–PRESENT From Goods to Culture

Unfortunately, much of Japan's rapid growth in the 1980s was unsustainable. By 1991 the bubble had burst, leading to 20 years of limited economic expansion. Japan avoided an economic crisis, and most people continued to lead comfortable, if somewhat simpler, lives. After decades of exporting goods, Japan has—particularly since 2000—become an exporter of culture in the form of animation, video games, and cuisine. Japan, famous for importing ideas, has begun to send its own culture to the world.

■ Shinjuku, Harajuku, and Shibuya, (Tokyo)
■ Akihabara (Tokyo)
■ Manga Museum (Kyoto)

Tokyo Neighborhoods

WORD OF MOUTH

"Shinjuku and Shibuya are arguably the brightest areas for food and entertainment. In Shinjuku and Shibuya you can walk out of the hotel lobby and be right in the middle of the action. Ginza's high-class shopping, Roppongi's nightlife, and Ikebukuro's shopping are also worth mentioning."

—Sydney2K

JAPANESE POP CULTURE

Step onto the streets of Shibuya—or brave the crowds of preening high school fashionistas populating Harujuku's Takeshita-dori—and you'll get a crash course on Japanese pop culture that extends way beyond familiar exports like Hello Kitty and Godzilla.

(top left) Manga is a Japan-wide obsession (top right) distinctive manga style (bottom right) matriarch of Japanese *kawaii*, Hello Kitty.

Japanese pop culture has long been a source of fascination—and sometimes bewilderment—for foreign visitors. New fashion styles, technology, and popular media evolve quickly here, and in something of a vacuum, which leads to a constant turnover of wholly unique, sometimes wacky trends you won't find anywhere outside Japan. Luckily, you don't have to go out of your way to explore Japan's popular obsessions. You can have an immersion experience just walking through neighborhoods like Shibuya, Shinjuku, Harujuku, and Akihabara.

DID YOU KNOW?

There are more than 5 million vending machines in Japan, making it the most dense population of machines, per capita, anywhere in the world. Here, automated machines sell everything from hot drinks to live lobsters. Some use facial recognition to verify age for tobacco and beer and even offer indecisive customers age-appropriate drink recommendations.

2

KAWAII

Kawaii, or "cute," isn't just a descriptor you'll hear coming out of the mouths of teenage girls, it's an aww-inducing aesthetic you'll see all over Tokyo; major airlines plaster depictions of adorable animation characters like Pikachu across the sides of their planes, and even at local police stations it's not unusual for a fluffy, stuffed-animal mascot to be on display. Duck into an arcade photo booth to take *purikura*—stickers pictures that let you choose your own kawaii background—or head to Sanrio Puroland, an entire theme park dedicated to cuteness.

KEITAI CULTURE

You can't visit Japan without marveling at the relationship people have with their cell phones or *keitai denwa*, which can operate as credit cards, TV-watching devices, and game consoles, just for starters. Japanese cell phones are so advanced, they're said to suffer from "Galapagos syndrome," a reference to the creatures of the Galapagos Islands that evolved in isolation, and subsequently have little relation to their mainland cousins. In 2003 the first novel written entirely on a cell phone was a big hit, and cell phone novels continue to be a popular literary subgenre.

J-POP IDOLS

The age of the boy band—or the girl band for that matter—is not over in

Japan. "Idol" groups are hot. Over-the-top outfits, sugar-sweet synthesized beats, and love-professing lyrics (with the occasional English word thrown in) dominate the Japanese pop charts. AKB-48, one of Tokyo's hottest groups of idols, is 48 girls strong, and performs daily at its own theater complex in Akihabara. Beloved pop groups like all-male SMAP have been pumping out hits for more than 20 years.

ANIME AND MANGA

Peek over the shoulder of a comic-book-reading businessman and you'll quickly discover that, in Japan, cartoons aren't just kids' stuff. Animation (*anime*) and comic books (*manga*) are extremely popular with readers both young and old. Comic book addicts, known as *otaku*, claim Tokyo's Akihabara as their home base. Though otaku can be translated as "nerd" or "obsessive," the term has been embraced by some. Former prime minister Taro Aso declared himself an otaku and confessed to reading 10 to 20 manga a week.

Updated by
Brett Bull

For many, the 2003 film *Lost in Translation* by Sophia Coppola was the first chance to see beyond Tokyo's historic temples and sushi to the modern, pulsating metropolis that it is today. But don't think that the temples and sushi stands have gone away. This is a city of old and new, where opposites attract and new trends come and go like the tide, but history and tradition continue to be held in utmost respect.

The city is also the center of design and cutting-edge fashion. One step into the hip neighborhoods of Harajuku and Shibuya and you'll know what we mean. Dining is also a study in contrasts. People can dine at a Michelin-starred restaurant one night, and then belly up to the counter at the local ramen joint the next. And the people are as varied as their city. Residents of Aoyama may wear European fashion and drive fancy imports but those residing in Asakusa prefer to be decidedly less flashy. Stop in a bar in Ginza and one might find groups of salarymen, flush with large (though not as hefty in decades past) expense accounts, entertaining clients, but down the Hibiya Line in Ebisu many of the cheap watering holes are filled with young office professionals.

Even the landscape is varied. The city hosts some of the most unsightly sprawls of concrete housing—extending for miles in all directions—in the world. But it's also home to some pretty tall buildings. In Roppongi, you'll find the city's tallest building, Tokyo Midtown (248 meters [814 feet]), and the 634-meter (2,080-foot) Tokyo Sky Tree transmission tower is now taking shape near the Sumida River (set for completion in 2012).

Whether you're gazing at the glow of Tokyo's evening lights or the green expanse of its parks or a plate of the freshest sushi imaginable or dramatically dressed people, this is a city of astonishing and intriguing beauty. If you're a foodie, artist, design lover, or cultural adventurer, then Tokyo, a city of inspiration and ideas, is for you.

IMPERIAL PALACE AND GOVERNMENT DISTRICT 皇居近辺

Sightseeing
★★★★★

Dining
★☆☆☆☆

Lodging
★★★☆☆

Shopping
★★☆☆☆

Nightlife
★☆☆☆☆

The Imperial Palace was built by the order of Ieyasu Tokugawa, who chose the site for his castle in 1590. The castle had 99 gates (36 in the outer wall), 21 watchtowers (of which 3 are still standing), and 28 armories. The outer defenses stretched from present-day Shimbashi Station to Kanda. Completed in 1640 (and later expanded), it was at the time the largest castle in the world.

This district is the core of Japan's government. It is primarily comprised of *Nagata-cho*, the Imperial Palace (*Kokyo-gaien*), the Diet (national parliament building), the Prime Minister's residence (*Kantei*), and the Supreme Court. The Imperial Palace and the Diet are both important to see, but the Supreme Court is nondescript. Unfortunately, the Prime Minister's residence is only viewable from afar, hidden behind fortified walls and trees.

The Japanese Imperial Family resides in heavily blockaded sections of the palace grounds. Tours are conducted by reservation only, and restricted to designated outdoor sections, namely, the palace grounds and the East Gardens. The grounds are open to the general public only twice a year, on January 2 and December 23 (the Emperor's birthday), when thousands of people assemble under the balcony to offer their good wishes to the Imperial Family.

GETTING ORIENTED

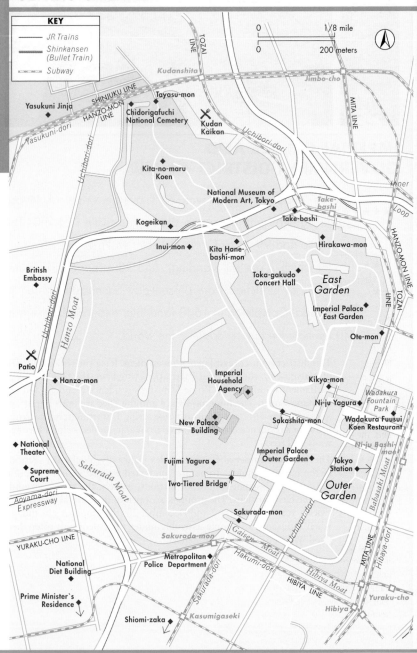

KEY
- JR Trains
- Shinkansen (Bullet Train)
- Subway

0 — 1/8 mile
0 — 200 meters

Yasukuni Jinja

SHINJUKU LINE
HANZO-MON LINE
TOZAI LINE

Kudanshita

Jimbo-cho

MITA LINE

Tayasu-mon

Yasukuni-dori

Chidorigafuchi National Cemetery

Kudan Kaikan

Uchibori-dori

Uchibori-dori

Kita-no-maru Koen

National Museum of Modern Art, Tokyo

Take-bashi

Inner

Loop

Kogeikan

Take-bashi

HANZO-MON LINE

Inui-mon

Kita Hane-bashi-mon

Hirakawa-mon

British Embassy

Toka-gakudo Concert Hall

East Garden

Uchibori-dori

Hanzo Moat

Imperial Palace East Garden

TOZAI LINE

Ote-mon

Patio

Hanzo-mon

Imperial Household Agency

Kikyo-mon

Wadakura Fountain Park

Ni-ju Yagura

Wadakura Fuusui Koen Restaurant

New Palace Building

Sakashita-mon

National Theater

Supreme Court

Sakurada Moat

Fujimi Yagura

Imperial Palace Outer Garden

Ni-ju Bashi-mae

Tokyo Station

Babasaki Moat

Two-Tiered Bridge

Outer Garden

Aoyama-dori Expressway

Sakurada-mon

YURAKU-CHO LINE

Sakurada-mon

Gaisen Moat

Hakumi-dori

National Diet Building

Metropolitan Police Department

Sakurada-dori

Uchibori-dori

Hibiya Moat

MITA LINE

Hibiya-dori

Prime Minister's Residence

HIBIYA LINE

Yuraku-cho

Shiomi-zaka

Kasumigaseki

Hibiya

ORIENTATION

The Imperial Palace is located in the heart of central Tokyo, and the city's other neighborhoods branch out from here. The palace, where the Imperial Family still resides, is surrounded by a moat that connects through canals to Tokyo Bay and Sumida River (Sumida-gawa) to the east. Outside the moat, large four-lane roads trace its outline, as if the city expanded from this primary location.

PLANNING

The best way to discover the Imperial Palace is to take part in one of the free tours offered by the **Imperial Household Agency** (☎ 03/3213–1111 ⊕ www.kunaicho.go.jp). There are four different tours: Imperial Palace Grounds, the East Gardens (*Higashi Gyo-en*), Sannomaru Shozokan, and Gagaku Performance (autumn only). Tour registration is required a day in advance; hours change according to the season.

If going on your own, allow at least an hour for the East Garden and Outer Garden. Visit Yasukuni Jinja after lunch and spend at least an hour there, taking half an hour each for the small Yushukan (at Yasukuni Jinja) and Kogeikan museums. The modern art museum requires a more leisurely visit.
■TIP→ Avoid visiting the Imperial Palace on Monday, when the East Garden and museums are closed; the East Garden is also closed Friday. In July and August, heat will make the palace walk grueling—bring a hat and bottled water.

GETTING HERE AND AROUND

The best way to get to the Imperial Palace is by subway. Take the Chiyoda Line to Nijubashimae Station (Exit 6) or the JR lines to Tokyo Station (Marunouchi Central Exit). There are three entrance gates—Ote-mon, Hirakawa-mon, and Kita-hane-bashi-mon. You can also easily get to any of the three from the Ote-machi or Takebashi subway stations.

QUICK BITES

Before exploring the Imperial Palace enjoy breakfast at **Patio** (⊠ 1-1 Hayabusa-cho), the restaurant inside the Grand Arc Hanzomon hotel, where ham, toast, eggs, and juice are just ¥1,050. In summer spend the early evening at **Kudan Kaikan** (⊠ 1-6-5 Kudanshita ☎ 03/3261–5521). The rooftop beer garden is one of the best in the city, offering a huge seating area and light pub fare to go with cold beer. Certain days feature female servers in bunny costumes. Ask ahead.

TOP REASONS TO GO

A City Oasis. Located in the middle of the city, the Imperial Palace East Garden is a wonderful place to escape the hustle and bustle of the city.

House of Parliament. Looking something like a squat pyramid, the National Diet Building houses Japan's parliament.

A Controversial Shrine. The Yasukuni Shrine (Shrine of Peace for the Nation), which represents Japan's militaristic past, has long been the source of political tension between Japan, Korea, and China.

Art Abounds. The finest collection of Japanese modern art is housed in the National Museum of Modern Art, including works by such renowned painters as Taikan Yokoyama, Gyoshu Hayami, Kokei Kobayashi, and Gyokudo Kawai.

TOP ATTRACTIONS

Chidorigafuchi National Cemetery 千鳥ヶ淵戦没者墓苑 (*Chidorigafuchi Senbotsusha Boen*). High on the edge of the Imperial Palace moat, the park at this cemetery, which holds the remains of thousands of unknown soldiers, is famous for its springtime cherry tree blossoms. The most popular activity in this garden is renting rowboats on the moat at the **Chidorigafuchi Boathouse.** The entrance to the garden is near Yasukuni Jinja. ✉ *2 Sanban-cho, Chiyoda-ku* ☎ *03/3234–1948* 🎫 *Park free, boat rental ¥500 for 30 mins during regular season, ¥800 for 30 mins during cherry blossom season* ⊙ *Park daily sunrise–sunset; boathouse early Apr.–late Nov., Tues.–Sun. 11–5:30* Ⓜ *Hanzo-mon and Shinjuku subway lines, Kudanshita Station (Exit 2).*

Fodor'sChoice ★ **Imperial Palace East Garden** 皇居東御苑 (*Kokyo Higashi Gyo-en*). The entrance to the East Garden is the Ote-mon (⇨ *below*), once the main gate of Ieyasu Tokugawa's castle. Here, you will come across the National Police Agency *dojo* (martial arts hall) and the Ote Rest House, where for ¥100 you can buy a simple map of the garden.

The **Hundred-Man Guardhouse** was once defended by four shifts of 100 soldiers each. Past it is the entrance to what was once the *ni-no-maru,* the "second circle" of the fortress. It's now a grove and garden. At the far end is the **Suwa Tea Pavilion,** an early-19th-century building relocated here from another part of the castle grounds.

The steep stone walls of the **hon-maru** (the "inner circle"), with the Moat of Swans below, dominate the west side of the garden. Halfway along is **Shio-mi-zaka,** which translates roughly as "Briny View Hill," so named because in the Edo period the ocean could be seen from here.

Head to the wooded paths around the garden's edges for shade, quiet, and benches to rest your weary feet. In the southwest corner is the Fujimi Yagura, the only surviving watchtower of the hon-maru; farther along the path, on the west side, is the **Fujimi Tamon,** one of the two remaining armories.

The odd-looking octagonal tower is the **Tokagakudo Concert Hall.** Its mosaic tile facade was built in honor of Empress Kojun in 1966. ✉ *1–1 Chiyoda, Chiyoda-ku* ☎ *03/3213–1111* 🎫 *Free* ⊙ *Mar.–Apr. 14 and Sep.–Oct., daily 9–4:30; Apr. 15–Aug. until 5; Nov.–Feb. until 4; closed Mon. and Fri.* Ⓜ *Tozai, Marunouchi, and Chiyoda subway lines, Ote-machi Station (Exit C13B).*

National Diet Building 国会議事堂 (*Kokkai-Gijido*). This building, which houses the Japanese parliament, is the perfect example of post–World War II Japanese architecture; on a gloomy day it seems as if it might have sprung from the screen of a German Expressionist movie. Started in 1920, construction took 17 years to complete. The Prime Minister's residence, Kantei, is across the street. ✉ *1–7–1 Nagata-cho, Chiyoda-ku* ☎ *03/3581–3100* Ⓜ *Marunouchi subway line, Kokkai-Gijido-mae Station (Exit 2).*

National Theater 国立劇場 (*Kokuritsu Gekijo*). Architect Hiroyuki Iwamoto's winning entry in the design competition for the National Theater building (1966) is a rendition in concrete of the ancient *azekura*

Once the site of the Imperial Palace's innermost defense circles, the East Garden now offers respite in a beautiful setting.

(storehouse) style, invoking the 8th-century Shosoin Imperial Repository in Nara. The large hall seats 1,610 and presents primarily Kabuki theater, ancient court music, and dance. The small hall seats 590 and is used mainly for *bunraku* puppet theater and traditional music. The building is worth a look, but all performances are in Japanese, so it can be difficult to sit through an entire show. ✉ *4–1 Hayabusa-cho, Chiyoda-ku* ☎ *03/3265–7411* ⊕ *www.ntj.jac.go.jp* ✉ *Varies depending on performance* Ⓜ *Hanzo-mon subway line, Hanzo-mon Station (Exit 1).*

Tokyo Station 東京駅 *(Tokyo Eki).* The work of Kingo Tatsuno, one of Japan's first modern architects, Tokyo Station was completed in 1914. Tatsuno modeled his creation on the railway station of Amsterdam. The building lost its original top story in the air raids of 1945, but was promptly repaired. In the late 1990s, a plan to demolish the station was impeded by public outcry. Inside, it has been deepened and tunneled and redesigned any number of times to accommodate new commuter lines, but the lovely old redbrick facade remains. While the historical Tokyo Station Hotel is closed for renovation (set for completion in 2012) one of the more popular attractions is the Gran Tokyo North Tower. The 200-meter-tall (656-foot-tall) glass-and-steel office building includes a branch of the high-end department store chain Daimaru. ✉ *1–9–1 Marunouchi, Chiyoda-ku* ☎ *03/3212–8011* ⊕ *www.grantokyo-nt.com* Ⓜ *Marunouchi subway line and JR lines.*

★ **Yasukuni Jinja** 靖国神社 *(Shrine of Peace for the Nation).* This shrine is not as impressive as Asakusa Shrine and Meiji Jingu, but it is still worth a visit. Founded in 1869, this shrine is dedicated to approximately 2.5 million Japanese, Taiwanese, and Koreans who have died since then in war or military service. Since 1945 Yasukuni has been a center of stubborn political debate given that the Japanese constitution expressly renounces both militarism and state sponsorship of religion. Several prime ministers have visited the shrine since 1979, causing a political chill between Japan and its close neighbors, Korea and China—who suffered under Japanese colonialism. Despite all this, hundreds of thousands of Japanese come here every year, simply to pray for the repose of friends and relatives they have lost. These pilgrimages are most frenzied on August 15, the anniversary of the conclusion of World War II, when former soldiers and ultra-right-wing groups descend upon the shrine's grounds en masse.

> ## THE GRUTT PASS
>
> If you plan on visiting a lot of the city's sites, purchasing a **GRUTT Pass** (⊕ www.museum.or.jp/grutto) is the way to go. The pass, which is only ¥2,000, gives visitors free or discounted admission to 70 sites throughout the city including museums, zoos, aquariums, and parks. Passes can be purchased at all participating sites, as well as the Tokyo Tourist Information Center, or Family Mart and Lawson convenience stores. Keep in mind that passes expire two months after date of purchase.

The shrine is not one structure but a complex of buildings that include the **Main Hall** and the **Hall of Worship**—both built in the simple, unadorned style of the ancient Shinto shrines at Ise—and the **Yushukan,** a museum of documents and war memorabilia. Also here are a Noh theater and, in the far western corner, a sumo-wrestling ring. Sumo matches are held at Yasukuni in April, during the first of its three annual festivals. You can pick up a pamphlet and simplified map of the shrine, both in English, just inside the grounds.

Refurbished in 2002, the Yushukan presents Japan at its most ambivalent—if not unrepentant—about its more recent militaristic past. Critics charge that the newer exhibits glorify the nation's role in the Pacific War as a noble struggle for independence; certainly there's an agenda here that's hard to reconcile with Japan's firm postwar rejection of militarism as an instrument of national policy. Many Japanese visitors are moved by such displays as the last letters and photographs of young kamikaze pilots; visitors from other countries tend to find the Yushukan a cautionary, rather than uplifting, experience.

Although some of the exhibits have English labels and notes, the English is not very helpful; most objects, however, speak clearly enough for themselves. Rooms on the second floor house an especially fine collection of medieval swords and armor. Visiting on a Sunday gives one the option of foraging at the flea market that runs from morning until sundown (⇨ *Chapter 6, Shopping*). ⊠ *3–1–1 Kudankita, Chiyoda-ku* ☎ *03/3261–8326* ⊕ *www.yasukuni.or.jp* 🖃 *¥800* ☉ *Grounds Mar.–Oct., daily 8:15–5; Nov–Feb., daily 8:15–4; Museum Apr.–Sept., daily 9–5:30; Oct.–Mar., daily 9–5* Ⓜ *Hanzo-mon and Shinjuku subway lines, Kudanshita Station (Exit 1).*

Stretch Your Legs

CLOSE UP

The venue of choice for runners is the **Imperial Palace Outer Garden.** At the west end of the park, Sakurada-mon's (Gate of the Field of Cherry Trees) small courtyard is the traditional starting point for the 5-km (3-mi) run around the palace—though you can join in anywhere along the route. Jogging around the palace is a ritual that begins as early as 6 am and goes on throughout the day, no matter what the weather. Almost everybody runs the course counter-clockwise, but now and then you may spot someone going the opposite way.

Looking for a challenge? Japan hosts a number of marathons throughout

the year and one of the most famous is the **Tokyo Marathon** (⊕ *www.tokyo42195.org*), which is held in February. Plan ahead if you're going to sign up, because the registration deadline is at the end of August of the previous year (most of the country's running events require signing up and qualifying far more in advance than their counterparts on other shores). The marathon starts at one of Tokyo's most prominent landmarks, the Tokyo Metropolitan Government Office in Shinjuku-ku, winds its way through the Imperial Palace, past the Tokyo Tower and Asakusa Kaminari-mon Gate, and finishes at Tokyo Big Sight Exhibition Center in Koto Ward.

WORTH NOTING

Hanzo-mon 半蔵門 *(Hanzo Gate).* The house of Hattori Hanzo (1541–96) once sat at the foot of this small wooden gate. Hanzo was a legendary leader of Ieyasu Tokugawa's private corps of spies and infiltrators—and assassins, if need be. They were the menacing, black-clad ninja—perennial material for historical adventure films and television dramas. The gate is a minute's walk from the subway. ⊠ *Chiyoda-ku* Ⓜ *Hanzo-mon subway line, Hanzo-mon Station (Exit 3).*

Hirakawa-mon 平川門 *(Hirakawa Gate).* The approach to this gate crosses the only wooden bridge that spans the Imperial Palace moat. The gate and bridge are reconstructions, but Hirakawa-mon is especially beautiful, looking much as it must have when the shogun's wives and concubines used it on their rare excursions from the seraglio. ⊠ *Chiyoda-ku* Ⓜ *Tozai subway line, Takebashi Station (Exit 1A).*

Imperial Palace Outer Garden 皇居外苑 *(Kokyo-Gaien).* When the office buildings of the Meiji government were moved from this area in 1899, the whole expanse along the east side of the palace was turned into a public promenade and planted with 2,800 pine trees. The Outer Garden affords the best view of the castle walls and their Tokugawa-period fortifications: Ni-ju-bashi and the Sei-mon, the 17th-century Fujimi Yagura watchtower, and the Sakurada-mon gate. ⊠ *Chiyoda-ku* ✉ *Free* Ⓜ *Chiyoda subway line, Ni-ju-bashi-mae Station (Exit 2).*

NEED A BREAK?

Stop by the **Wadakura Funsui Koen Restaurant** 和田倉噴水公園 飲食店 for pasta, sandwiches, and soup with lovely water fountain views. English menus are available upon request, but the signs are only in Japanese.

Lunch set menus range from ¥1,200 to ¥2,400. ⊠ *3–1 Kokyo Gaien, Chiyoda-ku* ☎ *03/3214–2286* Ⓜ *Ote-machi Station (Exit D2 or D3).*

Kogeikan 工芸館 *(Crafts Gallery at the National Museum of Modern Art).* For those who are interested in modern and traditional Japanese crafts, this museum is worth seeing. Built in 1910, the Kogeikan, once the headquarters of the Imperial Guard, is a Gothic Revival redbrick building. The exhibits are all too few, but many master artists are represented here in the traditions of lacquerware, textiles, pottery, bamboo, and metalwork. ⊠ *1–1 Kita-no-maru Koen, Chiyoda-ku* ☎ *03/3211–7781* ⊕ *www.momat.go.jp* ᠍ *¥200; additional fee for special exhibits; free 1st Sun. of month; admission to National Museum of Modern Art is separate* ⊙ *Thurs.–Tues. 10–5* Ⓜ *Hanzo-mon and Shinjuku subway lines, Kudanshita Station (Exit 2); Tozai subway line, Takebashi Station (Exit 1B).*

National Museum of Modern Art, Tokyo 国立近代美術館 *(Tokyo Kokuritsu Kindai Bijutsukan).* Founded in 1952 and moved to its present site in 1969, this was Japan's first national art museum. Twentieth- and 21st-century Japanese and Western art is featured throughout the year, but the museum tends to be rather lackadaisical about how these exhibitions are organized and presented, and the exhibitions are seldom on the cutting edge. The second through fourth floors house the permanent collection, which includes the painting, prints, and sculpture by Rousseau, Picasso, Tsuguji Fujita, Ryuzaburo Umehara, and Taikan Yokoyama. ⊠ *3–1 Kita-no-maru Koen, Chiyoda-ku* ☎ *03/5777–8600* ⊕ *www.ntj. jac.go.jp* ᠍ *¥420, includes admission to the Kogeikan; free 1st Sun. of month* ⊙ *Tues.–Thurs. and weekends 10–5, Fri. 10–8* Ⓜ *Tozai subway line, Takebashi Station (Exit 1B); Hanzo-mon and Shinjuku subway lines, Kudanshita Station (Exit 2).*

Ote-mon 大手門 *(Ote Gate).* The main entrance to the Imperial Palace East Garden, Ote-mon was in former days the principal gate of Ieyasu Tokugawa's castle. Most of the gate was destroyed in 1945 but was rebuilt in 1967 on the original plans. The outer part of the gate survived, and today it houses a fascinating photo collection of before-and-after photographs of the castle, taken about 100 years apart. ⊠ *Chiyoda-ku* Ⓜ *Tozai, Marunouchi, and Chiyoda subway lines, Ote-machi Station (Exit C10).*

Two-Tiered Bridge 二重橋 *(Ni-ju-bashi).* Making a graceful arch across the moat, this bridge is surely the most photogenic spot on the grounds of the former Edo Castle. Mere mortals may pass through only on December 23 (the Emperor's birthday) and January 2 to pay their respects to the Imperial Family. The guards in front of their small, octagonal, copper-roof sentry boxes change every hour on the hour— alas, with nothing like the pomp and ceremony at Buckingham Palace. ⊠ *Chiyoda-ku* Ⓜ *Chiyoda subway line, Ni-ju-bashi-mae Station (Exit 2).*

2

AKIHABARA 秋葉原 AND JIMBO-CHO 神保町

Sightseeing
★★★☆☆

Dining
★★☆☆☆

Lodging
★★☆☆☆

Shopping
★★★★☆

Nightlife
★☆☆☆☆

Akihabara is techno-geek heaven. Also known as Akihabara Electric Town, this district, which was once all about electronics, is becoming a wacky fetish district where *otaku* (nerds) can indulge in computer-game fantasies, hang out in kinky cafés, and buy *manga* (comics). Visitors don't just come here to purchase digital cameras, but to also observe one of the nation's subcultures.

If you're looking for something a little more cerebral, head to Jimbo-cho where family-run specialty bookstores of every genre abound including rare antiquarian and Japanese manga. The area is also home to Meiji University and Nihon University.

Akihabara is one of the best places in Tokyo to go if you want to buy manga comics or get a costume so you can dress up on Halloween as your favorite anime character. However, if you aren't interested in manga or anime, you can also buy the latest wacky Japanese electronics at duty-free prices in the neighborhood's stores.

The area is also a draw for those interested in the phenomenon of the "maid café." The servers in these cafés—they are all women—dress up in frilly maid uniforms, addressing patrons as "master" (or in rare cases "mistress"). The first of these cafés opened in Akihabara in early 2001, catering primarily to men who are obsessed with the type of young, innocent-looking girls predominantly featured in Japanese anime.

GETTING ORIENTED

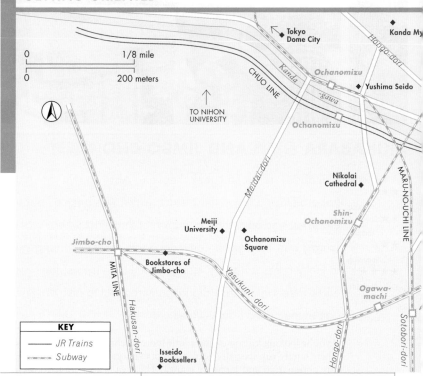

```
0        1/8 mile
0        200 meters
```

Tokyo Dome City

Kanda My

Hongo-dori

CHUO LINE

Kanda

Ochanomizu

-gawa

Yushima Seido

TO NIHON UNIVERSITY

Ochanomizu

MARUNOUCHI LINE

Meidai-dori

Nikolai Cathedral

Shin-Ochanomizu

Meiji University

Ochanomizu Square

Jimbo-cho

MITA LINE

Bookstores of Jimbo-cho

Yasukuni-dori

Hakusan-dori

Hongo-dori

Ogawa-machi

Sotobori-dori

KEY
— JR Trains
⋯⋯ Subway

Isseido Booksellers

ORIENTATION

Akihabara is east of the Imperial Palace, right below Ueno and Asakusa. Akihabara Station is located north of Tokyo Station, on the JR Yamanote, Hibiya, and Tsukuba lines. It's right below Asakusa and Ueno districts.

Located just to the west of Akihabara, Jimbo-cho should be a very short stopover either before or after an excursion to Akihabara. The best way to get there is by taxi, which should cost about ¥800 to or from Akihabara Station.

GETTING HERE AND AROUND

Take the train to Akihabara Station on the JR Yamanote Line. Akihabara is a 20- to 30-minute ride from most hotels in Shinjuku or Minato-ku.

PLANNING

Credit cards are accepted at all major electronics superstores, but bring enough cash to get around, because ATMs are difficult to find. Keep in mind that most stores in Akihabara do not open until 10 am. Weekends draw hordes of shoppers, especially on Sunday, when the four central blocks of Chuo-dori are closed to traffic and become a pedestrian mall.

2

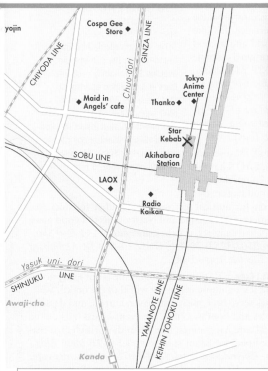

QUICK BITES

If you need a break from shopping for electronics and games, a spicy kebab sandwich from **Star Kebab** (⊕ *www.kebab.co.jp*) should do the trick. There are three outlets in the area, offering beef strips, lettuce, and tomatoes in pita pockets (¥500, unless you choose the "big boy" option for ¥100 more). Lines at the take-out store (⊠ *3–15–5 Soto-Kanda*) get long, so consider taking a seat at the terrace branch (⊠ *1–13–1 Soto-Kanda*). The third branch is near the Akihabara JR Station.

TOP REASONS TO GO

Hello Master. At maid cafés, largely popularized in Akihabara, waitresses dress in maid costumes, address patrons as "*master*," and cater to the fetishes of Japanese otaku (nerds).

Dancing in the Streets. A visit in May must include the Kanda Festival—one of Tokyo's major street celebrations. More than 200 portable shrines are carried in a parade towards the ground of the Kanda Myojin.

Toys without Tax. Purchase the best and most up-to-date electronics at the LAOX duty-free store.

Want to be a Superhero? See the greatest collection of Japanese comic character costumes at Cospa Gee Store.

An Eccentric Collection. Check out the toys, electronic gadgets, and hobby items at Radio Kaikan.

Read All About It. Browse an impressive variety of specialty bookstores in Jimbo-cho.

TOP ATTRACTIONS

Cospa Gee Store ジーストア. Fans of anime will enjoy this zany Japanese costume-shop experience. It's like no other in the world and a good place to pick up an original costume for Halloween. ⊠ *2F MN Bldg., 3–15–5 Soto-Kanda, Chiyoda-ku* ☎ *03/3526–6877* ⊙ *Mon.–Sat. 11–8, Sun. and holidays 11–7* Ⓜ *JR Yamanote Line, Akihabara Station (Akihabara Electric Town Exit).*

LAOX ラオックス. Of all the discount stores in Akihabara, LAOX has the largest and most comprehensive selection, with four buildings in this area—one exclusively for musical instruments, another for duty-free appliances—and outlets in Yokohama and Narita. This is a good place to find the latest in digital cameras, watches, and games. ⊠ *1–2–9 Soto-Kanda, Chiyoda-ku* ☎ *03/3253–7111* ⊙ *Daily 10–8* Ⓜ *JR Akihabara Station (Akihabara Electric Town Exit).*

Maid in Angels' (M.I.A.) Cafe ミアカフェ. This maid café is not exceptional by any standard, but it's a glimpse inside the world of the otaku. Waitresses in frilly dresses serve beer, juice, tea, pasta, curries, and desserts at simple wood tables and booths. Check the event board outside the front door for special café happenings, like when the girls change costumes based on the holidays. Santa suits anyone? ⊠ *1F Meiji Bldg., 3–1–2 Soto-Kanda, Chiyoda-ku* ☎ *03/5294–0078* ⊕ *www.mia-café. com* ⊙ *Mon.–Sat. noon–10, Sun. and holidays 11–10* Ⓜ *JR Yamanote Line, Akihabara Station (Akihabara Electric Town Exit).*

Radio Kaikan ラジオ会館. Eight floors featuring a variety of vendors selling mini-spy cameras, cell phones disguised as stun guns, manga comics, adult toys, gadgets, and oddball hobby supplies draw otaku, other shoppers, and visitors alike. Start browsing from the top floor and work your way down. ⊠ *1–15–16 Soto-Kanda, Chiyoda-ku* ☎ *03/3251–3711* ⊙ *Daily 10–7* Ⓜ *JR Yamanote Line, Akihabara Station (Akihabara Electric Town Exit).*

Thanko サンコー. As the king of wacky electronics from Japan, Thanko sells everything from recording binoculars to a smokeless ashtray to a flowerpot with a speaker mounted on its side. This showroom is a must-see for gadget geeks. ⊠ *1F Machida Bldg., 3–9–10 Soto-Kanda, Chiyoda-ku* ☎ *03/3526–5472* ⊕ *www.thanko.jp* ⊙ *Mon.–Sat. 11–8, Sun. 11–7* Ⓜ *JR Yamanote Line, Akihabara Station (Akihabara Electric Town Exit).*

DID YOU KNOW?

Space is the greatest luxury in Tokyo and affordable housing is found only in the suburbs. An average Tokyo family probably lives in a cramped apartment that averages 80 square meters (860 square feet). A one-bedroom apartment situated inside the Roppongi Hills residential complex is approximately ¥600,000 (around $7,000) per month to rent.

WORTH NOTING

Bookstores of Jimbo-cho 神保町書店街. For the ultimate browse through art books, catalogs, scholarly monographs, secondhand paperbacks, and dictionaries in almost any language, the bookstores of Jimbo-cho are the place to go. A number of the antiquarian booksellers here carry rare typeset editions, wood-block-printed books of the Edo period, and individual prints. At shops like **Isseido** and **Ohya Shobo** (both are open Monday–Saturday 10–6) it's still possible to find genuine 19th- and 20th-century prints—not always in the best condition—at affordable prices. Many of Japan's most prestigious publishing houses make their home in this area as well. The bookstores run for ½ km (¼ mi) on Yasukuni-dori beginning at the Surugadai-shita intersection. ✉ *Isseido: 1–7–4 Kanda Jimbo-cho, Chiyoda-ku* ☏ *03/3292–0071* ⊕ *www.isseido-books.co.jp* ✉ *Ohya Shobo: 1–1 Kanda Jimbo-cho, Chiyoda-ku, Jimbo-cho* ☏ *03/3291–0062* ⊕ *www.ohya-shobo.com* Ⓜ *Shinjuku and Mita subway lines, Jimbo-cho Station (Exit A7).*

Kanda Myojin 神田明神 *(Kanda Shrine).* This shrine is said to have been founded in 730 in a village called Shibasaki, where the Ote-machi financial district stands today. The shrine itself was destroyed in the Great Kanto Earthquake of 1923, and the present buildings reproduce in concrete the style of 1616.

You will never be able to see every shrine in the city and the ones in Akihabara are of minor interest, unless you are around for the **Kanda Festival**—one of Tokyo's three great blowouts—in mid-May. (The other two are the Sanno Festival of Hie Jinja in Nagata-cho and the Sanja Festival of Asakusa Shrine.) Some of the smaller buildings you see as you come up the steps and walk around the Main Hall contain the *mikoshi*—the portable shrines that are featured during the festival. Kanda Myojin is on Kuramae-bashi-dori, about a five-minute walk west of the Suehiro-cho subway stop. ✉ *2–16–2 Soto-Kanda, Chiyoda-ku* ☏ *03/3254–0753* Ⓜ *Ginza subway line, Suehiro-cho Station (Exit 3).*

Nikolai Cathedral ニコライ堂. It's curious that a Russian Orthodox cathedral was built in Tokyo's Electric Town, but it's a place to stop for a quick snapshot. Formally, this is the Holy Resurrection Cathedral, derived from its founder, St. Nikolai Kassatkin (1836–1912), a Russian missionary who came to Japan in 1861 and spent the rest of his life here. The building, planned by a Russian engineer and executed by a British

---

SHRINE FESTIVAL 411

Every town, city, or village in Japan has a shrine festival at least once a year that essentially airs out their gods. The mid-May Kanda Festival began in the early Edo period. The floats that lead the procession today move in stately measure on wheeled carts, attended by the shrine's priests and officials. The portable Shinto shrines (*mikoshi*), some 70 of them, follow behind, carried on the shoulders of the townspeople. Shrine festivals are a peculiarly competitive form of worship: piety is a matter of who can shout the loudest, drink the most beer, and have the best time.

architect, was completed in 1891. Heavily damaged in the earthquake of 1923, the cathedral was restored with a dome much more modest than the original. Even so, it endows this otherwise featureless part of the city with unexpected charm. ⊠ *4–1–3 Surugadai, Chiyoda-ku* ☎ *03/3291–1885* Ⓜ *Chiyoda subway line, Shin-Ochanomizu Station (Exit B1).*

Tokyo Anime Center 東京アニメセンター. As an information source and exhibitor of images and films, the center attracts tens of thousands of visitors each year. A shop sells a wide range of anime goods that will satisfy even the most ardent of fans. ⊠ *4F UDX Bldg., 4–14–1 Soto-Kanda, Chiyoda-ku* ☎ *03/5298–1188* ⊕ *www.animecenter.jp* ☉ *Tues.–Sun. 11–7* Ⓜ *JR Yamanote Line, Akihabara Station (Akihabara Electric Town Exit).*

☺ **Tokyo Dome City** 東京ドームシティ. The Korakuen stop on the Marun-ouchi subway line, about 10 minutes from Tokyo Station, lets you out in front of the Tokyo Dome, Japan's first air-supported indoor stadium, built in 1988 and home to the Yomiuri Giants baseball team. Across from the stadium is Tokyo Dome City, a combination of family amusement park, shopping mall, restaurants, and a natural-spring spa. The **Baseball Hall of Fame and Museum** (⊕ *www.baseball-museum.or.jp* ⊠ *¥500* ☉ *Mar.–Sept., daily 10–6; Oct.–Feb., daily 10–5)* 野球体育博物館 offers a chance to see some of the bats, balls, and gloves of the legends that made Japanese Pro Baseball the game it is today. **LaQua Amusement Park** (⊠ *Roller-coaster rides ¥600–¥1,000* ☉ *Daily 10–10)* has a stomach-churning roller coaster, a Ferris wheel, and a merry-go-round. The **LaQua Shopping Center** (☉ *Shops daily 11–9; restaurants daily 11–11)* holds more than 50 clothing and beauty shops and restaurants. **LaQua Spa** (⊠ *¥2,565; ¥315 more on holi-days; and ¥1,890 surcharge 1 am–6 am; ¥525 surcharge for Healing Room* ☉ *Daily 11 am–9 am)* is a natural hot spring for adults, more like an amusement park in itself. There are four floors of pampering and hot springs with high concentrations of sodium chloride, which is believed to increase blood circulation. ⊠ *1–3–61 Koraku, Bunkyo-ku* ☎ *03/5800–9999* ⊕ *www.tokyo-dome.co.jp.*

Yushima Seido 湯島 *(Yushima Shrine)*. Akihabara shrines are of minor interest in comparison to the Asakusa Shrine, Yasukuni Shrine, and Meiji Jingu. If you have time to kill, then perhaps a short stroll through this shrine will do. Its origins date to a hall, founded in 1632, for the study of the Chinese Confucian classics. Its headmaster was Hayashi Razan, the official Confucian scholar to the Tokugawa government. Moved to its present site in 1691 (and destroyed by fire and rebuilt six times), the hall became an academy for the ruling elite. In a sense, nothing has changed: in 1872 the new Meiji government established the country's first teacher-training institute here, and that, in turn, evolved into Tokyo University—the graduates of which still make up much of the ruling elite. The hall looks like nothing else you're likely to see in Japan: painted black, weathered, and somber, it could almost be in China. ⊠ *1–4–25 Yushima, Bunkyo-ku* ☎ *03/3251–4606* ⊕ *www.seido. or.jp* ⊠ *Free* ☉ *Weekdays 9–5, weekends 10–5; closed Aug. 13–17 and Dec. 29–31* Ⓜ *Marunouchi subway line, Ochanomizu Station (Exit B2).*

2

UENO 上野

Sightseeing
★★★★☆

Dining
★★★★☆

Lodging
★★★☆☆

Shopping
★★★☆☆

Nightlife
★★☆☆☆

JR Ueno Station is Tokyo's version of the Gare du Nord: the gateway to and from Japan's northeast provinces. Since its completion in 1883, the station has served as a terminus in the great migration to the city by villagers in pursuit of a better life.

Ueno was a place of prominence long before the coming of the railroad. Since Ieyasu Tokugawa established his capital here in 1603, 36 subsidiary temples were erected surrounding the Main Hall, and the city of Edo itself expanded to the foot of the hill where the main gate of the Kan-ei-ji temple once stood.

The Meiji government turned Ueno Hill into one of the nation's first public parks. It would serve as the site of trade and industrial expositions; it would have a national museum, a library, a university of fine arts, and a zoo. The modernization of Ueno still continues, but the park is more than the sum of its museums. The Shogitai warriors failed to take everything with them: some of the most important buildings in the temple complex survived or were restored and should not be missed.

GETTING ORIENTED

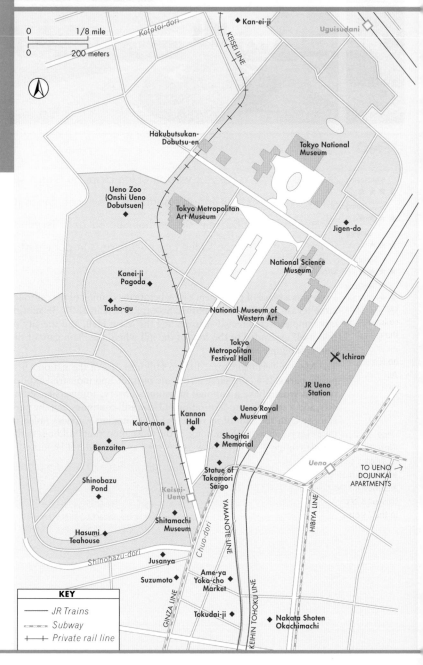

Kan-ei-ji

Uguisudani

Kototoi-dori

KEISEI LINE

0 — 1/8 mile
0 — 200 meters

Hakubutsukan-
Dobutsu-en

Tokyo National
Museum

Ueno Zoo
(Onshi Ueno
Dobutsuen)

Tokyo Metropolitan
Art Museum

Jigen-do

Kanei-ji
Pagoda

National Science
Museum

Tosho-gu

National Museum of
Western Art

Tokyo
Metropolitan
Festival Hall

Ichiran

JR Ueno
Station

Kannon
Hall

Ueno Royal
Museum

Kuro-mon

Shogitai
Memorial

Benzaiten

Statue of
Takamori
Saigo

Ueno

TO UENO
DOJUNKAI
APARTMENTS

Shinobazu
Pond

Keisei-
Ueno

YAMANOTE LINE

HIBIYA LINE

Hasumi
Teahouse

Shitamachi
Museum

Chuo-dori

Shinobazu-dori

Jusanya

Suzumoto

Ame-ya
Yoko-cho
Market

GINZA LINE

Tokudai-ji

KEIHIN TOHOKU LINE

Nakata Shoten
Okachimachi

KEY

—— JR Trains
⬚⬚ Subway
+—+ Private rail line

ORIENTATION

Ueno, along with Asakusa, makes up the historical enclave of Tokyo. Though the Tokyo Sky Tree transmission tower (slated for completion in 2012) can be seen from nearly all parts of these neighborhoods, traditional architecture and way of life are preserved here at the northeastern reaches of the city. Both areas can be explored in a single day, though if you have the time, it's also a good idea to devote an entire day to this place to fully appreciate its many museum exhibits and shrines.

PLANNING

Exploring Ueno can be one excursion or two: an afternoon of cultural browsing or a full day of cultural discoveries in one of the great centers of the city. ■TIP→ **Avoid Monday, when most of the museums are closed.** Ueno out of doors is no fun at all in February or the rainy season (late June–mid-July); mid-August can be brutally hot and muggy. In April, the cherry blossoms of Ueno Koen are glorious.

GETTING HERE AND AROUND

Ueno Station can be accessed by train on the Hibiya Line, Ginza Line, and JR Yamanote Line (Koen Entrance). Be sure to avoid rush hours in the morning (8–9) and evening (6–9) and bring plenty of cash for admission fees to museums and food for the day as finding an ATM may be challenging. Museums accept some major credit cards for admission and in their stores.

TOP REASONS TO GO

All That Art! If you want to explore Tokyo's top museums, then head to Ueno where you'll find the Tokyo National Museum and the National Museum of Western Art.

Shining Shrine. Dating back to 1627, the Tosho-gu Shrine is a National Treasure that houses a priceless collection of historical art and is one of the few remaining early-Edo-period buildings in Tokyo—it survived the 1868 revolt, the 1923 earthquake, and the 1945 bombings. The shrine is under renovation until December 2013 but the grounds are open.

Beautiful Bloom. From mid-June through August, *Shinobazu-ike* (Shinobazu Pond) is the only place in Tokyo where you'll see such a vast expanse of lotus flowers in bloom—the flowers stretch over the entire pond.

QUICK BITES

At Ueno Station is a branch of Japan's most amusing ramen chain. **Ichiran** (⊠ *7–1–1 Ueno*) serves *tonkotsu* (pork broth) noodles. Rather than receiving a menu upon entry, guests are given survey sheets (English forms are available) on which they tick boxes expressing the flavor, appearance, and style they desire in the meal. Then they settle down in a stall with a curtain. Like magic—presto!—the curtain rises and made-to-order steaming bowls appear.

TOP ATTRACTIONS

Ame-ya Yoko-cho Market アメヤ横丁. Not much besides Ueno Station survived the bombings of World War II, and anyone who could make it here from the countryside with rice and other small supplies of food could sell them at exorbitant black-market prices. Sugar was a commodity that couldn't be found at any price in postwar Tokyo. Before long, there were hundreds of stalls in the black market selling various kinds of *ame* (confections), most made from sweet potatoes. These stalls gave the market its name, Ame-ya Yoko-cho (often shortened to Ameyoko), which means "Confectioners' Alley." Shortly before the Korean War, the market was legalized, and soon the stalls were carrying watches, chocolate, ballpoint pens, blue jeans, and T-shirts that had somehow been "liberated" from American PXs. In years to come the merchants of Ameyoko diversified still further—to fine Swiss timepieces and fake designer luggage, cosmetics, jewelry, fresh fruit, and fish. The market became especially famous for the traditional prepared foods of the New Year, and, during the last few days of December, as many as half a million people crowd into the narrow alleys under the railroad tracks to stock up for the holiday. For a break, the area also features numerous small restaurants specializing in raw slices of tuna over rice (*maguro-don*)—cheap, quick, and very good. ⊠ *Ueno 4-chome, Taito-ku* ⊗ *Most shops and stalls daily 10–7* Ⓜ *JR Ueno Station (Hiroko-ji Exit).*

Benzaiten 弁財天. Perched in the middle of Shinobazu Pond, this shrine is dedicated to the goddess Benten, one of the Seven Gods of Good Luck that evolved from a combination of Indian, Chinese, and Japanese mythology. As matron goddess of the arts, she is depicted holding a lute-like musical instrument called a *biwa*. The shrine, which was built by Abbot Tenkai, was destroyed in the bombings of 1945; the present version, with its distinctive octagonal roof, is a faithful copy. You can rent rowboats and pedal boats at a nearby boathouse. ⊠ *2–1 Ueno Koen, Taito-ku* ☎ *03/3828–9502 for boathouse* 🚣 *Rowboats ¥600 for 1 hr, pedal boats ¥600 for 30 mins, swan boats ¥700 for 30 mins* ⊗ *Boathouse daily 9–5* Ⓜ *JR Ueno Station (Koen-guchi/Park Exit); Keisei private rail line, Keisei-Ueno Station (Ikenohata Exit).*

Kannon Hall 清水観音堂 (*Kiyomizu Kannon-do*). This National Treasure was a part of Abbot Tenkai's attempt to build a copy of Kyoto's magnificent Kiyomizu-dera in Ueno. His attempt was honorable, but failed to be as impressive as the original. The principal Buddhist image of worship here is the Senju Kannon (Thousand-Armed Goddess of Mercy). Another figure, however, receives greater homage. This is the Kosodate Kannon, who is believed to answer the prayers of women having difficulty conceiving children. If their prayers are answered, they return to Kiyomizu and leave a doll, as both an offering of thanks and a prayer for the child's health. In a ceremony held every September 25, the dolls that have accumulated during the year are burned in a bonfire. ⊠ *1–29 Ueno Koen, Taito-ku* ☎ *03/3821–4749* 🎟 *Free* ⊗ *Daily 7–5* Ⓜ *JR Ueno Station (Koen-guchi/Park Exit).*

★ **National Museum of Western Art** 国立西洋美術館 (*Kokuritsu Seiyo Bijutsukan*). Along with castings from the original molds of Rodin's *Gate*

The "ame" in Ame-ya Yoko-cho Market also means "American," referencing the many American products sold during the area's black-market era.

of Hell, *The Burghers of Calais,* and *The Thinker,* the wealthy businessman Matsukata Kojiro (1865–1950) acquired some 850 paintings, sketches, and prints by such masters as Renoir, Monet, Gauguin, van Gogh, Delacroix, and Cézanne. Matsukata kept the collection in Europe, but he left it to Japan in his will. The French government sent the artwork to Japan after World War II, and the collection opened to the public in 1959 in a building designed by Swiss-born architect Le Corbusier. Since then, the museum has diversified a bit; more recent acquisitions include works by Reubens, Tintoretto, El Greco, Max Ernst, and Jackson Pollock. The Seiyo is one of the best-organized, most pleasant museums to visit in Tokyo. ⊠ *7–7 Ueno Koen, Taito-ku* ☎ *03/3828–5131* ⊕ *www.nmwa.go.jp* ⊠ *¥420; additional fee for special exhibits* ⊗ *Tues.–Thurs. and weekends 9:30–5:30, Fri. 9:30–8* Ⓜ *JR Ueno Station (Koen-guchi/Park Exit).*

☼ **Shinobazu Pond** 不忍池. Shinobazu was once an inlet of Tokyo Bay. When the area was reclaimed, it became a freshwater pond. Abbot Tenkai, founder of Kan-ei-ji on the hill above the pond, had an island made in the middle of it, which he built for **Benzaiten** (⇨ *above*), the goddess of the arts. Later improvements included a causeway to the island, embankments, and even a racecourse (1884–93). Today the pond is in three sections. The first, with its famous lotus plants, is a wildlife sanctuary. Some 5,000 wild ducks migrate here from as far away as Siberia, sticking around from September to April. The second section, to the north, belongs to Ueno Zoo; the third, to the west, is a small lake for boating. In July, the Ueno *matsuri* (festival) features food stalls and music events in the small at the pond's edge. ⊠ *Shinobazu-dori, Taito-ku*

The Tokyo National Museum offers not only a huge collection of Japanese artifacts, but its buildings are a study in traditional and foreign architecture.

✉ *Free* ☉ *Daily sunrise–sunset* Ⓜ *JR Ueno Station (Koen-guchi/Park Exit); Keisei private rail line, Keisei-Ueno Station (Higashi-guchi/East Exit).*

NEED A BREAK?

Hasumi Teahouse 蓮見茶屋, a charming Japanese teahouse located on the bank of Shinobazu Pond, is only open in summer, when the lotus flowers cover the water. It's an open, airy café that offers perfect views of the lotus flowers in bloom and serves lunch and dinner sets: for lunch, you can get a set of tea and snacks for ¥900; for dinner you can get a set of cold beer and snacks for ¥1,000. English is not spoken, but sets are displayed in plastic models at the entrance to make ordering easier. ✉ *3 Ueno KoenTaito-ku* ☎ *03/3833–0030 (Mon.–Sat.)* ☉ *Early July–late Sept., Thurs.–Tues. noon–9* Ⓜ *Toei Oedo Line, Ueno-Okachi-machi Station (Exit 2); JR Yamanote Line, Ueno Station (Exit 6).*

Tokudai-ji 徳大寺 *(Tokudai Temple).* This is a curiosity in a neighborhood of curiosities: a temple on the second floor of a supermarket. Two deities are worshipped here. One is the bodhisattva Jizo, and the act of washing this statue is believed to safeguard your health. The other is of the Indian goddess Marici, a daughter of Brahma; she is believed to help worshippers overcome difficulties and succeed in business. ✉ *4–6–2 Ueno, Taito-ku* ☎ *03/3831–7926* Ⓜ *JR Yamanote and Keihin-tohoku lines, Okachi-machi Station (Higashi-guchi/East Exit) or Ueno Station (Hiroko-ji Exit).*

Tokyo Metropolitan Art Museum 東京都美術館 *(Tokyo-to Bijutsukan).*
■**TIP→** **At this writing, the museum is closed for renovations until April 2012. Check with the museum for updates.** The museum displays its own collection of modern Japanese art on the lower level and rents out the remaining two floors to various art institutes and organizations. At any given time, there can be a variety of exhibits in the building: international exhibitions, work by local young painters, or new forms and materials in sculpture or modern calligraphy. ⊠ *8–36 Ueno Koen, Taito-ku* ☎ *03/3823–6921* ⊕ *www.tobikan.jp* ✉ *Permanent collection free; fees vary for other exhibits (usually ¥800–¥1,400)* ⊘ *Daily 9–5; closed 3rd Mon. of month* Ⓜ *JR Ueno Station (Koen-guchi/Park Exit).*

Fodor's Choice **Tokyo National Museum** 東京国立博物館 *(Tokyo Kokuritsu Hakubutsu-*
★ *kan).* This complex of four buildings grouped around a courtyard is one of the world's great repositories of East Asian art and archaeology. Altogether, the museum has some 87,000 objects in its permanent collection, with several thousand more on loan from shrines, temples, and private owners.

The Western-style building on the left (if you're standing at the main gate), with bronze cupolas, is the **Hyokeikan.** Built in 1909, it was devoted to archaeological exhibits; aside from the occasional special exhibition, the building is closed today. The larger **Heiseikan,** behind the Hyokeikan, was built to commemorate the wedding of crown prince Naruhito in 1993 and now houses Japanese archaeological exhibits. The second floor is used for special exhibitions.

In 1878, the 7th-century Horyu-ji (Horyu Temple) in Nara presented 319 works of art in its possession—sculpture, scrolls, masks, and other objects—to the Imperial Household. These were transferred to the National Museum in 2000 and now reside in the **Horyu-ji Homotsukan** (Gallery of Horyu-ji Treasures), which was designed by Yoshio Tanigu-chi. There's a useful guide to the collection in English, and the exhibits are well explained. Don't miss the hall of carved wooden *gigaku* (Buddhist processional) masks.

The central building in the complex, the 1937 **Honkan,** houses Japanese art exclusively: paintings, calligraphy, sculpture, textiles, ceramics, swords, and armor. Also here are 84 objects designated by the government as National Treasures. The Honkan rotates the works on display several times during the year. It also hosts two special exhibitions annually (April and May or June, and October and November), which feature important collections from both Japanese and foreign museums. These, unfortunately, can be an ordeal to take in: the lighting in the Honkan is not particularly good, the explanations in English are sketchy at best, and the hordes of visitors make it impossible to linger over a work you especially want to study. As of this writing, more attractive **Toyokan,** to the right of the Honkan, is closed for renovation and is slated to reopen in 2012. Completed in 1968, it is devoted to the art and antiquities of China, Korea, Southeast Asia, India, the Middle East, and Egypt. ⊠ *13–9 Ueno Koen, Taito-ku* ☎ *03/3822–1111* ⊕ *www.tnm.go.jp* ✉ *Regular exhibits ¥600, special exhibits approx. ¥1,500* ⊘ *Tues.–Sun. 9:30–5, times vary during special exhibitions* Ⓜ *JR Ueno Station (Koen-guchi/Park Exit).*

★ **Tosho-gu** 東照宮 (*Tosho Shrine*). ■TIP→ At this writing, the shrine closed for renovations until December 2013, but the outdoor areas are still accessible. This shrine, built in 1627, is dedicated to Ieyasu, the first Tokugawa shogun. It miraculously survived all major disasters that destroyed most of Tokyo's historical structures—the fires, the 1868 revolt, the 1923 earthquake, the 1945 bombings—making it one of the few early-Edo-period buildings left in Tokyo. The shrine and most of its art are designated National Treasures.

Two hundred *ishidoro* (stone lanterns) line the path from the stone entry arch to the shrine itself. One of them, just outside the arch to the left, and more than 18 feet high, is called *obaketoro* (ghost lantern). Legend has it that one night a samurai on guard duty slashed at a ghost (*obake*) that was believed to haunt the lantern. His sword was so strong, it left a nick in the stone, which can be seen today.

The first room inside the shrine is the **Hall of Worship;** the four paintings in gold on wooden panels are by Tan'yu, a member of the famous Kano family of artists, dating from the 15th century. Behind the Hall of Worship, connected by a passage called the *haiden*, is the sanctuary, where the spirit of Ieyasu is said to be enshrined.

The real glory of Tosho-gu is its so-called **Chinese Gate,** at the end of the building, and the fence on either side that has intricate carvings of birds, animals, fish, and shells of every description. The two long panels of the gate, with their dragons carved in relief, are attributed to Hidari Jingoro—a brilliant sculptor of the early Edo period whose real name is unknown (*hidari* means "left"; Jingoro was reportedly left-handed). The lifelike appearance of his dragons has inspired a legend. Every morning they were found mysteriously dripping with water and it was believed that the dragons were sneaking out at night to drink from the nearby Shinobazu Pond. Wire cages were put up to curtail this disquieting habit. ⊠ *9–88 Ueno Koen, Taito-ku* ☎ *03/3822–3455* 🖃 *¥200* ⊙ *Daily 9–5* Ⓜ *JR Ueno Station (Koen-guchi/Park Exit).*

WORTH NOTING

Kan-ei-ji 寛永寺 (*Kan-ei Temple*). In 1638 the second Tokugawa shogun, Hidetada, commissioned the priest Tenkai to build a temple on the hill known as Shinobu-ga-oka in Ueno to defend his city from evil spirits. The only remarkable remaining structure here is the ornately carved vermilion gate to what was the mausoleum of Tsunayoshi, the fifth shogun. Tsunayoshi is famous for his disastrous fiscal mismanagement and his *Shorui Awaremi no Rei* (Edicts on Compassion for Living Things), which, among other things, made it a capital offense for a human being to kill a dog. ⊠ *1–14–11 Ueno Sakuragi, Taito-ku* ☎ *03/3821–1259* 🖃 *Free, contributions welcome* ⊙ *Daily 9–4* Ⓜ *JR Ueno Station (Koen-guchi/Park Exit), JR Uguisudani Station.*

Nakata Shoten Okachimachi 中田商店 御徒町店. This store probably has more shades of green than the average Tokyo park. Stuffed with cargo pants, camouflage jackets, military uniforms, and ammo boxes, Nakata Shoten is more about outfitting its customers in funky fashion than resurrecting Imperial militarism. The watches make interesting souvenirs.

The National Museum of Western Art pays homage to great painters and sculptors from Europe and the United States.

✉ *6–2–14 Ueno, Taito-ku* ☎ *03/3839–6866* ⏱ *Daily 10–8* Ⓜ *JR lines, Okachi-machi Station (North Exit); Toei Oedo subway line, Ueno Okachi-machi Station (Exit A7).*

☪ **National Science Museum** 国立科学博物館 *(Kokuritsu Kagaku Hakubutsukan).* The six buildings of the complex house everything from fossils to moon rocks—the 30-meter (98-foot) model of a blue whale perched at the entrance is a huge hit with kids. And what self-respecting science museum wouldn't have dinosaurs? Look for them in the B2F Exhibition Hall, in the newest annex. Although the museum occasionally outdoes itself with special exhibits, it's pretty conventional and provides few hands-on learning experiences. Kids seem to like it, but this is not a place to linger if your time is short. ✉ *7–20 Ueno Koen, Taito-ku* ☎ *03/3822–0111* ⊕ *www.kahaku. go.jp* 🎫 *¥600; additional fee for special exhibits* ⏱ *Tues.–Sun. 9–5* Ⓜ *JR Ueno Station (Koen-guchi/ Park Exit).*

☪ **Shitamachi Museum** 下町風俗資料館
★ *(Shitamachi Fuzoku Shiryokan).* Japanese society in the days of the Tokugawa shoguns was rigidly stratified. Some 80% of the city's land was allotted to the warrior class, temples, and shrines. The remaining 20%—between Ieyasu's

fortifications on the west, and the Sumida-gawa on the east—was known as *shitamachi*, or "downtown" or the "lower town" (as it expanded, it came to include what today constitutes the Chuo, Taito, Sumida, and Koto wards). It was here that the common, hardworking, free-spending folk, who made up more than half the population, lived. The Shitamachi Museum preserves and exhibits what remained of that way of life as late as 1940.

The two main displays on the first floor are a merchant house and a tenement, intact with all their furnishings. This is a hands-on museum: you can take your shoes off and step up into the rooms. On the second floor are displays of toys, tools, and utensils donated, in most cases, by people who had grown up with them and used them all their lives. There are also photographs and video documentaries of craftspeople at work. Occasionally various traditional skills are demonstrated, and you're welcome to take part. This don't-miss museum makes great use of its space, and there are even volunteer guides (available starting at 10) who speak passable English. ⊠ *2–1 Ueno Koen, Taito-ku* ☎ *03/3823–7451* 🏷 *¥300* ☉ *Tues.–Sun. 9:30–4:30* Ⓜ *JR Ueno Station (Koen-guchi/Park Exit).*

Shogitai Memorial 彰義隊の墓. Time seems to heal wounds quickly in Japan. Only six years after the Shogitai had destroyed most of Ueno Hill in 1868, the Meiji government permitted Tokugawa loyalists to be honored with a gravestone, erected on the spot where their bodies had been cremated. ⊠ *Taito-ku* Ⓜ *JR Ueno Station (Koen-guchi/Park Exit); Keisei private rail line, Keisei-Ueno Station (Higashi-guchi/East Exit).*

Statue of Takamori Saigo 西郷隆盛像. As chief of staff of the Meiji Imperial army, Takamori Saigo (1827–77) played a key role in forcing the surrender of Edo and the overthrow of the shogunate. Ironically, Saigo himself fell out with the other leaders of the new Meiji government and was killed in an unsuccessful rebellion of his own. The sculptor Takamura Koun's bronze, made in 1893, sensibly avoids presenting Saigo in uniform. ⊠ *Taito-ku* Ⓜ *JR Ueno Station (Koen-guchi/Park Exit); Keisei private rail line, Keisei-Ueno Station (Higashi-guchi/East Exit).*

Suzumoto 鈴本演芸場. Originally built around 1857 for Japanese comic-monologue performances called *rakugo* and since rebuilt, the 285-seat Suzumoto is the oldest theater operation of its kind in Tokyo. The theater is on Chuo-dori, a few blocks north of the Ginza Line's Ueno Hiroko-ji stop. For a slice of traditional pop culture, rakugo at Suzumoto is worth seeing, even if you don't understand a word. ⊠ *2–7–12 Ueno, Taito-ku* ☎ *03/3834–5906* 🏷 *¥2,800* ☉ *Continual performances daily 12:30–4:30 and 5:30–8:40* Ⓜ *Ginza subway line, Ueno Hiroko-ji Station (Exit 3).*

Ueno Dojunkai Apartments 上野下アパートメント. The historic Dojunkai apartments comprised one residential block of a series of 16 built in and around Tokyo following the Great Kanto Earthquake of 1923. They featured such innovations as gas lines and trash chutes. In 2006 Tadao Ando's Omotesando Hills complex in Aoyama famously replaced most of the apartments. Few realize, however, that one Dojunkai block still remains. For architecture buffs or the curious, the tiny units are well

CLOSE UP

A Day on the Green

Tokyo has 21 golf courses within its borders and a vast selection beyond city limits. Some are private, but that doesn't always mean nonmembers can't play. Bear in mind that you may pay twice what you would on weekdays for weekends and holidays, and just because facilities are open to tourists doesn't mean they have bilingual staff. Luckily, most have self-service systems or friendly staff. You can book tee times at *Golf in Japan* (⊕ www.golf-in-japan.com), an online guide to the country's courses.
■TIP➔ Most courses rent sets so you don't have to lug yours.

IN TOKYO

Showanomori Golf Course, Akishima. Built during the U.S. occupation, this public course offers wide fairways, a remote-control monorail cart, and some English-speaking staff, but no caddies. ⊠ *1–1–7 Tsutsujigaoka, Akishima* ♟ *18 holes, Par 72* ☎ *042/543–1273* ⛳ *Fees ¥13,000–¥18,000; club rentals ¥2,000* Ⓜ *JR Ome Line, Akishima Station.*

Wakasu Golf Links. If convenience is what you seek, this centrally located public course is for you. Reservations are required, but carts and caddies are optional. (⊠ *3–1–2 Wakasu, Koto-ku* ♟ *18 holes, Par 72* ⛳ *Fees ¥13,475–¥22,745; club rentals ¥3,150* ☎ *03/3522–3221* Ⓜ *Yuraku-cho Line, Shin Kiba Station.*

Yomiuri Golf Club, Inagi. Expect a strict dress code at this private club, which hosts the annual Salonpas World Ladies Championships in May. It's open to the public, you can rent golf carts, and caddies are a must, but don't count on a bilingual staff. ⊠ *3376–1 Yanokuchi, Inagi* ♟ *18 holes, Par 72* ⛳ *Fees*
¥25,200–¥35,700; club rentals ¥5,250 ☎ *044/966–1141* Ⓜ *Odakyu Line Semi Express, Shin Yurigaoka Station.*

OUTSIDE TOKYO

Gotemba and Belle View Nagao golf clubs, Gotemba, Shizuoka. At the foot of Mt. Fuji, these courses will challenge your skills and stamina, especially on foggy days. ⊠ *1924–2 Koyama, Gotemba* ♟ *18 holes, Par 72* ⛳ *Fees ¥5,000 for 9 holes; ¥19,000 for 18 holes; club rentals ¥3,675* ☎ *0550/87–1555* Ⓜ *Odakyu Asagiri Romance car from Shinjuku Station to Gotemba Station, 1 hr and 40 mins.*

Kasumigaura Country Club, Kasumigaura, Ibaraki. Loaded with water hazards and sand traps, this course will make you curse and sweat. The spacious clubhouse, high-end restaurant, and other luxurious facilities will make up for it though. ⊠ *1000 Serizawa Tamatsukuri-machi, Namegata* ♟ *18 holes, Par 72* ⛳ *Fees ¥7,800–¥18,000; club rentals ¥4,200* ☎ *0299/55–2311* Ⓜ *JR Joban from Ueno Station to Ishioka Station, 1 hr, plus taxi (30 mins, ¥6,000) to club.*

DRIVING RANGES

Lottè Kasai Golf. The granddaddy of Tokyo driving ranges sports 300 bays and a 250-yard field. ⊠ *2–4–2 Rinkai-cho, Edogawa-ku* ☎ *03/5658–5600* ⛳ *Varies but about ¥18 per ball; prepaid cards ¥3,000–¥20,000* ☉ *Daily 24 hrs* Ⓜ *JR Keiyo Line, Kasai-Rinkai-Koen Station.*

Meguro Gorufu-jo. There is no weekday wait and an easy-to-navigate self-service system at this driving range. ⊠ *5–6–22 Kami-Meguro, Meguro-ku* ☎ *03/3713–2805* ⛳ *About ¥14 per ball* Ⓜ *Hibiya Line, Naka-Meguro Station).*

2

worth a trip. Don't expect to go inside though; the apartments are occupied so only glimpses of the outside are possible ✉ *5–4 Higashi Ueno, Taito-ku* Ⓜ *Ginza subway line, Inari-cho Station (Exit 3).*

Ueno Royal Museum 上野の森美術館 *(Ueno-no-Mori Bijutsukan).* Although the museum has no permanent collection of its own, it makes its galleries available to various groups, primarily for modern painting and calligraphy. Café Mori is a great place to stop for coffee and cake. ✉ *1–2 Ueno Koen, Taito-ku* ☎ *03/3833–4191* ⊕ *www.ueno-mori.org* 💰 *Prices vary depending on exhibit, but usually ¥300–¥500* ⊙ *Daily 10–5* Ⓜ *JR Ueno Station (Koen-guchi/Park Exit).*

Ⓒ **Ueno Zoo** 上野動物園 *(Ueno Dobutsuen).* First built in 1882, this is Japan's first zoo. Its two main gardens host an exotic mix of more than 900 species of animals. The deaths of its two giant pandas—Tong Tong and Ling Ling—have left the zoo without a large tourist draw, but the tigers from Sumatra, gorillas from the lowland swamp areas of western Africa, and numerous monkeys, some from Japan, make a visit to the East Garden worthwhile. The West Garden is highlighted by rhinos, zebras, and hippopotamuses, and a children's area. The process of the zoo's expansion somehow left within its confines the 120-foot, five-story Kan-ei-ji Pagoda. Built in 1631 and rebuilt after a fire in 1639, the building offers traditional Japanese tea ceremony services. ✉ *9–83 Ueno Koen, Taito-ku* ☎ *03/3828–5171* ⊕ *www.tokyo-zoo.net/zoo/ueno* 💰 *¥600, free on Mar. 20, May 4, and Oct. 1* ⊙ *Tues.–Sun. 9:30–5* Ⓜ *JR Ueno Station (Koen-guchi/Park Exit).*

2

ASAKUSA 浅草

Sightseeing
★★★★☆
Dining
★★★★☆
Lodging
★★★☆☆
Shopping
★★★☆☆
Nightlife
★★☆☆☆

Historically, Asakusa has been the city's entertainment hub. The area blossomed when Ieyasu Tokugawa made Edo his capital and it became the 14th-century city that never slept. For the next 300 years it was the wellspring of almost everything we associate with Japanese culture. In the mid-1600s, it became a pleasure quarter in its own right with stalls selling toys, souvenirs, and sweets; acrobats, jugglers and strolling musicians; and sake shops and teahouses—where the waitresses often provided more than tea. Then, in 1841, the Kabuki theaters moved to Asakusa.

The theaters were here for a short time, but it was enough to establish Asakusa as *the* entertainment quarter of the city—a reputation it held unchallenged until World War II, when most of the area was destroyed. Though it never fully recovered as an entertainment district, the area today is home to artisans and small entrepreneurs, children and grandmothers, hipsters, hucksters, and priests. If you have any time to spend in Tokyo, make sure you devote at least a day to exploring Asakusa.

Asakusa is not merely a shopping district. The Senso-ji Complex is a group of temples and shrines devoted to the goddess Kannon, a Buddhist figure closely associated with compassion. But given Asakusa's long association with the arts and theater, kabuki actors, sumo wrestlers, and geishas all come here to pay their respects at the Senso-ji Main Hall. Many of the original temple structures were destroyed during World War II, so most of what you see was rebuilt in the 1950s, although a few structures—including Asakusa Jinja—survived.

GETTING ORIENTED

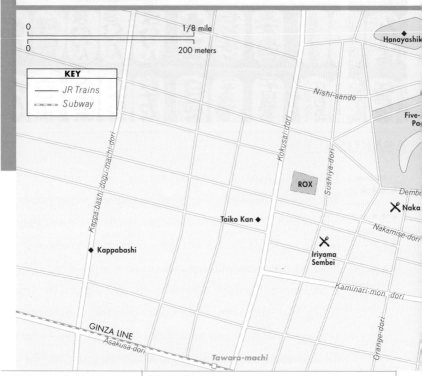

ORIENTATION

Rich in traditional culture, this northeastern area of Tokyo should be top on your list of destinations. Asakusa is a border city ward that separates central Tokyo from its suburban areas. It's a unique spiritual and commercial, tourist, and residential area, where locals walk their dogs on the Asakusa Jinja grounds or give offerings and pray at Kannon Temple. Asakusa is just east of Ueno and can be explored in a half day, whether you go straight from Ueno or on a separate excursion.

PLANNING

Unlike most of the other areas to explore on foot in Tokyo, Senso-ji is admirably compact. You can easily see the temple and environs in a morning. The garden at Dembo-in is worth a half hour. If you decide to include Kappabashi, allow yourself an hour more for the tour. Some of the shopping arcades in this area are covered, but Asakusa is essentially an outdoor experience. Be prepared for rain in June and heat and humidity in July and August.

The Asakusa Tourist Information Center (Asakusa Bunka Kanko Center) is across the street from Kaminari-mon. A volunteer with some English knowledge is on duty here daily 10–5 and will happily load you down with maps and brochures.

2

GETTING HERE AND AROUND

Getting here by subway from Ueno Station (Ginza Line, Ueno Station to Asakusa Station, ¥160) or taxi (approximately ¥900) is most convenient. Asakusa is the last stop (eastbound) on the Ginza line.

Another way get to Asakusa is by river-bus ferry from Hinode Pier, which stops at the southwest corner of Sumida Koen.

QUICK BITES

For a little local flavor, stop at **Iriyama Sembei** (⌧ 1–13–4 Asakusa) for a baked rice cracker. Dried for three days and baked for a few minutes, the soy-dipped snacks are a real treat. Should a cocktail be on your mind, hit up **Bar Six** (⌧ 2–34–3 Asakusa), on the sixth floor of the Amuse Museum, and enjoy the views of the Senso-ji Complex.

TOP REASONS TO GO

Make a Wish. Visit the Asakusa Jinja where the souls of the three men who built Senso-ji are enshrined. If you have a special wish, purchase a wooden placard, write your message on it, and leave it for the gods.

A Japanese Party. Half-naked drunken people? Loud crowds? Brilliant colors? It's all part of the Sanja Festival, which happens every May in the streets of Asakusa.

Photo Op. Want to show your friends that you saw the Thunder God Gate? Then make sure you take a photograph in front of the giant red-paper lantern of Kaminari-mon.

Don't Eat That! Discover the delight of Japanese plastic food in Kappabashi.

Shop 'Til You Drop. Looking for trinkets or gifts to bring home? Visit more than 80 shops on Nakamise-dori that sell everything from rice crackers to *kiriko* (traditionally cut and colored glassware whose style was developed in the Edo period).

Asakusa's heart and soul is the Senso-ji Complex, famous for its 17th-century Shinto shrine, Asakusa Shrine, as well as its garden and the wild Sanja Festival in May.

TOP EXPERIENCES: THE SENSO-JI COMPLEX 浅草寺

Fodor's Choice
★

Dedicated to the goddess Kannon, the **Senso-ji Complex** is the heart and soul of Asakusa. Come for its local and historical importance, its garden, its 17th-century Shinto shrine, and the wild Sanja Festival in May. ✉ *2–3–1 Asakusa, Taito-ku* ☎ *03/3842–0181* ✉ *Free* ⊙ *Temple grounds daily 6–sunset* Ⓜ *Ginza subway line, Asakusa Station (Exit 1/ Kaminari-mon Exit).*

Asakusa Jinja 浅草神社 *(Asakusa Shrine).* Several structures in the Senso-ji temple complex survived the bombings of 1945. The largest, to the right of the Main Hall, is this Shinto shrine to the Hikonuma brothers and their master, Naji-no-Nakamoto—the putative founders of Senso-ji. In Japan, Buddhism and Shintoism have enjoyed a comfortable coexistence since the former arrived from China in the 6th century. The shrine, built in 1649, is also known as Sanja Sama (Shrine of the Three Guardians). Near the entrance to Asakusa Shrine is another survivor of World War II: the east gate to the temple grounds, **Niten-mon,** built in 1618 for a shrine to Ieyasu Tokugawa and designated by the government as an Important Cultural Property. ✉ *2–3–1 Asakusa, Taito-ku* ☎ *03/3844–1575* ⊕ *www.asakusajinja.jp.*

Belfry 時の鐘鐘楼 *(Toki-no-kane Shoro).* The tiny hillock Benten-yama, with its shrine to the goddess of good fortune, is the site of this 17th-century belfry. The bell here used to toll the hours for the people of the district, and it was said that you could hear it anywhere within a radius of some 6 km (4 mi). The bell still sounds at 6 am every day, when the temple grounds open. It also rings on New Year's Eve—108 strokes in all, beginning just before midnight, to "ring out" the 108 sins and frailties of humankind and make a clean start for the coming year. Benten-yama and the belfry are at the beginning of the narrow street that parallels Nakamise-dori. ✉ *Taito-ku.*

NEED A BREAK?

Originally a teahouse, **Waentei-Kikko** 和えん亭 吉幸 is now a cozy, country-style Japanese restaurant and bar. The owner, Fukui Kodai, is a traditional Japanese *Tsugaru Shamisen* (string instrument) musician, who performs at scheduled times throughout the day. Narrow your field of vision, shut out the world outside, and you could be back in the waning days of Meiji-period Japan. This pub specializes in premium sake, with set courses of food and drink for lunch (¥2,500 to ¥3,500) and dinner (¥6,825 to ¥14,175). There's a 10% service charge for dinner. ✉ *2–2–13 Asakusa, Taito-ku* ☎ *03/5828–8833* ⊕ *www.waentei-kikko.com* ⊘ *Thurs.–Tues. 11:30–2 and 5–10* Ⓜ *Ginza subway line, Asakusa Station (Exit 1/Kaminari-mon Exit).*

> **THREE WISE MEN**
>
> The Sanja Festival, held annually over the third weekend of May, is said to be the biggest, loudest, wildest party in Tokyo. Each of the areas in Asakusa has its own mikoshi, and, on the second day of the festival, are paraded through the streets of Asakusa to the shrine. Many of the "parishioners" take part naked to the waist, or with the sleeves of their tunics rolled up, to expose fantastic red-and-black tattoo patterns that sometimes cover their entire backs and shoulders. These are the markings of the Japanese underworld.

★ **Dembo-in** 伝法院 *(Dembo Temple).* Believed to have been made in the 17th century by Kobori Enshu, the genius of Zen landscape design, the garden of Dembo-in, part of the living quarters of the abbot of Senso-ji, is the best-kept secret in Asakusa. The garden of Dembo-in is usually empty and always utterly serene, an island of privacy in a sea of pilgrims. Spring, when the wisteria blooms, is the ideal time to be here.

A sign—you'll find the sign about 150 yards west of the intersection with Naka-mise-dori—in English on Dembo-in-dori leads you to the entrance, which is a side door to a large wooden gate. ■ TIP→ For permission to see the abbot's garden, you must first apply at the temple administration building, between Hozo-mon and the Five-Story Pagoda, in the far corner. ✉ *2–3–1 Asakusa, Taito-ku* ☎ *03/3842–0181 for reservations* ☑ *Free* ⊘ *Daily 9–4; may be closed if abbot has guests* Ⓜ *Ginza subway line, Asakusa Station (Exit 1/Kaminari-mon Exit).*

NEED A BREAK?

Nakase 中瀬. This is a lovely retreat from the overbearing crowds at Asakusa Kannon. The building, which is 130 years old, lends a truly authentic Japanese experience: food is served in lacquerware bento boxes and there are an interior garden and a pond, which is filled with carp and goldfish. Across Orange-dori from the redbrick Asakusa Public Hall, Nakase is expensive (lunch starts at ¥2,625; more elaborate dinner courses top out at ¥14,700), but the experience is worth it. ✉ *1–39–13*

The Dembo Shrine offers a bit of solitude inside the otherwise bustling Senso-ji Complex.

Asakusa, Taito-ku ☎ *03/3841–4015* 🚫 *No credit cards* ⊘ *Wed.–Mon.*
11:30–2 and 5–10, weekends 5–8 Ⓜ *Ginza subway line, Asakusa Station*
(Exit 1/Kaminari-mon Exit).

Kaminari-mon 雷門 *(Thunder God Gate).* This is the proper Senso-ji entrance, with its huge red-paper lantern hanging in the center—a landmark of Asakusa, and picture perfect. The original gate was destroyed by fire in 1865; the replica you see today was built after World War II. Traditionally, two fearsome guardian gods are installed in the alcoves of Buddhist temple gates to ward off evil spirits. The Thunder God (Kaminari-no-Kami) is on the left with the Wind God (Kaze-no-Kami) on the right. ■ TIP➔ **Want to buy some of Tokyo's most famous souvenirs? Stop at Tokiwa-do, the shop on the west side of the gate for *kaminari okoshi* (thunder crackers), made of rice, millet, sugar, and beans.**

Kaminari-mon also marks the southern extent of **Nakamise-dori,** the Street of Inside Shops. The area from Kaminari-mon to the inner gate of the temple was once composed of stalls leased to the townspeople who cleaned and swept the temple grounds. This is now kitsch-souvenir central, so be prepared to buy a few key chains, dolls, and snacks. ✉ *1 Asakusa, Taito-ku* Ⓜ *Ginza subway line, Asakusa Station (Exit 1/ Kaminari-mon Exit).*

Senso-ji Main Hall 浅草観音堂. The Main Hall and Five-Story Pagoda of Senso-ji are both faithful copies in concrete of originals that burned down in 1945. During a time when most of the people of Asakusa were still rebuilding after the fire raids, it took 13 years to raise money for the restoration of their beloved Senso-ji. To them, and those in the entertainment world, this is much more than a tourist attraction: Kabuki actors still come here before a new season of performances, and sumo wrestlers visit before a tournament to pay their respects. The large lanterns in the Main Hall were donated by the geisha associations of Asakusa and nearby Yanagi-bashi. Most Japanese stop at the huge bronze incense burner, in front of the Main Hall, to bathe their hands and faces in the smoke—it's a charm to ward off illnesses—before climbing the stairs to offer their prayers.

The Main Hall, about 115 feet long and 108 feet wide, is not an especially impressive work of architecture. Unlike in many other temples, however, part of the inside has a concrete floor, so you can come and go without removing your shoes. In this area hang Senso-ji's chief claims to artistic importance: a collection of 18th- and 19th-century votive paintings on wood. Plaques of this kind, called *ema,* are still offered to the gods at shrines and temples, but they are commonly simpler and smaller. The worshipper buys a little tablet of wood with the picture already painted on one side and inscribes a prayer on the other. The temple owns more than 50 of these works, which were removed to safety in 1945 to escape the air raids. Only eight of them, depicting scenes from Japanese history and mythology, are on display. A catalog of the collection is on sale in the hall, but the text is in Japanese only.

Lighting is poor in the Main Hall, and the actual works are difficult to see. One thing that visitors cannot see at all is the holy image of Kannon itself, which supposedly lies buried somewhere deep under the temple. Not even the priests of Senso-ji have ever seen it, and there is in fact no conclusive evidence that it actually exists.

Hozo-mon, the gate to the temple courtyard, is also a repository for sutras (Buddhist texts) and other treasures of Senso-ji. This gate, too, has its guardian gods; should either god decide to leave his post for a stroll, he can use the enormous pair of sandals hanging on the back wall—the gift of a Yamagata Prefecture village famous for its straw weaving. ⊠ *2–3–1 AsakusaTaito-ku.*

TOP ATTRACTIONS

☼ ★ **Hanayashiki** 花やしき. Dubbing itself as "the old park with a smile," Hanayashiki, established in 1853, is Tokyo's premier retro amusement park—think Coney Island. A haunted house, Ferris wheel, and merry-go-round await the kids who will likely be a little tired of Asakusa's historic areas. ⊠ *2–28–1 Asakusa, Taito-ku* ☎ *03/3842–8780* ⊕ *www.hanayashiki.net* ⏱ *¥900–¥2,200* ☉ *Daily 10–6, but check schedule for later closing times* Ⓜ *Ginza subway line, Asakusa Station (Exit 1/ Kaminari-mon Exit).*

★ **Kappabashi** かっぱ橋. In the 19th century, according to local legend, a river ran through the present-day Kappabashi district. The surrounding area was poorly drained and was often flooded. A local shopkeeper began a project to improve the drainage, investing all his own money, but met with little success until a troupe of *kappa*—mischievous green water sprites—emerged from the river to help him. A more prosaic explanation for the name of the district points out that the

CLOSE UP

Is That Edible?

The custom of putting models of the food served in the restaurant's windows dates back to the Meiji Restoration period, but the food wasn't always plastic. In fact, the idea first came to Japan from the wax models that were used as anatomical teaching aids in the new schools of Western medicine. A businessman from Nara decided that wax models would also make good point-of-purchase advertising for restaurants. He was right: the industry grew in a modest way at first, making models mostly of Japanese food. In the boom years after 1960, restaurants began to serve all sorts of dishes most people had never seen before, and the models provided much-needed reassurance: "So *that's* a cheeseburger. It doesn't look as bad as it sounds. Let's go in and try one." By the mid-1970s, the makers of plastic food were turning out creations of astonishing virtuosity and realism. If you're looking for what some have deemed a form of pop art, then head to Kappabashi.

lower-ranking retainers of the local lord used to earn extra money by making straw raincoats, also called *kappa*, that they spread to dry on the bridge.

Today, Kappabashi's more than 200 wholesale dealers sell everything the city's restaurant and bar trade could possibly need to do business, from paper supplies and steam tables to the main attraction, plastic food. It is baffling to most Japanese that Kappabashi is a hot tourist attraction. ⊠ *Nishi-Asakusa 1-chome and 2-chome, Taito-ku* ⊙ *Most shops daily 9–6* Ⓜ *Ginza subway line, Tawara-machi Station (Exit 1).*

WORTH NOTING

☺ **Taiko Kan** 太皷館 *(Drum Museum).* Become a *taiko* (drum) master for a day as you pound away on the exhibits at this fourth-floor museum dedicated to traditional Japanese and foreign drums. More than 200 instruments can be played, making it a great place for kids. Just make sure their hands remain off the antique instruments, which are carefully marked. Should you feel inspired, there is a shop on the ground floor of the same building that sells various Japanese drums and festival accessories, which make great souvenirs. ⊠ *2–1–1 Asakusa, Taito-ku* ☎ *03/3842–5622* ⊞ *¥300* ⊙ *Wed.–Sun. 10–5* Ⓜ *Ginza subway line, Tawara-machi Station.*

2

TSUKIJI 築地 AND SHIODOME 汐留

Sightseeing
★★★☆☆
Dining
★★★★☆
Lodging
★★★★☆
Shopping
★★★☆☆
Nightlife
★★☆☆☆

Although it's best known today as the site of the largest wholesale fish market in the world, Tsukiji is also a reminder of the awesome disaster of the great fire of 1657. In the space of two days, it killed more than 100,000 people and leveled almost 70% of Ieyasu Tokugawa's new capital. Ieyasu was not a man to be discouraged by mere catastrophe, however; he took it as an opportunity to plan an even bigger and better city, one that would incorporate the marshes east of his castle. Tsukiji, in fact, means "reclaimed land," and a substantial block of land it was, laboriously drained and filled, from present-day Ginza to the bay.

To the west of Tsukiji lies Shiodome (literally "where the tide stops"), an area of saltwater flats on which in 1872 the Meiji government built the Tokyo terminal—the original Shimbashi Station—on Japan's first railway line. By 1997, long after the JR had run out of use for the land, an urban renewal plan for the area evolved, and the land was auctioned off. Among the buyers were Nippon Television and Dentsu, the largest advertising agency in Asia.

In 2002 Dentsu consolidated its scattered offices into the centerpiece of the Shiodome project: a 47-story tower and annex designed by Jean Nouvel. With the annex, known as the Caretta Shiodome, Dentsu created an "investment in community": a complex of cultural facilities, shops, and restaurants that has turned Shiodome into one of the most fashionable places in the city. The 1,200-seat Dentsu Shiki Theater SEA here has become one of Tokyo's major venues for live performances; its resident repertory company regularly brings long-running Broadway hits to eager Japanese audiences.

GETTING ORIENTED

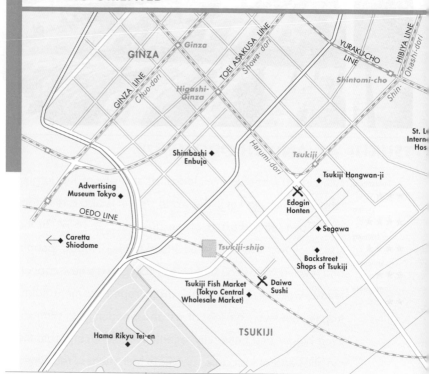

ORIENTATION

Shiodome is the southeastern transportation hub of central Tokyo. Tsukiji is a sushi-lover's dream. Perhaps getting up at 5 am to eat fish at the market isn't your idea of breakfast, but this is definitely an excellent place taste the freshest sushi on Earth, located just east of Shiodome.

PLANNING

Tsukiji has few places to spend time *in*; getting from point to point, however, can consume most of a morning. The backstreet shops will probably require no more than an hour. Allow yourself about an hour to explore the fish market; if fish in all its diversity holds a special fascination for you, take two hours. Remember that in order to see the fish auction in action, you need to get to the market before 6:30 am; by 9 am the business of the market is largely finished for the day. Sushi and sashimi will be cheaper here than in other parts of Tokyo, with sushi sets at most sushi stalls costing between ¥1,000 to ¥2,100.

This part of the city can be brutally hot and muggy in August; during the O-bon holiday, in the middle of the month, Tsukiji is comparatively lifeless. Mid-April and early October are best for strolls in the Hama Rikyu Tei-en.

MINATO

Luke's national spital

Sumida-gawa

◆ Tsukugen

TSUKUDA-JIMA

TSUKI-SHIMA

Tsukishima

KEY

Subway

GETTING HERE AND AROUND

Shidome's easily accessed by public transport: JR lines and Yurikamome Line at Shimbashi Station, Toei Oedo Line to Shiodome Station, and Asakusa Line and Ginza Line to Shimbashi Station. The connection station to the Yurikamome Monorail, a scenic ride that takes you to Odaiba in approximately 30 minutes, is also here. You can also get around quite easily on foot. There are elevated walkways that connect all the major buildings and subway and train stations.

To visit the fish market, take the subway to Tsukiji Station, which will always be the more dependable and cost-efficient option.

QUICK BITES

After traipsing through the fish market, a sushi breakfast is a great idea. **Daiwa Sushi** (✉ 5–2–1 *Tsukiji*) offers delicious course menus starting around ¥2,000. Grab a counter seat and let the chef serve what might be the freshest raw tuna in town. Lines can be long, but the wait is worth it.

TOP REASONS TO GO

Urban Oasis. Discover a lovely traditional garden oasis and old teahouse surrounded by skyscrapers and concrete at Hama Rikyu Tei-en.

Got Fish? You'll dine on the freshest sushi in the world at Tsukiji fish market.

Off the Beaten Path. Discover the local charm of old sushi and sashimi restaurants, and small markets in the backstreets of Tsukiji.

Ads as Art. Get a glimpse at ad formats, from radio to magazines, dating back to the Edo period (1603–1867) at the Advertising Museum Tokyo.

TOP ATTRACTIONS

Advertising Museum Tokyo アド・ミュージアム東京. ADMT puts the unique Japanese gift for graphic and commercial design into historical perspective, from the sponsored "placements" in 18th-century wood-block prints to the postmodern visions of fashion photographers and video directors. The museum is maintained by a foundation established in honor of Hideo Yoshida, fourth president of the mammoth Dentsu Advertising Company, and includes a digital library of some 130,000 entries on everything you ever wanted to know about hype. There are no explanatory panels in English—but this in itself is a testament to how well the visual vocabulary of consumer media can communicate across cultures. ⊠ *B1F–B2F Caretta Shiodome, 1–8–2 Higashi-Shimbashi, Chuo-ku* ☎ *03/6218–2500* ⊕ *www.admt.jp* 🚇 *Free* ☉ *Tues.–Fri. 11–6:30, weekends 11–4:30* Ⓜ *Toei Oedo subway line, Shiodome Station (Exit 7); JR (Shiodome Exit) and Asakusa and Ginza lines (Exit 4), Shimbashi Station.*

Fodor'sChoice ★ **Backstreet shops of Tsukiji** 築地6丁目. Tokyo's markets provide a vital counterpoint to the museums and monuments of conventional sightseeing: they let you see how people really live in the city. If you have time for only one market, this is the one to see. The three square blocks between the Tokyo Central Wholesale Market and Harumi-dori have, naturally enough, scores of fishmongers, but also shops and restaurants. Stores sell pickles, tea, crackers and snacks, cutlery (what better place to pick up a professional sushi knife?), baskets, and kitchenware. Hole-in-the-wall sushi bars here have set menus ranging from ¥1,000 to ¥2,100; look for the plastic models of food in glass cases out front. The area includes the row of little counter restaurants, barely more than street stalls, under the arcade along the east side of Shin-Ohashi-dori, each with its specialty. If you haven't had breakfast by this point in your walk, stop at **Segawa** for *maguro donburi*—a bowl of fresh raw tuna slices served over rice and garnished with bits of dried seaweed (Segawa is in the middle of the arcade, but without any distinguishing features or English signage; your best bet is to ask someone). ■TIP→ **Some 100 of the small retailers and restaurants in this area are members of the Tsukiji Meiten-kai (Association of Notable Shops) and promote themselves by selling illustrated maps of the area for ¥50; the maps are all in Japanese, but with proper frames they make great souvenirs.** ⊠ *Tsukiji 4-chome, Chuo-ku* Ⓜ *Toei Oedo subway line, Tsukiji-shijo Station (Exit A1); Hibiya subway line, Tsukiji Station (Exit 1).*

★ **Hama Rikyu Tei-en** 浜離宮庭園 *(Detached Palace Garden)*. Like a tiny sanctuary of Japanese tradition and nature that's surrounded by towering glass buildings, this garden is worth a visit. The land here was originally owned by the Owari branch of the Tokugawa family from Nagoya, and it extended to part of what is now the fish market. When one of the family became shogun in 1709, his residence was turned into a shogunal palace—with pavilions, ornamental gardens, pine and cherry groves, and duck ponds. The garden became a public park in 1945, although a good portion of it is fenced off as a nature preserve. None of the original buildings have survived, but on the island in the

Join the throngs of people waiting for a fresh sushi breakfast at the Tsukiji Fish Market.

large pond is a reproduction of the pavilion where former U.S. president Ulysses S. Grant and Mrs. Grant had an audience with the emperor Meiji in 1879. The building can now be rented for parties. The stone linings of the saltwater canal work and some of the bridges underwent a restoration project that was completed in 2009. The path to the left as you enter the garden leads to the "river bus" ferry landing, from which you can leave this excursion and begin another: up the Sumidagawa to Asakusa. ⚠ Note that you must pay the admission to the garden even if you're just using the ferry. ✉ *1–1 Hamarikyu–Teien, Chuo-ku* ☎ *03/3541–0200* 💴 *¥300* 🕐 *Daily 9–4:30* Ⓜ *Toei Oedo subway line, Shiodome Station (Exit 8).*

★ **Tsukiji Fish Market** 中央卸売市場 *(Tokyo Metropolitan Central Wholesale Market, Tsukiji Shijo).* The city's fish market used to be farther uptown, in Nihombashi. It was moved to Tsukiji after the Great Kanto Earthquake of 1923, and it occupies the site of what was once Japan's first naval training academy. Today the market sprawls over some 54 acres of reclaimed land and employs approximately 15,000 people, making it the largest fish market in the world. Its warren of buildings houses about 1,200 vendors, supplying 90% of the seafood (and some of the vegetables, meat, and fruit) consumed in Tokyo every day—some 2,000 metric tons of it. Most of the seafood sold in Tsukiji comes in by truck, arriving through the night from fishing ports all over the country. ⇨ *For more information see the feature in Chapter 3, Where to Eat.* ✉ *5–2–1 Tsukiji, Chuo-ku* ☎ *03/3542–1111* ⊕ *www.shijou.metro. tokyo.jp* 💴 *Free* 🕐 *Business hrs Mon.–Sat. (except 2nd and 4th Wed.*

Cherry blossoms bloom at Hama Rikyu garden.

of month) 5 am–3 pm Ⓜ *Toei Oedo subway line, Tsukiji-shijo Station (Exit A1); Hibiya subway line, Tsukiji Station (Exit 1).*

WORTH NOTING

Caretta Shiodome. This 51-story skyscraper houses the offices of advertising giant Dentsu, as well as other offices, restaurants, and shops. The sky restaurants on the building's top floors have scenic views of Tokyo Bay and are a good place to have lunch or dinner. Try **Bice Tokyo** (☎ *03/5537–1926* ⊕ *www.bicetokyo.com* ⊘ *Weekdays lunch 11:30–3:30, dinner 5:30–11:30*) on the 47th floor, which serves a European set lunch (¥3,675) and dinner (¥9,450) menus. ✉ *1–8–1 Higashi-Shimbashi, Minato-ku* ⊕ *www.caretta.jp* ⊘ *Daily 11–8.*

Tsukiji Hongan-ji 築地本願寺 *(Tsukiji Hongan Temple).* Disaster seemed to follow this temple, which is an outpost of Kyoto's Nishi Hongwan-ji. Since it was first located here in 1657, it was destroyed at least five times, and reconstruction in wood was finally abandoned after the Great Kanto Earthquake of 1923. The present stone building dates from 1935. It was designed by Chuta Ito, a pupil of Tokyo Station architect Tatsuno Kingo. Ito's other credits include the Meiji Shrine in Harajuku; he also lobbied for Japan's first law for the preservation of historic buildings. Ito traveled extensively in Asia; the evocations of classical Hindu architecture in the temple's domes and ornaments were his homage to India as the cradle of Buddhism. But with stained-glass windows and a pipe organ as well, the building is nothing if not eclectic. Talks in English are held on the third Saturday of the month at 5:30. ✉ *3–15–1 Tsukiji, Chuo-ku* ☎ *03/3541–1131* ⊕ *www.tsukijihongwanji.*

CLOSE UP

Cruising Like a Samurai

As during the time of the samurai, cruising in a roof-topped boat, or *yakatabune*, is the perfect means to relax amid bursting fireworks or cherry blossoms. The charm remains intact: guests are treated like royalty and are entertained while floating on the gentle waves of the Sumida or Arakawa River. Hosts within the cabin serve multiple courses of tempura and sushi and pour beer and whiskey while the boats cruise past historic bridges and along the riverbanks that make up the bay front. When the shoji (paper blinds) are opened, panoramic views of the illuminated Tokyo nightscape are a sight to behold. Observation decks offer even better viewing opportunities.

Harumiya, whose servers speak English, is a popular yakatabune company. Their boats accommodate groups of 20 to 350 and tours are run day and night, year-round. Nighttime is the best time to take a ride because of the nightscape view. Spring features the cherry blossoms in bloom; in summer, catch a break from the sweltering heat; and winter is when the year-end parties are in full swing. There are launch locations on the bay and the Arakawa River. ✉ *6–17–12 Higashisuna, Koto-ku* ☎ *03/3644–1344* ⊕ *www.harumiya. co.jp* 🍴 *Around ¥10,000 per person for 2 hrs of touring* Ⓜ *Tozai subway line, Minamisuna-cho Station (East Exit).*

2

jp 🍴 *Free* ⊗ *Daily services at 7 am and 4 pm* Ⓜ *Hibiya subway line, Tsukiji Station (Exit 1).*

NEED A BREAK?

Edogin Honten. One of the area's older sushi bars, founded in 1924, it is legendary for its portions—slices of raw fish that almost hide the balls of rice on which they sit. The set menu at lunch is a certifiable bargain, ranging between ¥1,050 and ¥1,470, and sushi dinner sets start at ¥3,700. Take note: it's often jam-packed. For access, walk southwest on Shin-Ohashi-dori from its intersection with Harumi-dori. Take the first right and look for Edogin just past the next corner, on the left. ✉ *4–5–1 Tsukiji, Chuo-ku* ☎ *03/3543–4401* ▭ *AE, MC, V* ⊗ *Closed early Jan.* Ⓜ *Hibiya subway line, Tsukiji Station (Exit 1); Toei Oedo subway line, Tsukiji-shijo Station (Exit A1).*

NIHOMBASHI日本橋, GINZA
銀座, AND MARUNOUCHI 丸の内

Sightseeing
★★☆☆☆

Dining
★★★★☆

Lodging
★★★★★

Shopping
★★★★★

Nightlife
★★★★☆

Tokyo is a city of many centers. The municipal administrative center is in Shinjuku. The national government center is in Kasumigaseki. Nihombashi is the center of banking and finance, and Ginza is the center of commerce.

When Ieyasu Tokugawa had the first bridge constructed at Nihombashi, he designated it the starting point for the five great roads leading out of his city, the point from which all distances were to be measured. His decree is still in force: the black pole on the present bridge, erected in 1911, is the Zero Kilometer marker for all the national highways and is considered the true center of Tokyo.

When Japan's first corporations were created and the Meiji government developed a modern system of capital formation, the Tokyo Stock Exchange (Shoken Torihikijo) was established on the west bank of the Nihombashi-gawa (Nihombashi River). The home offices of most of the country's major securities companies are nearby.

In the Edo period there were three types of currency in circulation: gold, silver, and copper. Ieyasu Tokugawa started minting his own silver coins in 1598 in his home province of Suruga, even before he became shogun. In 1601 he established a gold mint on the site of what is now the Bank of Japan. In 1612 he relocated the Suruga plant to a patch of reclaimed land west of his castle. The area soon came to be known informally as Ginza (Silver Mint).

Marunouchi lies west of Tokyo Station and extends between Hibiya Park and the Outer Garden of the Imperial Palace. In the late 19th century, Iwasaki Yanosuke, the second president of Mitsubishi Corporation, bought the land. Today it houses numerous office and retail complexes and the headquarters of various companies within the Mitsubishi group.

The clock atop Ginza's Wako department store commemorates the Hattori Clock Tower, which stood at the same location from 1894 to 1921.

TOP ATTRACTIONS

Bridgestone Museum of Art ブリヂストン美術館 *(Burijisuton Bijutsukan)*. This is one of Japan's best private collections of French impressionist art and sculpture and of post-Meiji Japanese painting in Western styles by such artists as Shigeru Aoki and Tsuguji Fujita. The collection, assembled by Bridgestone Tire Company founder Shojiro Ishibashi, also includes works by Rembrandt, Picasso, Utrillo, and Modigliani. The small gallery devoted to ancient art has a breathtaking Egyptian *Sacred Cat* sculpture dating to between 950 and 660 bc. The Bridgestone also puts on major exhibits from private collections and museums abroad. ⊠ *1–10–1 Kyo-bashi, Chuo-ku* ☎ *03/3563–0241* ⊕ *www.bridgestone-museum.gr.jp* 🖼 *¥1,000* 🕙 *Tues.–Sat. 10–8, Sun. 10–6 (entrance up to 30 mins before closing)* Ⓜ *Ginza subway line, Kyo-bashi Station (Meijiya Exit) or Nihombashi Station (Takashimaya Exit).*

Ginza 銀座. With more history as a shopping district than trendier Omotesando and Harajuku, Ginza is where high-end shopping first took root in Japan, but the area has yielded somewhat to the "fast fashion" of midlevel clothing chains. Yet even before this shift, Ginza didn't always have the cachet of wealth and style. In fact, it wasn't until a fire in 1872 destroyed most of the old houses here that the area was rebuilt as a Western quarter. It had two-story brick houses with balconies, the nation's first sidewalks and horse-drawn streetcars, gaslights, and, later, telephone poles. Before the turn of the 20th century, Ginza was home to the great mercantile establishments that still define its character. The **Wako** department store, for example, on the northwest corner of the

GETTING ORIENTED

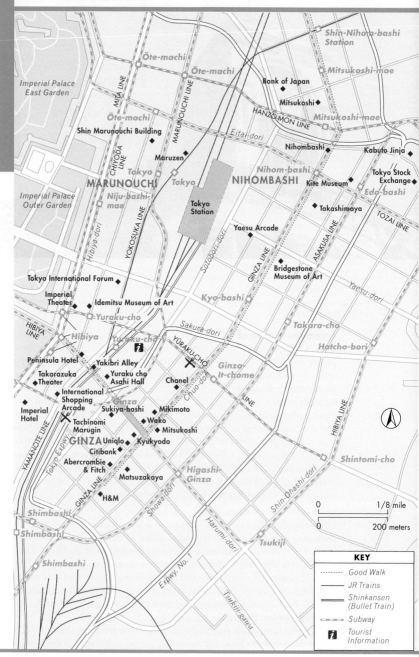

Shin-Nihom-bashi
Station

Ōte-machi

Ōte-machi

Mitsukoshi-mae

*Imperial Palace
East Garden*

MITA LINE

MARUNOUCHI LINE

Bank of Japan

Mitsukoshi ◆

HANZO-MON LINE

Ōte-machi

Mitsukoshi-mae

Shin Marunouchi Building ◆

CHIYODA LINE

Eitai-dori

Nihombashi ◆

Kabuto Jinja ◆

Maruzen ◆

Tokyo

Nihom-bashi

Tokyo Stock
Exchange ◆

MARUNOUCHI

Tokyo

NIHOMBASHI

Kite Museum ◆

Edo-bashi

*Imperial Palace
Outer Garden*

Niju-bashi-
mae

YOKOSUKA LINE

Tokyo
Station

Takashimaya ◆

TOZAI LINE

Hibiya-dori

Yaesu Arcade ◆

GINZA LINE

ASAKUSA LINE

Sotobori-dori

Bridgestone
Museum of Art ◆

Yaesu-dori

Tokyo International Forum ◆

Imperial
Theater ◆

◆ Idemitsu Museum of Art

Kyo-bashi

HIBIYA
LINE

Yuraku-cho

Sakura-dori

Takara-cho

Hibiya

Yuraku-cho

YŪRAKU-CHO

Hatcho-bori

Peninsula Hotel ◆

Yakibri Alley ◆

Ginza-
It-chome

Chuo-dori

Takarazuka
Theater ◆

◆ Yuraku cho
Asahi Hall

Chanel ◆

HIBIYA LINE

International
Shopping ◆
Arcade

Sukiya-bashi ◆

Mikimoto ◆

Imperial
Hotel ◆

Tachinomi ◆
Marugin

GINZA

◆ Wako

Mitsukoshi ◆

Shintomi-cho

Uniqlo ◆ Kyukyodo ◆

Citibank ◆

Abercrombie ◆
& Fitch

Higashi-
Ginza

Matsuzakaya ◆

GINZA LINE

Showa-dori

H&M ◆

Shimbashi

Shin-Ohashi-dori

Harumi-dori

0 ──────── 1/8 mile

0 ──────── 200 meters

Shimbashi

Shimbashi

Tsukiji

Expwy. No. 1

Tsukiji-gawa

KEY	
┈┈┈┈	*Good Walk*
────	*JR Trains*
════	*Shinkansen (Bullet Train)*
⊏⊐⊏⊐	*Subway*
🛈	*Tourist Information*

PLANNING

There's something about this part of Tokyo—the traffic, the crowds, the way it urges you to keep moving—that can make you feel you've covered more ground than you really have. Attack this area early in the morning but avoid rush hour (8–9) if you plan on taking the subway. None of the area's sites, with the possible exception of the Bridgestone and Idemitsu museums, should take you more than 45 minutes; the time you spend shopping is up to you. In summer start early or in the late afternoon, because by midday the heat and humidity can be brutal. On weekend afternoons (October–March, Saturday 3–5 and Sunday noon–5; April–September, Saturday 2–6 and Sunday noon–6), Chuo-dori is closed to traffic from Shimbashi to Kyo-bashi and becomes a pedestrian mall with tables and chairs set out along the street. Note that some museums and other sights in the area close Sunday.

TOP REASONS TO GO

A Yen for Yen. See where the history of the yen began, in the Bank of Japan and Currency Museum.

Japanese Impressions. Go to the Bridgestone Museum of Art, one of Japan's best private collections of French Impressionist art and post-Meiji Japanese painting in Western styles.

Tang and Song. The Idemitsu Museum of Art houses a collection of Tang- and Song-dynasty Chinese porcelain and Japanese ceramics. Also on display are masterpieces of Old Seto, Oribe, Old Kutani, Karatsu, and Kakiemon ware.

A Leisurely Stroll. On weekends, see the historic Wako department store, and explore the small side streets of this old shopping district without fear of traffic.

Feeding Frenzy. Check out the basement food halls in Mitsukoshi department store in Nihombashi and Ginza, where you will find hundreds of delicious desserts and prepared foods.

ORIENTATION

The combined areas of Marun-ouchi, Ginza, and Nihombashi are located beside the Imperial Palace district, to the southeast of central Tokyo. Marunouchi lies west of Tokyo Station and extends between Hibiya Park and the Outer Garden of the Imperial Palace.

GETTING HERE AND AROUND

To access Marunouchi, multiple north-south-running JR lines run between Tokyo and Yurakucho stations (¥130). The Yuraku-cho subway line, too, rolls through from Nagata-cho and Shin Kiba. To the east, the Ginza and Hibiya subway lines stop at Ginza Station. Slightly north is Nihombashi, which is also on the Ginza Line and only a few minutes from the bustling Ote-machi Station on the Tozai Line (¥160). By walking west from Yuraku-cho, Hibiya Park is reachable in five minutes. So is Ginza, in the opposite direction.

QUICK BITES

The Ginza corridor, which is surrounded on three sides by a freeway, is one of Tokyo's more lively areas. An ideal place inside this area for a short stop is the yakitori (grilled chicken) restaurant **Tachinomi Marugin** (✉ *7–1–105 Ginza*). Skewered chicken breasts, small salads, and sausages are sure to put a smile on the face of even the weariest shopper.

4-chome intersection, established itself here as Hattori, purveyors of clocks and watches. The clock on the present building was first installed in the Hattori clock tower, a Ginza landmark, in 1894.

Many of the nearby shops have lineages almost as old, or older, than Wako's. A few steps north of the intersection, on Chuo-dori, **Mikimoto** sells the famous cultured pearls first developed by Kokichi Mikimoto in 1883. His first shop in Tokyo dates to 1899. South of the intersection, next door to the San-ai Building, **Kyukyodo** carries a variety of hand-made Japanese papers and traditional stationery goods. Kyukyodo has been in business since 1663 and on Ginza since 1880. Across the street and one block south is the **Matsuzakaya** department store, which began as a kimono shop in Nagoya in 1611. And connected to the Ginza Line Ginza Station is the **Mistukoshi** department store, where the basement food markets are a real attraction. Stores like **H&M** and **Uniqlo** offer simple jeans and T-shirts to those seeking less traditional wares.

There's even a name for browsing this area: Gin-bura, or "Ginza wandering." The best times to wander here are Saturday afternoons and Sunday from noon to 5 or 6 (depending on the season), when Chuo-dori is closed to traffic between Shimbashi and Kyo-bashi. ⊠ *Chuo-ku* Ⓜ *Ginza and Hibiya subway lines, Ginza Station.*

★ **Idemitsu Museum of Art** 出光美術館 *(Idemitsu Bijutsukan)*. The strength of the collection in these four spacious, well-designed rooms lies in the Tang- and Song-dynasty Chinese porcelain and in the Japanese ceramics—including works by Nonomura Ninsei and Ogata Kenzan. On display are masterpieces of Old Seto, Oribe, Old Kutani, Karatsu, and Kakiemon ware. The museum also houses outstanding examples of Zen painting and calligraphy, wood-block prints, and genre paintings of the Edo period. Of special interest to scholars is the resource collection of shards from virtually every pottery-making culture of the ancient world. The museum is on the ninth floor of the Teikoku Gekijo building, which looks down upon the lavish Imperial Garden. ⊠ *3–1–1 Marunouchi, Chiyoda-ku* ☎ *03/3213–9402* 💴 *¥1,000* 🕐 *Tues.–Thurs. and weekends 10–5, Fri. 10–7* Ⓜ *Yuraku-cho subway line, Yuraku-cho Station (Exit A1).*

★ **Mitsukoshi** 三越. Takatoshi Mitsui made his fortune by revolutionizing the retail system for kimono fabrics. The emergence of Mitsukoshi as Tokyo's first *depato* (department store), also called *hyakkaten* (hundred-kinds-of-goods emporium), actually dates to 1908, with the construction of a three-story Western building modeled on Harrods of London. This was replaced in 1914 by a five-story structure with Japan's first escalator. The present flagship store is vintage 1935. Even if you don't plan to shop, this branch merits a visit. Two bronze lions, modeled on those at London's Trafalgar Square, flank the main entrance and serve as one of Tokyo's best-known meeting places. Inside, a sublime statue of Magokoro, a Japanese goddess of sincerity, rises four stories through the store's central atrium. Check out the basement floors for a taste of the food-market culture of Japanese department stores and grab a quick meal-to-go while you're there. Delicious local and international prepared food is sold here at premium prices: intricately designed *mochi*

The Tokyo International Forum's glass atrium is the centerpiece of this arts- and culture-oriented building.

(sweet red bean) cakes, Japanese bento boxes, sushi sets, and square watermelons all sell for approximately ¥10,000. ⊠ *1–4–1 Nihombashi Muro-machi, Chuo-ku* ☎ *03/3241–3311* ⊕ *www.mitsukoshi.co.jp* ☯ *Daily 10–7, basements until 8* Ⓜ *Ginza and Hanzo-mon subway lines, Mitsukoshi-mae Station (Exits A3 and A5).*

Sukiya-bashi 数寄屋橋. The side streets of the Sukiya-bashi area are full of art galleries, which operate a bit differently here than they do in most of the world's art markets. A few, like the venerable **Nichido** (⊠ *5–3–16 Ginza*), **Gekkoso** (⊠ *7–2–8 Ginza*), **Yoseido** (⊠ *5–5–15 Ginza*), and **Kabuto-ya** (⊠ *8–8–7 Ginza*), actually function as dealers, representing particular artists, as well as acquiring and selling art. The majority, however, are rental spaces. Artists or groups pay for the gallery by the week, publicize their shows themselves, and in some cases even hang their own work. You might suspect, and with good reason, that some of these shows are vanity exhibitions by amateurs with money to spare, even in a prestigious venue like Ginza; thankfully, that's not always the case. ⊠ *Chiyoda-ku* Ⓜ *Ginza, Hibiya, and Marunouchi subway lines, Ginza Station (Exit C4).*

★ **Tokyo International Forum** 東京国際フォーラム. This postmodern masterpiece, the work of Uruguay-born American architect Raphael Viñoly, is the first major convention and art center of its kind in Tokyo. Viñoly's design was selected in a 1989 competition that drew nearly 400 entries from 50 countries. The plaza of the Forum is that rarest of Tokyo rarities: civilized open space. There's a long central courtyard with comfortable benches shaded by trees. Freestanding sculpture, triumphant architecture, and people strolling are all here. The first and third Sunday

A GOOD WALK: NIHOMBASHI AND GINZA

Tokyo's east side routinely plays second fiddle to the trendier and hipper areas out west. That, however, shouldn't stop you from wandering through the ever-changing streets of Nihombashi and Ginza.

NIHOMBASHI

Nihombashi was the commercial center of Tokyo during the Edo Period. For a peek at a company that started during that time, enter Mitsukoshi department store, which is the original outlet in this venerable chain. Check out the massive supermarket in the basement—perfect for a snack to take with you. From there head south on Chuo-dori to the Nihombashi Bridge, which was build during the Edo period to be the origin of five national highways. Unfortunately, it is also well known for being obscured by an overhead freeway built for the 1964 Olympics. A few more minutes south is the Bridgestone Museum of Art.

GINZA

Farther south the intersection of Harumi-dori and Chuo-dori will be swamped with visitors on weekends, when he area becomes as a pedestrian mall (known as a Pedestrian Paradise) and benches and umbrellas spring up in the street. Historically Ginza has been regarded Tokyo's ritziest area, and it still is, but the landscape has changed. Yes, Wako (identifiable by the large clock on top) still has its legendary luxury-goods store positioned proudly at the intersection, but retailers like Uniqlo and Abercrombie & Fitch have opened outlets a bit farther south.

CHICKEN UNDER THE TRACKS

Move back up at the intersection, turn left, and keep going until you pass beneath the large freeway overpass. Off to the right is the Yuraku-cho Mullion Building, which includes the Yuraku-cho Asahi Hall film theater—a great place to catch a Japanese or imported movie. Hungry? Stop in at one of the *yakitori* restaurants in Yakatori Alley, the area underneath railroad tracks running next to the Mullion.

HIBIYA PARK

If tea is more on your mind, stop in the lobby of Peninsula Hotel for the famous Peninsula Traditional Afternoon Tea. When finished, cross Hibiya-dori. Hibiya Park, which was converted from a military facility over 100 years ago, is off to the left. Nearly each weekend, the park hosts a festival, fair, or music event. Cap off the day with a stroll through its meandering paths while viewing its ponds, greenery, and fountain.

of each month feature an antiques flea market in the plaza's courtyard. The Forum itself is actually two buildings. On the east side of the plaza is Glass Hall, the main exhibition space, and the west building has six halls for international conferences, exhibitions, receptions, and concert performances. Transit fans should take a stroll up the catwalks to the top, which concludes with a view of the Tokyo Station JR lines. ✉ *3–5–1 Marunouchi, Chiyoda-ku* ☎ *03/5221–9000* ⊕ *www.t-i-forum. co.jp* Ⓜ *Yuraku-cho subway line, Yuraku-cho Station (Exit A-4B).*

NEED A BREAK? Amid all of Tokyo's bustle and crush, you actually can catch your breath in the **Tokyo International Forum**—cafés and Italian, Japanese, and French

Even in hyper-modern Tokyo, women still dress in traditional kimono on special occasions.

restaurants are located throughout the complex. A reasonably priced and delicious Kyoto-style vegetarian restaurant to try is **Tsuruhan.** Lunch sets start at ¥1,050 and dinner ¥3,000. Maps are available, so pick and choose. There are also ATM machines on the third floor. ⊠ *3–5–1 Marunouchi, Chiyoda-ku* ☎ *03/3214–2260* ⊘ *Daily 11–3 and 5–11.*

WORTH NOTING

Bank of Japan 日本銀行 *(Nihon Ginko).* The older part of the Bank of Japan is the work of Tatsuno Kingo, who also designed Tokyo Station. Completed in 1896, on the site of what had been the Edo-period gold mint, the bank is one of the few surviving Meiji-era Western-style buildings in the city. The annex building houses the **Currency Museum,** a historical collection of rare gold and silver coins from Japan and other East Asian countries. There's little English information here, but the setting of muted lighting and plush red carpets evokes the days when the only kind of money around was heavy, shiny, and made of precious metals. ⊠ *2–1–1 Nihombashi Hongoku-cho, Chuo-ku* ☎ *03/3279–1111 bank, 03/3277–3037* ⊕ *www.imes.boj.or.jp* ✉ *Free* ⊘ *Tues.–Sun. 9:30–4:30* Ⓜ *Ginza (Exit A5) and Hanzo-mon (Exit B1) subway lines, Mitsukoshi-mae Station.*

Kabuto Jinja 兜神社 *(Kabuto Shrine).* This is a minor shrine, so if you have had your fill of shrine-viewing, this one can be overlooked. But like the Nihombashi itself, it is another bit of history lurking in the shadows of the expressway. Legend has it that a noble warrior of the 11th century, who had been sent by the Imperial Court in Kyoto to subdue the barbarians of the north, stopped here and prayed for assistance. His expedition was successful, and on the way back he buried a *kabuto,* a golden helmet, on this spot as an offering of thanks. Few Japanese are aware of this legend, and the monument of choice in Kabuto-cho today is the nearby Tokyo Stock Exchange. ⊠ *1–8 Kabuto-cho, Nihombashi, Chuo-ku* Ⓜ *Tozai subway line, Kayaba-cho Station (Exit 10).*

🐣 **Kite Museum** 凧の博物館 *(Tako no Hakubutsukan).* Kite flying is an old tradition in Japan. The collection here includes examples of every shape and variety from all over the country, hand-painted in brilliant colors with figures of birds, geometric patterns, and motifs from Chinese and Japanese mythology. You can call ahead to arrange a kite-making workshop (in Japanese) for groups of children. ⊠ *1–12–10 Nihombashi, Chuo-ku* ☎ *03/3271–2465* ⊕ *www.tako.gr.jp* 💰 *¥210* 🕙 *Mon.–Sat. 11–5* Ⓜ *Tozai subway line, Nihombashi Station (Exit C5).*

Nihombashi 日本橋 *(Bridge of Japan).* Why the expressway *had* to be routed directly over this lovely old landmark back in 1962 is one of the mysteries of Tokyo and its city planning—or lack thereof. There were protests and petitions, but they had no effect. At that time, Tokyo had only two years left to prepare for the Olympics, and the traffic congestion was out of control. So the bridge, originally built in 1603, with its graceful double arch, ornate lamps, and bronze Chinese lions and unicorns, was doomed to bear the perpetual rumble of trucks overhead—its claims overruled by concrete ramps and pillars. ⊠ *Chuo-ku* Ⓜ *Tozai and Ginza subway lines, Nihombashi Station (Exits B5 and B6); Ginza and Hanzo-mon subway lines, Mitsukoshi-mae Station (Exits B5 and B6).*

Shin Marunouchi Building 新丸の内ビルディング. Starting in the late 1990s, Mitsubishi Estate has been aggressively reshaping the area just to the west of Tokyo Station with sparkling mixed-use complexes–and the 38-floor Shin Marunouchi Building is the best example. Largely European in style, including arching steel and high windows, the first seven floors have over 150 shops and restaurants. The wood-deck terrace on the seventh floor is the best choice for a bite as it affords a very nice view of Tokyo Station. For the weary, all public areas of the building have massive amounts of benches—a rarity in Tokyo. ⊠ *1–5–1 Marunouchi, Chiyoda-ku* ☎ *03/5218–5100* ⊕ *www.marunouchi.com/shinmaru* 🕙 *Shops Mon. 11–9, Sun. and holidays 11–8; restaurants Mon. 11–11, Sun. and holidays 11–10* Ⓜ *JR lines, Tokyo Station (Marunouchi North Exit); Chiyoda Line, Nijubashimae Station (Exit 7).*

AOYAMA 青山, HARAJUKU 原宿, AND SHIBUYA 渋谷

Sightseeing
★★★★☆
Dining
★★★★☆
Lodging
★★★★★
Shopping
★★★★★
Nightlife
★★★★★

Who would have known? As late as 1960, this was as unlikely a candidate as any area in Tokyo to develop into the chic capital of Tokyo. Between Meiji shrine and the Aoyama Cemetery to the east, the area was so boring that the municipal government zoned a chunk of it for low-cost public housing. Another chunk, called Washington Heights, was being used by U.S. occupation forces who spent their money elsewhere. The few young Japanese people in Harajuku and Aoyama were either hanging around Washington Heights to practice their English or attending the Methodist-founded Aoyama University—seeking entertainment farther south in Shibuya.

When Tokyo won its bid to host the 1964 Olympics, Washington Heights was turned over to the city for the construction of Olympic Village. Aoyama-dori, the avenue through the center of the area, was renovated and the Ginza and Hanzo-mon subway lines were built under it. Suddenly, Aoyama became attractive for its Western-style fashion houses, boutiques, and design studios. By the 1980s the area was positively *smart*. Today, most of the low-cost public housing along Omotesando are long gone, and in its place are the glass-and-marble emporia of *the* preeminent fashion houses of Europe: Louis Vuitton, Chanel, Armani, and Prada. Their showrooms here are cash cows of their worldwide empires. Superb shops, restaurants, and amusements in this area target a population of university students, wealthy socialites, young professionals, and people who like to see and be seen.

GETTING ORIENTED

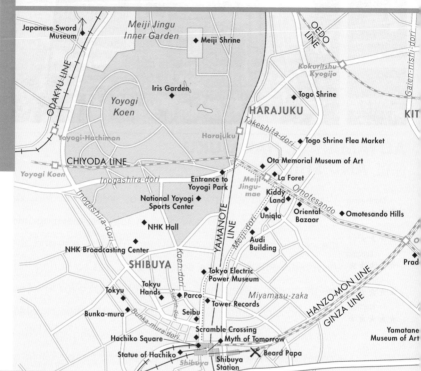

ORIENTATION

Aoyama and Harajuku, west of the Imperial Palace and just north of Roppongi, are the trendsetting areas of youth culture and fashion. Aoyama and nearby Omotesando contain European fashion houses' flagship stores. Harajuku is a young, bohemian fashion district. Its Meiji Jingu is a famous hangout for dressed-up teens.

Shibuya, an entertainment district, is not as clean or sophisticated as Tokyo's other neighborhoods. Shops, cheap restaurants, karaoke lounges, bars, and nightclubs are everywhere.

PLANNING

Trying to explore Aoyama and Harajuku together will take a long time because there is a lot of area to cover. Ideally, spend an entire day here, allowing for plenty of time to browse the shops. You can see Meiji Shrine in less than an hour; the Nezu Museum and its gardens warrant a leisurely two-hour visit. The best way to enjoy this area is to explore the tiny shops, restaurants, and cafés in the backstreets.

Shibuya seems chaotic and intimidating at first, but it is fairly compact. You can easily cover it in about two hours. Be prepared for huge crowds: Shibuya crossing is one of the busiest intersections in the world and at one light change, hundreds rush to reach the other side. Unless you are shopping, no particular stop should occupy you for more than a half hour; allow an hour for the NHK Broadcasting Center if you decide to take the guided tour. Sunday is the best day to visit Shibuya and Yoyogi Koen, as it affords the best opportunity to observe Japan's younger generation.

2

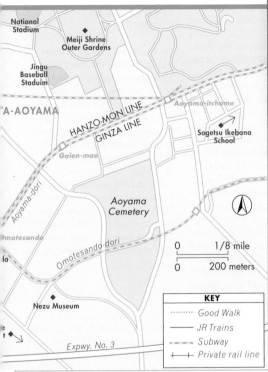

National Stadium

Meiji Shrine Outer Gardens

Jingu Baseball Staduim

A-AOYAMA

Aoyama-itchome

HANZO-MON LINE

GINZA LINE

Sogetsu Ikebana School

Gaien-mae

Aoyama-dori

Aoyama Cemetery

'motesando

Omotesando-dori

la

Nezu Museum

Expwy. No. 3

0   1/8 mile
0   200 meters

KEY
.... *Good Walk*
—— *JR Trains*
⊂==⊃ *Subway*
+——+ *Private rail line*

GETTING HERE AND AROUND

Primary access to Shibuya is via the looping JR Yamanote Line, but the most recent point of passage is via the Fukutoshin subway line, which opened in 2008 and goes north from Shibuya up through Shinjuku and onto Ikebukuro. Old stand-bys are the Hanzo-mon and Ginza lines, both of which stop in Omotesando Station (¥160). The Inokashira railway goes toward Kichijoji, home to Ino-kashira Park, and the Toyoko railway reaches Yokohama in about 30 minutes. Hachiko Exit will be swarmed with people. Just next to it is the "scramble crossing," which leads from the station to the area's concentration of restaurants and shops. Two bus stops provide service to Roppongi to the east and Meguro and Setagaya wards to the west. On Meiji-dori, Hara-juku is walkable to the north in 15 minutes, and Ebisu takes about the same going south.

TOP REASONS TO GO

Trendy Togs and Tots. Observe the trendy Japanese youth street fashions of Takeshita-dori Street.

National Treasures. Stop inside Shibuya Station for a peek at "Myth of Tomorrow," the large, 14-panel mural by avant-garde artist Taro Okamoto.

Hobby Shop. Whether you're a fan of woodworking, painting, DIY home-improvement projects, or even jewelry making, you'll find something you need at Tokyu Hands.

You Ain't Nothing But a Hound Dog. Every Sunday watch large groups of dancing Elvis impersonators at Yoyogi Koen.

QUICK BITES

Judging by the line in front of **Beard Papa** (⊠ *2–24–1 Shibuya*) at Shibuya Station, these must be the world's best cream puffs. Pick up a single or a six-pack of piping-hot pastries. Follow the vanilla smell near the Toyoko Line ticket gate.

TOP ATTRACTIONS

★ **Japanese Sword Museum** 刀剣博物館 *(Token Hakabutsukan)*. It's said that in the late 16th century, before Japan closed its doors to the West, the Spanish tried to establish a trade here in weapons made from famous Toledo steel. The Japanese were politely uninterested; they had been making blades of incomparably better quality for more than 600 years. At one time there were some 200 schools of sword making in Japan; swords were prized not only for their effectiveness in battle but for the beauty of the blades and fittings and as symbols of the higher spirituality of the warrior caste. There are few inheritors of this art today. ✉ *4–25–10 Yoyogi, Shibuya-ku* ☎ *03/3379–1386* ⊕ *www.touken. co.jp* 🎫 *¥600* ⏱ *Tues.–Sun. 10–4:30* Ⓜ *Odakyu private rail line, Sangubashi Station.*

> ### TEENYBOPPER SHOPPERS
>
> On weekends the heart of Harajuku, particularly the street called Takeshita-dori, belongs to high school and junior high school shoppers, who flock there for the latest trends. Entire industries give themselves convulsions just trying to keep up with adolescent styles. Stroll through Harajuku—with its outdoor cafés, designer-ice-cream and Belgian-waffle stands, profusion of stores with names like A Bathing Ape and the Virgin Mary—and you may find it impossible to believe that Japan's most rapidly aging society in the industrial world.

★ **Meiji Shrine** 明治神宮 *(Meiji Jingu)*. The Meiji Shrine honors the spirits of Emperor Meiji, who died in 1912, and Empress Shoken. It was established by a resolution of the Imperial Diet the year after the Emperor's death to commemorate his role in ending the long isolation of Japan under the Tokugawa Shogunate and setting the country on the road to modernization. Completed in 1920 and virtually destroyed in an air raid in 1945, it was rebuilt in 1958.

A wonderful spot for photos, the mammoth entrance gates (*torii*), rising 40 feet high, are made from 1,700-year-old cypress trees from Mt. Ari in Taiwan; the crosspieces are 56 feet long. Torii are meant to symbolize the separation of the everyday secular world from the spiritual world of the Shinto shrine. The buildings in the shrine complex, with their curving, green, copper roofs, are also made of cypress wood. The surrounding gardens have some 100,000 flowering shrubs and trees.

An annual festival at the shrine takes place on November 3, Emperor Meiji's birthday, which is a national holiday. On the festival and New Year's Day, as many as 1 million people come to offer prayers and pay their respects. Several other festivals and ceremonial events are held here throughout the year; check by phone or on the shrine Web site to see what's scheduled during your visit. Even on a normal weekend the shrine draws thousands of visitors, but this seldom disturbs its mood of quiet serenity.

The peaceful **Inner Garden** (Jingu Nai-en), where the irises are in full bloom in the latter half of June, is on the left as you walk in from the main gates, before you reach the shrine. Beyond the shrine is the

Meiji Shrine provides a large green oasis of calm near Harajuku's frenetic Takeshita Street.

Treasure House, a repository for the personal effects and clothes of Emperor and Empress Meiji—perhaps of less interest to foreign visitors than to the Japanese. ✉ *1–1 Kamizono-cho, Yoyogi, Shibuya-ku* ☎ *03/3379–9222* ⊕ *www.meijijingu.or.jp* ✉ *Shrine free, Inner Garden ¥500, Treasure House ¥500* ☉ *Shrine daily sunrise–sunset; Inner Garden Mar.–Nov., daily 9–4; Treasure House daily 10–4; closed 3rd Fri. of month* Ⓜ *Chiyoda and Fukutoshin subway lines, Meiji-Jingu-mae Station; JR Yamanote Line, Harajuku Station (Exit 2).*

Meiji Shrine Outer Gardens 明治神宮外苑 *(Meiji Jingu Gai-en).* This rare expanse of open space is devoted to outdoor sports of all sorts. The Yakult Swallows play at **Jingu Baseball Stadium** (✉ *13 Kasumigaoka, Shinjuku-ku* ☎ *03/3404–8999*); the Japanese baseball season runs from April to October. The main venue of the 1964 Summer Olympics, **National Stadium** (✉ *10 Kasumigaoka, Shinjuku-ku* ☎ *03/3403–1151*) now hosts soccer matches. Some of the major World Cup matches were played here when Japan cohosted the event with Korea in autumn 2002. The **Meiji Memorial Picture Gallery** (*Kaigakan* ✉ *1–1 Kasumigaoka, Shinjuku-ku, Aoyama* ☎ *03/3401–5179*), across the street from the National Stadium, doesn't hold much interest unless you're a fan of Emperor Meiji and don't want to miss some 80 otherwise distinguished paintings depicting events in his life. It's open daily 9–5 and costs ¥500. ✉ *Shinjuku-ku* ⊕ *www.meijijingugaien.jp* Ⓜ *Ginza and Hanzo-mon subway lines, Gaien-mae Station (Exit 2); JR Chuo Line, Shina-no-machi Station.*

Fodor's Choice ★ **Myth of Tomorrow** 明日の神話. This once-lost mural by avant-garde artist Taro Okamoto has been restored and mounted inside Shibuya Station.

Commuters arriving at Shibuya Station view Taro Okamoto's *Myth of Tomorrow*.

Often compared to Picasso's *Guernica*, the 14 colorful panels depict the moment of an atomic bomb detonation. The painting was discovered in 2003 in Mexico City, where in the late '60s it was originally set to be displayed in a hotel but wound up misplaced following the bankruptcy of the developer. Walk up to the Inokashira Line entrance; the mural is mounted along the hallway that overlooks Hachiko plaza. ⊠ *2 Dogen-zaka, Shibuya-ku* Ⓜ *JR Shibuya Station (Hachikō Exit)*.

Fodor'sChoice
★ **Nezu Museum** 根津美術館 *(Nezu Bijutsukan)*. This recently rebuilt museum houses the private collection of traditional Japanese and Asian works of art owned by Meiji-period railroad magnate and politician Kaichiro Nezu. For the main building, architect Kengo Kuma designed an arched roof that rises two floors and extends roughly half a block through this upscale Minami Aoyama neighborhood. Inside, the 5,000-square-meter space offers a portion of the 7,000 works of calligraphy, paintings, sculptures, bronzes, and lacquerware that comprise the Nezu's collection. The museum is also home to one of Tokyo's finest gardens, featuring 5 acres of ponds, rolling paths, waterfalls, and teahouses. ⊠ *6–5–1 Minami-Aoyama, Minato-ku* ☎ *03/3400–2536* ⊕ *www.nezu-muse.or.jp* 💴 *¥1,000* ⊙ *Tues.–Sun. 10–5* Ⓜ *Ginza and Hanzo-mon subway lines, Omotesando Station (Exit A5)*.

★ **Ota Memorial Museum of Art** 太田記念美術館 *(Ota Kinen Bijutsukan)*. The gift of former Toho Mutual Life Insurance chairman Seizo Ota, this is probably the city's finest private collection of *ukiyo-e*, traditional Edo-period wood-block prints. Ukiyo-e (pictures of the floating world) flourished in the 18th and 19th centuries. The works on display are selected and changed periodically from the 12,000 prints in the collection, which include some extremely rare work by artists such as Hiroshige, Hokusai, Sharaku, and Utamaro. ✉ *1–10–10 Jingu-mae, Shibuya-ku* ☎ *03/3403–0880* ⊕ *www.ukiyoe-ota-muse.jp* 🎟 *¥700– ¥1,000, depending on exhibit* ⊗ *Tues.–Sun. 10:30–5:30; closed a few days at the end of each month; call ahead or check Web site* Ⓜ *Chiyoda and Fukutoshin subway lines, Meiji-Jingu-mae Station (Exit 5); JR Yamanote Line, Harajuku Station (Omotesando Exit).*

★ **Tokyu Hands** 東急ハンズ. This is a hobbyist's fantasy store, with everything people could ever need, and plenty of things they don't: tools for woodworking, painting, do-it-yourself home improvement, and jewelry making, as well as travel accessories and bicycle parts. Its slogan is "creative life store," and it truly is: seven floors of cool stuff that takes at least two hours to browse. This superstore is worth a visit, especially for souvenir shopping. ✉ *12–18 Udagawacho, Shibuya-ku* ☎ *03/5489–5111* ⊗ *Daily 10–8:30.*

🕓 **Yoyogi Koen** 代々木公園 *(Yoyogi Park).* This is the perfect spot to have a picnic on a sunny day. On Sunday, people come here to play music, practice martial arts, and ride bicycles on the bike path (rentals are available). Be sure to look out for a legendary group of dancing Elvis impersonators, who meet at the concrete entry plaza every Sunday and dance to classic rock-and-roll music. On Sunday there's a flea market along the main thoroughfare that runs through the park, opposite the National Yoyogi Sports Center. ✉ *Jinnan 2-chome, Shibuya-ku* ☎ *03/3469–6081* Ⓜ *Chiyoda and Fukutoshin subway lines, Meiji-Jingu-mae Station (Exit 2); JR Yamanote Line, Harajuku Station (Omotesando Exit).*

WORTH NOTING

Bunkamura 文化村. One of the liveliest venues in Tokyo for music and art, this six-story theater-and-gallery complex, a venture of the next-door Tokyu department store, hosts everything from acrobat performances and opera to ballet and big bands. The museum on the lower-level Garden Floor often has well-planned, interesting exhibits on loan from major European museums. ✉ *2–24–1 Dogen-zaka, Shibuya-ku* ☎ *03/3477–9111, 03/3477–9999 ticket center* ⊕ *www. bunkamura.co.jp* 🎟 *Theater admission and exhibit prices vary with events* ⊗ *Lobby ticket counter daily 10–7* Ⓜ *JR Yamanote Line, Ginza and Hanzo-mon subway lines, and private rail lines; Shibuya Station (Exits 5 and 8 for Hanzo-mon subway line, Kita-guchi/North Exit for all others).*

NEED A BREAK?

Les Deux Magots デュ・マゴ・パリ, sister of the famed Paris café, on the Garden Floor of the Bunkamura complex, serves a good selection of beers and wines, sandwiches, salads, quiches, tarts, and coffee. There's a fine-arts bookstore next door, and the tables in the courtyard are perfect for people-watching. ✉ *Bunka-mura, lower courtyard, 2–24–1 Dogen-zaka, Shibuya-ku* ☎ *03/3477–9124* ⊕ *www.bunkamura.co.jp* ⊗ *Daily 11–7:30* Ⓜ *JR Yamanote Line, Ginza and Hanzo-mon subway lines, and private*

A GOOD WALK: SHIBUYA AND HARAJUKU

Shibuya and Harajuku are extremely popular with teenagers, hipsters, and those who love to watch the latest fashions walk by.

SHIBUYA

Begin at Shibuya Station, where the once-lost mural *Myth of Tomorrow* is mounted inside the plaza that leads to the Keio Inokashira Line. Hachiko Square is at street level below. Made famous for its statue of loyal dog Hachiko, the plaza is Shibuya's most common meeting place, and to say it is usually packed would be an understatement. The intersection fronting the plaza is the famous Scramble Crossing, which at peak times accommodates more than a thousand people during a single light change. Cross with the masses and turn right onto the adjoining street to get to Seibu Department. Stop inside for whatever clothing and footwear you may fancy. Tower Records—go for the selection of J-pop—is on the opposite side of the street. Up a little further, where the road bends, is the distinctive Tokyo Electric Power museum. The shiny, lipstick-shaped structure offers multiple floors of displays to depict how electricity gets from generation facilities to Tokyo's homes.

ON TO MEIJI-DORI

At Meiji-dori go left towards Harajuku. This area is known for its high-end boutiques from international and domestic clothing makers. After a few minutes, you'll see the Audi Building, whose multi-sloped glass exterior, resembling an iceberg, ought to catch the eye of any fan of architecture. Further north is a large outlet for clothing chain Uniqlo, a very popular label that offers inexpensive jeans, T-shirts, and jackets.

UP TO HARAJUKU

The intersection where Meiji-dori meets Omotesando-dori presents several possibilities. In the direction of Omotesando, Oriental Bazaar is a great place to shop for souvenirs, including dolls, decorative pens, and tableware. On Sunday head the other direction, to the entrance of Yoyogi Park, and check out the leather-clad, 1960s-styled street dancers, who offer no shortage of photo ops. The huge park is worth a visit any day of the week. Another option is to cross the intersection and head to the Laforet building on the left, which has many small boutiques filled the trendiest fashions in the city.

rail lines; Shibuya Station (Exits 5 and 8 for Hanzo-mon subway line, Kitaguchi/North Exit for all others).

☺ **Kiddy Land** キデイランド. First opened in 1950, this Harajuku landmark has moved around the corner from its prominent position on Omotesando-dori while the original shop is rebuilt (expected summer 2012). The temporary three-floor store is still full of enough toys and trinkets to put a smile on any kid's face. You might grin, too: there's something for the kid in all of us, including a complete collection of Hello Kitty and Mickey Mouse paraphernalia, as well as home planetariums. ✉ 6–14–2 Jingu-mae, Shibuya-ku ☎ 03/3409–3431 ⊕ www.kiddyland.co.jp ⏰ Weekdays 11–9, weekends 10:30–9 Ⓜ Ginza, Chiyoda, Hanzo-mon subway line, Omotesando Station (Exit A1).

Gothic styles influence the striking outfits worn by Harajuku Girls.

Omotesando Hills 表参道ヒルズ. This curious shopping mall was designed by Pritzker Prize–winning architect Tadao Ando. Despised and adored with equal zeal, this controversial project demolished the charming yet antiquated Dojunkai Aoyama Apartments along Omotesando Avenue. Filled with high-end boutiques and stores for such brands as Dolce & Gabbana and Yves Saint Laurent, it's worth a stroll to see the latest in Japanese haute couture. Restaurants and cafés can also be found here, but beware of long lines. ⊠ *4–12–10 Jingu-mae, Shibuya-ku* ☎ *03/3497–0310* ⊕ *www.omotesandohills.com* ⊘ *Daily 11–9* Ⓜ *Ginza, Chiyoda, Hanzo-mon subway lines, Omotesando Station (Exit A2).*

NEED A BREAK?

Anniversaire Café. Relax "Omotesando-style" at this Parisian-style café. This charming venue is part of a wedding center and hall and has outdoor seating under a red awning. It's a perfect resting spot in spring and early summer. On weekends, the sidewalk is jammed and newlyweds walk in procession in front of onlookers sitting in the café. Champagne by the glass costs ¥1,400; soup sets, ¥1,000; delicious salads, ¥1,200; and desserts, ¥1,100. ⊠ *3–5–30 Kita Aoyama, Minato-ku* ☎ *03/5411–5988* ⊕ *www.anniversaire.co.jp* ⊘ *Daily 10 am–11:30 pm* Ⓜ *Ginza, Chiyoda, and Hanzo-mon subway lines, Omotesando Station (Exit A2).*

Sogetsu Ikebana School 草月会館 *(Sogetsu Kaikan).* The schools of *Ikebana*, like those of other traditional arts, are highly stratified organizations. Students rise through levels of proficiency, paying handsomely for lessons and certifications as they go, until they can become teachers themselves. At the top of the hierarchy is the *iemoto*, the head of the school, a title usually held within a family for generations. The Sogetsu school of flower arrangement is a relative newcomer to all this. It was founded by Sofu Teshigahara in 1927, and, compared to the older schools, it espouses a style flamboyant, free-form, and even radical. Two-hour introductory lessons in flower arrangement are given in English a few times each month. Reservations must be made in advance. The main hall of the Sogetsu Kaikan, created by the late Isamu Noguchi, one of the masters of modern sculpture, is well worth a visit. Sogetsu Kaikan is a 10-minute walk west on Aoyama-dori from the Akasaka-mitsuke intersection or east from the Aoyama-itchome subway stop. ✉ *7–2–21 Akasaka, Minato-ku* ☎ *03/3408–1151* ⊕ *www.sogetsu.or.jp* Ⓜ *Ginza and Marunouchi subway lines, Akasaka-mitsuke Station; Ginza and Hanzo-mon subway lines, Aoyama-itchome Station (Exit 4).*

Statue of Hachiko ハチ公像. Hachiko is the Japanese version of Lassie; he even starred in a few heart-wrenching films. Every morning, Hachiko's master, a professor at Tokyo University, would take the dog with him as far as Shibuya Station and Hachiko would go back to the station every evening to greet him on his return. In 1925 the professor died of a stroke. Every evening for the next seven years, Hachiko would go to Shibuya and wait there until the last train had pulled out of the station. When loyal Hachiko died, his story made headlines. A handsome bronze statute of Hachiko was installed in front of the station, funded by fans from all over the country. The present version is a replica—the original was melted down for its metal in World War II. This Shibuya landmark is one of the most popular meeting places in the city. Look for the green train car fronting the JR station; the statue is off the side, where everyone is standing. ✉ *2 Dogenzaka, Shibuya-ku* Ⓜ *JR Shibuya Station (Hachikō Exit).*

Togo Shrine Flea Market 東郷神社骨董市. You'll find Japanese antiques, old movie posters, books, and knickknacks at this flea market. It's located near the intersection of Takeshita-dori Street and Meiji-dori in Harajuku. ✉ *1–5–3 Jingu-mae, Shibuya-ku* ☎ *03/3425–7965* 🕑 *1st and 4th Sat. of month 5–3* Ⓜ *JR Yamanote Line, Harajuku Station (Takeshita Exit).*

Yamatane Museum of Art 山種美術館 *(Yamatane Bijutsukan).* Relocated from the Government district to this location in swanky Hiroo, the museum, which specializes in *Nihon-ga*—traditional Japanese painting—from the Meiji period and later, has a private collection of masterpieces by such painters as Taikan Yokoyama, Gyoshu Hayami, Kokei Kobayashi, and Gyokudo Kawai. The exhibits, which sometimes include works borrowed from other collections, change seven or eight times a year. Visitors can take a break at Café Tsubaki, which offers coffee and cake sets. ✉ *3–12–36 Hiroo, Shibuya-ku* ☎ *03/5777–8600* ⊕ *www.yamatane-museum.or.jp* 🎫 *¥1,000* 🕑 *Tues.–Sun. 10–5* Ⓜ *Hibiya subway line, Ebisu Station (Exit 2); JR Yamanote Line, Ebisu Station (West Exit).*

2

ROPPONGI 六本木

Sightseeing
★★☆☆☆
Dining
★★★☆☆
Lodging
★★★★★
Shopping
★★☆☆☆
Nightlife
★★★★★

During much of the last decade of the 20th century, Roppongi was a better-heeled, better-behaved version of Shinjuku or Shibuya, without the shopping: not much happens by day, but by night the area is an irresistible draw for young clubbers with foreign sports cars and wads of disposable income. Today, this area has become an entertainment capital, attracting tourists to its bustling bar, restaurant, and nightclub scenes; English is spoken at most restaurants and shops.

Ritzy developments like Roppongi Hills and Tokyo Midtown have revitalized the area. However, since opening in 2003, the loss of some of its high-rolling tenants—the now-defunct Lehman Brothers Japan and tech company Livedoor, founded by disgraced renegade businessman Takafumi Horie—has taken a bit of the shine off Mori Tower, the main building in Roppongi Hills. Tokyo Midtown, which was completed in 2007, is home to the headquarters of Cisco Japan, FujiFilm, and game maker Konami. Further separating Roppongi from its wild ways is "Art Triangle Roppongi," a promotion campaign for three of the area's museums: the National Art Center, Tokyo; Mori Art Museum; and Suntory Museum of Art.

Azabu Juban is a prestigious residential district with many embassies in Minato-ku. Before the fire raids of 1945, Azabu Juban, like Roppongi, was a famous entertainment district with department stores, a red-light quarter, and theaters. The fires destroyed the entire neighborhood, and it was reborn as a residential area. Though the apartments may be small, this is one of the most expensive areas of the city and many celebrities, artists, and businesspeople reside here.

GETTING ORIENTED

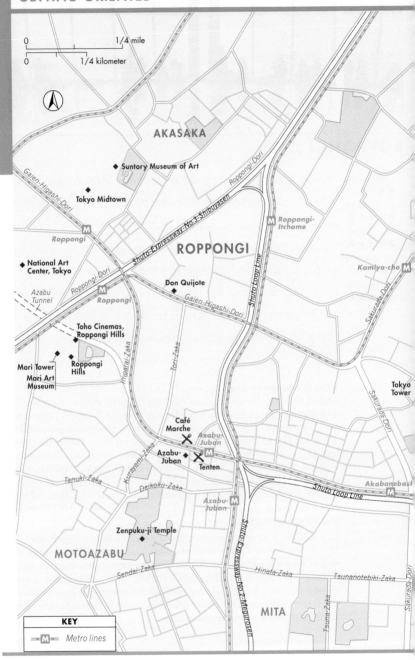

0   1/4 mile

0   1/4 kilometer

AKASAKA

◆ Suntory Museum of Art

◆ Tokyo Midtown

Gaien-Higashi-Dori

Ⓜ Roppongi

◆ National Art Center, Tokyo

Shuto-Expressway-No.3-Shibuyasen

Roppongi-Dori

ROPPONGI

Ⓜ Roppongi-Itchome

Kamiya-cho Ⓜ

Sakurada-Dori

Azabu Tunnel

Roppongi-Dori

Ⓜ Roppongi

◆ Don Quijote

Gaien-Higashi-Dori

Shuto Loop Line

Toho Cinemas, Roppongi Hills

Imoarai-Zaka

Tori-Zaka

Mori Tower
Mori Art Museum

◆ Roppongi Hills

Tokyo Tower

Sakurada-Dori

Kurayami-Zaka

Café Marche ✗

Azabu-Juban

Azabu-Juban ✗ Ⓜ

Tenten

Akabanebashi Ⓜ

Shuto Loop Line

Tanuki-Zaka

Daikoku-Zaka

Azabu-Juban Ⓜ

Shuto-Expressway-No.2-Megurosen

Zenpuku-ji Temple ◆

MOTOAZABU

Sendai-Zaka

Hinata-Zaka

Tsunanotebiki-Zaka

Tsuna-Zaka

Sakurada-Dori

MITA

KEY
═Ⓜ═ Metro lines

PLANNING

There are ATMs and currency-exchange services at Roppongi Hills and Tokyo Midtown, as well as family- and kid-friendly activities, such as small parks and sculpture.

Azabu Juban is a quick visit, and a good place to sit in a café and people-watch. The best time to visit is in August, during the **Azabu Juban Summer Festival,** one of the biggest festivals in Minato-ku. The streets, which are closed to car traffic, are lined with food vendors selling delicious international fare and drinks. Everyone wears their nicest summer *yukatas* (robes) and watches live performances. Check the online *Minato Monthly* newsletter (⊕ *www.city.minato.tokyo.jp*) in August for a list of summer festivals.

TOP REASONS TO GO

A Day's Trip. Visit Mori Building company's apex development, Roppongi Hills, to see the Mori Art Museum, watch a film, do some shopping, have a bite to eat, see some art, or see one of the best views of Tokyo on the observation deck.

Lofty Aspirations. The main tower at nearby Tokyo Midtown is the tallest building in Tokyo. The complex's attractions include excellent restaurants, art exhibitions, and numerous shopping choices.

How the Locals Do It. Enjoy observing everyday life for Tokyo residents in Azabu Juban, where good food and cafés are plentiful.

ORIENTATION

Roppongi is located just east of Shibuya and Aoyama, and south of the Imperial Palace. Azabu Juban is located just south of Roppongi, within a seven-minute walk from Roppongi Hills, or a short subway ride on the Toei Oedo Line to Azabu Juban Station.

GETTING HERE AND AROUND

The best way to get to Roppongi is by subway, and there are two lines that'll take you to Roppongi Station: the Hibiya Line, which takes you right into the complex of Roppongi Hills, or the Oedo Line, with exits convenient to Tokyo Midtown.

Azabu Juban is only a short 10-minute walk from Roppongi. You can also take the Oedo Line from Roppongi to Azabu Juban Station (Exit 5), just one stop away, for ¥170.

QUICK BITES

For a taste of Osaka in Azabu Juban stop at **Tenten** (✉ *1–3–8 Azabu Juban*) for the panfried gyoza dumplings. Most gyoza require a few bites but these are small enough for a single chomp. To get a little fancier, try the version garnished with shredded daikon radish. Tofu and shrimp dishes are also available.

The Mori Art Museum curates temporary contemporary art exhibitions in a sky-high space.

TOP ATTRACTIONS

Mori Art Museum 森美術館. Occupying the 52nd and 53rd floors of Mori Tower, Mori Art Museum is one of the leading contemporary art show-cases in Tokyo. Though lacking a permanent collection, the space is well designed (by American architect Richard Gluckman), intelligently curated, diverse in its media, and hospitable to big crowds. The nine galleries occupy 2,875 square meters for exhibits that rotate every few months and tend to focus on contemporary architecture (Le Corbus-ier), fashion, design, and photography. ✉ *6–10–1 Roppongi, Minato-ku* ☎ *03/5777–8600* ⊕ *mori.art.museum/jp* 🗁 *Admission fee varies with exhibit* ⊙ *Wed.–Mon. 10–10, Tues. 10–5* Ⓜ *Hibiya subway line, Roppongi Station (Exit 1C).*

National Art Center, Tokyo 国立新美術館. Tokyo's nightlife-happy Rop-pongi neighborhood has never been an art lover's destination—until now. The debut of the National Art Center adds to this town's newly burgeoning intellectual heft. Architect Kisho Kurokawa's stun-ning facade shimmers in undulating waves of glass. The cavernous 171,000-square-foot space houses seven exhibition areas; a library; restaurant Brasserie Paul Bocuse Le Musée, offering fine French dishes; and a museum shop. The center features traveling exhibitions that focus on modern and contemporary art. ✉ *7–22–2 Roppongi, Minato-ku* ☎ *03/5777–8600* ⊕ *www.nact.jp* ⊙ *Mon., Wed., Thurs., and weekends 10–6; Fri. 10–8* 🗁 *Admission fee varies with exhibit* Ⓜ *Toei Oedo and Hibiya lines, Roppongi Station (Exit 7).*

Suntory Museum of Art サントリー美術館. Based on the principle of dividing profits three ways, Suntory, Japan's beverage giant, has committed a third of its profits to what it feels is its corporate and social responsibility to provide the public with art, education, and environmental conservation. The establishment of the Suntory Art Museum in 1961 was just one of the fruits of this initiative. The museum's new home at Tokyo Midtown Gardenside is a beautiful place to view some of Tokyo's finest fine art exhibitions. Past displays have included everything from works by Picasso and Toulouse-Lautrec to fine kimonos from the Edo period. ✉ *Tokyo Midtown Gardenside, 9–7–4 Akasaka, Minato-ku* ☎ *03/3479–8600* ⊕ *www.suntory.com/culture-sports/sma* ⊙ *Wed.–Sat. 10–8, Sun. and Mon. 10–6* 💴 *Around ¥1,300 but varies by exhibit* Ⓜ *Toei Oedo Line, Roppongi Station; Hibiya Line, Roppongi Station (Exit 8).*

Tokyo Midtown 東京ミッドタウン. The trend towards luxury, mini-city development projects, which started with Roppongi Hills in 2003, is changing the dynamic of the city. With Tokyo Midtown, Mitsui Fudosan created the tallest building in Tokyo—the 248-meter main tower rises 10 meters higher than Mori Tower at Roppongi Hills. Office, residential, and retail spaces fill out the development. Inside the complex's park is architect Tadao Ando's slope-roof design center 21_21 Design Sight, a gallery and exhibition space that covers 1,700 square meters. ✉ *9 Akasaka, Minato-ku* ☎ *03/5413–8485* ⊕ *www.tokyo-midtown.com* Ⓜ *Toei Oedo Line, Roppongi Station; Hibiya Line, Roppongi Station.*

NEED A BREAK?

A popular local hangout in Azabu Juban at all hours of the day, Café Marche カフェロリータ **is open until late. The multiple reflective wall decorations and chrome piping give a retro feel, and street-level seating allows perfect people-watching vantage points while you enjoy well-prepared pasta dishes (less than ¥1,000) and beer (Japanese or imported), cocktails, and champagne.** ✉ *1F Mademoiselle Bldg., 1–4–8 Azabu Juban, Minato-ku* ☎ *03/6234–0122* ⊙ *Mon.–Thurs. 11–2, Fri. and Sat. 11–4, Sun. 11–midnight.*

☽ **Tokyo Tower** 東京タワー. In 1958 Tokyo's fledgling TV networks needed a tall antenna array to transmit signals. Trying to emerge from the devastation of World War II, the nation's capital was also hungry for a landmark—a symbol for the aspirations of a city still without a skyline. The result was the 333-meter-high (1,093-foot-high) Tokyo Tower, an unabashed knockoff of Paris's Eiffel Tower, and with great views of the city. The Main Observatory, set at 492 feet above ground, and the Special Observatory, up an additional 100 meters, quickly became major tourist attractions; they still draw many visitors a year, the vast majority of them Japanese youngsters on their first trip to the big city. A modest art gallery, the Guinness Book of World Records Museum Tokyo, and a wax museum round out the tower's appeal as an amusement complex. Enjoy live music and stunning views on the main observation-floor café during **Club 333** (⊙ *Wed. and Thurs. 7–9 pm, Fri. 7–9:30 pm*), featuring live jazz, R&B, and bossa nova performances at no extra charge. ✉ *4–2–8 Shiba-Koen, Minato-ku* ☎ *03/3433–5111* 💴 *Main*

Observatory ¥820, Special Observatory ¥600 extra ☉ Tower, daily 9 am–10 pm. Museums and art gallery, daily 10–9 ⊕ www.tokyotower. co.jp Ⓜ Hibiya subway line, Kamiyacho Station (Exit 2).

WORTH NOTING

Don Quijote ドンキホーテ. This is perhaps the weirdest 24-hour discount store on Earth, complete with aquariums featuring the ugliest giant fish you've ever seen; a half-pike roller coaster on the rooftop that has never operated (angry neighbors signed a petition, forcing the owners to drop the idea); the constantly looping "Don Quixote" theme song; and cheesy merchandise like vinyl pants and wigs. Not convinced that you can find almost anything here? It also has secondhand iPhone cases and deodorant. ✉ *3–14–10 Roppongi, Minato-ku* ☏ *03/5786–0811* ⊕ *www. donki.com* ☉ *Daily 11–10.*

Mori Tower 森タワー. When it opened in 2003, the Roppongi Hills complex was the center of Tokyo opulence, with the shimmering, 54-story Mori Tower as its main showpiece. Though no longer a special skyscraper, the tower still outclasses most with the Tokyo City View observation promenade on the 52nd floor, from where wonderful views of Mt. Fuji are possible on a clear day. On the same floor, Café Mado Lounge is the perfect place to recline with a beer or cocktail as the Tokyo night unfolds outside the window. ✉ *6–10–1 Roppongi, Minato-ku* ☏ *03/5777–8600* ⊕ *www.roppongihills.com/tcv/jp* 🎫 *¥1,500* ☉ *Daily 10 am–11 pm* Ⓜ *Hibiya subway line, Roppongi Station (Exit 1C).*

☼ **Roppongi Hills** 六本木ヒルズ. In 2003, Mori Building Company—Japan's biggest commercial landlord—created Roppongi Hills, a complex of shops, restaurants, residential and commercial towers, a nine-screen cineplex, the Grand Hyatt Tokyo hotel, and a major art museum—all wrapped around the TV Asahi studios and sprawled out in five zones located between the Roppongi intersection and Azabu Juban. To navigate this mini-city, go to the information center to retrieve a floor guide with color-coded maps in English; most of the staff members speak English as well. ✉ *6–10–1 Roppongi, Minato-ku* ⊕ *www.roppongihills. com* Ⓜ *Hibiya subway line, Roppongi Station (Exit 1C).*

Toho Cinemas Roppongi Hills TOHO シネマズ 六本木ヒルズ. If you want to catch a movie in English, this is the place to go for the most posh cinema seats in town. On the 1st and 14th of each month, all tickets are ¥1,000. For films in 3-D, an added charge of ¥400 applies. ✉ *Keyakizaka Complex, 6–10–2 Roppongi, Minato-ku* ☏ *03/5775–6090* 🎫 *Regular admission ¥1,800* Ⓜ *Hibiya subway line, Roppongi Station (Exit 1C).*

Zenpuku-ji Temple 麻布山善福寺. This temple, just south of the Ichinohashi Crossing, dates back to the 800s. In the 1200s, the temple was converted to the Shinran school of Buddhism. When Consul-General Townsend Harris arrived from the Americas in 1859, he lived on the temple grounds. ✉ *1–6–21 Moto-Azabu, Minato-ku* ☏ *03/3451–7402* Ⓜ *Toei Oedo and Namboku subway lines, Azabu Juban Station (Exits 1 and 7).*

2

SHINJUKU 新宿

Sightseeing
★★★☆☆

Dining
★★★☆☆

Lodging
★★★★★

Shopping
★★★☆☆

Nightlife
★★★★★

If you have a certain sort of love for big cities, you're bound to love Shinjuku. Come here, and for the first time Tokyo begins to seem *real:* all the celebrated virtues of Japanese society—its safety and order, its grace and beauty, its cleanliness and civility—fray at the edges.

To be fair, the area has been on the fringes of respectability for centuries. When Ieyasu, the first Tokugawa shogun, made Edo his capital, Shinjuku was at the junction of two important arteries leading into the city from the west. It became a thriving post station, where travelers would rest and refresh themselves for the last leg of their journey; the appeal of this suburban pit stop was its "teahouses," where the waitresses dispensed a good bit more than sympathy with the tea.

When the Tokugawa dynasty collapsed in 1868, 16-year-old Emperor Meiji moved his capital to Edo, renaming it Tokyo, and modern Shinjuku became the railhead connecting it to Japan's western provinces. It became a haunt for artists, writers, and students; in the 1930s Shinjuku was Tokyo's bohemian quarter. The area was virtually leveled during the firebombings of 1945—a blank slate on which developers could write, as Tokyo surged west after the war.

Now, by day the east side of Shinjuku Station is an astonishing concentration of retail stores, vertical malls, and discounters of every stripe and description. By night much of the activity shifts to the nearby redlight quarter of Kabuki-cho, which is an equally astonishing collection of bars and clubs, strip joints, hole-in-the-wall restaurants, *pachinko* parlors (an upright pinball game), and peep shows—just about anything that amuses, arouses, alters, or intoxicates is for sale. Recent crackdowns by police have limited this sort of adult activity but whatever you are after is probably still there if you know where to look.

GETTING ORIENTED

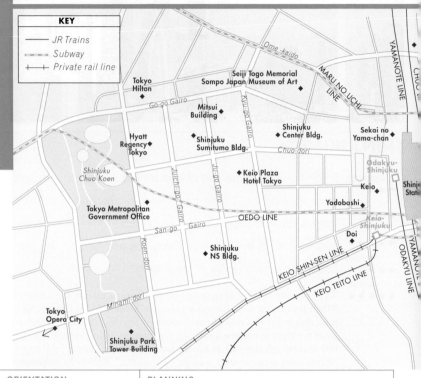

KEY

── JR Trains
═══ Subway
+—+ Private rail line

Ome-kaido

YAMANOTE LINE

CHUO

MARU NO UCHI LINE

Tokyo Hilton

Seiji Togo Memorial
Sompo Japan Museum of Art

Go-go Gairo

Kyu-go Gairo

Mitsui Building

Shinjuku Center Bldg.

Sekai no Yama-chan

Hyatt Regency Tokyo

Shinjuku Sumitumo Bldg.

Chuo-dori

Odakyu-Shinjuku

Shinjuku Chuo Koen

Ju-go Gairo

Keio Plaza Hotel Tokyo

Keio

Shinj Stati

Tokyo Metropolitan Government Office

Juichi-go Gairo

Yodobashi

OEDO LINE

Keio-Shinjuku

San-go Gairo

Koen-dori

Doi

Shinjuku NS Bldg.

ODAKYU LINE

YAMANO

KEIO SHIN-SEN LINE

Minami-dori

KEIO TEITO LINE

Tokyo Opera City

Shinjuku Park Tower Building

ORIENTATION

By day, Shinjuku is a bustling center of business and government where office workers move in droves during rush hour. By night, people are inundated with flashing signs, and a darker side of Tokyo emerges, where drunken hordes leave their offices to go out for drinks, food, and sometimes, sex. Perhaps this is a rougher side of town, but Shinjuku is a fascinating place to discover at night.

PLANNING

Every day three subways, seven railway lines, and more than 3 million commuters converge on Shinjuku Station, making this the city's busiest and most heavily populated commercial center. The hub at Shinjuku—a vast, interconnected complex of tracks and terminals, department stores and shops—divides the area into two distinctly different subcities, Nishi-Shinjuku (West Shinjuku) and Higashi-Shinjuku (East Shinjuku).

Plan at least a full day for Shinjuku if you want to see both the east and west sides. Subway rides can save you time and energy as you're exploring, but don't rule out walking. The Shinjuku Gyo-en National Garden is worth at least an hour, especially if you come in early April during *sakura* (cherry blossom) season. The Tokyo Metropolitan Government Office complex can take longer than you might expect; lines for the elevators to the observation decks are often excruciatingly long. Sunday, when shopping streets are closed to traffic, is the best time to tramp around Higashi-Shinjuku.

2

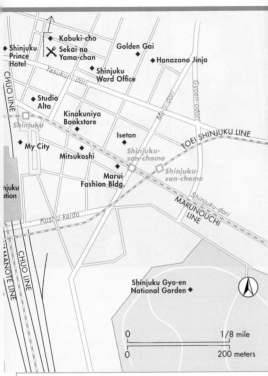

GETTING HERE AND AROUND

From Shibuya to the south and Ikebukuro to the north, the JR Yamanote Line is one of the more common ways to reach Shinjuku Station. The Saikyo Line travels the same path but less frequently. The Keio and Odakyu lines serve destinations to the west. Subway lines, like the Marunouchi, Shinjuku, and Toei Oedo, are best used to move to destinations in the center of the city, such as Ote-machi, Kudanshita, and Roppongi. On foot, Kabuki-cho is accessible in minutes to the east. For the forest of office-building skyscrapers, go through the underground passage to the west.

QUICK BITES

Chicken wings, or *tebasaki*, are not rare in Tokyo. But the basket (¥400) served up by Nagoya-based *izakaya* (traditional bar) chain **Sekai no Yama-chan** (⊠ *2–45–13 Kabuki-cho*) is perhaps the spiciest. In Kabuki-cho, the outlet near the Seibu Shinjuku Station ticket gate is often crowded but the food is delicious, fast, and cheap.

TOP REASONS TO GO

On a Clear Day. The observation deck of Tokyo Metropolitan Government Office has a great view of Mt. Fuji, and the complex hosts open-air concerts and exhibitions.

Priceless Art. The Seiji Togo Memorial Sompo Japan Museum of Art has van Gogh's *Sunflowers*, and the work of Japanese painter Seiji Togo.

Take a Wrong Turn? No, you haven't fallen down the rabbit hole: the famous New York Bar now calls the Park Hyatt home. You might recognize it from the movie *Lost in Translation*.

Among the bright lights of Kabuki-cho you may glimpse Yakuza members in the crowds of revelers.

TOP ATTRACTIONS

Kabuki-cho 歌舞伎町. Kabuki-cho is the vice capital of Japan. When laws got stricter, prostitution just went a bit deeper underground here, where it remains—widely tolerated. ⚠ Despite recent crackdowns by police on sex shops and hostess clubs, Kabuki-cho remains Japan's most vast adult entertainment quarter. Neon signs flash; shills proclaim the pleasures of the places you particularly want to shun. Even when a place looks respectable, ask about prices first: bottakuri—overcharging for food and drink—is indeed a possibility, and watered-down drinks can set you back ¥5,000 or more in a hostess or host club. You needn't be intimidated by the area though. Stop in to a street-level bar (that clearly indicates its pricing) and watch out the window as the hosts, hostesses, and local denizens shuffle on past. In an attempt to change the area's image after World War II, plans were made to replace Ginza's fire-gutted Kabuki-za with a new one in Shinjuku. The plans were never realized, however, as the old theater was rebuilt. But the project gave the area its present name.

Shinjuku Park Tower Building 新宿パークタワー. Kenzo Tange's Shinjuku Park Tower has in some ways the most arrogant, hard-edged design of any of the skyscrapers in Nishi-Shinjuku, but it does provide any number of opportunities to rest and refuel. Some days there are free chamber-music concerts in the atrium. There are many restaurants to choose from in the building, with a variety of international and Japanese restaurants. Take a ride up to the skylighted bamboo garden of the Peak Lounge on the 41st floor of the Park Hyatt Hotel, which was the set location of the Oscar-winning film *Lost in Translation*.

Order a Suntory whiskey at the New York Bar 11 floors above, and you might feel a little like Bill Murray's character in the movie. Also come for brunch at Giranole, a French brasserie with a fantastic view of the city. ✉ *3–7–1 Nishi-Shinjuku, Shinjuku-ku* Ⓜ *JR Shinjuku Station (Nishi-guchi/West Exit).*

NEED A BREAK? **Humax Pavilion. Need a break from the sensory overload? At the Humax Pavilion** (✉ *1–20–1 Kabuki-cho, Shinjuku-ku* Ⓜ *JR Shinjuku Station [Higashi-guchi/East Exit] and Marunouchi subway line [Exits B10, B11, B12, and B13], Shinjuku Station* ☎ *03/3200–2213* ⊕ *www.humax.co.jp*)**, you can shoot a few games of pool, recline in a sauna, relax in a karaoke box, or sharpen your skills at Grand Theft Auto. This multifloor entertainment center is smack dab in the middle of Kabuki-cho's chaos.**

WORTH NOTING

Hanazono Jinja 花園神社 *(Hanazono Shrine).* Constructed in the early Edo period, Hanazono is not among Tokyo's most imposing shrines, but it does have one of the longest histories. Prayers offered here are believed to bring prosperity in business. The shrine is a five-minute walk north on Meiji-dori from the Shinjuku-san-chome subway station. The shrine grounds are at their most lively during the spring and autumn festivals. The block just to the west (5-chome 1) has the last, embattled, remaining bars of the "Golden-Gai" (⇨ *See Golden Gai in Chapter 5*), a district of tiny, somewhat seedy *nomiya* (bars) that in the '60s and '70s commanded the fierce loyalty of fiction writers, artists, freelance journalists, and expat Japanophiles—the city's hard-core outsiders. ✉ *5–17–3 Shinjuku, Shinjuku-ku* ☎ *03/3209–5265* 🎫 *Free* 🕐 *Daily sunrise–sunset* Ⓜ *Marunouchi and Fukutoshin subway lines, Shinjuku-san-chome Station (Exits B2 and B3).*

Seiji Togo Memorial Sompo Japan Museum of Art 東郷青児美術館 *(Sompo Japan Togo Seiji Bijutsukan).* The painter Seiji Togo (1897–1978) was a master of putting on canvas the grace and charm of young maidens. More than 100 of his works from the museum collection are on display here at any given time, along with works by other Japanese and Western artists, such as Gauguin and Cezanne. The museum also houses van Gogh's *Sunflowers.* The gallery includes an especially good view of the old part of Shinjuku. ✉ *42F Sompo Japan Headquarters Bldg., 1–26–1 Nishi-Shinjuku, Shinjuku-ku* ☎ *03/3349–3591* ⊕ *www.sompo-japan. co.jp/museum* 🎫 *¥1,000; additional fee for special exhibits* 🕐 *10–6* Ⓜ *Marunouchi and Shinjuku subway lines, JR rail lines; Shinjuku Station (Exit A18 for subway lines, Nishi-guchi/West Exit or Exit N4 from the underground passageway for all others).*

Shinjuku Gyo-en National Garden 新宿御苑. This lovely 150-acre park was once the estate of the powerful Naito family of feudal lords, who were among the most trusted retainers of the Tokugawa shoguns. After World War II, the grounds were finally opened to the public. It's a perfect place for leisurely walks: paths wind past ponds and bridges, artificial hills, thoughtfully placed stone lanterns, and more than 3,000 kinds of plants, shrubs, and trees. There are different gardens in Japanese, French, and English styles, as well as a greenhouse (the nation's first, built in 1885) filled with tropical plants. ■TIP→ The best times to visit are April, when 75 different species of cherry trees—some 1,500 trees in all—are in bloom, and the first two weeks of November, during the chrysanthemum exhibition. ⊠ *11 Naito-cho, Shinjuku-ku* ☎ *03/3350–0151* ☞ *¥200* ⊗ *Tues.–Sun. 9–4:30; also Mon. 9–4:30 in cherry-blossom season (late Mar.–early Apr.)* Ⓜ *Marunouchi subway line, Shinjuku Gyo-en-mae Station (Exit 1).*

> **HE SAID WHAT?**
>
> Yasuda Fire & Marine Insurance Company (now Sompo Japan Insurance) CEO Yasuo Goto acquired van Gogh's *Sunflowers* in 1987 for ¥5.3 billion—at the time the highest price ever paid at auction for a work of art. He later created considerable stir in the media with the ill-considered remark that he'd like the painting cremated with him when he died.

Tokyo Metropolitan Government Office 東京都庁 *(Tokyo Tocho).* Dominating the western Shinjuku skyline and built at a cost of ¥157 billion, this Kenzo Tange–designed, grandiose, city-hall complex is clearly meant to remind observers that Tokyo's annual budget is bigger than that of the average developing country. The late-20th-century complex consists of a main office building, an annex, the Metropolitan Assembly building, and a huge central courtyard, often the venue of open-air concerts and exhibitions. The building design has raised some debate: Tokyoites either love it or hate it. On a clear day, from the observation decks on the 45th floors of both towers (663 feet above ground), you can see all the way to Mt. Fuji and to the Boso Peninsula in Chiba Prefecture. Several other skyscrapers in the area have free observation floors—among them the Shinjuku Center Building and the Shinjuku Sumitomo Building—but city hall is the best of the lot. The Metropolitan Government Web site, incidentally, is an excellent source of information on sightseeing and current events in Tokyo. ⊠ *2–8–1 Nishi-Shinjuku, Shinjuku-ku* ☎ *03/5321–1111* ⊕ *www.metro.tokyo.jp* ☞ *Free* ⊗ *North and south observation decks daily 9:30–5:30* Ⓜ *Toei Oedo subway line, Tocho-mae Station (Exit A4).*

Tokyo Opera City 東京オペラシティ. Completed in 1997, this mixed-use office and entertainment complex is home to the New National Theater, Tokyo (Shin Kokuritsu Gekijo Tokyo), consisting of the 1,814-seat Opera house, the 1,038-seat Playhouse, and an intimate performance space called the Pit, with seating for up to 468. Architect Helmut Jacoby's design for this building, with its reflecting pools, galleries, and granite planes of wall, deserves real plaudits.

Its east side consists of a 54-story office tower flanked by a sunken garden and art museum on one side and a concert hall on the other. The museum focuses rather narrowly on post–World War II Japanese abstract painting. The 1,632-seat concert hall is arguably the most impressive classical-music venue in Tokyo, with tiers of polished-oak panels, and excellent acoustics despite the venue's daring vertical design. ⊠ *3–20–2 Nishi-Shinjuku, Shinjuku-ku* ☎ *03/5353–0788 concert hall, 03/5351–3011 New National Theater* ⊕ *www.tokyooperacity.co.jp* Ⓜ *Keio private rail line, Hatsudai Station (Higashi-guchi/East Exit).*

DID YOU KNOW?

In the 1970s, the first major skyscraper construction began in Shinjuku, a then-undeveloped tract of land at the city's edge. Today the neighborhood is considered the new city center, with its collection of malls and government buildings, as well as one of the world's busiest train stations. The Gyoen National Garden provides a calm space to recover from the densely packed, bustling crowds.

ODAIBA お台場

Odaiba is a man-made peninsula in Tokyo Bay. Its beginnings date back to the Edo Period (1603-1868), when various fortifications were constructed for protection from attacks by ships.

As a result of Japan's rapidly expanding economy in the 1980s, the area became a target location for a number of flamboyant and futuristic-looking development projects. Today, 1,000 acres of landfill are home to various leisure, corporate, and commercial complexes.

Connected to the city by the Yurikamome monorail from Shimbashi and the Rinkai Line from Osaki, Odaiba is known to tourists for its arcades, hotels, shopping malls, and museums, as well as the city's longest (albeit artificial) stretch of sandy beach, along the boat harbor—swimming is not recommended because of high levels of pollution. There's also a large Ferris wheel, a neon phantasmagoric beacon for anyone driving into the city across the Rainbow Bridge. The exhibition halls at the Tokyo Big Sight, the entrance of which is beneath four large upside-down pyramids, hosts numerous conventions, trade shows, and fairs. For one day in the spring and fall, the Nagisa Music Festival turns an open field near the tip of Odaiba into a frenzied party for thousands of fans of rock, trance, and techno.

At the foot of the Rainbow Bridge, one can walk out onto the diamond-shaped Odaiba Park that juts out into the bay or stroll over the bridge itself to get an amazing view of what is certainly one of the most diverse megaprojects in Tokyo.

TOP ATTRACTIONS

Aqua City アクアシティお台場. This massive shopping complex has six floors of boutiques, cafés, and eateries—including a branch of the hamburger chain Kua' Aina on the fourth level and the excellent noodle house Sapporo Ramen Daishin one floor above. ⊠ *1–7–1 Daiba,*

Head to the beach without leaving town at Odaiba's Decks Tokyo Beach.

Minato-ku ☎ *03/3599–4700* ⊕ *www.aquacity.jp* Ⓜ *Rinkai Line, Tokyo Teleport Station; Yurikamome Line, Daiba Station.*

Decks Tokyo Beach デックス東京ビーチ. Overlooking the harbor, this seven-story complex of shops, restaurants, and boardwalks is really two connected malls: Island Mall and Seaside Mall. Daiba Little Hong Kong, on the sixth and seventh floors of the Island Mall, has a collection of Cantonese restaurants and dim sum joints on neon-lighted "streets" designed to evoke the real Hong Kong. At the Seaside Mall, a table by the window in any of the restaurants affords a delightful view of the harbor, especially at sunset, when the *yakatabune* (traditional-roofed pleasure boats) drift down the Sumida-gawa from Yanagibashi and Ryogoku. ⊠ *1–6–1 Daiba, Minato-ku* ☎ *03/3599–6500* ⊕ *www. odaiba-decks.com* Ⓜ *Rinkai Line, Tokyo Teleport Station; Yurikamome Line, Odaiba-kaihin Koen Station.*

Fuji Television Building フジテレビ. Architecture buffs should make time for Daiba if only to contemplate this futuristic building, designed by Kenzo Tange and completed in 1996. From its fifth-floor Studio Promenade, you can watch television programs being produced. The observation deck on the 25th floor affords a spectacular view of the bay and the graceful curve of the Rainbow Bridge. ⊠ *2–4–8 Daiba, Minato-ku* ☎ *03/5500–8888* ⊕ *www.fujitv.co.jp* ⬛ *¥500* ⊗ *Tues.–Sun. 10–8* Ⓜ *Rinkai Line, Tokyo Teleport Station; Yurikamome Line, Odaiba-kaihin Koen Station.*

GETTING ORIENTED

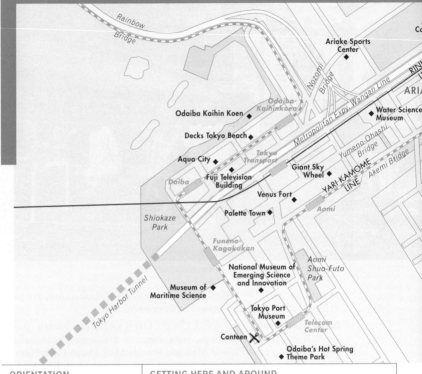

ORIENTATION

Located on the southernmost point of Tokyo, this is a popular weekend destination for families. The lack of historical monuments or buildings in Odaiba separates it from Tokyo's other districts.

PLANNING

If you can, visit Odaiba during the week, as weekends are frenzied and crammed with families. Though a bit isolated, its entertainment facilities make for a good half-day excursion.

GETTING HERE AND AROUND

The best way to get here is via the fully automated Yurikamome Line. From Shimbashi Station you can take the JR, Karasumori Exit; Asakusa subway line, Exit A2; or the Ginza subway line, Exit 4—follow the blue seagull signs to the station entrance. You can pick up a map of Odaiba in English at the entrance. The Yurikamome Line makes 10 stops between Shimbashi and the terminus at Ariake; fares range from ¥310 to ¥370, but the best strategy is to buy a ¥800 one-day unlimited-use pass that allows you to make multiple stops at different points. The line runs every three to five minutes. The JR Rinkai Line also serves the area from Osaki Station, which is a part of the Yamanote Line loop. Perhaps the most interesting means of arrival is via the Tokyo Cruise Ship, which operates a boat service between Hinode Pier (at Hinode Station on the Yurikamome Line) and the Odaiba Seaside Park.

2

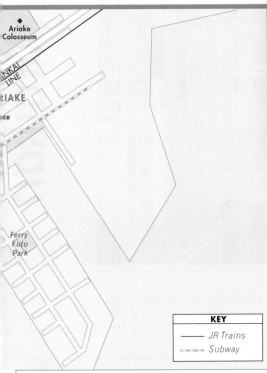

Ariake Colosseum

RINKAI LINE

RIAKE
ce

Ferry Futo Park

KEY

—— *JR Trains*

═ ═ ═ *Subway*

QUICK BITES

Shopping and entertainment are two attractive points for Odaiba, but the chance for a short escape from Tokyo's madness is another. To enhance that, stop in at **Canteen** (⊠ *2–7-4 Aomi*), a café operated by Transit General Office. The terrace seating is a fine choice for enjoying a cup of coffee and an ice-cream cake (¥580).

TOP REASONS TO GO

Fun in the Sun. Decks Tokyo Beach has shopping, arcades, and great Chinese food, while Odaiba Kaihin Koen offers a sandy beach, a small knockoff of the Statue of Liberty, and a view of the Rainbow Bridge.

Lights, Camera, Action. Don't miss the Fuji Television Building, Odaiba's modern architectural landmark.

Buff Bathing. Odaiba's Hot Spring Theme Park is a memorable *onsen* experience in Edo-era surroundings; that is, if you don't mind being naked in a crowd.

Amazing ASIMO. Meet Honda's famous humanoid robot at the National Museum of Emerging Science and Innovation.

The National Museum of Emerging Science and Innovation educates the public about new technology in this innovative space.

Odaiba Kaihin Koen お台場海浜公園. This artificial beach and its board-walk are home to a small replica of the Statue of Liberty and, for many strolling couples, a wonderful evening view of the Rainbow Bridge. Ⓜ *Yurikamome Line, Odaiba-kaihin Koen Station.*

Palette Town. This complex of malls and amusements is located at the east end of the island. The uncontested landmark here is the 377-foot-high Palette Town Ferris Wheel, one of the world's largest. It was modeled after the London Eye; it's open daily 10–10 and costs ¥900. Just opposite is Mega Web, a complex of rides and multimedia amusements that's also a showcase for the Toyota Motor Corporation. You can ride a car (hands off—the ride is electronically controlled) over a 1-km (½-mi) course configured like a roller coaster but moving at a stately pace. You can drive any car you want, of course, as long as it's a Toyota. The shopping mall **Venus Fort** (✉ *Palette Town 1-chome, Aomi, Koto-ku* ☎ *03/3599–0700*) at Aomi consists of galleries designed to suggest an Italian Renaissance palazzo, with arches and cupolas, marble fountains and statuary, and painted vault ceilings. The mall is chock-full of boutiques by the likes of Folli Follie, Diesel, Max & Co., and all the other usual suspects. Ⓜ *Yurikamome Line, Odaiba-kaihin Koen Station.*

WORTH NOTING

Museum of Maritime Science 船の科学館 *(Fune-no-Kagakukan)*. This museum houses an impressive collection of models and displays on the history of Japanese shipbuilding and navigation. Built in the shape of an ocean liner, the museum is huge; if you're interested in ships, plan at least an hour here to do it justice. There are no English-language explanations at the museum. Anchored alongside the museum are the ferries: *Yotei-maru*, which for some 30 years plied the narrow straits between Aomori and Hokkaido, and the icebreaker *Soya-maru*, the first Japanese ship to cross the Arctic Circle. ⊠ *3–1 Higashi-Yashio, Shinagawa-ku* ☎ *03/5500–1111* ⊕ *www.funenokagakukan.or.jp* ⊠ *¥700* ☉ *Tues.–Sun. 10–5* Ⓜ *Yurikamome Line, Funeno-Kagakukan Station.*

National Museum of Emerging Science and Innovation 日本科学未来館 *(Nihon Gagaku Miraikan)*. Make sure to stop by the third floor of this museum, known locally as Miraikan, where you will meet the most famous intelligent robot in the world, ASIMO, and a host of other experimental robots in development. This museum has four different themes: "Earth Environment and Frontiers," "Innovation and the Future," "Information Science and Technology for Society," and "Life Science." The rest of the museum is what the Japanese call *o-majime* (deeply sincere)—five floors of thematic displays on environment-friendly technologies, life sciences, and the like with high seriousness and not much fun. The director of this facility, Dr. Mamoru Mohri, was Japan's first astronaut, who in 1992 logged some 460 hours in space aboard the NASA Spacelab-J *Endeavor*. Some of the exhibits have English-language explanations. It's a short walk here from the Museum of Maritime Science. ⊠ *2–3–6 Aomi, Koto-ku* ☎ *03/3570–9151* ⊕ *www.miraikan.jst.go.jp* ⊠ *¥600* ☉ *Wed.–Mon. 10–5* Ⓜ *Yuri-kamome Line, Funeno-Kagakukan Station.*

Odaiba's Hot Spring Theme Park 大江戸温泉物語 *(Oedo Onsen Mono-gatari)*. Once upon a time, when bathtubs in private homes were a rarity, the great defining social institution of Japanese urban life was the relaxing *sento*: the local public bath. And if the sento was also an *onsen*—a thermal spring—with waters drawn from some mineral-rich underground supply, the delight was even greater. No more than a handful of such places survive in Tokyo, but the Oedo Onsen managed to tap a source some 4,600 feet below the bay. A two-minute walk south from the Telecom Center, visitors can choose from several indoor and outdoor pools, each with different temperatures and motifs—but remember that you must soap up and rinse off (including your hair) before you enter any of them. Follow your soak with a massage and a stroll through the food court—modeled after a street in Yoshiwara, the licensed red-light district of the Edo period—for sushi or noodles and beer. Charges include the rental of a yukata and a towel. ⊠ *2–57 Aomi, Koto-ku* ☎ *03/5500–1126* ⊕ *www.ooedoonsen.jp* ⊠ *¥2,900; surcharge for entrance after midnight* ☉ *Daily 11 am–9 am; front desk closes at 2 am* Ⓜ *Rinkai Line, Tokyo Teleport Station; Yurikamome Line, Odaiba-kaihin Koen Station.*

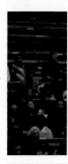

GREATER TOKYO

Sightseeing
★★★☆☆
Dining
★★☆☆☆
Lodging
★★☆☆☆
Shopping
★★☆☆☆
Nightlife
★☆☆☆☆

The sheer size of the city and the diversity of its institutions make it impossible to fit all of Tokyo's interesting sights into neighborhoods. Plenty of worthy places—from Tokyo Disneyland to sumo stables to the old Oji district—fall outside the city's neighborhood repertoire. Yet no guide to Tokyo would be complete without them.

The 23 wards of Tokyo border four prefectures and a bay. The sheer size of the space in between those borders and the diversity of its institutions make it impossible to fit all of Tokyo's interesting sights into its neighborhoods. A number of historically and culturally important sights require a special trek off the Yamanote line. Yet no guide to Tokyo would be complete without them.

Central Tokyo is routinely described as a concrete haven that lacks greenery. Yet the Kasai Seaside Park offers numerous flora at the edge of Tokyo Bay. Tokyo has a few traditional areas remaining, but if the sport of sumo tickles your fancy, the most extensive collection of training stables is in the Ryogoku area. There are also theme parks, like the conventional Tokyo Disneyland and Sanrio Puroland, whose numerous kitsch attractions celebrate Japan's love for all that is cute. Creatures from the sea abound at the Shinagawa Aquarium and Sunshine International Aquarium. If land mammals are more to your liking, the Tama Zoo is a fine choice for kids.

TOP ATTRACTIONS

Fodor's Choice
★

Ryogoku 両国. Two things make this working-class Shitamachi neighborhood worth a special trip: this is the center of the world of sumo wrestling as well as the site of the extraordinary Edo-Tokyo Museum. Five minutes from Akihabara on the JR Sobu Line, Ryogoku is easy to get to, and if you've budgeted a leisurely stay in the city, it's well worth a morning's expedition.

A sumo wrestler makes his way to an event in Ryogoku's Kokugikan (National Sumo Arena).

The **Edo-Tokyo Museum** (✉ *1–4–1 Yokoami, Sumida-ku* ☎ *03/3626–9974* ⊕ *www.edo-tokyo-museum.or.jp* ✉ *¥600; additional fees for special exhibits* ☉ *Tues.–Fri. and Sun. 9:30–5:30, Sat. 9:30–7:30*) rises from an open plaza on massive pillars to the permanent exhibit areas on the fifth and sixth floors. The escalator takes you directly to the sixth floor—and back in time 300 years. You cross a replica of the Edo-period Nihombashi Bridge into a truly remarkable collection of dioramas, scale models, cutaway rooms, and even whole buildings: an intimate and convincing experience of everyday life in the capital of the Tokugawa shoguns. Equally elaborate are the fifth-floor re-creations of early modern Tokyo, the "enlightenment" of Japan's headlong embrace of the West, and the twin devastations of the Great Kanto Earthquake and World War II. If you only visit one non-art museum in Tokyo, make this it.

To get to the museum, leave Ryogoku Station by the West Exit, immediately turn right, and follow the signs. The moving sidewalk and the stairs bring you to the plaza on the third level; to request an English-speaking volunteer guide, use the entrance to the left of the stairs instead, and ask at the General Information counter in front of the first-floor Special Exhibition Gallery.

GETTING ORIENTED

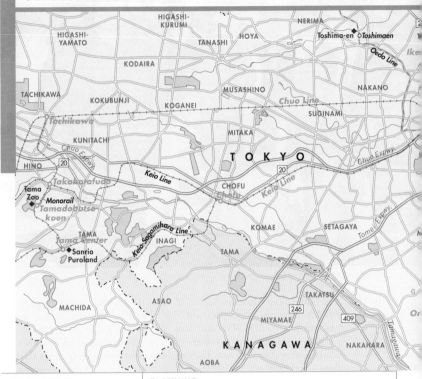

ORIENTATION

Since it they are so accessible, the central wards of Tokyo are often the focus for visitors. Of course, there is much more to discover in the city. The areas that lie to the west of Shibuya, south of Shinagawa, north of Ikebukuro, and east of Tokyo Station offer amusement parks, zoos, galleries, and museums.

PLANNING

For the amusement parks and zoos, visitors will want to plan to spend the entire day. The galleries and parks will only take a few hours. Be sure to plan ahead: some destinations can take over an hour to reach by train. Also keep in mind that the farther away from the city one moves the more spread out the city becomes, so plan on taking a taxi from the train station.

TOP REASONS TO GO

Mickey Mousing. Tokyo Disneyland mimics the California original in amazing detail. It also adds Tokyo Disney Sea, a park with a nautical theme.

Supersize Me. Head to Ryogoku to see sumo wrestlers grapple in the ring. There's also a wonderful museum dedicated to Tokyo's history (The Edo-Tokyo Museum) just around the corner.

Samurai Spirit. At Sengaku-ji, learn the story of the deaths of 47 samurai, often portrayed in Kabuki theater plays, and visit a museum dedicated to the men.

GETTING HERE AND AROUND

From central Tokyo, the city spreads out like the spokes of a wheel; various railways serve areas in all cardinal directions. For Chiba Prefecture, where Tokyo Disneyland is located, take Keiyo Line, which originates at Tokyo Station. Use the same line to access Kasai Seaside Park. Multiple JR lines and the Keihin Kyuko Line chug south from Shinagawa Station in the direction of Yokohama and to the Shinagawa Aquarium. To the west, the Chuo Line passes through Shinjuku to reach Tachikawa Station; transfer to the Tama Monorail here for the Tama Zoo. The Keio Line, too, starts at Shinjuku Station; Sanrio Puroland is accessible from Tama Center Station on this line. The Namboku Line is a subway line that moves north through Komagome Station on the Yamanote Line before reaching the throwback town of Oji.

Walk straight out to the main street in front of the West Exit of Ryogoku Station, turn right, and you come almost at once to the Kokugikan (National Sumo Arena), with its distinctive copper-green roof.

If you can't attend one of the Tokyo sumo tournaments, you may want to at least pay a short visit to the **Sumo Museum** (✉ *1–3–28 Yokoami, Sumida-ku* ☎ *03/3622–0366* ⊕ *www.sumo.or.jp* 🖃 *Free* ⊗ *Weekdays 10–4:30*), in the south wing of the arena. There are no explanations in English, but the museum's collection of sumo-related wood-block prints, paintings, and illustrated scrolls includes some outstanding examples of traditional Japanese fine art.

★ **Sengaku-ji** 泉岳寺 *(Sengaku Temple)*. In 1701, a young provincial baron named Asano Takumi-no-Kami attacked and seriously wounded a courtier named Yoshinaka Kira. Asano, for daring to draw his sword in the confines of Edo Castle, was ordered to commit suicide, so his family line was abolished and his fief confiscated. Forty-seven of Asano's loyal retainers vowed revenge; the death of their leader made them *ronin*—masterless samurai. On the night of December 14, 1702, Asano's ronin stormed Kira's villa in Edo, cut off his head, and brought it in triumph to Asano's tomb at Sengaku-ji, the family temple. The ronin were sentenced to commit suicide—which they accepted as the reward, not the price, of their honorable vendetta—and were buried in the temple graveyard with their lord.

Through the centuries this story has become a national epic and the last word on the subject of loyalty and sacrifice, celebrated in every medium from Kabuki to film. The temple still stands, and the graveyard is wreathed in smoke from the bundles of incense that visitors still lay reverently on the tombstones. There is a collection of weapons and other memorabilia from the event in the temple's small museum. One of the items dispels forever the myth of Japanese vagueness and indirection in the matter of contracts and formal documents. Kira's family, naturally, wanted to give him a proper burial, but the law insisted this could not be done without his head. They asked for it back, and Oishi—pillar of chivalry that he was—agreed. He entrusted it to the temple, and the priests wrote him a receipt, which survives even now in the corner of a dusty glass case. "Item," it begins, "One head."

Take the Asakusa subway line to Sengaku-ji Station (Exit A2), turn right when you come to street level, and walk up the hill. The temple is past the first traffic light, on the left. ✉ *2–11–1 Takanawa, Minato-ku* ☎ *03/3441–5560* 🖃 *Temple and grounds free, museum ¥200* ⊗ *Temple Apr.–Sept., daily 7–6; Oct.–Mar., daily 7–5. Museum daily 9–4* Ⓜ *Asakusa subway line, Sengakuji Station (Exit A2).*

☾ **Tokyo Disneyland** 東京ディズニーランド. At Tokyo Disneyland, Mickey-san and his coterie of Disney characters entertain just the way they do in the California and Florida Disney parks. When the park was built in 1983 it was much smaller than its counterparts in the United States, but the construction in 2001 of the adjacent DisneySea, with its seven "Ports of Call" with different nautical themes and rides, added more than 100 acres to this multifaceted Magic Kingdom.

CLOSE UP

A Mostly Naked Free-For-All

Sumo wrestling dates back some 1,500 years. Originally a religious rite performed at shrines to entertain the harvest gods, a match may seem like a fleshy free-for-all to the casual spectator, but to the trained eye, it's a refined battle. Two wrestlers square off in a dirt ring about 15 feet in diameter and charge straight at each other in nothing but silk loincloths. There are various techniques of pushing, gripping, and throwing, but the rules are simple: except for hitting below the belt, grabbing your opponent by the hair (which would certainly upset the hairdresser who accompanies every sumo ringside), or striking with a closed fist, almost anything goes. If you're thrown down or forced out of the ring, you lose. There are no weight divisions and a runt of merely 250 pounds can find himself facing an opponent twice his size.

You must belong to one of the roughly two dozen *heya* (stables) based in Tokyo to compete. Stables are run by retired wrestlers who have purchased the right from the Japan Sumo Association. Hierarchy and formality rule in the sumo world. Youngsters recruited into the sport live in the stable dormitory, do all the community chores, and wait on their seniors. When they rise high enough in tournament rankings, they acquire their own servant-apprentices.

Most of the stables are concentrated on both sides of the Sumida-gawa near the Kokugikan. Wander this area when the wrestlers are in town (January, May, and September) and you're more than likely to see some of them on the streets, in their wood clogs and kimonos. Come 7 am–11 am, and you can peer through the doors and windows of the stables to watch them in practice sessions. One that offers tours is the **Michinoku Stable** (✉ *1–18–7 Ryogoku*). Have a Japanese speaker complete the application form on the Web site in advance (⊕ *michinokubeya.com*) and you might be able to gain access. Another offering tours, also requiring advance reservation via the Web, is the **Kasugano Stable** (✉ *1–7–11 Ryogoku* ⊕ *www.kasuganobeya.com*).

When: Of the six Grand Sumo Tournaments (called *basho*) that take place during the year, Tokyo hosts three: in early January, mid-May, and mid-September. Matches go from early afternoon, when the novices wrestle, to the titanic clashes of the upper ranks at around 6 pm.

Where: Tournaments are held in the Kokugikan, the National Sumo Arena, in Ryogoku, a district in Sumida-ku also famed for its clothing shops and eateries that cater to sumo sizes and tastes. ✉ *1–3–28 Yokoami, Sumida-ku* ☎ *03/3623–5111* ⊕ *www.sumo.or.jp* Ⓜ *JR Sobu Line, Ryogoku Station (West Exit).*

How: The most expensive seats, closest to the ring, are tatami-carpeted loges for four people, called *sajiki*. The loges are terribly cramped and cost ¥9,200–¥11,300 per person. Cheap seats start as low as ¥3,600 for advance sales, ¥2,100 for same-day box office sales for general admission seats. For same-day box office sales you should line up an hour before the tournament. You can also get tickets through Family Mart, Circle K Sunkus, and Lawson convenience stores.

There are several types of admission tickets. Most people buy the One-Day Passport (¥5,800), which gives you unlimited access to the attractions and shows at one or the other of the two parks. See the park Web site for other ticketing options. You can buy tickets in advance from any local travel agency, such as the Japan Travel Bureau (JTB).

The simplest way to get to Disneyland is by JR Keiyo Line from Tokyo Station to Maihama; the park is just a few steps from the station exit. From Nihombashi you can also take the Tozai subway line to Urayasu and walk over to the Tokyo Disneyland Bus Terminal for the 25-minute ride, which costs ¥230. ✉ *1–1 Maihama, Urayasu* ☎ *0570/00–8632 information, 047/729–0733 guest relations* ⊕ *www.tokyodisneyresort. co.jp* ⊙ *Daily 9 am–10 pm; seasonal closings in Dec. and Jan. may vary, so check before you go.*

🕒 **Tokyo Sea Life Park** 葛西臨海水族館. The three-story cylindrical complex of this aquarium houses more than 540 species of fish and other sea creatures within three different areas: "Voyagers of the Sea" ("Maguro no Kaiyu"), with migratory species; "Seas of the World" ("Sekai no Umi"), with species from foreign waters; and the "Sea of Tokyo" ("Tokyo no Umi"), devoted to the creatures of the bay and nearby waters. To get here, take the JR Keiyo Line local train from Tokyo Station to Kasai Rinkai Koen Station; the aquarium is a 10-minute walk or so from the South Exit. ✉ *6–2–3 Rinkai-cho, Edogawa-ku* ☎ *03/3869–5152* 🎫 *¥700* ⊙ *Thurs.–Tues. 9:30–5* Ⓜ *JR Keiyo Line, Kasai Rinkai Koen Station.*

WORTH NOTING

🕒 **Kasai Seaside Park** 葛西臨海公園. The **Diamonds and Flowers Ferris Wheel** (Daia to Hana no Dai-kanransha) takes passengers on a 17-minute ride to the apex, 384 feet above the ground, for a spectacular view of the city. On a clear day you can see all the way to Mt. Fuji; at night, if you're lucky, you reach the top just in time for a bird's-eye view of the fireworks over the Magic Kingdom, across the river. To get here, take the JR Keiyo Line local train from Tokyo Station to Kasai Rinkai Koen Station; the park is a five-minute walk from the South Exit. ✉ *6–2–1 Rinkai-cho, Edogawa-ku* ☎ *03/5696–1331* 🎫 *Free, Ferris wheel ¥700* ⊙ *Most park attractions closed Wed.; Ferris wheel Sept.–July, weekdays 10–8, weekends 10–9.*

Oji. Take the JR Yamanote Line to Otsuka, cross the street in front of the station, and change to the Toden Arakawa Line—Tokyo's last surviving trolley. Heading east, for ¥160 one way, the trolley takes you through the back gardens of old neighborhoods on its way to Oji—once the site of Japan's first Western-style paper mill, built in 1875 by Oji Paper Company, the nation's oldest joint-stock company. The mill is long gone, but the memory lingers on at the **Asuka-yama Oji Paper Museum** (✉ *1–1–3 Oji, Kita-ku* ☎ *03/3916–2320* ⊕ *www.papermuseum.jp* 🎫 *¥300* ⊙ *Tues.–Sun. 10–5*). Exhibits—covering 2,000 years of the history of paper—show the processes for milling paper from pulp and recycling and include a number of machines used. Others illustrate the astonishing variety of products that can be made from paper. The

Join the crowds waiting for a coveted photo op with Minnie Mouse at Tokyo Disneyland.

museum is a minute's walk from the trolley stop at Asuka-yama Koen; you can also get here from the JR Oji Station (Minami-guchi/South Exit) on the Keihin–Tohoku Line, or the Nishigahara Station (Asuka-yama Exit) on the Namboku subway line.

Sanrio Puroland サンリオピューロランド. As a theme park dedicated to the world's most famous white cat with no mouth—Hello Kitty, of course—Sanrio Puroland is effectively a shrine to the concept of cuteness. An all-day passport allows for unlimited use of multiple attractions, including three theaters, a boat ride, and the Kitty Lab, where guests are allowed to experiment with what exactly is "cute." Pens, packaged snacks, and plush toys are readily available so guests don't leave empty-handed. ⊠ *1–31 Ochiai, Tama-shi* ☎ *042/339–1111* ☒ *¥3,000–¥4,000* ⊕ *www. puroland.co.jp* ⊙ *Weekdays 10–5, summer until 6 pm; weekends 10–8; closed Thurs.* Ⓜ *Keio Line, Tama Center Station.*

Ⓒ **Shinagawa Aquarium** 品川水族館 *(Shinagawa Suizokukan)*. The fun part of this aquarium in southwestern Tokyo is walking through an under-water glass tunnel while some 450 species of fish swim around and above you. There are no pamphlets or explanation panels in English, however, and do your best to avoid Sunday, when the dolphin and sea lion shows draw crowds in impossible numbers. Take the local Keihin-Kyuko private rail line from Shinagawa to Omori-kaigan Station. Turn left as you exit the station and follow the ceramic fish on the sidewalk to the first traffic light; then turn right. ⊠ *3–2–1 Katsushima, Shinagawa-ku* ☎ *03/3762–3431* ☒ *¥1,300* ⊙ *Wed.–Mon. 10–5; dolphin and sea lion shows 3 times daily, on varying schedule* Ⓜ *Keihin Kyuko Line, Omori Kaigan Station.*

Ↄ **Sunshine International Aquarium** サンシャイン国際水族館. ■TIP→ The aquarium is closed for renovations and is slated to reopen in summer 2012. Check with the aquarium before planning a visit. This aquarium has some 750 kinds of sea creatures on display, plus sea lion performances four times a day (except when it rains). An English-language pamphlet is available, and most of the exhibits have some English explanation. If you get tired of the sea life, head to the Sunshine Starlight Dome planetarium, where you can see 400,000 stars. And if that still isn't enough to keep you occupied, try the 60th-floor observatory for great views of the city. To get here, take the JR Yamanote Line to Ikebukuro Station (Exit 35) and walk about eight minutes west to the Sunshine City complex. You can also take the Yuraku-cho subway to Higashi-Ikebukuro Station (Exit 2); Sunshine City and the aquarium are about a three-minute walk north. ⊠ *3–1–3 Higashi-Ikebukuro, Toshima-ku* ☎ *03/3989–3331* ⊕ *www.sunshinecity.co.jp* 🎫 *Aquarium ¥1,800, planetarium ¥900, observatory ¥620; tickets may be purchased in combination* ☉ *Aquarium weekdays 10–6, weekends 10–6:30; planetarium daily 11–7; observation deck daily 10–9:30* Ⓜ *Yuraku-cho subway line, Ikebukuro Station (Exit 35).*

Ↄ **Tama Zoo** 多摩動物園 *(Tama Dobutsu Koen).* More a wildlife park than a zoo, this facility in western Tokyo gives animals room to roam; moats typically separate them from you. You can ride through the Lion Park in a minibus. To get here, take a Keio Line train toward Takao from Shinjuku Station and transfer at Takahata-Fudo Station for the one-stop branch line that serves the park. ⊠ *7–1–1 Hodokubo, Hino* ☎ *0425/91–1611* ⊕ *www.tokyo-zoo.net/zoo/tama* 🎫 *¥700* ☉ *Thurs.–Tues. 9:30–5* Ⓜ *From JR Tachikawa Station, take the Tama Monorail, and get off at Tama Dobutsu Koen Station.*

Ↄ **Toshima-en** としまえん. This large, well-equipped amusement park in the northwestern part of Tokyo has four thrill rides, a haunted house, and six swimming pools. What makes it special is the authentic Coney Island carousel—left to rot in a New York warehouse, discovered and rescued by a Japanese entrepreneur, and lovingly restored down to the last gilded curlicue on the last prancing unicorn. From Shinjuku, the Toei Oedo Line goes directly to the park. ⊠ *3–25–1 Koyama, Nerima-ku* ☎ *03/3990–8844* ⊕ *www.toshimaen.co.jp* 🎫 *Day pass ¥3,900* ☉ *Thurs.–Mon. 10–6* Ⓜ *Toei Oedo subway line, Toshimaen Station.*

Where to Eat

WORD OF MOUTH

"It's very easy to order food in Japan—most restaurants have pictures or plastic models of the food. Unlike in the U.S., these are not tourist restaurants, just normal places. Japanese people check out the window display rather than consulting the menu when choosing among restaurants in an area, and so can you."

—Therese

Updated by
Kevin Mcgue

Though Tokyoites still stubbornly resist foreign concepts in many fields, the locals have embraced outside culinary styles with gusto. While newer restaurants targeting younger diners strive for authenticity in everything from New York–style bagels to Neapolitan pizza, it is still not uncommon to see menus offering East-meets-West concoctions such as spaghetti topped with cod roe and shredded seaweed. That said, the city's best French and Italian establishments can hold their own on a global scale, with high prices to match. There is also excellent Japanese food available throughout the city, ranging from the traditional to nouveau cuisine that can be shockingly expensive.

That is not to imply that every meal in the city will drain your finances—the current rage is all about "B-class gourmet," restaurants that fill the gap between nationwide chains and fine cuisine, offering tasty Japanese and Asian food without the extra frills of tablecloths and lacquerware. All department stores and most skyscrapers have at least one floor of restaurants which, while not amazing, are accessible and affordable.

Asakusa is known for its tempura, and Tsukiji prides itself on its fresh sashimi, which is available in excellent quality throughout the city. Ramen is a passion for many locals, who will travel across town or stand in line for an hour in order to sit at the counter of a shop rumored to offer the perfect balance of noodles and broth. There have been good and affordable Indian and Chinese restaurants in the city for decades. As a result of increased travel by the Japanese to more exotic locations, Thai, Vietnamese, and Turkish restaurants have popped up around the city. ■TIP➜ When in doubt, note that Tokyo's top-rated international hotels also have some of the city's best places to eat and drink.

DINING PLANNER

DRESS

Dining out in Tokyo does not ordinarily demand a great deal in the way of formal attire. If you are attending a business meal with Japanese hosts or guests, dress conservatively: for men, a suit and tie; for women, a dress or suit in a basic color and minimal jewelry. On your own, follow the unspoken dress codes you'd observe at home. We mention dress only when men are required to wear a jacket or a jacket and tie.

> ### CHECK IT OUT!
>
> **English OK!** (⊕ *www.englishok.jp*) lists restaurants where English is spoken so people with limited or no Japanese can order food without worrying about the language barrier. Before heading out, check the Web site for maps, sample menus, and printable coupons.

For Japanese-style dining on tatami floors, keep two things in mind: wear shoes that slip on and off easily and presentable socks, and choose clothing you'll be comfortable in for a few hours with your legs gathered under you.

QUICK BITES

If you're in a hurry, visit a branch of one of the nationwide burger chains: MOS Burger, Freshness Burger, or First Kitchen. Yoshinoya is another popular chain, serving grilled salmon, rice, and miso soup for breakfast (until 10), and then hearty portions of rice and beef for the rest of the day.

PRICES

Eating at hotels and famous restaurants is costly; however, you can eat well and reasonably at standard restaurants that may not have signs in English. Good places to look for moderately priced dining spots are in the restaurant concourses of department stores and larger office buildings, usually on the basement levels and the top floors.

All restaurants charge 5% tax, and by law, the price on the menu includes tax. Izakaya often charge a flat table charge (around ¥500 per person), which includes the tiny appetizer that's served to all guests. Some restaurants add a service charge of 10% on large parties, which is usually indicated at the bottom of menus.

Japanese-style restaurants often serve set meals, which may include rice, soup, and pickled vegetables in addition to the main course—this can drive up the cost. You can sometimes request the main dish without the sides, but then you'd be missing out on the beauty and harmony of a Japanese meal.

WHAT IT COSTS IN YEN					
	¢	$	$$	$$$	$$$$
AT DINNER	under ¥800	¥800–¥1,000	¥1,000–¥2,000	¥2,000–¥3,000	over ¥3,000

Prices are per person for a main course.

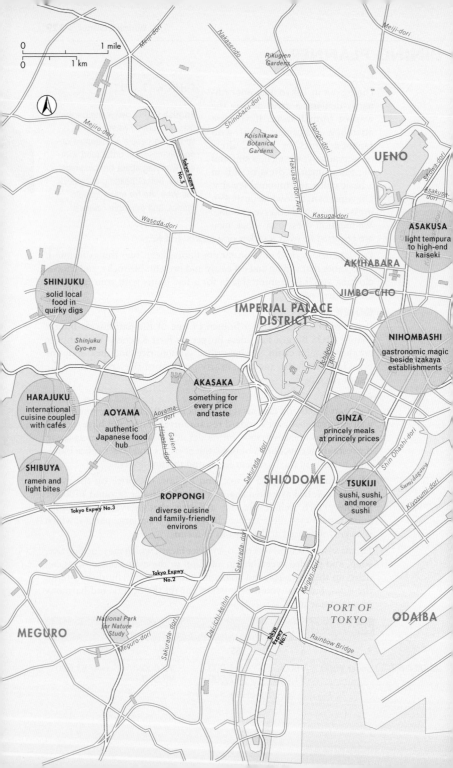

SHINJUKU
solid local food in quirky digs

HARAJUKU
international cuisine coupled with cafés

SHIBUYA
ramen and light bites

AOYAMA
authentic Japanese food hub

AKASAKA
something for every price and taste

ROPPONGI
diverse cuisine and family-friendly environs

ASAKUSA
light tempura to high-end kaiseki

NIHOMBASHI
gastronomic magic beside izakaya establishments

GINZA
princely meals at princely prices

TSUKIJI
sushi, sushi, and more sushi

UENO

AKIHABARA

JIMBO-CHO

IMPERIAL PALACE DISTRICT

SHIODOME

MEGURO

ODAIBA

PORT OF TOKYO

Rainbow Bridge

National Park for Nature Study

Shinjuku Gyo-en

Koishikawa Botanical Gardens

Rikugien Gardens

0 1 mile
0 1 km

Meiji-dori

Nakasendo

Meiji-dori

Mejiro-dori

Waseda-dori

Shinobazu-dori

Hakusan-dori Ave.

Hongo-dori

Kasuga-dori

Showa-dori

Asakusa-dori

Tokyo Expwy No.5

Aoyama-dori

Gaien-Higashi-dori

Sakurada-dori

Uchibori-dori

Shin Ohashi-dori

Sumidagawa

Kiyosumi-dori

Tokyo Expwy No.3

Tokyo Expwy No.2

Tokyo Expwy No.1

Sakurada-dori

Dai-ichi-keihin

Meguro-dori

Kaigan-dori

BEST BETS FOR TOKYO DINING

With hundreds of restaurants to choose from, how will you decide where to eat? Fodor's writers and editors have selected their favorite restaurants by price, cuisine, and experience in the Best Bets lists here. In the first column, Fodor's Choice properties represent the "best of the best" in every price category. You can also search by neighborhood for excellent eats—just peruse our reviews on the following pages.

3

LATE-NIGHT DINING

Sawanoi, p. 137
Tableaux, p. 140

MOST ROMANTIC

Aquavit, p. 144
Azure 45, p. 151

Fodor'sChoice ★

Ganchan, p. 153
Inakaya, p. 155
Robata, p. 164
Tableaux, p. 140
Ume no Hana, p. 139

Best by Price

$

Afuri, p. 157
Homeworks, p. 153
Takeno, p. 162

$$

Heiroku-zushi, p. 145
Maisen, p. 139
Mist, p. 145
Sakuratei, p. 147

$$$$

Aquavit, p. 144
Jidaiya, p. 136
Signature, p. 151

Best by Experience

BEST SUSHI

Edo-gin, p. 162
Heiroku-zushi, p. 145
Takeno, p. 162

BEST RAMEN

Afuri, p. 157
Darumaya, p. 138
Kohmen, p. 155
Mist, p. 145
Suzuran, p. 157

BEST TEMPURA

Daikokuya Tempura, p. 139
Tenmatsu, p. 158

BEST BURGER

Homeworks, p. 153
Towers Grill, p. 157

MOST UNIQUE

Ninja, p. 137
Ryoma no Sora, p. 161
Tapas Molecular Bar, p. 151

HOTEL DINING

Azure 45, p. 151
Gordon Ramsay, p. 141
Toh-Ka-Lin, p. 138

GREAT VIEW

Gordon Ramsay, p. 141
Towers Grills, p. 157
T.Y. Harbor Brewery, p. 160
Wa no Mori Sumika, p. 144

BEST BRUNCH

Ben's Café, p. 160
Good Honest Grub, p. 157
Roti, p. 156

LUNCH PRIX FIXE

Aquavit, p. 144
Mist, p. 145
Pizza Salvatore Cuomo, p. 137
Tenmatsu, p. 158

CHILD-FRIENDLY

Ninja, p. 137
Pizza Salvatore Cuomo, p. 137
Tony Roma's, p. 157

AMERICAN

Homeworks, p. 153
Roti, p. 156
Tony Roma's, p. 157
T.Y. Harbor Brewery, p. 160

SOUTH ASIAN

Moti, p. 136
Sanko-en, p. 156
Tonki, p. 147

TOKYO'S VENDING MACHINES AND CONVENIENCE STORES

With a brightly lit convenience store on practically every corner and a few well-stocked vending machines in between, quick shopping is truly hassle-free in Tokyo—and with the offerings ranging from novel to bizarre, an impulse buy can turn into a journey of discovery.

(top left) Ubiquitous vending machines provide fast, cheap snacks (top right) limited-edition potato chip flavors (bottom right) convenience stores offer a taste of Japanese culture.

While vending machines and convenience stores did not originate in Japan, their popularity in the country seems to have no limit. Today Japan has the world's highest density of vending machines per capita, with one machine for every 23 people. Those looking for a wider selection can head to one of the 42,000 convenience stores in the country. Canned drinks, both cold and hot, are the main staple of vending machines, but it is not uncommon to find ones offering cigarettes, batteries, snacks, ice-cream cones, toiletries, fresh fruit, customized business cards, or even potted flowers. For North Americans used to convenience stores that offer little more than a candy shelf and a magazine rack, the Japanese equivalent can be a source of amazement, boasting everything from postal and courier services and digital photo printing to full hot meals.

DID YOU KNOW?

Many vending machine offerings aren't exactly healthful—sugar-laden coffee, colas, and alcohol. However, new machines are geared toward the health-conscious. Dole installed banana dispensers around Shibuya train station, targeting hurried commuters with no time for breakfast. The fruit is lightly refrigerated and gently lowered to the opening to avoid bruising. Single bananas and bunches are available.

VENDING MACHINES

If you visit Tokyo during the hot and humid summer months, it will not take long for you to understand why there is a machine selling cool drinks on every sidewalk. In winter, hot drinks warm both the stomach and hands. Long-popular drinks include Pocari Sweat, a noncarbonated sports drink with a very mild grapefruit taste; Aquarius, a comparable drink manufactured by Coca-Cola; and *Marocha Chaba no Ko*, a cold green tea available in both cans and plastic bottles. Machines sell beer and other alcoholic beverages, but you may want to avoid *shochu* alcohol sold in glass jars or paper cartons—it is overpoweringly strong. Coffee—both hot and cold—comes in small cans. Don't be surprised to see locals buy one, suck it down, and dispose of the can all during the two-minute wait for the subway. If some Japanese writing below an item is lighted in red, the machine is sold out of it. Hot drinks have a red strip below them and cold drinks are marked with blue. Automation has even spread to religion, as shrines and temples use vending machines to sell *omikuji*, fortunes written on slips of paper.

CONVENIENCE STORES

For the visitor to Tokyo, the nearest *konbini* is a treasure trove of new—and often surprising—experiences. The first convenience store opened in Japan in 1973, and like so many other concepts that have been imported into the country, the Japanese have embraced the konbini, turning it into something of their own. Beyond the usual products you might expect, Japanese convenience stores also carry full hot *bento* (boxed meal), basic clothing items, and event tickets. Services available include digital photo printing, faxing, and utility bill payments. Step into a 7-Eleven, ampm, or Family Mart and you will see familiar brands such as Pepsi and Pringles, but you are not likely to know Pepsi flavored with *shiso*, a Japanese herb, or soy sauce Pringles. Many locals indulge in the practice of *tachiyomi*, standing in front of a magazine rack and browsing the selections without actually buying anything. This practice is accepted and, for visitors, is a good way to get a sense of current trends.

TOP BUYS

Japanese Pringles potato chips have come in flavors such as cheese and bacon and seaweed, and new surprising combinations are rolled out every season. Another international brand that often adds a local twist is Kit Kat, which in the past has released grilled corn, Camembert cheese, and Earl Grey tea versions of its candy bars. The Japanese pronunciation, *kitto katsu*, sounds like the phrase "you are sure to pass," and so make popular gifts to students during entrance exam season. New varieties of Kit Kat debut in spring. If you are traveling with children, a fun purchase is *ramune*, a carbonated drink sold in a glass bottle sealed with a glass marble held in place by the pressure of the gas—push the marble down with your thumb to break the seal. One convenience store treat you cannot leave Japan without trying at least once is *onigiri*, a triangular rice ball containing tuna, pickled plum, or other fillings, and wrapped in sheets of dried seaweed.

TSUKIJI FISH MARKET

The fresh sashimi, grilled fish, and other seafood seen on sale from Tokyo's street-side food stalls to its award-winning restaurants all have one thing in common: it all passes through the largest seafood market in the world; a lively center of unforgettable sights, sounds, and smells.

(top left) Vendors bid on the freshest fish in the world (top right) tuna sells for as much as $20,000 (bottom right) scope out the goods along with wholesalers.

It comes as no surprise that in Japan, an island nation, seafood has been a staple for centuries, and this remains just as true today even though beef and pork consumption have skyrocketed. Completed in 1935, Tsukiji Market is the main conduit through which the bounty of the oceans pass into the country. Seen from above, Tsukiji Market resembles a quarter circle. Several small city blocks at the point of the circle constitute the outer market or the *jogai shijo*. Radiating around this is the vast inner market, or *jonai shijo*. Every day over 2,000 metric tons of seafood, worth 1.5 billion yen changes hands here. The adventurous—and lucky—traveler can walk among the fast-dealing wholesalers at the pre-dawn market. A more leisurely visit will include a stroll through the outer market and a fresh sushi breakfast.

CONTACT INFORMATION

✉ 5–2–1 Tsukiji, Chuo-ku ☎ 03/3542–1111 ⊕ www.shijou.metro.tokyo.jp ⊠ Free ⊘ Mon.–Sat. (except 2nd and 4th Wed. of month) 5 am–3 pm Ⓜ Toei Oedo subway line, Tsukiji-shijo Station (Exit A1); Hibiya subway line, Tsukiji Station (Exit 1).

INNER MARKET

Professional buyers and resellers deftly move through the hundreds of varieties seafood and assess them with a glance of an expert's eye at the inner market. Visitors may make purchases, but should be careful not to get in the way of the pros. Only licensed buyers can bid at the famed tuna auction, exchanging rapid-fire hand gestures with a fast-talking auctioneer. The prized catches can sell for upwards of $20,000 each.

OUTER MARKET

When Japanese consumers go to Tsukiji, they generally shop for seafood in the outer market, a collection of more than 100 separate shops, stands, and sushi restaurants. Retailers also sell dried fish, *nerimono* (fish cakes), fruits and vegetables, meat, beans, and grains. For a practical and unique souvenir, browse the shops offering Japanese kitchen utensils, both traditional wood and bamboo items and modern, cleverly designed tools. Ornately decorated dishware and chopsticks are also available. Nori (sheets of dry seaweed), essential for making sushi rolls at home, and Japanese green tea can be easily packed away to bring home.

EATING IN THE MARKET

Enjoying a sushi breakfast is an integral part of any trip to Tsukiji. There are dozens of sushi restaurants scattered throughout the outer market and it is easy to tell which are the best—they have the longest queues outside. It is well worth the wait—and the cost—as the area has the freshest sushi in the world. Daiwa Sushi (✉ *Tsukiji Oroshiurishijo 6 Bldg.*), just inside the inner market, has only one item, the chef's set (¥3,500), but it is a perennial favorite. A cheaper and quicker option is sashimi donburi, an oversized bowl of steamed rice topped with slices of raw fish, omelet, and piquant wasabi paste. Kaisendon Oedo (✉ *Tsukiji Oroshiurishijo 8 Bldg.*) is a no-frills restaurant that specializes in the dish, offering more than 30 different combinations of sashimi toppings.

3

TIPS

Get to the market by 5 am if you want to see the tuna auction, and by 7 am if you want to browse the inner market.

In busy seasons (including December), visitors are completely barred from the auctions. At other times 140 are admitted between 5 am and 6:15 am on a first-come basis.

There is pungent water on the ground, so wear hiking boots or waterproof sneakers and casual clothing.

In the inner market, be especially careful of the delivery carts that zip around, rarely slowing down when someone gets in their way.

Photography is allowed in the auction, but flashes are strictly forbidden. Taking pictures in the inner market is acceptable, but it is good practice to ask the stall keeper before snapping away.

Never touch any seafood in the auction or anywhere in the inner market.

The inner market officially closes to visitors at 9 am, and the outer market is mostly closed down by 11 am.

RESTAURANT REVIEWS

Restaurant reviews are listed in alphabetical order within neighborhood. Use the coordinate (✛ B2) at the end of each listing to locate a site on the Where to Eat in Tokyo map.

AKASAKA 赤坂

$$ ✕**Ajanta** アジャンタ. In the mid-20th century, the owner of Ajanta came
INDIAN to Tokyo to study electrical engineering. He ended up changing careers and establishing what is today one of the oldest and best Indian restaurants in town. There's no decor to speak of at this restaurant which stays open until 4 am. The emphasis instead is on the variety and intricacy of South Indian cooking—and none of its dressier rivals can match Ajanta's menu for sheer depth. The curries are hot to begin with, but you can order them even hotter. Try the *masala dosa* (a savory crepe), *keema* (minced beef), or mutton curry. A small boutique in one corner sells saris and imported Indian foodstuffs. ✉ *3–11 Niban-cho, Chiyoda-ku* ☎ *03/3264–6955* Ⓜ *Yuraku-cho subway line, Koji-machi Station (Exit 5)* ✛ *E2.*

$$$$ ✕**Jidaiya** 時代屋. Like the Jidaiya in Roppongi, these two Akasaka
JAPANESE branches serve various prix fixe courses, including shabu-shabu, tempura, sushi, and steamed rice with seafood. The food isn't fancy, but it's delicious and filling. The rustic interior makes for a good atmosphere. ✉ *1F Naritaya Bldg., Akasaka 3–14–3, Minato-ku* ☎ *03/3588–0489* ⊘ *No lunch weekends* Ⓜ *Ginza and Marunouchi subway lines, Akasaka-mitsuke Station (Belle Vie Akasaka Exit)* ✉ *B1 Isomura Bldg., Akasaka 5–1–4, Minato-ku* ☎ *03/3224–1505* ⊕ *tokyo-jidaiya.jp/en* Ⓜ *Chiyoda subway line, Akasaka Station (Exit 1A)* ✛ *D4.*

$$$$ ✕**Kisoji** 木曽路. The specialty here is shabu-shabu: thin slices of beef
JAPANESE cooked in boiling water at your table and dipped in sauce. Normally this is an informal, if pricey, sort of meal; after all, you do get to play with your food a bit. Kisoji, which has been serving the dish for more than 60 years, adds a dimension of posh to the experience, with all the tasteful appointments of a traditional *ryotei*—private dining rooms with tatami seating (at a 10% surcharge), elegant little rock gardens, and alcoves with flower arrangements. ✉ *3–10–4 Akasaka, Minato-ku* ☎ *03/3588–0071* Ⓜ *Ginza and Marunouchi subway lines, Akasaka-mitsuke Station (Belle Vie Akasaka Exit)* ✛ *D4.*

$$ ✕**Moti** モティ. Vegetarian dishes at Moti, especially the lentil and egg-
INDIAN plant curries, are very good; so is the chicken masala, cooked in butter
★ and spices. The chefs here are recruited from India by a family member who runs a restaurant in Delhi. As its reputation for reasonably priced North Indian cuisine grew, Moti established branches in nearby Akasaka-mitsuke, Roppongi, and farther away in Yokohama. They all have the inevitable Indian friezes, copper bowls, and white elephants, but this one—popular at lunch with the office crowd from the nearby Tokyo Broadcasting System headquarters—puts the least effort into decor. ✉ *3F Kimpa Bldg., 2–14–31 Akasaka, Minato-ku* ☎ *03/3584–6649* Ⓜ *Chiyoda subway line, Akasaka Station (Exit 2)* ✛ *D4.*

3

$$$–$$$$
JAPANESE

✗ **Ninja** 忍者. In keeping with the air of mystery you'd expect from a ninja-themed restaurant, a ninja-costumed waiter leads you through a dark underground maze to your table in an artificial cave. The menu has more than 100 choices, including some elaborate set courses that are extravagant in both proportion and price. Among the impressively presented dishes are "jack-in-the-box" seafood salad—a lacquerware box overflowing with seasonal seafood and garnished with mustard, avocado tartar, and miso paste—and the life-size bonsai-tree dessert made from cookies and green-tea ice cream. Magical tricks are performed at your table during dinner—it's slightly kitschy but entertaining nonetheless. ⊠ *Akasaka Tokyu Plaza, 2–14–3 Nagata-cho, Minato-ku* ☎ *03/5157–3936* ⚑ *Reservations essential* Ⓜ *Ginza and Marunouchi subway lines, Akasaka-mitsuke Station (Tokyu Plaza Exit)* ✛ *D4.*

$$–$$$
ITALIAN

✗ **Pizza Salvatore Cuomo** ピッツアサルヴァトーレクオモ. Visitors to Pizza Salvatore Cuomo instantly catch the rich aroma of the wood-burning oven that is the centerpiece of this homey, spacious restaurant. Chef Salvatore Cuomo adheres to traditional Neapolitan methods, while updating recipes with dough infused with spinach, herbs, and even squid ink. Lunch courses are filling, affordable, and quick. Though seating space is ample, expect a full house on weekdays. For dinner, classic antipasto dishes such as Caprese make for an authentic Italian meal. ⊠ *Prudential Plaza Bldg., 2–13–10 Nagata-cho, Chiyoda-ku* ☎ *03/3500–5700* Ⓜ *Chiyoda and Marunouchi subway lines, Akasaka-mitsuke Station* ✛ *D4.*

$$
ITALIAN

✗ **Ristorante Carmine** カルミネ. Everybody pitched in, so the story goes, when chef Carmine Cozzolino left his job at an upscale restaurant in Aoyama and opened this unpretentious neighborhood bistro in 1987: friends designed the logo and the interior, painted the walls (black and white), and hung the graphics, swapping their labor for meals. The five-course dinner (¥3,990–¥5,250) here could be the best deal in town. The menu changes weekly; specialties of the house include risotto primavera and Tuscan-style *filetto di pesce* (fish fillet) parmigiano. The wine list is well chosen, and the *torta al cioccolata* (chocolate cake) is a serious dessert. ⊠ *1F Nishikawa Bldg., 1–19 Saiku-cho, Shinjuku-ku* ☎ *03/3260–5066* Ⓜ *Oedo subway line, Ushigome-Kagurazaka Station (Exit 1)* ✛ *D2.*

$–$$
JAPANESE

✗ **Sawanoi** 澤乃井. The homemade udon noodles, served in a broth with seafood, vegetables, or chicken, make a perfect light meal or midnight snack. Try the *inaka* (country-style) udon, which has bonito, seaweed flakes, radish shavings, and a raw egg dropped in to cook in the hot broth. For a heartier meal, chose the *tenkama* set: hot udon and shrimp tempura with a delicate soy-based sauce. A bit run-down, Sawanoi is one of the last remaining neighborhood shops in what is now an upscale business and entertainment district. It stays open until 3 am, and a menu is available in English. ⊠ *1F Shimpo Bldg., 3–7–13 Akasaka, Minato-ku* ☎ *03/3582–2080* ▭ *No credit cards* ☾ *Closed Sun.* Ⓜ *Ginza and Marunouchi subway lines, Akasaka-mitsuke Station (Belle Vie Akasaka Exit)* ✛ *D3.*

$$$$
SUSHI

✗ **Sushi Saito** 鮨さいとう. No trip to Tokyo is complete without sampling the freshest sushi available in the world. The award-winning

Sushi Saito, situated just across the street from the U.S. embassy, has only six counter seats and a discreet sign out front, but it is always fully booked. And for good reason—it has some of the best sushi in town. ✉ *1F Jidousha kaikan Bldg., 1–9–15 Akasaka, Minato-ku* ☎ *03/3589–4412* 👝 *Reservations essential* 🕐 *Closed Sun. and holidays* Ⓜ *Ginza subway line, Tameike-Sanno Station (Exit 9)* ✛ *D4.*

$$$–$$$$ ✕ **Toh-Ka-Lin** 桃花林. Business travel-
CHINESE ers consider the Okura to be one of the best hotels in Asia. That judgment has to do with its polish, its human scale, its impeccable standards of service, and, to judge by Toh-Ka-Lin, the quality of its restaurants. The style of the cuisine here is eclectic; two stellar examples are the Peking duck and the sautéed quail wrapped in lettuce leaf. The restaurant also has a not-too-expensive mid-afternoon meal ($$) of assorted dim sum and other delicacies—and one of the most extensive wine lists in town. ✉ *6F Hotel Okura Main Bldg., 2–10–4 Tora-no-mon, Minato-ku* ☎ *03/3505–6068* Ⓜ *Hibiya subway line, Kamiya-cho Station (Exit 4B); Ginza subway line, Tora-no-mon Station (Exit 3)* ✛ *D4.*

AOYAMA 青山

$–$$ ✕ **Darumaya** だるまや. The classic bowl of ramen is topped with slices
RAMEN of pork, but Darumaya, in the fashion district of Omotesando, offers a slightly different take, topping its noodles with grilled vegetables. Vegetarians beware: the soups and sauces are not meat-free. ✉ *1F Murayama Bldg., 5–9–5 Minami-Aoyama, Minato-ku* ☎ *03/3499–6295* ▭ *No credit cards* Ⓜ *Ginza, Chiyoda, and Hanzo-mon subway lines, Omotesando Station (Exit B1)* ✛ *B4.*

$$$ ✕ **Higo-no-ya** 肥後の屋. The specialty of the house is *kushi-yaki*: small
JAPANESE servings of meat, fish, and vegetables cut into bits and grilled on bamboo skewers. There's nothing ceremonious or elegant about kushi-yaki; it resembles the more familiar yakitori, with somewhat more variety to the ingredients. Higo-no-ya's helpful English menu guides you to other delicacies like shiitake mushrooms stuffed with minced chicken; bacon-wrapped scallops; and bonito, shrimp, and eggplant with ginger. The restaurant is a postmodern–traditional cross, with wood beams painted black, paper lanterns, and sliding paper screens. There's tatami, table, and counter seating. ✉ *B1 AG Bldg., 3–18–17 Minami-Aoyama, Minato-ku* ☎ *03/3423–4461* 🕐 *No lunch* Ⓜ *Ginza, Chiyoda, and Hanzo-mon subway lines, Omotesando Station (Exit A4)* ✛ *B4.*

Tofu is top dog at Ume no Hana in Aoyama.

$$-$$$
JAPANESE

✕ **Maisen** まい泉. Converted from a *sento* (public bathhouse), Maisen still has the old high ceiling (built for ventilation) and the original signs instructing bathers where to change. Bouquets of seasonal flowers help transform the large, airy space into a pleasant dining room. Maisen's specialty is the *tonkatsu* set: tender, juicy, deep-fried pork cutlets served with a spicy sauce, shredded cabbage, miso soup, and rice. A popular alternative is the *Suruga-zen* set, a main course of fried fish served with sashimi, soup, and rice. There are no-smoking rooms upstairs. ⊠ *4–8–5 Jingu-mae, Shibuya-ku* ☎ *03/3470–0071* Ⓜ *Ginza, Chiyoda, and Hanzo-mon subway lines, Omotesando Station (Exit A2)* ✛ *B4*.

$$$
JAPANESE
Fodor'sChoice
★

✕ **Ume no Hana** 梅の花. The exclusive specialty here is tofu, prepared in more ways than you can imagine—boiled, steamed, stir-fried with minced crabmeat, served in a custard, and wrapped in thin layers around a delicate whitefish paste. Tofu is touted as the perfect high-protein, low-calorie health food; at Ume no Hana it's raised to the elegance of haute cuisine. Remove your shoes when you step up to the main room of the elegant restaurant. Latticed wood screens separate the tables, and private dining rooms with tatami seating are available. Prix fixe meals include a complimentary aperitif. ⊠ *2F Aoyama M's Tower, 2–27–18 Minami-Aoyama, Minato-ku* ☎ *03/5412–0855* Ⓜ *Ginza Line, Gaien-mae Station (Exit 1A)* ✛ *C4*.

ASAKUSA 浅草

$$
JAPANESE

✕ **Daikokuya Tempura** 大黒家天麩羅. Although tempura is available throughout the city, Asakusa prides itself on its battered, deep-fried seafood and vegetables. Daikokuya, in the center of Asakusa's historic district, is a point of pilgrimage for both locals and tourists. The menu choices are simple—*tendon* is tempura served over rice, and the tempura meal includes rice, pickled vegetables, and miso soup. Famished diners can add additional pieces of tempura for an additional fee. The light, fluffy tempura is made to order. When the line of waiting customers outside is too long, head to the shop's annex (*bekkan*) just around the corner. ✉ *1–38–10 Asakusa, Taito-ku* ☎ *03/3844–1111* 🚇 *No credit cards* Ⓜ *Ginza and Asakusa subway lines, Asakusa Station* ✚ *H1.*

$$
JAPANESE

✕**Tatsumiya** たつみ屋. Here's a restaurant that's run like a formal ryotei but has the feel of a rough-cut *izakaya* (Japanese pub). Neither inaccessible nor outrageously expensive, Tatsumiya is adorned—nay, cluttered—with antique chests, braziers, clocks, lanterns, bowls, utensils, and craft work, some of it for sale. The evening meal is in the *kaiseki* style, with seven courses: tradition demands that the meal include something raw, something boiled, something vinegary, and something grilled. The kaiseki dinner is served only until 8:30, and you must reserve ahead for it. Tatsumiya also serves a light lunch, plus a variety of *nabe* (one-pot seafood and vegetable stews, prepared at your table) until 10. The pork nabe is the house specialty. ✉ *1–33–5 Asakusa, Taito-ku* ☎ *03/3842–7373* Ⓜ *Ginza and Asakusa subway lines, Asakusa Station (Exits 1 and 3)* ✚ *H1.*

DAIKANYAMA 代官山

$$$–$$$$
ITALIAN

✕**Eataly** イータリー. The Italian luxury supermarket chain that originated in Turin has come to Tokyo. The complex, the first of its kind in Japan, is dedicated to all things Italian. In addition to shopping, there is a gelato and cake bar with outdoor seating, casual pasta and pizza restaurants open for lunch and dinner, and Guido, an elegant "slow food" dinner restaurant. ✉ *20–23 Daikanyama-cho, Shibuya-ku* ☎ *03/5784–2736* Ⓜ *Tokyu Toyoko private rail line, Daikanyama Station (Kita-guchi/North Exit)* ✚ *A5.*

$
PAN-ASIAN

✕**Monsoon Cafe** モンスーンカフェ. With several locations, Monsoon Cafe meets the demand in Tokyo for "ethnic" food—which by local definition means spicy and primarily Southeast Asian. Complementing the eclectic Pan-Asian food are rattan furniture, brass tableware from Thailand, colorful papier-mâché parrots on gilded stands, Balinese carvings, and ceiling fans. Here, at the original Monsoon, the best seats in the house are on the balcony that runs around the four sides of the atrium-style central space. Try the satay (grilled, skewered cubes of meat) platter, steamed shrimp dumplings, or *nasi goring* (Indonesian fried rice). ✉ *15–4 Hachiyama-cho, Shibuya-ku* ☎ *03/5489–3789* ⊕ *www.monsoon-cafe.jp* Ⓜ *Tokyu Toyoko private rail line, Daikanyama Station (Kita-guchi/North Exit)* ✚ *A6.*

$$$–$$$$
ECLECTIC
Fodor's Choice
★

✕**Tableaux** タブロー. The mural in the bar depicts the fall of Pompeii, the banquettes are upholstered in red leather, and the walls are papered in antique gold. Tableaux may lay on more glitz than is necessary, but the service is cordial and professional, and the food is superb. Try Zuwai-crab-and-red-shrimp spring rolls; filet mignon with creamed potatoes, seasonal vegetables, and merlot sauce; or, for dessert, the chocolate soufflé cake. The bar is open until 1:30 am. ✉ *B1 Sunroser Daikanyama*

The opulent décor matches Tableaux's decadent dishes.

Bldg., 11–6 Sarugaku-cho, Shibuya-ku ☎ *03/5489–2201* 🏛 *Jacket and tie* 🕐 *No lunch* Ⓜ *Tokyu Toyoko private rail line, Daikanyama Station (Kita-guchi/North Exit)* ✛ *A5.*

GINZA 銀座

$$$–$$$$
INDIAN
✕ **Ashoka** アショカ. Since 1968, Ashoka has staked out the high ground for Indian cuisine in Tokyo—with a dining room suited to its fashionable Ginza location. The room is hushed and spacious, incense perfumes the air, the lighting is recessed, the carpets are thick, and the servers wear spiffy uniforms. The best thing to order here is the *thali*, a selection of curries, tandoori chicken, and naan served on a figured brass tray. The Goan fish curry is also excellent, as is the chicken tikka: boneless chunks marinated and cooked in the tandoor. ✉ *2F Ginza Inz Bldg. 1, 3–1 Nishi Ginza, Chuo-ku* ☎ *03/3567–2377* Ⓜ *Marunouchi and Ginza subway lines, Ginza Station (Exit C9)* ✛ *E4.*

$$$$
FRENCH
✕ **Gordon Ramsay at the Conrad Hotel** ゴードン・ラムゼイ. This luxurious French restaurant in the Conrad Hotel offers breathtaking views of the Hamarikyu Gardens and Tokyo Bay 37 floors below. There's also plenty to see inside, as the chef prepares dishes such as roasted scallops with mushroom tortellini, peas, and mint velouté with great élan in the open kitchen. Guests may even spot Ramsay himself in the kitchen during one of his frequent visits to Tokyo. ✉ *37F Conrad Tokyo, 1–9–1 Higashi-Shinbashi, Minato-ku* ☎ *03/3688–8000* ⊕ *www.gordonramsay. com* 🍴 *Reservations essential* 🕐 *No lunch* Ⓜ *Toei Oedo subway line, Shiodome Station (Exit 3)* ✛ *F5.*

DINING ON A BUDGET

Tokyo offers an astounding array of top-notch Japanese and international cuisines, but quality comes at a price. However, it's possible to eat well on a budget, and the recent trend for *B-kyu gurume* ("B-grade Gourmet") is making it even easier. These restaurants forgo the frills and just serve good food for affordable prices. Wallet-friendly establishments such as these can be found across the city. Here are a few of the best.

✕ **Kanda Matsuya** 神田まつや (¢–$). Udon—thick noodles served chilled in summer and hot in winter—are available everywhere, even convenience stores. Matsuya offers authentic udon in a rustic atmosphere. A simple udon meal costs ¥600, or, for a bit more, get noodles topped with tempura or other goodies. ⊠ *1–3 Kanda Sudacho, Chiyoda-ku* ☎ *03/3251–1556* ▭ *No credit cards* Ⓜ *Marunouchi Line, Awajicho Station (Exit A3).*

✕ **Kanda Yabu Soba** かんだ やぶそば (¢–$). Soba—thin noodles made from buckwheat flour and quickly dipped into a hot broth or cold dipping sauce—are the lighter cousin of udon. Because it can be eaten so quickly, soba is often sold at small stands in train stations, where it can be slurped down while waiting to change trains. Kanda Yabu Soba, set in a Japanese garden, offers a place to sit down and savor the dish. A basic soba meal costs just ¥700, but the *shun* (seasonal meal), which change 10 times a year, are excellent and affordable. ⊠ *2–10 Kanda Awajicho, Chiyoda-ku* ☎ *03/3251–0287* ▭ *No credit cards* Ⓜ *JR and Marunouchi lines, Awajicho Station (Exit A3).*

✕ **Santa** とんかつ三田 ($). Tonkatsu, breaded, deep-fried pork cutlets, are synonymous with cheap but filling meals. Santa offers some of the best tonkatsu in the city in large portions for affordable prices. ⊠ *3–33–10 Shinjuku, Shinjuku-ku* ☎ *03/3351–5861* Ⓜ *Shinjuku Station (East Exit).*

✕ **Umenoki** 梅乃木 ($$). At an izakaya, food and drink are equally important and equally good. Umenoki, in Shibuya, specializes in sashimi, which can be astronomically expensive in award-winning restaurants, but is surprisingly affordable here. You will most likely share one of the long, sunken tables with a number of other diners, which is all part of the experience. ⊠ *2–11–1 Dogenzaka, Shibuya-ku* ☎ *03/5428–6707* Ⓜ *Shibuya Station (Hachiko Exit).*

$$
IZAKAYA
✕ **Kanemasu** かねます. Unlike most izakaya, which stay open to the wee hours of the morning, Kanemasu is open only a few hours in the evening, from 4 until around 8. There are no tables or chairs, and patrons stand around the counter while they eat and drink. So what is the attraction? The father-and-son cooking team raises izakaya fare to a new level by creating novel combinations such as *uni* (sea urchin) wrapped in strips of raw beef. The daily menu is scrawled in chalk on a blackboard, but you can always ask for *osusume* (chef's recommendation). ⊠ *1–10–4 Kachidoki, Chuo-ku* ☎ *03/3531–8611* ▭ *No credit cards* ⊙ *Closed Sun. and holidays* Ⓜ *Oedo subway line, Kachidoki Station (Exit A4)* ✛ *G5.*

Save your yen and slurp up Kanda Yabu Soba's budget-friendly noodles and broth.

$$$$ ✕**Kappo-Ajioka** 割烹味岡. When prepared incorrectly, fugu, the highly
JAPANESE poisonous puffer fish, is fatal, yet this doesn't stop people from trying it
at this Tokyo branch of the Kansai fugu ryotei (puffer-fish restaurant).
Licensed chefs prepare the fish in every way imaginable—raw, fried,
stewed—using the fresh catch flown in straight from Shimonoseki, a
prime fugu-fishing region. The overall flavor is subtle and somewhat
nondescript—people are drawn more to the element of danger than the
taste (fatalities are rare, but a few people in Japan die each year from
fugu poisoning). Try the house specialty of *suppon* (Japanese turtle) and
fugu nabe, fugu sashimi, or fugu *no arayaki* (grilled head and cheeks).
■TIP→ Reservations must be made two days in advance to order fugu.
⊠ *6F New Comparu Bldg., 7–7–12 Ginza, Chuo-ku* ☎ *03/3574–8844*
Ⓜ *Ginza, Hibiya, and Marunouchi subway lines, Ginza Station (Exit
A5)* ✛ *F4.*

$$$$ ✕**Oshima** 大志満. The draw at Oshima is the *Kaga ryori* cooking of
KAISEKI Kanazawa, a small city on the Sea of Japan known as "Little Kyoto"
for its rich craft traditions. Waitresses dress in kimonos of Kanazawa's
famous Yuzen dyed silk; Kutani porcelain and Wajima lacquerware
grace the exquisite table settings. Seafood at Oshima is superb, but
don't ignore the specialty of the house: a stew of duck and potatoes
called *jibuni.* Kaiseki full-course meals are pricey, but there's a reasonable lunchtime set menu for ¥2,625. ⊠ *9F Ginza Core Bldg., 5–8–20
Ginza, Chuo-ku* ☎ *03/3574–8080* Ⓜ *Ginza, Hibiya, and Marunouchi
subway lines, Ginza Station (Exit A5)* ✛ *F4.*

$$$–$$$$ ✕**Rangetsu** らん月. Japan enjoys a special reputation for its lovingly
JAPANESE raised, tender, marbled domestic beef. Try it, if your budget will bear
the weight, at Rangetsu, in the form of this elegant Ginza restaurant's

signature shabu-shabu or sukiyaki course. Call ahead to reserve a private alcove, where you can cook for yourself, or have a kaiseki meal brought to your table by kimono-clad attendants. A lunch course is available for ¥1,800 on weekends. Rangetsu is a block from the Ginza 4-chome crossing, opposite the Matsuya Department Store. ⊠ *3–5–8 Ginza, Chuo-ku* ☎ *03/3567–1021* Ⓜ *Marunouchi and Ginza subway lines, Ginza Station (Exits A9 and A10)* ✣ *F4.*

$$$$

JAPANESE

✕ **Wa no Mori Sumika** 和の杜すみか. A short walk from the heart of Ginza, this respite from the haute cuisine of Ginza specializes in vegetables shipped directly from farms around Japan, reflecting a recent movement in Japan toward healthier, safer eating. There are private dining rooms with tatami seating, and sunken counter seats at the window, affording a beautiful night view of lights of Ginza. The seasonal vegetables and fresh fish course (¥8,400) is like taking a tour of Japan, with the best and freshest produce from around the country appearing on your plate. ⊠ *8F Duplex Bldg., 5–13–19 Ginza, Chuo-ku* ☎ *03/3547–8383* 🍴 *Reservations essential* Ⓜ *Marunouchi and Ginza subway lines, Ginza Station (Exits A9 and A10)* ✣ *F4.*

$$

JAPANESE

✕ **Yumeya**夢や. Tsukishima ("moon island") is a small man-made island a stone's throw from the upscale Ginza district, which takes its name from its crescent-moon shape and is the birthplace of *monjayaki*. The watery batter is mixed with shredded cabbage and other ingredients, fried on a griddle built into the table, and eaten directly from the grill with metal spatulas. The main street in Tsukishima is filled with monjayaki establishments, and one of the best is Yumeya, which can be identified by the line of waiting patrons often outside. It can be a bit tricky to make monjayaki yourself—you need to form a ring of dry ingredients on the grill and pour the batter into the middle. The servers can also make it for you at your table. ⊠ *3–18–4 Tsukishima, Chuo-ku* ☎ *03/3536–7870* 🖃 *No credit cards* 🕙 *Closed Mon. No lunch weekdays* Ⓜ *Oedo and Yuraku-cho subway lines, Tsukishima Station (Exit 7)* ✣ *G5.*

HARAJUKU 原宿

$$$$

SCANDINAVIAN

✕ **Aquavit** アクアビット. One of the handful of authentic Swedish restaurants in Tokyo, Aquavit offers a reasonably priced prix fixe dinner (and lunch). A good appetizer to try is herring sampler, which includes pickled herring and sweet varieties that change seasonally. Good main dish choices include smoked trout with celery puree, white beech mushrooms, and apple-horseradish sauce or the venison loin served with cured ham, potato dumplings, and lingonberry sauce. Got room for dessert? Don't pass up the scrumptious Swedish pancakes, which are served with ginger confit, fresh cream, and raspberries. Everything is served in a romantic dining room with ultramodern design and furniture by Friz Hansen of Denmark. ⊠ *1F Shimizu Bldg., 2–5–8 Kita-Aoyama, Minato-ku* ☎ *03/5413–3300* ⊕ *www.aquavit-japan.com* Ⓜ *Ginza subway line, Gaien-mae Station (Exit 1B)* ✣ *B4.*

$$$$

BRAZILIAN

✕ **Barbacoa Grill** バルバッコアグリル. Carnivores flock here for the great-value all-you-can-eat Brazilian grilled chicken and barbecued beef, which the efficient waiters will keep bringing to your table on skewers until you tell them to stop. Those with lighter appetites can choose the less-expensive salad buffet and *feijoada* (pork stew with black beans); both are bargains. Barbacoa has hardwood floors, lithographs of bull motifs, warm lighting, salmon-color tablecloths, and roomy seating. This popular spot is just off Omotesando-dori on the Harajuku 2-chome shopping street (on the north side of Omotesando-dori), about 50 yards down on the left. ⊠ *4–3–24 Jingu-mae, Shibuya-ku* ☎ *03/3796–0571* Ⓜ *Ginza, Chiyoda, and Hanzo-mon subway lines, Omotesando Station (Exit A2)* ✛ *B4.*

> ### AVOID THE CROWD
>
> Chances are that when you're hungry for dinner, so are hundreds of other people who will flock to the same restaurant districts. It's not uncommon to wait for a table for up to an hour, especially on Friday and Saturday nights. Go a little early, say around 5:30, to bypass the crowds, or reserve ahead to avoid disappointment.

$$
SUSHI
✕ **Heiroku-zushi** 平禄寿司. Ordinarily, a meal of sushi is a costly indulgence. The rock-bottom alternative is a *kaiten-zushi,* where sushi is literally served assembly-line style. The chefs inside the circular counter maintain a constant supply on the revolving belt on plates color-coded for price; just choose whatever takes your fancy as dishes pass by. Heiroku-zushi is a bustling, cheerful example of the genre, with fresh fish and no pretensions at all to decor. When you're done, the server counts up your plates and calculates your bill (¥126 for staples like tuna and squid to ¥367 for delicacies like eel and salmon roe). ⊠ *5–8–5 Jingu-mae, Shibuya-ku* ☎ *03/3498–3968* ▭ *No credit cards* Ⓜ *Ginza, Chiyoda, and Hanzo-mon subway lines, Omotesando Station (Exit A1)* ✛ *B4.*

$$–$$$
RAMEN
✕ **Mist** ミスト. Exercising your plastic in Tokyo's Omotesando Hills shopping complex can be tiring. Refuel at Mist, a 21-seat "noodle studio" inside the Tadao Ando–designed complex. The look is minimalist-chic, with counter seats, a stainless-steel kitchen, and burgundy banquettes. The food, as lovely as the space, includes homemade ramen—springy, firm, and served with a savory broth. The menu boasts two styles of ramen and three optional toppings. At lunch, gourmet ramen and one beverage will set you back at least ¥1,700. ⊠ *4–12–10 Jingu-mae, Shibuya-ku* ☎ *03/5410–1368* Ⓜ *Ginza, Chiyoda, and Hanzo-mon subway lines, Omotesando Station (Exit A2)* ✛ *B4.*

$–$$
CAFÉ
✕ **Montoak** モントーク. If you're into people-watching, then this two-story café on Omotesando street in the heart of one of the most fashion-conscious areas of Tokyo is the perfect place to relax on an afternoon. Order one of the scrumptious homemade tarts or cakes and a coffee, and watch the trendiest Tokyoites stroll by the full-length windows. ⊠ *6–1–9 Jingu-mae, Shibuya-ku* ☎ *03/5468–5928* Ⓜ *Ginza, Chiyoda, and Hanzo-mon subway lines, Omotesando Station (Exit A1); Chiyoda subway line, Meiji-Jingu-mae (Harajuku) Station (Exit 5)* ✛ *B4.*

$$
FRENCH
✕ **Red Pepper** レッドペッパー. This cozy bistro is a short walk down a narrow alley from Omotesando Crossing, the trendy shopping district. The atmosphere is homey, and guests squeeze into tiny antique school chairs and desks topped with candles. The cuisine is constantly

The Essentials of a Japanese Meal

The basic formula for a traditional Japanese meal is deceptively simple. It starts with soup, followed by raw fish, then the entrée (grilled, steamed, simmered, or fried fish, chicken, or vegetables), and ends with rice and pickles, with perhaps fresh fruit for dessert, and a cup of green tea. It's as simple as that—almost.

There are, admittedly, a few twists to the story. Beyond the raw fish, it's the incredible variety of vegetation used in Japanese cooking that still surprises the Western palate: take-no-ko (bamboo shoots), renkon (lotus root), and the treasured matsutake mushrooms (which grow wild in jealously guarded forest hideaways and sometimes sell for more than $60 apiece), to name a few.

There are also ground rules. Absolute freshness is first. To a Japanese chef, this is an unparalleled virtue, and much of a chef's reputation relies on the ability to obtain the finest ingredients at the peak of season: fish brought in from the sea this morning (not yesterday) and vegetables from the earth (not the hothouse), if at all possible.

Simplicity is next. Rather than embellishing foods with heavy spices and rich sauces, the Japanese chef prefers flavors au naturel. Flavors are enhanced, not elaborated, accented rather than concealed. Without a heavy sauce, fish is permitted a degree of natural fishiness—a garnish of fresh red ginger will be provided to offset the flavor rather than to disguise it.

The third prerequisite is beauty. Simple, natural foods must appeal to the eye as well as to the palate. Green peppers on a vermilion dish, perhaps, or an egg custard in a blue bowl. Rectangular dishes for a round eggplant. So important is the seasonal element in Japanese cooking that maple leaves and pine needles will be used to accent an autumn dish. Or two small summer delicacies, a pair of freshwater ayu fish, will be grilled with a purposeful twist to their tails to make them "swim" across a crystal platter and thereby suggest the coolness of a mountain stream on a hot August night.

Not to be forgotten is mood, which can make or break the entire meal. Japanese connoisseurs will go to great lengths to find the perfect yakitori stand—a smoky, lively place—an environment appropriate to the occasion, offering a night of grilled chicken, cold beer, and camaraderie. In fancier places, mood becomes a fancier problem, to the point of quibbling over the proper amount of "water music" trickling in the basin outside your private room.

---

changing, and most dinners ignore the printed menu in favor of the daily recommendations chalked on blackboards (mostly in Japanese) propped up here and there. You might find dishes such as button mushrooms grilled in garlic and olive oil, or porcini-and-cream-sauce fettuccine. ⊠ 1F Shimizu Bldg., 3–5–25 Kita-Aoyama, Shibuya-ku ☎ 03/3478–1264 Ⓜ Ginza, Chiyoda, and Hanzo-mon subway lines, Omotesando Station (Exit A3) ⊕ B4.

¢–$ ✕ R Style アールスタイル. Even in some of the swankiest restaurants, Jap-
JAPANESE anese wagashi (sweets) aren't up to par. To sample authentic handmade

wagashi while sipping green tea, head to this café. The main ingredients in wagashi are adzuki beans, rice, and other grains sweetened slightly by sugarcane—making these treats a fairly healthful dessert. The intricate morsels of edible art are almost too perfectly presented to eat—almost, but not quite. Try the *konomi* (rice dumpling with adzuki conserve) or *koyomi* (bracken dumpling with soy custard) set. ✉ *3F Omotesando Hills Main Bldg., 4–12–10 Jingu-mae, Shibuya-ku* ☎ *03/3423–1155* Ⓜ *Ginza, Chiyoda, and Hanzo-mon subway lines, Omotesando Station (Exit A2); Chiyoda subway line, Meiji-Jingu-mae (Harajuku) Station (Exit 5)* ⊹ *B4.*

$$–$$$ ✕ **Sakuratei** さくら亭. Tucked away between two art galleries that feature
JAPANESE works by young Japanese artists, Sakuratei defies other conventions as well: eating here doesn't always mean you don't have to cook. At this do-it-yourself *okonomiyaki* (a kind of pancake made with egg, meat, and vegetables) restaurant, you choose ingredients and cook them on the *teppan* (grill). Okonomiyaki is generally easy to make, but flipping the pancake to cook the other side can be challenging—potentially messy but still fun. Fortunately, you're not expected to do the dishes. Okonomiyaki literally means "as you like it," so experiment with your own recipe or try the house special, *sakurayaki* (with pork, squid, and onions), or *monjayaki* (a watered-down variation of okonomiyaki from the Kanto region). ✉ *3–20–1 Jingu-mae, Shibuya-ku* ☎ *03/3479–0039* Ⓜ *Chiyoda subway line, Meiji-Jingu-mae (Harajuku) Station (Exit 5)* ⊹ *B4.*

MEGURO 目黒

$$ ✕ **Keawjai** ゲウチャイ. Blink and you might miss the faded sign of this
THAI little basement restaurant a minute's walk from Meguro Station. Keaw-
★ jai is one of the few places in Tokyo to specialize in the subtle complexities of Royal Thai cuisine, and despite its size—only eight tables and four banquettes—it serves a remarkable range of dishes in different regional styles. The spicy beef salad is excellent (and *really* spicy), as are the baked rice and crabmeat served in a whole pineapple, and the red-curry chicken in coconut milk with cashews. The service is friendly and unhurried. There is also a branch in Shinjuku. ✉ *B1 Meguro Kowa Bldg., 2–14–9 Kami Osaki, Meguro-ku* ☎ *03/5420–7727* Ⓜ *JR Yamanote and Namboku subway lines, Meguro Station (Higashi-guchi/East Exit)* ⊹ *B5.*

$–$$ ✕ **Tonki** とんき. Meguro, a neighborhood distinguished for almost noth-
JAPANESE ing else culinary, has arguably the best tonkatsu restaurant in Tokyo. It's
★ a family joint, with Formica-top tables and a server who comes around to take your order while you wait the requisite 10 minutes in line. And people do wait in line, every night until the place closes at 10:45. Tonki is a success that never went conglomerate or added frills to what it does best: deep-fried pork cutlets, soup, raw-cabbage salad, rice, pickles, and tea. That's the standard course, and almost everybody orders it, with good reason. ✉ *1–1–2 Shimo-Meguro, Meguro-ku* ☎ *03/3491–9928* ⊙ *Closed Tues. and 3rd Mon. of month* Ⓜ *JR Yamanote and Namboku subway lines, Meguro Station (Nishi-guchi/West Exit)* ⊹ *B5.*

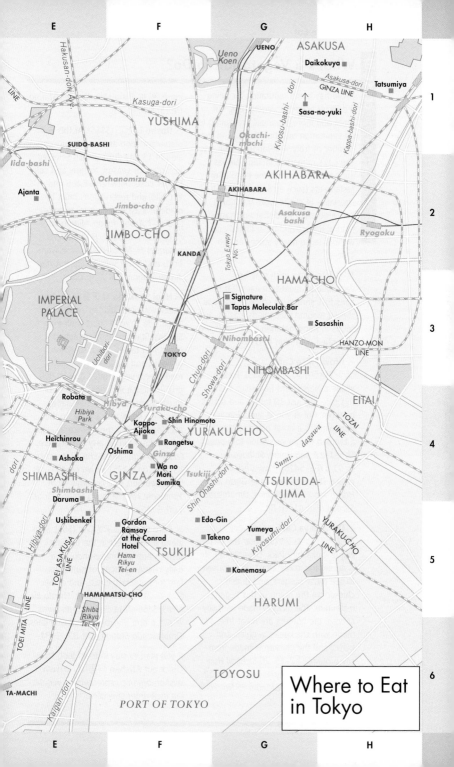

Where to Eat in Tokyo

What's a Vegetarian to Do?

Tokyo has had a reputation for being a difficult place for vegetarians, but more and more Japanese are opting to go vegetarian resulting in a rise in the number of truly vegetarian restaurants. The city's numerous Indian eateries are a safe bet, as are the handful of restaurants (such as Sasa-no-yuki) that specialize in *shojin ryori*, traditional Zen vegetarian food that emphasizes natural flavors and fresh ingredients without using heavy spices or rich sauces.

Take note that a dish may be described as meat-free even if it contains fish, shrimp, or chicken. And one should assume that salads, pastas, and soups in nonvegetarian restaurants are garnished with ham or bacon.

✕ **Brown Rice Café** ブラウンライス カフェ($$$). Tucked inside a Neal's Yard Remedies store, this café has just 10 tables and closes by 9 pm. But, if you're shopping in Harajuku, it's a great place to stop for a tempeh burger or stuffed tofu pouch. ⊠ 5–1–17 Jingu-mae, Shibuya-ku ☎ 03/5778–5416 ⊕ www.brown. co.jp ▭ No credit cards Ⓜ Ginza and Hanzo-mon subway lines, Omotesando Station (Exit A1) ⊹ B4.

✕ **Deva Deva Café** デヴァデヴァカフェ($). Near the picturesque Inokashira Park, Deva Deva Cafe is an organic oasis. Don't be surprised to see pizza, burgers, and grilled chicken on the menu of this vegan restaurant. The pizza is made with soy cheese; the burgers are meat-free, made with chickpeas, veggies, and herbs; and the chicken is made from soy protein. ⊠ 2–15–26 Kichijoji Hon-cho, Musashino City ☎ 042/221 6220 ⊕ www.devadevacafe.com ▭ No credit

cards Ⓜ JR Chuo Line, Kichijoji Station (North Exit) ⊹ A1.

✕ **Itosho** いと正 ($$$$). At this Zen restaurant, food arrives in a procession of 13 tiny dishes, each selected according to season, texture, and color. Dinner costs between ¥8,400 and ¥10,500, and reservations must be made at least two days in advance. ⊠ 3–4–7 Azabu Juban, Minato-ku ☎ 03/3454–6538 ⬧ Reservations essential ▭ No credit cards Ⓜ Nam-boku and Oedo subway lines, Azabu Juban Station (Exit 1) ⊹ C5.

✕ **Nagi Shokudo** なぎ食堂 ($). This small restaurant hidden away on a small side street a short walk from Shibuya Station has mismatched chairs and tables and a selection of books and magazines you can read over a vegan meal. The ¥1,000 prix fixe lunch includes a choice of three dishes, which change daily, rice, miso soup, and a drink. In the evening, this is a great place to enjoy a light dinner in an arty atmosphere. ⊠ 15–10 Uguisudani-cho, Shibuya-ku ☎ 050/1043–7751 ▭ No credit cards ⊗ Closed Sun. and holidays Ⓜ JR Yamanote Line, Shibuya Station (South Exit) ⊹ A5.

✕ **Pure Café** ピュアカフェ ($$$). Stop along a backstreet in the upscale fashion hub of Omotesando for a daily changing menu of nutritious fare for breakfast, lunch, and dinner. ⊠ 5–5–21 Minami-Aoyama, Minato-ku ☎ 03/5466–2611 ▭ No credit cards Ⓜ Ginza and Hanzo-mon subway lines, Omotesando Station (Exit B3) ⊹ B4.

If you plan to stay in town long term, check out **Alishan** 阿里山 (⊕ www. alishan-organic-center.com), a vegetarian mail-order specialist.

NIHOMBASHI 日本橋

$$
IZAKAYA

✕ **Sasashin** 笹新. Like most izakaya, Sasashin spurns the notion of decor: there's a counter laden with platters of the evening's fare, a clutter of rough wooden tables, and not much else. It's noisy, smoky, crowded—and great fun. Like izakaya fare in general, the food is best described as professional home cooking, and is meant mainly as ballast for the earnest consumption of beer and sake. Try the sashimi, the grilled fish, or the fried tofu; you really can't go wrong by just pointing your finger at anything on the counter that takes your fancy. Unlike some izakaya that stay open into the wee hours, this one winds down around 10:30. ✉ *2–20–3 Nihombashi-Ningyocho, Chuo-ku* ☎ *03/3668–2456* ⌂ *Reservations not accepted* ▭ *No credit cards* ⊗ *Closed Sun. and 3rd Sat. of month. No lunch* Ⓜ *Hanzo-mon subway line, Suitengu-mae Station (Exit 7); Hibiya and Asakusa subway lines, Ningyocho Station (Exits A1 and A3)* ✛ *G3.*

$$$$
FRENCH

✕ **Signature** シグネチャー. This elegant, award-wining French restaurant on the 37th floor of the Mandarin Oriental Hotel offers wonderful views of the Tokyo skyline as well an open kitchen where diners can see the masterful chef Olivier Rodriguez and his staff at work. The prix fixe lunch menu offers dishes that blend French and Japanese influences, such as fillet of sole dusted with nori (dried seaweed). The dinner menu includes inspired creations such as roasted veal rack with pumpkin gnocchi and espresso-flavored gravy. A sommelier is on hand, and the wine list includes biodynamic and organic offerings. ✉ *37F Mandarin Oriental Tokyo, 2–1–1 Nihonbashi, Chuo-ku* ☎ *03/3270–8188* ⊕ *www.mandarinoriental.com/tokyo/dining/signature* ⌂ *Reservations essential* Ⓜ *Ginza subway lines, Mitsukoshi-mae Station (Exit A7)* ✛ *G3.*

$$$$
JAPANESE

✕ **Tapas Molecular Bar** タパス モラキュラーバー. This award-wining restaurant occupies a mysterious place between a traditional sushi counter, a tapas bar, a science lab, and a magic show. "Chief Culinary Engineer" Jeff Ramsey, a former sushi chef, dazzles dinners with a live performance in which he creates more than 15 courses that surprise and delight. Nothing on the seasonally changing menu is what it seems, including sweet lemon slices, and the Emperor's New Mojito, an "invisible" cocktail. There are only eight seats, and seatings are at 6 and 8:30 only, so reserve as early as possible. ✉ *38F Mandarin Oriental, 2–1–1 Nihonbashi, Chuo-ku* ☎ *03/3270–8188* ⊕ *www.mandarinoriental.com/tokyo/dining/molecular* ⌂ *Reservations essential* ⊗ *No lunch* Ⓜ *Ginza subway lines, Mitsukoshi-mae Station (Exit A7)* ✛ *G2.*

ROPPONGI 六本木

$$$$
FRENCH

✕ **Azure 45** アジュール フォーティーファイブ. French restaurants in Japan often focus on famous beef and poultry dishes, ignoring the fresh seafood and vegetables that are plentiful though out the country. Executive sous chef Kiyonari Araki amends this oversight at this restaurant in the Ritz-Carlton specializing in seafood. Prix fixe lunch courses offer a choice of three, four, or five dishes from a monthly changing menu. For dinner there is a "chef's tasting" menu, which is paired with wine

CLOSE UP

Kanpai!

Whether you're out with friends, clients, or belting out a tune at the local karaoke bar, you're sure to have a drink at least once during your stay. Things may look a little different, even before you start knocking back a few, so take note of the liquors of this island nation. And remember, shout *Kanpai!* (sounds like "kaan-pie") instead of *Cheers!* when you raise your glass.

THE SACRED DRINK

Sake, pronounced *sa*-kay, is Japan's number one alcoholic beverage. There are more than 2,000 different brands of sake produced throughout Japan. Like other kinds of wine, sake comes in sweet (*amakuchi*) and dry (*karakuchi*) varieties; these are graded *tokkyu* (superior class), *ikkyu* (first class), and *nikkyu* (second class) and are priced accordingly. (Connoisseurs say this ranking is for tax purposes and is not necessarily a true indication of quality.)

Best drunk at room temperature (*nurukan*) so as not to alter the flavor, sake is also served heated (*atsukan*) or with ice (*rokku de*). It's poured from *tokkuri* (small ceramic vessels) into tiny cups called *choko*. The diminutive size of these cups shouldn't mislead you into thinking you can't drink too much. The custom of making sure that your companion's cup never runs dry often leads the novice astray.

Junmaishu is the term for pure rice wine, a blend of rice, yeast, and water to which no extra alcohol has been added. Junmaishu sake has the strongest and most distinctive flavor, compared with various other methods of brewing, and is preferred by the sake *tsu*, as connoisseurs are known.

Apart from the *nomiya* (bars) and restaurants, the place to sample sake is the izakaya, a drinking establishment that usually serves dozens of different kinds of sake, including a selection of *jizake*, the kind produced in limited quantities by small regional breweries throughout the country.

HEAVENLY SPIRITS

Shochu is made from grain and particularly associated with the southern island of Kyushu. It's served either on the rocks or mixed with water and can be hot or cold. Sometimes a wedge of lemon or a small pickled apricot, known as *umeboshi*, is added as well. It can also be mixed with club soda and served cold.

HAVIN' A BIIRU

Japan has four large breweries: Asahi, Kirin, Sapporo, and Suntory. Asahi and Kirin are the two heavyweights, constantly battling for the coveted title of "Japan's No. 1 Brewery," but many beer fans rate Suntory's Malts brand and Sapporo's Yebisu brand as the tastiest brews in the land. In recent years, Belgian beers have grown in popularity and are available in specialty shops and even supermarkets; the products of Japanese microbreweries have also become easier to find.

selected by the hotel's sommelier. ⊠ *Tokyo Midtown, 9-7-1 Akasaka, Minato-ku* ☎ *01/20798-688* Ⓜ *Hibiya subway line, Roppongi Station (Exit 4A); Toei Oedo Line, Roppongi Station (Exit 7)* ✛ *D4.*

\$\$–\$\$\$

THAI

✕**Erawan** エラワン. Window tables at this sprawling Thai "brasserie" on the top floor of a popular Roppongi vertical mall afford a wonderful view of the Tokyo skyline, including Tokyo Tower, at night. Black-painted wood floors, ceiling fans, Thai antiques, and rattan chairs establish the mood, and the space is nicely broken up into large and small dining areas and private rooms. The service is cheerful and professional. Specialties of the house include deep-fried prawn and crabmeat cakes, spicy roast-beef salad, sirloin tips with mango sauce, and a terrific dish of stir-fried lobster meat with cashews. For window seating, it's best to reserve ahead. ⊠ *13F Roi Bldg., 5-5-1 Roppongi, Minato-ku* ☎ *03/3404-5741* Ⓜ *Hibiya subway line, Roppongi Station (Exit 3)* ✛ *C5.*

\$\$

JAPANESE

Fodor's Choice

★

✕**Ganchan** がんちゃん. The Japanese expect their yakitori joints—restaurants that specialize in bits of charcoal-broiled chicken and vegetables—to be just like Ganchan: smoky, noisy, and cluttered. The counter here seats barely 15, and you have to squeeze to get to the chairs in back. Festival masks, paper kites and lanterns, and greeting cards from celebrity patrons adorn the walls. The cooks yell at each other, fan the grill, and serve up enormous schooners of beer. Try the *tsukune* (balls of minced chicken) and the fresh asparagus wrapped in bacon. The place stays open until 1:30 am (midnight on Sunday). ⊠ *6-8-23 Roppongi, Minato-ku* ☎ *03/3478-0092* ◷ *No lunch* Ⓜ *Hibiya subway line, Roppongi Station (Exit 1A)* ✛ *D4.*

\$–\$\$

AMERICAN

✕**Homeworks** ホームワークス. Every so often, even on alien shores, you've got to have a burger. When the urge strikes, the Swiss-and-bacon special at Homeworks is an incomparably better choice than anything you can get at one of the global chains. Hamburgers come in three sizes on white or wheat buns, with a variety of toppings. There are also hot teriyaki chicken sandwiches, pastrami sandwiches, and vegetarian options like a soybean veggie burger or a tofu sandwich. Desserts, alas, are so-so. With its hardwood banquettes and French doors open to the street in good weather, Homeworks is a pleasant place to linger over lunch. There's also a branch in Hiro-o. ⊠ *1F Vesta Bldg., 1-5-8 Azabu Juban, Minato-ku* ☎ *03/3405-9884* Ⓜ *Namboku and Oedo subway lines, Azabu Juban Station (Exit 4)* ✛ *D5.*

\$\$\$\$

FRENCH

✕**Hortensia** オルタシア. French restaurants in Tokyo tend to offer little in terms of variety or customer choice. This restaurant in trendy Azabu Juban rectifies that situation by offering a prix fixe lunch which allows diners to choose four dishes, even if it is a quartet of mains or four desserts. For dinner, the varieté meal offers eight courses, with each course's main ingredient meticulously prepared in two or three ways, such as a lobster claw served with mango confit and lobster meat paired with caviar. The sommelier Kazuto Chiba spent years researching in Napa Valley, and the wine list includes new entries from California, Oregon, and Washington in addition to old French standards. ⊠ *B1F NS Azabu Juban, 3-6-2 Azabu Juban, Minato-Ku* ☎ *03/5419-8455* ⊕ *www.lahortensia.com/en* ✛ *C5.*

CLOSE UP

The Kitchen Magician

At the tender age of 34, Jeff Ramsey is the chef of an award-winning restaurant he started in 2005, and he nightly dazzles diners—and other chefs—with his innovative creations. The Japanese-American has come a long way since he got his start as a teenager washing dishes in a sushi restaurant in the Washington, DC, area. As the "Chief Culinary Engineer" at Tapas Molecular Bar in the Mandarin Oriental Hotel, Ramsey uses experimentation, innovation, and deception to create dishes that challenge common perceptions of what it means to dine and drink.

Here, Ramsey shares his Tokyo recommendations for dining, both fine and casual.

Fodor's: Tell me about your restaurant, Tapas Molecular Bar.

JR: We have eight seats set up at a counter that was originally destined to be a sushi bar. We do a live cooking show that lasts about an hour and a half. We try to be very creative in terms of the ingredients and the presentation. But we try to make the food still recognizable to people, either through deconstruction, or using ingredients or combinations that people know, and applying modern techniques to get interesting effects. It is a food journey in which we are able to present points of modern cooking that people do not get a chance to see otherwise in Tokyo.

Fodor's: If someone is in Tokyo only for a few days, what do you recommend they try?

JR: Abroad, people's perception of Japanese food is often one restaurant that has a little bit of everything—some tempura, some yakitori, some

udon, etc. In Tokyo, people should definitely try specialty restaurants that only serve one type of cuisine. In winter, they should try fugu. One thing that fits in well with people's conception of Japanese food is izakaya. There is a standing izakaya called Kanematsu run by a father-son team in Kachidoki. The dishes are simple, with only three or four ingredients, but they are phenomenal.

Fodor's: What is one dish everyone should try before they leave Tokyo?

JR: Really nice wagyu (Japanese beef) seared on a teppanyaki grill is really unlike anything you can try outside Japan. Also, sushi in Tsukiji has a nice romantic value because you are at the fish market, but it is not the best Japan has to offer. My favorite place is Sushi Shomasa in Nishi-Azabu. That dining experience changed my opinion on how good food can taste.

Fodor's: What is comfort food for you on your day off?

JR: I love soba. I'm Japanese-American, and I grew up eating soba. We are all tied to the foods of our childhood.

Fodor's: Where do you go for inspiration?

JR: It is great to go to a bookstore and browse through food books and magazines. There are tons of books and magazines with a really wide coverage and high-quality photography and layout. Even if you cannot read them, they still make good coffee table pieces.

—Kevin Mcgue

Get a quintessential robatayaki experience with the delectable grilled dishes at Inayaka.

$$$

JAPANESE

Fodor's Choice
★

✕**Inakaya** 田舍屋. The style here is *robatayaki*, a dining experience that segues into pure theater. Inside a large U-shape counter, two cooks in traditional garb sit on cushions behind a grill, with a cornucopia of food spread out in front of them: fresh vegetables, seafood, skewers of beef and chicken. You point to what you want, and your server shouts out the order. The cook bellows back your order, plucks your selection up out of the pit, prepares it, and hands it across on an 8-foot wooden paddle. Inakaya is open from 5 pm to 5 am, and fills up fast after 7. If you can't get a seat here, there is now another branch on the other side of Roppongi Crossing. ⊠ *1F Reine Bldg., 5–3–4 Roppongi, Minato-ku* ☎ *03/3408–5040* ⏴ *Reservations not accepted* ☉ *No lunch* Ⓜ *Hibiya subway line, Roppongi Station (Exit 3)* ✛ *C5.*

$$$$

JAPANESE

✕**Jidaiya** 時代屋. Entering Jidaiya, which loosely translates as "period house," is like stepping into an Edo-period tavern. Most locals order from ornately drawn strips of paper that hang from high on the walls. If you are not sure what to order, leave it up to the chef (order the omakase) and you will be served a selection of shabu-shabu, tempura, sushi, rice dishes, and grilled fish. The food's not so fancy, but it's filling and delicious. ⊠ *B1 Yuni Roppongi Bldg., 7–15–17 Roppongi, Minato-ku* ☎ *03/3403–3563* Ⓜ *Hibiya subway line, Roppongi Station (Exit 2)* ✛ *C5.*

¢–$

RAMEN

✕**Kohmen** 光麺. This always-busy ramen shop near Roppongi Crossing sets itself apart with a polished, stainless-steel-and-glass interior, but that does not mean it is any less authentic or tasty. Kohmen is known for its *tonkotsu* (pork bone) soup, and yelling "tonkotsu" over the counter will get you a basic bowl of soup with noodles topped with a slice of barbecued pork. Adding *zen bu no say* (with the works), will get you a side dish of hard-boiled egg, vegetables, dried seaweed, and other good-ies you dump over your soup before eating. Kohmen is open until 6 am, making it the perfect place to stop after a night in Roppongi's entertain-ment district. ⊠ *7–14–3 Roppongi, Minato-ku* ☎ *03/6406–4565* ▤ *No credit cards* ✛ *C5.*

$$$$
ECLECTIC
✕ **Lovenet** ラブネット. Within the 33 private, themed rooms of Lovenet, you can dine and enjoy Japan's national pastime: karaoke. Go not just for the food but the entire experience. Request the intimate Morocco suite, the colorful Candy room, or the Aqua suite, where you can eat, drink, and take a dip in the hot tub while belting out '80s hits. The Italian-trained chefs prepare Mediterranean and Japanese cuisine in the form of light snacks and full-course meals, which you order via a phone intercom system. Try the duck confit with wine sauce or a salmon-roe rice bowl. The bill is calculated based on what room you use, how long you stay, and what you order. Note that there's a two-person mini-mum for each room. ⊠ *3F–4F Hotel Ibis, 7–14–4 Roppongi, Minato-ku* ☎ *03/5771–5511* ⊕ *www.lovenet-jp.com* ⌛ *Reservations essential* Ⓜ *Oedo and Hibiya subway lines, Roppongi Station (Exit 4A)* ✛ *C5.*

$$–$$$
AMERICAN
✕ **Roti** ロティ. Billing itself a "modern American brasserie," Roti takes pride in the creative use of simple, fresh ingredients, and a fusing of Eastern and Western elements. For an appetizer, try the falafel and char-grilled vegetables on flat bread, or shoestring french fries with white truffle oil and Parmigiano-Reggiano cheese. Don't neglect dessert: the espresso-chocolate tart is to die for. Roti stocks some 60 California wines, microbrewed ales from the famed Rogue brewery in Oregon, and Cuban cigars. There is also a fantastic weekend brunch menu. The best seats in the house are, in fact, outside, at one of the dozen tables around the big glass pyramid on the terrace. ⊠ *1F Piramide Bldg., 6–6–9 Rop-pongi, Minato-ku* ☎ *03/5785–3671* Ⓜ *Hibiya subway line, Roppongi Station (Exit 1A); Toei Oedo Line, Roppongi Station (Exit 1A)* ✛ *C5.*

$$–$$$
KOREAN
✕ **Sanko-en** 三幸園. With the embassy of South Korea a few blocks away, Sanko-en stands out in a neighborhood thick with Korean-barbecue joints. Customers—not just from the neighborhood but from nearby trendy Roppongi as well—line up at all hours (from 11:30 am to mid-night) to get in. Korean barbecue is a smoky affair; you cook your own food, usually thin slices of beef and vegetables, on a gas grill at your table. The *karubi* (brisket), which is accompanied by a great salad, is the best choice on the menu. If you like kimchi (spicy pickled cabbage), Sanko-en's is considered by some to be the best in town. ⊠ *1–8–7 Azabu Juban, Minato-ku* ☎ *03/3585–6306* ⌛ *Reservations not accepted* ⊗ *Closed Wed.* Ⓜ *Namboku and Oedo subway lines, Azabu Juban Station (Exit 4)* ✛ *C5.*

$$$$
SUSHI
✕ **Sushiso Masa** すし匠 まさ. If you are lucky enough to get a reserva-tion for a few of the seven counter seats and willing to pay top dollar for it, Sushiso Masa offers a sublime sushi experience. The interior is unpretentious, and the presentation gorgeous as it is at any sushi shop. What really sets this apart is cuts of fish of the highest quality avail-able and garnishes of rare ingredients such as *zha cai* (pickled stem of the mustard plant). ⊠ *B1F Seven Nishi-Azabu Bldg., 4–1–15 Nishi-Azabu, Minato-ku* ☎ *03/3499–9178* ⌛ *Reservations essential* ⊗ *Closed*

Mon. No lunch Ⓜ *Hibiya subway line, Roppongi Station (Exit 1B); Toei Oedo Line, Roppongi Station (Exit 1A)* ✛ *C5.*

$–$$ ✕ **Tony Roma's** トニーローマ. If your kids flee in terror when a plate
AMERICAN of sushi is placed in front of them, you may want to take them for a
ⓒ taste of home at this American chain world-famous for its barbecued
ribs. Started in Miami, Florida, in the 1970s, this casual place—one of
five in Tokyo—serves kid-size portions of ribs, burgers, chicken strips,
and fried shrimp. ✉ *5–4–20 Roppongi, Minato-ku* ☎ *03/3408–2748*
🌐 *www.tonyromas.jp/en* ☉ *No lunch Sun. and holidays* Ⓜ *Hibiya subway line, Roppongi Station (Exit 3); Toei Oedo Line, Roppongi Station
(Exit 3)* ✛ *C5.*

$$$$ ✕ **Towers Grill** タワーズグリル. While Tokyo obviously offers the best Jap-
AMERICAN anese food in the world, visitors may want to take a break and visit an
American-style grill. Towers Grill on the 45th floor of the Ritz-Carlton
Hotel provides meals made from high-quality ingredients from around
Japan including A-4-rank Tankaku beef and abalone from Sanriku.
There's a great view which includes the Tokyo Sky Tree and Tokyo
Tower, from which the eatery takes its name. A prix fixe lunch includes
a choice of three items from a seasonally changing menu, and there
are dinners with three, four, and five courses. Brunch is also available
weekends and holidays. Visitors who plan to return to Tokyo may want
to join the "Knife for Life" club, which provides a Laguiole steak knife
engraved with the user's name. ✉ *Tokyo Midtown, 9–7–1 Akasaka,
Minato-ku* ☎ *01/2079–8688* Ⓜ *Hibiya subway line, Roppongi Station
(Exit 4A); Toei Oedo Line, Roppongi Station (Exit 7)* ✛ *D4.*

SHIBUYA 原宿

$ ✕ **Afuri** 阿夫利/あふり. Ramen is the quintessential Japanese fast food
RAMEN in a bowl: thick Chinese noodles in a savory broth, with soybean paste,
diced leeks, grilled *chashu* (pork loin), and spinach. No neighborhood
in Tokyo is without at least one ramen joint—often serving only at a
counter. In Ebisu, the hands-down favorite is Afuri. Using the picture
menu, choose your ramen by inserting coins into a ticket machine, find
a seat, and hand over your ticket to the cooks who will prepare your
ramen then and there. There's limited seating, and at lunch and dinner,
the line of waiting customers extends down the street. ✉ *1–1–7 Ebisu,
Shibuya-ku* ☎ *03/5795–0750* 🖃 *No credit cards* ☉ *Closed Wed.* Ⓜ *JR
Yamanote Line (Nishi-guchi/West Exit) and Hibiya subway line (Exit
1), Ebisu Station* ✛ *B5.*

$$ ✕ **Good Honest Grub** グッドオネストグラブ. This airy, laid-back restaurant
CAFÉ has the feel of enjoying a home-cooked meal at a friend's house. Brunch
is served 10:30–4:30 on weekends and national holidays, and includes
offerings such as Greek omelets, wraps, and perhaps the best eggs Bene-
dict in town. Everything comes from the restaurant's own organic farm.
✉ *2–20–8 Higashi, Shibuya-ku* ☎ *03/3797–9877* ✍ *Reservations not
accepted for brunch* 🖃 *No credit cards* Ⓜ *JR Yamanote, Shibuya Sta-
tion (South Exit)* ✛ *B4.*

$–$$ ✕ **Suzuran** すずらん. It's said that you can judge the quality of a Tokyo
RAMEN ramen restaurant by the number of people lined up out front. If that's
true, Suzuran, a short walk from Shibuya Station, must be one of the

best in town, as people begin lining up before the restaurant opens its doors at 11:30. Expect excellent ramen, as well as *tsukemen* (wide noodles in a light, vinegary sauce) topped with boiled fish. Don't be afraid of the long line outside, it moves quickly and the ramen is worth the wait. ⊠ *3–7–5 Shibuya, Shibuya-ku* ☎ *03/3499–0434* ▭ *No credit cards* Ⓜ *JR Yamanote, Shibuya Station (South Exit)* ✛ *B5.*

\$\$–\$\$\$
JAPANESE
★

✕ **Tenmatsu** 天松. The best seats in the house at Tenmatsu, as in any tempura-*ya*, are at the immaculate wooden counter, where your tidbits of choice are taken straight from the oil and served immediately. You also get to watch the chef in action. Tenmatsu's brand of good-natured professional hospitality adds to the enjoyment of the meal. Here you can rely on a set menu or order à la carte tempura delicacies like lotus root, shrimp, *unagi* (eel), and kisu. Call ahead to reserve counter seating or a full-course kaiseki dinner in a private tatami room. ⊠ *1–6–1 Dogen-zaka, Shibuya-ku* ☎ *03/3462–2815* Ⓜ *JR Yamanote Line, Shibuya Station (Minami-guchi/South Exit); Ginza and Hanzo-mon subway lines, Shibuya Station (Exit 3A)* ✛ *A5.*

SHIMBASHI 新橋

\$\$\$
JAPANESE

✕ **Daruma** 黒達磨. This casual eatery takes its name from the hollow wooden dolls—talismans of good luck for the Japanese—that decorate the interior. The specialty here is yakitori, bits of chicken meat and cartilage grilled on skewers. Daruma serves yakitori in the style of Hakata, an area of Fukuoka city in southern Japan, where the dish is not limited to poultry, but includes pork and vegetables. The menu also includes horse sashimi and *mentaiko*, a marinated fish roe which is another famous delicacy from Hakata. ⊠ *2–15–8 Shimbashi, Minato-ku* ☎ *03/5512–2778* ☉ *No lunch* ✛ *E4.*

\$\$\$
JAPANESE

✕ **Ushibenkei** 牛弁慶. Japan prides itself on producing high-quality marbleized beef. Cuts are ranked based on the ratio, distribution, and sweetness of the fat in relation to the meat, and some of the highest ranks are available for reasonable prices at this new eatery with a rustic atmosphere. For the full experience select a *gyu-nabe* ("beef pot") course, and your server will move a *shichirin*, a portable coal-burning stove, to your table and prepare a range of cow tongue, beef, tofu, and vegetables in front of your eyes. The meat is fresh enough to be safely eaten raw, so don't be surprised if you are given paper-thin cuts of beef that are only lightly seared. There are à la carte options, too. ⊠ *3–18–7 Shimbashi, Minato-ku* ☎ *03/3459–9318* ▭ *No credit cards* Ⓜ *JR Yamanote Line, Shimbashi Station (Kasumori Exit)* ✛ *E5.*

SHINAGAWA AND 品川 AND SHIROKANEDAI 白金台

\$\$\$\$
JAPANESE

✕ **Enju** 槐樹. Happo-en, a 300-year-old-Japanese garden wrapped around a lake, is the setting for the palatial complex that houses this upscale restaurant, a shrine, and a traditional teahouse. Beautiful scenery aside, the food is what draws locals and visitors again and again. The grand exterior and pristine banquet rooms are somewhat uninviting and overly formal, but the tables overlooking the garden are a tranquil backdrop for an unforgettable meal. Among the pricey prix fixe dinners

Outdoor restaurants around Tokyo offer casual meals and camaraderie among diners.

are kaiseki, shabu-shabu, sukiyaki, and tempura, and there's also a buffet dinner. Go in the afternoon for a tour of the grounds, *sado* (tea ceremony), and a seasonal Japanese set lunch for ¥2,625 or ¥3,675. For more casual dining, Café Thrush, in the same complex, has an open-air terrace with a stunning view of the garden. ⊠ *1–1–1 Shirokanedai, Minato-ku* ☎ *03/3443–3125* ⌕ *Reservations essential* Ⓜ *Mita and Namboku subway lines, Shirokanedai Station (Exit 2)* ✛ C6.

$$$ ✕ **Manhattan Grill** マンハッタングリル. Only in hyper-eclectic Japan can
ECLECTIC   you have a French-Indonesian meal at a restaurant called the Manhattan Grill in a food court dubbed the "Foodium." Chef Wayan Surbrata, who trained at the Four Seasons Resort in Bali, has a delicate, deft touch with such dishes as spicy roast-chicken salad, and steak marinated in cinnamon and soy sauce, served with shiitake mushrooms and *gado-gado* (shrimp-flavor rice crackers). One side of the minimalist restaurant is open to the food court; the floor-to-ceiling windows on the other side don't afford much of a view. The square black-and-white ceramics set off the food especially well. ⊠ *4F Atré Shinagawa, 2–18–1 Konan, Minato-ku* ☎ *03/6717–0922* Ⓜ *JR Shinagawa Station (Higashi-guchi/ East Exit)* ✛ D6.

$$ ✕ **Sabado Sabadete** サバドサバデテ. Catalan jewelry designer Mañuel
SPANISH   Benito used to rent a bar in Aoyama on Saturday nights and cook for his friends, just for the fun of it. Word got around: eventually there wasn't room in the bar to lift a fork. Inspired by this success, Benito opened this Spanish restaurant. The highlight of every evening is still the moment when the chef, in his bright red cap, shouts out "Gohan desu yo!"—the Japanese equivalent of "Soup's on!"—and dishes out his bubbling-hot paella. Don't miss the empanadas or the *escalivada* (Spanish ratatouille

As microbrews become more ubiquitous in Tokyo, restaurants like T.Y. Brewery grow more popular.

with red peppers, onions, and eggplant). ⊠ *2F Genteel Shirokanedai Bldg., 5–3–2 Shirokanedai, Minato-ku* ☎ *03/3445–9353* ⊟ *No credit cards* ⊘ *Closed Sun. and Mon.* Ⓜ *Mita and Namboku subway lines, Shirokanedai Station (Exit 1)* ✛ *C6.*

$$$ ✕ **T. Y. Harbor Brewery** T.Y.ハーバーブルワリーレストラン. A converted
ECLECTIC warehouse on the waterfront houses this restaurant, a Tokyo hot spot
★ for private parties. Chef David Chiddo refined his signature California-
Thai cuisine at some of the best restaurants in Los Angeles. Don't miss
his grilled mahimahi with green rice and mango salsa, or the grilled
jumbo-shrimp brochettes with tabbouleh. True to its name, T. Y. Har-
bor brews its own beer in a tank that reaches all the way to the 46-foot-
high ceiling. The best seats in the house are on the bay-side deck, open
from May to October. Reservations are a good idea on weekends.
⊠ *2–1–3 Higashi-Shinagawa, Shinagawa-ku* ☎ *03/5479–4555* Ⓜ *To-
kyo Monorail or Rinkai Line, Ten-nozu Isle Station (Exit B)* ✛ *D6.*

SHINJUKU 新宿

$$ ✕ **Ben's Café** ベンズカフェ. This artsy café in the student town of
CAFÉ Takadanobaba is one of the few locations in Tokyo that serves a full
English breakfast, available weekends 11:30–3. ⊠ *1–29–21 Takadanobaba, Shinjuku-ku* ☎ *03/3202–2445* ⊟ *No credit cards* Ⓜ *JR Yamanote Line, Takadanobaba Station (Waseda-guchi/Waseda Exit)* ✛ *B1.*

$$$ ✕ **Nanairo Temari Uta**七色てまりうた. Traditionally, *temari* were toys
SUSHI made from the remnants of old kimono by mothers for their children.
Today they are a prime example of Japanese folk art. This restaurant is
all about temari—booths are shaped like giant temari balls, and smaller

FAMILY-FRIENDLY DINING

Tokyo can be a challenging place to travel with children, and this is especially true when the little ones get hungry. Many Japanese parents opt to take young children to *famiresu*, or "family restaurants," such as Denny's, Jonathan's, or Saizeria. These chains are located all over the city and will do in a pinch. Be forewarned that Denny's in Japan bears only a fleeting resemblance to its American counterpart, and all family restaurants refuse substitutions or à la carte orders. But if you look beyond the chains you'll find some memorable dining experiences for the whole family. These are some of our favorites:

✕ **57**($$). This New York–style lounge usually has a decidedly adult atmosphere, but during the famous Sunday brunch, family-friendly meals are served and the lounge area is transformed into a playpen. ✉ *4-2-35 Roppongi, Minato-ku*

☎ *03/5775–7857* Ⓜ *Hibiya and Toei Oedo lines, Roppongi Station (Exit 6).*

✕ **Baseball Café** ベースボールカフェ($$). Located in the shadow of Tokyo Dome, the primary baseball stadium in Tokyo, this theme restaurant features sports memorabilia, waitstaff dressed in athletic uniforms, and a menu full of fun selections such as "home-run pizza" and the ridiculously oversize "world champion burger." This is the perfect place for sports-loving kids. ✉ *1-3 Koraku, Bunkyo-ku* ☎ *03/3817–6262* Ⓜ *JR Sobu Line; Toei Mita Line, Suidobashi Station (Exit A5).*

✕ **Garden Café** ガーデンカフェ($$). Located within the beautiful grounds of the Tokyo American Club, this eatery offers kids plenty of room to run around and healthful food to eat. ✉ *4-25-46 Takanawa, Minato-ku* ☎ *03/4588–0705* Ⓜ *JR Shinagawa Station (Takanawa Exit).*

versions decorate the interior. The design motif even extends to the food, which includes sushi shaped like colorful balls rather than the usual rectangles. It is fun, if a bit kitschy. ✉ *5F Humax Pavillion, 3–28– 10 Shinjuku, Shinjuku-ku* ☎ *03/3226-8070* 🕙 *No lunch* Ⓜ *JR Shinjuku Station (Higashi-guchi/East Exit); Marunouchi and Fukutoshin subway lines, Shinjuku Sanchome Station (Exit A5)* ✛ *B2.*

$$ ✕ **Ryoma no Sora Bettei** 龍馬の空別邸. Tokyoites love unique dining expe-
JAPANESE riences and are also fascinated by their own history—they can revel in both in this eatery which is a tribute to Ryoma Sakamoto, a hero who helped overthrow the feudal Tokugawa Shogunate in the 1860s. When you enter from the ultramodern streets of Shinjuku, slide off your shoes, stash them in a wooden locker, and walk by a statute of the sword-wielding Sakamoto as you step into the Japan of the past. You can sit in the main dining hall, which resembles a bustling historic inn, or you can phone ahead to reserve a private tatami-mat dining room. The cuisine also harkens back to the traditional rural cooking, popu- lar before Japan opened up to the West. The house specialty is *seiro- mushi*, a bamboo box filled with carefully arranged seafood, poultry, or meat, steamed over a pot, served piping hot, and quickly shared with everyone at the table. ✉ *B2 141 Shinjuku Bldg., 1–4–2 Nishi-Shinjuku, Shinjuku-ku* ☎ *03/3347–2207* 🌐 *www.diamond-dining.com/shop_info/*

ryomanosora-bettei ⊘ *No lunch* Ⓜ *JR Shinjuku Station (Nishi-guchi/ West Exit)* ✛ *A2.*

TSUKIJI 築地

$$–$$$ ✕ **Edo-Gin** 江戸銀. In an area that teems with sushi bars, this one main-
SUSHI   tains its reputation as one of the best. Edo-Gin serves generous slabs of
★   fish that drape over the vinegared rice rather than perch demurely on
top. The centerpiece of the main room is a huge tank where the day's
ingredients swim about until they are required; it doesn't get any fresher
than this. Set menus here are reasonable, especially for lunch, but a big
appetite for specialties like sea urchin and *otoro* tuna can put a dent
in your budget. ⊠ *4–5–1 Tsukiji, Chuo-ku* ☎ *03/3543–4401* ⊘ *Closed
Sun. and Jan. 1–4* Ⓜ *Hibiya subway line, Tsukiji Station (Exit 1); Oedo
subway line, Tsukiji-shijo Station (Exit A1)* ✛ *E5.*

¢–$ ✕ **Takeno** たけの. Just a stone's throw from the Tokyo fish market, Tak-
JAPANESE eno is a rough-cut neighborhood restaurant that tends to fill up at noon
with the market's wholesalers and auctioneers and personnel from the
nearby Asahi newspaper offices. There's nothing here but the freshest and the best—big portions of it, at very reasonable prices. Sushi
and sashimi are the staples, but there's also a wonderful *tendon* bowl,
with shrimp and eel tempura on rice. Prices are not posted because
they vary with the costs that morning in the market. ■TIP➔ Reservations can only be made for large parties, or if you plan to dine before 6:30
pm. ⊠ *6–21–2 Tsukiji, Chuo-ku* ☎ *03/3541–8698* ⊟ *No credit cards*
⊘ *Closed Sun.* Ⓜ *Hibiya subway line, Tsukiji Station (Exit 1); Oedo
subway line, Tsukiji-shijo Station (Exit A1)* ✛ *F5.*

HIBIYA 内幸町

$$$–$$$$ ✕ **Heichinrou** 聘珍楼. A short walk from the Imperial Hotel, this branch
CHINESE of one of Yokohama's oldest and best Chinese restaurants commands a
★   spectacular view of the Imperial Palace grounds. Call ahead to reserve a
table by the window. The cuisine is Cantonese; pride of place goes to the
kaisen ryori, a banquet of steamed sea bass, lobster, shrimp, scallops,
abalone, and other seafood dishes. Much of the clientele comes from
the law offices, securities firms, and foreign banks in the building. The
VIP room at Heichinrou, with its soft lighting and impeccable linens, is
a popular venue for power lunches. ⊠ *28F Fukoku Seimei Bldg., 2–2–2
Uchisaiwai-cho, Chiyoda-ku* ☎ *03/3508–0555* ⊘ *Closed Sun.* Ⓜ *Mita
Line, Uchisaiwai-cho Station (Exit A6)* ✛ *E4.*

UENO 上野

$$$$ ✕ **Sasa-no-yuki** 笹の雪. In the heart of one of Tokyo's old working-class
JAPANESE Shitamachi (downtown) neighborhoods, Sasa-no-yuki has been serv-
ing meals based on homemade tofu for the past 315 years. The food is
inspired in part by shojin ryori (Buddhist vegetarian cuisine). The basic
three-course set menu includes *ankake* (bean curd in sweet soy sauce),
uzumi tofu (scrambled with rice and green tea), and *unsui* (a creamy
tofu crepe filled with sea scallops, shrimp, and minced red pepper).

CLOSE UP

On the Menu

Sushi—slices of raw fish or shellfish on hand-formed portions of vinegared rice, with a dab of wasabi for zest—is probably the most well-known Japanese dish in the Western world. The best sushi restaurants in Tokyo send buyers early every morning to the Central Wholesale Market in Tsukiji for the freshest ingredients: *maguro* (tuna), *hamachi* (yellowtail), *tako* (octopus), *ika* (squid), *ikura* (salmon roe), *uni* (sea urchin), *ebi* (shrimp), and *anago* (conger eel).

Sushi's cousin sashimi consists of fresh, thinly sliced seafood served with soy sauce, wasabi paste, ginger root, and a simple garnish like shredded daikon. Though most seafood is served raw, some sashimi ingredients, like octopus, may be cooked. Less common ingredients are vegetarian items such as *yuba* (bean-curd skin) and raw red meats such as beef or even horse.

Another Japanese dish that may be familiar to you is tempura: fresh fish, shellfish, and vegetables delicately batter-fried in oil. Tempura dates to the mid-16th century, with the earliest influences of Spanish and Portuguese culture on Japan, and you'll find it today all over the world. But nowhere is it better than in Tokyo, and nowhere in Tokyo is it better than in the tempura stalls and restaurants of *Shitamachi*—the older commercial and working-class districts of the eastern wards—or in the restaurants that began there in the 19th century and moved upscale. Typical ingredients are shrimp, *kisu* (smelt), *shirauo* (whitebait), shiitake mushrooms, lotus root, and green peppers. To really enjoy tempura, sit at the counter in front of the chef: these individual portions should be served and eaten the moment they emerge from the oil.

Sukiyaki is a popular beef dish that is sautéed with vegetables in an iron skillet at the table. The tenderness of the beef is the determining factor here, and many of the best sukiyaki houses also run their own butcher shops so that they can control the quality of the beef they serve—the Japanese are justifiably proud of their notorious beer-fed and hand-massaged beef.

Shabu-shabu is another possibility, though this dish has become more popular with tourists than with the Japanese. It's similar to sukiyaki because it's prepared at the table with a combination of vegetables, but the cooking methods differ: shabu-shabu is swished briefly in boiling water (the word *shabu-shabu* is onomatopoeic for this swishing sound), whereas sukiyaki is sautéed in oil and, usually, a slightly sweetened soy sauce.

Nabemono (one-pot dishes), commonly known as nabe, may not be familiar to Westerners, but the possibilities are endless. Simmered in a light, fish-based broth, these stews can be made of almost anything: chicken (*tori-nabe*), oysters (*kaki-nabe*), or the sumo wrestler's favorite, the hearty *chanko-nabe*—with something in it for everyone. Nabemono is a popular family or party dish. The restaurants specializing in nabe-mono often have a casual, country atmosphere.

3

For bigger appetites, there's also an eight-course banquet. There's both tatami and table seating, and the dining room includes a view of the Japanese garden complete with waterfall. ⊠ *2–15–10 Negishi, Taito-ku* ☎ *03/3873–1145* ⊗ *Closed Mon.* Ⓜ *JR Uguisudani Station (Kita-guchi/ North Exit)* ✢ *H1.*

YURAKU-CHO 有楽町

$$ ✕ **Robata** 炉端. Old, funky, and more than a little cramped, Robata is
JAPANESE a bit daunting at first. But fourth-generation chef-owner Takao Inoue
Fodor's Choice holds forth here with an inspired version of Japanese home cooking.
★ He's also a connoisseur of pottery; he serves his food on pieces acquired at famous kilns all over the country. There's no menu; just tell Inoue-san (who speaks some English) how much you want to spend, and leave the rest to him. A meal at Robata—like the pottery—is simple to the eye but subtle and fulfilling. Typical dishes include steamed fish with vegetables, stews of beef or pork, and seafood salads. ⊠ *1–3–8 Yuraku-cho, Chiyoda-ku* ☎ *03/3591–1905* ⊟ *No credit cards* ⊗ *Closed some Sun. each month. No lunch* Ⓜ *JR Yuraku-cho Station (Hibiya Exit); Hibiya, Chiyoda, and Mita subway lines, Hibiya Station (Exit A4)* ✢ *E4.*

$$ ✕ **Shin Hinomoto** 新日の基. This izakaya is located directly under the
IZAKAYA tracks of the Yamanote Line, making the wooden interior shudder each time a train passes overhead. It's a favorite with local and foreign journalists, as the Foreign Correspondents Club is just across the street, and is actually run by a Brit, who travels down the road to Tsukiji Market every morning to buy seafood. Don't miss the fresh sashimi and buttered scallops. ⊠ *2–4–4 Yuraku-cho, Chiyoda-ku* ☎ *03/3214– 8021* ⊟ *No credit cards.* ⊗ *No lunch* Ⓜ *JR Yuraku-cho Station (Hibiya Exit); Hibiya, Chiyoda, and Mita subway lines, Hibiya Station (Exit A2)* ✢ *F4.*

Where to Stay

WORD OF MOUTH

"I visited Tokyo for the first time in October and was overwhelmed by the choice of neighborhoods. I stayed at the Granbell Hotel Shibuya. It has a wonderful location for catching trains . . . It was clean and quiet in a bustling, fun neighborhood."

—m_bran

Updated by
Brett Bull

Japan may have experienced two decades of stagnation following the collapse of the asset-inflated "bubble" economy of the late '90s, but one wouldn't know it from the steadily increasing number of high-end hotels throughout the metropolis. As land prices subsequently fell, Tokyo's developers seized the chance to construct centrally located skyscrapers. Oftentimes hotels from international brands were installed on the upper floors of these glimmering towers. This boom has complemented the spare-no-expense approach taken by many of the domestic hoteliers a decade earlier, when soaring atriums, elaborate concierge floors, and oceans of marble were all the rage. The result: Tokyo's present luxury accommodations rival those of any big city in the world.

Are there bargains to be had? Absolutely, but you'll have to do your homework. Lower-profile business and boutique hotels are decent bets for singles or couples who do not need a lot of space, and, in addition to hostels, exchanges, and rentals, the budget-conscious traveler can utilize plenty of Japanese accommodations: ryokan, minshuku, "capsule" hotels, homes, and temples.

A number of boutique hotels—typified by small rooms, utilitarian concepts, and quirky, stylish elements—have popped up in Tokyo. Room interior furnishings of blacks and varying browns are prevalent, but so are such Japanese touches as paper lanterns and tatami flooring. Reception areas are simple spaces bathed in dim lights and surrounded by earth-tone wall panels. Given that these accommodations often contain only a few floors, their locations are likely not easy to find. But when priced at around ¥20,000 a night, they can offer some of the best bargains in a city known for being incredibly expensive.

LODGING PLANNER

⇨ *See the Hotel Primer in Experience Tokyo for information on types of hotels.*

WHAT TO EXPECT

There are three things you can take for granted almost anywhere you set down your bags in Tokyo: cleanliness, safety, and good service. Unless otherwise specified, all rooms at the hotels listed in this book have private baths and are Western style. In listings, we always name the facilities that are available, but we don't always specify whether they cost extra. When pricing accommodations, try to find out what's included and what entails an additional charge.

PRICES

Deluxe hotels charge a premium for good-size rooms, lots of perks, great service, and central locations. More-affordable hotels that cost less aren't always in the most convenient places, and have disproportionately small rooms as well as fewer amenities. That said, a less-than-ideal location should be the least of your concerns. Many moderately priced accommodations are still within the central wards; some have an old-fashioned charm and personal touch the upscale places can't offer. And, wherever you're staying, Tokyo's subway and train system—comfortable (except in rush hours), efficient, inexpensive, and safe—will get you back and forth.

WHAT IT COSTS IN YEN					
	¢	$	$$	$$$	$$$$
FOR TWO PEOPLE	under ¥10,000	¥10,000– ¥20,000	¥20,000– ¥30,000	¥30,000– ¥40,000	over ¥40,000

Price categories are assigned based on the range between the least and most expensive standard double rooms in nonholiday high season. Taxes (5%, plus 3% for bills over ¥15,000) are extra.

RESERVATIONS

The Japanese Inn Group is a nationwide association of small ryokan and family-owned tourist hotels. Because they tend to be slightly out of the way and provide few amenities, these accommodations are priced to attract budget-minded travelers. The association has the active support of JNTO.

The JNTO Tourist Information Center publishes a listing of some 700 reasonably priced accommodations in Tokyo and throughout Japan. To be listed, properties must meet Japanese fire codes and charge less than ¥8,000 per person without meals. For the most part, the properties charge ¥5,000–¥6,000. These properties welcome foreigners. Properties include business hotels, ryokan of a very rudimentary nature, and minshuku. It's the luck of the draw whether you choose a good or less-than-good property. In most cases rooms are clean but very small. Except in business hotels, shared baths are the norm, and you are expected to have your room lights out by 10. The JNTO's downtown Tokyo office is open daily 9 to 5.

WHERE SHOULD I STAY?

	NEIGHBORHOOD VIBE	PROS	CONS
Akasaka	Business area with lively nightlife scene	Located in central Tokyo; many restaurant and bar choices	Can be noisy and crowded
Asakusa	Historic temple area with quaint shops and restaurants	Plenty of shops selling souvenirs; historic area	Not exactly central
Ginza	High-end area with shopping and restaurants	Numerous gallery, restaurant, and shopping options	Generally expensive; a bit sterile
Marunouchi	Business area with numerous shopping and restaurant options	Convenient access to transportation; plenty of shops and restaurants	Business area with a businesslike feel
Meguro	Upscale residential area	Quiet; numerous restaurant choices	Pricey compared to other nearby areas
Mejiro	Residential area	Pleasant, often overlooked area of Tokyo	Surrounding neighborhoods might offer little of interest
Nihombashi	Historic district that has grown into a trendy dining and shopping spot	Traditional area with numerous restaurant choices	Not central
Odaiba	Man-made island popular with tourists	Amusement parks in area; views of Tokyo Bay	Not located in a central location; touristy
Roppongi	Entertainment and business district	Plenty of bars and restaurants; central location	Oftentimes crowded and noisy
Shiba Koen	Quiet area near Tokyo Tower	Pleasant area; easy access to a park	Surrounding neighborhoods offer little of interest
Shibuya	Shopping and dining playground for young people	Fashionable; many shops, bars, and restaurants	Can be noisy and crowded; Ebisu section can be pricey
Shinagawa	Bay-side rail hub with large office district	Easy access to transportation	Few entertainment options
Shinjuku	Large business and entertainment area	Lively entertainment; many hotel choices; convenient access to transportation	Can be noisy and crowded
Shiodome	Bay-side district of office towers	Numerous hotel options; nearby park	Access for pedestrians can be confusing
Suido-bashi	Business district	Easy access to Tokyo Dome; convenient rail access	Surrounding areas might be of little interest
Ueno	Entertainment area with rail hub	Large park in area; convenient access to Narita airport	Few entertainment options in surrounding area

The nonprofit Welcome Inn Reservation Center can help you reserve many of the establishments on JNTO's list—and many that are not. Reservation forms are available from the JNTO office. The center must receive reservation requests at least one week before your departure to allow processing time. ■ TIP → If you are already in Tokyo, JNTO's Tourist Information Centers (TICs) at Narita Airport, Kansai International Airport, and downtown can make immediate reservations for you.

Contacts JNTO Tourist Information Center (☎ 03/3201–3331 ⊕ www. ntainbound.com). **Welcome Inn Reservation Center** (☎ 03/6902–5081 ⊕ www.itcj.or.jp).

Japan Travel Agents IACE Travel (☎ 800/872–4223 ⊕ www.iace-usa.com). **JTB Sunrise Tours** (☎ 03/5796–5454 ⊕ www.jtbgmt.com). **Nippon Travel Agency** (⊕ www.nta.co.jp/english/index.htm ☎ 310/768–0017 in the U.S.).

Online Accommodations Budget Japan Hotels (⊕ www.budgetjapanhotels. com). **Japan Hotel.net** (⊕ www.japanhotel.net). **J-Reserve** (⊕ www.j-reserve. com). **Rakuten Travel** (⊕ travel.rakuten.co.jp/en).

LODGING REVIEWS

Hotel reviews have been abbreviated in this book. For expanded reviews, please go to Fodors.com. Use the coordinate (✛ B2) at the end of each listing to locate a site on the Where to Stay in Tokyo map.

AKASAKA 赤坂

$$$–$$$$ **ANA InterContinental Tokyo** *(ANA)インターコンチネンタルホテル東京*.
HOTEL The ANA typifies the ziggurat-atrium style that seems to have been a requirement for hotel architecture from the mid-1980s. **Pros:** great concierge; wonderful city views; spacious lobby. **Cons:** there's a charge to use the pool and gym; room bathrooms are a bit small. ⊠ *1–12–33 Akasaka, Minato-ku* ☎ *03/3505–1111* ⊕ *www.anaintercontinental-tokyo.jp* 🖙 *800 rooms, 43 suites* ⌂ *In-room: safe, refrigerator, Internet. In-hotel: 7 restaurants, room service, bars, pool, gym, laundry service, parking* ❮O❯ *No meals* Ⓜ *Ginza and Namboku subway lines, Tameike-Sanno Station (Exit 13); Namboku subway line, Roppongi-itchome Station (Exit 3)* ✛ *D4.*

$$ **the b akasaka** *ザ・ビー赤坂*. Part of the boutique chain that promotes
HOTEL its ability to deliver balance, breakfast, bedrooms, and business, the b akasaka is a stylish option for the business traveler in the heart of the city. **Pros:** near large entertainment area; affordable. **Cons:** difficult to find; single rooms can be confining. ⊠ *7–6–13 Akasaka, Minato-ku* ☎ *03/3586–0811* ⊕ *www.ishinhotels.com* 🖙 *156 rooms* ⌂ *In-room: safe, refrigerator, Wi-Fi. In-hotel: restaurant, room service, spa, laundry service* ❮O❯ *No meals* Ⓜ *Chiyoda subway line, Akasaka Station (Exit 3B)* ✛ *D4.*

$$$$ **The Capitol Hotel Tokyu** *ザ・キャピトルホテル東急*. In a break from the
HOTEL trend over the past decade, the newest player in the market for high-end lodging in Tokyo is a domestic chain. Tokyu reopened its Capitol hotel, whose original incarnation enjoyed a 43-year history, inside a

BEST BETS FOR TOKYO LODGING

Fodor's offers a selective listing of quality lodging in every price range, from Tokyo's best budget beds to its most sophisticated luxury hotels. Here, we've compiled our top recommendations by price and experience. The best properties—in other words, those that provide a particularly remarkable experience in their price range—are designated in the listings with the Fodor's Choice logo.

Fodor's Choice ★

Claska, p. 176
Ginza Yoshimizu, p. 172
Granbell Hotel Shibuya, p. 180
Park Hotel Tokyo, p. 186
Park Hyatt Tokyo, p. 185
Prince Park Tower, p. 178
Shangri-La Hotel Tokyo, p. 174

Best by Price

¢

Capsule Inn Akasaka, p. 171
Green Plaza Shinjuku, p. 181
Ryokan Mikawaya Honten, p. 172
Sawanoya Ryokan, p. 187

$

Claska, p. 176

Hotel Arca Torre, p. 178
Hotel Asia Center of Japan, p. 178
Ryokan Asakusa Shigetsu, p. 172

$$

the b akasaka, p. 169
Ginza Yoshimizu, p. 172
Granbell Hotel Shibuya, p. 180
Mitsui Garden Hotel Ginza Premier, p. 173
Park Hotel Tokyo, p. 186

$$$

ANA InterContinental Tokyo, p. 169
Hotel Century Southern Tower, p. 181

$$$$

Grand Hyatt Tokyo at Roppongi Hills, p. 177
Mandarin Oriental, p. 176

Park Hyatt, p. 185
The Ritz-Carlton, p. 178
Shangri-La Hotel Tokyo, p. 174

Best by Experience

BEST CONCIERGE

Four Seasons Hotel, Marunouchi, p. 174
Hotel Seiyo Ginza, p. 173
Mandarin Oriental, Tokyo, p. 176
The Ritz-Carlton, p. 178
Shangri-La Hotel Tokyo, p. 174
Westin Tokyo, p. 185

BEST HOTEL BARS

Conrad Tokyo, p. 185
Grand Hyatt Tokyo at Roppongi Hills, p. 177
Imperial Hotel, p. 173
Park Hyatt, p. 185
The Peninsula Tokyo, p. 174

MOST KID-FRIENDLY

Asakusa View Hotel, p. 172
Prince Hotel Shinagawa, p. 180
The Prince Park Tower Tokyo, p. 178

BEST FOR ROMANCE

Four Seasons Hotel Chinzan-so, p. 176
Grand Pacific Le Daiba, p. 177
Hotel Nikko Tokyo, p. 177
Park Hyatt Tokyo, p. 185
The Ritz-Carlton, p. 178

BEST LOCATION

Four Seasons Hotel Tokyo at Marunouchi, p. 174
Granbell Hotel Shibuya, p. 180
Hotel Century Southern Tower, p. 181
The Peninsula Tokyo, p. 174
Shibuya Excel Hotel Tokyu, p. 180

BEST-KEPT SECRETS

Claska, p. 176
Hotel Century Southern Tower, p. 181
Mitsui Garden Hotel Ginza Premier, p. 173
Park Hotel Tokyo, p. 186
The Strings by Inter-Continental Tokyo, p. 180

boxy 29-floor commercial complex designed by architect Kengo Kuma in 2010. **Pros:** convenient location; beautiful and spacious pool. **Cons:** pricey; government district might not appeal to tourists. ✉ *2–10–3 Nagata-cho, Minato-ku* ☎ *03/3477–6355* ⊕ *www.capitolhoteltokyu. com* ⇲ *238 rooms, 13 suites* ⚭ *In-room: refrigerator, safe, Wi-Fi. In-hotel: 3 restaurants, room service, bar, pool, gym, spa, laundry service, business center, parking* ⏣ *No meals* Ⓜ *Ginza and Namboku subway lines, Tameike-Sanno Station (Exit 5)* ✛ *D4.*

¢ 🏨 **Capsule Inn Akasaka** かぷせ
HOTEL るイン赤坂. The Capsule Inn is a good option if you're shaking off a few drinks once the trains stop running. **Pros:** reservations made via the Internet get a ¥500 discount; convenient location; unique experience. **Cons:** small sleeping spaces; few services; women are not allowed; communal Japanese baths only. ✉ *6–14–1 Akasaka, Minato-ku* ☎ *03/3588–1811* ⊕ *www.marroad.jp/capsule* ⇲ *201 capsules* ⚭ *In-room: no phone. In-hotel: laundry facilities* ⏣ *No meals* Ⓜ *Chiyoda subway line, Akasaka Station (Exit 6)* ✛ *D4.*

$$$–$$$$ 🏨 **Hotel New Otani Tokyo** ホテルニューオータニ東京. Opened in 1964 just
HOTEL prior to the Olympics and used as a setting for the 1967 James Bond film *You Only Live Twice*, the New Otani is a bustling complex in the center of Tokyo. **Pros:** beautiful garden; first-rate concierge; convenient location. **Cons:** complex layout could be off-putting; charge for Internet in some rooms. ✉ *4–1 Kioi-cho, Chiyoda-ku* ☎ *03/3265–1111* ⊕ *www. newotani.co.jp* ⇲ *1,479 rooms, 61 suites* ⚭ *In-room: safe, refrigerator, Internet. In-hotel: 34 restaurants, room service, bars, pool, gym, laundry service, parking* ⏣ *No meals* Ⓜ *Ginza and Marunouchi subway lines, Akasaka-mitsuke Station (Exit 7)* ✛ *D3.*

$$$$ 🏨 **Hotel Okura Tokyo** ホテルオークラ東京. Conservative dark wood in the
HOTEL lobby and the tiered exterior architecture at the entry have helped the
★ Okura achieve an understated sophistication, dating back to its opening in 1962. **Pros:** friendly staff; one of Tokyo's older hotels that has kept its throwback design and feel intact; large rooms. **Cons:** navigating between buildings is confusing; a tad pricey. ✉ *2–10–4 Tora-no-mon, Minato-ku* ☎ *03/3582–0111* ⊕ *www.okura.com/tokyo* ⇲ *779 rooms, 51 suites* ⚭ *In-room: safe, refrigerator, DVD, Wi-Fi. In-hotel: 10 restaurants, room service, bars, pool, gym, spa, laundry service, parking* ⏣ *No meals* Ⓜ *Hibiya subway line, Kamiya-cho Station (Exit 4B); Ginza subway line, Tora-no-mon Station (Exit 3)* ✛ *D4.*

KNOW BEFORE YOU GO

Some useful words when checking into a hotel:

air-conditioning: *eakon*

double beds: *daburu-beddo*

king bed: *kingu saizu-no-beddo*

one night: *ippaku*

private baths: *o-furo*

queen bed: *kuin saizu-no-beddo*

reservation: *yoyaku*

separate beds: *betsu beddo*

showers: *shawa*

television: *terebi*

twin beds: *tsuin-beddo*

4

ASAKUSA 浅草

$$$
HOTEL
☾

🏠 **Asakusa View Hotel** 浅草ビューホテル. Upscale Western-style accommodations are rare in Asakusa, so the Asakusa View pretty much has this end of the market to itself. **Pros:** affordable; free in-room Wi-Fi; located in a historic temple area, Japanese baths available. **Cons:** room interiors are generally basic; not near central Tokyo. ⊠ *3–17–1 Nishi-Asakusa, Taito-ku* ☎ *03/3847–1111* ⊕ *www.viewhotels.co.jp/asakusa* ⇗ *330 Western-style rooms, 7 Japanese-style suites* ⚍ *In-room: safe, refrigerator, Wi-Fi. In-hotel: 5 restaurants, room service, bars, pool, gym, laundry service, parking* �│⊙│ *No meals* Ⓜ *Ginza subway line, Tawara-machi Station (Exit 3)* ✛ *H1.*

$
RYOKAN
★

🏠 **Ryokan Asakusa Shigetsu** 旅館浅草 指月. Just off Nakamise-dori and inside the Senso-ji grounds, this small inn, with both Japanese- and Western-style rooms, could not be better located for a visit to the temple. **Pros:** affordable rooms; located in a historic temple area; close to subway station. **Cons:** futons and tatami might not be suitable for those accustomed to Western-style beds; not convenient to central Tokyo; some might not feel comfortable with Japanese baths. ⊠ *1–31–11 Asakusa, Taito-ku* ☎ *03/3843–2345* ⊕ *www.shigetsu.com/e/index.html* ⇗ *6 Western-style rooms, 16 Japanese-style rooms, 1 suite* ⚍ *In-room: Internet. In-hotel: restaurant, laundry facilities, business center* �│⊙│ *No meals* Ⓜ *Ginza subway line, Asakusa Station (Exit 1/Kaminari-mon Exit)* ✛ *H1.*

¢
RYOKAN
★

🏠 **Ryokan Mikawaya Honten** 旅館三河屋本店. In the heart of Asakusa, this concrete ryokan is just behind the Kaminari-mon, the gateway leading to the Senso-ji complex. **Pros:** affordable accommodations; traditional Japanese experience; interesting shopping in the area. **Cons:** futons and tatami might not be suitable for those accustomed to Western-style beds; small rooms; staff is English-challenged. ⊠ *1–30–12 Asakusa, Taito-ku* ☎ *03/3844–8807* ⇗ *19 Japanese-style rooms, 1 Western-style room* ⚍ *In-room: Internet. In-hotel: laundry facilities, business center* �│⊙│ *No meals* Ⓜ *Ginza subway line, Asakusa Station (Exit 1/Kaminari-mon Exit)* ✛ *H1.*

GINZA 銀座

$$
RYOKAN
Fodor's Choice
★

🏠 **Ginza Yoshimizu** 銀座吉水. With meals cooked from organic ingredients and chemical-free tatami mats in the rooms, the Yoshimizu is an environmentally friendly ryokan in the middle of Ginza. **Pros:** many shopping options nearby; central location; opportunity to have the traditional ryokan experience. **Cons:** often fully booked; Japanese baths, futon, and tatami might not suit everyone. ⊠ *3–11–3 Ginza, Chuo-ku* ☎ *03/3248–4432* ⊕ *www.yoshimizu.com* ⇗ *11 Japanese-style rooms without bath* ⚍ *In-room: no phone, no TV. In-hotel: restaurant* �│⊙│ *Breakfast* Ⓜ *Hibiya subway line, Higashi-Ginza Station (Exit 3 or A2)* ✛ *F4.*

$$
HOTEL

🏠 **Hotel Monterey Ginza** ホテルモントレー銀座. With a somewhat cheesy, faux-stone exterior that attempts to replicate 20th-century Europe, the Monterey's a bargain in the middle of Ginza. **Pros:** multiple shopping choices in area; central location; reasonable prices considering the area. **Cons:** rooms are a tad small; in-hotel dining options are limited. ✉ *1–10–18 Ginza, Chuo-ku* ☎ *03/3562–0111* ⊕ *www.hotelmonterey. co.jp* ⤵ *224 rooms* ⌂ *In-room: safe, refrigerator, Internet. In-hotel: 2 restaurants, bar, laundry service* ⅋ *No meals* Ⓜ *Ginza subway line, Ginza Station (Exit A13)* ✛ *F4.*

$$$$
HOTEL
⌂ **Hotel Seiyo Ginza** ホテル西洋銀座. The grand marble staircase, the profusion of cut flowers, the reception staff in coats and tails: all combine to create an atmosphere more like an elegant private club than a hotel. **Pros:** convenient for public transport; many shopping options nearby; helpful staff. **Cons:** not suitable for children; smallish rooms. ✉ *1–11–2 Ginza, Chuo-ku* ☎ *03/3535–1110* ⊕ *www.seiyo-ginza.com* ⤵ *51 rooms, 26 suites* ⌂ *In-room: safe, refrigerator, DVD, Internet. In-hotel: 3 restaurants, room service, bars, gym, laundry service, parking* ⅋ *No meals* Ⓜ *Ginza subway line, Kyo-bashi Station (Exit 2); Yuraku-cho Line, Ginza-Itchome Station (Exit 7)* ✛ *F4.*

$$
HOTEL
⌂ **Mitsui Garden Hotel Ginza Premier** 三井ガーデンホテル銀座プレミア. Chic and reasonable, this hotel, occupying the top of the 38-floor Nihonbashi Mitsui Tower, is a winner at the edge of bustling Ginza. **Pros:** affordable; convenient location. **Cons:** rooms are small; in-hotel restaurant a tad pricey; geared toward business rather than leisure travelers. ✉ *8–13–1 Ginza, Chuo-ku* ☎ *03/3543–1131* ⊕ *www.gardenhotels.co.jp* ⤵ *361 rooms* ⌂ *In-room: safe, refrigerator, Wi-Fi. In-hotel: restaurant, room service, bar, parking* ⅋ *No meals* Ⓜ *Ginza subway line, Ginza Station (A3) or JR Shimbashi Station (Ginza Exit)* ✛ *F4.*

HAKOZAKI 箱崎

$$$–$$$$
HOTEL
⌂ **Royal Park Hotel** ロイヤルパークホテル. A passageway connects this hotel to the Tokyo City Air Terminal, where you can easily catch a bus to Narita Airport, making the Royal Park a great one-night stopover point. **Pros:** convenient airport access; nice lobby; good service. **Cons:** not located near downtown; non–Executive Floors charged to use pool and gym. ✉ *2–1–1 Nihombashi, Kakigara-cho, Chuo-ku* ☎ *03/3667– 1111* ⊕ *www.rph.co.jp* ⤵ *395 rooms, 11 suites* ⌂ *In-room: safe, refrigerator, Internet. In-hotel: 6 restaurants, room service, bars, pool, gym, laundry service, parking* ⅋ *No meals* Ⓜ *Hanzo-mon subway line, Suitengu-mae Station (Exit 4)* ✛ *H3.*

HIBIYA 日比谷

$$$$
HOTEL
⌂ **Imperial Hotel** 帝国ホテル. Though not as fashionable or spanking new as its neighbor, the Peninsula, the venerable Imperial can't be beat for traditional elegance. **Pros:** this is an old Japanese hotel with a long history; great service; large rooms. **Cons:** layout can be confusing; some rooms have dated interiors. ✉ *1–1–1 Uchisaiwai-cho, Chiyoda-ku* ☎ *03/3504–1111* ⊕ *www.imperialhotel.co.jp* ⤵ *931 rooms, 67 suites* ⌂ *In-room: safe, refrigerator, Internet. In-hotel: 13 restaurants, room service, bars, pool, gym, laundry service, parking* ⅋ *No meals* Ⓜ *Hibiya subway line, Hibiya Station (Exit 5)* ✛ *E4.*

$$$$
HOTEL
★

🏨 **The Peninsula Tokyo** ザ・ペニンシュラ東京. From the staff in caps and sharp suits, often assisting guests from a Rolls-Royce shuttling to and from Narita, to the shimmering gold glow emitting from the top floors, the 24-floor Peninsula Tokyo exudes elegance and grace. **Pros:** first-class room interiors; wonderful spa; great service. **Cons:** high prices; located near a business district. ⊠ *1–8–1 Yuraku-cho, Chiyoda-ku* ☎ *03/6270–2888* ⊕ *www.peninsula.com* ⤶ *267 rooms, 47 suites* ⌂ *In-room: safe, refrigerator, DVD, Wi-Fi. In-hotel: 4 restaurants, room service, bars, pool, gym, spa, laundry service, parking* �| *No meals* Ⓜ *JR Yamanote Line, Yuraku-cho Station (Hibiya-guchi/Hibiya Exit); Mita, Chiyoda, and Hibiya subway lines, Hibiya Station (Exits A6 and A7)* ⊹ *F4.*

MARUNOUCHI 丸の内

$$$$
HOTEL

🏨 **Four Seasons Hotel Tokyo at Marunouchi** フォーシーズンズホテル丸の内東京. A departure from the typical large scale of most properties in the chain, this Four Seasons, set within the glistening Pacific Century Place, has the feel of a boutique hotel. **Pros:** convenient airport access; central location; helpful, English-speaking staff. **Cons:** high priced; the only views are those of nearby Tokyo Station, but such proximity makes catching the Narita Express a snap. ⊠ *1–11–1 Marunouchi, Chiyoda-ku* ☎ *03/5222–7222* ⊕ *www.fourseasons.com/marunouchi* ⤶ *48 rooms, 9 suites* ⌂ *In-room: safe, refrigerator, DVD, Wi-Fi. In-hotel: restaurant, room service, bar, gym, spa, laundry service, parking* ⊘O| *No meals* Ⓜ *JR Tokyo Station (Yaesu South Exit)* ⊹ *F3.*

$$$
HOTEL

🏨 **Marunouchi Hotel** 丸ノ内ホテル. Convenience is one reason to choose the Marunouchi Hotel, occupying the upper 11 floors of the Marunouchi Oazo Building and joining Tokyo Station via an underground walkway. **Pros:** convenient airport access; central location; helpful concierge. **Cons:** designed for business travelers; rooms are smallish; limited dining choices. ⊠ *1–6–3 Marunouchi, Chiyoda-ku* ☎ *03/3217–1111* ⊕ *www.marunouchi-hotel.co.jp* ⤶ *204 rooms, 1 suite* ⌂ *In-room: safe, refrigerator, DVD, Internet. In-hotel: 3 restaurants, room service, bar, laundry service, parking* ⊘O| *No meals* Ⓜ *JR Tokyo Station (Marunouchi North Exit)* ⊹ *F3.*

$$$$
HOTEL
Fodor's Choice
★

🏨 **Shangri-La Hotel Tokyo** シャングリ・ラ ホテル 東京. The Shangri-La Hotel Tokyo, which opened in 2009, offers high-end luxury, lavish interiors, and superb views of Tokyo Bay and the cityscape from the top 11 floors of Marunouchi Trust Tower Main, a 37-floor building conveniently located near Tokyo Station. **Pros:** convenient location; lavish service. **Cons:** pricey; located in a business district. ⊠ *Marunouchi Trust Tower Main, 1–8–3 Marunouchi, Chiyoda-ku* ☎ *03/6739–7888* ⊕ *www.shangri-la.com* ⤶ *194 rooms, 6 suites* ⌂ *In-room: safe, refrigerator, DVD, Wi-Fi. In-hotel: 2 restaurants, room service, bar, pool, gym, spa, laundry service, parking* ⊘O| *No meals* Ⓜ *JR Tokyo Station (Yaesu North Exit)* ⊹ *F3.*

Ginza Yoshimizu

Claska

MEGURO 目黒

$–$$
HOTEL
Fodor's Choice
★

🏨 **Claska** クラスカ. Hip, modern, and Japanese, Claska is Tokyo's premier boutique hotel. **Pros:** Japanese aesthetics in a modern setting; great staff; cool gift shop. **Cons:** it's five minutes by taxi from Meguro Station; dining options in immediate area are limited; often fully booked. ✉ *1–3–18 Chuo-cho, Meguro-ku* ☎ *03/3719–8121* ⊕ *www.claska.com* 🛏 *9 Western rooms, 3 Japanese rooms, 3 weekly residence rooms, 3 suites* ⚒ *In-room: DVD, Internet. In-hotel: restaurant, room service, laundry service, parking* ⊚ *No meals* Ⓜ *Toyoko Line, Gakugeidaigaku Station (Higashi-guchi/East Exit); 5 mins by taxi from JR Meguro Station* ✚ *B6.*

MEJIRO 目白

$$$$
HOTEL
★

🏨 **Four Seasons Hotel Chinzan-so** フォーシーズンズホテル椿山荘. Boasting a European flair amid a 17-acre garden setting, the elegant and isolated Four Seasons is like a sheltered haven in the busy metropolis. **Pros:** stunning rooms; nice pool; garden views; shuttle service to subway and Tokyo Station. **Cons:** expensive room rates; isolated location. ✉ *2–10–8 Sekiguchi, Bunkyo-ku* ☎ *03/3943–2222* ⊕ *www.fourseasons. com/tokyo* 🛏 *215 rooms, 44 suites* ⚒ *In-room: safe, refrigerator, DVD, Wi-Fi. In-hotel: 3 restaurants, room service, pool, gym, spa, laundry service, parking* ⊚ *No meals* Ⓜ *Yuraku-cho subway line, Edogawabashi Station (Exit 1A)* ✚ *C1.*

NIHOMBASHI 日本橋

$$$$
HOTEL
★

🏨 **Mandarin Oriental, Tokyo** マンダリン オリエンタル 東京. Occupying the top nine floors of the glistening Nihombashi Mitsui Tower is this hotel, a blend of harmony and outright modernity. **Pros:** wonderful spa and concierge service; nice city views; amazing room interiors. **Cons:** pricey; quiet area on the weekends; no pool. ✉ *2–1–1 Nihombashi Muromachi, Chuo-ku* ☎ *03/3270–8950* ⊕ *www.mandarinoriental. com/tokyo* 🛏 *157 rooms, 21 suites* ⚒ *In-room: safe, refrigerator, DVD, Wi-Fi. In-hotel: 4 restaurants, room service, bars, gym, spa, laundry service, parking* ⊚ *No meals* Ⓜ *Ginza and Hanzo-mon subway lines, Mitsukoshi-mae Station (Exit A7)* ✚ *G3.*

$
HOTEL
★

🏨 **Sumisho Hotel** 住庄ほてる. This hotel, in a down-to-earth, friendly neighborhood, is popular with budget-minded foreign visitors who prefer to stay near the small Japanese restaurants and bars of Ningyo-cho area of Nihombashi.

ODAIBA

A commercial and entertainment development on reclaimed land within Tokyo Bay, Odaiba is a bit off the beaten track; although the Rinkai and Yurikamome lines serve the area, Odaiba isn't convenient to the heart of the city. That said, the attractions of the area are of resort quality—with shopping, museums, amusement complexes, and a beach—and proximity to several convention centers. Note that the Hotel InterContinental is near rather than in Odaiba, though it's also accessible by the Yurikamome Line.

Pros: nicely priced; friendly staff; neighborhood has small restaurants and pubs that offer great food for a good price. **Cons:** small rooms and baths; quiet area on weekends. ✉ *9–14 Nihombashi-Kobunacho, Chuo-ku* ☎ *03/3661–4603* ⊕ *www.sumisho-hotel.co.jp* ⤳ *72 Western-style rooms, 11 Japanese-style rooms* ♿ *In-room: Internet. In-hotel: restaurant, laundry facilities, laundry service* ❖ *No meals* Ⓜ *Hibiya and Asakusa subway lines, Ningyo-cho Station (Exit A5)* ✛ *G3.*

ODAIBA お台場

$$$$
HOTEL

🏨 **Grand Pacific Le Daiba** グランパシフィックル ダイバ. A sprawling complex at the tip of a human-made peninsula in Tokyo Bay, the Grand Pacific's a good choice for conventioneers at the nearby Tokyo Big Site. **Pros:** great views of Tokyo Bay; large, nicely appointed rooms; romantic setting. **Cons:** isolated location; numerous weddings booked on weekends. ✉ *2–6–1 Daiba, Minato-ku* ☎ *03/5500–6711* ⊕ *www. grandpacific.jp* ⤳ *860 rooms, 24 suites* ♿ *In-room: safe, refrigerator, Internet. In-hotel: 8 restaurants, room service, bars, pool, gym, laundry service, parking* ❖ *No meals* Ⓜ *Yurikamome rail line, Daiba Station* ✛ *F6.*

$$$
HOTEL

🏨 **Hotel InterContinental Tokyo Bay** ホテル インターコンチネンタル東京ベイ. Wedged between Tokyo Bay and an expressway, the InterContinental affords pleasant views, albeit in a slightly isolated setting. **Pros:** great views of the Rainbow Bridge and Tokyo Bay; large, nicely appointed rooms; quiet area. **Cons:** no pool; location might be out-of-the-way for the sightseer. ✉ *1–16–2 Kaigan, Minato-ku* ☎ *03/5404–2222* ⊕ *www.interconti-tokyo.com* ⤳ *331 rooms, 8 suites* ♿ *In-room: safe, refrigerator, Internet. In-hotel: 4 restaurants, room service, bar, gym, laundry service, parking* ❖ *No meals* Ⓜ *Yurikamome rail line, Takeshiba Station* ✛ *F5.*

$$$–$$$$
HOTEL

🏨 **Hotel Nikko Tokyo** ホテル日航東京. Like the nearby Grand Pacific hotel, the 16-story Nikko, whose facade follows the curve of the Tokyo Bay shoreline, presents itself as an "urban resort" with European style. **Pros:** great views of Tokyo Bay; friendly staff; romantic setting. **Cons:** isolated location might not be ideal for the sightseer; room interiors are a tad bland. ✉ *1–9–1 Daiba, Minato-ku* ☎ *03/5500–5500* ⊕ *www.hnt. co.jp* ⤳ *436 rooms, 17 suites* ♿ *In-room: safe, refrigerator, Internet. In-hotel: 8 restaurants, room service, bar, pool, gym, spa, laundry service, parking* ❖ *No meals* Ⓜ *Yurikamome rail line, Daiba Station* ✛ *F6.*

ROPPONGI 六本木

$$$$
HOTEL
★

🏨 **Grand Hyatt Tokyo at Roppongi Hills** グランドハイアット東京. Japanese refinement and a contemporary design come together perfectly at the Grand Hyatt—a truly classy hotel that provides every imaginable convenience and comfort. **Pros:** great spa; wide range of restaurants; stunning rooms. **Cons:** pricey; the complicated layout of the complex can make moving around seem like a game of Chutes and Ladders. ✉ *6–10–3 Roppongi, Minato-ku* ☎ *03/4333–1234* ⊕ *www.tokyo.grand.hyatt.com* ⤳ *361 rooms, 28 suites* ♿ *In-room: safe, refrigerator, DVD, Wi-Fi. In-hotel: 6 restaurants, room service, bars, pool, gym, spa, laundry service,* *parking* ❌*No meals* Ⓜ*Hibiya subway line, Roppongi Station (Exit 1A); Oedo subway line, Roppongi Station (Exit 3)* ✛ *D5.*

$ 　🏨 **Hotel　　　Arca　　　Torre**
HOTEL　ホテルアルカトーレ. This European-inspired hotel sits on a coveted location in the heart of one of Tokyo's premier nightlife quarters, just a few minutes' walk from the Tokyo Midtown and Roppongi Hills shopping-and-entertainment complexes. **Pros:** affordable; convenient access to nightlife. **Cons:** no room service; small rooms; neighborhood's plethora of bars and clubs makes the area noisy. ✉ *6–1–23 Roppongi, Minato-ku* ☎ *03/3404–5111* ⊕ *www.arktower.co.jp* 🛏 *76 rooms* ⚿ *In-room: refrigerator, Internet. In-hotel: 2 restaurants, laundry service* ❌*No meals* Ⓜ*Hibiya and Oedo subway lines, Roppongi Station (Exit 3)* ✛ *C5.*

¢–$ 　🏨 **Hotel Asia Center of Japan** ホテルアジア会館. Established mainly for
HOTEL　Asian students and travelers on limited budgets, these accommoda-
★　tions have become popular due to their good value and easy access (a 15-minute walk) to the nightlife of Roppongi. **Pros:** affordable; this area is great for those who love the nightlife; complimentary Internet. **Cons:** just one restaurant; no room service; small rooms. ✉ *8–10–32 Akasaka, Minato-ku* ☎ *03/3402–6111* ⊕ *www.asiacenter.or.jp* 🛏 *172 rooms, 1 suite* ⚿ *In-room: refrigerator, Internet. In-hotel: restaurant, laundry service, business center* ❌*No meals* Ⓜ*Ginza and Hanzo-mon subway lines, Aoyama-itchome Station (Exit 4)* ✛ *C4.*

$$$$ 　🏨 **The Ritz-Carlton, Tokyo** ザ・リッツ・カールトン東京. Installed in the
HOTEL　top floors of the 53-story Midtown Tower, the Ritz-Carlton provides
★　Tokyo's most luxurious accommodations in the middle of the city. **Pros:** great views of Tokyo; romantic setting; convenient access to nightlife; stunning rooms. **Cons:** high prices; immediate area is somewhat grungy. ✉ *9–7–1 Akasaka, Minato-ku* ☎ *03/3423–8000* ⊕ *www.ritzcarlton.com* 🛏 *212 rooms, 36 suites* ⚿ *In-room: safe, refrigerator, DVD, Wi-Fi. In-hotel: 7 restaurants, room service, bar, pool, spa, laundry service, parking* ❌*No meals* Ⓜ*Hibiya subway line, Roppongi Station (Exit 4); Oedo subway line, Roppongi Station (Exit 7)* ✛ *D4.*

SHIBA KOEN 芝公園

$$$ 　🏨 **The Prince Park Tower Tokyo** ザ・プリンス パークタワー東京. The sur-
HOTEL　rounding parkland and the absence of any adjacent buildings make the
☺　Park Tower a peaceful setting. **Pros:** park nearby; guests have a choice
Fodor'sChoice　of bed pillows for the large beds; there's a bowling alley and wedding
★　chapel in the hotel; ladies-only floor comes with nice amenities. **Cons:** a tad isolated; there's an extra fee to use the pool and fitness center; expensive room service. ✉ *4–8–1 Shiba-koen, Minato-ku* ☎ *03/5400–1111* ⊕ *www.princehotels.com/en/parktower* 🛏 *639 rooms, 34 suites* ⚿ *In-room: safe, refrigerator, Internet. In-hotel: 7 restaurants, room*

Prince Park Tower Tokyo

Granbell Hotel Shibuya

service, bars, pool, gym, spa, laundry service, parking ▮◎▮ *No meals* Ⓜ *Oedo subway line, Akabanebashi Station (Akabanebashi Exit)* ✛ *E5.*

SHIBUYA 渋谷

$$$$ ▦ **Cerulean Tower Tokyu Hotel** セルリアンタワー東急ホテル. The pricey
HOTEL   Cerulean Tower, perched on a slope above Shibuya's chaos, has a cavernous yet bustling lobby filled with plenty of attentive, English-speaking
staffers. **Pros:** friendly, attentive service; great city views; convenient
location. **Cons:** pricey rates; Shibuya is one of Tokyo's more popular
(read: crowded) areas; charge to use Internet, gym, and pool. ⊠ *26–1
Sakuragaoka-cho, Shibuya-ku* ☎ *03/3476–3000* ⊕ *www.ceruleantower-
hotel.com* ⇀ *402 rooms, 9 suites* ⚲ *In-room: refrigerator, DVD, Internet. In-hotel: 6 restaurants, room service, bars, pool, gym, laundry
service, parking* ▮◎▮ *No meals* Ⓜ *JR Shibuya Station (South Exit)* ✛ *A5.*

$$ ▦ **Granbell Hotel Shibuya** 渋谷グランベルホテル. Location, location, loca-
HOTEL   tion—that's the Granbell, and with a minimalist pop-art style to boot.
Fodor's Choice **Pros:** reasonable rates; great location; funky design. **Cons:** small rooms;
★   neighborhood can be noisy. ⊠ *15–17 Sakuragaoka–cho, Shibuya-ku*
☎ *03/5457–2681* ⊕ *www.granbellhotel.jp* ⇀ *98 rooms, 7 suites* ⚲ *In-
room: refrigerator, Internet. In-hotel: 2 restaurants, bar, laundry service*
▮◎▮ *No meals* Ⓜ *JR Shibuya Station (West Exit)* ✛ *A5.*

$$$ ▦ **Shibuya Excel Hotel Tokyu** 渋谷エクセル東急. The key to this unremark-
HOTEL   able but very convenient hotel, which is within the towering Mark
City complex, is access: local shopping and cheap dining options are
aplenty, Shinjuku is a five-minute train ride to the north, and the Narita
Express departs from nearby Shibuya Station frequently each morning. **Pros:** affordable; convenient location; friendly staff. **Cons:** small,
uninspired rooms; crowds in the area can be intimidating. ⊠ *1–12–2
Dogenzaka, Shibuya-ku* ☎ *03/5457–0109* ⊕ *www.tokyuhotelsjapan.
com* ⇀ *407 rooms, 1 suite* ⚲ *In-room: refrigerator, Internet. In-hotel:
3 restaurants, room service, laundry service, parking* ▮◎▮ *No meals* Ⓜ *JR
Shibuya Station (Hachiko Exit)* ✛ *A5.*

SHINAGAWA 品川

$–$$ ▦ **Prince Hotel Shinagawa** 品川プリンスホテル. Just a three-minute walk
HOTEL   from JR Shinagawa Station, the Prince is a sprawling complex that's
ℭ   part hotel (with four towers) and part entertainment village, featuring
everything from a bowling alley to tennis courts to a 10-screen movie
theater. **Pros:** affordable rates; multiple entertainment choices including
a bowling alley and an IMAX theater; nice view of Tokyo Bay from
lounge. **Cons:** complicated layout; crowded on weekends; charge for
Internet. ⊠ *4–10–30 Takanawa, Minato-ku* ☎ *03/3440–1111* ⊕ *www.
princehotels.co.jp/shinagawa-e* ⇀ *3,679 rooms* ⚲ *In-room: refrigerator, Internet. In-hotel: 12 restaurants, room service, bar, tennis courts,
pool, gym, laundry service, parking* ▮◎▮ *No meals* Ⓜ *JR Yamanote Line,
Shinagawa Station (Nishi-guchi/West Exit)* ✛ *D6.*

$$$$ ▦ **The Strings by InterContinental Tokyo** ストリングスホテル東
HOTEL   京インターコンチネンタル. Like the Conrad Tokyo up the road in
★   Shiodome, the Strings is all about blending modernity with traditional

Japanese aesthetics. **Pros:** great lobby; convenient location; nice view of the Tokyo skyline. **Cons:** expensive rates; finding elevator entrance can be challenging; no pool or spa. ⊠ *2–16–1 Konan, Minato-ku* ☏ *03/4562–1111* ⊕ *www.intercontinental-strings.jp* ⇌ *200 rooms, 6 suites* ⌂ *In-room: safe, refrigerator, Internet. In-hotel: 2 restaurants, room service, bars, gym, laundry service, parking* ⓘⓞⓘ *No meals* Ⓜ *JR Yamanote Line, Shinagawa Station (Konan Exit)* ⚓ *F6.*

SHINJUKU 新宿

♺ 🏨 **Green Plaza Shinjuku** グリーンプラザ新宿. Male budget travelers in Shinjuku willing to throw claustrophobia to the wind can settle in for a night at the Green Plaza, a capsule hotel in the entertainment district of Kabuki-cho. As with most capsule hotels, there are no accommodations for women. **Pros:** if you want to try a capsule hotel this is the place to do it as it's fairly priced; convenient location; public bath area offers mineral baths and saunas. **Cons:** small and limited accommodations; noisy neighborhood. ⊠ *1–29–2 Kabuki-cho, Shinjuku-ku* ☏ *03/3207–5411* ⊕ *www.hgpshinjuku.jp* ⇌ *660 capsules without bath* ⌂ *In-room: no phone. In-hotel: restaurant, laundry service* ⓘⓞⓘ *No meals* Ⓜ *Shinjuku Station (Higashi-guchi/East Exit)* ⚓ *A2.*

HOTEL ★

$$–$$$ 🏨 **Hilton Tokyo** ヒルトン東京. The Hilton, which is a short walk from the megalithic Tokyo Metropolitan Government Office, is a particular favorite of Western business travelers. **Pros:** great gym; convenient location; free shuttle to Shinjuku Station. **Cons:** in-room Internet is not free; restaurants are pricey. ⊠ *6–6–2 Nishi-Shinjuku, Shinjuku-ku* ☏ *03/3344–5111* ⊕ *www.hilton.com* ⇌ *688 rooms, 127 suites* ⌂ *In-room: safe, refrigerator, Wi-Fi. In-hotel: 6 restaurants, room service, bars, pool, gym, laundry service, parking* ⓘⓞⓘ *No meals* Ⓜ *Shinjuku Station (Nishi-guchi/West Exit); Marunouchi subway line, Nishi-Shinjuku Station (Exit C8); Oedo subway line, Tocho-mae Station (all exits)* ⚓ *A2.*

HOTEL

$$–$$$ 🏨 **Hotel Century Southern Tower** 小田急ホテルセンチュリーサザンタワー. The sparse offerings at the Century (i.e., no room service, empty refrigerators) are more than compensated for by the hotel's reasonable prices and wonderful location atop the 35-floor Odakyu Southern Tower, minutes by foot from Shinjuku Station. **Pros:** affordable; convenient location; great views. **Cons:** room amenities are basic; no room service or pool. ⊠ *2–2–1 Yoyogi, Shibuya-ku* ☏ *03/5354–0111* ⊕ *www.southerntower.co.jp* ⇌ *375 rooms* ⌂ *In-room: refrigerator, Wi-Fi. In-hotel: 3 restaurants, bar, gym, laundry service, parking* ⓘⓞⓘ *No meals* Ⓜ *Shinjuku Station (Minami-guchi/South Exit); Oedo and Shinjuku subway lines, Shinjuku Station (Exit A1)* ⚓ *A3.*

HOTEL ★

$$–$$$ 🏨 **Hyatt Regency Tokyo** ハイアットリージェンシー 東京. The Hyatt Regency, set amid Shinjuku's skyscrapers, has the trademark Hyatt atrium-style lobby: seven stories high, with open-glass elevators soaring upward and three huge chandeliers suspended from above. **Pros:** friendly staff; affordable room rates; spacious rooms. **Cons:** rather bland exteriors and common areas; restaurant options are limited outside hotel. ⊠ *2–7–2 Nishi-Shinjuku, Shinjuku-ku* ☏ *03/3348–1234* ⊕ *tokyo.regency.hyatt.com* ⇌ *726 rooms, 18 suites* ⌂ *In-room: safe,*

HOTEL

4

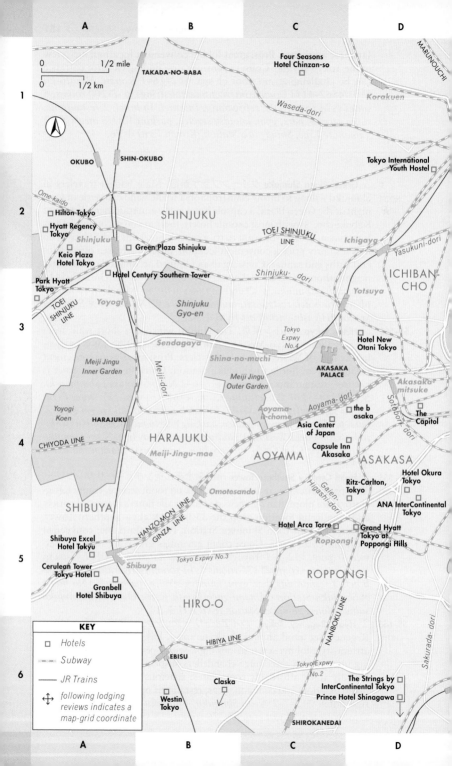

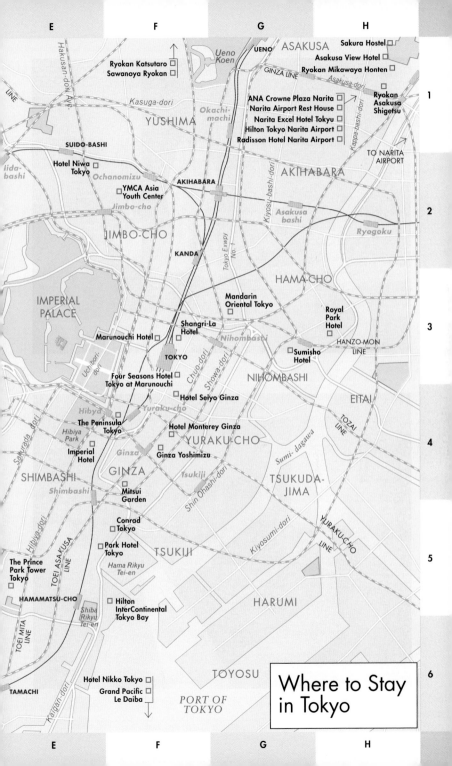

Where to Stay in Tokyo

Park Hyatt Tokyo

Park Hotel Tokyo

refrigerator, Internet. In-hotel: 6 restaurants, room service, bars, pool, gym, spa, laundry service, parking |O| *No meals* M *Marunouchi subway line, Nishi-Shinjuku Station (Exit C8); Oedo subway line, Tocho-mae Station (all exits)* ✛ *A2.*

$$$
HOTEL

Keio Plaza Hotel Tokyo 京王プラザホテル. This hotel, composed of two cereal-box-shape towers, has a reputation as a business destination that serves its guests with a classic touch. **Pros:** nice pools; affordable nightly rates; convenient location. **Cons:** rather bland exteriors and common areas; restaurant options are limited outside hotel; can be crowded if there are conventions or large groups in residence. ⊠ *2–2–1 Nishi-Shinjuku, Shinjuku-ku* ☎ *03/3344–0111* ⊕ *www.keioplaza.com* ⤴ *1,431 rooms, 19 suites* ⌂ *In-room: refrigerator, Internet. In-hotel: 13 restaurants, room service, bars, pool, gym, laundry service, parking* |O| *No meals* M *Shinjuku Station (Nishi-guchi/West Exit)* ✛ *A2.*

$$$$
HOTEL
Fodor's Choice
★

Park Hyatt Tokyo パークハイアット東京. The elevator inside the sleek, Kenzo Tange–designed Shinjuku Park Tower whisks you to the 41st floor, where this stunning hotel—immortalized in the 2003 film *Lost in Translation*—begins with an atrium lounge enclosed on three sides by floor-to-ceiling plate-glass windows. **Pros:** wonderful room interiors; great city views; top-class restaurants; discounts provided via Twitter (@ParkHyattTokyo). **Cons:** pricey; taxi is best way to get to Shinjuku Station; restaurant options are limited outside hotel. ⊠ *3–7–1–2 Nishi-Shinjuku, Shinjuku-ku* ☎ *03/5322–1234* ⊕ *tokyo.park.hyatt.com* ⤴ *155 rooms, 23 suites* ⌂ *In-room: safe, refrigerator, DVD, Wi-Fi. In-hotel: 4 restaurants, room service, bars, pool, gym, spa, laundry service, parking* |O| *No meals* M *JR Shinjuku Station (Nishi-guchi/West Exit)* ✛ *A3.*

$$$$
HOTEL

Westin Tokyo ウェスティンホテル東京. In the Yebisu Garden Place development, the Westin provides easy access to Mitsukoshi department store, the Tokyo Metropolitan Museum of Photography, the elegant Ebisu Garden concert hall, and the award-winning Taillevent-Robuchon restaurant (in a full-scale reproduction of a Louis XV château). **Pros:** beds really are heavenly; large rooms; great concierge. **Cons:** walk from station is more than 10 minutes; Internet is not free. ⊠ *1–4 Mita 1-chome, Meguro-ku* ☎ *03/5423–7000* ⊕ *www.westin-tokyo.co.jp* ⤴ *418 rooms, 20 suites* ⌂ *In-room: safe, refrigerator, DVD, Wi-Fi. In-hotel: 5 restaurants, room service, bars, gym, laundry service, parking* |O| *No meals* M *JR, Yamanote Line and Hibiya subway line, Ebisu Station (Higashi-guchi/East Exit)* ✛ *B6.*

SHIODOME 汐留

$$$$
HOTEL

Conrad Tokyo コンラッド東京. The Conrad, part of the Hilton family, welcomes you to the space age with a Japanese twist. **Pros:** modern design; fantastic bay view; fine restaurants. **Cons:** expensive; finding entrance to elevator is troublesome; charge to use pool and gym. ⊠ *1–9–1 Higashi-Shimbashi, Minato-ku* ☎ *03/6388–8000* ⊕ *conradtokyo.co.jp* ⤴ *222 rooms, 68 suites* ⌂ *In-room: safe, refrigerator, DVD, Wi-Fi. In-hotel: 4 restaurants, room service, bar, pool, gym, spa, laundry service, parking* |O| *No meals* M *JR Yamanote Line, Shimbashi Station (Shiodome Exit); Oedo subway line, Shiodome Station (Exit 9)* ✛ *F5.*

NARITA DAY ROOMS AND SHOWERS

Narita Airport is the hub between Asia and North America, so it sees many weary travelers transiting through. Since passengers on long-haul trips appreciate the chance to freshen up, the airport provides dayrooms and showers located in both terminals. Shower units can be rented for ¥500 for 30 minutes. A lounge and soaps and towels are provided. Single and twin dayrooms start at ¥1,000 per hour. Units are open from 7 am to 9 pm (9:30 in Terminal 1), and advance reservations are not accepted. ☎ *0476/33–2190 (Terminal 1), 0476/34-8537 (Terminal 2)* ⊕ *www.narita-airport.jp* ⤴ *18 shower units (8 in Terminal 1, 10 in Terminal 2), 24 dayrooms (10 singles and 3 twins in Terminal 1, 8 singles and 3 twins in Terminal 2).*

$$
HOTEL
Fodor's Choice
★

Park Hotel Tokyo パークホテル東京. A panorama of Tokyo or a bay view, comfortable beds, and large bathrooms greet you in the rooms of this reasonably priced boutique hotel. **Pros:** the guest rooms and public areas are stylish; affordable room rates; great concierge service. **Cons:** small rooms; few in-room frills; no pool or gym. ⊠ *1–7–1 Higashi Shimbashi, Minato-ku* ☎ *03/6252–1111* ⊕ *www.parkhoteltokyo.com* ⤴ *272 rooms, 1 suite* � *In-room: safe, refrigerator, Internet. In-hotel: 5 restaurants, room service, bar, laundry service, parking* ⦿| *No meals* Ⓜ *JR Yamanote Line, Shimbashi Station (Shiodome Exit); Oedo subway line, Shiodome Station (Exit 10)* ✛ *E5.*

SUIDO-BASHI 水道橋

$$
HOTEL

Hotel Niwa Tokyo庭のホテル 東京. Traditional and contemporary elements come together to make the Hotel Niwa Tokyo a hidden boutique gem in the middle of the city. **Pros:** affordable; quiet area; central location. **Cons:** rooms are a bit small; finding entrance is a bit challenging. ⊠ *1–1–16 Misaki-cho, Chiyoda-ku* ☎ *03/3293–0028* ⊕ *www.hotelniwa.jp* ⤴ *238 rooms* ⚑ *In-room: safe, refrigerator, Internet. In-hotel: 2 restaurants, room service, gym, laundry service* ⦿| *No meals* Ⓜ *JR Chuo or Sobu lines, Suido-bashi Station (East Exit); Mita subway line, Suido-bashi Station (Exit A1)* ✛ *E2.*

UENO 上野

¢
RYOKAN

Ryokan Katsutaro 旅館勝太郎. Established four decades ago, this small, simple, economical hotel is a five-minute walk from the entrance to Ueno Koen (Ueno Park) and a 10-minute walk from the Tokyo National Museum. **Pros:** a traditional and unique Japanese experience; reasonably priced room rates; free use of computers in lobby. **Cons:** no breakfast served; baths are small; some rooms have shared Japanese baths. ⊠ *4–16–8 Ikenohata, Taito-ku* ☎ *03/3821–9808* ⊕ *www.katsutaro.com* ⤴ *7 Japanese-style rooms, 4 with bath* ⚑ *In-room: Internet. In-hotel: Business center, bicycles, laundry facilities* ⦿| *No meals* Ⓜ *Chiyoda subway line, Nezu Station (Exit 2)* ✛ *F1.*

¢ HOSTEL 🏠 **Sakura Hostel** サクラホステル浅草. Located at the edge of the historic "six districts" entertainment area of Asakusa, the clean and cheap accommodations of the Sakura provide easy access to many film and performance theaters and dozens of quaint bars. **Pros:** multiple entertainment options in neighborhood; complimentary Wi-Fi; no curfew for night owls. **Cons:** a little more than 10 minutes by foot from subway station; in-house meals are limited. ✉ *2–24–2 Asakusa, Taito-ku* ☎ *03/3847–8112* ⊕ *www.sakura-hostel.co.jp* 🛏 *162 beds* 🛌 *In-room: safe. In-hotel: laundry facilities* 🍴 *No meals* Ⓜ *Asakusa or Ginza subway line, Asakusa Station (Exit A4)* ✛ *H1.*

¢–$ RYOKAN 🏠 **Sawanoya Ryokan** 澤の屋旅館. The Shitamachi area is known for its down-to-earth friendliness, which you get in full measure at Sawanoya. **Pros:** traditional Japanese experience; affordable rates; friendly management. **Cons:** rooms are on the small side; it's a bit of a hike to the subway station; must book well in advance; many rooms share Japanese baths. ✉ *2–3–11 Yanaka, Taito-ku* ☎ *03/3822–2251* ⊕ *www.sawanoya. com* 🛏 *12 Japanese-style rooms, 2 with bath* 🛌 *In-room: Internet. In-hotel: bicycles, laundry facilities, business center* 🍴 *No meals* Ⓜ *Chiyoda subway line, Nezu Station (Exit 1)* ✛ *F1.*

¢ HOSTEL 🏠 **Tokyo International Hostel** 東京国際ホステル. In typical hostel style, you're required to be off the premises between 10 am and 3 pm. Less typical is the fact that for an additional ¥1,350 over the standard rate, you can eat breakfast and dinner in the hostel cafeteria. **Pros:** affordable room rates; good location; nice view from public areas of Tokyo's skyline. **Cons:** overnight curfew; entrance is hard to find; Japanese baths. ✉ *18F Central Plaza Bldg., 1–1 Kagura-kashi, Shinjuku-ku* ☎ *03/3235– 1107* ⊕ *www.tokyo-ih.jp* 🛏 *158 beds (12 Japanese-style)* 🛌 *In-room: Internet.* 🍴 *No meals* Ⓜ *JR; Tozai, Namboku, and Yuraku-cho subway lines, Iidabashi Station (Exit B2)* ✛ *D5.*

¢–$ HOSTEL 🏠 **YMCA Asia Youth Center** YMCAアジア青少年センター. Both men and women can stay at this hostel, and all rooms are private and have private baths. **Pros:** reasonably priced rooms; convenient access to train station; discounts for YMCA members, students taking entrance exams, and clergy. **Cons:** small rooms; hotel has a limited selection of restaurants. ✉ *2–5–5 Saragaku, Chiyoda-ku* ☎ *03/3233–0611* ⊕ *ymcajapan. org/ayc* 🛏 *55 rooms* 🛌 *In-hotel: restaurant, laundry facilities, business center* 🍴 *No meals* Ⓜ *JR Mita Line, Suido-bashi Station* ✛ *F1.*

NEAR NARITA AIRPORT

Transportation between Narita Airport and Tokyo proper takes at least an hour and a half. In heavy traffic, a limousine bus or taxi ride, which could set you back ¥30,000, can stretch to two hours or more. A sensible strategy for visitors with early-morning flights home would be to spend the night before at one of the hotels near the airport, all of which have courtesy shuttles to the departure terminals; these hotels are also a boon to visitors en route elsewhere with layovers in Narita. Many of them have soundproof rooms to block out the noise of the airplanes.

$$ HOTEL 🏠 **ANA Crowne Plaza Narita** ANAクラウンプラザホテル成田. With its brass-and-marble detail in the lobby, this hotel replicates the grand style

of other hotels in the ANA chain. **Pros:** convenient location; pleasant staff, airport shuttle. **Cons:** small rooms; charge to use pool; in-house restaurants are the only nearby dining options. ⊠ *68 Hori-no-uchi, Narita, Chiba-ken* ☎ *0476/33–1311, 0120/029–501 toll-free* ⊕ *www. anahotel-narita.com* ↝ *389 rooms, 7 suites* ⚲ *In-room: safe, refrigerator, Internet. In-hotel: 3 restaurants, room service, pool, gym, parking* ⏐◎⏐ *No meals* ✢ *H1.*

$
HOTEL
🏨 **Hilton Tokyo Narita Airport** ヒルトン成田. Given its proximity to the airport (a 10-minute drive), this C-shape hotel is a reasonable choice for a one-night visit. **Pros:** reasonably priced rooms; spacious lobby; airport shuttle. **Cons:** charge to use the pool and gym; standard rooms have dated furnishings. ⊠ *456 Kosuge, Narita, Chiba-ken* ☎ *0476/33–1121* ⊕ *www.hilton.com* ↝ *537 rooms, 11 suites* ⚲ *In-room: safe, refrigerator, Internet. In-hotel: 3 restaurants, room service, bar, golf, tennis court, pool, gym, spa, laundry service, parking* ⏐◎⏐ *No meals* ✢ *H1.*

$
HOTEL
🏨 **Narita Airport Rest House.** A basic business hotel without much in the way of frills, the Rest House offers the closest accommodations to the airport itself, less than five minutes away by shuttle bus. **Pros:** day rooms available; closest rooms to the airport; hotel provides a shuttle to the airport. **Cons:** few dining choices outside the hotel; in-room furnishings are dated. ⊠ *Narita International Airport, Narita, Chiba-ken* ☎ *0476/32–1212* ⊕ *www.apo-resthouse.com* ↝ *209 rooms* ⚲ *In-room: refrigerator. In-hotel: restaurant, bar, laundry service, business center* ⏐◎⏐ *No meals* ✢ *H1.*

$$
HOTEL
🏨 **Narita Excel Hotel Tokyuo** 成田エクセル東急. Airline crews rolling their bags through the lobby are a common sight at the Excel, a hotel with reasonable prices and friendly service. **Pros:** nice concierge; view of runway from bar; nice Japanese garden. **Cons:** small bathrooms; no outside dining options in immediate area. ⊠ *31 Oyama, Narita, Chiba-ken* ☎ *0476/33–0109* ⊕ *www.tokyuhotelsjapan.com* ↝ *706 rooms, 2 suites* ⚲ *In-room: safe, refrigerator, Internet. In-hotel: 4 restaurants, room service, bar, golf, tennis court, pool, gym, laundry service, parking* ⏐◎⏐ *No meals* ✢ *H1.*

$
HOTEL
🏨 **Radisson Hotel Narita Airport** ラディソンホテル成田エアポート. Set on 28 spacious, green acres, this modern hotel feels somewhat like a resort, with massive indoor and outdoor pools. All told, it's probably the best bet for an airport stopover. **Pros:** reasonably priced rooms; high-quality bathroom toiletries by Shiseido; nice-size rooms; airport shuttle available. **Cons:** a 15-minute drive by car to the airport; no outside restaurants in the immediate area. ⊠ *650–35 Nanae, Tomisato, Chiba-ken* ☎ *0476/93–1234* ⊕ *www.radisson.com/tokyojp_narita* ↝ *488 rooms, 2 suites* ⚲ *In-room: safe, refrigerator, Internet. In-hotel: 2 restaurants, room service, bar, tennis court, pool, gym, laundry service, parking* ⏐◎⏐ *No meals* ✢ *H1.*

Nightlife and the Arts

WORD OF MOUTH

"Kabuki can include double entendres, puns, etc. But no more so, for example, than in Shakespeare's plays. At least this was true of the 3 kabuki plays I've attended."

—Paul1950

Updated by
Nicholas
Coldicott

As Tokyo's rich cultural history entwines itself with an influx of foreign influences, Tokyoites get the best of both worlds. An evening out can be as civilized as a night of Kabuki or as rowdy as a Roppongi nightclub. In between there are dance clubs, a swingin' jazz scene, theater, cinema, live venues, and more than enough bars to keep the social lubricant flowing past millions of tonsils nightly.

The sheer diversity of nightlife is breathtaking. Rickety street stands sit yards away from luxury hotels, and wallet-crunching hostess clubs can be found next to cheap and raucous rock bars. Whatever your style, you'll find yourself in good company if you venture out after dark.

Metropolis is a free English-language weekly magazine that has up-to-date listings of what's going on in the city; it's available at hotels, book and music stores, some restaurants and cafés, and other locations. The English-language daily newspapers *The Japan Times* and *The Daily Yomiuri* have decent entertainment features and listings in their Friday editions.

If your hotel can't help you with concert and performance bookings, call **Ticket Pia** (☎ *03/5237–9999*) for assistance in English. The **Playguide Agency** (✉ *Playguide Bldg., 2–6–4 Ginza, Chuo-ku* ☎ *03/3561–8821* Ⓜ *Yuraku-cho subway line, Ginza Itchome Station, Exit 4*) sells tickets to cultural events via outlets in most department stores and in other locations throughout the city; you can stop in at the main office and ask for the nearest counter, but be aware that you may not find someone who speaks English. Note that agencies normally do not have tickets for same-day performances but only for advance booking.

For information on jazz events at small venues, a visit to the record shop **Disk Union** (✉ *3–31–2 Shinjuku, Shinjuku-ku* ☎ *03/5379–3551* Ⓜ *Marunouchi subway line, Shinjuku-san-chome Station [Exit A1]*) is essential. The store has flyers (sometimes in English) for smaller gigs, and the staff can make recommendations.

THE ARTS

An astonishing variety of dance and music, both classical and popular, can be found in Tokyo, alongside the must-see traditional Japanese arts of Kabuki, Noh, and Bunraku. The city is a proving ground for local talent and a magnet for orchestras and concert soloists from all over the world. Tokyo also has modern theater—in somewhat limited choices, to be sure, unless you can follow dialogue in Japanese, but Western repertory companies can always find receptive audiences here for plays in English. And it doesn't take long for a hit show from New York or London to open. Musicals such as *Mamma Mia* and *Wicked* have found enormous popularity here—although you'll find the protagonists speaking Japanese.

Tokyo movie theaters screen a broad range of films—everything from big Asian hits to American blockbusters and Oscar nominees. The increased diversity brought by smaller distributors, and an increased appetite for Korean, Chinese, and Hong Kong cinema have helped to develop vibrant small theaters that cater to art-house fans. New multiplexes have also brought new screens to the capital, offering a more comfortable film-going experience than some of the older Japanese theaters.

SHIBUYA

FILM

Bunkamura. This complex in Shibuya has two movie theaters, a concert auditorium (Orchard Hall), and a performance space (Theater Cocoon); it's the principal venue for many of Tokyo's film festivals. ⊠ *2–24–1 Dogen-zaka, Shibuya-ku* ☎ *03/3477–9999* Ⓜ *JR Yamanote Line, Ginza and Hanzo-mon subway lines, and private rail lines, Shibuya Station (Exits 5 and 8 for Hanzo-mon Line, Kita-guchi/North Exit for all others).*

Cine Saison Shibuya. In addition to popular films, this theater occasionally screens recent releases by award-winning directors from such countries as Iran, China, and South Korea. ⊠ *Prime Bldg., 2–29–5 Dogenzaka, Shibuya-ku* ☎ *03/3770–1721* Ⓜ *JR Yamanote Line, Shibuya Station (Hachiko Exit).*

MUSIC

NHK Hall. The home base for the Japan Broadcasting Corporation's NHK Symphony Orchestra is probably the auditorium most familiar to Japanese lovers of classical music, as performances here are routinely rebroadcast on the national TV station. ⊠ *2–2–1 Jinnan, Shibuya-ku* ☎ *03/3465–1751* Ⓜ *JR Yamanote Line, Shibuya Station (Hachiko Exit); Ginza and Hanzo-mon subway lines, Shibuya Station (Exits 6 and 7).*

TRADITIONAL THEATER

NOH **Kanze No-gakudo.** Founded in the 14th century, this is among the most important of the Noh family schools in Tokyo. The current *iemoto* (head) of the school is the 26th in his line. ⊠ *1–16–4 Shoto, Shibuya-ku* ☎ *03/3469–5241* Ⓜ *Ginza and Hanzo-mon subway lines, Shibuya Station (Exit 3A).*

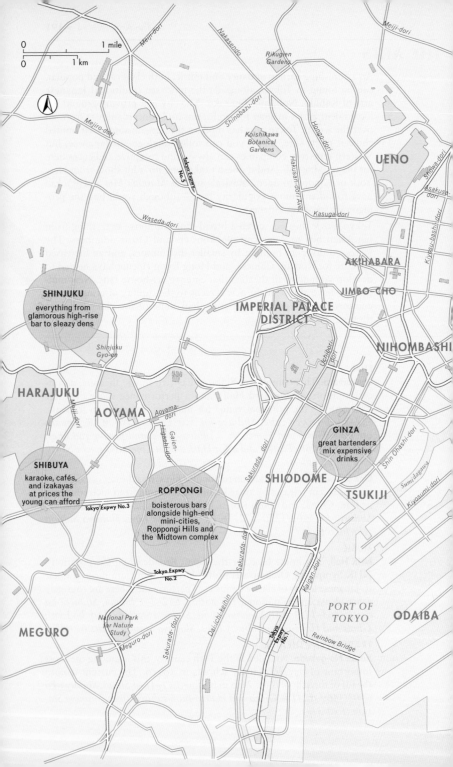

0 | 1 mile
0 | 1 km

Meiji-dori

Nakasendo

Rikugien Gardens

Meijiro-dori

Tokyo Expwy No.5

Shinobazu-dori

Koishikawa Botanical Gardens

Hakusan-dori Ave.

Hongo-dori

UENO

Showa-dori

Asakusa-dori

Waseda-dori

Kasuga-dori

Kiyosu-bashi-dori

AKIHABARA

JIMBO-CHO

SHINJUKU
everything from glamorous high-rise bar to sleazy dens

Shinjuku Gyo-en

IMPERIAL PALACE DISTRICT

Uchibori-dori

NIHOMBASHI

HARAJUKU

Meiji-dori

AOYAMA

Aoyama-dori

Gaien-Higashi-dori

GINZA
great bartenders mix expensive drinks

Shin Ohashi-dori

Sumidagawa

SHIBUYA
karaoke, cafés, and izakayas at prices the young can afford

Tokyo Expwy No.3

ROPPONGI
boisterous bars alongside high-end mini-cities, Roppongi Hills and the Midtown complex

Sakurada-dori

SHIODOME

TSUKIJI

Kiyosumi-dori

Tokyo Expwy No.2

Sakurada-dori

Kaigan-dori

PORT OF TOKYO

ODAIBA

National Park for Nature Study

MEGURO

Meguro-dori

Sakurada-dori

Daiichi-keihin

Tokyo Expwy No.1

Rainbow Bridge

CLOSE UP

Traditional Japanese Theater

Gorgeous costumes, sword fights and tearful reunions, acrobatics and magical transformations, spectacular makeup and masks, singing and dancing, ghosts and goblins, and star-crossed lovers: never let it be said that traditional Japanese culture is short on showmanship.

KABUKI

Tradition has it that Kabuki was created around 1600 by an Izumo shrine maiden named Okuni; it was then performed by troupes of women, who were often also prostitutes. The authorities soon banned women from the stage as a threat to public order. Eventually Kabuki cleaned up its act and female impersonators, who train for years to project a seductive, dazzling femininity, found roles as professional actors. Kabuki had spectacle; it had pathos and tragedy; it had romance and social satire. Though the Kabuki repertoire does not really grow or change, it still has superstars and quick-change artists. Stars like Ennosuke Ichikawa and Tamasaburo Bando still draw fans, who stay all day.

NOH

Noh is a dramatic tradition far older than Kabuki: it reached a point of formal perfection in the 14th century and survives virtually unchanged from that period. Many of the plays in the repertoire are drawn from classical literature or tales of the supernatural, and the texts are richly poetic. The principal character in a Noh play brings a carved wooden mask to life, conveying a considerable range of emotions. Some understanding of the plot of each play is necessary to enjoy a performance, which moves at a glacial pace. The major Noh theaters often provide synopses of the plays in English. The best way to enjoy Noh is in the open air, at torchlight performances called Takigi Noh, held in the courtyards of temples. Tickets to Takigi Noh sell out quickly and are normally available only through the temples.

■TIP→ Kyogen are shorter, lighter plays that are often interspersed in between Noh performances and are much more accessible.

BUNRAKU

The third major form of traditional Japanese drama is Bunraku. In the late 16th century, a narrative ballad form called *joruri*, accompanied by a *shamisen* (three-string banjo-like instrument), was grafted onto puppet theater, and Bunraku was born. The golden age of Bunraku came some 200 years later, when most of the great plays were written and the puppets themselves evolved to their present form. The most important Bunraku troupe is the government-supported National Bunraku Theatre in Osaka, but there are occasional performances at Tokyo's National Theater.

RAKUGO

A *rakugo* comedian sits on a cushion and, ingeniously using a fan as a prop for all manner of situations, relates stories that have been handed down for centuries. With different voices and facial expressions, the storyteller acts out the parts of different characters. There's generally no English interpretation, and the monologues, filled with puns and expressions in dialect, can even be difficult for the Japanese. A performance of rakugo is still worth seeing, however, for a slice of traditional pop culture.

—Jared Lubarsky

GINZA

TRADITIONAL THEATER

KABUKI **Shimbashi Enbujo.** Dating to 1925, this theater was built for the geisha of the Shimbashi quarter to present their spring and autumn performances of traditional music and dance. Since the Kabuki-za was razed, Shimbashi Enbujo has become the top spot in Tokyo to

KABUKI-ZA

Kabuki-za, once the place to see a Kabuki show in Tokyo, has been torn down because of structural concerns. It will reopen on the same spot in spring of 2013.

see the nation's favorite traditional performing art. This is also the home of "Super Kabuki," a faster, jazzier modern version. Reserved seats commonly run ¥2,100–¥16,800, and there's no gallery. ⊠ *6–18–2 Ginza, Chuo-ku* ☎ *03/5565–6000* Ⓜ *Hibiya and Asakusa subway lines, Higashi-Ginza Station (Exit A6).*

YURAKU-CHO

FILM

Chanter Cine. A three-screen cinema complex, Chanter Cine tends to show British and American films by independent producers but also showcases fine work by filmmakers from Asia and the Middle East. ⊠ *1–2–2 Yuraku-cho, Chiyoda-ku* ☎ *03/3591–1511* Ⓜ *Hibiya, Chiyoda, and Mita subway lines, Hibiya Station (Exit A5).*

MODERN THEATER

Takarazuka. Japan's all-female theater troupe was founded in the Osaka suburb of Takarazuka in 1913 and has been going strong ever since. Today it has not one but five companies, one of which has a permanent home in Tokyo at the 2,069-seat Tokyo Takarazuka Theater. Where else but at the Takarazuka could you see *Gone With the Wind,* sung in Japanese, with a young woman in a mustache and a frock coat playing Rhett Butler? ■TIP➔ Advance tickets are available only through the Playguide agency (☎ *03/3561–8821*), with any remaining tickets sold at the theater box office on the second day. ⊠ *1–1–3 Yuraku-cho, Chiyoda-ku* ☎ *03/5251–2001* ☜ *¥3,500–¥11,000* Ⓜ *JR Yamanote Line, Yuraku-cho Station (Hibiya Exit); Hibiya subway line, Hibiya Station (Exit A5); Chiyoda and Mita subway lines, Hibiya Station (Exit A13).*

ROPPONGI

FILM

Haiyuza. This is primarily a repertory theater, but on the irregularly scheduled Haiyuza Talkie Nights it screens notable foreign films. ⊠ *4–9–2 Roppongi, Minato-ku* ☎ *03/3401–4073* Ⓜ *Hibiya subway line, Roppongi Station (Exit 4A).*

Toho Cinemas. In Roppongi Hills, this complex offers comfort, plus six screens, VIP seats, and late shows on weekends. There are plenty of bars in the area for post-movie discussions. ⊠ *Keyakizaka Complex, 6–10–2 Roppongi, Minato-ku* ☎ *03/5775–6090* ☜ *Regular theater ¥1,800,*

Premier theater ¥3,000 Ⓜ *Hibiya and Oedo subway lines, Roppongi Station (Roppongi Hills Exit).*

MUSIC

Suntory Hall. This lavishly appointed concert auditorium in the Ark Hills complex has one of the best locations for theatergoers who want to extend their evening out: there's an abundance of good restaurants and bars nearby. ✉ *1–13–1 Akasaka, Minato-ku* ☎ *03/3505–1001* Ⓜ *Ginza and Namboku subway lines, Tameike-Sanno Station (Exit 13).*

SHINJUKU

MUSIC

Nakano Sun Plaza. Everything from rock to Argentine tango is staged at this hall, located five minutes by train from Shinjuku Station. ✉ *4–1–1 Nakano, Nakano-ku* ☎ *03/3388–1151* Ⓜ *JR and Tozai subway lines, Nakano Station (Kita-guchi/North Exit).*

New National Theater and Tokyo Opera City Concert Hall. With its 1,810-seat main auditorium, this venue nourishes Japan's fledgling efforts to make a name for itself in the world of opera. The Opera City Concert Hall has a massive pipe organ and hosts visiting orchestras and performers. Large-scale operatic productions such as *Carmen* draw crowds at the New National Theater's Opera House, while the Pit and Playhouse theaters showcase musicals and more-intimate dramatic works. Ticket prices range from ¥1,500 to ¥21,000. The complex also includes an art gallery. ✉ *3–20–2 Nishi-Shinjuku, Shinjuku-ku* ☎ *03/5353–0788, 03/5353–9999 for tickets* ⊕ *www.operacity.jp* Ⓜ *Keio Shin-sen private rail line, Hatsudai Station (Higashi-guchi/East Exit).*

IMPERIAL PALACE AND GOVERNMENT DISTRICT

TRADITIONAL THEATER

KABUKI   **National Theater** *(Kokuritsu Gekijo).* This theater hosts Kabuki companies based elsewhere; it also has a training program for young people who may not have one of the hereditary family connections but want to break into this closely guarded profession. Debut performances, called *kao-mise*, are worth watching to catch the stars of the next generation. Reserved seats are usually ¥1,500–¥9,000. Tickets can be reserved by phone up until the day of the performance by calling the theater box office between 10 and 5. ✉ *4–1 Hayabusa-cho, Chiyoda-ku* ☎ *05/7007–9900* ⊕ *www.ntj.jac.go.jp/kokuritsu* Ⓜ *Hanzo-mon subway line, Hanzo-mon Station (Exit 1).*

CENTRAL TOKYO

NOH   **National Noh Theater.** One of the few public halls to host Noh performances, this theater provides English-language summaries of the plots at performances. ✉ *4–18–1 Sendagaya, Shibuya-ku* ☎ *03/3423–1331* Ⓜ *JR Chuo Line, Sendagaya Station (Minami-guchi/South Exit); Oedo subway line, Kokuritsu-Kyogijo Station (Exit A4).*

UENO

MUSIC

Tokyo Metropolitan Festival Hall *(Tokyo Bunka Kaikan).* In the 1960s and '70s this hall was one of the city's premier showcases for orchestral music and visiting soloists. It still gets major bookings. ✉ *5–45 Ueno Koen, Taito-ku* ☎ *03/3828–2111* Ⓜ *JR Yamanote Line, Ueno Station (Koen-guchi/Park Exit).*

TRADITIONAL THEATER

RAKUGO **Suzumoto.** Built around 1857 and later rebuilt, Suzumoto is the oldest rakugo theater in Tokyo. It's on Chuo-dori, a few blocks north of the Ginza Line's Ueno Hiroko-ji stop. Tickets cost ¥2,800, and performances run continually throughout the day 12:20–4:30 and 5:20–9:10. ✉ *2–7–12 Ueno, Taito-ku* ☎ *03/3834–5906* Ⓜ *Ginza subway line, Ueno Hiroko-ji Station (Exit 3).*

GREATER TOKYO

MODERN THEATER

Cirque du Soleil. The acrobatic superstars are so popular in Japan that they have their own purpose-built theater on the edge of the Tokyo Disneyland complex. The show, *Zed,* is bigger and flashier than most temporary Cirque shows. Check any major ticket vendor for current shows and locations. The theater is located in Chiba Prefecture, 15 minutes by train from Tokyo Station. ■ TIP→ **If you're going to Disneyland, too, a combined ticket offers big savings.** ✉ *1–1 Maihama, Urayasu, Chiba* ☎ *05/7002–8666* 🗁 *¥7,800–¥18,000* ⊕ *www.cirquedusoleil.co.jp* Ⓜ *JR Keiyo, Musashino lines, Maihama Station (South Exit).*

Tokyo Dome. A 55,000-seat sports arena, the dome also hosts big-name Japanese pop acts as well as the occasional international star. ✉ *1–3–61 Koraku, Bunkyo-ku* ☎ *03/5800–9999* Ⓜ *Marunouchi and Namboku subway lines, Koraku-en Station (Exit 2); Oedo and Mita subway lines, Kasuga Station (Exit A2); JR Suido-bashi Station (Nishi-guchi/West Exit).*

NIGHTLIFE

Most bars and clubs in the main entertainment districts have printed price lists, often in English. Drinks generally cost ¥700–¥1,200, although some small exclusive bars and clubs will set you back a lot more. Be wary of establishments without visible price lists. Hostess clubs and small backstreet bars known as "snacks" or "pubs" can be particularly treacherous territory for the unprepared. That drink you've just ordered could set you back a reasonable ¥1,000; you might, on the other hand, have wandered unknowingly into a place that charges you ¥30,000 up front for a whole bottle—and slaps a ¥20,000 cover charge on top. If the bar has hostesses, it's often unclear what the companionship of one will cost you, but as an unfamiliar face, you can bet it will cost you a lot. Ignore the persuasive shills on the streets of Roppongi and Kabuki-cho, who will try to hook you into their establishment.

The Red Lights of Kabuki-cho

Tokyo has more than its fair share of red-light districts, but the leader of the pack is unquestionably Kabuki-cho, located just north of Shinjuku Station. The land was once a swamp, although its current name refers to an aborted post–World War II effort to bring culture to the area in the form of a landmark Kabuki theater. Nowadays, most of the entertainment is of the insalubrious kind, with strip clubs, love hotels, host and hostess clubs, and thinly disguised brothels all luridly advertising their presence.

The area's also home to throngs of Japanese and Chinese gangsters, giving rise to its image domestically as a danger zone. But in truth, Kabuki-cho poses little risk even to the solo traveler. The sheer volume of people in the area each night, combined with a prominent security-camera presence, means that crime stays mostly indoors.

Despite its sordid reputation, Kabuki-cho does offer something beyond the red lights. There are eateries galore ranging from chain diners to designer restaurants. The impressive 16th-century shrine **Hanazono Jinja** (✉ 5–17–3 Shinjuku, Shinjuku-ku ☎ 03/3209–5265 📷 Free ◷ Daily sunrise–sunset Ⓜ Marunouchi subway line, Shinjuku-san-chome Station [Exits B2 and B3]) hosts several events throughout the year, but comes alive with two must-see colorful festivals on its grounds. The weekend closest to May 28 brings the Hanazono shrine festival, in which portable shrines are paraded through the streets. The November Tori-no-Ichi festival (the exact days in November vary each year) is held here and at several shrines throughout Tokyo, but Hanazono is the most famous place to buy the festival's *kumade*: big rakes decorated with money, mock fruit, and other items people would like to "rake in." People buy them for luck, and replace them every year.

Also here is Golden Gai, probably Tokyo's most atmospheric drinking area.

—Nicholas Coldicott

There is, of course, plenty of safe ground: hotel lounges, jazz clubs, and the rapidly expanding Irish pub scene are pretty much the way they are anywhere else. But elsewhere it's best to follow the old adage: if you have to ask how much it costs, you probably can't afford it.

Major nightlife districts in Tokyo include Aoyama, Ginza, Harajuku, Roppongi, Shibuya, and Shinjuku. Each has a unique atmosphere, clientele, and price level.

AOYAMA

BARS

Radio. Koji Ozaki is the closest thing Tokyo has to a superstar bartender. This demure septuagenarian has been crafting cocktails for half a century, and he's known for both his perfectionism and creativity. Ozaki not only designed the bar he works behind and the glasses he serves his creations in (some of the best in the city), he also arranges the bar's flowers. ✉ 3–10–34 Minami-Aoyama, Minato-ku ☎ 03/3402–2668 ⊕ www.

bar-radio.com ⊙ *Mon.–Sat. 6 pm–1 am* Ⓜ *Chiyoda, Ginza, and Hanzomon subway lines, Omotesando Station (Exit A4).*

Two Rooms. Aoyama's dressed-up drinkers hang out on the stylish terrace. Drinks are big, pricey, and modern—think martinis in multiple flavors. It adjoins a popular grill restaurant. ⊠ *3–11–7 Kita-Aoyama, Minato-ku* ☎ *03/3498–0002* ⊕ *www.tworooms.jp.*

DANCE CLUBS

Le Baron de Paris. The Tokyo branch of the Paris and New York club is partly owned by superstar designer Marc Newson. As you might expect, it draws a fashionable crowd and plays host to events by trendy magazines and visiting musicians. Expect an eclectic mix of nostalgic and modern party music. Hours and prices vary greatly, so check the Web site for info. ⊠ *B1, 3–8–40 Minami-Aoyama, Minato-ku* ☎ *03/3408–3665* ⊕ *www.lebaron.jp* Ⓜ *Chiyoda, Ginza, and Hanzomon subway lines, Omotesando Station (Exit A4).*

JAZZ CLUBS

Blue Note Tokyo. The Blue Note isn't for everyone: prices are high, sets are short, and patrons are packed in tight, often sharing a table with strangers. But if you want to catch the legends—those of Herbie Hancock and Sly & the Family Stone caliber—you'll have to come here. Expect to pay upwards of ¥12,000 to see major acts, and put another ¥4,000–¥5,000 on the budget for food and drink. ⊠ *6–3–16 Minami-Aoyama, Minato-ku* ☎ *03/5485–0088* ⊕ *www.bluenote.co.jp* ⊙ *Shows usually Mon.–Sat. at 7 and 9:30, Sun. at 6:30 and 9* Ⓜ *Chiyoda, Ginza, and Hanzo-mon subway lines, Omotesando Station (Exit A3).*

HARAJUKU

BARS

Harajuku Taproom. Expat Bryan Baird runs an acclaimed microbrewery in the shadow of Mt. Fuji. In 2010 he opened this great taproom that serves his range of brews, as well as decent Japanese-style pub grub. ⊠ *1–20–13 Jingu-mae, Shibuya-ku* ☎ *03/6438–0450* ⊕ *www.bairdbeer. com* ⊙ *Weekdays 5–midnight., weekends noon–midnight.*

Montoak. Positioned halfway down the prestigious shopping street Omotesando-dori, within spitting distance of such fashion giants as Gucci, Louis Vuitton, and Tod's, this hip restaurant-bar is a great place to rest after testing the limits of your credit card. With smoky floor-to-ceiling windows, cushy armchairs, and a layout so spacious you won't believe you're sitting on one of Tokyo's most exclusive streets, the place attracts a hipper-than-thou clientele but never feels unwelcoming. The bar food consists of canapés, salads, cheese plates, and the like. Drinks start at ¥700. ⊠ *6–1–9 Jingu-mae, Shibuya-ku* ☎ *03/5468–5928* ⊕ *www.montoak.com* ⊙ *Daily 11 am–3 am* Ⓜ *Chiyoda subway line, Meiji-Jingu-mae Station (Exit 4).*

Go techno in Shibuya at Womb.

SHIBUYA

BEER HALLS AND PUBS

What the Dickens. This spacious pub, in the Ebisu section of Shibuya, feels more authentically British than many of its rivals, thanks partly to a menu of traditional pub grub. It hosts regular live music (funk, folk, jazz, rock, reggae—anything goes here) and other events. ⊠ *4F, 1–13–3 Ebisu-Nishi, Shibuya-ku* ☎ *03/3780–2099* ⊕ *www.whatthedickens.jp* ⊗ *Tues. and Wed. 5 pm–1 am, Thurs.–Sat. 5 pm–2 am, Sun. 5 pm– midnight* Ⓜ *Hibiya subway line, Ebisu Station (Nishi-guchi/West Exit).*

DANCE CLUBS

★ **Womb.** Well-known techno and break-beat DJs make a point of stopping by this Shibuya überclub on their way through town. The turntable talent, local and international, and four floors of dance and lounge space make Womb Tokyo's most consistently rewarding club experience. ⊠ *2–16 Maruyama-cho, Shibuya-ku* ☎ *03/5459–0039* ⊕ *www. womb.co.jp* 🖃 *Around ¥3,500* ⊗ *Daily 10 pm–early morning* Ⓜ *JR Yamanote Line, Ginza and Hanzo-mon subway lines, Shibuya Station (Hachiko Exit for JR and Ginza, Exit 3A for Hanzo-mon).*

GAY BARS

Chestnut & Squirrel. Chestnut & Squirrel (the name translates in Japanese as a certain female body part) is the place to be for lesbians on Wednesday nights in Tokyo. The bar's cheap drinks (cocktails and most beers ¥500), friendly, unpretentious vibe, and mix of foreign and Japanese customers give it the feel of a friendly neighborhood bar. ⊠ *3F O-ishi Bldg., 3–7–8 Shibuya, Shibuya-ku* ☎ *No phone* ⊕ *www. chestnutandsquirrel.com* ⊗ *Wed. 7:30 pm–late.*

CLOSE UP

Tokyo-Style Nightlife

Tokyo has a variety of nightlife options, so don't limit yourself to your hotel bar in the evenings. Spend some time relaxing the way the locals do at izakaya, karaoke, and live houses—three unique forms of contemporary Japanese entertainment.

IZAKAYA

Izakaya (literally "drinking places") are Japanese pubs that can be found throughout Tokyo. If you're in the mood for elegant decor and sedate surroundings, look elsewhere; these drinking dens are often noisy, bright, and smoky. But for a taste of authentic Japanese-style socializing, a visit to an izakaya is a must—this is where young people start their nights out, office workers gather on their way home, and students take a break to grab a cheap meal and a drink.

Typically, izakaya have a full lineup of cocktails, a good selection of sake, draft beer, and lots of cheap, greasy Japanese and Western food; rarely does anything cost more than ¥1,000. Picture menus make ordering easy, and because most cocktails retain their Western names, communicating drink preferences shouldn't be difficult.

KARAOKE

In buttoned-down, socially conservative Japan, karaoke is one of the safety valves. Employees, employers, husbands, wives, teenage romancers, and good friends all drop their guard when there's a microphone in hand. The phenomenon started in the 1970s when cabaret singer Daisuke Inoue made a coin-operated machine that played his songs on tape so that his fans could sing along. Unfortunately for Inoue, he neglected to patent his creation, thereby failing to cash in

as karaoke became one of Japan's favorite pastimes. Nowadays it's the finale of many an office outing, a cheap daytime activity for teens, and a surprisingly popular destination for dates.

Unlike most karaoke bars in the United States, in Japan the singing usually takes place in the seclusion of private rooms that can accommodate groups. Basic hourly charges vary but are usually less than ¥1,000. Most establishments have a large selection of English songs, stay open late, and serve inexpensive food and drink, which you order via a telephone on the wall. Finding a venue around one of the major entertainment hubs is easy—there will be plenty of young touts eager to escort you to their employer. And unlike with most other touts in the city, you won't end up broke by following them.

LIVE HOUSES

Tokyo has numerous small music clubs known as "live houses." These range from the very basic to miniclub venues, and they showcase the best emerging talent on the local scene. Many of the best live houses can be found in the Kichijoji, Koenji, and Nakano areas, although they are tucked away in basements citywide. The music could be gypsy jazz one night and thrash metal the next, so it's worth doing a little research before you turn up. Cover charges vary depending on who's performing but are typically ¥3,000–¥5,000 ($25–$41).

IZAKAYA

Tachimichiya. With its traditional Japanese dishes, wide range of sakes and shochus, and rustic interior, Tachimichiya is a classic izakaya in all ways but one: its love of punk rock. The wall is adorned with posters of the Sex Pistols, the Ramones, and the Clash, who also provide the sound track. The theme is fun rather than overbearing, and the food alone is good enough to warrant a visit. It's located in Daikanyama, two minutes by train from Shibuya Station. ⊠ *B1, 30–8 Sarugaku-cho, Shibuya-ku* ☎ *03/5459–3431* ⊗ *Weekdays 6 pm–4 am, weekends 6 pm–midnight* Ⓜ *Tokyu Toyoko Line, Daikanyama Station.*

Watami. One of Tokyo's big izakaya chains—with a half dozen branches in the youth entertainment district of Shibuya alone—Watami is popular for its seriously inexpensive menu. Seating at this location ranges from a communal island bar to Western-style tables to more-private areas. ⊠ *4F Satose Bldg., 13–8 Udagawacho, Shibuya-ku* ☎ *03/6415–6516* ⊗ *Sun.–Thurs. 5 pm–3 am, Fri. and Sat. 5 pm–5 am* Ⓜ *JR Yamanote Line, Ginza and Hanzo-mon subway lines, Shibuya Station (Hachiko Exit for JR and Ginza, Exit 6 for Hanzo-mon).*

KARAOKE

Shidax. The Shidax chain's corporate headquarters—in an excellent Shibuya location, across from Tower Records—has 130 private karaoke rooms, a café, and a restaurant. ⊠ *1–12–13 Jinnan, Shibuya-ku* ☎ *03/5784–8881* 🖳 *¥760 per hr* ⊗ *Daily 11 am–8 am* Ⓜ *JR, Ginza, and Hanzo-mon subway lines, Shibuya Station (Exit 6).*

ASAKUSA

BARS

Fodor'sChoice ★ **Kamiya Bar.** Tokyo's oldest Western-style bar hasn't had a face-lift for decades, and that's part of what draws so many drinkers to this bright, noisy venue. The other major attraction is the Denki Bran, a delicious but hangover-inducing liquor (comprising gin, red wine, brandy, and curaçao) that was invented here and is now stocked by bars throughout Japan. ⊠ *1–1–1 Asakusa, Taito-ku* ☎ *03/3841–5400* ⊗ *Daily 11:30 am–10 pm* Ⓜ *Asakusa and Ginza subway lines, Asakusa Station (Exit A5).*

GINZA

BARS

Star Bar. It's often said that Ginza has all the best bars, and Star Bar may be the best of the lot. Owner-bartender Hisashi Kishi is the Director of Technical Research for the Japan Bartenders Association, and his attention to detail is staggering. The drinks aren't cheap, but you get what you pay for. Try one of Kishi's Sidecars. ⊠ *B1, 1–5–13 Ginza, Chuo-ku* ☎ *03/3535–8005* ⊕ *www.starbarginza.com* ⊗ *Weekdays 6 pm–2 am; Sat. 6 pm–midnight* Ⓜ *JR Yamanote Line, Yuraku-cho Station (Kyobashi Exit).*

5

In such a dense city, narrow bars crop up anywhere they can find space, including under a railway arch.

BEER HALLS AND PUBS

Ginza Lion. This bar, in business since 1899 and occupying the same stately Chuo-dori location since 1934, is remarkably inexpensive for one of Tokyo's toniest addresses. Ginza shoppers and office workers alike drop by for beer and ballast—anything from yakitori to spaghetti. Beers start at ¥590. ⊠ 7–9–20 Ginza, Chuo-ku ☎ 03/3571–2590 ⊘ Daily 11:30 am–11 pm Ⓜ Ginza, Hibiya, and Marunouchi subway lines, Ginza Station (Exit A3).

YURAKU-CHO

BARS

Fodor's Choice
★

Peter. Like most of Tokyo's high-end hotels, the Peninsula has a high-rise bar. But unlike many hotel bars, especially the high-rise, five-star varieties that are dimly lighted with a jazz piano and ultracomposed staff, Peter has an entrance in a rainbow of colors, eye-catching cocktails, and occasional DJs. This 24th-floor spot's decor of chrome trees and rainbow lights is defiantly anti-zeitgeist, but lots of fun. ⊠ 24F Peninsula Tokyo, 1–8–1 Yuraku-cho, Chiyoda-ku ☎ 03/6270–2763 ⊕ www.tokyo.peninsula.com ⊘ Daily 11:30 am–10 pm Ⓜ Hibiya and Mita subway lines, Hibiya Station (Exit A6).

IZAKAYA

Takara. This high-class izakaya in the sumptuous Tokyo International Forum is a favorite with foreigners because of its English-language menu and extensive sake list. ⊠ B1, 3–5–1 Marunouchi, Chiyoda-ku ☎ 03/5223–9888 ⊘ Weekdays 11:30 am–2:30 pm and 5:30 pm–11 pm,

CLOSE UP

Tokyo Rocks!

First the bad news: Most of the biggest and best music festivals take place outside Tokyo. But the good news is that many of them are in easy-to-get-to, often stunning countryside locations, and are well worth the trip. Most festivals take place in the summer months, and though tickets aren't cheap, they usually sell out fast. If you can't purchase tickets directly from the organizers, Ticket Pia or Lawson's convenience stores should stock them.

Fuji Rock Festival. Despite the name, Japan's most popular festival takes place far from Mt. Fuji in the picturesque ski resort of Naeba, about two hours from Tokyo. On a good year, more than 100,000 music lovers attend this three-day event that runs, like so much in Japan, with stunning efficiency. Though rock dominates the lineup, you'll also find jazz, world music, techno, pop, and folk on the bill. ⊠ Naeba Ski Resort, Niigata-ken ⊕ www.fujirockfestival.com ⊗ Last weekend in July.

Metamorphose. Japan's premier dance music festival is held annually on the Izu Peninsula, close to Mt. Fuji. The lineup has diversified slightly from its techno origins and recently saw Afrobeat pioneer Tony Allen and Japanese jazzy hip-hop DJ Nujabes on the bill. ⊠ Cycle Sports Center, Shuzenji, Shizuoka-ken410-2416 ⊕ www.metamo.info ⊗ 4th weekend of Aug.

Summer Sonic. This annual two-day festival takes place in a baseball stadium and convention center an hour outside Tokyo. The rock- and pop-centric lineup usually boasts major stars and a selection of up-and-coming acts, but the drab setting and cavernous acoustics really dent the vibe. The festival also takes place in Osaka on the same weekend, with Saturday's Tokyo lineup playing Osaka on Sunday, and vice versa. ⊠ Chiba Marine Stadium and Makuhari Messe Convention Center, Mihama-ku, Nakano, Chiba-ken ⊕ www.summersonic.com ⊗ 2nd weekend in Aug.

—Nicholas Coldicott

5

weekends 11:30 am–3:30 pm and 5:30 pm–10 pm Ⓜ Yuraku-cho subway line, Yuraku-cho Station (Exit A-4B).

ROPPONGI

BARS

A971. With a plum spot on the edge of Roppongi's Midtown complex, A971 has been popular right from its opening. It has an airy, modern feel, faces a spacious patio, and often hosts house music DJs. It's standing room only on the weekends, which means plenty of socializing, usually of the flirtatious kind. ⊠ Tokyo Midtown East, 9–7–2 Akasaka, Minato-ku ☎ 03/5413–3210 ⊕ www.a971.com ⊗ Mon.–Thurs. 10 am–5 am, Sun. 10 am–midnight Ⓜ Hibiya and Oedo subway lines, Roppongi Station (Exit 8).

Agave. In most Roppongi hot spots, tequila is pounded one shot at a time. Not so at Agave: this authentic Mexican cantina treats the spirit with a little more respect, and your palate will be tempted by a choice of more than 400 tequilas and mescals. A single shot can cost between ¥800 and ¥10,000, but most of the varieties here aren't available anywhere else in Japan, so the steep prices are worth paying. ⊠ *7–15–10 Roppongi, Minato-ku* ☎ *03/3497–0229* ⊘ *Mon.–Thurs. 6:30 pm–2 am, Fri. and Sat. 6:30 pm–4 am* Ⓜ *Hibiya and Oedo subway lines, Roppongi Station (Exit 3).*

DANCE CLUBS

★ **Eleven.** One of Tokyo's top clubs, Eleven occupies two basement floors and hosts the best of Tokyo's homegrown DJs as well as big names like Francois K, Frankie Knuckles, and Joaquin Joe Claussell. ⊠ *1–10–11 Nishi-Azabu, Minato-ku* ☎ *03/5775–6206* ⊕ *www.go-to-eleven.com* 💳 *¥3,000–¥3,500* ⊘ *10 pm–5 am.*

Super-Deluxe. This isn't quite a dance club. You could call it an experimental party space, with each night hosting a different kind of event. It's home to Pecha Kucha, a popular evening of presentations by creative types; but you might also find a techno night, underground-film screenings, a performance-art event, or anything else the imagination can conjure up. ⊠ *B1, 3–1–25 Nishi-Azabu, Minato-ku* ☎ *03/5412–0516* ⊕ *www.super-deluxe.com* ⊘ *Daily 6 pm–late* Ⓜ *Hibiya and Oedo subway lines, Roppongi Station (Exit 1C).*

Warehouse 702. Nightlife in Roppongi tends to be raucous and lowbrow, so serious clubbers should head to nearby Azabu Juban for this spacious subterranean venue with a great sound system and consistently high-quality DJs. ⊠ *B1, 1–4–5 Azabu Juban, Minato-ku* ☎ *03/6230–0343* ⊕ *www.warehouse702.com* 💳 *Around ¥3,500* ⊘ *Wed.–Mon. 11 pm–5 am* Ⓜ *Nanboku and Oedo subway lines, Azabu Juban Station (Exit 7).*

JAZZ CLUBS

Fodor's Choice
★ **Sweet Basil 139.** An upscale jazz club near Roppongi Crossing, Sweet Basil 139 (no relation to the famous New York Sweet Basil) is renowned for local and international acts that run the musical gamut from smooth jazz and fusion to classical. A large, formal dining area serves Italian dishes that are as good as the jazz, making this spot an excellent choice for a complete night out. With a spacious interior and standing room for 500 on the main floor, this is one of the largest and most accessible jazz bars in town. Prices range from ¥2,857 to ¥12,000 depending on who's headlining. ⊠ *6–7–11 Roppongi, Minato-ku* ☎ *03/5474–0139* ⊕ *stb139.co.jp* ⊘ *Mon.–Sat. 6–11 pm; shows at 8* Ⓜ *Hibiya and Oedo subway lines, Roppongi Station (Exit 3).*

KARAOKE

Big Echo. One of Tokyo's largest karaoke chains, Big Echo has dozens of locations throughout the city. Cheap hourly rates and late closing times make it popular with youngsters. The Roppongi branch is spread over three floors. ⊠ *7–14–12 Roppongi, Minato-ku* ☎ *03/5770–7700* 💳 *¥500–¥600 per hr* ⊘ *Daily 6 pm–5 am* Ⓜ *Hibiya and Oedo subway lines, Roppongi Station (Exit 4).*

★ **Lovenet.** Despite the misleading erotic name, Lovenet is actually the fanciest karaoke box in town. Luxury theme rooms of all descriptions create a fun and classy setting for your dulcet warbling. Mediterranean and

TOKYO'S GAY BARS

Gay culture in Japan is a little different than that in the West. Most of it takes place well under the radar, which can be both a blessing and a curse; there are fewer options, but there's also less of the prejudice you might experience elsewhere. People are more likely to be baffled than offended by gay couples and some hotels may "not compute" that a same-sex couple would like a double bed. Still it's a very safe city to visit and with a little digging you'll find a scene more vibrant than you—or many Tokyoites—might expect. The city's primary queer hub is Ni-chome in the Shinjuku district. Take the Shinjuku or Marunouchi subway line to Shinjuku-Sanchome Station (Exit C7). Ni-chome is sometimes likened to its more notorious neighbor Kabuki-cho, its name also spoken in hushed tones and accompanied by raised eyebrows. Ni-chome, however, is more subtle in its approach. Although queer and queer-friendly establishments can be found sprinkled in other areas (Shibuya, Daikanyama Shinbashi, and Ebisu), none quite match Ni-chome for variety or accessibility.

Japanese food is served. ✉ 7–14–4 Roppongi, Minato-ku ☎ 03/5771–5511 ⊕ www.lovenet-jp.com ✒ From ¥2,000 per hr ⊗ Daily 6 pm–5 am Ⓜ Hibiya and Oedo subway lines, Roppongi Station (Exit 4A).

Pasela. This 10-story entertainment complex on the main Roppongi drag of Gaien-Higashi-dori has seven floors of karaoke rooms with more than 10,000 foreign-song titles. A Mexican-themed bar and a restaurant are also on-site. ✉ 5–16–3 Roppongi, Minato-ku ☎ 0120/911–086 ⊕ www.pasela.co.jp ✒ ¥400–¥1,260 per hr ⊗ Mon.–Thurs. 5 pm–10 am, Fri.–Sun. 2 pm–8 am Ⓜ Hibiya and Oedo subway lines, Roppongi Station (Exit 3).

SHINJUKU

BARS

Donzoko. This venerable bar claims to be Shinjuku's oldest—established in 1951—and has hosted Yukio Mishima and Akira Kurosawa among many other luminaries. It's also one of several bars that claim to have invented the popular *chu-hai* cocktail (*shochu* with juice and soda). But for all its history, Donzoko has a young and vibrant atmosphere, with its five floors usually packed. ✉ 3–10–2 Shinjuku, Shinjuku-ku ☎ 03/3354–7749 ⊗ Weekdays 6 pm–1 am; weekends 5 pm–midnight Ⓜ Marunouchi and Shinjuku subway lines, Shinjuku-san-chome Station (Exit C3).

★ **New York Bar.** Even before *Lost in Translation* introduced the Park Hyatt's signature lounge to filmgoers worldwide, New York Bar was a local Tokyo favorite. All the style you would expect of one of the city's top hotels combined with superior views of Shinjuku's skyscrapers and neon-lighted streets make this one of the city's premier nighttime venues. The quality of the jazz on offer equals that of the view. Drinks start at ¥800, and there's a cover charge of ¥2,000 after 8 pm

Kabuki-cho, in Shinjuku, is a brightly lit hub for bars, pachinko parlors, and restaurants, as well as tattooed Yakuza.

(7 pm on Sunday). ⊠ *52F Park Hyatt Hotel, 3–7–1–2 Nishi-Shinjuku, Shinjuku-ku* ☎ *03/5322–1234* ⊙ *Sun.–Wed. 5 pm–midnight, Thurs.–Sat. 5 pm–1 am* Ⓜ *JR Shinjuku Station (Nishi-guchi/West Exit).*

GAY BARS

Advocates Cafe. Almost every great gay night out begins at this welcoming street-corner pub, where the patrons spill out onto the street. This is the perfect place to put back a few cocktails (¥700–¥900), meet new people, and get a feeling for where to go next. The crowd is mixed and very foreigner friendly. ⊠ *2–18–1 Shinjuku, Shinjuku-ku* ☎ *03/3358–3988* ⊕ *www.advocates-cafe.com* ⊙ *Mon.–Sat. 6 pm–4 am, Sun. 6 pm–1 am.*

Arty Farty. Cheap and cheesy, Arty Farty is a fun club, complete with a ministage and stripper pole. Those with aversions to Kylie or Madonna need not bother. Draft beer starts at ¥500, and the alcohol selection is comprehensive. The crowd is mixed and foreigner friendly. ⊠ *2F Dai 33 Kyutei Bldg., 2–11–7 Shinjuku, Shinjuku-ku* ☎ *03/5362–9720* ⊙ *Sun.–Thurs. 7 pm–3 am, Fri. and Sat. 7 pm–5 am.*

Dragon Men. Despite the name, Tokyo's swanky gay lounge Dragon Men also welcomes women. Remodeled in 2007, Dragon is a neon-deco space that would look right at home in New York or Paris. The location could be better: it's behind a drugstore, and the outdoor tables face a ramshackle wall, but when the place is crammed on weekends with cuties of all persuasions, who's looking? ⊠ *1F Stork Nagasaki, 2–11–4 Shinjuku, Shinjuku-ku* ☎ *03/3341–0606* ⊙ *Sun.–Thurs. 6 pm–3 am, Fri. and Sat. 6 pm–4 am.*

CLOSE UP

Golden Gai

Tucked away on the eastern side of Tokyo's sordid Kabuki-cho district (near Shinkuku), Golden Gai is a ramshackle collection of more than 200 Lilliputian bars that survived the rampant construction of Japan's bubble-economy years, thanks to the passion of its patrons. In the 1980s, when the *yakuza*, Japan's crime syndicate, was torching properties to sell the land to big-thinking developers, Golden Gai's supporters took turns guarding the area each night.

Each bar occupies a few square yards, and some accommodate fewer than a dozen drinkers. With such limited space, many of the bars rely on their regulars—and give a frosty welcome and exorbitant bill to the casual visitor. And although the timeworn look of Golden Gai captures the imagination of most visitors, many of the establishments are notoriously unfriendly to foreigners. But times change, as do leases, and a new generation of owners is gradually emerging to offer the same intimate drinking experience and cold beers without the unwelcome reception.

Albatross G. When it opened in summer 2005, Albatross G quickly built a following with its friendliness and, in Golden Gai terms, affordability. The ¥300 seating charge and drinks starting at ¥600 are a marked contrast to most of its neighbors. ✉ *2F 5th Ave., 1–1 Kabuki-cho, Shinjuku-ku* ☎ *03/3203–3699* ⊕ *www.alba-s.com* ☉ *Daily 8 pm–5 am* Ⓜ *Marunouchi and Shinjuku subway lines, Shinjuku-san-chome Station (Exit B3).*

La Jetée. It should come as no surprise that French cinema is the proprietor's big passion: a film lover's paradise, La Jetée is covered in Euro-cinema posters and was named after a French movie. It struggles to seat 10 customers, but that means intimate conversations—in Japanese, French, and sometimes English—usually about movies. If you want to discuss European cinema with Wim Wenders or sit toe-to-toe with Quentin Tarantino, this is your best bet. The music, naturally, comes exclusively from film sound tracks. The seating charge is ¥1,000. ✉ *2F, 1–1–8 Kabuki-cho, Shinjuku-ku* ☎ *03/3208–9645* ☉ *Mon.–Sat. 7 pm–early morning* Ⓜ *Marunouchi and Shinjuku subway lines, Shinjuku-san-chome Station (Exit B3).*

Sumire no Tenmado. Tim Burton's favorite Tokyo bar is a tiny shrine to the gothloli (Gothic Lolita) subculture, and you'll find the director's skeletal drawings on the pitch-black walls. It's eerie but friendly, dark but fun, and even the signature cocktail— *Ankoku Sumire le poison* (Sumire's pitch-black poison)—is as black as the decor. ✉ *2F, 1–1–7 Kabukicho, Shinjuku-ku* ☎ *03/3209–1204* ⊕ *www. kokusyokusumire.net* ☉ *Weekdays 4:30–11:30, weekends 11:30–11:30* Ⓜ *Marunouchi and Shinjuku subway lines, Shinjuku-san-chome Station (Exit B3).*

—Nicholas Coldicott

5

All That Tokyo Jazz

The Tokyo jazz scene is one of the world's best, far surpassing that of Paris and New York with its number of venues playing traditional, swing, bossa nova, rhythm and blues, and free jazz. Though popular in Japan before World War II, jazz really took hold of the city after U.S. forces introduced Charlie Parker and Thelonius Monk in the late 1940s. The genre had been banned in wartime Japan as an American vice, but even at the height of the war, fans were able to listen to their favorite artists on Voice of America radio. In the 1960s Japan experienced a boom in all areas of the arts, and jazz was no exception. Since then, the Japanese scene has steadily bloomed, with several local stars—such as Sadao Watanabe in the 1960s and contemporary favorites Keiko Lee and Hiromi Uehara—gaining global attention.

Today there are more than 120 bars and clubs that host live music, plus hundreds that play recorded jazz. Shinjuku, Takadanobaba, and Kichijoji are the city's jazz enclaves. Famous international acts regularly appear at big-name clubs such as the Blue Note, but the smaller, lesser-known joints usually have more atmosphere. With such a large jazz scene, there's an incredible diversity to enjoy, from Louis Armstrong tribute acts to fully improvised free jazz—sometimes on successive nights at the same venue.

If you time your visit right, you can listen to great jazz at one of the city's more than 20 annual festivals dedicated to this adopted musical form. The festivals vary in size and coverage, but two to check out are the Tokyo Jazz Festival and the Asagaya Jazz Street Festival.

Tokyo Jazz Festival. On the last weekend in September, the festival takes over the Tokyo International Forum in Marunouchi. Though the 5,000-seat hall lacks the intimacy you might seek in a jazz show, the lineup is usually an impressive mix of local talent and international stars. ☎ 03/5777–8600 ⊕ www.tokyo-jazz. com

Asagaya Jazz Street Festival. Held the last weekend of October, the predominantly mainstream affair takes places in some less-than-mainstream places, with venues ranging from a Shinto shrine to a Lutheran church (most within walking distance of Asagaya Station). Look for festival staff at the station to help guide you, but they may not speak English. Previous headliners have included the Mike Price Jazz Quintet and vocalist Masamichi Yano. The festival gets crowded, so come early to ensure entry. ☎ 03/5305–5075

—James Catchpole

GB. The men-only GB has been running for two decades, and carries a whiff of the old days when things were less mainstream. Video monitors blast contemporary and classic dance hits. On weekends the place is packed with gentlemen in their twenties through fifties cruising via strategically placed mirrors. ⊠ *B1 Shinjuku Plaza Bldg., 2–12–3 Shinjuku, Shinjuku-ku* ☎ *03/3352–8972* ⊕ *gb-tokyo.tripod.com* ☉ *Sun.–Thurs. 8 pm–2 am, Fri. and Sat. 8 pm–3 am.*

Motel #203. One of Ni-chome's newest bars, Motel is a posh but relaxed bar for "women who love women." It's a cozy den of vintage lamps, leather sofas, and plush cushions, with no cover charge. The bar's owner is an icon in the Tokyo lesbian scene and also runs a popular monthly dance party, called "Girlfriend," usually the last Saturday of every month at nearby Bar Hijo-guchi, or Bar Exit. Motel is women-only except Thursday, which is mixed. ⊠ *203 Sunnocorpo Shinjuku Bldg., 2–7–2 Shinjuku, Shinjuku-ku* ☎ *03/6383–4649* ⊕ *www.bar-motel.com* ⊙ *Wed.–Mon. 8 pm–4 am.*

JAZZ CLUBS

Intro. This small basement bar features one of the best jazz experiences in Tokyo: a Saturday "jam session" that stretches until 5 *am* (¥1,000 entry fee). Other nights of the week occasionally bring unannounced live sets by musicians just dropping by, but usually it's the owner's extensive vinyl and CD collection that the regulars are listening to. Simple Japanese and Western food is available. ⊠ *B1 NT Bldg., 2–14–8 Takadanobaba, Shinjuku-ku* ☎ *03/3200–4396* ⊕ *www.intro.co.jp* ⊙ *Sun.–Thurs. 6:30 pm–midnight, Fri. 6:30 pm–1 am, Sat. 5 pm–5 am* Ⓜ *JR Takadanobaba Station (Waseda Exit).*

Shinjuku Pit Inn. Most major jazz musicians have played at least once in this classic Tokyo club. The veteran Shinjuku Pit stages mostly mainstream fare with the odd foray into the avant-garde. Afternoon admission is ¥1,300 weekdays, ¥2,500 weekends; evening entry is typically ¥3,000. Better-known local acts often cost a little more. ⊠ *B1 Accord Shinjuku Bldg., 2–12–4 Shinjuku, Shinjuku-ku* ☎ *03/3354–2024* ⊙ *Daily, hrs vary* ⊕ *www.pit-inn.com* Ⓜ *Marunouchi subway line, Shinjuku-san-chome Station.*

CENTRAL TOKYO

KARAOKE

Smash Hits. If karaoke just isn't karaoke to you without drunken strangers to sing to, Smash Hits has the answer. An expat favorite, it offers thousands of English songs and a central performance stage. The cover charge gets you two drinks and no time limit. ⊠ *5–2–26 Hiro-o, Shibuya-ku* ☎ *03/3444–0432* ⊕ *www.smashhits.jp* ⊠ *¥3,500* ⊙ *Tues.–Sat. 7 pm–3 am* Ⓜ *Hibiya Line, Hiroo Station (Exit 2).*

ELSEWHERE IN TOKYO

BEER HALLS AND PUBS

Popeye. Of the staggering 70 beers on tap here, most are top-quality Japanese microbrews, from pilsners to IPAs to barley wines. The owner is one of Japan's leading authorities on beer, and his passion is reflected in the quality of the brews. Popeye is always packed, so get there early or be prepared to wait. ⊠ *2–18–7 Ryogoku, Sumida-ku* ☎ *03/3633–2120* ⊕ *www.40beersontap.com* ⊙ *Mon.–Sat. 5 pm–11:30 pm.*

DANCE CLUBS

Ageha. This massive bay-side venue has the city's best sound system and most diverse musical lineup. The cavernous Arena hosts well-known house and techno DJs, the bar plays hip-hop, a summer-only swimming-pool area has everything from reggae to break beats, and inside a chill-out tent there's usually ambient or trance music. Because of its far-flung location and enormous capacity, Ageha can be either a throbbing party or an embarrassingly empty hall, depending on the caliber of the DJ. Free buses to Ageha depart every half hour between 11 pm and 4:30 am from the stop opposite the Shibuya police station on Roppongi-dori, a three-minute walk from Shibuya Station (there are also return buses every half hour from 11:30 pm to 5 am). ⊠ *2–2–10 Shin-Kiba, Koto-ku* ☎ *03/5534–1515* ⊕ *www.ageha.com* 🍸 *Around ¥3,500* Ⓜ *Yuraku-cho subway line, Shin-Kiba Station.*

JAZZ CLUBS

Hot House. This could very well be the world's smallest jazz club. An evening here is like listening to live jazz in your living room with five or six other jazz lovers on your sofa. It's so small, in fact, that you can't get through the front door once the pianist is seated, so don't show up late. Live acts are trios at most, with no space for drums or amplifiers. Simple, home-style Japanese cooking helps make this a truly intimate experience. ⊠ *B1 Liberal Takadanobaba, 2–14–8 Takadanobaba, Shinjuku-ku* ☎ *03/3367–1233* 🕐 *Show times vary from 8:30 pm to early morning* Ⓜ *JR Takadanobaba Station (Waseda Exit).*

LIVE HOUSES

Showboat. A small, basic venue in western Tokyo that's been going strong for more than a decade, Showboat attracts both amateur and semiprofessional performers. Ticket prices vary by act but are typically around ¥2,000 and often include one drink. ⊠ *B1 Oak Hill Koenji, 3–17–2 Koenji Kita, Suginami-ku* ☎ *03/3337–5745* ⊕ *www.showboat. co.jp* 🕐 *Daily 6 pm–early morning* Ⓜ *JR Sobu and JR Chuo lines, Koenji Station (Kita-guchi/North Exit).*

GREATER TOKYO

LIVE HOUSES

Manda-la 2. Relaxed and intimate, this local favorite in the bustling western suburb of Kichijoji attracts an eclectic group of performers. Cover charges range from ¥1,800 to ¥4,000. ⊠ *2–8–6 Kichijoji-Minami-cho, Musashino* ☎ *0422/42–1579* 🕐 *Daily 6:30 pm to varying closing times* Ⓜ *Keio Inokashira private rail line, JR Chuo and JR Sobu lines, Kichijoji Station (Koen-guchi/Park Exit, on Suehiro-dori).*

Shelter. An ever-popular, long-running venue in Shimo-Kitazawa, an area just west of Shibuya dominated by people in their late teens and early twenties, Shelter is a great place to catch promising local bands of all genres. ⊠ *B1F, 2–6–10 Kitazawa, Setagaya-ku* ☎ *03/3466–7430* 🕐 *Daily 6:30 pm to varying closing times; some daytime shows on weekends* Ⓜ *Keio Inokashira, Odakyu private rail lines, Shimo-Kitazawa Station (North Exit).*

Shopping

WORD OF MOUTH

"You can get brushes such as those for calligraphy and . . . paper at Ito-ya and Kyukyodo stores both on the Ginza."

— Mara

Updated by
Misha Janette

You didn't fly all the way to Tokyo to buy European designer clothing, so shop for items that are Japanese-made for Japanese people and sold in stores that don't cater to tourists. This city is Japan's showcase. The crazy clothing styles, obscure electronics, and new games found here are capable of setting trends for the rest of the country—and perhaps the rest of Asia.

Also, don't pass up the chance to purchase Japanese crafts. Color, balance of form, and superb workmanship make these items exquisite and well worth the price you'll pay. Some can be quite expensive; for example, Japanese lacquerware carries a hefty price tag. But if you like the shiny boxes, bowls, cups, and trays and consider that quality lacquerware is made to last a lifetime, the cost is justified.

The Japanese approach to shopping can be feverish; on the weekends, some of the hipper, youth-oriented stores will have lines that wind down the street as kids wait patiently to pick up the latest trend. But shopping here can also be an exercise in elegance and refinement. Note the care taken with items after you purchase them, especially in department stores and boutiques. Goods will be wrapped, wrapped again, bagged, and sealed. Sure, the packaging can be excessive—does anybody really need three plastic bags for one croissant?—but such a focus on presentation has deep roots in Japanese culture.

This focus on presentation also influences salespeople who are invariably helpful and polite. In the larger stores they greet you with a bow when you arrive, and many of them speak at least enough English to help you find what you're looking for. There's a saying in Japan: *o-kyaku-sama wa kami-sama*, "the customer is a god"—and since the competition for your business is fierce, people do take it to heart.

Horror stories abound about prices in Japan—and some of them are true. Yes, a cup of coffee can cost $10, if you pick the wrong coffee shop. A gift-wrapped melon from a department-store gourmet counter can cost $150. And a taxi ride from the airport to central Tokyo does cost about $200. But most people take the convenient airport train for $9, and if you shop around, you can find plenty of gifts and souvenirs at fair prices.

Japan has been slow to embrace the use of credit cards, and even though plastic is now accepted at big retailers, some smaller shops only take cash. So when you go souvenir hunting, be prepared with a decent amount of cash; Tokyo's low crime rates make this a low-risk proposition. The dishonor associated with theft is so strong, in fact, that it's considered bad form to conspicuously count change in front of cashiers.

Japan has an across-the-board 5% value-added tax (V.A.T.) imposed on luxury goods as well as on restaurant and hotel bills. This tax can be avoided at some duty-free shops in the city (don't forget to bring your passport). It's also waived in the duty-free shops at the international airports, but because these places tend to have higher profit margins, your tax savings there are likely to be offset by the higher markups.

Stores in Tokyo generally open at 10 or 11 am and close at 8 or 9 pm.

AKIHABARA AND JIMBO-CHO

Akihabara was at one time the only place Tokyoites would go to buy cutting-edge electronic gadgets, but the area has lost its aura of exclusivity thanks to the Internet and the big discount chains that have sprung up around the city. Still, for its sheer variety of products and foreigner-friendliness, Akihabara has the newcomers beat—and a visit remains essential to any Tokyo shopping spree. Salesclerks speak decent English at most of the major shops (and many of the smaller ones), and the big chains offer duty-free and export items. Be sure to poke around the backstreets for smaller stores that sell used and unusual electronic goods. The area has also become the center of the *otaku* (nerd) boom, with loads of shops offering enough video games and *manga* (sophisticated comic books) to satisfy even the most fastidious geek. West of Akihabara, in the used-book store district of Jimbo-cho, you'll find pretty much whatever you're looking for in dictionaries and art books, rare and out-of-print editions (Western and Japanese), and prints. Ⓜ *For Akihabara: JR Yamanote, Keihin Tohoku, and Sobu lines, Akihabara Station (Electric Town Exit); Hibiya subway line, Akihabara Station. For Jimbo-cho: Hanzo-mon, Shinjuku, and Mita subway lines, Jimbo-cho Station.*

SPECIALTY STORES
ANTIQUES
Yasukuni Jinja. Every Sunday, from sunrise to sunset, antiques-hunters can search and explore this flea market, which boasts 100 booths run by professional collectors. It's located near the Yasukuni Jinja, so when you're finished shopping, stroll over to the shrine to learn about the controversy that surrounds it. ✉ *3–1–1 Kudan-Kita, Chiyoda-ku* ☎ *03/3261–8326* Ⓜ *Hanzo-mon and Shinjuku subway lines, Kudan-shita Station (Exit 1).*

6

IKEBUKURO
northern hub of Shinjuku-based department stores

Rikugien Gardens

Koishikawa Botanical Gardens

ASAKUSA AND UENO
traditional crafts and kitschy souvenirs

AKIHABARA AND JIMBO-CHO
gadgets galore and rare books

SHINJUKU
deparment stores dominate

Shinjuku Gyo-en

IMPERIAL PALACE DISTRICT

NIHOMBASHI
department stores, both historic and hyper-modern

HARAJUKU
funky shops for the young and hip

AOYAMA
high fashion showcased in boutique settings

GINZA
world-renowned high-end shopping and fashion chains

SHIBUYA
reasonably priced small shops for young shoppers

ROPPONGI
new crop of high-end shops

SHIODOME

TSUKIJI

DAIKANYAMA AND NAKAMEGURO
fashionistas and bohemiam types mingle

National Park for Nature Study

MEGURO

PORT OF TOKYO

ODAIBA

Rainbow Bridge

Meijiro-dori
Meji-dori
Nakasendo
Meiji-dori
Shinobazu-dori
Hondo-dori
Kasuga-dori
Waseda-dori
Tokyo Expwy No.5
Meiji-dori
Aoyama-dori
Gaien-Higashi-dori
Sakurada-dori
Uchibori-dori
Shin Ohashi-dori
Sumidagawa
Kiyosumi-dori
Kiyosu-bashi-dori
Hakusan-dori Ave.
Tokyo Expwy No.3
Tokyo Expwy No.2
Tokyo Expwy No.1
Daiichi-keihin
Sakurada-dori
Kaigan-dori
Meguro-dori

0   1 mile
0   1 km

BOOKS

Bookstores of Jimbo-cho. The site of one of the largest concentrations of used-book stores in the world, the Jimbo-cho area is a bibliophile's dream. In the ½-km (¼-mi) strip along Yasukuni-dori and its side streets you can find centuries-old Japanese prints, vintage manga, and even complete sets of the *Oxford English Dictionary*. Most shops have predominately Japanese-language selections, but almost all stock some foreign titles, with a few devoting major floor space to English books. Kitazawa Shoten, recognizable by its stately entranceway, carries lots of humanities titles. Tokyo Random Walk is the retail outlet of Tuttle Publishing, which puts out books on Japanese language and culture. The large Japanese publisher Sanseido has its flagship store here; the fifth floor sells magazines and postcards in addition to books. The stores in the area are usually open 9 or 9:30 to 5:30 or 6, and many of the smaller shops close Sunday or Monday. Ⓜ *Mita, Shinjuku, and Hanzo-mon subway lines, Jimbo-cho Station (Exit A5).*

DOLLS

Beishu. Colorful and often made from precious metals, the delicate dolls handcrafted at this shop have found their way into some of Japan's larger department stores, museums, and even the Imperial Palace. ✉ *1–23–3 Yanagibashi, Taito-ku* ☎ *03/3834–3501* ⊙ *Daily 9:30–5:30* Ⓜ *JR Sobu Line, Asakusa subway line, Asakusa-bashi Station (Exit A3).*

Kyugetsu. In business for more than a century, Kyugetsu sells every kind of doll imaginable. ✉ *1–20–4 Yanagibashi, Taito-ku* ☎ *03/5687–5176* ⊙ *Weekdays 9:15–6, weekends 9:15–5:15* Ⓜ *Asakusa subway line, JR Sobu Line, Asakusa-bashi Station (Exit A3).*

ELECTRONICS

LAOX. One of the big Akihabara chains, LAOX has several locations in the area. The seven-story main branch is duty free, with three floors dedicated to export models. English-speaking staff members are always on call. ✉ *1–2–9 Soto-Kanda, Chiyoda-ku* ☎ *03/3253–7111* ⊙ *Sun.–Thurs. 10–8, Fri. and Sat. 10–9* Ⓜ *JR Yamanote Line, Akihabara Station (Electric Town Exit).*

Sofmap. One Akihabara retailer that actually benefited from the bursting of Japan's economic bubble in the early '90s is Sofmap, once known as a used-PC and software chain with a heavy presence in Tokyo. Now its multiple branches also sell electronics, music, and mobile phones. Most are open daily until 7:30 or 8. ✉ *3–13–8 Soto-Kanda, Chiyoda-ku* ☎ *03/3253–3399* ⊙ *Daily 11–8* Ⓜ *JR Yamanote Line, Akihabara Station (Electric Town Exit).*

AOYAMA AND OMOTESANDO

You can find boutiques by many of the leading Japanese and Western designers in Aoyama, as well as elegant, but pricey, antiques shops on Kotto-dori. Aoyama tends to be a showcase not merely of high fashion but also of the latest concepts in commercial architecture and interior design. The centerpiece of Omotesando (a short stroll from Aoyama) is the long, wide avenue running from Aoyama-dori to Meiji Jingu.

High-end goods fill the stores at Omotesando Hills mall.

Known as the Champs-Elysées of Tokyo, the sidewalks are lined with cafés and designer boutiques, both foreign and domestic. There are also several antiques and souvenir shops here. Omotesando is perfect for browsing, window-shopping, and lingering over a café au lait before strolling to your next destination. Ⓜ *Chiyoda, Ginza, and Hanzo-mon subway lines, Omotesando Station (Exits A4, A5, B1, B2, and B3).*

MALLS AND SHOPPING CENTERS

Glassarea. Virtually defining Aoyama elegance is this small cobblestone shopping center, which draws well-heeled young professionals to its boutiques, restaurants, and housewares shops. ✉ *5–4–41 Minami-Aoyama, Minato-ku* ☏ *03/5778–4450* ⊙ *Most shops daily 11–8* Ⓜ *Ginza, Chiyoda, and Hanzo-mon subway lines, Omotesando Station (Exit B1).*

Gyre. Near the Harajuku end of Omotesando, this mall houses luxury-brand shops such as Chanel and Bulgari as well as the only MoMA design store outside New York City. ✉ *5–10–1 Jingu-mae, Shibuya-ku* ☏ *03/5468–5801* ⊙ *Daily 11–10* Ⓜ *Chiyoda and Fukutoshin subway lines, Meiji-Jingu-mae Station (Exit 4).*

Omotesando Hills. Architect Tadao Ando's latest adventure in concrete is Tokyo's newest monument to shopping. The six wedge-shape floors include some brand-name heavy hitters (Yves Saint Laurent and Harry Winston) and a wide range of smaller stores whose shelves showcase mid- to high-end shoes and bags. ✉ *4–12–10 Jingu-mae, Shibuya-ku* ☏ *03/3497–0293* ⊙ *Daily 11–9* Ⓜ *Hanzo-mon, Ginza, and Chiyoda subway lines, Omotesando Station (Exit A2).*

SPECIALTY STORES
ANTIQUES

★ **Fuji-Torii.** An English-speaking staff, a central Omotesando location, and antiques ranging from ceramics to swords are the big draws at this shop, in business since 1948. In particular, Fuji-Torii has an excellent selection of folding screens, lacquerware, painted glassware, and *ukiyo-e* (wood-block prints). ✉ *6–1–10 Jingu-mae, Shibuya-ku* ☎ *03/3400–2777* ⊘ *Wed.–Mon. 11–6; closed 3rd Mon. of month* Ⓜ *Chiyoda and Fukutoshin subway lines, Meiji-Jingu-mae Station (Exit 4).*

Morita. This Aoyama shop carries antiques and new *mingei* (Japanese folk crafts) in addition to a large stock of textiles from throughout Asia. ✉ *5–12–2 Minami-Aoyama, Minato-ku* ☎ *03/3407–4466* ⊘ *Daily 10–7* Ⓜ *Ginza, Chiyoda, and Hanzo-mon subway lines, Omotesando Station (Exit B1).*

CERAMICS

Tsutaya. *Ikebana* (flower arrangement) and *sado* (tea ceremony) goods are the only items sold at this Kotto-dori shop, but they come in such stunning variety that a visit is definitely worthwhile. Colorful vases in surprising shapes and traditional ceramic tea sets make for unique souvenirs. ✉ *5–10–5 Minami-Aoyama, Minato-ku* ☎ *03/3400–3815* ⊘ *Daily 10–6:30* Ⓜ *Ginza, Chiyoda, and Hanzo-mon subway lines, Omotesando Station (Exit B3).*

CLOTHING BOUTIQUES

10 Corso Como Comme des Garçons. Milanese lifestyle guru Carla Sozzani helped create this spacious boutique for designer Rei Kawakubo's Comme des Garçons lines, which include Junya Watanabe men's and women's wear. Also on offer are local cult brands like Toga. The staff isn't too busy being hip to help you out. ✉ *5–3 Minami-Aoyama, Minato-ku* ☎ *03/5774–7800* ⊘ *Daily 11–8* Ⓜ *Ginza, Chiyoda, and Hanzo-mon subway lines, Omotesando Station (Exit A5).*

Bape Exclusive Aoyama. Since the late 1990s, no brand has been more coveted by Harajuku scenesters than the A Bathing Ape label (shortened to Bape) from DJ–fashion designer Nigo. At the height of the craze, hopefuls would line up outside Nigo's well-hidden boutiques for the chance to plop down ¥7,000 for a T-shirt festooned with a simian visage or a *Planet of the Apes* quote. Bape has since gone aboveground, with Nigo expanding his business empire to Singapore, Hong Kong, New York, Paris, Los Angeles, and London. Here in Tokyo, you can see what all the fuss is about at a spacious boutique that houses the Bape Gallery on the second floor. ✉ *5–5–8 Minami-Aoyama, Minato-ku* ☎ *03/3407–2145* ⊘ *Daily 11–7* Ⓜ *Ginza and Hanzo-mon subway lines, Omotesando Station (Exit A5).*

★ **Comme des Garçons.** Sinuous low walls snake through Rei Kawakubo's flagship store, a minimalist labyrinth that houses the designer's signature clothes, shoes, and accessories. Staff members will do their best to ignore you, but that's no reason to stay away from one of Tokyo's funkiest retail spaces. ✉ *5–2–1 Minami-Aoyama, Minato-ku* ☎ *03/3406–3951* ⊘ *Daily 11–8* Ⓜ *Ginza, Chiyoda, and Hanzo-mon subway lines, Omotesando Station (Exit A5).*

Mix with Tokyo's most glamorous residents at Prada's architecturally dazzling Omotesando store.

Issey Miyake. The otherworldly creations of internationally renowned designer Miyake are on display at his flagship store in Aoyama, which carries the full Paris line. Keep walking on the same street away from Omotesando Station and you'll find his menswear, Pleats Please, Haat and Me stores just a stone's throw away. ⊠ *3–18–11 Minami-Aoyama, Minato-ku* ☎ *03/3423–1408* ⊗ *Daily 11–8* Ⓜ *Ginza, Chiyoda, and Hanzo-mon subway lines, Omotesando Station (Exit A4).*

Fodor'sChoice
★
Prada. This fashion "epicenter," built in 2003 and designed by Herzog & de Meuron, is one of the most buzzed-about architectural wonders in the city. Its facade is comprised of a mosaic of green glass "bubble" windows: alternating convex and concave windows create distorted reflections of the surrounding area. Many world-renowned, nearby boutiques have tried to replicate the significant impact the Prada building has had on the Omotesando, but none have been unable to match this tower. Most visitors opt for a photo in front of the cavelike entrance that leads into the basement floor. ⊠ *5–2–6 Minami-Aoyama, Minato-ku* ☎ *03/6418–0400* ⊗ *Daily 11–8* Ⓜ *Ginza, Chiyoda, and Hanzo-mon subway lines, Omotesando Station (Exit A5).*

Undercover. This stark shop houses Paris darling Jun Takahashi's cult clothing. Racks of men's and women's punkish duds sit under a ceiling made of a sea of thousands of hanging lightbulbs. ⊠ *5–3–18 Minami-Aoyama, Minato-ku* ☎ *03/3407–1232* ⊗ *Daily 11–8* Ⓜ *Ginza, Chiyoda, and Hanzo-mon subway lines, Omotesando Station (Exit A5).*

THE ARCHITECTURE OF OMOTESANDO

With Tokyo's impressive array of high-end fashion and jewelry stores have come an equally astonishing collection of beautiful buildings. A 20-minute walk along the Omotesando promenade from Aoyama to Harajuku will take you past several stand-out structures. Start at the **Prada** flagship on the south-east end of Omotesando. The Swiss-based Herzog & de Meuron team created this building of concave and protruding diamond-shaped glass panels that gives it a honeycomb-like effect. Next door are the similar glass-and-metal buildings for **Chloé** and **Cartier**. Part of Chloé's facade is hidden behind wooden bamboo-like slits that tilt and jut high into the air at random.

Walk toward Shibuya on Aoyama-dori—on the right is the Ao Building.

At night, the glass exterior becomes a curtain of blue, green, and purple lights, recalling the Aurora Borealis. Or walk on Omotesando toward Harajuku, where on the left side you will see the white translucent box that is **Dior**. It was designed by Kazuyo Sejima and Ryue Nishizawa of SANAA, 2010 Pritzker Architecture Prize recipients. Moving projections play on the building during most of the year. Hang a left on Meiji-dori and you won't miss the **Audi Forum's** "Iceberg" Building. The sharp geometry of the blue, glass structure was inspired by ice, crystal, and plastic bottles. Finally, just on the north side of Meiji-jingu crossing is the **H&M** building, which appears to be a tower of stacked ice cubes. The cubes glow softly from day to night and reflect the dynamic design of the city that surrounds it.

FOLK CRAFTS

★ **Oriental Bazaar.** The four floors of this popular tourist destination are packed with just about anything you could want as a traditional Japanese (or Chinese or Korean) handicraft souvenir: painted screens, pottery, chopsticks, dolls, and more, all at very reasonable prices. ✉ *5–9–13 Jingu-mae, Shibuya-ku* ☎ *03/3400–3933* ⊙ *Fri.–Wed. 10–7* Ⓜ *Chiyoda and Fukutoshin subway lines, Meiji-Jingu-mae Station (Exit 4).*

FOODSTUFFS AND WARES

☾ **Ginza Natsuno.** This two-story boutique sells an incredible range of chopsticks, from traditional to pop-motifs, and wooden to crystal-encrusted sticks that can be personalized. Children's chopsticks and dishes are available here, too. ✉ *4–2–17 Jingu-mae, Shibuya-ku* ☎ *03/3403–6033* ⊙ *Mon.–Sat. 10–8, Sun. 10–7* Ⓜ *Ginza, Chiyoda, and Hanzo-mon subway lines, Omotesando Station (Exit A2).*

Tea-Tsu. Some people ascribe Japanese longevity to the beneficial effects of green tea. Tea-Tsu sells a variety of leaves in attractive canisters that make unique gifts. Customers can sample tea and tea-flavored desserts while browsing the leaves and tea sets. ✉ *5–10–17 Minami-Aoyama, Minato-ku* ☎ *03/3498–5300* ⊙ *Tues.–Sun. 11–7* Ⓜ *Ginza, Chiyoda, and Hanzo-mon subway lines, Omotesando Station (Exit B1).*

HOUSEWARES

Franc Franc Village. This concept shop by the popular interior chain sells fun, colorful goods like place mats, rice bowls, and stationery for reasonable prices. It also houses the mini Monocle shop, curated by the culture magazine of the same name, which has a selection of small goods for the person who already has everything, like smartphone accessories and obscure coffee-table books. ⊠ *3–11–13 Minami-Aoyama, Minato-ku* ☎ *03/5413–2511* ⊘ *Daily 11–10* Ⓜ *Ginza, Chiyoda, and Hanzo-mon subway lines, Omotesando Station (Exit A3).*

Sempre. Playful, colorful, and bright describe both the products and the space of this Kotto-dori housewares dealer. Among the great finds here are interesting tableware, glassware, lamps, office goods, and jewelry. ⊠ *5–13–3 Minami-Aoyama, Minato-ku* ☎ *03/5464–5655* ⊘ *Mon.–Sat. 11–8, Sun. 11–7* Ⓜ *Ginza, Chiyoda, and Hanzo-mon subway lines, Omotesando Station (Exit B3).*

KIMONO

Gallery Kawano. Kawano, in the high-fashion district of Omotesando, sells kimonos and kimono fabric in a variety of patterns. ⊠ *4–4–9 Jingu-mae, Shibuya-ku* ☎ *03/3470–3305* ⊘ *Daily 11–6* Ⓜ *Ginza, Chiyoda, and Hanzo-mon subway lines, Omotesando Station (Exit A2).*

TOYS

☺ **Kiddy Land.** Commonly regarded as Tokyo's best toy store, Kiddy Land also carries kitsch items that draw in Harajuku's teen brigade. As of this writing, the store is in a temporary location while the original building gets a face-lift. It is expected to return to 6–1–9 Jingu-mae by fall of 2012. Check with the store for updates (the phone number, station, and business times will all remain the same despite the move). ⊠ *6–14–2 Jingu-mae, Shibuya-ku* ☎ *03/3409–3431* ⊘ *Weekdays 11–9, weekends 10:30–9* Ⓜ *JR Yamanote Line, Harajuku Station (Omotesando Exit); Chiyoda and Fukutoshin subway lines, Meiji-Jingu-mae Station (Exit 4).*

ASAKUSA AND UENO

While sightseeing in Asakusa and Ueno, take time to stroll through its arcades. At first glance, many of the goods sold here are the kinds of souvenirs you can find in any tourist trap. Look a little harder and you can find small backstreet shops that have been making beautiful wooden combs, delicate fans, and other items of fine traditional craftsmanship for generations. Also here are the cookware shops of Kappabashi, where you can load up on everything from sushi knives to plastic lobsters. Ⓜ *Asakusa subway line, Asakusa Station (Kaminari-mon Exit); Ginza subway line, Asakusa Station (Exit 1) and Tawara-machi Station (Exit 3).*

SHOPPING STREETS AND ARCADES

Ame-ya Yoko-cho Market. Everything from fresh fish to cheap import clothing is for sale at this bustling warren of side streets between Okachi-machi and Ueno stations. In the days leading up to New Years, the area turns into mosh-pit mayhem as shoppers fight for fish and

CLOSE UP

Traditional Crafts

The Japanese take pride in their *monozukuri*: a gift for making things. Well they might, with traditions of craftsmanship centuries old to draw on: an itch for perfection, a loving respect for materials, and a profound aesthetic sense of what can be done with them. Each region has its own traditional crafts, but you can find exquisite pieces from all over the country with some focused shopping in Tokyo.

Ceramics: Most Japanese pottery, apart from some porcelain and earthenware, is stoneware—formed into a wonderful variety of vases, cups, bowls and platters and fired in climbing kilns on the slopes of hills. At first glance, Japanese ceramics seem priced for a prince's table, but keep an eye out for seasonal sales; you can often find affordable pieces. Department stores and Tokyo specialty shops like **Kuroda Toen** (⊠ *7-8-6 Ginza* ☎ *03/3571–3223* ⊠ *1-16-14 Shibuya* ☎ *03/3499–3225*) have extensive selections of these and other wares.

Dolls: Traditional dolls, meant primarily for display and not as playthings, come in many different styles: the long, cylindrical Kokeshi; red, round papier-mâché Daruma; and ceramic figurines in the traditional costumes of geisha, samurai, and festival dancers, called Hakata. The best area to shop for dolls in Tokyo is **Asakusabashi,** by the Sumida River.

Printed Fabrics: Stencil-dyed fabrics date to the Edo period and survive in a range of motifs and intricate geometric designs—especially for light summer kimonos, room dividers, and cushion covers. *Furoshiki*—large cotton squares for wrapping, storing, and carrying things—make great wall hangings, as do the smaller cotton hand towels called *tenugui*. Look for the latter at **Fujiya,** in Asakusa (⊠ *2-2-15 Asakusa* ☎ *03/3841–2283*).

Kimono: A new kimono, in brocaded silk, can cost ¥1 million or more. Consider a secondhand version—about ¥10,000 in a flea market, for one in decent condition—or look instead for cotton summer kimonos, called *yukata*, in a wide variety of colorful designs, you can buy new for ¥7,000–¥10,000. In Tokyo browse the **Oriental Bazaar** (⊠ *5-9-13 Jingumae, Shibuya-ku* ☎ *03/3400–3933*).

Lacquerware: For its history, diversity, and fine workmanship, lacquerware rivals ceramics as the traditional Japanese craft nonpareil. Cheaper pieces usually have plastic rather than wood underneath, and because these won't shrink and crack in dry climates, they make safer—but no less attractive—buys.

Paper: The Japanese make *washi* (handmade paper, usually of mulberry fibers) in a myriad of colors, textures, and designs and fashion it into an astonishing number of useful and decorative objects. Look for stationery, greeting cards, single sheets for gift wrapping and origami, and washi-covered jewelry boxes, at **Kyukyodo** (⊠ *5-7-4 Ginza* ☎ *03/3571–4429* ⊕ *www.kyukyodo.co.jp*).

Find it All: The **Japan Traditional Craft Center** (⊠ *Metropolitan Plaza 1-3F, 1-11-1 Nishi-Ikebukuro* ☎ *03/5954–6066* ⊕ *www.kougei.or.jp* ☉ *Daily 11–7, closed Dec. 19–Jan. 4*) sells the best of the craft work from all over the country, in most of the important categories from paper to tools to pottery.

6

snacks to serve over the holidays. The name of the market is often short-ened to Ameyoko. Most shops and stalls are open daily 10–7. ⊠ *Ueno 4-chome, Taito-ku* Ⓜ *JR Ueno Station (Hiroko-ji Exit), JR Okachi-machi Station (Exit A7).*

Nakamise-dori. This narrow street is heaven for those seeking out tra-ditional knickknacks and souvenirs. It is just as lively as it was when it was established in the Edo period, although now shops sells cheap sushi key chains and T-shirts alongside traditional hairpieces and silk screens. The entrance is marked by the giant red lantern at the Kaminari-mon, and ends at the grounds of the Senso-ji Complex. Most shops are open daily 10–6. ⊠ *Asakusa 2-chome, Taito-ku* ☎ *03/3844–3350* Ⓜ *Ginza subway line, Asakusa Station (Exit 1).*

Nishi-Sando. Kimono and *yukata* (cotton kimono) fabrics, traditional accessories, swords, and festival costumes at very reasonable prices are all for sale at this Asakusa arcade. It runs east of the area's movie the-aters, between Rok-ku and the Senso-ji Complex. ⊠ *Asakusa 2-chome, Taito-ku* Ⓜ *Ginza subway line, Asakusa Station (Exit 1).*

SPECIALTY STORES

FOODSTUFFS AND WARES

Tokiwa-do. Come here to buy some of Tokyo's most famous souvenirs: *kaminari okoshi* (thunder crackers), made of rice, millet, sugar, and beans. The shop is on the west side of Asakusa's Thunder God Gate, the Kaminari-mon entrance to Senso-ji. ⊠ *1–3–2 Asakusa, Taito-ku* ☎ *03/3841–5656* ⊙ *Daily 9–8:30* Ⓜ *Ginza subway line, Asakusa Sta-tion (Exit 1).*

PAPER

Origami Kaikan. In addition to shopping for paper goods at Yushima no Kobayahi's store, you can also tour a papermaking workshop and learn the art of origami. ⊠ *1–7–14 Yushima, Bunkyo-ku* ☎ *03/3811–4025* ⊙ *Mon.–Sat. 9–6* Ⓜ *JR Chuo and Sobu lines, Ochanomizu Station (West Exit); Chiyoda subway line, Yushima Station (Exit 5).*

SWORDS AND KNIVES

Ichiryo-ya Hirakawa. A small, cluttered souvenir shop in the Nishi-Sando arcade, Ichiryo-ya carries antique swords and reproductions and has some English-speaking salesclerks. ⊠ *2–7–13 Asakusa, Taito-ku* ☎ *03/3843–0051* ⊙ *Wed. and Fri.–Mon. 11–6* Ⓜ *Ginza subway line, Asakusa Station (Exit 1) or Tawara-machi Station (Exit 3).*

TRADITIONAL WARES

★ **Fuji-ya.** Master textile creator Keiji Kawakami's cotton *tenugui* (teh-noo-goo-ee) hand towels are collector's items, often framed instead of used as towels. Kawakami is an expert on the hundreds of traditional towel motifs that have come down from the Edo period: geometric pat-terns, plants and animals, and scenes from Kabuki plays and festivals. When Kawakami feels he has made enough of one pattern of his own design, he destroys the stencil. The shop is near the corner of Dembo-in Dori, on the street that runs parallel behind Naka-mise dori. ⊠ *2–2–15 Asakusa, Taito-ku* ☎ *03/3841–2283* ⊙ *Fri.–Wed. 10–6* Ⓜ *Ginza subway line, Asakusa Station (Exit 6).*

Hyaku-suke. This is the last place in Tokyo to carry government-approved skin cleanser made from powdered nightingale droppings. Ladies of the Edo period—especially the geisha—swore by the cleanser. These days this 100-year-old-plus cosmetics shop sells little of the nightingale powder, but its theatrical makeup for Kabuki actors, geisha, and traditional weddings—as well as unique items like seaweed shampoo, camellia oil, and handcrafted combs and cosmetic brushes—makes it a worthy addition to your Asakusa shopping itinerary. ✉ *2–2–14 Asakusa, Taito-ku* ☎ *03/3841–7058* ⏱ *Wed.–Mon. 11–5* Ⓜ *Ginza subway line, Asakusa Station (Exit 6).*

Jusan-ya. A shop selling handmade boxwood combs, this business was started in 1736 by a samurai who couldn't support himself as a feudal retainer. It has been in the same family ever since. Jusan-ya is on Shinobazu-dori, a few doors west of its intersection with Chuo-dori in Ueno. ✉ *2–12–21 Ueno, Taito-ku* ☎ *03/3831–3238* ⏱ *Mon.–Sat. 10–6:30* Ⓜ *Ginza subway line, Ueno Hiroko-ji Station (Exit 3); JR Yamanote Line, Ueno Station (Shinobazu Exit).*

Naka-ya. If you want to equip yourself for Senso-ji's annual Sanja Festival in May, this is the place to come. Best buys here are *sashiko hanten,* which are thick, woven, firemen's jackets, and *happi* coats, cotton tunics printed in bright colors with Japanese characters. Some items are available in children's sizes. ✉ *2–2–12 Asakusa, Taito-ku* ☎ *03/3841–7877* ⏱ *Daily 10–6:30* Ⓜ *Ginza subway line, Asakusa Station (Exit 6).*

Yono-ya. Traditional Japanese coiffures and wigs are very complicated, and they require a variety of tools to shape them properly. Tatsumi Minekawa, the current master at Yono-ya—the family line goes back 300 years—deftly crafts and decorates very fine boxwood combs. Some combs are carved with auspicious motifs, such as peonies, hollyhocks, or cranes, and all are engraved with the family benchmark. ✉ *1–37–10 Asakusa, Taito-ku* ☎ *03/3844–1755* ⏱ *Thurs.–Tues. 10:30–6* Ⓜ *Ginza subway line, Asakusa Station (Exit 1).*

DAIKANYAMA AND NAKAMEGURO

Unleash your inner fashionista in Daikanyama. Wedged between Shibuya and Ebisu, this area is a boutique heaven: see stacks of retro T-shirts, assortments of skate-punk wear, and a concentration of premium denim shops that will make jeans fans giddy. Nakameguro lies just beyond it marked by the sakura-tree-lined Meguro River that explodes with pink blossoms in spring. It attracts an organic-living-oriented crowd whose aesthetic is reflected in the bohemian clothing sold at the laid-back shops. Ⓜ *Tokyu Toyoko Line, Daikanyama Station*; *Tokyu Toyoko and Hibiya subway lines, Nakameguro Station.*

SHOPPING STREETS AND ARCADES

Boutiques along Meguro River. Just one block behind Nakameguro Station is the Meguro River, a canal beside which a number of hip cafés and clothing boutiques are concentrated. The crowd here is decidedly artsy and ecologically minded. There's barely a chain store to be found, and many of the cozy shops tout locally sourced vegan and organic food and clothing. Many are also open until 10 for the nighttime strolling clientele. ✉ *Between Kami-meguro 1-chome and Aobadai 1-chome, Meguro-ku* Ⓜ *Tokyu Toyoko and Hibiya subway lines, Nakameguro Station (Main Exit).*

SPECIALTY STORES

CLOTHING BOUTIQUES

Harcoza. This is one of those "only in Tokyo" shops, with a quirky selection of clothing and accessories such as a Bonsai tree watch and rings made of solidified croissants and desserts. Downstairs is a gallery that features work from underground artists. ✉ *2–15–9 Ebisu-nishi, Shibuya-ku* ☎ *03/6416–0725* ☯ *Wed.–Mon. 11–7:30* Ⓜ *Tokyu Toyoko Line, Daikanyama Station (West Exit).*

CLOTHING CHAINS

Mangart Beams T. This small but intriguing boutique sells manga along-side designer-made T-shirts inspired by the comic books. Even better, new designs rotate overhead on a conveyor belt. ✉ *2F, 19–6 Saru-gakucho, Shibuya-ku* ☎ *03/5428–5952* ☯ *Daily 11–8* Ⓜ *Tokyu Toyoko Line, Daikanyama Station (Komazawa-dori Exit).*

HOUSEWARES

Zero First Design. Kyu-Yamate-dori at Daikanyama is a well-known hub of interior goods stores, and this one is full of unique and modern pieces from both local and international designers. And even though it is a fair walk from Daikanyama Station it is still the go-to place for local discerning style aficionados. ✉ *2–3–1 Aobadai, Meguro-ku* ☎ *03/5489–6101* ☯ *Daily 11–8* Ⓜ *Tokyu Toyoko Line, Daikanyama Station (Komazawa-dori Exit).*

LACQUERWARE

Fodor's Choice
★

Yamada Heiando. With a spacious, airy layout and lovely lacquerware goods, this fashionable Daikanyama shop is a must for souvenir hunt-ers—and anyone else who appreciates fine design. Rice bowls, sushi trays, *bento* lunch boxes, *hashioki* (chopstick rests), and jewelry cases come in traditional blacks and reds, as well as patterns both subtle and bold. Prices are fair—many items cost less than ¥10,000—but these are the kinds of goods for which devotees of Japanese craftsmanship would be willing to pay a lot. ✉ *Hillside Terrace G Block # 202, 18–12 Sarugakucho, Shibuya-ku* ☎ *03/3464–5541* ☯ *Mon.–Sat. 10:30–7, Sun. 10:30–6:30* Ⓜ *Tokyu Toyoko Line, Daikanyama Station (Komazawa-dori Exit).*

GINZA

This world-renowned entertainment and shopping district dates back to the Edo period (1603–1868), when it consisted of long, willow-lined avenues. The willows have long since gone, and the streets are now lined with department stores and boutiques. The exclusive shops in this area—including flagship stores for major jewelers like Tiffany & Co., Harry Winston, and Mikimoto—sell quality merchandise at high prices. Now many affordable fashion and goods chains have built towers in the area creating a mix of high- and lowbrow style that defines modern

Shopping in Kappabashi

CLOSE UP

A wholesale-restaurant-supply district might not sound like a promising shopping destination, but Kappabashi, about a 10-minute walk west of the temples and pagodas of Asakusa, is worth a look. Ceramics, cutlery, cookware, folding lanterns, and even kimono can all be found here, along with the kitschy plastic food models that appear in restaurant windows throughout Japan. The best strategy is to stroll up and down the 1-km (½-mi) length of Kappabashi-dogu-machi-dori and visit any shop that looks interesting. Most stores here emphasize function over charm, but some manage to stand out for their stylish spaces as well. Most Kappabashi shops are open until 5:30; some close Sunday. To get here, take the Ginza subway line to Tawara-machi Station.

Kappabashi Soshoku. Come here for *aka-chochin* (folding red-paper lanterns) like the ones that hang in front of inexpensive bars and restaurants. ⊠ *3–1–1 Matsugaya, Taito-ku* ☎ *03/3844–1973* ⏱ *Mon.–Sat. 9:30–5:30.*

Kawahara Shoten. The brightly colored bulk packages of rice crackers, shrimp-flavored chips, and other Japanese snacks sold here make offbeat gifts. ⊠ *3–9–2 Nishi-Asakusa, Taito-ku* ☎ *03/3842–0841* ⏱ *Mon.–Sat. 9–5:30.*

⏱ **Maizuru.** This perennial tourist favorite manufactures the plastic food that's displayed outside almost every Tokyo restaurant. Ersatz sushi, noodles, and even beer cost just a few thousand yen. You can buy tiny plastic key holders and earrings, or splurge on a whole Pacific lobster, perfect in coloration and detail down to the tiniest spines on its legs. ⊠ *1–5–14 Nishi-*

Asakusa, Taito-ku ☎ *03/3843–1686* ⏱ *Daily 9–6.*

Noren-no-Nishimura. This Kappabashi shop specializes in *noren*—the curtains that shops and restaurants hang to announce they're open. The curtains are typically cotton, linen, or silk, most often dyed-to-order for individual shops. Nishimura also sells premade noren of an entertaining variety—from white-on-blue landscapes to geisha and sumo wrestlers in polychromatic splendor—for home decorating. They make wonderful wall hangings and dividers. ⊠ *1–10–10 Matsugaya, Taito-ku* ☎ *03/3841–6220* ⏱ *Mon.–Sat. 10–5.*

Soi Furniture. The selection of lacquerware, ceramics, and antiques sold at this Kappabashi shop is modest, but Soi displays the items in a primitivist setting of stone walls and wooden floor planks, with up-tempo jazz in the background. ⊠ *3–17–3 Matsugaya, Taito-ku* ☎ *03/3843–9555* ⏱ *Daily 10–6.*

★ **Tsubaya Hochoten.** Tsubaya sells high-quality cutlery for professionals. Its remarkable selection is designed for every imaginable use, as the art of food presentation in Japan requires a great variety of cutting implements. The best of these carry the Traditional Craft Association seal: hand-forged tools of tempered blue steel, set in handles banded with deer horn to keep the wood from splitting. Be prepared to pay the premium for these items: a cleaver just for slicing soba can cost as much as ¥50,000. ⊠ *3–7–2 Nishi-Asakusa, Taito-ku* ☎ *03/3845–2005* ⏱ *Mon.–Sat. 9–5:45, Sun. 9–5.*

Tokyo's taste. On Sunday the main strip of Chuo-dori is closed to car traffic and umbrella-covered tables dot the pavement; it's a great place for shoppers to rest their weary feet. Ⓜ *Marunouchi, Ginza, and Hibiya subway lines, Ginza Station (Exits A1–A10); Yuraku-cho subway line, Ginza Itchome Station; JR Yamanote Line, Yuraku-cho Station.*

SHOPPING STREETS AND ARCADES

International Shopping Arcade. A somewhat ragtag collection of shops in Hibiya, this arcade holds a range of goods, including cameras, electronics, pearls, and kimonos. The shops are duty-free, and most of the sales staff speaks decent English. If you listen carefully you'll hear the rumble of cars passing above on the freeway that is the roof of the building. ☒ *1–7–23 Uchisaiwai-cho, Chiyoda-ku* Ⓜ *Chiyoda and Hibiya subway lines, Hibiya Station (Exit A13).*

DEPARTMENT STORES

Fodor's Choice ★ **Matsuya.** On the fourth floor, the gleaming Matsuya houses an excellent selection of Japanese fashion, including Issey Miyake, Yohji Yamamoto, and Comme Ça Du Mode. The Louis Vuitton shops on the first and second floors are particularly popular with Tokyo's brand-obsessed shoppers. ☒ *3–6–1 Ginza, Chuo-ku* ☎ *03/3567–1211* ☉ *Daily 10–8* Ⓜ *Ginza, Marunouchi, and Hibiya subway lines, Ginza Station (Exits A12 and A13).*

Matsuzakaya. The Matsuzakaya conglomerate was founded in Nagoya and still commands the loyalties of shoppers with origins in western Japan. It houses affordable fashion chains like Forever21 and Muji with less emphasis on luxury. ☒ *6–10–1 Ginza, Chuo-ku* ☎ *03/3572–1111* ☉ *Daily 10:30–7:30* Ⓜ *Ginza, Marunouchi, and Hibiya subway lines, Ginza Station (Exits A3 and A4).*

★ **Mitsukoshi.** Mitsukoshi was Japan's first department-store chain, and this Ginza branch has been open since 1930. It is the largest department store in the area, with a sprawling grass-covered terrace on the ninth floor that provides a respite from the shopping bustle and the modern architecture of a glittery annex. ☒ *4–6–16 Ginza, Chuo-ku* ☎ *03/3562–1111* ☉ *Daily 10–8* Ⓜ *Ginza, Marunouchi, and Hibiya subway lines, Ginza Station (Exits A6, A7, and A8).*

Fodor's Choice ★ **Muji.** This chain features generically branded housewares and clothing at reasonable prices. You'll find a large selection of Bauhaus-influenced furniture, appliances, and bedding at the massive flagship branch in Yuraku-cho. If you're a bit overwhelmed by all the options, relax at the dining area that boasts—what else?—Muji meals. ☒ *3–8–3 Marunouchi, Chiyoda-ku* ☎ *03/5208–8241* ☉ *Daily 10–9* Ⓜ *JR Yamanote Line,*

Muji offers youthful styles at refreshingly low prices.

Yuraku-cho subway line, Yuraku-cho Station (JR Kyobashi Exit, subway Exit D9).

Wako. Wako is well known for its high-end watches, glassware, jewelry, and accessories, as well as having some of the handsomest, most sophisticated window displays in town. The clock atop this curved 1930s-era building is illuminated at night, making it one of Tokyo's more recognized landmarks. ⊠ *4–5–11 Ginza, Chuo-ku* ☎ *03/3562–2111* ⊗ *Mon.–Sat. 10:30–6* Ⓜ *Ginza, Marunouchi, and Hibiya subway lines, Ginza Station (Exits A9 and A10).*

SPECIALTY STORES
CLOTHING CHAINS

Uniqlo. Uniqlo offers customers a chance to wrap themselves in simple, low-priced items from the company's own brand. This supersize location sells men's, women's, and children's clothing right on the main Ginza drag. ⊠ *5–7–7 Ginza, Chuo-ku* ☎ *03/3569–6781* ⊗ *Daily 11–9* Ⓜ *Ginza, Hibiya, and Marunouchi subway lines, Ginza Station (Exit A2).*

ELECTRONICS

★ **Apple Store.** This very stylish showroom displays the newest models from Apple's line of computer products. The Genius Bar on the second floor offers consulting services should you need advice on how to resuscitate a comatose iPad or MacBook. ⊠ *3–5–12 Ginza, Chuo-ku* ☎ *03/5159–8200* ⊗ *Daily 10–9* Ⓜ *Ginza, Hibiya, and Marunouchi subway lines, Ginza Station (Exit A13).*

Ⓒ **Sony Building.** Test drive the latest Sony gadgets at this retail and entertainment space in the heart of Ginza. The first- to fourth-floor

The Power of Tea

Green tea is ubiquitous in Japan. But did you know that besides being something of a national drink, it's also good for you? Green tea contains antioxidants twice as powerful as those in red wine; these help reduce high blood pressure, lower blood sugar, and fight cancer. A heightened immune system and lower cholesterol are other benefits attributed to this beverage.

Whether drinking green tea for its healing properties, good taste, or as a manner of habit, you'll have plenty of choices in Japan. Pay attention to tea varietals, which are graded by the quality and parts of the plant used, because price and quality runs the spectrum within these categories. For the very best Japanese green tea, take a trip to the Uji region of Kyoto.

Bancha (common tea). This second-harvest variety ripens between summer and fall, producing leaves larger than those of sencha and a weaker-tasting tea.

Genmai (brown rice tea). This is a mixture, usually in equal parts, of green tea and roasted brown rice.

Genmaicha (popcorn tea). This is a blend of bancha and genmai teas.

Gyokuro (jewel dew). Derived from a grade of green tea called *tencha* (divine tea), the name comes from the light-green color the tea develops when brewed. Gyokuro is grown in the shade, an essential condition to develop just this type and grade.

Hojicha (panfried tea). A panfried or oven-roasted green tea.

Kabusecha (covered tea). Similar to gyokuru, kabusecha leaves are grown in the shade, though for a shorter period, giving it a refined flavor.

Kukicha (stalk tea). A tea made from stalks by harvesting one bud and three leaves.

Matcha (rubbed tea). Most often used in the tea ceremony, matcha is a high-quality, hard-to-find powdered green tea. It has a thick, paintlike consistency when mixed with hot water. It is also a popular flavor of ice cream and other sweets in Japan.

Sencha (roasted tea). This is the green tea you are most likely to try at the local noodle or bento shop. Its leaves are grown under direct sunlight, giving it a different flavor from cousins like gyokuro.

---

showrooms allows parents to fiddle with digital cameras and computers from Japan's electronics leader while kids will enjoy playing with interactive displays of electric trains and weight-sensitive musical stairs. The Opus theater on the eighth floor shows movie trailers on a super-high-definition 3-D screen that also features games and events to coincide with movie releases. Take a break by browsing the Internet for free or at one of the cafés or pubs on the floors above the showroom. ⊠ *5–3–1 Ginza, Chuo-ku* ☎ *03/3573–2371* ⊘ *Daily 11–7* Ⓜ *JR Yamanote Line, Yuraku-cho Station (Ginza Exit); Ginza, Hibiya, and Marunouchi subway lines, Ginza Station (Exit B9).*

Sukiya Camera. The cramped Nikon House branch of this two-store operation features enough Nikons—old and new, digital and film—that it could double as a museum to the brand. Plenty of lenses and flashes are available as well. ✉ *4–2–13 Ginza, Chuo-ku* ☎ *03/3561–6000* 🕐 *Mon.–Sat. 10–7:30, Sun. 10–7* Ⓜ *JR Yamanote Line, Yuraku-cho Station (Ginza Exit); Ginza, Hibiya, and Marunouchi subway lines, Ginza Station (Exit B10).*

JEWELRY

Ginza Tanaka. From necklaces to precious metals shaped into statues, this chain of jewelry stores has crafted a reputation as one of Japan's premier jewelers since its founding in 1892. ✉ *1–7–7 Ginza, Chuo-ku* ☎ *03/5561–0491* 🕐 *Daily 10:30–7* Ⓜ *Yuraku-cho subway line, Ginza 1-Chome Station (Exit 7).*

Fodor's Choice ★ **Mikimoto.** Kokichi Mikimoto created his technique for cultured pearls in 1893. Since then his name has been associated with the best quality in the industry. Mikimoto's tower in Ginza is a boutique devoted to nature's ready-made gems; the building, like the pearls it holds, dazzles visitors with its facade that resembles Swiss cheese. ✉ *2–4–12 Ginza, Chuo-ku* ☎ *03/3562–3130* 🕐 *Mon.–Sat. 11–7:30, Sun. 11–7* Ⓜ *Ginza, Hibiya, and Marunouchi subway lines, Ginza Station (Exit C8).*

KIMONO

Hayashi. This store in the Yuraku-cho International Arcade, under the train tracks, specializes in ready-made kimono, sashes, and dyed yukata. ✉ *2–1–1 Yuraku-cho, Chiyoda-ku* ☎ *03/3501–4012* 🕐 *Mon.–Sat. 10–7, Sun. 10–6* Ⓜ *JR Yamanote Line, Yuraku-cho Station (Ginza Exit); Hibiya subway line, Hibiya Station (Exit A5).*

Tansu-ya. This small but pleasant Ginza shop, part of a chain with locations throughout Japan and abroad, has attractive used kimono, yukata, and other traditional clothing in many fabrics, colors, and patterns. The helpful staff can acquaint you with the somewhat complicated method of putting on the garments. ✉ *3–4–5 Ginza, Chuo-ku* ☎ *03/3561–8529* 🕐 *Mon.–Sat. 11–7, Sun. 1..1–6* Ⓜ *Ginza, Hibiya, and Marunouchi subway lines, Ginza Station (Exit A13).*

PAPER

Itoya. The 10 stories of this paper emporium are filled with locally crafted and import stationery, much of which is designed to translate traditional motifs onto contemporary office tools. ✉ *2–7–15 Ginza, Chuo-ku* ☎ *03/3561–8311* 🕐 *Mon.–Sat. 10:30–8, Sun. 10:30–7* Ⓜ *Ginza, Hibiya, and Marunouchi subway lines, Ginza Station (Exit A2).*

★ **Kyukyodo.** Kyukyodo has been in business since 1663—and in Ginza since 1880—selling its wonderful handmade Japanese papers, paper products, incense, brushes, and other materials for calligraphy. ✉ *5–7–4 Ginza, Chuo-ku* ☎ *03/3571–4429* 🕐 *Mon.–Sat. 10–7:30, Sun. 11–7* Ⓜ *Ginza, Hibiya, and Marunouchi subway lines, Ginza Station (Exit A2).*

SWORDS AND KNIVES

Fodor's Choice ★ **Nippon Token** *(Japan Sword).* Wannabe samurai can learn how to tell their *toshin* (blades) from their *tsuka* (sword handles) with help from the English-speaking staff at this small shop, which has been open since the Meiji era (1868–1912). Items that range from a circa-1390 samurai sword to inexpensive reproductions will allow you to take a trip back in time, but make sure your wallet is ready for today's prices. ⊠ *3–8–1 Toranomon, Minato-ku* ☎ *03/3434–4321* ◷ *Weekdays 9:30–6, Sat. 9:30–5* Ⓜ *Hibiya and Ginza subway lines, Tora-no-mon Station (Exit 2).*

Token Shibata. A tiny, threadbare shop incongruously situated near Ginza's glittering department stores, Token Shibata sells well-worn antique swords. ⊠ *5–6–8 Ginza, Chuo-ku* ☎ *03/3573–2801* ◷ *Mon.– Sat. 9:30–6:30* Ⓜ *Ginza, Hibiya, and Marunouchi subway lines, Ginza Station (Exit A1).*

HARAJUKU

The average shopper in Harajuku is under 20; a substantial percentage is under 16. Most stores focus on moderately priced clothing and accessories, with a lot of kitsch mixed in, but there are also several upscale fashion houses in the area—and more on the way. This shopping and residential area extends southeast from Harajuku Station along both sides of Omotesando and Meiji-dori; the shops that target the youngest consumers concentrate especially on the narrow street called Takeshita-dori. Tokyo's most exciting neighborhood for youth fashion and design lies beyond that, in the maze of backstreets called Ura-hara and along the promenade known as Cat Street that runs parallel to Meiji-dori. Ⓜ *Chiyoda and Fukutoshin subway lines, Meiji-Jingu-mae Station (Exits 1–5); JR Yamanote Line, Harajuku Station.*

MALLS AND SHOPPING CENTERS

★ **Laforet.** This mall is so earnest about staying on the tip of Harajuku fashion trends that it changes out stores every six months. While shop genres vary, from Gothic Lolita to bohemian chic, they all target fashion-conscious teenagers. Rumor has it that many of the West's top fashion designers still come here to look for inspiration for their next collections. ⊠ *1–11–6 Jingu-mae, Shibuya-ku* ☎ *03/3475–0411* ◷ *Daily 11–9* Ⓜ *Chiyoda and Fukutoshin subway lines, Meiji-Jingu-mae Station (Exit 5).*

SHOPPING STREETS AND ARCADES

Cat Street. With its avant-garde crafts stores, funky T-shirt shops, and hipster boutiques, this pedestrian strip serves as a showcase for Japan's au courant designers and artisans. Cat Street is the place to experience bohemian Tokyo in all its exuberance. ⊠ *Between Jingu-mae 3-chome and Jingu-mae 6-chome, Shibuya-ku* Ⓜ *Chiyoda and Fukutoshin subway lines, Meiji-Jingu-mae Station (Exits 4 and 5).*

Takeshita-dori. Teenybopper fashion is all the rage along this Harajuku mainstay, where crowds of schoolkids look for the newest, low-priced addition to their ever-changing, outrageous wardrobes. ⊠ *Jingu-mae 1-chome, Shibuya-ku* Ⓜ *JR Harajuku Station (Takeshita-Dori Exit).*

SPECIALTY STORES

CLOTHING CHAINS

Beams. Harajuku features a cluster of no fewer than 11 Beams stores that provide Japan's younger men and women with extremely hip threads. With branches ranging from street wear to high-end import brands as well as a record store, uniform gallery, and funky "from

Tokyo" souvenir shop that sells anime figurines, shopping here will ensure that you or your kids will be properly stocked with the coolest wares from the city. ✉ *3–24–7 Jingu-mae, Shibuya-ku* ☏ *03/3470–3947* ⊗ *Daily 11–8* Ⓜ *JR Harajuku Station (Takeshita-Dori Exit); Chiyoda and Fukutoshin subway lines, Meiji-Jingu-mae Station (Exit 4).*

Uniqlo UT Store. This Harajuku post takes a fashion-forward approach by housing its large variety of T-shirts in a space that resembles a futuristic convenience store or vending machine. The shirts are stuffed into plastic canisters and lined up on shelves that reach the ceiling. ✉ *6–10–8 Jingu-mae, Shibuya-ku* ☏ *03/5468–7313* ⊗ *Daily 11–9* Ⓜ *Chiyoda and Fukutoshin subway lines, Meiji-Jingu-mae Station (Exit 4).*

SHIBUYA

This is primarily an entertainment and retail district geared toward teenagers and young adults. The shopping scene in Shibuya caters to these groups with many reasonably priced smaller shops and a few department stores that are casual yet chic. Ⓜ *JR Yamanote Line, Tokyu and Keio lines, Ginza, Fukutoshin, and Hanzo-mon subway lines, Shibuya Station (Nishi-guchi/West Exit for JR, Exits 3–8 for subway lines).*

MALLS AND SHOPPING CENTERS

Parco. Parco, owned by the Seibu conglomerate, is actually a gathering of vertical malls filled with small retail shops and boutiques, all in walking distance of one another in the commercial heart of Shibuya. Parco Part 1 caters to a young crowd and stocks many casual brands from the local runways for men and women. Part 3 sells a mixture of fashion and hip interior goods. The nearby Zero Gate complex houses the basement restaurant-nightclub La Fabrique, and Quattro, behind it, is a popular concert venue. ✉ *15–1 Udagawa-cho, Shibuya-ku* ☏ *03/3464–5111* ⊗ *Daily 10–9* Ⓜ *Ginza, Fukutoshin, and Hanzo-mon subway lines, Shibuya Station (Exits 6 and 7).*

Shibuya 109. This nine-floor outlet is a teenage girl's dream. It's filled with small stores whose merchandise screams kitsch and trend. Many weekend afternoons will see dance groups and fashion shows on the stage at the front entrance. ✉ *2–29–1 Dogenzaka, Shibuya-ku* ☏ *03/3477–5111* ⊗ *Daily 10–9* Ⓜ *JR Yamanote Line, Ginza, Fukutoshin, and Hanzo-mon subway lines, Shibuya Station (Hachiko Exit for JR, Exit 3 for subway lines).*

SPECIALTY STORES

BOOKS

Tower Records. This branch of the U.S.-based chain carries an eclectic collection of English-language books at more reasonable prices than most bookstores in town. It also has one of the best selections of foreign magazines in Tokyo. ✉ *1–22–14 Jinnan, Shibuya-ku* ☏ *03/3496–3661* ⊗ *Daily 10–11* Ⓜ *JR Yamanote Line, Hanzo-mon, Fukutoshin, and Ginza subway lines, Shibuya Station (Hachiko Exit for JR, Exit 6 for subway).*

CLOTHING CHAINS

★ **Journal Standard.** This is not a chain dedicated to outfitting copy editors and reporters in shirts and ties. In fact, this branch is frequented by young couples looking for the season's *it* fashions. To the south of it is the Journal Standard Café with a bakery and an outside terrace that is perfect for people-watching. ⊠ *1–5–6 Jinnan, Shibuya-ku* ☎ *03/5457–0700* ⊙ *Daily 11:30–8* Ⓜ *JR Yamanote Line, Ginza, Fukutoshin, and Hanzo-mon subway lines, Shibuya Station (Hachiko Exit for JR, Exits 6 and 7 for subways).*

HOUSEWARES

Ⓒ **Tokyu Hands.** This housewares chain is dedicated to providing the do-it-yourselfer with all the tools, fabrics, and supplies he or she may need to tackle any job. There's a selection of plastic models and rubber Godzilla action figures on the seventh floor of the Shibuya branch. It's not unusual to see Japanese hobbyists spending an entire afternoon browsing in here. ⊠ *12–18 Udagawa-cho, Shibuya-ku* ☎ *03/5489–5111* ⊙ *Daily 10–8:30* Ⓜ *JR Yamanote Line, Ginza, Fukutoshin, and Hanzo-mon subway lines, Shibuya Station (Hachiko Exit for JR, Exits 6 and 7 for subway).*

Fodor's Choice ★

RECORD STORES

Manhattan Records. The hottest hip-hop, reggae, and R&B vinyl can be found here, and a DJ booth pumps out the jams from the center of the room. Don't expect a lot advice from the staff—no one can hear you over the throbbing tunes. ⊠ *10–1 Udagawa-cho, Shibuya-ku* ☎ *03/3477–7166* ⊙ *Daily noon–9* Ⓜ *JR Yamanote Line, Ginza, Fukutoshin, and Hanzo-mon subway lines, Shibuya Station (Hachiko Exit for JR, Exits 6 and 7 for subway).*

IKEBUKURO

Ikebukuro is a bustling neighborhood situated north of Shinjuku that is the nearest urban center to the northern outlying suburbs of Tokyo. Because of this many Shinjuku stores have set up shop in Ikebukuro, but here they are often supersize to accommodate the weekend crowds. The Ikebukuro Seibu department store is one of the biggest in the city. Ⓜ *JR Yamanote Line, Marunouchi, Fukutoshin, and Yurakucho subway lines, Seibu Ikebukuro and Tobu Tojo lines, Ikebukuro Station.*

DEPARTMENT STORES

Seibu. Even Japanese customers have been known to get lost in this mammoth department store; the main branch is in Ikebukuro. The Shibuya branch, which still carries an impressive array of merchandise, is smaller and more manageable. Seibu has an excellent selection of household goods, from furniture to lacquerware and quirky interior design pieces, in its stand-alone Loft shops (often next door to Seibu branches, or occasionally within the department store itself). ⊠ *1–28–1 Minami Ikebukuro, Toshima-ku* ☎ *03/3981–0111* ⊙ *Mon.–Sat. 10–9, Sun. 10–8* Ⓜ *JR Yamanote Line, Marunouchi, Fukutoshin, and Yurakucho subway lines, Ikebukuro Station (Minami-guchi/South Exit); Seibu Ikebukuro Line, Seibu Ikebukuro Station (Seibu Department*

Continued on page 241

 # SHOP TOKYO   By Misha Janette

Tokyo, the most retail-dense city in the world, lures even the most reluctant shoppers with promises of every product imaginable. Travel back in time at department and specialty stores selling traditional ceramics and lacquerware, or leap into the future in Akihabara and other gadget-oriented neighborhoods. Fashionistas watch trends in Harajuku morph before their eyes, while those with more highbrow sensibilities browse the jewelry at stalwarts like Mikimoto.

Each Tokyo neighborhood has its own specialty, style, mood, and type of customer. Local production still thrives in the city's backstreets despite an influx of global chains and mega-corporations. Keep in mind, however, that nearly all of the locally produced goods will cost a pretty penny; the Japanese are meticulous in design and quality, and tend to prefer small-scale production to large output. Here in Tokyo you will find that one-offs and limited-edition items are often the norm rather than the exception.

For clothing, sizing is still the biggest roadblock to really getting the most from Tokyo boutiques. But with the abundance of quirky trends sometimes it's enough just to window-shop.

Above: A Harajuku boutique shows off wild new trends.

WHAT TO BUY

MANGA

Manga, or Japanese comic books, have had an incredible influence on pop culture around the world. The inherently Japanese-style illustrations are fun to look at, and the simple language is great for studying. Book-Off, a well-known used manga chain, sells comics at rock-bottom prices, sometimes ¥100 each.

INNERWEAR

The Japanese are known for their electronics, but did you know their textile and fiber industry is also one of the most advanced in the world? The sweat-repelling, heat-conducting, UBAV/UVB-blocking and aloe-vera dispensing underthings available at Tokyo department stores are probably already in every Japanese person's top drawer at home.

FLAVORED SNACKS

Japan is the land of limited-edition products, and every season brings new, adventurous flavors in finite quantities. All it takes is a trip to the local convenience store to find melon- or Sakura-flavored Kit-Kat bars, or sweet Mont Blanc-flavored Pepsi. We dare you to try them.

PHONE ACCESSORIES

Cell phones and their accoutrement have become a fashion statement all their own. Phone straps, small plastic models that hang from one's phone, are the most popular. They come in all forms, from Asahi beer bottles to Hello Kitty dolls. There are also matching plastic "no peek" sheets that prevent others from spying on your phone's screen.

HOUSEWARES

Tokyoites appreciate fine design, and this passion is reflected in the exuberance of the city's *zakka* shops—retailers that sell small housewares. The Daikanyama and Aoyama areas positively brim with these stores, but trendy zakka can be found throughout the city. Handmade combs, chopsticks, and towels are other uniquely Japanese treasures to consider picking up while in Tokyo.

RECORDS

Tokyo's small specialty music stores are a real treat: local music and imports from around the world are usually available on both vinyl and CD. Out-of-print or obscure vinyl editions can run well over ¥10,000, but collectors will find the condition of the jackets to be unmatched.

SOCKS

As it's customary in Japanese houses to remove one's shoes, socks are more than mere padding between foot and shoe. It's no surprise, then, that the selection of socks goes well beyond black and white. Stripes, polka-dots, Japanese scenery, and monograms are just some of the depictions you'll find at the high-end sock boutiques. The complicated weaving techniques mean they will also cost more than the average cotton pair.

SAKE SETS

Sake is a big deal here, and the type of sake presented to another can make or break business deals and friendships. Better than just a bottle are the gift sets that include the short sake glasses and oversized bottles in beautiful packaging fit for royalty.

JEWELRY

Japan has always been known for its craftsmen who possess the ability to create finely detailed work. Jewelry is no exception, especially when cultured pearls are used. Pearls, which have become something of a national symbol, are not inexpensive, but they are much cheaper in Japan than elsewhere.

WASHLETTE TOILET SEATS

It may seem ludicrous, but the Japanese "washlette" toilet seat is perhaps the best innovation of this millennium. The seats are heated, come with deodorizers, and may even play music to mask any "rude" sounds. Even better, some can be retrofitted to old toilets—just be sure to check your seat measurements before leaving home.

CHARCOAL

Japanese women have been using charcoal, or *takesumi*, in their beauty routines for centuries, believing it cleans out the pores and moisturizes the skin. Charcoal-infused formulas are used in soaps, cleansers, cremes, and masques, and often are naturally colored pitch-black like squid ink.

FOLK CRAFTS

Japanese folk crafts, called *mingei*—among them bamboo vases and baskets, fabrics, paper boxes, dolls, and toys—achieve a unique beauty in their simple and sturdy designs. Be aware, however, that simple does not mean cheap. Long hours of labor go into these objects, and every year there are fewer craftspeople left, producing their work in smaller and smaller quantities. Include these items in your budget ahead of time: The best—worth every cent—can be fairly expensive.

EXPERIENCING JAPANESE DEPATO

The impressive architecture at the Prada flagship matches the designer wares inside.

A visit to a Japanese *depato* (department store) is the perfect Cliff's Notes introduction to Japanese culture. Impeccable service combines with the best luxury brands, gourmet food, and traditional goods—all displayed as enticing eye candy.

These large complexes are found around major train stations and are often owned by the conglomerate rail companies who make their profit when visitors take the train to shop there. The stores themselves commonly have travel agencies, theaters, and art galleries on the premises, as well as reasonably priced and strategically placed restaurants and cafés.

ARRIVE EARLY
The best way to get the full experience is to arrive just as the store is opening. Err on the early side: Tokyo's department stores are exacting in their opening times. White-gloved ladies and gents bow to waiting customers when the doors open on the hour. Early birds snatch up limited-edition food and goods before they sell out. There's never a dearth of reasons to come: local celebrity appearances, designer Q&A sessions, and fairs.

ANATOMY OF A DEPATO
The first floors typically house cosmetics, handbags, and shoes, with the next few floors up going to luxury import brands. On many a top floor you'll find gift packages containing Japan's best-loved brands of sake, rice crackers, and other foods. Department stores also typically devote one floor to traditional Japanese crafts, including ceramics, paintings, and lacquerware.

Don't miss the *depachika* (food departments) on the basement levels, where an overwhelming selection of expensive Japanese and Western delicacies are wrapped with the utmost care. More affordable versions come packed deli-style to be taken home for lunch or dinner.

Shibuya's depato attract trendsetters.

BEST DEPATO FOR...

Most department stores are similar and house the same brands. But some have distinctive characteristics.

The Trendy Dresser: Seibu in Shibuya and Ikebukuro is known for its collection of fashion-forward tenants.

Emerging Designers: Isetan in Shinjuku oozes style and has ample space on the fourth floor dedicated to up-and-coming designers.

Gifts: Shinjuku's Takashimaya is the place to buy souvenirs for discerning friends back home.

Traditional Crafts: Mitsukoshi in Nihombashi will leave those looking for a bit of Old Japan wide-eyed.

Depato interiors are often dramatic.

TIPS FOR DEPATO SHOPPING

■ Major department stores accept credit cards and provide shipping services.

■ It's important to remember that, unlike most of the Western world, goods must be purchased in the department where they were found. This goes for nearly every multilevel shop in Japan.

■ Nowadays, most salesclerks speak some English. If you're having communication difficulties, someone will always come to the rescue.

■ On the first floor you'll invariably find a general information booth with maps of the store in English.

■ Some department stores close one or two days a month. To be on the safe side, call ahead.

FASHIONABLE TOKYO

The Japanese fashion scene has gone through many changes since Yohji Yamamoto's solemn, deconstructed garments and Rei Kawakubo's Comme des Garçons clothing lines challenged norms in the 1980s. While these designers and their ilk are still revered, it's Tokyo's street fashion that keeps the city on the world's radar.

Clockwise from top left: An orange-haired Harajuku Girl; manga-influenced street fashion; girls from Shibuya ogle a mobile phone.

Thanks to Gwen Stefani's "Harajuku Girls" and Quentin Tarantino's *Kill Bill*, images of the Gothic Lolita—a fashion subculture typified by a Victorian porcelain-doll look punctuated by dark makeup and macabre accessories—have seeped into Western popular culture. New subcultures, or "tribes," like the Harajuku Girls emerge, take hold in Tokyo, and evolve (or get thrown aside) with blazing speed. The "forest girl" tribe's aesthetic draws from sources such as the American prairie and traditional German attire in loose layers, often in organic and vintage materials. The "skirt boys" are among the mens' tribes. These cool boys stomp around in boots and skirts that Japanese menswear designers have been favoring on the runway in recent years.

Japanese fashion continues to awe and inspire; international designers come to Tokyo for ideas. This means you might already be wearing something from Tokyo without even knowing it!

SIZING UP JAPANESE SIZES

Japanese garments, even if they are not a troublesome and common "one-size-fits-all," run considerably smaller than American items. The female aesthetic tends to favor loose and roomy shapes so is far more forgiving than the menswear, which is often cut impossibly small and tight.

Shibuya brands often carry items in nothing more than an arbitrary "one-size-only" on the racks that may not fit many Westerners at all. Many designers, in deference to the growing foreign market, are starting to offer larger sizes. The internationally recognized brands, department stores, and bigger boutiques, including Opening Ceremony in Shibuya, are the best bets for finding a range of sizes.

Shoes tend to run small, often stopping at 27 cm (U.S. size 9) for men and 24 cm (U.S. size 8) for women. What's more, Japanese shoes are often made a little wider than their Western counterparts.

Above: Harajuku Girls wear dramatic costume-like outfits.

A TALE OF TWO NEIGHBORHOOD STYLES

You don't need to be an industry insider attending Japan's Fashion Week shows to get a sense of Tokyo's multiple styles; you just need to stroll the neighborhoods where every sidewalk is a catwalk.

Japanese street fashion begins and ends along the maze-like backstreets of **Harajuku**, referred to as "Ura-Hara." You'll find many of Tokyo's most popular and promising up-and-coming brands' boutiques, although it might take sharp eyes to spot the often-obstructed store signs. Tokyo's youngest shoppers come for the newest fashions and to show off their costume-like vestments. Visit on a Sunday to see them in full regalia. If the throngs of tweens prove too much, there are other incredible street-fashion shopping areas. Shimokitazawa and Koenji are known for their used-clothing shops and a young fashion scene that's just as lively as that of Harajuku.

For a different take, go to **Shibuya**, where women and men have cultivated a distinctive fashion and lifestyle. The so-called Shibuya style is vivid, brash, and hyper, and comes with its own idols, models, and magazines. Malls such as 109, which is the center of this movement's universe, dedicate their retail space wholly to this world.

More than 50,000 people, including many visitors to Tokyo, attend the biannual **Tokyo Girls Collection**, daylong events of Shibuya-style fashion shows and musical performances by pop big acts. JTB offers full package tours around the event starting at ¥8,000 per person.

FIVE EMERGING DESIGNERS

Limi Feu: Limi, Yohji Yamamoto's daughter, takes a hint from him in her loose, monotone, punk attire, but injects it with a cool, feminine touch. ⊕ www.limifeu.com

Matohu: This unisex brand creates looks based on traditional and colorful Japanese clothing, namely robes, by incorporating ancient dye and weaving techniques into 21st-century designs. ⊕ www.matohu.com/en

N. Hoolywood: Daisuke Obana's menswear line has been on the top of Japanese editors' lists since 2002. He adds contemporary design elements to used clothing, and his attire tends to be loose and casual. ⊕ www.n-hoolywood.com

Tao Comme des Garçons: The youngest in line to the avant-garde Comme des Garçons throne is a wunderkind with knitwear. Expect ingenious mixed-and-matched textures, vivid colors, and patterns.

Somarta: This brand is known for its intricate, seamless knitwear and other experimental textiles developed using Japanese technology. The new menswear line called Molfic follows the same innovative ethos in its seasonless designs. ⊕ www.somarta.jp

Top to bottom: Limi Feu, N. Hoolywood, Somarta

Store Exit); Tobu Tojo Line, Tobu Ikebukuro Station (Minami-guchi/ South Exit) ✉ *1–1 Udagawa-cho, Shibuya-ku* ☎ *03/3462–0111* ⊘ *Sun.–Wed. 10–8, Thurs.–Sat. 10–9* Ⓜ *JR Yamanote Line, Ginza and Hanzo-mon subway lines, Shibuya Station (Hachiko Exit for JR, Exits 6 and 7 for subway lines).*

SPECIALTY STORES

PAPER

Kami-no-Takamura. Specialists in washi and other papers printed in traditional Japanese designs, this shop also carries brushes, inkstones, and other tools for calligraphy. At the entrance is a gallery showcasing seasonal traditional stationery and the work of local artists. ✉ *1–1–2 Higashi-Ikebukuro, Toshima-ku* ☎ *03/3971–7111* ⊘ *Daily 11–6:45* Ⓜ *JR Yamanote Line, Marunouchi and Fukutoshin subway lines, Ikebukuro Station (East Exit for JR, Exit 35 for subway).*

SHINJUKU

Shinjuku is not without its honky-tonk and sleaze, but it also has some of the city's most popular department stores. The shopping crowd is a mix of Tokyo youth and office ladies. Surrounding the station are several discount electronics and home-appliance outlets. The area's abundant array of shopping, business, politics, and entertainment forms a microcosm of Tokyo culture. Ⓜ *JR Yamanote Line, Odakyu and Keio lines, Marunouchi, Shinjuku, Fukutoshin, and Oedo subway lines, Shinjuku Station.*

DEPARTMENT STORES

Isetan. One of Tokyo's oldest and largest department stores, Isetan is known for its high-end fashions, including a selection of larger sizes not found in most Tokyo stores. The basement's food court, which includes both traditional and modern prepared cuisine, is one of the city's largest in a department store. ✉ *3–14–1 Shinjuku, Shinjuku-ku* ☎ *03/3352–1111* ⊘ *Daily 10–8* Ⓜ *JR Yamanote Line, Marunouchi subway line, Shinjuku Station (Higashi-guchi/East Exit for JR, Exits B2, B3, B4, and B5 for subway line).*

Marui. Marui, easily recognized by its red-and-white logo, burst onto the department store scene in the 1980s by introducing an in-store credit card—one of the first stores in Japan to do so. Newly remodeled, the five Marui buildings together comprise the largest department store in the area by a large margin. This includes Marui Curren, Marui Annex, and Marui Men where youngsters flock to the stores in search of petite clothing, accessories, and sportswear. Marui Honkan is the chain's main location. ✉ *3–30–13 Shinjuku, Shinjuku-ku* ☎ *03/3354–0101* ⊘ *Mon.–Sat. 11–9, Sun. 11–8:30* Ⓜ *JR Yamanote Line, Shinjuku Station (Higashi-guchi/East Exit); Marunouchi, Shinjuku, and Fukutoshin subway lines, Shinjuku San-chome Station (Exit A1).*

★ **Takashimaya.** In Japanese, *taka* means "high"—a fitting word for this store, which is beloved for its superior quality and prestige. Gift-givers all over Japan seek out this department store; a present that comes in a Takashimaya bag makes a statement regardless of what's inside.

The third floor, with shops by Prada, Celine, Fendi, Cartier, and many others, is one of the toniest retail spaces in the district. The lower-level food court carries every gastronomic delight imaginable, from Japanese crackers and Miyazaki beef to one of the largest gourmet dessert courts in the city. The annexes boast a large-scale Tokyu Hands and Kinokuniya bookstore as well. *Takashimaya Times Sq., 5–24–2 Sendagaya, Shibuya-ku* ☎ *03/5361–1111* ☉ *Sun.–Fri. 10–8, Sat. 10–8:30* Ⓜ *JR Yamanote Line, Shinjuku Station (Minami-guchi/South Exit); Fukutoshin subway line, Shinjuku San-chome Station (Exit E8).*

SPECIALTY STORES

BOOKS

Kinokuniya. The mammoth Kinokuniya bookstore, an annex of Takashimaya (⇨ *above*) devotes most of its sixth floor to English titles, with an excellent selection of travel guides, magazines, and books on Japan. ✉ *Takashimaya Times Sq., 5–24–2 Sendagaya, Shibuya-ku* ☎ *03/5361–3300* ☉ *Sun.–Fri. 10–8, Sat. 10–8:30* Ⓜ *JR Yamanote Line, Shinjuku Station (Minami-guchi/South Exit); Fukutoshin subway line, Shinjuku San-chome Station (Exit E8).*

CLOTHING CHAINS

Don Quixote. This 24-hour discount store has chains all around the country. The generally tight quarters aren't recommended for those with claustrophobia, but junk collectors will love the costumes, odd cosmetics, family-size bags of Japanese snacks, and used luxury handbags and watches. It's all haphazardly stacked from the floor to the ceiling. ✉ *1–16–5 Kabuki-cho, Shinjuku-ku* ☎ *03/5291–9211* ☉ *Daily 24 hrs* Ⓜ *Marunouchi, Oedo, and Shinjuku subway lines, JR Yamanote Line, Keio and Odakyu lines, Shinjuku Station (Higashi-guchi/East Exit).*

ELECTRONICS

Bic Camera. This large discount-electronics chain in the Odakyu Halc building sells far more than just cameras. Bic is well known for its vast selection of energy- and economically efficient electronics at extremely competitive prices. ✉ *1–5–1 Nishi-Shinjuku, Shinjuku-ku* ☎ *03/5326–1111* ☉ *Daily 10–9* Ⓜ *Marunouchi, Oedo, and Shinjuku subway lines, JR Yamanote Line, Keio and Odakyu lines, Shinjuku Station (Nishi-guchi/West Exit).*

Yodobashi Camera. This discount-electronics superstore near Shinjuku Station carries a selection comparable to that of Akihabara's big boys. It is comprised of a number of annexes, including a watch, hobby, and professional camera building, that together span an entire block. ✉ *1–11–1 Nishi-Shinjuku, Shinjuku-ku* ☎ *03/3346–1010* ☉ *Daily 9:30 am–10 pm* Ⓜ *Marunouchi, Shinjuku, and Oedo subway lines, JR Yamanote Line, Keio and Odakyu lines, Shinjuku Station (Nishi-guchi/West Exit).*

FOLK CRAFTS

Bingo-ya. Although it is a good taxi ride away from Shinjuku, this tasteful four-floor shop allows you to complete your souvenir shopping in one place. The store carries traditional handicrafts—including ceramics, toys, lacquerware, Noh masks, fabrics, and lots more—from all over Japan. ✉ *10–6 Wakamatsu-cho, Shinjuku-ku* ☎ *03/3202–8778*

⊘ *Tues.–Sun. 10–7* Ⓜ *Oedo sub-way line, Wakamatsu Kawada Station (Kawada Exit).*

RECORD STORES

Fodor's Choice **Disk Union.** Vinyl junkies rejoice.
★ The Shinjuku flagship of this chain offers Latin, rock, and indie at 33 rpm. Other stores clustered within the nearby blocks have punk, metal, and jazz. Be sure to grab a store flyer that lists all of its branches since each usually specializes in one music genre or other. Oh, and for you digital folk: CDs are available, too. ⊠ *3–31–4 Shinjuku, Shinjuku-ku* ☎ *03/3352–2691* ⊘ *Mon.–Sat. 11–9, Sun. 11–8* Ⓜ *Marun-ouchi, Oedo, and Shinjuku subway lines, JR Yamanote Line, Keio and Odakyu lines, Shinjuku Station (Higashi-guchi/East Exit).*

ROPPONGI

6

Roppongi's reputation has traditionally been marred by the being a vortex of riffraff populating the neighborhood day or night, and there certainly are a number of dingy clubs and bars. But in recent years it has seen shopping complexes, luxury condominiums, and parks pop up that have given it a new high-end image. What's more, the addition of a handful of grade-A museums such as the new National Art Center with its undulating all-glass facade, the Mori Art Museum on the 50th floor of Roppongi Hills, the Suntory Museum of Art, and the Issey Miyake-produced 21_21 Design Sight in the Midtown Tokyo complex transformed this into an area to see and be seen.

MALLS AND SHOPPING CENTERS

⟳ **Axis.** Classy and cutting-edge housewares, fabrics, and ceramics are sold at this multistory design center on the main Roppongi drag of Gaien-Higashi-dori. Savoir Vivre has an excellent selection of ceramics. Kids can play at the basement toy store or on the miniature replica cars on the first floor. The JIDA Gallery on the fourth floor shows the best of what's current in Japanese industrial design. ⊠ *5–17–1 Roppongi, Minato-ku* ☎ *03/3587–2781* ⊘ *Most shops Mon.–Sat. 11–7* Ⓜ *Hibiya and Oedo subway lines, Roppongi Station (Exit 3); Namboku subway line, Roppongi Itchome Station (Exit 1).*

★ **Midtown Tokyo.** Opened in 2007, it is one of the newer shopping and business multiplexes in the city. An airy, open structure houses exclu-sive boutiques such as Restir and hotels like the Ritz Carlton, and it is also known for its concentration of cafés by the world's top pâtissiers. ⊠ *9–7–3 Akasaka, Minato-ku* ☎ *03/3475–3100* ⊘ *Most shops daily 11–9* Ⓜ *Hibiya and Oedo subway lines, Roppongi Station (Exit 8); Chiyoda subway line, Nogizaka Station (Exit 3).*

Roppongi Hills. You could easily spend a whole day exploring the retail areas of this minicity. The shops here emphasize eye-catching design and chichi brands. Finding a particular shop, however, can be a hassle

DID YOU KNOW?

Most of Tokyo's malls carry both foreign and Japanese brands and, like the city's department stores, house cafés, bars, and restaurants. Midtown Tokyo (pictured here), for example, is known for its concentration of patisseries. If you don't have the time or energy to dash about Tokyo in search of the perfect gifts, consider visiting one of these shopping centers, where you can find a wide selection of merchandise.

TSUKIJI

Best known for its daily fish-market auctions, Tsukiji also has a warren of streets that carry useful, everyday items that serve as a window into the lives of the Japanese. This is a fascinating area to poke around after seeing the fish auction held at the crack of dawn and before stopping in the neighborhood for an early fresh-as-can-be sushi lunch (⇨ *Tsukiji Fish Market feature in Chapter 3: Where to Eat*). Get there before December 2014 when it will be dismantled and moved to a new complex in Toyosu. Ⓜ *Oedo subway line, Tsukiji-shijo Station (Exit A1); Hibiya subway line, Tsukiji Station (Exit 1).*

After exploring the "inside" fish market, make time to wind through the backstreet shops of Tsukiji. Between the Central Wholesale Market and Harumi-dori, among the many fishmongers, is the "outside" market where you can also find stores selling pickles, tea, crackers, kitchen knives, baskets, and crockery. The area is a real slice of Japanese life, and while some of these shops are said to be sticking around, many will be moving along with the "inside" market to Toyosu in 2014—so think about patronizing them sooner than later. ⊠ *Tsukiji 4-chome, Chuo-ku* Ⓜ *Oedo subway line, Tsukiji-shijo Station (Exit A1); Hibiya subway line, Tsukiji Station (Exit 1).*

given the building's Escher-like layout. ⊠ *6–10–1 Roppongi, Minato-ku* ☏ *03/6406–6000* ◷ *Most shops daily 11–9* Ⓜ *Hibiya and Oedo subway lines, Roppongi Station (Roppongi Hills Exit).*

SPECIALTY STORES

ANTIQUES

Nogi Jinja. This antiques fair at the Nogi shrine is the longest running in the city with a history of over 35 years. On the second Sunday of every month (except November) about 40 veteran dealers offer their traditional wares at negotiable prices. ⊠ *8–11–27 Akasaka, Minato-ku* ☏ *04/2691–4687* ◷ *5–3:30* Ⓜ *Chiyoda subway line, Nogizaka Station (Exit 1).*

CERAMICS

Noritake. The Akasaka showroom of this internationally renowned brand carries fine china and glassware in a spacious setting. ⊠ *7–8–5 Akasaka, Minato-ku* ☏ *03/3586–0059* ◷ *Weekdays 10–6* Ⓜ *Chiyoda subway line, Akasaka Station (Exit 7).*

Savoir Vivre. In Roppongi's swanky Axis Building, this store sells contemporary and antique tea sets, cups, bowls, and glassware. ⊠ *3F Axis Bldg., 5–17–1 Roppongi, Minato-ku* ☏ *03/3585–7365* ◷ *Daily 11–7* Ⓜ *Hibiya and Oedo subway lines, Roppongi Station (Exit 3).*

CLOTHING BOUTIQUES

Restir. In the Midtown Tokyo complex, this is possibly the most exclusive and fashion-forward boutique in the city. The first floor is decorated in graphite and black mirrors and comes replete with a DJ booth for private parties. ⊠ *9–7–4 Akasaka, Minato-ku* ☏ *03/5413–3708* ◷ *Daily 11–9* Ⓜ *Hibiya and Oedo subway lines, Roppongi Station (Exit 8); Chiyoda subway line, Nogizaka Station (Exit 3).*

JEWELRY

Tasaki Pearl Gallery. Tasaki sells pearls at slightly lower prices than Miki-moto. The store has several showrooms and hosts an English-language tour that demonstrates the technique of culturing pearls and explains how to maintain and care for them. ☒ *1–3–3 Akasaka, Minato-ku* ☎ *03/5561–8880* ☯ *Weekdays 9–7, weekends 9–6* Ⓜ *Ginza subway line, Tameike-Sanno Station (Exit 9).*

NIHOMBASHI AND TOKYO

Tokyo, and its namesake train station, is for all intents and purposes the entranceway to the city. To the north is Nihombashi, which sees historic department stores facing off with 21st-century malls; only a few mom-and-pop shops still stand their ground. To the west of Tokyo Station is Marunouchi, which is all about modernity. It attracts sophisticated professionals who look for no-fuss quality. They also know how to let loose at the neighborhood's lounges and bars when the work day is done.

MALLS AND SHOPPING CENTERS

Coredo. Unlike other big stores in the Nihombashi area, this sparkling mall has a contemporary feel thanks to an open layout and extensive use of glass and wood. Housewares shops cover the third floor and fashion can be found on the first two floors. ☒ *1–4–1 Nihombashi, Chuo-ku* ☎ *03/3272–4939* ☯ *Mon.–Sat. 11–9, Sun. 11–8* Ⓜ *Ginza, Tozai, and Asakusa subway lines, Nihombashi Station (Exit B12).*

Marunouchi and Shin-Marunouchi Buildings. These neighboring shopping, office, and dining mega-complexes have brought some much-needed retail dazzle to the area. Between the two of them are about 300 stores, covering clothing, jewelry, housewares, and more. ☒ *2–4–1 Marun-ouchi, Chiyoda-ku* ☎ *03/5218–5100* ☯ *Mon.–Sat. 11–9, Sun. 11–8* Ⓜ *Marunouchi subway line, Tokyo Station (Marunouchi Bldg. Exit); JR Yamanote Line, Tokyo Station (Marunouchi Minami-guchi/South Exit).*

DEPARTMENT STORES

Fodor's Choice
★

Mitsukoshi. Founded in 1673 as a dry-goods store, Mitsukoshi later played one of the leading roles in introducing Western merchandise to Japan. It has retained its image of quality and excellence, with a particularly strong representation of Western fashion designers. The store also stocks fine traditional Japanese goods—don't miss the art gallery and the crafts area on the sixth floor. With its own subway stop, bronze lions at the entrance, and an atrium sculpture of the Japanese goddess Magokoro, this flagship store merits a visit even if you're not planning on buying anything. ☒ *1–4–1 Nihombashi Muro-machi, Chuo-ku* ☎ *03/3241–3311* ☯ *Daily 10–7* Ⓜ *Ginza and Hanzo-mon subway lines, Mitsukoshi-mae Station (Exits A3 and A5).*

SPECIALTY STORES

BOOKS

Maruzen. There are English titles on the fourth floor as well as art books; this flagship branch of the Maruzen chain also hosts the occasional art exhibit. ☒ *1–6–4 Marunouchi, Chiyoda-ku* ☎ *03/5288–8881* ☯ *Daily*

An art gallery and impressive sculptures at Mitsukoshi department store entertain even those uninterested in the fine Western fashions for sale.

9–9 Ⓜ *JR Yamanote Line, Tokyo Station (North Exit); Tozai subway line, Otemachi Station (Exit B2C).*

Yaesu Book Center. English-language paperbacks, art books, and calendars are available on the seventh floor of this celebrated bookstore. ✉ *2–5–1 Yaesu, Chuo-ku* ☎ *03/3281–1811* ⊘ *Mon.–Sat. 10–9, Sun. 10–8* Ⓜ *JR Yamanote Line, Tokyo Station (Yaesu South Exit 5).*

FOODSTUFFS AND WARES

Yamamoto Noriten. The Japanese are resourceful in their uses of products from the sea. Nori, the paper-thin dried seaweed used to wrap maki sushi and *onigiri* (rice balls), is the specialty here. If you plan to bring some home with you, buy unroasted nori and toast it yourself at home; the flavor will be far better than that of the preroasted sheets. ✉ *1–6–3 Nihombashi Muro-machi, Chuo-ku* ☎ *03/3241–0261* ⊘ *Daily 9–6:30* Ⓜ *Hanzo-mon and Ginza subway lines, Mitsukoshi-mae Station (Exit A1).*

HOUSEWARES

Pass the Baton. *Zakka* is what the Japanese call small knickknacks and gifts, and this eccentric store is brimming with zakka that are donated from the coffers of local fashion designers, artists, magazine editors, and celebrities. The goods are fixed up and resold, with a portion of the profit going to charity. It is tucked inside the Brick Square complex, next to an English rose garden. ✉ *2–6–1 Marunouchi, Chiyoda-ku* ☎ *03/6269–9555* ⊘ *Mon.–Sat. 11–9, Sun. 11–8* Ⓜ *Marunouchi subway line, Tokyo Station (Marunouchi Bldg. Exit); JR Yamanote Line, Tokyo Station (Marunouchi Minami-guchi/South Exit).*

CLOSE UP

Day Spa Escape: May's Garden Spa

It's all about personalized service at **May's**, which has been in business for over 80 years. Located on the third floor of the swanky Roppongi Hills complex, it has catered to big-name clients, such as the Japanese Royal Family, Grace Kelly, and Mariah Carey. Herbs used in the footbath are from the facility's own herb gardens right outside the windows, and much of the nail and hair work is done from seats with views of Roppongi Hills. The full facial treatment includes a one-on-one consultation with a professional aesthetician, as well as a full-body immersion in a hydro-jet bath of oxygen foam for some serious cleansing of your pores. Enzyme packs are applied to bring the glow back to your complexion. A gentle facial massage completes the service. Though the package does include a few back rubs, full bodywork is also available, as are hair, nail, bridal prep, and kimono dressing services.

Services: Facial treatments, body treatments, waxing, aroma massage, and aroma and geranium baths.

Package Picks: Facial treatments range from ¥13,650 to ¥24,150, depending on the treatment. Body treatments are 120 minutes for ¥21,000, and 150 minutes for ¥23,100. Waxing ranges from ¥1,050 to ¥16,800, depending on the time and the body part.

General Info: ⊠ 6–4–1 Roppongi, Minato-ku ☎ 03/3408–1613 ⊕ www. hollywoodsalon.co.jp ⊗ Daily 9–7 Ⓜ Hibiya and Oedo subway lines, Roppongi Station (Roppongi Hills Exit).

PAPER

Ozu Washi. This shop, which was opened in the 17th century, has one of the largest washi showrooms in the city and its own gallery of antique papers. ⊠ 3–6–2 Nihombashi-Honcho, Chuo-ku ☎ 03/3662–1184 ⊗ Mon.–Sat. 10–7 Ⓜ Ginza and Hanzo-mon subway lines, Mitsukoshi-mae Station (Exit A4).

SWORDS AND KNIVES

Kiya. Workers shape and hone blades in one corner of this shop, which carries cutlery, pocketknives, saws, and more. Scissors with handles in the shape of Japanese cranes are among the many unique gift items sold here, and custom-made knives are available, too. Kiya is located in the Coredo Muro-machi complex. ⊠ 2–2–1 Nihombashi-Muromachi, Chuo-ku ☎ 03/3241–1333 ⊗ Daily 10–8 Ⓜ Ginza subway line, Mitsu-koshi-mae Station (Exit A4).

Side Trips from Tokyo

WORD OF MOUTH

"I had a wonderful time visiting Mt Fuji. Magnificent! And it was only one of the 60 days a year where you got a clear view, so I was very fortunate. Beautiful cruise on a volcanic lake and amazing cable car ride too. . . . It would be criminal not to take a day trip to Mt Fuji!"

—Hagan

SIDE TRIPS FROM TOYKO

TOP REASONS TO GO

★ **Peerless Fuji:** Climb Japan's tallest mountain or catch a glimpse of it from Fuji-Hakone-Izu National Park.

★ **Rustic Japan:** Escape the endless modernity of Tokyo in Nikko, where the Tosho-gu area shrines and temples transport you centuries back into the country's past and the Kegon Falls just transport you.

★ **Zen and the Art of Travel:** Kita-Kamakura is home to two preeminent Zen temples, Engaku and Kencho. In Hase gaze on the Great Buddha or explore inside the giant statue.

★ **Go to China Without Boarding a Plane:** In Yokohama, a port city, sample authentic Chinese goods, spices, and crafts in Chinatown. For a bit of whimsy and a great view, ride Yokohama's Ferris wheel.

1 Fuji-Hakone-Izu National Park and Mt. Fuji. Fuji-Hakone-Izu National Park lies southwest of Tokyo. Its chief attraction, of course, is Mt. Fuji. South of it, the Izu Peninsula projects out into the Pacific, with Suruga Bay to the west and Sagami Bay to the east. The beaches and rugged shoreline of Izu, its forests and highland meadows, and its numerous hot-springs inns and resorts make the region a favorite destination for the Japanese.

2 Nikko. Nikko is not simply the site of the Tokugawa Shrine but also of a national park, Nikko Kokuritsu Koen, on the heights above it. The centerpiece of the park is Chuzenji-ko, a deep lake some 21 km (13 mi) around, and the 318-foot-high Kegon Falls, Japan's most famous waterfall.

3 Kamakura. Kamakura is an ancient city—the birthplace, one could argue, of the samurai way of life. Minamoto no Yoritomo, the country's first shogun, chose this site, with its rugged hills and narrow passes, as the seat of his military government. The warrior elite took much of their ideology—and their aesthetics—from Zen Buddhism, endowing splendid temples that still exist today. A walking tour of Kamakura's Zen temples and Shinto shrines is a must for anyone with a day to spend out of Tokyo.

4 Yokohama. Yokohama is Japan's largest port and has an international character that rivals—if not surpasses—that of Tokyo. Its waterfront park and its ambitious Minato Mirai bay-side development project draw visitors from all over the world.

GETTING ORIENTED

Kamakura and Yokohama are close enough to Tokyo to provide ideal day trips, and as it's unlikely that you'll stay overnight in either city, no accommodations are listed for them. Mt. Takao, less than an hour from Shinjuku, can be visited in one day. Nikko is something of a toss-up: you can easily see Tosho-gu and be back in Tokyo by evening. But when the weather turns glorious in spring or autumn, why not spend some time in the national park, staying overnight at Chuzenji, and returning to the city the next day? Mt. Fuji and Hakone, on the other hand—and more especially the Izu Peninsula—are pure resort destinations. Staying overnight is an intrinsic part of the experience, and it makes little sense to go without hotel reservations confirmed in advance.

7

Map labels

Mt. Nantai
Nikko **2**
Imaichi
Daigo
Karasuyama
Numata
Ashio
Utsunmiya
4
Shibukawa
Kiryu
Maebashi
Tochigi
Kasama
Mito
50
Ashikaga
50
Oyama
Shimodate
Honjo
Isezaki
Kurogo
Ishioka
Kumagaya
Koga
17
Konosu
4
Noda
Matsuyama
6
Kawagoe
Omiya
Narita Int'l Airport
Hanno
Ichikawa
Sakura
Tako
Tachikawa
16
Hachioji
TOKYO
Chiba
Naruto
Katakai
Kawasaki
Tokyo Bay
Haneda Int'l Airport
Oami
16
Atsugi
Yokohama
Mobara
4
Kisarazu
Fujisawa
Kisarazu
Hiratsuka
Kamakura
3
Yokosuka
Fujioayashi
Ohara
1
Odawara
Kazusaminato
Sagami Bay
Misaki
Atami
Kamogawa
Ito
Sagaminada Sea
Tateyama
Chikura
Fuji-Hakone-Izu National Park
Okata
O-SHIMA
TO-SHIMA
HONSHU ISLAND
PACIFIC OCEAN

Updated by
Kevin Mcgue

While there's plenty to keep you occupied in Tokyo for days, the urge to get out and explore beyond the city limits should not be ignored. The city's a great base for numerous day trips including visits to the iconic Fuji-san (Mt. Fuji) in Fuji-Hakone-Izu National Park, one of Japan's most popular resort areas; Nikko, a popular vacation destination for Tokyo residents and the home of Tosho-gu, the astonishing shrine to the first Tokugawa shogun Ieyasu; the ancient city of Kamakura which has great historical and cultural sights; and Yokohama, a port city with an international character all its own—it's home to the country's largest Chinatown.

One caveat: the term "national park" does not quite mean what it does elsewhere in the world. In Japan, pristine grandeur is hard to come by; there are few places in this country where intrepid hikers can go to contemplate the beauty of nature for very long in solitude. If a thing's worth seeing, it's worth developing. This world view tends to fill Japan's national parks with bus caravans, ropeways, and gondolas, scenic overlooks with coin-fed telescopes, signs that tell you where you may or may not walk, fried-noodle joints and vending machines, and shacks full of kitschy souvenirs. That's true of Nikko, and it's true as well of Fuji-Hakone-Izu National Park.

PLANNING

RESTAURANTS

The local specialty in Nikko is a soybean-based concoction known as *yuba* (tofu skin); dozens of restaurants in Nikko serve it in a variety of dishes you might not have believed possible for so prosaic an ingredient. Other local favorites are *soba* (buckwheat) and *udon* (wheat-flour) noodles—both inexpensive, filling, and tasty options for lunch.

Three things about Kamakura make it a good place to dine. It's on the ocean (properly speaking, on Sagami Bay), which means that fresh seafood is everywhere; it's a major tourist stop; and it has long been a prestigious place to live among Japan's worldly and well-to-do (many successful writers, artists, and intellectuals call Kamakura home). On a day trip from Tokyo, you can feel confident picking a place for lunch almost at random.

Yokohama, as befits a city of more than 3 million people, lacks little in the way of food: from quick-fix lunch counters to elegant dining rooms, you'll find almost every imaginable cuisine. Your best bet is Chinatown—Japan's largest Chinese community—with more than 100 restaurants representing every regional style. If you fancy Italian, Indian, or even Scandinavian, this international port is still guaranteed to provide an eminently satisfying meal.

HOTELS

In both Nikko and the Fuji-Hakone-Izu area, there are modern, Western-style hotels that operate in a fairly standard international style. More common, however, are the traditional *ryokan* (inns). The main difference between these lodging options is that Western-style hotels are situated in prime tourist locations whereas ryokans stick strictly to Japanese-style rooms and are found in less touristy locations. The undisputed pleasure of a ryokan is to return to it at the end of a hard day of sightseeing, luxuriate for an hour in a hot bath with your own garden view, put on the *yukata* (cotton kimono) provided for you (remember to close your right side first and then the left), and sit down to a catered private dinner party. There's little point to staying at a Western-style hotel, unless you want to say you've had the experience and survived. These places do most of their business with big, boisterous tour groups; the turnover is ruthless and the cost is way out of proportion to the service they provide.

The price categories listed here are for double occupancy, but you'll find that most kanko and ryokan normally quote per-person rates, which include breakfast and dinner. Remember to stipulate whether you want a Japanese or Western breakfast. If you don't want dinner at your hotel, it's usually possible to renegotiate the price, but the management will not be happy about it; the two meals are a fixture of their business. The typical ryokan takes great pride in its cuisine, usually with good reason: the evening meal is an elaborate affair of 10 or more different dishes, based on the fresh produce and specialties of the region, served to you—nay, *orchestrated*—in your room on a wonderful variety of trays and tableware designed to celebrate the season.

WHAT IT COSTS IN YEN					
	¢	$	$$	$$$	$$$$
Restaurants	under ¥800	¥800–¥1,000	¥1,000–¥2,000	¥2,000–¥3,000	over ¥3,000
Hotels	under ¥8,000	¥8,000–¥12,000	¥12,000–¥18,000	¥18,000–¥22,000	over ¥22,000

Restaurant prices are per person for a main course at dinner. Hotel price categories reflect the range of least- to most-expensive standard double rooms in nonholiday high season, with no meals, unless otherwise noted. Taxes (5%) are included.

FUJI-HAKONE-IZU NATIONAL PARK 富士箱根伊豆国立公園

Fuji-Hakone-Izu National Park, southwest of Tokyo between Suruga and Sagami bays, is one of Japan's most popular resort areas. The region's main attraction, of course, is Mt. Fuji, a dormant volcano—it last erupted in 1707—rising to a height of 12,388 feet. The mountain is truly beautiful; utterly captivating in the ways it can change in different light and from different perspectives. Its symmetry and majesty have been immortalized by poets and artists for centuries. ■TIP➔ **In spring and summer, Mt. Fuji often hides behind a blanket of clouds. Keep this in mind if seeing the mountain is an important part of your trip.**

Apart from Mt. Fuji itself, each of the three areas of the park—the Izu Peninsula, Hakone and environs, and the Five Lakes—has its own unique appeal. Izu is defined by its dramatic rugged coastline, beaches, and *onsen* (hot springs). Hakone has mountains, volcanic landscapes, and lake cruises, plus onsen of its own. The Five Lakes form a recreational area with some of the best views of Mt. Fuji. And in each of these areas there are monuments to Japan's past.

Although it's possible to make a grand tour of all three areas at one time, most people make each of them a separate excursion from Tokyo.

Trains will serve you well in traveling to major points anywhere in the northern areas of the national-park region and down the eastern coast of the Izu Peninsula. For the west coast and central mountains of Izu, there are no train connections; unless you are intrepid enough to rent a car, the only way to get around is by bus.

Especially in summer and fall, the Fuji-Hakone-Izu National Park area is one of the most popular vacation destinations in the country, so most towns and resorts have local visitor information centers. Few of them have staff members who speak fluent English, but you can still pick up local maps and pamphlets, as well as information on low-cost inns, pensions, and guesthouses.

FUJI-SAN (MT. FUJI) 富士山

Fodor's Choice ★

Fuji-san. There are six routes to the summit of the 12,388-foot-high mountain but only two, both accessible by bus, are recommended: from Go-gome (Fifth Station), on the north side, and from Shin-Go-gome (New Fifth Station), on the south. The climb to the summit from Go-gome takes five hours and is the shortest way up; the descent takes three hours. From Shin-Go-gome the ascent is slightly longer and stonier, but the way down, via the *sunabashiri*, a volcanic sand slide, is faster. The quickest route is to ascend from Go-gome and descend to Shin-Go-gome via the sunabashiri. ⇨ *For more information on Mt. Fuji, see Peerless Fuji in this chapter.*

GETTING HERE AND AROUND

Take one of the daily buses directly to Go-gome from Tokyo; they run July through August and leave from Shinjuku Station. The journey takes about two hours and 40 minutes from Shinjuku and costs ¥2,600.

Continued on page 264

Fuji-Hakone-Izu National Park

Mt. Kanayama

Shoji Trail

Shoji-ko (Lake Shoji)

Sai-ko (Lake Sai)

Kawaguchi-ko (Lake Kawaguchi)

Fuji Museum

Fuji-Yoshida

Fuji-Kyu Highland

Motosu-ko (Lake Motosu)

52

FUJI GO-KO

Tenjo-san

Yamanaka-ko (Lake Yamanaka)

Fuji-san (Mt. Fuji)

Fuji-Hakone-Izu National Park

1

Matsuda

Kozu

Gotemba

Gora

Hakone Ropeway

Miyanoshita

Odawara

52

Mt. Ashitaka

Owaku-dani

Togendai

Soun-zan (Mt. Soun)

Hakone-machi

Lake Ashi

Sagami Bay

Fuji

Susono

Kanbara

Hara

Numazu

Mishima

MOA Museum of Art

1

Nirayama

Oyu Geyser

Atami

Atami Bai-en (Atami Plum Garden)

Kinomiya Station

Izu-Nagaoka

Hatsu-Shima

Mita

Usami

Heda

Shuzenji

Ito

Suruga Bay

Ikeda 20th Century Art Museum

Komuro-san Koen

Toi

Tsukigase

Izu Cactus Park

Joren Falls

Fuji-Hakone-Izu National Park

Kamo

IZU PENINSULA

Mt. Amagi

Atagawa

Nishi-Izu Tourist Office

Dogashima

Matsuzaki

Mizukuri

Kawazu

Sagaminada Sea

Shimoda

Yumi-ga-hama

Iro-zaki (Iro Point)

0   5 mi

0   5 km

KEY

Shinkansen (Bullet Trains)

JR Trains or Private Trains

Cable Car

Beaches

PEERLESS FUJI

by Peter MacMillan

Climbing Mt. Fuji

Mount Fuji greets hikers who arrive at its summit just before dawn with the *go-raiko*, or the Honorable Coming of the Light. The reflection of this light shimmers across the sky just before the sun first appears, giving the extraordinary sunrise a mystical feel. Fuji-san's early morning magic is just one of the characteristics of the mountain that has captured the collective imagination of the Japanese, along with its snowy peak, spiritual meaning, and propensity to hide behind clouds. The close-to-perfectly symmetrical cone is an object to conquer physically and to admire from afar.

Japan is more than 70% mountainous, and Fuji is its tallest mountain. It appears in literature, art, and culture from the highest level to the most ordinary in countless ways. In a word, Fuji is ubiquitous.

Since ancient times Mt. Fuji has been an object of worship for both Shinto and Buddhist practitioners. Shrines devoted to Konohana-Sakuya Hime, Mt. Fuji's goddess, dot the trails. So sacred is Fuji that the mountaintop torii gate at the Okumiya of Sengen Taisha Shrine (though at Fuji's foot, the shrine also encompasses the mountain above the 8th station) states that this is the greatest mountain in the world. Typically the gate would provide the shrine's name. Here, the torii defines not the shrine but the sacred space of the mountain.

Rising to 12,385 feet (3,776 meters) Mt. Fuji is an active volcano, but the last eruption was in 1707. Located on the boundaries of Shizuoka and Yamanashi prefectures, the mountain is an easy day trip west of Tokyo, and on clear days you can see the peak from the city. In season, hikers clamber to the peak, but it is gazing upon Fuji that truly inspires awe and wonder. No visit to Japan would be complete without at least a glimpse of this beautiful icon.

(top left) Mt. Fuji's famous morning light draws visitors, (top right) the summit is often surrounded by clouds, (bottom right) the trails are rocky and rugged at tiimes.

THE SYMBOLISM OF FUJI-SAN

ARTISTIC FUJI

Mt. Fuji is one of the world's most painted and photographed mountains. But rising above all the visual depictions are Katsushika Hokusai's *Thirty-six Views of Mt. Fuji* and his *One Hundred Views of Mt. Fuji*. The latter is a stunning work and considered his masterpiece. However, the *Thirty-Six Views* is more famous because the images were printed in full color, while the *One Hundred Views* was printed in monochrome black and gray. His *Great Wave off Kanagawa* is one of the most famous prints in the history of art.

Hokusai believed that his depictions would get better and better as he got older, and they did; his *One Hundred*

Views was completed when he was 75. He was also obsessed with achieving immortality. In creating the *One Hundred Views of Mt. Fuji*, a mountain always associated with immortality, he hoped to achieve his own. History proved him right.

LITERARY FUJI

There are thousands of literary works related to Fuji, including traditional and modern poems, haiku, Noh dramas, novels, and plays. In the Man'yoshu, 8th-century poet Yamabe no Akahito famously extolled Fuji: "When I sail out/on the Bay of Tago/every where's white-/Look! Snow's piling up/ on the peak of Fuji." Matsuo Basho, in another well known poem, wrote about not being able to see the mountain: "How lovely and intriguing!/ Covered in drifting fog,/ the day I could not see Fuji." There are many times of the year when Fuji hides behind the clouds, so don't be disappointed if you miss it. Like the great haiku poet, see the mountain in the eye of your heart.

(top) Katsushika Hokusai's *Red Fuji*, (bottom) *Great Wave off Kanagawa* by Katsushika Hokusai

SEE FUJI-SAN FROM AFAR

Like the poets and artists who have found inspiration in gazing at Fuji-san, you, too, can catch a glimpse of the snow-capped cone on the horizon. On a clear day, most likely in winter when the air is dry and the clouds lift, the following experiences provide some of the best Fuji views.

SEE FUJI

Atop Tokyo. Visit the Tokyo City View observation promenade on the 52nd floor of the Mori Tower in Roppongi. You can walk all around this circular building and take in the spectacular views of Tokyo and, when the weather is fine, Fuji. While you're here, don't miss the sky-high Mori Art Museum, a contemporary art space on the 52nd and 53rd floors. The evening view of the city is also splendid, but Fuji will be slumbering under the blanket of nightfall.

From Hakone. Part of Fuji-Hakone-Izu National Park, the same park Fuji calls home, and an easy day trip from Tokyo, Hakone is a playground of hiking trails, small art museums, an onsen, and more. Head to the beautiful garden at Hakone Detached Palace for scenic views of Fuji-san. Early morning and late evening will provide the best chance for clear skies.

Speeding out of town. The classic view of Fuji is from the Shinkansen traveling from Tokyo to Kyoto. Some of the world's fastest transportation technology hums beneath you when, suddenly, the world's most beautiful and sacred mountain appears on the left. This striking combination of the ancient and cutting-edge is at the heart of understanding Japan. Make sure not to fall asleep!

(top) Shinkansen speeding past Fuji, (bottom) Fuji from inside Hakone National Park i

7

IN FOCUS PEERLESS FUJI

CLIMBING FUJI-SAN
FROM KAWAGUCHIKO TRAIL

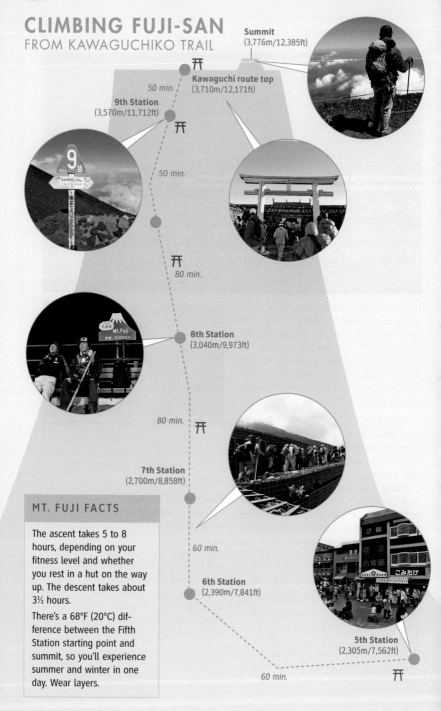

Summit
(3,776m/12,385ft)

Kawaguchi route top
(3,710m/12,171ft)

50 min.

9th Station
(3,570m/11,712ft)

50 min.

80 min.

8th Station
(3,040m/9,973ft)

80 min.

7th Station
(2,700m/8,858ft)

MT. FUJI FACTS

The ascent takes 5 to 8 hours, depending on your fitness level and whether you rest in a hut on the way up. The descent takes about 3½ hours.

There's a 68°F (20°C) difference between the Fifth Station starting point and summit, so you'll experience summer and winter in one day. Wear layers.

60 min.

6th Station
(2,390m/7,841ft)

5th Station
(2,305m/7,562ft)

60 min.

A photographer capturing view from Mt. Fuji

Although many Japanese like to climb Mt. Fuji once in their lives, there's a saying in Japanese that only a fool would climb it twice. You, too, can make a once-in-a-lifetime climb during the mountain's official open season from July through August. Unless you're an experienced hiker, do not attempt to make the climb at another time of year.

TRAIL CONDITIONS

Except for the occasional cobblestone path, the routes are unpaved and at times steep, especially toward the top. Near the end of the climb there are some rope banisters to steady yourself, but for the most part you'll have to rely on your own balance.

Fuji draws huge crowds in season, so expect a lot of company on your hike. The throngs grow thicker in August during the school break and reach their peak during the holiday Obon week in mid-August; it gets so crowded that hikers have to queue up at certain passes. Trails are less crowded overnight. Go during the week and in July for the lightest crowds (though the weather is less reliable). Or accept the crowds and enjoy the friendships that spring up among strangers on the trails.

TRAILS OVERVIEW

If you're in good health you should be able to climb from the base to the summit. That said, the air is thin, and it can be humbling to struggle for oxygen while some 83-year-old Japanese grandmother blithely leaves you in her dust (it happens).

Most visitors take buses as far as the Fifth Station and hike to the top from there (⇨ *See Mt. Fuji listing in this chapter for more information on buses*). The paved roads end at this halfway point.

Four routes lead to Mt. Fuji's summit—the **Kawaguchiko, Subashiri, Gotemba,** and **Fujinomiya**—and each has a corresponding Fifth Station that serves as the transfer point between bus and foot. Depending on which trail you choose, the ascent takes between 5 and 10 hours. Fujinomiya is closest to the summit; Gotemba is the farthest.

We recommend Kawaguchiko (Fuji-Yoshida) Trail in Yamanashi, as its many first-aid centers and lodging facilities (huts) ensure that you can enjoy the climb.
■ TIP → Those interested in experiencing Fuji's religious and spiritual aspects should walk this trail from the mountain's foot. Along the way are small shrines that lead to the torii gate at the top, which signifies Fuji's sacred status. While the food and cleanliness standards at mountain huts are subpar, they provide valuable rest spots and even more valuable camaraderie and good will among travelers. For further details on mountain huts and the climb see the Fuji-Yoshida City Official Web site: ⊕ *www.city. fujiyoshida.yamanashi.jp/div/ english/html/index.html*

AT THE TOP

Once you reach the top of Mt. Fuji, you can walk along the ridge of the volcano. A torii gate declares that Fuji is the greatest mountain in the world. It also marks the entrance to the **Fuji-san Honmiya Sengen Taisha Shrine** (at the foot of the mountain near the Kawaguchiko Trail is the shrine's other facility). Inside the shrine, head to the post office where you can mail letters and postcards with a special Mt. Fuji stamp. There's also a chalet at the top for those captivated enough to stay the night.

NIGHT HIKES

The most spectacular way to hike Mt. Fuji is to time the climb so that you arrive at sunrise. Not only is the light famously enchanting, but the sky is also more likely to be clear, allowing for views back to Tokyo. Those who choose this have a few options. Start from the Kawaguchiko Fifth Station on the Kawaguchi Trail around 10 PM (or later, depending on the sunrise time) and hike through the night, arriving at the summit between 4:30 and 5 AM, just as the sun begins to rise. A better alternative is to begin in the afternoon or evening and hike to the Seventh or Eighth Station, spend a few hours resting there, and then depart very early in the morning to see the sun rise. ■TIP→ The trail isn't lit at night, so bring a headlamp to illuminate the way. Avoid carrying flashlights, though, as it is important to keep your hands free in case of a fall.

COMMEMORATE YOUR VISIT

Purchase a walking stick at the base of Mt. Fuji and, as you climb, have it branded at each station. By the time you reach the top you'll have the perfect souvenir to mark your achievement.

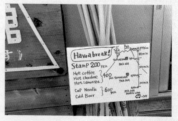

(top) First glimpse of the go-raiko, (bottom) Mt. Fuji at dawn

Walking sticks for sale

DID YOU KNOW?

Although earlier meanings of the word *Fuji* include "peer-less," and "immortal one," the current way of writing Fuji implies "wealthy persons of military status." The mountain called *fuji-san* (not *fuji-yama*) in Japanese.

Mt. Fuji is one of the world's most symmetrical mountains.

Reservations are required; book seats through the Fuji Kyuko Highway Bus Reservation Center, the Keio Highway Bus Reservation Center, the Japan Travel Bureau (which should have English-speaking staff), or any major travel agency.

To return from Mt. Fuji to Tokyo, take an hour-long bus ride from Shin-Go-gome to Gotemba (¥1,500). From Gotemba take the JR Tokaido and Gotemba lines to Tokyo Station (¥1,890), or take the JR Line from Gotemba to Matsuda (¥480) and change to the private Odakyu Line from Shin-Matsuda to Shinjuku (¥750).

ESSENTIALS

Buses from Tokyo Fuji Kyuko Highway Bus Reservation Center (☎ 03/5376–2222). **Japan Travel Bureau** (☎ 03/5796–5454). **Keio Highway Bus Reservation Center** (☎ 03/5376–2222). **Tokai Bus Company** (☎ 0557/36–1112 for main office, 0558/22–2511 Shimoda Information Center).

IZU PENINSULA 伊豆半島

GETTING HERE AND AROUND

Having your own car makes sense only for touring the Izu Peninsula, and only then if you're prepared to cope with less-than-ideal road conditions, lots of traffic (especially on holiday weekends), and the paucity of road markers in English. It takes some effort—but exploring the peninsula *is* a lot easier by car than by public transportation. From Tokyo take the Tomei Expressway as far as Oi-matsuda (about 84 km [52 mi]); then pick up Routes 255 and 135 to Atami (approximately

28 km [17 mi]). From Atami drive another 55 km (34 mi) or so down the east coast of the Izu Peninsula to Shimoda.

■TIP→ One way to save yourself some trouble is to book a car through the Nippon or Toyota rental agency in Tokyo and arrange to pick it up at the Shimoda branch. You can then simply take a train to Shimoda and use it as a base. From Shimoda you can drive back up the coast to Kawazu (35 minutes) and then to Shuzenji (30 minutes). It is possible to drop off the car in Tokyo but only at specific branches, so visit your rental-car company's Web site or call them in advance.

Once you are on the Izu Peninsula itself, sightseeing excursions by boat are available from several picturesque small ports. From Dogashima, you can take the Dogashima Marine short (20 minutes, ¥920) or long (45 minutes, ¥1,240) tours of Izu's rugged west coast. The Fujikyu Kogyo company operates a daily ferry to Hatsu-shima from Atami (25 minutes, ¥2,340 round-trip) and another to the island from Ito (23 minutes, ¥1,150). Izukyu Marine offers a 40-minute tour (¥1,530) by boat from Shimoda to the coastal rock formations at Iro-zaki.

Sunrise Tours operates a tour to Hakone, including a cruise across Lake Ashi and a trip on the gondola over Owaku-dani (¥15,000 includes lunch and return to Tokyo by Shinkansen; ¥12,000 includes lunch and return to Tokyo by bus). ■TIP→ These tours are an economical way to see the main sights all in one day and are ideal for travelers with limited time. Sunrise tours depart daily from Tokyo's Hamamatsu-cho Bus Terminal and some major hotels.

Trains are by far the easiest and fastest ways to get to the Fuji-Hakone-Izu National Park area. The gateway station of Atami is well served by comfortable express trains from Tokyo, on both JR and private railway lines. These in turn connect to local trains and buses that can get you anywhere in the region you want to go. Call the JR Higashi-Nihon Info Line (10–6 daily, except December 31–January 3) for assistance in English.

The *Kodama* Shinkansen from JR Tokyo Station to Atami costs ¥3,880 and takes 51 minutes; JR Passes are valid. The JR local from Atami to Ito takes 25 minutes and costs ¥320. Ito and Atami are also served by the JR Odoriko Super Express (not a Shinkansen train) also departing from Tokyo Station; for correct platform, check the schedule display board. The Tokyo–Ito run takes 1¾ hours and costs ¥4,190; you can also use a JR Pass. The privately owned Izukyu Railways, on which JR Passes are not valid, makes the Ito–Shimoda run in one hour for ¥1,570.

The Izu–Hakone Railway Line runs from Tokyo to Mishima (one hour, 36 minutes; ¥4,090), with a change at Mishima for Shuzenji (31 minutes, ¥500); this is the cheapest option if you don't have a JR Pass. With a JR Pass, a Shinkansen–Izu Line combination will save about 35 minutes and will be the cheapest option. The Tokyo–Mishima Shinkansen leg (62 minutes) costs ¥4,400; the Mishima–Shuzenji Izu Line leg (31 minutes) costs ¥500.

ESSENTIALS

Buses from Tokyo Fuji Kyuko Highway Bus Reservation Center
(☎ 03/5376–2222). **Keio Highway Bus Reservation Center** (☎ 03/5376–2222).
Tokai Bus Company (☎ 0557/36–1112 for main office, 0557/22–2511 Shimoda Information Center).

Rental-Car Contacts Nippon Rent-a-Car (☎ 03/3485–7196 English operator available on weekdays 10 am–5 pm ⊕ www.nipponrentacar.co.jp). **Toyota Rent-a-Car** (☎ 0070/800–0100 toll-free, 03/5954–8008 English operator available 8–8 ⊕ www.toyota-rl-tyo.co.jp/rentacar/syasyu/info-e.html).

Tour Contacts Dogashima Marine (☎ 0558/52–0013). **Fujikyu Kogyo** (☎ 0557/81–0541). **Izukyu Marine** (☎ 0558/22–1151). **Sunrise Tours** (☎ 03/5796–5454 ⊕ www.jtbgmt.com/sunrisetour).

Tourist Information Atami Tourist Association (⊠ 12–1 Ginza-cho, Atami ☎ 0557/85–2222). **Nishi-Izu Tourist Office** (⊠ Dogashima, Nishi-Izu-cho, Kamo-gu ☎ 0558/52–1268). **Shimoda Tourist Association** (⊠ 1–1 Soto-ga-oka, Shimoda ☎ 0558/22–1531).

Train Information Izukyu Corporation (☎ 0557/53–1111 for main office, 0558/22–3202 Izukyu Shimoda Station). **JR Higashi-Nihon Info Line** (☎ 03/3423–0111). **Odakyu Reservation Center** (☎ 03/3481–0130).

ATAMI 熱海

100 km (60 mi) southwest of Tokyo Station.

The gateway to the Izu Peninsula is Atami. Most Japanese travelers make it no farther into the peninsula than this town on Sagami Bay, so Atami itself has a fair number of hotels and traditional inns.

When you arrive, collect a map from the **Atami Tourist Information Office** at the train station.

GETTING HERE AND AROUND

From JR Tokyo Station, take the Tokaido Acty Express to Atami, which is the last stop (one hour, 34 minutes, ¥1,890) or the Kodama Shinkansen (49 minutes, ¥3,570).

ESSENTIALS

Visitor Information Atami Tourist Information Office (☎ 0557/85–2222).

WHAT TO SEE

Atami Plum Garden 熱海梅園 *(Atami Bai-en)*. The best time to visit the garden is in late January or early February, when its 850 trees bloom. If you do visit, also stop by the small shrine that's in the shadow of an enormous old camphor tree. The shrine is more than 1,000 years old and is popular spot for people who are asking the gods for help with alcoholism. The tree is more than 2,000 years old and has been designated a National Monument. It's believed that if you walk around the tree once, another year will be added to your life. Atami Bai-en is always open to the public and is 15 minutes by bus from Atami or an eight-minute walk from Kinomiya Station, the next stop south of Atami served by local trains. ⊠ 1169–1 Baien-cho, Atami ☎ 0557/85–2222 *Free.*

CLOSE UP

A Healing Headache

While earthquakes are an annoying, everyday fact of life in Japan, they also provide one of the country's greatest delights: thermal baths. Wherever there are volcanic mountains—and there are a lot—you're sure to find springs of hot water, called *onsen,* that are rich in all sorts of restorative minerals. Any place where lots of spas have tapped these sources is an *onsen chiiki* (hot-springs resort area). The Izu Peninsula is particularly rich in onsen. It has, in fact, one-fifth of the 2,300-odd officially recognized hot springs in Japan.

Spas take many forms, but the ne plus ultra is that small secluded Japanese mountain inn with a *rotemburo* (an open-air mineral-spring pool). For guests only, these pools are usually in a screened-off nook with a panoramic view. A room in one of these inns on a weekend or in high season should be booked months in advance. (High season is late December to early January, late April to early May, the second and third weeks of August, and the second and third weeks of October.) More typical is the large resort hotel, geared mainly to groups, with one or more large indoor mineral baths of its own. Where whole towns and villages have developed to exploit a local supply of hot water, there will be several of these large hotels, an assortment of smaller inns, and probably a few modest public bathhouses, with no accommodations, where you just pay an entrance fee for a soak of whatever length you wish.

7

Hatsu-shima 初島. If you have the time and the inclination for a beach picnic, it's worth taking the 25-minute high-speed ferry (round-trip ¥2,340) from the pier. There are nine departures daily between 7:30 and 5:20. You can easily walk around the island, which is only 4 km (2½ mi) in circumference, in less than two hours. Use of the **Picnic Garden** (open daily 10–3) is free. ☎ *0557/81–0541 for ferry.*

★ **MOA Museum of Art** 美術館 *(MOA Bijutsukan).* This museum houses the private collection of the messianic religious leader Mokichi Okada. Okada (1882–1955), who founded a movement called the Sekai Kyusei Kyo (Religion for the Salvation of the World), also acquired more than 3,000 works of art; some are from the Asuka period (6th and 7th centuries). Among these works are several particularly fine *ukiyo-e* (Edo-era wood-block prints) and ceramics. On a hill above the station and set in a garden full of old plum trees and azaleas, the museum also affords a sweeping view over Atami and the bay. ✉ *26–2 Momoyama, Atami* ☎ *0557/84–2511* ✆ *¥1,600* ⊙ *Fri.–Wed. 9:30–5.*

Oyu Geyser 大湯間欠泉 *(Oyu Kanketsusen).* Located just a 15-minute walk south east from Atami Station, the geyser used to gush on schedule once every 24 hours but stopped after the Great Kanto Earthquake of 1923. Not happy with this, the local chamber of commerce rigged a pump to raise the geyser every five minutes. ✉ *3 Kamijuku-cho, Atami.*

WHERE TO STAY

Hotel reviews have been abbreviated in this book. For expanded reviews, please go to Fodors.com.

$$$$
★
RYOKAN

🏯 **Atami Taikanso** 熱海大観荘. The views of the sea must have been the inspiration for Yokoyama Taikan, the Japanese artist who once owned this villa. **Pros:** spotlessly clean rooms. **Cons:** eating dinner may take most of your evening. ⊠ *7–1 Hayashi-ga-oka-cho, Atami* ☎ *0557/81–8137* ⊕ *www.atami-taikanso.com* ⤳ *44 Japanese-style rooms with bath* ⛄ *In-hotel: restaurant, pool* �🍴 *Some meals.*

$$$–$$$$
HOTEL

🏯 **New Fujiya Hotel** ニュー富士屋ホテル. Only the top rooms have a view of the sea at this modern, inland resort hotel that's a great base for sightseeing. **Pros:** a number of shared hot-spring baths. **Cons:** nothing of the comfortable, at-home service of a ryokan. ⊠ *1–16 Ginza-cho, Atami* ☎ *0557/81–0111* ⤳ *158 Western-style rooms with bath, 158 Japanese-style rooms with bath* ⛄ *In-hotel: 3 restaurants, bar, pool* ⍥ *Some meals.*

ITO 伊東

16 km (10 mi) south of Atami.

There are some 800 thermal springs in the resort area surrounding Ito, 16 km (10 mi) south of Atami. These springs—and the beautiful, rocky, indented coastline nearby—remain the resort's major attractions, although there are plenty of interesting sights here. Some 150 hotels and inns serve the area.

Ito traces its history of associations with the West to 1604, when William Adams (1564–1620), the Englishman whose adventures served as the basis for James Clavell's novel *Shogun,* came ashore.

Four years earlier Adams had beached his disabled Dutch vessel, *De Liefde,* on the shores of Kyushu and became the first Englishman to set foot on Japan. The authorities, believing that he and his men were Portuguese pirates, put Adams in prison, but he was eventually befriended by the shogun Ieyasu Tokugawa, who brought him to Edo (present-day Tokyo) and granted him an estate. Ieyasu appointed Adams his adviser on foreign affairs. The English castaway taught mathematics, geography, gunnery, and navigation to shogunal officials and in 1604 was ordered to build an 80-ton Western-style ship. Pleased with this venture, Ieyasu ordered the construction of a larger oceangoing vessel. These two ships were built at Ito, where Adams lived from 1605 to 1610.

This history was largely forgotten until British Commonwealth occupation forces began coming to Ito for rest and recuperation after World War II. Adams's memory was revived, and since then the Anjin Festival (the Japanese gave Adams the name *anjin,* which means "pilot") has been held in his honor every August. A monument to the Englishman stands at the mouth of the river.

GETTING HERE AND AROUND

From JR Tokyo Station or Shinagawa Station, take the Tokaido Line (2 hours, 15 minutes, ¥2,210) or the Super Odoriko Express (1 hour, 40 minutes, ¥4,190) to Ito Station.

ESSENTIALS

Visitor Information Ito Tourist Association (✉ *1–8–3 Yukawa, Ito* ☎ *0557/37–6105* ⊕ *www.itospa.com.*

WHAT TO SEE

Ikeda 20th-Century Art Museum 池田20世紀美術館 *(Ikeda 20-Seiki Bijut-sukan)*. The museum, which overlooks Lake Ippeki, houses works by Picasso, Dalí, Chagall, and Matisse, plus a number of wood-block prints. The museum is a 15-minute walk north west from Izu Cactus Park. ✉ *614 Totari* ☎ *0557/45–2211* 💴 *¥900* ⊘ *Thurs.–Tues. 10–4:30.*

Izu Cactus Park 伊豆シャボテン公園 *(Izu Shaboten Koen)*. The park consists of a series of pyramidal greenhouses that contain 5,000 kinds of cacti from around the world. At the base of Komuro-san (Mt. Komuro), the park is 20 minutes south of Ito Station by bus. ✉ *1317– 13 Futo* ☎ *0557/51–5553* 💴 *¥1,800* ⊘ *Mar.–Oct., daily 9–5; Nov.– Feb., daily 9–4.*

Komuro-san Koen 小室山公園 *(Mt. Komuro Park)*. On the east side of the park there are 3,000 cherry trees of 35 varieties that bloom at various times throughout the year. You can take a cable car to the top of the mountain. The park is about 20 minutes south of Ito Station by bus. ✉ *1428 Komuro-cho, Ito* ☎ *0557/45–1444* 💴 *Free; round-trip cable car to mountain top ¥400* ⊘ *Daily 9–4.*

WHERE TO STAY

Hotel reviews have been abbreviated in this book. For expanded reviews, please go to Fodors.com.

$$$–$$$$
RYOKAN

🏯 **Hanafubuki** 花吹雪. This traditional Japanese inn, which is located in the Jogasaki forest, has modern, comfortable rooms, but still retains classic elements like tatami mats, screen sliding doors, and *chabudai* (low dining tables) with *zabuton* (cushion seating). **Pros:** an authentic Japanese experience. **Cons:** meals are available to nonguests, so the dining room can be a bit crowded. ✉ *1041 Yawatano Isomichi, Ito* ☎ *0557/54–1550* ⊕ *www.hanafubuki.co.jp* 🛏 *12 Japanese-style rooms with bath, 2 Western-style rooms with bath, 3 family rooms with bath* ⌂ *In-hotel: restaurant, bar* ¶⊙ *Some meals.*

$$$$
HOTEL

🏯 **Hatoya Sun Hotel** ホテルサンハトヤ. Located along a scenic coastline, Hatoya Hotel is in the Ito onsen resort area. **Pros:** live entertainment at dinner. **Cons:** a lot of guests with children make this a bit noisy. ✉ *572–12 Yukawa Tateiwa, Ito* ☎ *057/38–4126* 🛏 *187 Japanese-style rooms with bath, 3 Western-style rooms with bath, 1 mixed Western-Japanese style room with bath* ⌂ *In-room: refrigerator (some). In-hotel: restaurant, bar, pool, parking (free)* ¶⊙ *Some meals.*

EN
ROUTE

South of Ito the coastal scenery is lovely—each sweep around a headland reveals another picturesque sight of a rocky, indented shoreline. There are several spa towns en route to Shimoda. Higashi-Izu (East Izu) has numerous hot-springs resorts, of which **Atagawa** is the most fashionable. South of Atagawa is **Kawazu,** a place of relative quiet and solitude, with pools in the forested mountainside and waterfalls plunging through lush greenery.

SHIMODA 下田

35 km (22 mi) south of Ito city.

Of all the resort towns south of Ito along Izu's eastern coast, none can match the distinction of Shimoda. Shimoda's encounter with the West began when Commodore Matthew Perry anchored his fleet of black ships off the coast here in 1853. To commemorate the event, the three-day Black Ship Festival (Kurofune Matsuri) is held here every year in mid-May. Shimoda was also the site, in 1856, of the first American consulate.

The **Shimoda Tourist Office**, in front of the station, has the easiest of the local English itineraries to follow. The 2½-km (1½-mi) tour covers most major sights. On request, the tourist office will also help you find local accommodations.

GETTING HERE AND AROUND

From JR Shinagawa Station, take the Tokaido Line to Atami, change to the Ito Line, and take it to the final stop, Izukyu Shimoda Station (three hours, ¥3,780).

ESSENTIALS

Visitor Information Shimoda Tourist Office (☎ *0558/22–1531*).

WHAT TO SEE

Hofuku-ji 宝福寺. The first American consul to Japan was New York businessman Townsend Harris. Soon after his arrival in Shimoda, Harris asked the Japanese authorities to provide him with a female servant; they sent him a young girl named Okichi Saito, who was engaged to be married. The arrangement brought her a new name, Tojin (the Foreigner's) Okichi, much disgrace, and a tragic end. When Harris sent her away, she tried, but failed to rejoin her former lover. The shame brought upon her for working and living with a Westerner and the pain of losing the love of her life drove Okichi to drown herself in 1892. Her tale is recounted in Rei Kimura's biographical novel *Butterfly in the Wind* and inspired Puccini's *Madame Butterfly*, although some skeptics say the story is more gossip than fact. Hofuku-ji was Okichi's family temple. The museum annex displays a life-size image of her, and just behind the temple is her grave—where incense is still kept burning in her memory. The grave of her lover, Tsurumatsu, is at Toden-ji, a temple about midway between Hofuku-ji and Shimoda Station. ✉ *18–26–1 Shimoda, Shimoda* ☎ *0558/22–0960* 🎫 *¥300* ☉ *Daily 8–5.*

Ryosen-ji 了仙寺. This is the temple in which the negotiations took place that led to the United States–Japan Treaty of Amity and Commerce of 1858. The **Treasure Hall** (Homotsu-den) contains more than 300 original artifacts relating to Commodore Perry and the "black ships" that opened Japan to the West. ✉ *3–12–12 Shimoda, Shimoda* ☎ *0558/22–2805* 🎫 *Treasure Hall ¥500* ☉ *Daily 8:30–5.*

WHERE TO STAY

Hotel reviews have been abbreviated in this book. For expanded reviews, please go to Fodors.com.

¢ 🏠 **Pension Sakuraya** ペンション桜家. There are a few Western-style bedrooms at this family-run inn just a few minutes' walk from Shimoda's

HOTEL

main beach, but the best lodgings are the Japanese-style corner rooms, which have nice views of the hills surrounding Shimoda. **Pros:** very homey atmosphere; Japanese bath available. **Cons:** rooms are a bit cramped. ✉ *2584–20 Shira-hama, Shimoda* ☎ *0558/23–4470* ➡ *4 Western-style rooms with bath, 5 Japanese-style rooms without bath* ⊕ *izu-sakuraya.jp/english* ⌂ *In-hotel: restaurant, laundry facilities, Internet terminal* ¶⊖ *Some meals.*

> **BATHING BEAUTIES**
>
> If you love the sun, make sure you stop at **Yumi-ga-hama** 弓ヶ浜. It's one of the prettiest sandy beaches on the whole Izu Peninsula. The bus from Shimoda Station stops here before continuing to Iro-zaki, the last stop on the route.

$$$-$$$$ ▦ **Shimoda Prince Hotel** 下田プリンスホテル. This modern V-shape resort
HOTEL hotel faces the Pacific and is steps away from a white-sand beach. **Pros:** an excellent view of the sea. **Cons:** the restaurants are on the pricey side. ✉ *1547–1 Shira-hama, Shimoda* ☎ *0558/22–2111* ⊕ *www.princehotels. co.jp* ➡ *70 Western-style rooms with bath, 6 Japanese-style rooms with bath* ⌂ *In-hotel: 2 restaurants, bar, tennis courts, pool* ¶⊖ *Some meals.*

$$$-$$$$ ▦ **Shimoda Tokyu Hotel** 下田東急ホテル. Perched just above the bay, the
HOTEL Shimoda Tokyu has impressive views of the Pacific from one side (where rooms cost about 10% more) and mountains from the other. **Pros:** nice views of the ocean. **Cons:** restaurants quite expensive compared to Tokyo standards. ✉ *5–12–1 Shimoda, Shimoda* ☎ *0558/22–2411* ⊕ *www.tokyuhotels.co.jp* ➡ *107 Western-style rooms with bath, 8 Japanese-style rooms with bath* ⌂ *In-hotel: 3 restaurants, bar, pool* ¶⊖ *Breakfast.*

IRO-ZAKI (IRO POINT) 石廊崎
11 km (8 mi) south of Shimoda.

If you visit Iro-zaki, the southernmost part of the Izu Peninsula, in January, you're in for a special treat: a blanket of daffodils covers the cape.

GETTING HERE AND AROUND
From Izukyu Shimoda Station on the Izu Kyuko Line, take Tokai Bus Minami Izu Line to Iro-zaki Minami-guchi Stop (15 minutes).

WHAT TO SEE
Iro-zaki Jungle Park 石廊崎ジャングルパーク. From the bus stop at the end of the line from Shimoda Station, it's a short walk to the park's 3,000 varieties of colorful tropical plants. Beyond the park you can walk to a lighthouse at the edge of the cliff that overlooks the sea; from here you can see the seven islands of Izu. ✉ *546–1 Iro-zaki, Minami-Izu* ☎ *0558/65–0050* 🎫 *¥900* 🕙 *Daily 8–5.*

DOGASHIMA 堂ヶ島
16 km (10 mi) northeast of Mishima.

The sea has eroded the coastal rock formations into fantastic shapes near the little port town of Dogashima, including a tombolo, or a narrow band of sand, that connects the mainland to a small peninsula with a scenic park.

7

The **Nishi-Izu Tourist Office** is near the pier, in the small building behind the bus station.

GETTING HERE AND AROUND

Dogashima is not directly accessible by train. From Shinjuku Station, take Odakyu Asagiri express train to Numazu Station (two hours, 1 minute, ¥3,280), and change to the Express Bus Super Romance (two hours, 15 minutes) to Dogashima. From Tokyo Station, take the JR Shinkansen to Mishima (44 minutes, ¥3,890), change to the Izu Hakone Line to Shuzenji (35 minutes, ¥5,000) and take the Tokai bus to the Dogashima stop. There is also an express Tokai Bus, Minami Izu Line, which will take you from Shimoda Station to Dogashima (55 minutes).

ESSENTIALS

Visitor Information Nishi-Izu Tourist Office (☎ *0558/52–1268*).

TOURS

Dogashima Marine Sightseeing Boat. Sightseeing boats from Dogashima Pier makes 20-minute runs to see the rocks (¥920). In an excess of kindness, a recorded loudspeaker—which you can safely ignore—recites the name of every rock you pass on the trip. ☎ *0558/52–0013*

WHERE TO STAY

Hotel reviews have been abbreviated in this book. For expanded reviews, please go to Fodors.com.

$$$$ 🏠 **Dogashima New Ginsui** 堂ヶ島ニュー銀水. Surrounded by its very own
HOTEL secluded beach, every guest room overlooks the sea at the New Ginsui, which sits atop cliffs above the water. *2977–1 Nishina, Nishi-Izu-cho* ☎ *0558/52–2211* ⊕ *www.dougashima-newginsui.jp* ⇗ *121 Japanese-style rooms with bath* ♿ *In-hotel: restaurant, pools, spa, laundry service* ❢⊙❢ *Some meals.*

SHUZENJI 修善寺

25 km (15 mi) south of Mishima by Izu-Hakone Railway.

Shuzenji—a hot-springs resort in the center of the peninsula, along the valley of the Katsura-gawa (Katsura River)—enjoys a certain historical notoriety as the place where the second Kamakura shogun, Minamoto no Yoriie, was assassinated early in the 13th century. Don't judge the town by the area around the station; most of the hotels and hot springs are 2 km (1 mi) to the west.

If you've planned a longer visit to Izu, consider spending a night at **Inoshishi-mura** いのしし村, en route by bus between Shimoda and Shuzenji. The scenery in this part of the peninsula is dramatic, and the dining specialty at the local inns is roast mountain boar. In the morning, a pleasant 15-minute walk from Inoshishi-mura brings you to **Joren Falls** (Joren-no-taki). Located on the upper part of the Kano River, these falls drop 82 feet into a dense forest below. This area has some nationally protected flora and fauna species, and because of the cool temperatures, hiking here is popular in summer.

GETTING HERE AND AROUND

The train is by far the easiest way to get to Shuzenji. The Izu–Hakone Railway Line runs from Tokyo to Mishima (one hour, 36 minutes, ¥4,090), with a change at Mishima for Shuzenji (31 minutes, ¥500);

CLOSE UP

Ryokan Etiquette

Guests are expected to arrive at ryokan in the late afternoon. When you do, put on the slippers that are provided and a maid will escort you to your room. Remember to remove your slippers before entering your room; never step on the tatami (straw mats) with shoes or slippers. Each room will be simply decorated—one small low table, cushions on the tatami, and a scroll on the wall—which will probably be shoji (sliding paper-paneled walls).

In ryokan with thermal pools, you can take to the waters anytime, although the pool doors are usually locked from 11 pm to 6 am. In ryokan without thermal baths or private baths in guest rooms, visits must be staggered. Typically the maid will ask what time you would like to bathe and fit you into a schedule. Make sure you wash and rinse off entirely before getting into the bath. Do not get soap in the tub. Other guests will be using the same bathwater, so it is important to observe this custom. After your bath, change into the yukata provided in your room. Don't worry about walking around in it—other guests will be doing the same.

Dinner is served around 6. At the larger, newer ryokan, meals will be in the dining room; at smaller, more personal ryokan, it is served in your room. When you are finished, a maid will clear away the dishes and lay out your futon. In Japan *futon* means bedding, and this consists of a thin cotton mattress and a heavy, thick comforter, which is replaced with a thinner quilt in summer. The small, hard pillow is filled with grain. The less expensive ryokan (under ¥7,000 for one) have become slightly lackadaisical in changing the quilt cover with each new guest; in an inoffensive a way as

possible, feel free to complain—just don't shame the proprietor. Around 8 am, a maid will gently wake you, clear away the futon, and bring in your Japanese-style breakfast, which will probably consist of fish, pickled vegetables, and rice. If this isn't appealing, politely ask if it's possible to have coffee and toast. Checkout is at 10 am.

Make sure you call or e-mail as far in advance as possible for a room—inns are not always willing to accept foreign guests because of language and cultural barriers. It is nearly impossible to get a room in July or August. Many top-level ryokan require new guests to have introductions and references from a respected client of the inn to get a room; this goes for new Japanese guests, too. On the other hand, inns that do accept foreigners without introduction sometimes treat them as cash cows, which means they might give you cursory service and a lesser room. If you don't speak Japanese, try to have a Japanese speaker reserve a room for you; this will convey the idea that you understand the customs of staying in a traditional inn.

7

this is the cheapest option if you don't have a JR Pass. With a JR Pass, a Shinkansen–Izu Line combination will save about 35 minutes and will be the least expensive. The Tokyo–Mishima Shinkansen leg (62 minutes) costs ¥4,400; the Mishima–Shuzenji Izu Line leg (31 minutes) costs ¥500.

WHERE TO STAY

Hotel reviews have been abbreviated in this book. For expanded reviews, please go to Fodors.com.

¢
RYOKAN

 Goyokan 五葉館. This family-run ryokan on Shuzenji's main street has rooms that look out on the Katsura-gawa, plus gorgeous stone-lined (for men) and wood-lined (for women) indoor hot springs. **Pros:** among the best-priced rooms in the area. **Cons:** doesn't have the cozy feel of a true ryokan. ⊠ *765–2 Shuzenji-cho, Tagata-gun* ☎ *05/5872–2066* ⊕ *www.goyokan.co.jp* ⟿ *11 Japanese-style rooms without bath* ⌂ *In-room: refrigerator* ⦿ *Breakfast.*

$$
RYOKAN

 Kyorai-An Matsushiro-kan 去来庵 松城館. Although this small family-owned inn is nothing fancy, the owners make you feel like a guest in their home. They also speak some English. **Pros:** nice shared hot-spring bath. **Cons:** the decor throughout is rather dated. ⊠ *55 Kona, Izunokuni* ☎ *05/5948–0072* ⟿ *16 Japanese-style rooms, 14 with bath* ⌂ *In-hotel: restaurant* ⊟ *No credit cards* ⦿ *Some meals.*

$$$$
RYOKAN

 Ochiairou Murakami 落合楼村上. This traditional ryokan was built in the Showa period and though it has been renovated and modernized, the main wooden structure remains true to its original design. **Pros:** there's free pickup from Yugashima bus terminal; there's a lovely garden on the grounds. **Cons:** you may have to wait for the shared baths. ⊠ *1887–1 Yugashima, Izu* ☎ *05/5885–0014* ⟿ *15 Japanese-style rooms with bath* ⌂ *In-hotel: restaurant* ⦿ *Some meals.*

$$$$
RYOKAN
★

 Ryokan Sanyoso 旅館三養荘. The former villa of the Iwasaki family, founders of the Mitsubishi conglomerate, is as luxurious and beautiful a place to stay as you'll find on the Izu Peninsula. **Pros:** a truly authentic ryokan and furnishings; Japanese bath available. **Cons:** the most expensive ryokan in the area. ⊠ *270 Mama-no-ue, Izunokuni* ☎ *05/5947–1111* ⟿ *3 Western-style, 30 Japanese-style, and 7 mixed Western-Japanese-style rooms with bath* ⌂ *In hotel: bar* ⦿ *Some meals.*

HAKONE 箱根

The national park and resort area of Hakone is a popular day trip from Tokyo and a good place for a close-up view of Mt. Fuji (assuming the mountain is not swathed in clouds, as often happens in summer). ■ **TIP→ On summer weekends it often seems as though all of Tokyo has come out to Hakone with you. Expect long lines at cable cars and traffic jams everywhere.**

TIMING

You can cover the best of Hakone in a one-day trip out of Tokyo, but if you want to try the curative powers of the thermal waters or do some hiking, then stay overnight. Two of the best areas are around the old hot-springs resort of Miyanoshita and the western side of Koma-ga-take-san (Mt. Koma-ga-take).

GETTING HERE AND AROUND

The typical Hakone route, outlined here, may sound complex, but this is in fact one excursion from Tokyo so well defined that you really can't get lost—no more so, at least, than any of the thousands of Japanese tourists ahead of and behind you. The first leg of the journey is from Odawara or Hakone-Yumoto by train and cable car through the mountains to Togendai, on the north shore of Ashi-no-ko (Lake Ashi). The long way around, from Odawara to Togendai by bus, takes about an hour—in heavy traffic, an hour and a half. The trip over the mountains, on the other hand, will take about two hours. Credit the difference to the Hakone Tozan Tetsudo Line—possibly the slowest train you'll ever ride. Using three switchbacks to inch its way up the side of the mountain, the train takes 54 minutes to travel the 16 km (10 mi) from Odawara to Gora (38 minutes from Hakone-Yumoto). The steeper it gets, the grander the view.

Trains do not stop at any station en route for any length of time, but they do run frequently enough to allow you to disembark, visit a sight, and catch another train.

Within the Hakone area, buses run every 15 to 30 minutes from Hakone-machi buses to Hakone-Yumoto Station on the private Odakyu Line (40 minutes, ¥930), and Odawara Station (one hour, ¥1,150), where you can take either the Odakyu Romance Car back to Shinjuku Station or a JR Shinkansen to Tokyo Station. The buses are covered by the Hakone Free Pass.

Sunrise Tours operates a tour to Hakone, including a cruise across Lake Ashi and a trip on the gondola over Owaku-dani (¥15,000 includes lunch and return to Tokyo by Shinkansen; ¥12,000 includes lunch and return to Tokyo by bus). ■TIP→ These tours are an economical way to see the main sights all in one day and are ideal for travelers with limited time. Sunrise Tours depart daily from Tokyo's Hamamatsu-cho Bus Terminal and some major hotels.

ESSENTIALS

Buses from Tokyo Fuji Kyuko Highway Bus Reservation Center (☎ *03/5376–2222*). Keio Highway Bus Reservation Center (☎ *03/5376–2222*). Tokai Bus Company (☎ *0557/36–1112 for main office, 0558/22–2511 Shimoda Information Center*).

Tour Contacts Sunrise Tours (☎ *03/5796–5454* ⊕ *www.jtbgmt.com/sunrisetour*).

Tourist Information Hakone-machi Tourist Association (✉ *698 Yumoto, Hakone-machi* ☎ *0460/5–8911*).

TOP ATTRACTIONS

Fodor's Choice
★

Hakone Kowakien Yunessun 箱根小涌園 ユネッサン. This complex on the hills overlooking Hakone offers more than the average onsen. There is a shopping mall modeled on a European outdoor market, a swimsuit rental shop, a massage salon, and game center in addition to all the water-based attractions. The park is divided into two main zones, called Yunessun and Mori no Yu ("Forest Bath"). In the Yunessun side, you need to wear a swimsuit, and can visit somewhat tacky re-creations of

Hakone Kowakien Yunessun offers a varied and unusual onsen experience.

Turkish and ancient Roman baths. You can also take a dip in coffee, green tea, sake, or red wine. It is all a bit corny, but fun. Younger visitors will enjoy the waterslides on "Rodeo Mountain." In the more secluded Mori no Yu side, you can go au naturel in a variety of indoor and outdoor, single-sex baths. When signing in at reception, get a waterproof digital wristband that allows you to pay for lockers and drink machines within the complex. ✉ *1297 Ninotaira Hakone-machi, Ashigarashimogun* ☎ *0460/82–4126* ⊕ *www.yunessun.com/english/* 💴 *¥3,500 for the Yunessun zone, ¥1,800 for the Mori no Yu zone, ¥4,000 for both* ⊙ *Mar.–Oct.: Yunessun daily 9–7, Mori no Yu daily 11–8. Nov.– Feb.: Yunessun daily 9–6, Mori no Yu daily 11–8.*

★ **Hakone Open-Air Museum** 箱根彫刻の森美術館 *(Hakone Chokoku-no-mori Bijutsukan).* Only a few minutes' walk from the Miyanoshita Station (directions are posted in English), the museum houses an astonishing collection of 19th- and 20th-century Western and Japanese sculpture, most of it on display in a spacious, handsome garden. There are works here by Rodin, Moore, Arp, Calder, Giacometti, Takeshi Shimizu, and Kotaro Takamura. One section of the garden is devoted to Emilio Greco. Inside are works by Picasso, Léger, and Manzo, among others. ✉ *1121 Ni-no-taira* ☎ *0460/82–1161* ⊕ *www.hakone-oam.or.jp* 💴 *¥1,600* ⊙ *Mar.–Nov., daily 9–5; Dec.–Feb., daily 9–4.*

★ **Hakone Ropeway.** At the cable-car terminus of Soun-zan, a gondola called the Hakone Ropeway swings up over a ridge and crosses the valley called **Owaku-dani,** also known as "Great Boiling Valley," on its way to Togendai. The landscape here is desolate, with sulfurous billows of steam escaping through holes from some inferno deep in the

The Road to the Shogun

In days gone by, the town of Hakone was on the Tokaido, the main highway between the imperial court in Kyoto and the shogunate in Edo (present-day Tokyo). The road was the only feasible passage through this mountainous country, which made it an ideal place for a checkpoint to control traffic. The Tokugawa Shogunate built the Hakone-machi here in 1618; its most important function was to monitor the *daimyo* (feudal lords) passing through—to keep track, above all, of weapons coming into Edo, and womenfolk coming out.

When Ieyasu Tokugawa came to power, Japan had been through nearly 100 years of bloody struggle among rival coalitions of daimyo. Ieyasu emerged supreme because some of his opponents had switched

sides at the last minute, in the Battle of Sekigahara in 1600. The shogun was justifiably paranoid about his "loyal" barons—especially those in the outlying domains—so he required the daimyo to live in Edo for periods of time every two years. When they did return to their own lands, they had to leave their wives behind in Edo, hostages to their good behavior. A noble lady coming through the Hakone Sekisho without an official pass, in short, was a case of treason.

The checkpoint served the Tokugawa dynasty well for 250 years. It was demolished only when the shogunate fell, in the Meiji Restoration of 1868. An exact replica, with an exhibition hall of period costumes and weapons, was built as a tourist attraction in 1965.

7

earth—yet another reminder that Japan is a chain of volcanic islands. At the top of the ridge is one of the two stations where you can leave the gondola. From here, a ¾-km (½-mi) walking course wanders among the sulfur pits in the valley. Just below the station is a restaurant; the food here is truly terrible, but on a clear day the view of Mt. Fuji is perfect. Remember that if you get off the gondola at any stage, you—and others in the same situation—will have to wait for someone to make space on a later gondola before you can continue down to Togendai and Ashi-no-ko (but again, the gondolas come by every minute). ⊠ *1–15–1 Shiroyama, Odawara* ☎ *0465/32–2205* ⊕ *www.hakoneropeway.co.jp* 🚡 *¥970 (without Hakone Free Pass)* ⊙ *Mar.–Nov., daily 8:45–5:15; Dec.–Feb., daily 9:15–4:15.*

Miyanoshita 宮ノ下. The first stop on the train route from Hakone-Yumoto, this is a small but very pleasant and popular resort. As well as hot springs, this village has antiques shops along its main road and several hiking routes up the ¾-km- (½-mi-) tall Mt. Sengen. If you get to the top, you'll be rewarded with a great view of the gorge.

WORTH NOTING

Ashi-no-ko 芦ノ湖 *(Lake Ashi).* From Owaku-dani, the descent by gondola to Togendai on the shore of Lake Ashi takes 25 minutes. There's no reason to linger at Togendai; it's only a terminus for buses to Hakone-Yumoto and Odawara and to the resort villages in the northern part of Hakone. Head straight for the pier, a few minutes' walk down the hill,

Passengers floating over the Owaku-dani valley on the Hakone Ropeway can see Fuji looming—on a clear day, of course.

where boats set out on the lake for Hakone-machi. Look for the **Hakone Sightseeing Cruise** (✉ *1–15–1 Shiroyama, Odawara* ☎ *0465/32–6830* ⊕ *www.hakone-kankosen.co.jp* ✆ *¥300* ⊙ *Summer, 40-min intervals; winter, 50-min intervals. Mar.–Nov., daily 9:30–5; Dec.–Feb., daily 9:30–4*). The ride is free with your Hakone Free Pass; otherwise, buy a ticket (¥970) at the office in the terminal. A few ships of conventional design ply the lake; the rest are astonishingly corny Disney knock-offs. One, for example, is rigged like a 17th-century warship. With still water and good weather, you'll get a breathtaking reflection of the mountains in the waters of the lake as you go. If a cruise is not what you're after, go exploring and fishing with hired boats from **Togen-dai Boat House** (☎ *090/1448–1834*) or **Ashinoko Fishing Center Oba** (☎ *0460/84–8984*) .

Gora 強羅. This small town is at the end of the train line from Odawara and at the lower end of the Hakone Tozan Cable Car. It's a good jumping-off point for hiking and exploring. Ignore the little restaurants and souvenir stands here: get off the train as quickly as you can and make a dash for the cable car at the other end of the station. If you let the rest of the passengers get there before you, and perhaps a tour bus or two, you may stand 45 minutes in line.

Hakone-machi 箱根町. The main attraction here is the **Hakone Barrier** (Hakone Sekisho). The barrier was built in 1618 and served as a checkpoint to control traffic until it was demolished during the Meiji Restoration of 1868. An exact replica was built as a tourist attraction in 1965 and is only a few minutes' walk from the pier, along the lakeshore in the direction of Moto-Hakone. Last entry is 30 minutes before closing time. ✉ *1 Hakone-machi* ☎ *0460/83–6635* 🎫 *¥300* 🕐 *Mar.–Nov., daily 9–5; Dec.–Feb., daily 9–4:30.*

Hakone Museum of Art 箱根美術館 *(Hakone Bijutsukan).* A sister institution to the MOA Museum of Art in Atami, Hakone Museum of Art is at the second stop of the Hakone Tozan Cable Car. The museum, which consists of two buildings set in a garden, houses a modest collection of porcelain and ceramics from China, Korea, and Japan. ✉ *1300 Gora* ☎ *0460/82–2623* 🌐 *www.moaart.or.jp* 🎫 *¥900* 🕐 *Apr.–Nov., Fri.–Wed. 9:30–4:30; Dec.–Mar., Fri.–Wed. 9:30–4.*

Soun-zan 早雲山 *(Mt. Soun).* The Hakone Tozan Cable Car travels from Gora to Soun-zan, departing every 20 minutes; it takes 10 minutes (¥410; free with the Hakone Free Pass) to get to the top. It's ideal for those wanting to spend a day hiking. There are four stops en route, and you can get off and reboard the cable car at any one of them if you've paid the full fare.

> **WHAT THE . . . ?**
>
> No, your eyes are not playing tricks on you. Those are in fact local entrepreneurs boiling eggs in the sulfur pits in Owaku-dani. Locals make a passable living selling the eggs, which turn black, to tourists at exorbitant prices. A popular myth suggests that eating one of these eggs can extend your life by seven years. What do you have to lose?

WHERE TO STAY

Hotel reviews have been abbreviated in this book. For expanded reviews, please go to Fodors.com.

GORA

$$$$
RYOKAN

🏯 **Gora Tensui** 強羅天翠. The Gora Tensui, which opened in 2007, is unique in that it's something of a cross between a boutique hotel and a Japanese-style inn. **Pros:** four rooms have a private onsen on a terrace. **Cons:** no Japanese food in the restaurant. ✉ *1320–276 Gora, Ashigarashimo-gun, Hakone-machi* ☎ *0460/86–1411* 🌐 *www.gora-tensui.com/index_english.html* ⤴ *17 rooms with private bath* 🛏 *In-hotel: restaurant* 🍴 *Some meals.*

LAKE ASHI

$$–$$$
HOTEL
★

🏯 **Hakone Prince Hotel** 箱根プリンスホテル. The location of this resort complex is perfect, with the lake in front and the mountains of Komaga-take in back. **Pros:** lovely quaint cottages surrounded by nature; Japanese bath available. **Cons:** a bit remote from nearby sightseeing spots. ✉ *144 Moto-Hakone, Hakone-machi* ☎ *0460/3–1111* 🌐 *www.princehotels.co.jp* ⤴ *142 Western-style rooms with bath, 116 Western-style cottages with bath* 🛏 *In-hotel: 2 restaurants, room service, bar, tennis courts, pools* 🍴 *Breakfast.*

MIYANOSHITA

$$$
HOTEL
★

🏯 **Fujiya Hotel** 富士屋ホテル. Built in 1878, this Western-style hotel with modern additions is showing signs of age, but that somehow adds to its charm. **Pros:** wonderful, friendly service. **Cons:** rooms and bath decor are rather dated. ✉ *359 Miyanoshita, Hakone-machi* ☎ *0460/2–2211* 🌐 *www.fujiyahotel.co.jp* ⤴ *149 Western-style rooms*

7

CLOSE UP

Hakone Freebies

Many places in Hakone accept the Hakone Free Pass. It's valid for three days and is issued by the privately owned Odakyu Railways. The pass covers the train fare to Hakone and allows you to use any mode of transportation including the Hakone Tozan Cable Car, the Hakone Ropeway, and the Hakone Cruise Boat. In addition to transportation, Free Pass holders get discounts at museums such as the Hakone Museum of Art, restaurants, and shops. The list of participants is pretty extensive and it always changes, so it's a good idea to check out the Web site for a complete list

of participating companies and terms and conditions.

The Hakone Free Pass (¥5,500) and the Fuji-Hakone Free Pass (¥7,200) can be purchased at the **Odakyu Sightseeing Service Center** (☎ 03/5321-7887 ⊕ www.odakyu-group.co.jp) inside JR Shinjuku Station, near the West Exit, or by credit card over the phone. Allow a couple of days for delivery to your hotel. If you have a JR Pass, it's cheaper to take a Kodama Shinkansen from Tokyo Station to Odawara and buy the Hakone Free Pass there (¥4,130) for travel within the Hakone region only.

---

with bath ☼ *In-hotel: 3 restaurants, room service, bar, golf course, pools* ⦿ *Some meals.*

SENGOKU

¢

HOTEL

⛩ **Fuji-Hakone Guest House** 富士箱根ゲストハウス. A small, family-run Japanese inn, this guesthouse has simple tatami rooms with the bare essentials. **Pros:** friendly staff; inexpensive rates. **Cons:** difficult to access from nearest transportation, especially at night. ✉ *912 Sengoku-hara (103 Moto-Hakone for Moto-Hakone Guest House), Hakone-machi* ☎ *0460/84–6577 for Fuji-Hakone, 0460/83–7880 for Moto-Hakone* ⤴ *14 Japanese-style rooms without bath in Fuji-Hakone, 5 Japanese-style rooms without bath in Moto-Hakone* ⦿ *Some meals.*

¢

RYOKAN

⛩ **Lodge Fujimien** ロッジ富士見苑. This traditional ryokan, complete with an on-site onsen, has all the trimmings of an expensive ryokan, for a fraction of the price. **Pros:** affordable rates; convenient location. **Cons:** its accessible location leads to occasional overcrowding. ✉ *1245 Sengoku-hara, Hakone* ☎ *0460/84–8675* ⊕ *www.fujimien.com* ⤴ *21 Japanese-style rooms with bath, 5 Western-style rooms with bath* ☼ *In-hotel: restaurant, parking (free)* ▤ *No credit cards* ⦿ *Some meals.*

FUJI GO-KO (FUJI FIVE LAKES) 富士五湖

To the north of Mt. Fuji, the Fuji Go-ko area affords an unbeatable view of the mountain on clear days and makes the best base for a climb to the summit. With its various outdoor activities, such as skating and fishing in winter and boating and hiking in summer, this is a popular resort area for families and business conferences.

The five lakes are, from the east, Yamanaka-ko, Kawaguchi-ko, Sai-ko, Shoji-ko, and Motosu-ko. Yamanaka and Kawaguchi are the largest and most developed as resort areas, with Kawaguchi more or less the centerpiece of the group.

TIMING

You can visit this area on a day trip from Tokyo, but unless you want to spend most of it on buses and trains, plan on staying overnight.

GETTING HERE AND AROUND

Direct bus service runs daily from Shinjuku Station in Tokyo to Lake Kawaguchi every hour between 7:10 am and 8:10 pm. Buses go from Kawaguchi-ko Station to Go-gome (the fifth station on the climb up Mt. Fuji) in about an hour; there are eight departures a day until the climbing season (July and August) starts, when there are 15 departures or more, depending on demand. The cost is ¥1,700.

The transportation hub, as well as one of the major resort areas in the Fuji Five Lakes area, is Kawaguchi-ko. Getting there from Tokyo requires a change of trains at Otsuki. The JR Chuo Line Kaiji and Azusa express trains leave Shinjuku Station for Otsuki on the half hour from 7 am to 8 pm (more frequently in the morning) and take approximately one hour. At Otsuki, change to the private Fuji-Kyuko Line for Kawaguchi-ko, which takes another 50 minutes. The total traveling time is about two hours, and you can use your JR Pass as far as Otsuki; otherwise, the fare is ¥1,280. The Otsuki–Kawaguchi-ko leg costs ¥1,110. Also available are two direct-service rapid trains for Kawaguchi-ko that leave Tokyo in the morning at 6:08 and 7:10 on weekdays, 6:09 and 7:12 on weekends and national holidays.

The Holiday Kaisoku Picnic-go, available on weekends and national holidays, offers direct express service from Shinjuku, leaving at 8:10 and arriving at Kawaguchi-ko Station at 10:37. From March through August, JR puts on additional weekend express trains for Kawaguchi-ko, but be aware that on some of them only the first three cars go all the way to the lake. Coming back, you have a choice of late-afternoon departures from Kawaguchi-ko that arrive at Shinjuku in the early evening. Check the express timetables before you go; you can also call either the JR Higashi-Nihon Info Line or Fuji-kyuuko Kawaguchi-ko Station for train information.

ESSENTIALS

Buses from Kawaguchi Fuji Kyuko Gotemba Reservation Center (☎ 0550/82–2555). Fuji Kyuko Lake Kawaguchi Reservation Center (☎ 0555/72–2922).

Buses from Tokyo Fuji Kyuko Highway Bus Reservation Center (☎ 03/5376–2222). Keio Highway Bus Reservation Center (☎ 03/5376–2222). Tokai Bus Company (☎ 0557/36–1112 for main office, 0558/22–2511 Shimoda Information Center).

Train Information Fuji-kyuuko Kawaguchi-ko Station (☎ 0555/72–0017). JR Higashi-Nihon Info Line (☎ 03/3423–0111). Odakyu Reservation Center (☎ 03/3481–0130).

Visitor Information Fuji-Kawaguchiko Tourist Association (✉ 890 Funatsu, Kawakuchiko-machi, Minami-Tsuru-gun ☎ 0555/72–2460).

WHAT TO SEE

Fuji-kyu Highland 富士急ハイランド. The largest of the recreational facilities at Lake Kawaguchi, Fuji-kyu Highland has an impressive assortment of rides, roller coasters, and other amusements, but it's probably not worth a visit unless you have children in tow. In winter there's superb skating here, with Mt. Fuji for a backdrop. Fuji-kyu Highland is about 15 minutes' walk east from Kawaguchi-ko Station. ⊠ *5–6–1 Shin Nishi Hara, Fujiyoshida* ☎ *0555/23–2111* 🖃 *Full-day Free Pass ¥4,800, entrance only ¥1,200* ⊙ *Weekdays 9–5, weekends 9–8.*

Fuji Museum 富士博物館 (*Fuji Hakubutsukan*). One of the little oddities at Lake Kawaguchi is this museum, located on the lake's north shore, next to the Fuji Lake Hotel. The first floor holds conventional exhibits of local geology and history, but upstairs is an astonishing collection of—for want of a euphemism—phalluses (you must be 18 or older to view the exhibit). Mainly made from wood and stone and carved in every shape and size, these figures played a role in certain local fertility festivals. ⊠ *3964 Funatsu, Fujikawaguchiko-machi, Minami Tsurugen* ☎ *0555/73–2266* 🖃 *1st fl. ¥200, 1st and 2nd fl. ¥500* ⊙ *Mar.–Oct., daily 9–4; Nov.–Feb., Sat.–Thurs. 9–4; closed 3rd Tues. of month.*

Kawaguchi-ko 河口湖 (*Lake Kawaguchi*). A 5- to 10-minute walk from Kawaguchi-ko Station, this is the most developed of the five lakes. It's ringed with weekend retreats and vacation lodges—many of them maintained by companies and universities for their employees. Excursion boats depart from a pier here on 30-minute tours of the lake. The promise, not always fulfilled, is to have two views of Mt. Fuji: one of the mountain itself and the other inverted in its reflection on the water.

Motosu-ko 本栖湖 (*Lake Motosu*). Lake Motosu is the farthest west of the five lakes. It's also the deepest and clearest of the Fuji Go-ko. It takes about 50 minutes to get here by bus.

Sai-ko 西湖 (*Lake Sai*). Between Lakes Shoji and Kawaguchi, Lake Sai is the third-largest lake of the Fuji Go-ko, with only moderate development. From the western shore there is an especially good view of Mt. Fuji. Near Sai-ko there are two natural caves, an ice cave and a wind cave. You can either take a bus or walk to them.

Shoji-ko 精進湖 (*Lake Shoji*). Many consider Lake Shoji, the smallest of the lakes, to be the prettiest. There are still remnants of lava flow jutting out from the water, which locals perch upon while fishing.

Shoji Trail 精進口ルート. This trail leads from Lake Shoji to Mt. Fuji through Aoki-ga-hara (Sea of Trees). Beware. This forest has an underlying magnetic lava field that makes compasses go haywire.

Tenjo-san 天上山 (*Mt. Tenjo*). A gondola along the shore of Lake Kawaguchi (near the pier) quickly brings you to the top of the 3,622-foot-tall mountain. From the observatory here the whole of Lake Kawaguchi lies before you, and beyond the lake is a classic view of Mt. Fuji.

Yamanaka-ko 山中湖 (*Lake Yamanaka*). The largest of the Fuji Go-ko, Lake Yamanaka) is 35 minutes by bus to the southeast of Kawaguchi. It's also the closest lake to the popular trail up Mt. Fuji that starts at Go-gome, and many climbers use this resort area as a base.

WHERE TO STAY

Hotel reviews have been abbreviated in this book. For expanded reviews, please go to Fodors.com.

KAWAGUCHI-KO

$$$–$$$$
HOTEL

⊡ **Fuji View Hotel** 富士ビューホテル. This hotel on Lake Kawaguchi is a little threadbare but comfortable. The terrace lounge affords fine views of the lake and of Mt. Fuji beyond. **Pros:** comparatively inexpensive lodgings. **Cons:** rooms are rather small. ⊠ *511 Katsuyama-mura, Fuji-Kawaguchiko-machi* ☎ *0555/83–2211* ⊕ *www.fujiyahotel.co.jp* ⬩ *40 Western-style rooms with bath, 30 Japanese-style rooms with bath* ⬩ *In-hotel: 2 restaurants, golf course, tennis courts* ◎ *Some meals.*

YAMANAKA-KO

$$
HOTEL

⊡ **Hotel Mount Fuji** 富士山ホテル. This is the best resort hotel on Lake Yamanaka and has all the facilities for a recreational holiday including on-site game and karaoke rooms and a nature walk on the grounds. **Pros:** comfortable rooms; convenient facilities. **Cons:** one of the more expensive options in the area. ⊠ *1360–83 Yamanaka, Yamanaka-ko-mura* ☎ *0555/62–2111* ⊕ *www.mtfuji-hotel.com* ⬩ *150 Western-style rooms with bath, 1 Japanese-style room with bath* ⬩ *In-hotel: 3 restaurants, pool, parking (free)* ◎ *Some meals.*

¢–$
HOTEL

⊡ **Inn Fujitomita** 旅館ふじとみた. One of the closest lodging options to the Mt. Fuji hiking trails, this inexpensive inn is a launching point for treks around the Fuji Go-ko area. **Pros:** spacious rooms; pleasant surrounding grounds. **Cons:** very crowded during climbing season. ⊠ *13235 Shibokusa, Oshinomura, Minami-Tsuru-gun* ☎ *0555/84–3359* ⊕ *www.tim.hi-ho.ne.jp/innfuji* ⬩ *10 Japanese-style rooms, 3 with bath* ⬩ *In-room: no TV (some). In-hotel: restaurant, tennis courts, pool, laundry facilities* ◎ *Some meals.*

THE SHOJI TRIANGLE

The Aoki-ga-hara Jukai (Sea of Trees) seems to hold a morbid fascination for the Japanese. Many people go into Aoki-ga-hara every year and never come out, some of them on purpose. If you're planning to climb Mt. Fuji from this trail, go with a guide.

NIKKO 日光

130 km (81 mi) north of Tokyo.

"Think nothing is splendid," asserts an old Japanese proverb, "until you have seen Nikko." Nikko, which means "sunlight," is a popular vacation spot for the Japanese, for good reason: its gorgeous sights include a breathtaking waterfall and one of the country's best-known shrines. In addition, Nikko combines the rustic charm of a countryside village (complete with wild monkeys that have the run of the place) with a convenient location not far from Tokyo.

GETTING HERE AND AROUND

Buses and taxis can take you from Nikko to the village of Chuzenji and nearby Lake Chuzenji; one-way cab fare from Tobu Nikko Station to Chuzenji is about ¥6,000. ⚠ There is no bus service between Tokyo and Nikko. Local buses leave Tobu Nikko Station for Lake Chuzenji,

7

stopping just above the entrance to Tosho-gu, approximately every 30 minutes from 6:15 am until 7:01 pm. The fare to Chuzenji is ¥1,100, and the ride takes about 40 minutes. The last return bus from the lake leaves at 7:39 pm, arriving back at Tobu Nikko Station at 9:17 pm.

It's possible, but unwise, to travel by car from Tokyo to Nikko. The trip will take at least three hours, and merely getting from central Tokyo to the toll-road system can be a nightmare. Coming back, especially on a Saturday or Sunday evening, is even worse.

The limited express train of the Tobu Railway has two direct connections from Tokyo to Nikko every morning, starting at 7:30 am from Tobu Asakusa Station, a minute's walk from the last stop on Tokyo's Ginza subway line; there are additional trains on weekends, holidays, and in high season. The one-way fare is ¥2,620. All seats are reserved. Bookings are not accepted over the phone; they can only be bought at Asakusa Station. During summer, fall, and weekends, buy tickets a few days in advance. The trip from Asakusa to the Tobu Nikko Station takes about two hours, which is quicker than the JR trains. If you're visiting Nikko on a day trip, note that the last return train is at 7:43 pm, requiring a quick and easy change at Shimo-Imaichi, and arrives at Asakusa at 9:35 pm. If you have a JR Pass, use JR (Japan Railways) service, which connects Tokyo and Nikko, from Ueno Station. Take the Tohoku–Honsen Line limited express to Utsunomiya (about 1½ hours) and transfer to the train for JR Nikko Station (45 minutes). The earliest departure from Ueno is at 5:10 am; the last connection back leaves Nikko at 8:03 pm and brings you into Ueno at 10:48 pm. (If you're not using the JR Pass, the one-way fare will cost ¥2,520.)

More expensive but faster is the Yamabiko train on the north extension of the Shinkansen; the one-way fare, including the surcharge for the express, is ¥4,920. The first one leaves Tokyo Station at 6:04 am (or Ueno at 6:10 am) and takes about 50 minutes to Utsunomiya; change there to the train to Nikko Station. To return, take the 9:46 pm train from Nikko to Utsunomiya and catch the last Yamabiko back at 10:37 pm.

VISITOR INFORMATION

You can do a lot of preplanning for your visit to Nikko with a stop at the Japan National Tourist Organization office in Tokyo, where the helpful English-speaking staff will ply you with pamphlets and field your questions about things to see and do. Closer to the source is the Tourist Information and Hospitality Center in Nikko itself, about halfway up the main street of town between the railway stations and Tosho-gu, on the left; don't expect too much in the way of help in English, but the center does have a good array of guides to local restaurants and shops, registers of inns and hotels, and mapped-out walking tours.

ESSENTIALS

Tourist Information Nikko Tourist Information and Hospitality Center (☎ 0288/54–2496).

Tours JTB Sunrise Tours (☎ 03/5796–5454 ⊕ www.jtbusa.com).

Train Contact Japan Railways (☎ 03/3423–0111 ⊕ www.japanrail.com).

> ## THE UBIQUITOUS TORII
>
> Wondering what those gatelike structures are with two posts and two crosspieces? They are torii and are used as gateways to Japanese Shinto temples.

EXPLORING

The town of Nikko is essentially one long avenue—Sugi Namiki (Cryptomeria Avenue)—extending for about 2 km (1 mi) from the railway stations to Tosho-gu. You can easily walk to most places within town. Tourist inns and shops line the street, and if you have time, you might want to make this a leisurely stroll. The antiques shops along the way may turn up interesting—but expensive—pieces like armor fittings, hibachi, pottery, and dolls. The souvenir shops here sell ample selections of local wood carvings.

TOSHO-GU 東照宮

The Tosho-gu area encompasses three UNESCO World Heritage sights—Tosho-gu Shrine, Futarasan Shrine, and Rinnoji Temple. These are known as *nisha-ichiji* (two shrines and one temple) and are Nikko's main draw. Signs and maps clearly mark a recommended route that will allow you to see all the major sights, which are within walking distance of each other. You should plan for half a day to explore the area.

A multiple-entry ticket is the best way to see the Tosho-gu precincts. The ¥1,000 pass gets you entrance to Rinno-ji (Rinno Temple), the Taiyu-in Mausoleum, and Futara-san Jinja (Futara-san Shrine); for an extra ¥300 you can also see the Sleeping Cat and Ieyasu's tomb at Taiyu-in (separate fees are charged for admission to other sights). There are two places to purchase the multiple-entry ticket: one is at the entrance to Rinno Temple, in the corner of the parking lot, at the top of the path called the Higashi-sando (East Approach) that begins across the highway from the Sacred Bridge; the other is at the entrance to Tosho-gu, at the top of the broad Omote-sando (Central Approach), which begins about 100 yards farther west.

TOP ATTRACTIONS

★ **Futara-san Jinja** 二荒山神社 *(Futara-san Shrine)*. Nikko's holy ground is far older than the Tokugawa dynasty, in whose honor it was improved upon. Futara-san is sacred to the Shinto deities Okuni-nushi-no-Mikoto (god of the rice fields, bestower of prosperity), his consort Tagorihime-no-Mikoto, and their son Ajisukitaka-hikone-no-Mikoto. Futara-san actually has three locations: the Main Shrine at Tosho-gu; the Chugu-shi (Middle Shrine), at Chuzenji-ko; and the Okumiya (Inner Shrine), on top of Mt. Nantai.

7

Ieyasu's Legacy

In 1600, Ieyasu Tokugawa (1543–1616) won a battle at a place in the mountains of south-central Japan called Seki-ga-hara that left him the undisputed ruler of the archipelago. He died 16 years later, but the Tokugawa Shogunate would last another 252 years.

The founder of such a dynasty required a fitting resting place. Ieyasu (ee-eh-*ya*-su) had provided for one in his will: a mausoleum at Nikko, in a forest of tall cedars, where a religious center had been founded more than eight centuries earlier. The year after his death, in accordance with Buddhist custom, he was given a *kaimyo*—an honorific name to bear in the afterlife. Thenceforth, he was Tosho-Daigongen: the Great Incarnation Who Illuminates the East. The imperial court at Kyoto declared him a god, and his remains were taken in a procession of great pomp and ceremony to be enshrined at Nikko.

The dynasty he left behind was enormously rich. Ieyasu's personal fief, on the Kanto Plain, was worth 2.5 million *koku* of rice. One koku, in monetary terms, was equivalent to the cost of keeping one retainer in the necessities of life for a year. The shogunate itself, however, was still an uncertainty. It had only recently taken control after more than a century of civil war. The founder's tomb had a political purpose: to inspire awe and to make manifest the power of the Tokugawas. It was Ieyasu's legacy, a statement of his family's right to rule.

Tosho-gu was built by his grandson, the third shogun, Iemitsu (it was Iemitsu who established the policy of national isolation, which closed the doors of Japan to the outside world for more than 200 years). The mausoleum and shrine required the labor of 15,000 people for two years (1634–36). Craftsmen and artists of the first rank were assembled from all over the country. Every surface was carved and painted and lacquered in the most intricate detail imaginable. Tosho-gu shimmers with the reflections of 2,489,000 sheets of gold leaf. Roof beams and rafter ends with dragon heads, lions, and elephants in bas-relief; friezes of phoenixes, wild ducks, and monkeys; inlaid pillars and red-lacquer corridors: Tosho-gu is everything a 17th-century warlord would consider gorgeous, and the inspiration is very Chinese.

The bronze torii at the entrance to the shrine leads to the **Chinese Gate** (Kara-mon), gilded and elaborately carved; beyond it is the **Hai-den**, the shrine's oratory. The Hai-den, too, is richly carved and decorated, with a dragon-covered ceiling. The Chinese lions on the panels at the rear are by two distinguished painters of the Kano school. From the oratory of the Taiyu-in a connecting passage leads to the **Sanctum** (Hon-den)—the present version of which dates from 1619. Designated a National Treasure, it houses a gilded and lacquered Buddhist altar some 9 feet high, decorated with paintings of animals, birds, and flowers, in which resides the object of all this veneration: a seated wooden figure of Iemitsu himself. ⊠ *Take the avenue to the left as you're standing before the stone torii at Tosho-gu and follow it to the end* ⌨ ¥200,

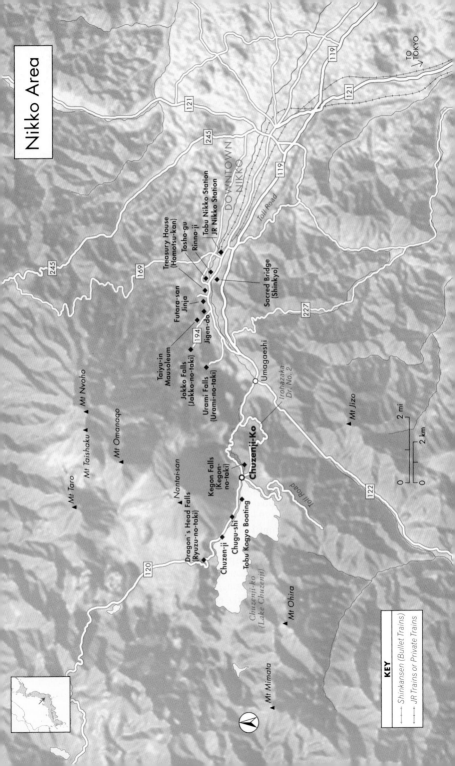

Nikko Area

TO TOKYO

119

121

121

119

245

DOWNTOWN NIKKO

Toll Road

Treasury House
(Homotsu-kan)
Tosho-gu
Rinno-ji
Tobu Nikko Station
JR Nikko Station

169

Futara-san
Jinja

Sacred Bridge
(Shinkyo)

227

194

Jigen-do

Taiyu-in
Mausoleum

Jakko Falls
(Jakko-no-taki)

Urami Falls
(Urami-no-taki)

245

Umagaeshi

Irohazaka
Dr. No. 2

Mt Jizo

Mt Nyoho

Mt Taishaku

Mt Omanago

Mt Taro

Nantai-san

Chuzenji-Ko

Kegon Falls
(Kegon-no-taki)

Chuzenji-ko
(Lake Chuzenji)

Tobu Kogyo Boating

Chugu-shi

Chuzen-ji

Dragon's Head Falls
(Ryuzu-no-taki)

120

Toll Road

122

Mt Ohira

Mt Mimata

2 mi

2 km

0

0

The gold-leaf detailing at Rinno Ji complements the gold on the three famed Buddhas in Sanbutsudoh Hall.

¥1,000 multiple-entry ticket includes admission to Rinno Temple and Taiyu-in Mausoleum ⏱ Apr.–Oct., daily 8–5; Nov.–Mar., daily 9–4.

★ **Rinno-ji** 輪王寺 *(Rinno Temple)*. This temple belongs to the Tendai sect of Buddhism, the head temple of which is Enryaku-ji, on Mt. Hiei near Kyoto. The main hall of Rinno Temple, called the **Sanbutsu-do,** is the largest single building at Tosho-gu; it enshrines an image of Amida Nyorai, the Buddha of the Western Paradise, flanked on the right by Senju (Thousand-Armed) Kannon, the goddess of mercy, and on the left by Bato-Kannon, regarded as the protector of animals. These three images are lacquered in gold and date from the early part of the 17th century. The original Sanbutsu-do is said to have been built in 848 by the priest Ennin (794–864), also known as Jikaku-Daishi. The present building dates from 1648.

In the southwest corner of the Rinno Temple compound, behind the abbot's residence, is an especially fine Japanese garden called **Shoyo-en,** created in 1815 and thoughtfully designed to present a different perspective of its rocks, ponds, and flowering plants from every turn on its path. To the right of the entrance to the garden is the **Treasure Hall** (Homotsu-den) of Rinno Temple, a museum with a collection of some 6,000 works of lacquerware, painting, and Buddhist sculpture. The museum is rather small, and only a few of the pieces in the collection— many of them designated National Treasures and Important Cultural Properties—are on display at any given time. ⊠ *2300 Yamauchi, Nikko* 🎫 *Rinno Temple ¥1,000, multiple-entry ticket includes admission to the Taiyu-in Mausoleum and Futara-san Shrine; Shoyo-en and Treasure*

Hall ¥400 ◷ Apr.–Oct., daily 8–5, last entry at 4; Nov.–Mar., daily 8–4, last entry at 3.

★ **Taiyu-in Mausoleum** 大猷院廟. This grandiose building is the resting place of the third Tokugawa shogun, Iemitsu (1604–51), who imposed a policy of national isolation on Japan that was to last more than 200 years. Iemitsu, one suspects, had it in mind to upstage his illustrious grandfather; he marked the approach to his own tomb with no fewer than six different decorative gates. The first is another Nio-mon—a Gate of the Deva Kings—like the one at Tosho-gu. The dragon painted on the ceiling

is by Yasunobu Kano. A flight of stone steps leads from here to the second gate, the Niten-mon, a two-story structure protected front and back by carved and painted images of guardian gods. Beyond it, two more flights of steps lead to the middle courtyard. As you climb the last steps to Iemitsu's shrine, you'll pass a bell tower on the right and a drum tower on the left; directly ahead is the third gate, the remarkable **Yasha-mon**, so named for the figures of *yasha* (she-demons) in the four niches. This structure is also known as the Peony Gate (Botan-mon) for the carvings that decorate it.

As you exit the shrine, on the west side, you come to the fifth gate: the **Koka-mon,** built in the style of the late Ming dynasty of China. The gate is normally closed, but from here another flight of stone steps leads to the sixth and last gate—the cast copper **Inuki-mon,** inscribed with characters in Sanskrit—and Iemitsu's tomb. ✉ 2300 Sannai, Nikko 🎫 ¥1,000 multiple-entry ticket includes admission to Rinno Temple and Futara-san Shrine ◷ Apr.–Oct., daily 8–5; Nov.–Mar., daily 8–4.

Fodor'sChoice **Tosho-gu** 東照宮. With its riot of colors and carvings, inlaid pillars,
★ red-lacquer corridors, and extensive use of gold leaf, this 17th-century shrine to Ieyasu Tokugawa is magnificent, astonishing, and never dull.

The west gate of Rinno Temple brings you to Omote-sando, which leads uphill to the stone torii of the shrine. The **Five-Story Pagoda** of Tosho-gu—a reconstruction dating from 1818—is on the left as you approach the shrine. The 12 signs of the zodiac decorate the first story. The black-lacquer doors above each sign bear the three hollyhock leaves of the Tokugawa family crest.

From the torii a flight of stone steps brings you to the front gate of the shrine—the Omote-mon, also called the Nio-mon (Gate of the Deva Kings), with its fearsome pair of red-painted guardian gods. From here the path turns to the left. In the first group of buildings you reach on the left is the **Sacred Stable** (Shinkyu). Housed here is the white horse—symbol of purity—that figures in many of the shrine's ceremonial events.

Tosho-gu honors Ieyasu Tokugawa, the first Shogun and founder of Tokyo.

Carvings of pine trees and monkeys adorn the panels over the stable. And where the path turns to the right, you'll find a granite font where visitors can purify themselves before entering the inner precincts of Tosho-gu. The **Sutra Library** (Rinzo), just beyond the font, is a repository for some 7,000 Buddhist scriptures, kept in a huge revolving bookcase nearly 20 feet high; it's not open to the public.

As you pass under the second (bronze) torii and up the steps, you'll see a belfry and a tall bronze candelabrum on the right and a drum tower and a bronze revolving lantern on the left. The two works in bronze were presented to the shrine by the Dutch government in the mid-17th century. Behind the drum tower is the **Yakushi-do,** which enshrines a manifestation of the Buddha as Yakushi Nyorai, the healer of illnesses. The original 17th-century building was famous for a huge India-ink painting on the ceiling of the nave, *The Roaring Dragon,* so named for the rumbling echoes it seemed to emit when visitors clapped their hands beneath it. The painting was by Yasunobu Enshin Kano (1613–85), from a family of artists that dominated the profession for 400 years. The Kano school was founded in the late 15th century and patronized by successive military governments until the fall of the Tokugawa Shogunate in 1868. The Yakushi-do was destroyed by fire in 1961, then rebuilt; the dragon on the ceiling now is by Nampu Katayama (1887–1980).

The centerpiece of Tosho-gu is the **Gate of Sunlight** (Yomei-mon), at the top of the second flight of stone steps. A designated National Treasure, it's also called the Twilight Gate (Higurashi-mon)—implying that you could gape at its richness of detail all day, until sunset. And rich it is indeed: 36 feet high and dazzling white, the gate has 12 columns, beams, and roof brackets carved with dragons, lions, clouds, peonies, Chinese sages, and demigods, painted vivid hues of red, blue, green, and gold. On one of the central columns, there are two carved tigers; the natural grain of the wood is used to bring out the "fur." As you enter the Yomei-mon, there are galleries running east and west for some 700 feet; their paneled fences are also carved and painted with nature motifs.

The portable shrines that appear in the Tosho-gu Festival, held yearly on May 17–18, are kept in the **Shinyo-sha,** a storeroom to the left as you come through the Twilight Gate into the heart of the shrine. The paintings on the ceiling, of *tennin* (Buddhist angels) playing harps, are by Tan-yu Kano (1602–74).

Mere mortals may not pass through the **Chinese Gate** (Kara-mon), which is the "official" entrance to the Tosho-gu inner shrine. Like its counterpart, the Yomei-mon, on the opposite side of the courtyard, the Kara-mon is a National Treasure—and, like the Yomei-mon, is carved and painted in elaborate detail with dragons and other auspicious figures. The Main Hall of Tosho-gu is enclosed by a wall of painted and carved panel screens; opposite the right-hand corner of the wall, facing the shrine, is the **Kito-den,** a hall where annual prayers were once offered for the peace of the nation. For a very modest fee, Japanese couples can be married here in a traditional Shinto ceremony, with an ensemble of drums and reed flutes and shrine maidens to attend them.

The **Main Hall** (Hon-den) of Tosho-gu is the ultimate purpose of the shrine. You approach it from the rows of lockers at the far end of the enclosure; here you remove and store your shoes, step up into the shrine, and follow a winding corridor to the Oratory (Hai-den)—the anteroom, resplendent in its lacquered pillars, carved friezes, and coffered ceilings bedecked with dragons. Over the lintels are paintings by Mitsuoki Tosa (1617–91) of the 36 great poets of the Heian period, with their poems in the calligraphy of Emperor Go-Mizuno-o. Deeper yet, at the back of the Oratory, is the Inner Chamber (Nai-jin)—repository of the Sacred Mirror that represents the spirit of the deity enshrined here. To the right is a room that was reserved for members of the three principal branches of the Tokugawa family; the room on the left was for the chief abbot of Rinno Temple, who was always chosen from the imperial line.

Behind the Inner Chamber is the Innermost Chamber (Nai-Nai-jin). No visitors come this far. Here, in the very heart of Tosho-gu, is the gold-lacquer shrine where the spirit of Ieyasu resides—along with two other deities, whom the Tokugawas later decided were fit companions. One was Hideyoshi Toyotomi, Ieyasu's mentor and liege lord in the long wars of unification at the end of the 16th century. The other was Minamoto no Yoritomo, brilliant military tactician and founder of the earlier (12th-century) Kamakura Shogunate (Ieyasu claimed Yoritomo for an ancestor).

■TIP→ Don't forget to recover your shoes when you return to the courtyard. Between the Goma-do and the **Kagura-den** (a hall where ceremonial dances are performed to honor the gods) is a passage to the **Gate at the Foot of the Hill** (Sakashita-mon). Above the gateway is another famous symbol of Tosho-gu, the Sleeping Cat—a small panel said to have been carved by Hidari Jingoro (Jingoro the Left-handed), a late-16th-century master carpenter and sculptor credited with important contributions to numerous Tokugawa-period temples, shrines, and palaces. A separate admission charge (¥520) is levied to go beyond the Sleeping Cat, up the flight of 200 stone steps through a forest of cryptomeria to **Ieyasu's tomb.** The climb is worth it for the view of the Yomei-mon and Kara-mon from above; the tomb itself is unimpressive. ✉ *Sannai, Nikko* 🖼 *Free, Ieyasu's tomb ¥520* ☉ *Apr.–Oct., daily 9–5; Nov.–Mar., daily 9–4.*

THREE LITTLE MONKEYS

While in the Sacred Stable, make sure to look at the second panel from the left. The three monkeys, commonly known as "Hear no evil, Speak no evil, See no evil," have become something of a Nikko trademark; the image has been reproduced on plaques, bags, and souvenirs. While the phrase's true origins are uncertain, scholars and legend suggest it originated from this shrine as a visual interpretation of the religious phrase, "If we do not hear, see, or speak evil, we ourselves shall be spared all evil." As for the monkeys, it's been said that a Chinese Buddhist monk introduced the image to Japan in the 8th century.

OFF THE BEATEN PATH

Located on the northern shore of peaceful Yunoko (Lake Yuno), these isolated hot springs were once a popular destination for 14th-century aristocrats. Today, the area is still known for its hot springs—being able to soak in an *onsen* (hot springs) all year long, even when temperatures drop below zero, will always be a major plus—but they are now controlled by separate resorts. Besides the healing and relaxing effects of the baths, visitors come for the hiking trails, fishing, camping, skiing, bird-watching, and mountain-climbing opportunities. ■TIP→ Try to avoid the fall season, as it's peak visitor time and there are always delays. You can get to the Yumoto onsen by taking the Tobu Operated Buses, which leave Tobu Nikko and JR Nikko stations. There are one or two services an hour depending on the time of the day. A one-way trip from central Nikko takes about 80 minutes and costs ¥1,650.

WORTH NOTING

☙ **Edo Wonderland** 日光江戸村 *(Nikko Edo Mura)*, a living-history theme park a short taxi ride from downtown, re-creates an 18th-century Japanese village. The complex includes sculpted gardens with waterfalls and ponds and 22 vintage buildings, where actors in traditional dress stage martial arts exhibitions, historical theatrical performances, and

The three monkeys, who "see no evil, speak no evil, hear no evil," perch on the paneling of Tosho-gu's Sacred Stable.

comedy acts. You can even observe Japanese tea ceremony rituals in gorgeous tatami-floor houses, as well as people dressed as geisha and samurai. Strolling stuffed animal characters and acrobatic ninjas keep kids happy. Nikko Edo Mura has one large restaurant and 15 small food stalls serving period cuisine like *yakisoba* (fried soba) and *dango* (dumplings). ✉ *470–20 Karakura, Nikko* ☎ *0288/77–1777* 🎫 *¥4,500 unlimited day pass includes rides and shows* 🕐 *Mid-Mar.–Nov., daily 9–5; Dec.–mid-Mar., daily 9:30–4.*

Jigen-do 慈眼堂. Tenkai (1536–1643), the first abbot of Rinno Temple, has his own place of honor at Tosho-gu: the Jigen-do. The hall, which was founded in 848, now holds many of Rinno Temple's artistic treasures. To reach it, take the path opposite the south entrance to Futara-san Shrine that passes between the two subtemples called Jogyo-do and Hokke-do. Connected by a corridor, these two buildings are otherwise known as the Futatsu-do (Twin Halls) of Rinno Temple and are designated a National Cultural Property. The path between the Twin Halls leads roughly south and west to the Jigen-do compound; the hall itself is at the north end of the compound, to the right. At the west end sits the Go-oden, a shrine to Prince Yoshihisa Kitashirakawa (1847–95), the last of the imperial princes to serve as abbot. Behind it are his tomb and the tombs of his 13 predecessors. ✉ *2300 Sannai, Nikko* 🎫 *Free* 🕐 *Apr.–Nov., daily 8–5; Dec.–Mar., daily 9–4.*

Monument to Masasuna Matsudaira 松平正綱の杉並木寄進碑. Opposite the Sacred Bridge, at the east entrance to the grounds of Tosho-gu, this monument pays tribute to one of the two feudal lords charged with the construction of Tosho-gu. Matsudaira's great contribution was the planting of the wonderful cryptomeria trees (Japanese cedars) surrounding the shrine and along all the approaches to it. The project took 20 years, from 1628 to 1648, and the result was some 36 km (22 mi) of cedar-lined avenues—planted with more than 15,000 trees in all. Fire and time have taken their toll, but thousands of these trees still stand in the shrine precincts, creating a setting of solemn majesty the buildings alone could never have achieved. Thousands more line Route 119 east of Nikko on the way to Shimo-Imaichi. ⊠ *Moritomo, Nikko.*

Sacred Bridge 神橋 *(Shinkyo).* Built in 1636 for shoguns and imperial messengers visiting the shrine, the original bridge was destroyed in a flood; the present red-lacquer wooden structure dates to 1907. Buses leaving from either railway station at Nikko go straight up the main street to the bridge, opposite the first of the main entrances to Tosho-gu. Open again after a year of renovation, the bridge is free to cross, but closes at 4 or 5 pm, depending on the season. The Sacred Bridge is just to the left of a modern bridge, where the road curves and crosses the Daiya-gawa (Daiya River). ⊠ *2307 Sannai, Nikko* 🕾 *¥500* 🕙 *Apr.– Oct., daily 9–5; Nov.–Mar., daily 9–4.*

Treasury House 宝物館 *(Homotsu-kan).* An unhurried visit to the precincts of Tosho-gu should definitely include the Treasury house as it contains a collection of antiquities from its various shrines and temples. From the west gate of Rinno Temple, turn left off Omote-sando, just below the pagoda, onto the cedar-lined avenue to Futara-san Jinja. A minute's walk will bring you to the museum, on the left. ⊠ *2280 Sannai, Nikko* 🕾 *0288/54–2558* 🕾 *¥500* 🕙 *Apr.–Oct., daily 9–5; Nov.–Mar., daily 9–4.*

CHUZENJI-KO 中禅寺湖

More than 3,900 feet above sea level, at the base of the volcano known as Nantai-san, is Chuzenji-ko (Lake Chuzenji), renowned for its clean waters and fresh air. People come to boat and fish on the lake and to enjoy the surrounding scenic woodlands, waterfalls, and hills.

TOP ATTRACTIONS

Fodor's Choice
★

Kegon Falls 華厳滝 *(Kegon-no-taki).* More than anything else, the country's most famous falls are what draw the crowds of Japanese visitors to Chuzenji. Fed by the eastward flow of the lake, the falls drop 318 feet into a rugged gorge; an elevator (¥530) takes you to an observation platform at the bottom. The volume of water over the falls is carefully regulated, but it's especially impressive after a summer rain or a typhoon. In winter the falls do not freeze completely but form a beautiful cascade of icicles. The elevator is just a few minutes' walk east from the bus stop at Chuzenji village, downhill and off to the right at the far end of the parking lot. ⊠ *2479–2 Chugushi, Nikko* 🕾 *0288/55–0030* 🕙 *Daily 8–5.*

NEED A BREAK?

Take a breather at the **Ryuzu-no-taki Chaya** (⊠ *2485 Chugushi, Nikko* 🕾 *0288/55–0157* 🕙 *Daily 11–5*), a charming, but rustic, tea shop near the waterfalls. Enjoy a cup of green tea, a light meal, or Japanese sweets like rice cakes boiled with vegetables and dango (sweet dumplings) while you gaze at the falling waters.

DID YOU KNOW?

The 97-meter-high Kegon Falls draws visitors from all over Japan and the world. The spectacular sight near Lake Chuzenji Lake is also home to 12 other waterfalls. Behind and next to Kegon, these falls drip out of cracks in the volcano, Nantai-san. Try to spot a few of them once you've taken in Kegon's grandeur.

Urami Falls 裏見滝 *(Urami-no-taki)*. "The water," wrote the great 17th-century poet Basho, "seemed to take a flying leap and drop a hundred feet from the top of a cave into a green pool surrounded by a thousand rocks. One was supposed to inch one's way into the cave and enjoy the falls from behind." ■TIP→ The falls and the gorge are striking—but you should make the climb only if you have good hiking shoes and are willing to get wet in the process. ⊠ *The steep climb to the cave begins at the Arasawa bus stop, with a turn to the right off the Chuzenji road.*

Tobu Kogyo Boating. Explore Lake Chuzenji on chartered 60-minute boat rides. ⊠ *2478 Chugushi, Nikko, Tochigi-ken* ☎ *0288/55–0360* ☎ *¥150–¥1,500 depending on route chosen* ⊙ *Dec.–Mar., daily 9:30–3:30.*

WORTH NOTING

Chugu-shi 中宮祠. A subshrine of the Futara-san Shrine at Tosho-gu, this is the major religious center on the north side of Lake Chuzenji, about 1½ km (1 mi) west of the village. The **Treasure House** (Homotsu-den) contains an interesting historical collection, including swords, lacquer-ware, and medieval shrine palanquins. ⊠ *Shrine free, Treasure House ¥300* ⊙ *Apr.–Oct., daily 8–5; Nov.–Mar., daily 9–4.*

Chuzen-ji 中禅寺 *(Chuzen Temple)*. A subtemple of Rinno Temple, at Tosho-gu, the principal object of worship here is the **Tachi-ki Kannon,** a 17-foot-tall standing statue of the Buddhist goddess of mercy, said to have been carved more than 1,000 years ago by the priest Shodo from the living trunk of a single Judas tree. The bus trip from Nikko to the national park area ends at Chuzenji village, which shares its name with the temple established here in 784. ⊠ *Turn left (south) as you leave the village of Chuzenji and walk about 1½ km (1 mi) along the eastern shore of the lake* ☎ *¥500* ⊙ *Apr.–Oct., daily 8–5; Mar. and Nov., daily 8–4; Dec.–Feb., daily 8–3:30.*

Dragon's Head Falls 竜頭滝 *(Ryuzu-no-taki)*. If you've budgeted an extra day for Nikko, you might want to consider a walk around the lake. A paved road along the north shore extends for about 8 km (5 mi), one-third of the whole distance, as far as the "beach" at Shobu-ga-hama. Here, where the road branches off to the north for Senjogahara, are the lovely cascades of Dragon's Head Falls. To the left is a steep footpath that continues around the lake to Senju-ga-hama and then to a campsite at Asegata. The path is well marked but can get rough in places. From Asegata it's less than an hour's walk back to Chuzenji village.

Jakko Falls 寂光滝 *(Jakko-no-taki)*. Falling water is one of the special charms of the Nikko National Park area; people going by bus or car from Tosho-gu to Lake Chuzenji often stop off en route to see these falls, which descend in a series of seven terraced stages, forming a sheet of water about 100 feet high. About 1 km (½ mi) from the shrine precincts, at the Tamozawa bus stop, a narrow road to the right leads to an uphill walk of some 3 km (2 mi) to the falls.

Umagaeshi 馬返し. In the old days, the road became too rough for horse riding, so riders had to alight and proceed on foot; the lake is 4,165 feet above sea level. From Umagaeshi the bus climbs a one-way toll road up the pass; the old road has been widened and is used for the traffic coming down. The two roads are full of steep hairpin turns, and on a clear day the view up and down the valley is magnificent—especially from the halfway point at **Akechi-daira** (Akechi Plain), from which you can see the summit of **Nantai-san** (Mt. Nantai), reaching 8,149 feet. Hiking season lasts from May through mid-October; if you push it, you can make the ascent in about four hours. ⚠ Wild monkeys make their homes in these mountains, and they've learned the convenience of mooching from visitors along the route. Be careful—they have a way of not taking no for an answer. Do not give in to the temptation to give them food—they will never leave you alone if you do. ⊠ *About 10 km (6 mi) from Tobu Station in Nikko, or 8 km (5 mi) from Tosho-gu.*

> **FEELING ADVENTUROUS?**
>
> If you want to avoid the hairpin turns, try the **ropeway** that runs from Akechi-daira Station directly to the Akechi-daira lookout. It takes three minutes and the panoramic views of Nikko and Kegon Falls are priceless. ⊠ *709–5 Misawa, Hosoo-machi, Nikko* ☎ *0288/55–0331* 🖃 *¥390* ⊘ *Apr.–Oct., daily 8:30–4; Nov.–Mar., daily 9–3.*

WHERE TO EAT

LAKE CHUZENJI

$$$
JAPANESE
✕ **Nantai** なんたい. The low tables, antiques, and pillows scattered on tatami flooring make visitors feel like they're dining in a traditional Japanese living room. Try the Nikko specialty, *yuba* (tofu skin), which comes with the *nabe* (hot pot) for dinner. It's the quintessential winter family meal. The seafood here is fresh and both the trout and salmon are recommended. Each meal comes with rice, pickles, and selected side dishes like soy-stewed vegetables, tempura, udon, and a dessert. ⊠ *2478–8 Chugushi, Nikko* ☎ *0288/55–0201.*

DOWNTOWN NIKKO

$$$$
FRENCH
✕ **Fujimoto** ふじもと. At what may be Nikko's most formal Western-style restaurant, finer touches include plush carpets, art deco fixtures, stained and frosted glass, a thoughtful wine list, and a maître d' in black tie. The menu combines elements of French and Japanese cooking styles and ingredients; the fillet of beef in mustard sauce is particularly excellent. Fujimoto closes at 7:30, so plan on eating early. ⊠ *2339–1 Sannai, Nikko* ☎ *0288/53–3754* ⊘ *Closed Thurs.*

$$$$
JAPANESE
✕ **Gyoshintei** 尭心亭. This is the only restaurant in Nikko devoted to *shojin ryori*, the Buddhist-temple vegetarian fare that evolved centuries ago into haute cuisine. Gyoshintei is decorated in the style of a *ryotei* (traditional inn), with all-tatami seating. It differs from a ryotei in that it has one large, open space where many guests are served at once, rather than a number of rooms for private dining. Dinner is served until 7. ⊠ *2339–1 Sannai, Nikko* ☎ *0288/53–3751* ⊘ *Closed Thurs.*

$$$$
KAISEKI
✕ **Masudaya** ゆば亭ますだや. Masudaya started out as a sake maker more than a century ago, but for four generations now, it has been the town's best-known restaurant. The specialty is yuba, which the chefs transform, with the help of local vegetables and fresh fish, into sumptuous high cuisine. The building is traditional, with a lovely interior

7

garden; the assembly-line-style service, however, detracts from the ambience. Masudaya serves a nine-course *kaiseki*-style meal at table seating for ¥3,990, and an 11-course meal at tatami seating for ¥5,450. Meals here are prix fixe. ☒ *439–2 Ishiya-machi, Nikko* ☎ *0288/54–2151* ⌂ *Reservations essential* ▭ *No credit cards* ⊘ *Closed Thurs. No dinner.*

$$$$
CONTINENTAL

✗ **Meiji-no-Yakata** 明治の館. Not far from the east entrance to Rinno Temple, Meiji-no-Yakata is an elegant 19th-century Western-style stone house, originally built as a summer retreat for an American diplomat. The food, too, is Western style; specialties of the house include fresh rainbow trout from Lake Chuzenji, roast lamb with pepper sauce, and melt-in-your-mouth filet mignon made from local Tochigi beef. High ceilings, hardwood floors, and an air of informality make this a very pleasant place to dine. The restaurant opens at 11 am in summer and 11:30 am in winter; it always closes at 7:30. ☒ *2339–1 Sannai, Nikko* ☎ *0288/53–3751* ⊘ *Closed Wed.*

$$$
JAPANESE

✗ **Sawamoto** 澤本. Charcoal-broiled *unagi* (eel) is an acquired taste, and there's no better place in Nikko to acquire it than at this restaurant. The place is small and unpretentious, with only five plain-wood tables, and service can be lukewarm, but Sawamoto is reliable for a light lunch or dinner of unagi on a bed of rice, served in an elegant lacquered box. Eel is considered a stamina builder: just right for the weary visitor on a hot summer day. ☒ *1019 Bandu, Kami Hatsuishi-machi, Nikko* ☎ *0288/54–0163* ▭ *No credit cards* ⊘ *No dinner.*

WHERE TO STAY

Hotel reviews have been abbreviated in this book. For expanded reviews, please go to Fodors.com.

LAKE CHUZENJI

$$$$
HOTEL

▣ **Chuzenji Kanaya** 中禅寺金谷ホテル. A boathouse and restaurant on the lake give this branch of the Nikko Kanaya on the road from the village to Shobu-ga-hama the air of a private yacht club. **Pros:** clean; Western-style rooms. **Cons:** the most expensive hotel in the area. ☒ *2482 Chu-gushi, Chuzen-ji, Nikko* ☎ *0288/51–0001* ⊕ *www.kanayahotel. co.jp/english/chuzenji/index.html* ⤶ *60 rooms, 54 with bath* ⌂ *In-hotel: restaurant* ⦿ *Some meals.*

$$–$$$
HOTEL

▣ **Nikko Lakeside Hotel** 日光レイクサイドホテル. In the village of Chuzenji at the foot of the lake, the Nikko Lakeside has no particular character, but the views are good and the transportation connections (to buses and excursion boats) are ideal. **Pros:** close to the lake and hot spring baths. **Cons:** room decor is a bit dated. ☒ *2482 Chu-gushi, Chuzen-ji, Nikko* ☎ *0288/55–0321* ⤶ *100 rooms with bath* ⌂ *In-hotel: 2 restaurants, bar, tennis court, bicycles* ⦿ *Some meals.*

DOWNTOWN NIKKO

$$$–$$$$
HOTEL
★

▣ **Nikko Kanaya Hotel** 日光金谷ホテル. This family-run operation is a little worn around the edges after a century of operation, but it still has the best location in town: across the street from Tosho-gu. ros: spacious; well-appointed. **Cons:** rooms are rather pricey. ☒ *1300 Kami Hatsuishi-machi, Nikko* ☎ *0288/54–0001* ⊕ *www.kanayahotel.co.jp/*

KUSATSU ONSEN

For an authentic Japanese experience and a bit of relaxation, head to the onsen of Kusatsu. Half a dozen hot springs dot the area. If you are traveling to Kusatsu from Nikko, you will need to backtrack to JR Omiya Station, where you can take the Kusatsu #3 Express to Naganohara-Kusatsuguchi Station (2 hours, ¥3,820). If you are coming from Tokyo, take the JR Kusatsu Limited Express from Ueno Station to Naganohara-Kusatsuguchi Station (2 hours, ¥4,620). From Naganohara-Kusatsuguchi Station take the JR bus to Kusatsu Onsen Bus Terminal (30 min, ¥1,000).

Kusatsu Onsen Center

草津温泉館. This onsen, surrounded by a wooded area, offers six different types of indoor and outdoor baths, including one in a cave, as well as steam baths. ✉ 464–35 Kusatasu, Kusatsu-cho, Azuma-gun ☎ 02/7988-2500 💰 ¥800 ⏱ Daily 10:30–7.

★ **Otaki no Yu** 大滝乃湯. Otaki no Yu is one of the biggest and most popular of the Kusatsu onsen. A wase-yu, one of the indoor bathing options, is comprised of three separate tubs of gradually increasing temperature, allowing your body to acclimate to the hottest temperature. Outside there is an enormous wooden bath that accommodates 1,000 (swim-suited) bathers. ✉ 596–13 Kusatasu, Kusatsu-machi, Azumagu ☎ 02/7988-2600 ⊕ www.kusatsu-onsen.ne.jp 💰 ¥800 ⏱ Daily 9–9.

Sai No Kawara Outdoor Bath

西の河原露天風呂. Sai No Kawara has giant outdoor baths, separated for men and women. The water creates a current—walk against the waves for a natural massage. The water temperature also varies from place to place, so if the water is too hot or cool for you, simply rove to another area. ✉ 521–3 Kusatsu, Kusatsu-cho , Azuma-gun ☎ 02/7988-6167 💰 ¥500 ⏱ Apr.–Nov., daily 7 am–8 pm; Dec.–Mar., daily 9–8.

english/nikko/index.html ⟿ 77 rooms, 62 with bath ♿ In-hotel: 2 restaurants, bar, pool ❙❀❙ Some meals.

HOTEL ¢ 🛏 **Turtle Inn Nikko** タートルイン日光. This Japanese Inn Group member provides friendly, modest, cost-conscious Western- and Japanese-style accommodations with or without a private bath. **Pros:** cozy atmosphere; English-speaking staff, Japanese bath available. **Cons:** rooms are a bit on the small side. ✉ 2–16 Takumi-cho, Nikko ☎ 0288/53–3168 ⟿ 7 Western-style rooms, 3 with bath; 5 Japanese-style rooms without bath ⊕ www.turtle-nikko.com ♿ In-room: Internet. In-hotel: restaurant ❙❀❙ Some meals.

KAMAKURA 鎌倉

Kamakura, about 40 km (25 mi) southwest of Tokyo, is an object lesson in what happens when you set the fox to guard the henhouse.

For the aristocrats of the Heian-era Japan (794–1185), life was defined by the imperial court in Kyoto. Who in their right mind would venture elsewhere? In Kyoto there was grace and beauty and poignant affairs of the heart; everything beyond was howling wilderness. Unfortunately, it was the howling wilderness that had all the estates: the large grants of land, called *shoen*, without which there would be no income to pay for all that grace and beauty.

By the 12th century two clans—the Taira (*ta*-ee-ra) and the Minamoto, themselves both offshoots of the imperial line—had come to dominate the affairs of the Heian court and were at each other's throats in a struggle for supremacy. In 1160 the Taira won a major battle that should have secured their absolute control over Japan, but in the process they made one serious mistake: having killed the Minamoto leader Yoshitomo (1123–60), they spared his 13-year-old son, Yoritomo (1147–99), and sent him into exile. In 1180 he launched a rebellion and chose Kamakura—a superb natural fortress, surrounded on three sides by hills and guarded on the fourth by the sea—as his base of operations.

The rivalry between the two clans became an all-out war. By 1185 Yoritomo and his half brother, Yoshitsune (1159–89), had destroyed the Taira utterly, and the Minamoto were masters of all Japan. In 1192 Yoritomo forced the imperial court to name him shogun; he was now de facto and de jure the military head of state. The emperor was left as a figurehead in Kyoto, and the little fishing village of Kamakura became—and for 141 years remained—the seat of Japan's first shogunal government.

The Minamoto line came to an end when Yoritomo's two sons were assassinated. Power passed to the Hojo family, who remained in control, often as regents for figurehead shoguns, for the next 100 years. In 1274 and again in 1281 Japan was invaded by the Mongol armies of China's Yuan dynasty. On both occasions typhoons—the original kamikaze (literally, "divine wind")—destroyed the Mongol fleets, but the Hojo family was still obliged to reward the various clans that had rallied to the defense of the realm. A number of these clans were unhappy with their portions—and with Hojo rule in general. The end came suddenly, in 1333, when two vassals assigned to put down a revolt switched sides. The Hojo regent committed suicide, and the center of power returned to Kyoto.

Kamakura reverted to being a sleepy backwater town on the edge of the sea, but after World War II, it began to develop as a residential area for the well-to-do. Nothing secular survives from the days of the Minamoto and Hojo; there wasn't much there to begin with. The warriors of Kamakura had little use for courtiers, or their palaces and gardened villas; the shogunate's name for itself, in fact, was the Bakufu—literally, the "tent government." As a religious center, however, the town presents an extraordinary legacy. Most of those temples and shrines are in settings of remarkable beauty; many are designated National Treasures. If you can afford the time for only one day trip from Tokyo, you should probably spend it here.

GETTING HERE AND AROUND

A bus from Kamakura Station (Sign 5) travels to most of the temples and shrines in the downtown Kamakura area, with stops at most access roads to the temples and shrines. However, you may want to walk out as far as Hokoku-ji and take the bus back; it's easier to recognize the end of the line than any of the stops in between. You can also go by taxi to Hokoku-ji—any cab driver knows the way—and walk the last leg in reverse.

Bus companies in Kamakura don't conduct guided English tours. However, if your time is limited or you don't want to do a lot of walking, the Japanese tours hit the major attractions. These tours depart from Kamakura Station eight times daily, starting at 9 am; the last tour leaves at 1 pm. Purchase tickets at the bus office to the right of the station.

On weekends the Kanagawa Student Guide Federation offers a free guide service. Students show you the city in exchange for the chance to practice their English. Arrangements must be made in advance through the Japan National Tourist Organization in Tokyo. You'll need to be at Kamakura Station between 10 am and noon.

Sunrise Tours runs daily English-language trips from Tokyo to Kamakura; these tours are often combined with trips to Hakone. You can book through, and arrange to be picked up at, any of the major hotels. Check to make sure that the tour covers everything you want to see, as many include little more than a passing view of the Great Buddha in Hase. Given how easy it is to get around—most sights are within walking distance of each other, and others are short bus or train rides apart—you're better off seeing Kamakura on your own.

Traveling by train is by far the best way to get to Kamakura. Trains run from Tokyo Station (and Shimbashi Station) every 10 to 15 minutes during the day. The trip takes 56 minutes to Kita-Kamakura and one hour to Kamakura. Take the JR Yokosuka Line from Track 1 downstairs in Tokyo Station (Track 1 upstairs is on a different line and does not go to Kamakura). The cost is ¥780 to Kita-Kamakura, ¥890 to Kamakura (or use your JR [Japan Railways] Pass). It's now also possible to take a train from Shinjuku, Shibuya, or Ebisu to Kamakura on the Shonan-Shinjuku Line, but these trains depart less frequently than those departing from Tokyo Station. Local train service connects Kita-Kamakura, Kamakura, Hase, and Enoshima.

To return to Tokyo from Enoshima, take a train to Shinjuku on the Odakyu Line. There are 11 express trains daily from here on weekdays, between 8:38 am and 8:45 pm; 9 trains daily on weekends and national holidays, between 8:39 am and 8:46 pm; and even more in summer. The express takes about 70 minutes and costs ¥1,220. Or you can retrace your steps to Kamakura and take the JR Yokosuka Line to Tokyo Station.

VISITOR INFORMATION

Both Kamakura and Enoshima have their own tourist associations, although it can be problematic getting help in English over the phone. Your best bet is the Kamakura Station Tourist Information Center, which has a useful collection of brochures and maps. And since Kamakura is in Kanagawa Prefecture, visitors heading here from Yokohama can preplan their excursion at the Kanagawa Prefectural Tourist Association office in the Silk Center, on the Yamashita Park promenade.

> **TIMING TIP**
>
> If your time is limited, you may want to visit only Engaku Temple and Tokei Temple in Kita-Kamakura before riding the train one stop to Kamakura. If not, follow the main road all the way to Tsuru-ga-oka Hachiman-gu and visit four additional temples en route.

ESSENTIALS

Tour Contacts Japan National Tourist Organization (✉ *Tokyo* ☎ *03/3201–3331* ⊕ *www.jnto.go.jp*). **Kanagawa Student Guide Federation** (☎ *03/3201–3331*). **Sunrise Tours** (☎ *03/5796–5454* ⊕ *www.jtbgmt.com/sunrisetour/index.aspx*).

Tourist Information Enoshima Tourist Association (☎ *0466/37–4141*). **Kamakura Station Tourist Information Center** (☎ *0467/22–3350*). **Kamakura Tourist Association** (☎ *0467/23–3050*). **Kanagawa Prefectural Tourist Association** (☎ *045/681–0007* ⊕ *www.kanagawa-kankou.or.jp*).

Train Contact Japan Railways (☎ *03/3423–0111* ⊕ *www.japanrail.com*).

EXPLORING

There are three principal areas in Kamakura, and you can easily get from one to another by train. From Tokyo head first to Kita-Kamakura for most of the important Zen temples, including Engaku-ji (Engaku Temple) and Kencho-ji (Kencho Temple). The second area is downtown Kamakura, with its shops and museums and the venerated shrine Tsuru-ga-oka Hachiman-gu. The third is Hase, a 10-minute train ride southwest from Kamakura on the Enoden Line. Hase's main attractions are the great bronze figure of the Amida Buddha, at Kotoku-in, and the Kannon Hall of Hase-dera. There's a lot to see in Kamakura, and even to hit just the highlights will take you most of a busy day.

KITA-KAMAKURA 北鎌倉

Hierarchies were important to the Kamakura Shogunate. In the 14th century it established a ranking system called Go-zan (literally, "Five Mountains") for the Zen Buddhist monasteries under its official sponsorship.

TOP ATTRACTIONS

★ **Engaku-ji** 円覚寺 *(Engaku Temple).* The largest of the Zen monasteries in Kamakura, Engaku-ji was founded in 1282 and ranks second in the Five Mountains hierarchy. Here, prayers were to be offered regularly for the prosperity and well-being of the government; Engaku Temple's special role was to pray for the souls of those who died resisting the Mongol invasions in 1274 and 1281. The temple complex currently

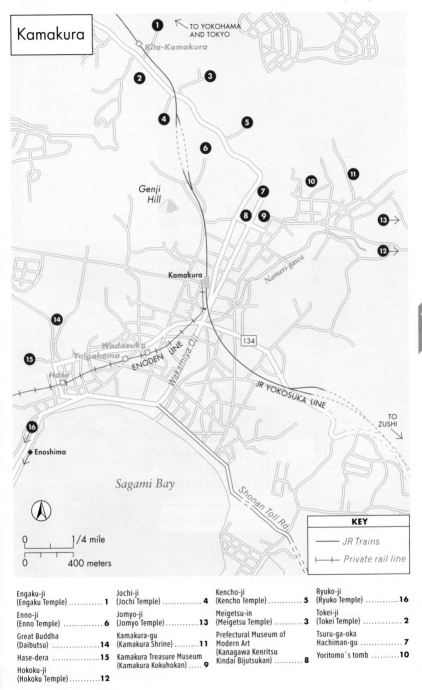

Kamakura

TO YOKOHAMA
AND TOKYO

Kita-Kamakura

Genji
Hill

Kamakura

Nameri-gawa

Wadezuka
Yuigahama

ENODEN LINE

Wakamiya Oji

Hase

134

JR YOKOSUKA LINE

TO
ZUSHI

Enoshima

Sagami Bay

Shonan Toll Rd.

0   1/4 mile
0   400 meters

KEY

— *JR Trains*
⊢—⊢ *Private rail line*

Engaku-ji (Engaku Temple) **1**	Jochi-ji (Jochi Temple) **4**
Enno-ji (Enno Temple) **6**	Jomyo-ji (Jomyo Temple) **13**
Great Buddha (Daibutsu) **14**	Kamakura-gu (Kamakura Shrine) **11**
Hase-dera **15**	Kamakura Treasure Museum (Kamakura Kokuhokan) **9**
Hokoku-ji (Hokoku Temple) **12**	

Kencho-ji (Kencho Temple) **5**	Ryuko-ji (Ryuko Temple) **16**
Meigetsu-in (Meigetsu Temple) **3**	Tokei-ji (Tokei Temple) **2**
Prefectural Museum of Modern Art (Kanagawa Kenritsu Kindai Bijutsukan) **8**	Tsuru-ga-oka Hachiman-gu **7**
	Yoritomo's tomb **10**

holds 18, but once contained as many as 50, buildings. Often damaged in fires and earthquakes, it has been completely restored.

Among the National Treasures at Engaku Temple is the **Hall of the Holy Relic of Buddha** (Shari-den), with its remarkable Chinese-inspired thatched roof. Built in 1282, it was destroyed by fire in 1558 but rebuilt in its original form soon after, in 1563. The hall is said to enshrine a tooth of the Gautama Buddha himself, but it's not on display. In fact, except for the first three days of the New Year, you won't be able to go any farther into the hall than the main gate. Such is the case, alas, with much of the Engaku Temple complex: this is still a functioning monastic center, and many of its most impressive buildings are not open to the public. The accessible National Treasure at Engaku Temple is the **Great Bell** (Kosho), on the hilltop on the southeast side of the complex. The bell—Kamakura's most famous—was cast in 1301 and stands 8 feet tall. It's rung only on special occasions, such as New Year's Eve. Reaching the bell requires a trek up a long staircase, but once you've made it to the top you can enjoy tea and traditional Japanese sweets at a small outdoor café. The views of the entire temple grounds and surrounding cedar forest from here are tremendous.

The two buildings open to the public at Engaku Temple are the **Butsunichi-an,** which has a long ceremonial hall where you can enjoy *sado* (Japanese tea ceremony), and the **Obai-in.** The latter is the mausoleum of the last three regents of the Kamakura Shogunate: Tokimune Hojo, who led the defense of Japan against the Mongol invasions; his son Sadatoki; and his grandson Takatoki. Off to the side of the mausoleum is a quiet garden with apricot trees, which bloom in February. As you exit Kita-Kamakura Station, you'll see the stairway to Engaku Temple just in front of you. ✉ *409 Yama-no-uchi, Kita-Kamakura* ☎ *0467/22–0478* 🖝 *Engaku Temple ¥300* 🕙 *Nov.–Mar., daily 8–4; Apr.–Oct., daily 8–5.*

★ **Enno-ji** 円応寺 *(Enno Temple)*. In the feudal period, Japan acquired from China a belief in Enma, the lord of hell, who, with his court attendants, judged the souls of the departed and determined their destination in the afterlife. Kamakura's otherwise undistinguished Enno-ji (Enno Temple) houses some remarkable statues of these judges—as grim and merciless a court as you're ever likely to confront. To see them is enough to put you on your best behavior, at least for the rest of your excursion. Enno Temple is a minute's walk or so from Kencho Temple, on the opposite (south) side of the main road to Kamakura. ✉ *A few minutes' walk along the main road to the south will bring you to Tsuru-ga-oka Hachiman-gu in downtown Kamakura. 1543 Yama-no-uchi, Kita-Kamakura* ☎ *0467/25–1095* 🖝 *¥200* 🕙 *Mar.–Nov., daily 9–4; Dec.–Feb., daily 9–3.*

★ **Kencho-ji** 建長寺 *(Kencho Temple)*. Founded in 1250, this temple was the foremost of Kamakura's five great Zen temples, and it lays claim to being the oldest Zen temple in all of Japan. It was modeled on one of the great Chinese monasteries of the time and built for a distinguished Zen master who had just arrived from China. Over the centuries, fires and other disasters have taken their toll on Kencho Temple, and although many buildings have been authentically reconstructed, the temple complex today is half its original size. Near the Main Gate (San-mon) is a bronze bell cast in 1255; it's the temple's most important treasure. The Main Gate and the Lecture Hall (Hatto) are the only two structures to have survived the devastating Great Kanto Earthquake of 1923. Like Engaku Temple, Kencho Temple is a functioning temple of the Rinzai sect, where novices train and laypeople can come to take part in Zen meditation. ⊠ *The entrance to Kencho Temple is about halfway along the main road from Kita-Kamakura Station to Tsuruga-oka Hachiman-gu, on the left.* 8 *Yama-no-uchi, Kita-Kamakura* ☎ *0467/22–0981* ✉ *¥300* ⊘ *Daily 8:30–4:30.*

★ **Tokei-ji** 東慶寺 *(Tokei Temple).* A Zen temple of the Rinzai sect, Tokei-ji holds special significance for the study of feminism in medieval Japan. More popularly known as the Enkiri-dera, or Divorce Temple, it was founded in 1285 by the widow of the Hojo regent Tokimune as a refuge for the victims of unhappy marriages. Under the shogunate, a husband of the warrior class could obtain a divorce simply by sending his wife back to her family. Not so for the wife: no matter what cruel and unusual treatment her husband meted out, she was stuck with him. If she ran away, however, and managed to reach Tokei Temple without being caught, she could receive sanctuary at the temple and remain there as a nun. After three years (later reduced to two), she was officially declared divorced. The temple survived as a convent through the Meiji Restoration of 1868. The last abbess died in 1902; her headstone is in the cemetery behind the temple, beneath the plum trees that blossom in February. Tokei Temple was later reestablished as a monastery.

The **Matsugaoka Treasure House** (Matsugaoka Hozo) of Tokei Temple displays several Kamakura-period wooden Buddhas, ink paintings, scrolls, and works of calligraphy, some of which have been designated by the government as Important Cultural Objects. The library, called the Matsugaoka Bunko, was established in memory of the great Zen scholar D. T. Suzuki (1870–1966).

Tokei Temple is on the southwest side of the JR tracks (the side opposite Engaku Temple), less than a five-minute walk south from the station on the main road to Kamakura (Route 21—the Kamakura Kaido), on the right. ⊠ *1367 Yama-no-uchi, Kita-Kamakura* ☎ *0467/22–1663* ✉ *Tokei Temple ¥100, Matsugaoka Treasure House additional ¥300* ⊘ *Tokei Temple Apr.–Oct., daily 8:30–5; Nov.–Mar., daily 8:30–4. Matsugaoka Treasure House Mon.–Thurs. 9:30–3:30.*

WORTH NOTING

Jochi-ji 浄智寺 *(Jochi Temple).* In the Five Mountains hierarchy, Jochi-ji was ranked fourth. The buildings now in the temple complex are reconstructions; the Great Kanto Earthquake of 1923 destroyed the originals. The garden here is exquisite. Jochi Temple is on the south side of the railway tracks, a few minutes' walk farther southwest of Tokei Temple in the direction of Kamakura. ⊠ *Turn right off the main road (Rte. 21) and cross over a small bridge; a flight of moss-covered steps leads up to the temple.* 1402 *Yama-no-uchi, Kita-Kamakura* ☎ *0467/22–3943* ✉ *¥200* ⊘ *Daily 9–4:30.*

Meigetsu-in 明月院 *(Meigetsu Temple)*. This temple is also known as Ajisai-dera (the hydrangeas temple), because when the flowers bloom in June, it becomes one of the most popular places in Kamakura. The gardens transform into a sea of color—pink, white, and blue—and visitors can number in the thousands. A typical Kamakura light rain shouldn't deter you; it only showcases this incredible floral display to its best advantage. Meigetsu-in features Kamakura's largest *yagura* (a tomb cavity enclosing a mural) on which 16 images of Buddha are carved. From Tokei Temple walk along Route 21 toward Kamakura for about 20 minutes until you cross the railway tracks; take the immediate left turn onto the narrow side street that doubles back along the tracks. This street bends to the right and follows the course of a little stream called the Meigetsu-gawa to the temple gate. ⊠ *189 Yama-no-uchi, Kita-Kamakura* ☎ *0467/24–3437* 🖅 *¥300* ⊙ *Nov.–May and July–Oct., daily 9–4; June, daily 8:30–5.*

DOWNTOWN KAMAKURA 鎌倉市

Downtown Kamakura is a good place to stop for lunch and shopping. Restaurants and shops selling local crafts, especially the carved and lacquered woodwork called Kamakura-*bori*, abound on Wakamiya Oji and the street parallel to it, Komachi-dori.

When the first Kamakura shogun, Minamoto no Yoritomo, learned he was about to have an heir, he had the tutelary shrine of his family moved to Kamakura from nearby Yui-ga-hama and ordered a stately avenue to be built through the center of his capital from the shrine to the sea. Along this avenue would travel the procession that brought his son— if there were a son—to be presented to the gods. Yoritomo's consort did indeed bear him a son, Yoriie (yo-*ree*-ee-eh), in 1182; Yoriie was brought in great pomp to the shrine and then consecrated to his place in the shogunal succession. Alas, the blessing of the gods did Yoriie little good. He was barely 18 when Yoritomo died, and the regency established by his mother's family, the Hojo, kept him virtually powerless until 1203, when he was banished and eventually assassinated. The Minamoto were never to hold power again, but Yoriie's memory lives on in the street that his father built for him: Wakamiya Oji, "the Avenue of the Young Prince."

TOP ATTRACTIONS

Hokoku-ji 報国寺 *(Hokoku Temple)*. Visitors to Kamakura tend to overlook this lovely little Zen temple of the Rinzai sect that was built in 1334, but it's worth a look. Over the years it had fallen into disrepair and neglect, until an enterprising priest took over, cleaned up the gardens, and began promoting the temple for meditation sessions, calligraphy exhibitions, and tea ceremony. Behind the main hall are a thick grove of bamboo and a small tea pavilion—a restful oasis and a fine place to go for *matcha* (green tea). The temple is about 2 km (1 mi) east on Route 204 from the main entrance to Tsuru-ga-oka Hachiman-gu; turn right at the traffic light by the Hokoku Temple Iriguchi bus stop and walk about three minutes south to the gate. ⊠ *2–7–4 Jomyo-ji* ☎ *0467/22–0762* 🖅 *¥200, tea ceremony ¥500* ⊙ *Daily 9–4.*

CLOSE UP

An Ancient Soap Opera

Once a year, during the Spring Festival (early or mid-April, when the cherry trees are in bloom), the Mai-den hall at Tsuru-ga-oka Hachiman-gu is used to stage a heartrending drama about Minamoto no Yoritomo's brother, Yoshitsune. Although Yoritomo was the tactical genius behind the downfall of the Taira clan and the establishment of the Kamakura Shogunate in the late 12th century, it was his dashing half brother who actually defeated the Taira in battle. In so doing, Yoshitsune won the admiration of many, and Yoritomo came to believe that his sibling had ambitions of his own. Despite Yoshitsune's declaration of allegiance, Yoritomo had him exiled and sent assassins to have him killed. Yoshitsune spent his life fleeing

from one place to another until, at the age of 30, he was betrayed in his last refuge and took his own life.

Earlier in his exile, Yoshitsune's lover, the dancer Shizuka Gozen, had been captured and brought to Yoritomo and his wife, Masako. They commanded her to dance for them as a kind of penance. Instead she danced for Yoshitsune. Yoritomo was furious, and only Masako's influence kept him from ordering her death. When he discovered, however, that Shizuka was carrying Yoshitsune's child, he ordered that if the child were a boy, he was to be killed. A boy was born. Some versions of the legend have it that the child was slain; others say he was placed in a cradle, like Moses, and cast adrift in the reeds.

★ **Tsuru-ga-oka Hachiman-gu** 鶴岡八幡宮 *(Minamoto Shrine)*. This shrine is dedicated to the legendary emperor Ojin, his wife, and his mother, from whom Minamoto no Yoritomo claimed descent. At the entrance, the small, steeply arched, vermilion **Drum Bridge** (Taiko-bashi) crosses a stream between two lotus ponds. The ponds were made to Yoritomo's specifications. His wife, Masako, suggested placing islands in each. In the larger **Genji Pond,** to the right, filled with white lotus flowers, she placed three islands. Genji was another name for clan, and three is an auspicious number. In the smaller **Heike Pond,** to the left, she put four islands. Heike (*heh*-ee-keh) was another name for the rival Taira clan, which the Minamoto had destroyed, and four—homophonous in Japanese with the word for "death"—is very unlucky indeed.

On the far side of the Drum Bridge is the **Mai-den.** This hall is the setting for a story of the Minamoto celebrated in Noh and Kabuki theater. Beyond the Mai-den, a flight of steps leads to the shrine's Main Hall (Hon-do). To the left of these steps is a ginkgo tree that—according to legend—was witness to a murder that ended the Minamoto line in 1219. From behind this tree, a priest named Kugyo leapt out and beheaded his uncle, the 26-year-old Sanetomo, Yoritomo's second son and the last Minamoto shogun. The priest was quickly apprehended, but Sanetomo's head was never found. Like all other Shinto shrines, the Main Hall is unadorned; the building itself, an 1828 reconstruction, is not particularly noteworthy. ⊠ *To reach Tsuru-ga-oka Hachiman-gu from the east side of Kamakura Station, cross the plaza, turn left, and walk north along Wakamiya Oji. Straight ahead is the first of three arches*

leading to the shrine, and the shrine itself is at the far end of the street.
2–1–31 Yuki-no-shita ☎0467/22–0315 ☑Free ☉ Daily 9–4.

Yoritomo's tomb 頼朝の墓. The man who put Kamakura on the map, so
to speak, chose not to leave it when he died: it's only a short walk from
Tsuru-ga-oka Hachiman-gu to the tomb of the man responsible for its
construction, Minamoto no Yoritomo. If you've already been to Nikko
and have seen how a later dynasty of shoguns sought to glorify its own
memories, you may be surprised at the simplicity of Yoritomo's tomb.
To get here, cross the Drum Bridge at Tsuru-ga-oka Hachiman-gu and
turn left. Leave the grounds of the shrine and walk east along the main
street (Route 204) that forms the T-intersection at the end of Wakamiya
Oji. A 10-minute walk will bring you to a narrow street on the left—
there's a bakery called Bergfeld (⇨ *see review below*) on the corner that
leads to the tomb, about 100 yards off the street to the north and up a
flight of stone steps. Yoritomo's tomb is located behind Tsuru-ga-oka
Hachiman-gu Yoritomo's tomb. ☑Free ☉ Daily 9–4.

WORTH NOTING

Jomyo-ji 浄明寺 *(Jomyo Temple)*. Founded in 1188, this one of the Five
Mountains Zen monasteries. Though it lacks the grandeur and scale
of the Engaku and Kencho, it still merits the status of an Important
Cultural Property. This modest single-story monastery belonging to the
Rinzai sect is nestled inside an immaculate garden that is particularly
beautiful in spring, when the cherry trees bloom. Its only distinctive
features are its green roof and the statues of Shaka Nyorai and Amida
Nyorai, who represent truth and enlightenment, in the main hall. To
reach it from Hokoku-ji, cross the main street (Route 204) that brought
you the mile or so from Tsuru-ga-oka Hachiman-gu, and take the first
narrow street north. A tea ceremony with Japanese green tea takes
place in this lovely setting. The monastery is about 100 yards from the
corner. ☒ 3–8–31 Jomyo-ji ☎0467/22–2818 ☑Jomyo Temple ¥100,
tea ceremony ¥500 ☉ Daily 9–4.

Kamakura-gu 鎌倉宮 *(Kamakura Shrine)*. This Shinto shrine was built
after the Meiji Restoration of 1868 and was dedicated to Prince Morinaga (1308–36), the first son of Emperor Go-Daigo. When Go-Daigo
overthrew the Kamakura Shogunate and restored Japan to direct imperial rule, Morinaga—who had been in the priesthood—was appointed
supreme commander of his father's forces. The prince lived in turbulent times and died young: when the Ashikaga clan in turn overthrew
Go-Daigo's government, Morinaga was taken into exile, held prisoner
in a cave behind the present site of Kamakura Shrine, and eventually beheaded. The **Treasure House** (Homotsu-den), on the northwest
corner of the grounds, next to the shrine's administrative office, is of
interest mainly for its collection of paintings depicting the life of Prince
Morinaga. To reach Kamakura Shrine, walk from Yoritomo's tomb to
Route 204, and turn left; at the next traffic light, a narrow street on the
left leads off at an angle to the shrine, about five minutes' walk west.
☒ 154 Nikaido ☎0467/22–0318 ☑Kamakura Shrine free, Treasure
House ¥300 ☉ Daily 9–4.

Kamakura Treasure Museum 鎌倉国宝館 *(Kamakura Kokuhokan)*. This museum was built in 1928 as a repository for many of the most important objects belonging to the shrines and temples in the area; many of these are designated Important Cultural Properties. The museum, located along the east side of the Tsuru-ga-oka Hachiman-gu shrine precincts, has an especially fine collection of devotional and portrait sculpture in wood from the Kamakura and Muromachi periods; the portrait pieces may be among the most expressive and interesting in all of classical Japanese art. ⊠ *2–1–1 Yuki-no-shita* ☎ *0467/22–0753* 🖂 *¥300* ☽ *Tues.–Sun. 9–4.*

Prefectural Museum of Modern Art 神奈川県立美術館 *(Kanagawa Kenritsu Kindai Bijutsukan)*. On the north side of the Heike Pond at Tsuru-ga-oka Hachiman-gu, this museum houses a collection of Japanese oil paintings and watercolors, wood-block prints, and sculpture. ⊠ *2–1–53 Yuki-no-shita* ☎ *0467/22–5000* 🖂 *¥800–¥1,200, depending on exhibition* ☽ *Tues.–Sun. 9:30–4:30.*

HASE 長谷
TOP ATTRACTIONS

Fodor's Choice
★

Great Buddha 大仏 *(Daibutsu)*. The single biggest attraction in Hase ("*ha*-seh") is the Great Buddha—sharing the honors with Mt. Fuji, perhaps, as the quintessential picture-postcard image of Japan. The statue of the compassionate Amida Buddha sits cross-legged in the temple courtyard, the drapery of his robes flowing in lines reminiscent of ancient Greece, his expression profoundly serene. The 37-foot bronze figure was cast in 1292, three centuries before Europeans reached Japan; the concept of the classical Greek lines in the Buddha's robe must have come over the Silk Route through China during the time of Alexander the Great. The casting was probably first conceived in 1180, by Minamoto no Yoritomo, who wanted a statue to rival the enormous Daibutsu in Nara. Until 1495 the Amida Buddha was housed in a wooden temple, which washed away in a great tidal wave. Since then the loving Buddha has stood exposed, facing the cold winters and hot summers, for more than five centuries.

■ TIP→ It may seem sacrilegious to walk inside the Great Buddha, but for ¥20 you can enter the figure from a doorway in the right side and explore his stomach, with a stairway that leads up to two windows in his back, offering a stunning view of the temple grounds (open until 4:15 pm). To reach Kotoku-in and the Great Buddha, take the Enoden Line from the west side of JR Kamakura Station three stops to Hase. From the East Exit, turn right and walk north about 10 minutes on the main street (Route 32). ⊠ *4–2–28 Hase, Hase* ☎ *0467/22–0703* 🖂 *¥200* ☽ *Apr.–Sept., daily 7–6; Oct.–Mar., daily 7–5:30.*

Fodor's Choice
★

Hase-dera 長谷寺. The only temple in Kamakura facing the sea, this is one of the most beautiful, and saddest, places of pilgrimage in the city. On a landing partway up the stone steps that lead to the temple grounds are hundreds of small stone images of Jizo, one of the bodhisattvas in the Buddhist pantheon. Jizo is the savior of children, particularly the souls of the stillborn, aborted, and miscarried; the mothers of these

Hase-dera, in Kamakura, is dedicated to unborn children. The beautiful temple faces the sea.

children dress the statues of Jizo in bright red bibs and leave them small offerings of food, heartbreakingly touching acts of prayer.

The **Kannon Hall** (Kannon-do) at Hase-dera enshrines the largest carved-wood statue in Japan: the votive figure of Juichimen Kannon, the 11-headed goddess of mercy. Standing 30 feet tall, the goddess bears a crown of 10 smaller heads, symbolizing her ability to search out in all directions for those in need of her compassion. No one knows for certain when the figure was carved. According to the temple records, a monk named Tokudo Shonin carved two images of the Juichimen Kannon from a huge laurel tree in 721. One was consecrated to the Hase-dera in present-day Nara Prefecture; the other was thrown into the sea in order to go wherever the sea decided that there were souls in need, and that image washed up on shore near Kamakura. Much later, in 1342, Takauji Ashikaga—the first of the 15 Ashikaga shoguns who followed the Kamakura era—had the statue covered with gold leaf.

The **Amida Hall** of Hase-dera enshrines the image of a seated Amida Buddha, who presides over the Western Paradise of the Pure Land. Minamoto no Yoritomo ordered the creation of this statue when he reached the age of 42; popular Japanese belief, adopted from China, holds that your 42nd year is particularly unlucky. Yoritomo's act of piety earned him another 11 years—he was 53 when he was thrown by a horse and died of his injuries. The Buddha is popularly known as the *yakuyoke* (good-luck) Amida, and many visitors—especially students facing entrance exams—make a point of coming here to pray. To the left of the main halls is a small restaurant where you can buy good-luck candy and admire the view of Kamakura Beach and Sagami Bay. ⊠ *To* reach Hase-dera from Hase Station, walk north about 5 mins on the main street (Rte. 32) towards Kotoku-in and the Great Buddha, and look for a signpost to the temple on a side street to the left. 3–11–2 Hase, Hase ☎0467/22–6300 ☞¥300 ⊗ Mar.–Sept., daily 8–5:30; Oct.–Feb., daily 8–4:30.

Kaiko-an 海光庵 is a spacious tearoom inside the temple grounds that offers dango (sweet rice dumplings on a stick), green tea, and sweets. Rest your feet, grab a table by the windows, and take in the breathtaking views of the ocean. ✉ 3–11–2 Hase, Hase ☎ 0467/22–6300 ☴ No credit cards ⊗ Mar.–Sept., daily 8–5:30; Oct.–Feb., daily 8–4:30.

WORD OF MOUTH

"From the Kamakura train station we boarded a local bus to Daibutsu—the Great Buddha. And great it was, an impressive 13 meter-high structure meditating in a lovely space surrounded by pine trees. Although we couldn't climb into the Buddha's ear, for a mere ¥20 each we were able to climb inside up to the Buddha's tummy (the statue is made of cypress wood with a copper patina), definitely a first for all of us!" —fourfortravel

---

RYUKO-JI AND ENOSHIMA 龍口寺・江ノ島

Ryuko-ji 龍口寺 (Ryuko Temple). The Kamakura story would not be complete without the tale of Nichiren (1222–82), the monk who founded the only native Japanese sect of Buddhism and who is honored here. Nichiren's rejection of both Zen and Jodo (Pure Land) teachings brought him into conflict with the Kamakura Shogunate, and the Hojo regents sent him into exile on the Izu Peninsula in 1261. Later allowed to return, he continued to preach his own interpretation of the Lotus Sutra—and to assert the "blasphemy" of other Buddhist sects, a stance that finally persuaded the Hojo regency, in 1271, to condemn him to death. The execution was to take place on a hill to the south of Hase. As the executioner swung his sword, legend has it that a lightning bolt struck the blade and snapped it in two. Taken aback, the executioner sat down to collect his wits, and a messenger was sent back to Kamakura to report the event. On his way he met another messenger, who was carrying a writ from the Hojo regents commuting Nichiren's sentence to exile on the island of Sado-ga-shima.

Followers of Nichiren built Ryuko Temple in 1337, on the hill where he was to be executed, marking his miraculous deliverance from the headsman. There are other Nichiren temples closer to Kamakura—Myohon-ji and Ankokuron-ji, for example. But Ryuko not only has the typical Nichiren-style main hall, with gold tassels hanging from its roof, but also a beautiful pagoda, built in 1904. To reach it, take the Enoden Line west from Hase to Enoshima—a short, scenic ride that cuts through the hills surrounding Kamakura to the shore. ✥ From Enoshima Station walk about 100 yards east, keeping the train tracks on your right, and you'll come to the temple. ✉ 3–13–37 Katase, Fujisawa ☎ 0466/25–7357 ☞ Free ⊗ Daily 6–4.

**OFF THE
BEATEN
PATH**

The Sagami Bay shore in this area has some of the closest beaches to Tokyo, and in the hot, humid summer months it seems as though all of the city's teeming millions pour onto these beaches in search of a vacant patch of rather dirty gray sand. Pass up this mob scene and press on instead to **Enoshima** 江ノ島. The island is only 4 km (2½ mi) around, with a hill in the middle. Partway up the hill is a shrine where the local fisherfolk used to pray for a bountiful catch—before it became a tourist attraction. Once upon a time it was quite a hike up to the shrine; now there's a series of escalators, flanked by the inevitable stalls selling souvenirs and snacks. The island has several cafés and restaurants, and on clear days some of them have spectacular views of Mt. Fuji and the Izu Peninsula. To reach the causeway from Enoshima Station to the island, walk south from the station for about 3 km (2 mi), keeping the Katase-gawa (Katase River) on your right. To return to Tokyo from Enoshima, take a train to Shinjuku on the Odakyu Line. From the island walk back across the causeway and take the second bridge over the Katase-gawa. Within five minutes you'll come to Katase-Enoshima Station. Or you can retrace your steps to Kamakura and take the JR Yokosuka Line to Tokyo Station.

> ### WHAT IS A BODHISATTVA?
>
> A bodhisattva is a being that has deferred its own ascendance into Buddhahood to guide the souls of others to salvation. It is considered a deity in Buddhism.

WHERE TO EAT

KITA-KAMAKURA

$$$$
JAPANESE
★

✕ **Hachinoki Kita-Kamakura-ten** 鉢の木北鎌倉店. Traditional shojin ryori (the vegetarian cuisine of Zen monasteries) is served in this old Japanese house on the Kamakura Kaido (Route 21) near the entrance to Jochi Temple. The seating is mainly in tatami rooms with beautiful antique wood furnishings. If you prefer table seating, visit the annex building. Allow plenty of time; this is not a meal to be hurried through. Meals, which are prix fixe only, are served Tuesday to Friday 11 to 2:30, weekends 11 to 3. ✉ *350 Yama-no-uchi, Kita-Kamakura* ☎ *0467/23–3722* ⊘ *Closed Wed.*

$$–$$$
JAPANESE

✕ **Kyorai-an** 去来庵. A traditional Japanese structure houses this restaurant known for its excellent Western-style beef stew. Also on the menu are pasta dishes, rice bouillon, homemade cheesecake, and wine produced in the Kita-Kamakura wine region. Half the seats are on tatami mats and half are at tables, but all look out on a peaceful patch of greenery. Kyorai-an is on the main road from Kita-Kamakura to Kamakura on the left side; it's about halfway between Meigetsu Temple and Kencho Temple, up a winding flight of stone steps. Meals are served Monday to Thursday 11:30 to 2:30, weekends and holidays 11 to 3 and 5 to 7. ✉ *157 Yamanouchi, Kamakura* ☎ *0467/24–9835* ⚫ *Reservations essential* ⊟ *No credit cards* ⊘ *No dinner Mon.–Thurs.*

DOWNTOWN KAMAKURA

¢
CAFÉ
✗**Bergfeld** ベルグフェルド . If you need to take a break during your walking tour of Kamakura, you may want to stop by this quaint café and bakery. It serves German cakes and cookies that are surprisingly authentic—the baker trained in Germany. There are a few small tables outside, and cozy tables inside where you can enjoy coffee and cakes before resuming your tour. Many Japanese who visit from other parts of the country bring back the bakery's butter cookies as souvenirs. ✉ *3–9–24 Yukinoshita, Kamakura* ☎ *0467/24–2706* ▭ *No credit cards* ✆ *Closed Tues. and the 3rd Thurs. of the month.*

¢
JAPANESE
✗**Kaisen Misaki-ko** 海鮮三崎港. This *kaiten-zushi* (sushi served on a conveyor belt that lets you pick the dishes you want) restaurant on Komachi-dori serves eye-poppingly large fish portions that hang over the edge of their plates. All the standard sushi creations, including tuna, shrimp, and egg, are prepared here. Prices range from ¥170 to ¥500. The restaurant is on the right side of the road just as you enter Komachi-dori from the East Exit of Kamakura Station. As in any kaiten-zushi joint, simply stack up your empty dishes to the side. When you are ready to leave, the dishes will be counted and you will be charged accordingly. ✉ *1–7–1 Komachi, Kamakura* ☎ *0467/22–6228* ▭ *No credit cards.*

$$–$$$
INDIAN
✗**T-Side** ティーサイド. Authentic, inexpensive Indian fare and a second-floor location that looks down upon Kamakura's main shopping street make this restaurant a popular choice for lunch and dinner. Curries are done well, the various *thali* (sets) are a good value, and the kitchen also serves some Nepalese dishes. T-Side is at the very top of Komachi-dori on the left as you enter from Kamakura Station. ✉ *2–11–11 Komachi, Kamakura* ☎ *0467/24–9572* ⊕ *www.kamakura-t-side.com* ▭ *No credit cards.*

HASE

$$$–$$$$
CHINESE
✗**Kaiserro** 華正樓. This establishment, in an old Japanese house, serves the best Chinese food in the city. The dining-room windows look out on a small, restful garden. Make sure you plan for a stop here on your way to or from the Great Buddha at Kotoku-in. ✉ *3–1–14 Hase, Hase* ☎ *0467/22–0280* ✍ *Reservations essential.*

> ## THE POWER OF THE JAPANESE BLADE
>
> In the corner of the enclosure where the Chinese Gate and Sanctum are found, an antique bronze lantern stands some 7 feet high. Legend has it that the lantern would assume the shape of a goblin at night; the deep nicks in the bronze were inflicted by swordsmen of the Edo period— on guard duty, perhaps, startled into action by a flickering shape in the dark. This proves, if not the existence of goblins, the incredible cutting power of the Japanese blade, a peerlessly forged weapon.

7

YOKOHAMA 横浜

In 1853, a fleet of four American warships under Commodore Matthew Perry sailed into the bay of Tokyo (then Edo) and presented the reluctant Japanese with the demands of the U.S. government for the opening of diplomatic and commercial relations. The following year

Perry returned and first set foot on Japanese soil at Yokohama—then a small fishing village on the mudflats of the bay, some 20 km (12½ mi) southwest of Tokyo.

Two years later New York businessman Townsend Harris became America's first diplomatic representative to Japan. In 1858 he was finally able to negotiate a commercial treaty between the two countries; part of the deal designated four locations—one of them Yokohama—as treaty ports. With the agreement signed, Harris lost no time in setting up his residence in Hangaku-ji, in nearby Kanagawa, another of the designated ports. Kanagawa, however, was also one of the 53 relay stations on the Tokaido, the highway from Edo to the imperial court in Kyoto, and the presence of foreigners—perceived as unclean barbarians—offended the Japanese elite. Die-hard elements of the warrior class, moreover, wanted Japan to remain in isolation and were willing to give their lives to rid the country of intruders. Unable to protect foreigners in Kanagawa, in 1859 the shogunate created a special settlement in Yokohama for the growing community of merchants, traders, missionaries, and other assorted adventurers drawn to this exotic new land of opportunity.

The foreigners (predominantly Chinese and British, plus a few French, Americans, and Dutch) were confined here to a guarded compound about 5 square km (2 square mi)—placed, in effect, in isolation—but not for long. Within a few short years the shogunal government collapsed, and Japan began to modernize. Western ideas were welcomed, as were Western goods, and the little treaty port became Japan's principal gateway to the outside world. In 1872 Japan's first railway was built, linking Yokohama and Tokyo. In 1889 Yokohama became a city; by then the population had grown to some 120,000. As the city prospered, so did the international community and by the early 1900s Yokohama was the busiest and most modern center of international trade in all of East Asia.

Then Yokohama came tumbling down. On September 1, 1923, the Great Kanto Earthquake devastated the city. The ensuing fires destroyed some 60,000 homes and took more than 40,000 lives. During the six years it took to rebuild the city, many foreign businesses took up quarters elsewhere, primarily in Kobe and Osaka, and did not return.

Over the next 20 years Yokohama continued to grow as an industrial center—until May 29, 1945, when in a span of four hours, some 500 American B-29 bombers leveled nearly half the city and left more than half a million people homeless. When the war ended, what remained became—in effect—the center of the Allied occupation. General Douglas MacArthur set up headquarters here, briefly, before moving to Tokyo; the entire port facility and about a quarter of the city remained in the hands of the U.S. military throughout the 1950s.

By the 1970s Yokohama was once more rising from the debris; in 1978 it surpassed Osaka as the nation's second-largest city, and the population is now inching up to the 3.5 million mark. Boosted by Japan's postwar economic miracle, Yokohama has extended its urban sprawl north to Tokyo and south to Kamakura—in the process creating a whole new subcenter around the Shinkansen Station at Shin-Yokohama.

The development of air travel and the competition from other ports have changed the city's role in Japan's economy. The great liners that once docked at Yokohama's piers are now but a memory, kept alive by a museum ship and the occasional visit of a luxury vessel on a Pacific cruise. Modern Yokohama thrives instead in its industrial, commercial, and service sectors—and a large percentage of its people commute to work in Tokyo. Is Yokohama worth a visit? Not, one could argue, at the expense of Nikko or Kamakura. But the waterfront is fun and the museums are excellent.

GETTING HERE AND AROUND

From Narita Airport, a direct limousine-bus service departs once or twice an hour between 6:45 am and 10:20 pm for Yokohama City Air Terminal (YCAT). YCAT is a five-minute taxi ride from Yokohama Station. JR Narita Express trains going on from Tokyo to Yokohama leave the airport every hour from 8:13 am to 1:13 pm and 2:43 pm to 9:43 pm. The fare is ¥4,180 (¥6,730 for the first-class Green Car coaches). Or you can take the limousine-bus service from Narita to Tokyo Station and continue on to Yokohama by train. Either way, the journey will take more than two hours—closer to three, if traffic is heavy.

The Airport Limousine Information Desk phone number provides information in English daily 9 to 6; you can also get timetables on its Web site. For information in English on Narita Express trains, call the JR Higashi-Nihon Info Line, available daily 10 to 6.

Most of the things you'll want to see in Yokohama are within easy walking distance of a JR or subway station, but this city is so much more negotiable than Tokyo that exploring by bus is a viable alternative. Buses, in fact, are the best way to get to Sankei-en. The city map available in the visitor centers in Yokohama has most major bus routes marked on it, and the important stops on the tourist routes are announced in English. The fixed fare is ¥210. One-day passes are also available for ¥600. Contact the Sightseeing Information Office at Yokohama Station (JR, East Exit) for more information and ticket purchases.

One subway line connects Azamino, Shin-Yokohama, Yokohama, Totsuka, and Shonandai. The basic fare is ¥200. One-day passes are also available for ¥740. The Minato Mirai Line, a spur of the Tokyu Toyoko Line, runs from Yokohama Station to all the major points of interest, including Minato Mirai, Chinatown, Yamashita Park, Moto-machi, and Basha-michi. The fare is ¥180–¥200, and one-day unlimited-ride passes are available for ¥450.

There are taxi stands at all the train stations, and you can always flag a cab on the street. ■ TIP→ Vacant taxis show a red light in the windshield. The basic fare is ¥710 for the first 2 km (1 mi), then ¥80 for every additional 350 meters (0.2 mi). Traffic is heavy in downtown Yokohama, however, and you will often find it faster to walk.

Teiki Yuran Bus offers a full-day (9–3:45) sightseeing bus tour that covers the major sights and includes lunch at a Chinese restaurant in Chinatown. The tour is in Japanese only, but pamphlets written in English are available at most sightseeing stops. Buy tickets (¥5,300) at the bus offices at Yokohama Station (east side) and at Kannai Station; the tour departs daily at 9:45 am from Bus Stop 14, on the east side of Yoko-hama Station. A half-day tour is also available, with lunch (9:30–1:20, ¥3,000) or without (2–5:45, ¥2,300).

The sightseeing boat *Marine Shuttle* makes 40-, 60-, and 90-minute tours of the harbor and bay for ¥1,000, ¥1,600, and ¥2,200, respectively. Boarding is at the pier at Yamashita Park. Boats depart roughly every hour between 10:20 am and 6:30 pm. Another boat, the *Marine Rouge,* runs 90-minute tours departing from the pier at 11, 1:30, and 4, and a special two-hour evening tour at 7 (¥2,800).

JR trains from Tokyo Station leave approximately every 10 minutes, depending on the time of day. Take the Yokosuka, the Tokaido, or the Keihin Tohoku Line to Yokohama Station (the Yokosuka and Tokaido lines take 30 minutes; the Keihin Tohoku Line takes 40 minutes and cost ¥450). From there the Keihin Tohoku Line (Platform 3) goes on to Kannai and Ishikawa-cho, Yokohama's business and downtown areas. If you're going directly to downtown Yokohama from Tokyo, the blue commuter trains of the Keihin Tohoku Line are best.

The private Tokyu Toyoko Line, which runs from Shibuya Station in Tokyo directly to Yokohama Station, is a good alternative if you leave from the western part of Tokyo. ■TIP➔ The term "private" is important because it means that the train does not belong to JR and is not a subway line. If you have a JR Pass, you'll have to buy a separate ticket. Depending on which Tokyu Toyoko Line you catch—the Limited Express, Semi Express, or Local—the trip takes between 25 and 44 minutes and costs ¥260.

Yokohama Station is the hub that links all the train lines and connects them with the city's subway and bus services. Kannai and Ishikawa-cho are the two downtown stations, both on the Keihin Tohoku Line; trains leave Yokohama Station every two to five minutes from Platform 3. From Sakuragi-cho, Kannai, or Ishikawa-cho, most of Yokohama's points of interest are within easy walking distance; the one notable exception is Sankei-en, which you reach via the JR Keihin Tohoku Line to Negishi Station and then a local bus.

VISITOR INFORMATION

The Yokohama International Tourist Association arranges visits to the homes of English-speaking Japanese families. These usually last a few hours and are designed to give *gaijin* (foreigners) a glimpse into the Japanese way of life.

The Yokohama Tourist Office, in the central passageway of Yokohama Station, is open daily 9 to 7 (closed December 28–January 3). The head office of the Yokohama Convention & Visitors Bureau, open weekdays 9 to 5 (except national holidays and December 29–January 3), is in the Sangyo Boeki Center Building, across from Yamashita Koen.

ESSENTIALS

Airport Transportation **Airport Limousine Information Desk** (☎ *03/3665–7220* ⊕ *www.limousinebus.co.jp*). **JR Higashi-Nihon Info Line** (☎ *03/3423–0111*).

Bus Information **Sightseeing Information Office** (☎ *045/465–2077*).

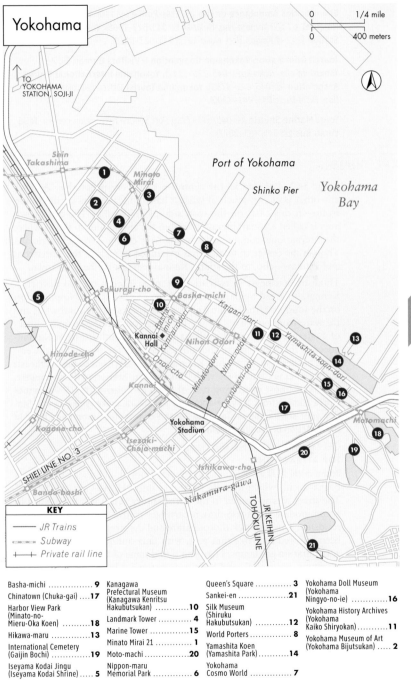

Yokohama

0 ——— 1/4 mile

0 ——— 400 meters

TO
YOKOHAMA
STATION, SOJI-JI

Port of Yokohama

Shinko Pier

*Yokohama
Bay*

Shin
Takashima

Minato
Mirai

Sakuragi-cho

Basha-michi

Kaigan-dori

Kannai
Hall

Nihon Odori

Yamashita-koen-dori

Basha-michi

Kannai-odori

Hinode-cho

Onoe-cho

Minato-dori

Nihon-dori

Osanbashi-dori

Kannai

Yokohama
Stadium

Motomachi

Kogane-cho

Isezaki-
Chojo-machi

SHIEL LINE NO. 3

Ishikawa-cho

Bando-bashi

Nakamura-gawa

JR KEIHIN TOHOKU LINE

KEY

——— *JR Trains*
○──○ *Subway*
+—+ *Private rail line*

Emergencies Ambulance or Fire (☎ 119). Police (☎ 110). Washinzaka Hospital (✉ 169 Yamate-cho, Naka-ku ☎ 045/623–7688). Yokohama Police Station (✉ 2-4 Kaigan-dori, Naka-ku ☎ 045/623–0110).

Tourist Information Yokohama Convention & Visitors Bureau (✉ 2 Yamashita-cho, Naka-ku ☎ 045/221–2111). Yokohama International Tourist Association (☎ 045/641–4759). Yokohama Tourist Office (✉ Yokohama Station, Nishi-ku ☎ 045/441–7300).

Tours Marine Shuttle (☎ 045/671–7719 Port Service reservation center). Teiki Yuran Bus (☎ 045/465–2077).

EXPLORING

Large as Yokohama is, the central area is very negotiable. As with any other port city, much of what it has to offer centers on the waterfront—in this case, on the west side of Tokyo Bay. The downtown area is called Kannai (literally, "within the checkpoint"); this is where the international community was originally confined by the shogunate. Though the center of interest has expanded to include the waterfront and Ishikawa-cho, to the south, Kannai remains the heart of town.

Think of that heart as two adjacent areas. One is the old district of Kannai, bounded by Basha-michi on the northwest and Nippon-odori on the southeast, the Keihin Tohoku Line tracks on the southwest, and the waterfront on the northeast. This area contains the business offices of modern Yokohama. The other area extends southeast from Nippon-odori to the Moto-machi shopping street and the International Cemetery, bordered by Yamashita Koen and the waterfront to the northeast; in the center is Chinatown, with Ishikawa-cho Station to the southwest. This is the most interesting part of town for tourists. ■TIP→ Whether you're coming from Tokyo, Nagoya, or Kamakura, make Ishikawa-cho Station your starting point. Take the South Exit from the station and head in the direction of the waterfront.

CENTRAL YOKOHAMA 横浜市街
TOP ATTRACTIONS
Basha-michi 馬車道. Running southwest from Shinko Pier to Kannai is Basha-michi, which literally translates into "Horse-Carriage Street." The street was so named in the 19th century, when it was widened to accommodate the horse-drawn carriages of the city's new European residents. This redbrick thoroughfare and the streets parallel to it have been restored to evoke that past, with faux-antique telephone booths and imitation gas lamps. Here you'll find some of the most elegant coffee shops, patisseries, and boutiques in town. On the block northeast of Kannai Station, as you walk toward the waterfront, is **Kannai Hall** (look for the red-orange abstract sculpture in front), a handsome venue for chamber music, Noh, classical recitals, and occasional performances by such groups as the Peking Opera. If you're planning to stay late in Yokohama, you might want to check out the listings. ✉ *Naka-ku* Ⓜ *JR Line, Kannai Station; Minato Mirai Line, Basha-michi Station.*

Get a taste of China in Japan with a visit to the restaurants and shops of Yokohama's Chinatown.

NEED A BREAK?
Japanese pâtissiers excel at making exquisite European sweets, occasionally giving them a new twist with Japanese ingredients such as sweet bean paste. The elegant **Keyuca Café and Sweets** (¢–$) is a good place to taste these skills while taking a break from your walking tour. The cappuccino is excellent, and there's a daily changing menu of bagel sandwiches and other light fare. ⊠ *B1 Queen's East, 2-3-2 Minato-Mirai, Nishi-ku* ☎ *045/640-1361* ⊟ *No credit cards* ⊘ *Daily 11–8.*

★ **Chinatown** 中華街 *(Chuka-gai)*. The largest Chinese settlement in Japan—and easily the city's most popular tourist attraction—Yokohama's Chinatown draws more than 18 million visitors a year. Its narrow streets and alleys are lined with some 350 shops selling foodstuffs, herbal medicines, cookware, toys and ornaments, and clothing and accessories. If China exports it, you'll find it here. Wonderful exotic aromas waft from the spice shops. Even better aromas drift from the quarter's 160-odd restaurants, which serve every major style of Chinese cuisine: this is the best place for lunch in Yokohama. Chinatown is a 10-minute walk southeast of Kannai Station. When you get to Yokohama Stadium, turn left and cut through the municipal park to the top of Nihon-odori. Then take a right, and you'll enter Chinatown through the Gembu-mon (North Gate), which leads to the dazzling red-and-gold, 50-foot-high Zenrin-mon (Good Neighbor Gate). ⊠ *Naka-ku* Ⓜ *JR Line, Ishikawa-cho Station; Minato Mirai Line, Motomachi-Chukagai Station.*

Harbor View Park 港の見える丘公園 *(Minato-no-Mieru-Oka Koen)*. The park—a major landmark in this part of the city, known, appropriately enough, as the Bluff *(yamate)*—was once the barracks of the British forces in Yokohama. Come here for spectacular nighttime views of the waterfront, the floodlit gardens of Yamashita Park, and the Bay Bridge. Foreigners were first allowed to build here in 1867, and it has been prime real estate ever since—an enclave of consulates, churches, international schools, private clubs, and palatial Western-style homes. ⊠ *Naka-ku* Ⓜ *JR Line, Ishikawa-cho Station; Minato Mirai Line, Motomachi-Chukagai Station.*

Hikawa-maru 氷川丸. Moored on the waterfront, more or less in the middle of Yamashita Park, is the *Hikawa-maru*. It was built in 1929 by Yokohama Dock Co. and was launched on September 30, 1929. For 31 years, she shuttled passengers between Yokohama and Seattle, Washington, making a total of 238 trips. A tour of the ship evokes the time when Yokohama was a great port of call for the transpacific liners. The *Hikawa-maru* has a French restaurant, and in summer there's a beer garden on the upper deck. ⊠ *Naka-ku* ☎ *045/641–4361* 🎫 *¥500* 🕙 *Apr.–June, Sept., and Oct., daily 9:30–7; July and Aug., daily 9:30–7:30; Nov.–Mar., daily 9:30–6:30* Ⓜ *JR Line, Ishikawa-cho Station; Minato Mirai Line, Motomachi-Chukagai Station.*

Silk Museum シルク博物館 *(Shiruku Hakubutsukan)*. The museum, which pays tribute to the period at the turn of the 20th century when Japan's exports of silk were all shipped out of Yokohama, houses an extensive collection of silk fabrics and an informative exhibit on the silk-making process. People on staff are very happy to answer questions. In the same building, on the first floor, are the main offices of the Yokohama International Tourist Association and the Kanagawa Prefectural Tourist Association. The museum is at the northwestern end of the Yamashita Park promenade, on the second floor of the Silk Center Building. ⊠ *1 Yamashita-cho, Naka-ku* ☎ *045/641–0841* 🎫 *¥500* 🕙 *Tues.–Sun. 9–4* Ⓜ *Minato Mirai Line, Nihon Odori Station (Exit 3).*

WORTH NOTING

International Cemetery 横浜山手外国人墓地 *(Gaikokujin Bochi)*. This Yokohama landmark is a reminder of the port city's heritage. It was established in 1854 with a grant of land from the shogunate; the first foreigners to be buried here were Russian sailors assassinated by xenophobes in the early days of the settlement. Most of the 4,500 graves on this hillside are English and American, and about 120 are of the Japanese wives of foreigners; the inscriptions on the crosses and headstones attest to some 40 different nationalities whose citizens lived and died in Yokohama. From Moto-machi Plaza, it's a short walk to the north end of the cemetery. ⊠ *Naka-ku* 🕙 *No entry after 4 pm* Ⓜ *JR Line, Ishikawa-cho Station; Minato Mirai Line, Motomachi-Chukagai Station.*

Kanagawa Prefectural Museum of Cultural History 神奈川県立歴史博物館 *(Kanagawa Kenritsu Rekishi Hakubutsukan)*. One of the few buildings in Yokohama to have survived both the Great Kanto Earthquake of 1923 and World War II, the museum is a few blocks north of Kannai Station (use Exit 8) on Basha-michi. Most exhibits here have no explanations in English, but the galleries on the third floor showcase some remarkable medieval wooden sculptures (including one of the first Kamakura shogun, Minamoto no Yoritomo), hanging scrolls, portraits, and armor. The exhibits of prehistory and of Yokohama in the early modern period are of much less interest. ✉ *5–60 Minami Naka-dori, Naka-ku* ☎ *045/201–0926* ✆ *¥300, special exhibits ¥800* ⊘ *Tues.–Sun. 9–4:30; closed last Tues. of month and the day after a national holiday* Ⓜ *JR Line, Sakuragi-cho and Kannai stations.*

Marine Tower マリンタワー. For an older generation of Yokohama residents, the 348-foot-high decagonal tower, which opened in 1961, was the city's landmark structure; civic pride prevented them from admitting that it falls lamentably short of an architectural masterpiece. The tower has a navigational beacon at the 338-foot level and purports to be the tallest lighthouse in the world. At the 328-foot level, an observation gallery provides 360-degree views of the harbor and the city, and on clear days in autumn or winter, you can often see Mt. Fuji in the distance. Marine Tower is in the middle of the second block northwest from the end of Yamashita Park, on the left side of the promenade. ✉ *15 Yamashita-cho, Naka-ku* ☎ *045/641–7838* ✆ *¥700* ⊘ *Jan. and Feb., daily 9–7; Mar.–May, Nov., and Dec., daily 9:30–9; June, July, Sept., and Oct., daily 9:30–9:30; Aug., daily 9:30 am–10 pm* Ⓜ *JR Line, Ishikawa-cho Station; Minato Mirai Line, Motomachi-Chukagai Station.*

Moto-machi 元町. Within a block of Ishikawa-cho Station is the beginning of this street, which follows the course of the Nakamura-gawa (Nakamura River) to the harbor where the Japanese set up shop 100 years ago to serve the foreigners living in Kannai. The street is now lined with smart boutiques and jewelry stores that cater to fashionable young Japanese consumers. ✉ *Naka-ku* Ⓜ *JR Line, Ishikawa-cho Station; Minato Mirai Line, Motomachi-Chukagai Station.*

Yamashita Koen 山下公園 *(Yamashita Park).* This park is perhaps the only positive legacy of the Great Kanto Earthquake of 1923. The debris of the warehouses and other buildings that once stood here were swept away, and the area was made into a 17-acre oasis of green along the waterfront. The fountain, representing the Guardian of the Water, was presented to Yokohama by San Diego, California, one of its sister cities. From Harbor View Park, walk northwest through neighboring French Hill Park and cross the walkway over Moto-machi. Turn right on the other side and walk one block down toward the bay to Yamashita-Koen-dori, the promenade along the park. ✉ *Naka-ku* Ⓜ *JR Line, Ishikawa-cho Station; Minato Mirai Line, Motomachi-Chukagai Station.*

☺ **Yokohama Doll Museum** 横浜人形の家 *(Yokohama Ningyo-no-ie).* This museum houses a collection of some 4,000 dolls from all over the world. In Japanese tradition, dolls are less to play with than to display—either in religious folk customs or as the embodiment of some spiritual quality. Japanese visitors to this museum never seem to outgrow their affection for the Western dolls on display here, to which they tend to assign the role of timeless "ambassadors of good will" from other cultures. The museum is worth a quick visit, with or without a child in tow. It's just across from the southeast end of Yamashita Park, on the left side of the promenade. ✉ *18 Yamashita-cho, Naka-ku* ☎ *045/671–9361* ✆ *¥500* ⊘ *Daily 10–6; closed 3rd Mon. of month* Ⓜ *JR Line, Ishikawa-cho Station; Minato Mirai Line, Motomachi-Chukagai Station.*

Landmark Tower and the Ferris wheel create a lovely skyline along Yokohama Bay.

Yokohama History Archives 横浜開港資料館 *(Yokohama Kaiko Shiryokan)*. Within the archives, housed in what was once the British Consulate, are some 140,000 items recording the history of Yokohama since the opening of the port to international trade in the mid-19th century. Across the street is a monument to the U.S.–Japanese Friendship Treaty. To get here from the Silk Center Building, at the end of the Yamashita Park promenade, walk west to the corner of Nihon-odori; the archives are on the left. ⊠ *3 Nihon-odori, Naka-ku* ☎ *045/201–2100* ⊡ *¥200* ⊙ *Tues.–Sun. 9:30–5* Ⓜ *Minato Mirai Line, Nihon-odori Station.*

AROUND YOKOHAMA

TOP ATTRACTIONS

Iseyama Kodai Jingu 伊勢山皇大神宮 *(Iseyama Kodai Shrine)*. A branch of the nation's revered Grand Shrines of Ise, this the most important Shinto shrine in Yokohama—but it's only worth a visit if you've seen most everything else in town. The shrine is a 10-minute walk west of Sakuragi-cho Station. ⊠ *64 Miyazaki-cho, Nishi-ku* ☎ *045/241–1122* ⊡ *Free* ⊙ *Daily 9–7* Ⓜ *JR Line, Sakuragi-cho Station; Minato Mirai Line, Minato Mirai Station.*

☺ **Landmark Tower** ランドマークタワー. The 70-story tower in Yokohama's Minato Mirai is Japan's tallest building, although the Tokyo Sky Tree broadcast tower is poised to take that title when construction is completed in 2011. The observation deck on the 69th floor has a spectacular view of the city, especially at night; you reach it via a high-speed elevator that carries you up at an ear-popping 45 kph (28 mph). The Yokohama Royal Park Hotel occupies the top 20 stories of the building. On the first level of the Landmark Tower is the **Mitsubishi Minato Mirai Industrial**

Museum, with rocket engines, power plants, a submarine, various gadgets, and displays that simulate piloting helicopters—great fun for kids.

The Landmark Tower complex's **Dockyard Garden,** built in 1896, is a restored dry dock with stepped sides of massive stone blocks. The long, narrow floor of the dock, with its water cascade at one end, makes a wonderful year-round open-air venue for concerts and other events; in summer (July–mid-August), the beer garden installed here is a perfect refuge from the heat. ⊠ *3–3–1 Minato Mirai, Nishi-ku* ☎ *045/224–9031* 🖱 *Elevator to observation deck ¥1,000, museum ¥300* ⊘ *Museum Tues.–Sun. 10–5* Ⓜ *JR Line, Sakuragi-cho Station; Minato Mirai Line, Minato Mirai Station.*

Minato Mirai 21 みなとみらい21. If you want to see Yokohama urban development at its most self-assertive, then this is a must. The aim of this project, launched in the mid-1980s, was to turn some three-quarters of a square mile of waterfront property, lying east of the JR Negishi Line railroad tracks between the Yokohama and Sakuragi-cho stations, into a model "city of the future." As a hotel, business, international exhibition, and conference center, it's a smashing success. ⊠ *Nishi-ku* Ⓜ *JR Line, Sakuragi-cho Station; Minato Mirai Line, Minato Mirai Station.*

★ **Sankei-en** 三渓園. Opened to the public in 1906, this was once the estate and gardens of Tomitaro Hara (1868–1939), one of Yokohama's wealthiest men, who made his money as a silk merchant before becoming a patron of the arts. On the extensive grounds of the estate he created is a kind of open-air museum of traditional Japanese architecture, some of which was brought here from Kamakura and the western part of the country. Especially noteworthy is **Rinshun-kaku,** a villa built for the Tokugawa clan in 1649. There's also a tea pavilion, Choshu-kaku, built by the third Tokugawa shogun, Iemitsu. Other buildings include a small temple transported from Kyoto's famed Daitoku-ji and a farmhouse from the Gifu district in the Japan Alps (around Takayama). ⊠ *58–1 Honmoku San-no-tani, Naka-ku* ☎ *045/621–0635* 🖱 *Inner garden ¥300, outer garden ¥300, farmhouse ¥100* ⊘ *Inner garden daily 9–4, outer garden and farmhouse daily 9–4:30* Ⓜ *JR Keihin Tohoku Line to Negishi Station and a local bus (number 54, 58, or 99) bound for Honmoku; Yokohama Station (East Exit) and take the bus (number 8 or 125) to Honmoku Sankei-en Mae. It will take about 35 mins.*

WORTH NOTING

Nippon-maru Memorial Park 日本丸メモリアルパーク. The centerpiece of the park, which is on the east side of Minato Mirai 21, where the O-oka-gawa (O-oka River) flows into the bay, is the *Nippon-maru,* a full-rigged three-masted ship popularly called the "Swan of the Pacific." Built in 1930, it served as a training vessel. The *Nippon-maru* is now retired, but it's an occasional participant in tall-ships festivals and is open for guided tours. Adjacent to the ship is the **Yokohama Maritime Museum,** a two-story collection of ship models, displays, and archival materials that celebrate the achievements of the Port of Yokohama from its earliest days to the present. ⊠ *2–1–1 Minato Mirai, Nishi-ku* ☎ *045/221–0280* 🖱 *Ship and museum ¥600, ship only ¥200* ⊘ *Mu-*

seum closed Mon. Ⓜ *JR Line, Sakuragi-cho Station; Minato Mirai Line, Minato Mirai Station.*

Queen's Square クイーンズスクエア. The courtyard on the northeast side of the Landmark Tower connects to this huge atrium-style vertical mall with dozens of shops (mainly for clothing and accessories) and restaurants. The complex also houses the Pan Pacific Hotel Yokohama and Yokohama Minato Mirai Hall, the city's major venue for classical music. ✉ *2–3–1 Minato-Mirai, Nishi-ku* ☎ *045/222–5015* ⊕ *www.qsy. co.jp* ⊘ *Shopping 11–8, restaurants 11 am–11 pm* Ⓜ *JR Line, Sakuragi-cho Station; Minato Mirai Line, Minato Mirai Station.*

World Porters ワールドポーターズ. This shopping center, on the opposite side of Yokohama Cosmo World, is notable chiefly for its restaurants that overlook the Minato Mirai area. Try arriving at sunset; the spectacular view of twinkling lights and the Landmark Tower, the Ferris wheel, and hotels will occasionally include Mt. Fuji in the background. Walking away from the waterfront area from World Porters will lead to **Aka Renga** (Redbrick Warehouses), two more shopping-and-entertainment facilities. ✉ *2–2–1 Shinko, Naka-ku* ☎ *045/222–2000* ☞ *Free* ⊘ *Daily 10–9, restaurants 10–11* Ⓜ *JR Line, Sakuragi-cho Station; Minato Mirai Line, Minato Mirai Station.*

ⓒ **Yokohama Cosmo World** よこはまコスモワールド. This amusement-park complex claims—among its 30 or so rides and attractions—the world's largest water-chute ride at 13 feet long and four stories high. The Ferris wheel towers over Yokohama. It's west of Minato Mirai and Queen's Square, on both sides of the river. ✉ *2–8–1 Shinko, Naka-ku* ☎ *045/641–6591* ☞ *Park free, rides ¥300–¥700 each* ⊘ *Mid-Mar.– Nov., weekdays 11–9, weekends 11–10; Dec.–mid-Mar., weekdays 11–8, weekends 11–9* Ⓜ *JR Line, Sakuragi-cho Station; Minato Mirai Line, Minato Mirai Station.*

Yokohama Museum of Art 横浜美術館 *(Yokohama Bijutsukan)*. Designed by Kenzo Tange and housed at Minato Mirai 21, the museum has 5,000 works in its permanent collection. Visitors will see paintings by both Western and Japanese artists, including Cézanne, Picasso, Braque, Klee, Kandinsky, Ryusei Kishida, and Taikan Yokoyama. ✉ *3–4–1 Minato Mirai, Nishi-ku* ☎ *045/221–0300* ☞ *¥500* ⊘ *Mon.–Wed. and weekends 10–5:30, Fri. 10–7:30 (last entry)* Ⓜ *JR Line, Sakuragi-cho Station; Minato Mirai Line, Minato Mirai Station.*

OFF THE BEATEN PATH

Soji-ji 総持寺. One of the two major centers of the Soto sect of Zen Buddhism, Soji-ji, in Yokohama's Tsurumi ward, was founded in 1321. The center was moved here from Ishikawa, on the Noto Peninsula (on the Sea of Japan, north of Kanazawa), after a fire in the 19th century. There's also a Soji-ji monastic complex at Eihei-ji in Fukui Prefecture. The Yokohama Soji-ji is one of the largest and busiest Buddhist institutions in Japan, with more than 200 monks and novices in residence. The 14th-century patron of Soji-ji was the emperor Go-Daigo, who overthrew the Kamakura Shogunate; the emperor is buried here, but his mausoleum is off-limits to visitors. However, you can see the **Buddha Hall,** the **Main Hall,** and the **Treasure House.** To get to Soji-ji, take the JR Keihin Tohoku Line two stops from Sakuragi-cho to Tsurumi. From the station walk five minutes south (back toward Yokohama), passing Tsurumi University on your right. Look out for the stone lanterns that mark the entrance to the temple complex. ✉ *2–1–1 Tsurumi, Tsurumi-ku* ☎ *045/581–6021* 🎫 *¥300* 🕐 *Daily dawn–dusk; Treasure House Tues.–Sun. 10–4.*

WHERE TO EAT

$$$–$$$$
SEAFOOD
★
✕ **Aichiya** 愛知屋. The "house of Aichi Prefecture" specializes in dishes of crab shipped in from Aichi. The merchandise is displayed in its pre-prepared state in cases and tanks at the front of the restaurant. There is crab soup, grilled crab, stewed crab, crab salad, and so on. A fall and winter course boasts *fugu* (blowfish), a delicacy that must be prepared by licensed experts, so as to avoid allowing the fish's poisonous organs from seeping into the meat. ✉ *7–156 Isezaki-cho, Naka-ku* ☎ *045/251–4163* 🚫 *No credit cards* 🕐 *Closed Mon. No lunch.*

$$$
JAPANESE
✕ **Chano-ma** 茶の間. This stylish eatery serves modern Japanese cuisine. There are bedlike seats that you can lounge on while eating and a house DJ spins tunes during dinner. While you're there, make sure you try the miso sirloin steak or grilled scallops with tasty citron sauce drizzled on top, served with a salad. It does get crowded here on the weekends, so come early to avoid a long wait. Try coming at lunchtime and you can take advantage of the ¥1,000 set-lunch special. ✉ *3F Red Brick Warehouse Bldg. 2, 1–1–2 Shinkou, Naka-ku* ☎ *045/650–8228* Ⓜ *Minato Mirai Line, Basha-michi Station; JR Negishi Line, Sakuragi-cho and Kannai stations.*

$$$$
CHINESE
★
✕ **Kaseiro** 華正樓. Surprisingly, Chinese food can be hit-or-miss in Japan, but not at Kaseiro. This elegant restaurant, with red carpets and gold-tone walls, is the best of its kind in the city, serving authentic Beijing cuisine, including, of course, Peking Duck and shark-fin soup. The consistently delicious dishes, combined with the fact that both the owner and chef are from Beijing, make this restaurant a well-known favorite among locals and travelers alike. ✉ *186 Yamashita-cho, Chinatown, Naka-ku* ☎ *045/681–2918* 🏛 *Jacket and tie.*

$$$$
JAPANESE
✕ **Motomachi Bairin** 元町梅林. The area of Motomachi is known as the wealthy, posh part of Yokohama; restaurants here tend to be exclusive and expensive, though the service and quality justify the price. This restaurant is an old-style Japanese house complete with a Japanese garden and five private tatami rooms. The ¥12,000, 27-course banquet includes some traditional Japanese delicacies such as sashimi, shiitake mushrooms, and chicken in white sauce; deep-fried burdock; and broiled sea bream. ✉ *1–55 Motomachi, Naka-ku* ☎ *045/662–2215* 🖊 *Reservations essential* 🚫 *No credit cards* 🕐 *Closed Mon.*

$$$$
JAPANESE
✕ **Rinka-en** 隣華苑. If you visit the gardens of Sankei-en, you might want to have lunch at this traditional country restaurant, which serves

kaiseki-style cuisine. Meals here are prix fixe. The owner is the grand-daughter of Hara Tomitaro, who donated the gardens to the city. ✉ *52–1 Honmoku San-no-tani, Naka-ku* ☎ *045/621–0318* ☖ *Reservations essential* 🏛 *Jacket and tie* 🚍 *No credit cards* ✪ *Closed Wed. and Aug.*

$$–$$$
ITALIAN
✕ **Roma Statione** ローマステーション. Opened more than 40 years ago, Roma Statione, between Chinatown and Yamashita Park, remains a popular venue for Italian food. The owner, whose father studied cooking in Italy before returning home to open this spot, is also the head chef and has continued using the original recipes. The house specialty is seafood: the spaghetti *vongole* (with clam sauce) is particularly good, as is the spaghetti *pescatora* and the seafood pizza. An added bonus is the impressive selection of Italian wines. ✉ *26 Yamashita-cho, Naka-ku* ☎ *045/681–1818* 🚍 *No credit cards* Ⓜ *Minato Mirai Line, Motomachi-Chukagai Station (Exit 1).*

$$$$
SCANDINAVIAN
✕ **Scandia** スカンディア. This Scandinavian restaurant near the Silk Center and the business district is known for its smorgasbord. It's popular for business lunches as well as for dinner. Scandia stays open until midnight, later than many other restaurants in the area. Expect dishes like steak tartare, marinated herring, and fried eel, and plenty of rye bread. ✉ *1–1 Kaigan-dori, Naka-ku* ☎ *045/201–2262* 🚍 *No credit cards.*

$$$$
STEAK
✕ **Serina Romanchaya** 瀬里奈 浪漫茶屋. The hallmarks of this restaurant are *ishiyaki* steak, which is grilled on a hot stone, and shabu-shabu—thin slices of beef cooked in boiling water at your table and dipped in one of several sauces; choose from sesame, vinegar, or soy. Fresh vegetables, noodles, and tofu are also dipped into the seasoned broth for a filling, yet healthful meal. ✉ *B1 Shin-Kannai Bldg., 4–45–1 Sumiyoshi-cho, Naka-ku* ☎ *045/681–2727.*

$$$
ITALIAN
✕ **Yokohama Cheese Cafe** 横浜チーズカフェ. This is a cozy and inviting casual Italian restaurant, whose interior looks like an Italian country home. There are candles on the tables and an open kitchen where diners can watch the cooks making pizza. On the menu: 18 kinds of Napoli-style wood-fire–baked pizzas, 20 kinds of pastas, fondue, and other dishes that include—you guessed it—cheese. The set-course menus are reasonable, filling, and recommended. ✉ *2–1–10 Kitasaiwai, Nishi-ku* ☎ *045/290–5656* Ⓜ *JR Yokohama Station.*

UNDERSTANDING TOKYO

THE EVOLUTION OF TOKYO

In the 12th century, Tokyo was a little fishing village called Edo (pronounced *eh*-doh). Over the next 400 years it was governed by a succession of warlords and other rulers. One of them, Dokan Ota, built the first castle in Edo in 1457. That act is still officially regarded as the founding of the city, but the honor really belongs to Ieyasu (ee-eh-*ya*-su), the first Tokugawa shogun, who arrived in 1590. On the site of Ota's stronghold, he built a fortress of his own—from which, 10 years later, he was effectively ruling the whole country.

By 1680 more than a million people lived here, and a great city had grown up out of the reeds in the marshy lowlands of Edo Bay. Tokyo is best understood as a *jo-ka-machi*—a castle town. Ieyasu had fought his way to the shogunate, and he had a warrior's concern for the geography of his capital. Edo Castle had the high ground, but all around it, at strategic points, he gave large estates to allies and trusted retainers. These lesser lords' villas also served as garrisons—outposts on a perimeter of defense.

Farther out, Ieyasu kept the barons he trusted least, and whom he controlled by bleeding their treasuries. He required them to keep large, expensive establishments in Edo; to contribute generously to the temples he endowed; to come and go in alternate years in great pomp and ceremony; and, when they returned to their estates, to leave their families—in effect, hostages—behind.

All the feudal estates, villas, gardens, and temples lay south and west of Edo Castle in an area known as Yamanote, where everything was about order, discipline, and ceremony. Every man had his rank and duties, and very few women were within the castle's garrisons. Those duties were less military than bureaucratic, and Ieyasu's precautions worked like a charm. The Tokugawa dynasty enjoyed some 250 years of nearly unbroken peace.

But Yamanote was only the demand side of the economy: somebody had to bring in the fish, weed the gardens, weave the mats, and entertain the bureaucrats. To serve the noble houses, common people flowed into Edo from all over Japan. Their allotted quarters of the city were jumbles of narrow streets, alleys, and cul-de-sacs in the low-lying estuarine lands to the north and east. Often the land assigned to them wasn't even there; they had to *make* it by draining and filling the marshes (the first reclamation project in Edo dates from 1457). The result was Shitamachi—literally "downtown"—the part below the castle. Bustling, brawling Shitamachi was the supply side: it had the lumberyards, markets, and workshops; the wood-block printers, kimono makers, and money lenders. The people gossiped over the back fence in the earthy, colorful Edo dialect. They went to Yoshiwara—a walled and moated area on the outskirts of Edo where prostitution was under official control. (Yoshiwara was for a time the biggest licensed brothel area in the world.) They supported the bathhouses and Kabuki theaters and reveled in their spectacular summer fireworks festivals. The city and spirit of the Edokko—the people of Shitamachi—have survived, while the great estates uptown are now mostly parks and hotels.

The shogunate was overthrown in 1867 by supporters of Emperor Meiji. The following year the emperor moved his court from Kyoto to Edo and renamed it Tokyo: the Eastern Capital. By now the city was home to nearly 2 million people, and the geography was vastly more complex than what Ieyasu had seen. As it grew, it became many smaller cities, with different centers of commerce, government, entertainment, and transportation. In Yamanote, the commercial emporia, office buildings, and public halls made up the architecture of an emerging modern state. The workshops of Shitamachi multiplied, some becoming small wholesalers and family-run factories. Still, there was no planning, no grid. The neighborhoods and subcenters were worlds unto themselves, and a traveler from one was soon hopelessly lost in another.

The fire-bombings of 1945 left Tokyo, for the most part, in rubble and ashes. That utter destruction could have been an opportunity to rebuild on the rational order of cities like Kyoto, Barcelona, or Washington. No such plan was ever made. Tokyo reverted to type: it became once again an aggregation of small towns and villages. One village was much like any other; the nucleus was always the *shoten-gai,* the shopping arcade. Each arcade had at least one fishmonger, grocer, rice dealer, mat maker, barber, florist, and bookseller. You could live your whole life in the neighborhood of the shoten-gai.

People seldom moved out of these villages. The vast waves of new residents who arrived after World War II—about three-quarters of the people in the Tokyo metropolitan area today were born elsewhere—just created more villages. People who lived in the villages knew their way around, so there was no particular need to name the streets. Houses were numbered in the order in which they were built, rather than in a spatial sequence.

No. 3 might well share a mailbox with No. 12. People still take their local geography for granted—the closer you get to the place you're looking for, the harder it is to get coherent directions. Away from main streets and landmarks even a taxi driver can get hopelessly lost.

Fortunately, there are the *koban:* small police boxes, or substations, usually with two or three officers assigned to each of them full-time, to look after the affairs of the neighborhood. You can't go far in any direction without finding a koban. The officer on duty knows where everything is and is glad to point the way. (The substation system, incidentally, is one important reason for the legendary safety of Tokyo: on foot or on white bicycles, the police are a visible presence, covering the beat. Burglaries are not unknown, of course, but street crime is very rare.)

Tokyo is still really two areas, Shitamachi and Yamanote. The heart of Shitamachi, proud and stubborn in its Edo ways, is Asakusa; the dividing line is Ginza, west of which lie the boutiques and department stores, the banks and engines of government, the pleasure domes and cafés. Today there are 13 subway lines in full operation that weave the two areas together.

JAPANESE GARDENS

Many of the principles that influence Japanese garden design come from religion. Shintoism, Taoism, and Buddhism, the three major religious influences in Japan, all stress the contemplation and re-creation of nature as part of the process of achieving understanding and enlightenment.

From Shintoism, Japan's ancient religion, comes *genus loci* (the spirit of place) and the search for the divine presence in remarkable natural features: special mountains, trees, rocks, and so forth. You can see the Taoist influence in islands, which act as a symbolic heaven for souls who achieve perfect harmony. Here sea turtles and cranes—creatures commonly represented in gardens—serve these enlightened souls.

Buddhist gardens function as settings for meditation, the goal of which is enlightenment. Shogun and samurai were strongly drawn to Zen Buddhism, so Zen gardens evolved as spaces to use almost exclusively for meditation and growth. The classic example is the *karesansui* (dry landscape) consisting of meticulously placed rocks and raked gravel.

The first garden designers in Japan were temple priests. Later, tea masters created gardens to refine the tea ceremony experience. A major contribution of the tea masters was the *roji*, the path or dewy ground that leads through the garden to the teahouse. The stroll along the roji prepares participants for the tea ceremony emotionally and mentally.

Gradually gardens moved out of the exclusive realm to which only nobles, *daimyo* (feudal lords), wealthy merchants, and poets had access, and the increasingly affluent middle class began to demand professional designers. In the process, aesthetic concerns came to override those of religion.

In addition to genus loci, karesansui style, and the roji mentioned above, here are a few terms that will help you more fully experience Japanese gardens.

Change and movement. Change is highlighted in Japanese gardens with careful attention to the seasonal variations that plants undergo: from cherry blossoms in spring to summer greenery to autumn leaf coloring to winter snow clinging to the garden's bare bones. A water element, real or abstract, often represents movement, as with the use of raked gravel or a stone "stream."

Mie gakure. The "reveal-and-hide" principle dictates that from no point should all of a garden be visible, that there is always mystery and incompleteness; viewers move through a garden to contemplate its changing perspectives.

Miniaturized landscapes. The depiction of celebrated natural and literary sites has been a frequent design technique in Japanese gardens—Fuji-san, represented by a truncated cone of stones; Ama-no-Hashidate, the famous spit of land, by a stone bridge; or a mighty forest by a lone tree.

Shakkei. "Borrowed landscape" extends the garden's boundaries by integrating a nearby mountain, grove of trees, or a sweeping temple roofline, and framing and capturing the view by echoing it with elements of similar shape or color inside the garden.

Symbolism. Abstract concepts and mythological legends are part of the garden vocabulary. The use of boulders in a streambed can represent life's surmountable difficulties, a pine tree can stand for stability, or islands in a pond for a far-away paradise.

BATHING: AN IMMERSION COURSE

Japanese cultural phenomena often confound first-time visitors, but few rituals are as opaque as those surrounding bathing. Baths in Japan are as much about pleasure and relaxation as they are about washing and cleansing. Traditionally, communal bathhouses served as centers for social gatherings, and even though most modern houses and apartments have bathtubs, many Japanese still prefer the pleasures of communal bathing—either at onsen while on vacation or in public bathhouses closer to home.

Japanese bathtubs are deep enough to sit in upright with (very hot) water up to your neck. It's not just the size of the tub that will surprise you; the procedures for using them are quite different from those in West. You wash yourself in a special area outside the tub first. The tubs are for soaking, not washing—soap must not get into the bathwater.

Many hotels in major cities have only Western-style reclining bathtubs, so to indulge in the pleasure of a Japanese bath you need to stay in a Japanese-style inn or find a *sento* (public bathhouse). The latter are clean but disappearing fast. Modern versions of the sento include saunas, steam rooms, and even a restaurant. Japanese bath towels, typically called *ta-o-ru,* are available for a fee at onsen and bathhouses. No larger than a hand towel, they have three functions: covering your privates, washing before and scrubbing while you bathe (if desired), and drying off (wring them out hard and they dry you quite well). If you want a larger towel to dry off, you have to bring one along.

You may feel apprehensive about bathing (and bathing *properly*) in an o-furo, but if you're well versed in bathing etiquette, you should soon feel at ease. And once you've experienced a variety of public baths—from the standard bathhouses to idyllic outdoor hot springs—you may find yourself a devotee of this ancient custom.

The first challenge in bathing is acknowledging that your Japanese bath mates will stare at your body. Take solace in the fact that their apparent voyeurism most likely stems from curiosity.

When you enter the bathing room, help yourself to two towels, soap, and shampoo (often included in the entry fee), and grab a bucket and a stool. At one of the shower stations around the edge of the room, use the handheld showers, your soap, and one of your towels to wash yourself thoroughly. A head-to-toe twice-over will impress onlookers. After rinsing, you may enter the public bath. You can use your one dry towel to cover yourself, or you can place it on your head (as many of your bath mates will do) while soaking. The water in the bath is as hot as the body can endure, and the reward for making it past the initial shock of the heat is the pleasure of a lengthy soak in water that is never tepid. All you need to do is lean back, relax, and experience the pleasures of purification.

THE TEA CEREMONY

The tea ceremony is a precisely choreographed program that started more than 1,000 years ago with Zen monks. The ritual begins as the server prepares a cup of tea for the first guest. This process involves a strictly determined series of movements and actions, which include cleansing each of the utensils to be used. One by one, the participants slurp up their bowl of tea, then eat a sweet confectionary served with it. Finally, comments about the beauty of the bowls used are exchanged. The entire ritual involves contemplating the beauty in the smallest actions, focusing on their meaning in the midst of the uncertainty of life.

The architecture of a traditional teahouse is also consistent. There are two entrances: a service entrance for the host and server and a low door that requires that guests enter on their knees, in order to be humbled. Tearooms often have tatami flooring and a flower arrangement or artwork in the alcove for contemplation and comment. The three best-known schools of tea ceremonies are the Ura Senke, the Omote Senke, and the Musha Kōji, each with its own styles, emphases, and masters.

Most of your tea experiences will be geared toward the uninitiated: the tea ceremony is a rite that requires methodical initiation by education. If you don't go for instruction before your trip, keep two things in mind: first, be in the right frame of mind when you enter the room. Though the tea ceremony is a pleasant event, some people take it quite seriously, and boisterous behavior is frowned upon. Instead, make conversation appropriate to a mood of serenity. Second, be sure to sit quietly through the serving and drinking—controlled slurping is expected—and openly appreciate the tools and cups afterward, commenting on their elegance and simplicity. This appreciation is the ritual's important final step. Above all, pay close attention to the perfect elements of the ceremony, from the art at the entryway and the kimono of the server to the quality of the utensils.

■TIP➜ Want to experience this ancient and highly ritualized art form firsthand? Stop by the Hotel Okura Tokyo in the heart of Roppongi (⇨ Chapter 4, Where to Stay), where one-hour and full-day sessions are available.

GEISHA

In modern Japan, geisha are an unusual sight outside of Kyoto, and their numbers have dwindled to around 10,000; in the 1920s there were more than 80,000 geisha in Japan. This is partly due to the increase of bar hostesses—who perform a similar function in nightclubs with virtually none of a geisha's training—not to mention the refinement and expense it takes to hire a geisha. Because she is essentially the most personal form of entertainer, the emphasis is on artistic and conversational skills, not solely on youth or beauty. Thus the typical geisha can work to an advanced age.

A geisha typically starts her career as a servant at a house until 13. She continues as a *maiko* (dancing child) until she masters the requisite accomplishments at about 18, including playing the *shamisen* (a traditional Japanese guitar-like instrument) and learning the proper hairstyles and kimono fittings. They are truly a sight to see strolling on the banks of the Kamo-gawa in the Gion district of Kyōto, or in Shimbashi, Akasaka, and Ginza in Tokyo, especially since these women are of a dying profession. Today geisha unions, restaurant unions, and registry offices regulate the times and fees of geisha. Fees are measured in "sticks"—generally, one hour—which is the time it would take a stick of *senko* (incense) to burn.

Geisha establish a variety of relations with men. Besides maintaining a dependable amount of favorite customers, one might choose a *danna*, one man for emotional, sexual, and financial gratification. Some geisha marry, most often to an intimate client. When they do, they leave the profession.

Although it's a common misconception in the West, geisha are not prostitutes. The character *gei* in *geisha* stands for arts and accomplishments (*sha* in this case means person); the public image of geisha in Japan is one of high status. To become a geisha, a woman must project perfect grace and have thorough mastery of etiquette. She should have an accomplished singing voice and dance beautifully. She needs a finely tuned aesthetic sense—with flower arranging and tea ceremony—and must excel at the art of conversation. In short, she should be the ultimate companion.

FILMS AND LITERATURE

Films

Western viewers have typically encountered Japanese cinema in the work of directors Mizoguchi Kenji, Ozu Yasujiro, and Kurosawa Akira. Three of Mizoguchi's finest films explore the role of women in feudal Japan: *The Life of Oharu* (1952), *Ugetsu* (1953), and *Sansho the Bailiff* (1954). Ozu's films—among them *Late Spring* (1949), *Early Summer* (1951), and *Tokyo Story* (1953)—explore traditional Japanese values in the everyday lives and relationships of middle-class families. Kurosawa's *Rashomon* (1950), a 12th-century murder story told by four different narrators, inspired a worldwide interest in Japanese cinema. Among his other classic period films are *Seven Samurai* (1954), *Yojimbo* (1961), *Red Beard* (1965), and *Kagemusha* (1980).

The next wave of postwar filmmakers include Ichikawa Kon, who directed two powerful antiwar movies, *The Burmese Harp* (1956) and *Fires on the Plain* (1959); Teshigahara Hiroshi, best known for his allegorical *Woman in the Dunes* (1964), based on a novel by Abe Kobo; and Imamura Shohei, who made *The Ballad of Narayama* (1983), about life and death in an Edo-period mountain village, and *Black Rain* (1989), which deals with the atomic bombing of Hiroshima.

More recent Japanese filmmakers winning acclaim abroad are Itami Juzo and Suo Masayuki. Itami's work includes *Tampopo* (1986), a highly original comedy about food; and *Minbo no onna* (1992), which dissects the world of Japanese gangsters. Suo's *Shall We Dance?* (1997) is a bittersweet comedy about a married businessman who escapes his daily routine by taking ballroom dance lessons.

Akin to the samurai films are Japanese gangster flicks. Though they date back to such Kurosawa classics as *Drunken Angel* (1948) and *Stray Dog* (1949), an edgy gangster genre emerged in the 1990s led by Beat Takeshi Kitano. His films *Fireworks* (1997) and *Zatoichi* (2003) have won awards at the Venice Film Festival. There are many Japanese gangster films, including a whole exploitative subset that mixes extreme violence with basically soft-core porn.

Those interested in Japanese anime should start with the Academy Award–winning picture *Spirited Away* (2002) by Hayao Miyazaki. Other modern anime pioneers include Tezuka Osamu, Mamoru Oshii, and Katsuhiro Otomo.

Recently, Japanese horror has also enjoyed international popularity. Focusing more on anticipation and psychological horror than blood-spurting special effects—though some can be quite gruesome, such as the hair-raising *Audition* (1999), directed by cult favorite Takashi Miike—Japanese horror tends to hinge on an eerie feeling of unseen threat and inescapable doom; they typically involve ghosts (by convention, women in white dresses and long hair) or poltergeists, seeking revenge for some wrong revealed as the movie progresses. The horror hits, *Ringu* (Nakata Hideo, 1998) and *Ju-on: The Grudge* (Shimizu Takashi, 2003) are representative of this genre; both have been remade by American directors for wider audiences.

Literature

Fiction and Poetry. The great classic of Japanese fiction is the *Tale of Genji*; written by Lady Murasaki Shikibu of the Heian court around the year 1000 and regarded by many as the world's first novel. From the same period is *The Pillow Book of Sei Shonagon*, the stylish and stylized diary of life at court. Required background reading for both is historian Ivan Morris's outstanding *The World of the Shining Prince*.

For the Edo period, Howard Hibbett's *Floating World in Japanese Fiction* gives an excellent selection with commentaries. The racy prose of late-17th-century Ihara

Saikaku is well translated in *Five Women Who Loved Love*.

The key figures in early modern Japanese fiction are Tanizaki Junchiro (*The Makioka Sisters* and *Some Prefer Nettles*), Nobel Prize winner Kawabata Yasunari (*Snow Country, The Sound of the Mountain, A Thousand Cranes*), and Soseki Natsume (*Botchan, I Am a Cat*). For the postwar period, read Mishima Yukio (*The Sea of Fertility, The Temple of the Golden Pavilion*), Abe Kobo (*Woman in the Dunes*), and Endo Shusaku (*The Samurai*).

Among the novelists at work in Japan today is Murakami Hiroki, whose *Wild Sheep Chase* and numerous short stories are often bizarre and humorous blends of magical realism and science fiction. Yoshimoto Banana's *Kitchen* and other novels are escapist fun. Nobel Prize winner Oe Kenzaburo's *A Personal Matter* is a compelling novelistic coming-to-terms with his relationship with his handicapped son.

Haiku, the 5-7-5 syllable form that the monk Matsuo Basho honed in the 17th century, especially in his *Narrow Road to the Deep North*, is perhaps the best known genre of Japanese poetry; two fine small collections of poems by Basho and other haiku masters are the beautifully illustrated *Monkey's Raincoat* and *A Net of Fireflies*. Three volumes of translations by Kenneth Rexroth, including *One Hundred Poems from the Japanese* and *Women Poets of Japan*, cover other genres of poetry and numerous authors from the last 1,000 years.

Travel Narratives. Two travel narratives stand out as superb introductions to Japanese history, culture, and people: Donald Richie's *The Inland Sea* and Leila Philip's eloquent *Road Through Miyama*.

History and Society. Two excellent surveys are Richard Storry's *A History of Modern Japan* and George Sansom's *Japan: A Short Cultural History*. Oliver Statler's *Japanese Inn* takes one family enterprise to trace 400 years of social change.

Yamamoto Tsunetomo's *Hagakure* is an 18th-century guide to the Way of the Samurai. Few books get closer to the realities of everyday life in early-modern rural Japan than Dr. Saga Junichi's 1970s collection of interviews, *Memories of Silk and Straw*.

Fine studies of the Japanese mind are to be found in Doi Takeo's *The Anatomy of Dependence*, and Nakane Chie's *Japanese Society*. Karel van Wolferen's *The Enigma of Japanese Power* is an enlightening book on the Japanese sociopolitical system. Alex Kerr's *Lost Japan*, the first work by a foreigner to win the Shincho Gakugei literature prize, examines the directions of Japanese society past and present.

Religion. The classic gateways to this subject are Suzuki Daisetsu's seminal *Introduction to Zen Buddhism* and *Zen and Japanese Culture*. Stuart D. Picken has written books on both major Japanese religions: *Shinto: Japan's Spiritual Roots* and *Buddhism: Japan's Cultural Identity*.

Art, Architecture, and Crafts. The *Japan Arts Library* series has separate volumes on castles, teahouses, screen painting, and wood-block prints. Nishi Kazuo and Hozumi Kazuo's *What Is Japanese Architecture?* treats the subject historically and has examples of buildings you will actually see on your travels.

Crafts and individual artisans are well-illustrated in the *Japan Crafts Sourcebook; Inside Japanese Ceramics*; in *Shoji Hamada*, on one of Japan's most revered potters; and in *The Living Traditions of Old Kyoto*.

ABOUT JAPANESE

To read and write Japanese you need a command of some 2,000 *kanji* (ideogram characters derived from Chinese) and two syllabic alphabets, called *hiragana* and *katakana*. The pronunciation of all the *kanji* and their various inflections can be rendered in either alphabet, although *katakana* is normally used for the spelling of foreign loan-words.

The alphabets are comprised of four types of syllables: the single vowels *a, i, u, e,* and *o* (pronounced ah, ee, ooh, eh, and oh); vowel-consonant pairs like *ka, ni, hu,* or *ro*; the single consonant *n* (which punctuates, for example, the upbeats of the word for bullet train, *Shinkansen: shee*-n-*ka*-n-*se*-n); and compounds like *kya, chu,* and *ryo*—also each one syllable. Thus Tōkyō, the capital city, has only two syllables—*tō* and *kyō*—not three. Likewise pronounce Kyōto *kyō-to,* not *kee-oh-to.* The Japanese *r* is rolled so that it sounds like a bounced *d.* There is no *l*-sound in the language, and the Japanese have great difficulty in distinguishing *l* from *r,* whether spoken or written.

No diphthongs. Paired vowels in Japanese words are not slurred together, as in the English *coin, brain,* or *stein.* The Japanese separate them, as in *mae* (*ma*-eh), which means in front of; *kōen* (*ko*-en); and *tokei* (to-*keh*-ee), which means clock or watch.

Macrons. Many Japanese words, when rendered in *romaji* (Roman letters) require a macron, or bar, over certain vowels to indicate whether it is pronounced long or short. The macrons in Tōkyō, for example, direct you to double the length of the *o,* as if you're saying it twice: *to-o-kyo-o.* Likewise, when you see double consonants, as in the city name Nikkō, double up on the *k*s—as you would with "bookkeeper"—and elongate the *o.*

Emphasis. Some books state that the Japanese emphasize all syllables in their words equally. This is not true. Take the words *sayōnara* and *Hiroshima.* Americans are likely to stress the downbeats: *sa*-yo-*na*-ra

and *hi*-ro-*shi*-ma. The Japanese actually emphasize the second beat in each case: sa-*yō*-na-ra (note the macron) and hi-ro-*shi*-ma. Metaphorically speaking, the Japanese don't so much stress syllables as pause over them or race past them: Emphasis is more a question of speed than weight. In the vocabulary below, we indicate emphasis by italicizing the syllable that you should stress.

Note also the unstressed pronunciations. The word *desu* roughly means "is." It looks like it has two syllables, but the Japanese race past the final *u* and just say "dess." Likewise, some verbs end in -*masu,* which is pronounced "mahss." Similarly, the character *shi* is often quickly pronounced "sh," as in the phrase meaning "pleased to meet you:" ha-ji-me-*mash(i)*-te.

Hyphens. Throughout this book we have hyphenated certain words to help you recognize meaningful patterns and vocabulary elements. This isn't conventional; it is practical. Seeing *Eki-mae-dōri* (literally "Station Front Avenue) this way instead of run together in a single word, for example, makes it easier to register the terms for "station" and "avenue" for use elsewhere. You'll also run across a number of sight names that end in -*jingu* or -*jinja* or –*taisha,* all of which mean "Shinto shrine."

Structure. Japanese sentences are structured back to front, i.e., subject-object-verb, instead of subject-verb-object as in English. "I am going to Tokyo" would translate literally in Japanese as "Tokyo to I'm going."

Note: placing an "o" before words like *tera* (*otera*) and *shiro* (*oshiro*) makes the word honorific. The meaning is clear enough without it, but omitting the polite form would be exceedingly un-Japanese.

ESSENTIAL PHRASES

BASICS

Yes/No	*ha-i*/*ii*-e	はい / いいえ
Please	o-ne-*gai* shi-masu	お願いします
Thank you (very much)	(*dō*-mo) a-*ri*-ga-tō go-*zai*-ma su	(どうも) ありがとうございます
You're welcome	*dō* i-ta-shi-ma-shi-te	どういたしまして
Excuse me	su-mi-ma-*sen*	すみません
Sorry	*go*-men na-*sai*	ごめんなさい
Good morning	o-*ha*-yō *go*-zai-ma-su	おはようございます
Good day/afternoon	kon-*ni*-chi-wa	こんにちは
Good evening	kom-*ban*-wa	こんばんは
Good night	o-*ya*-su-mi na-*sai*	おやすみなさい
Good-bye	sa-*yō*-na-ra	さようなら
Mr./Mrs./Miss	-san	〜さん
Pleased to meet you	*ha*-ji-me-*mashi*-te	はじめまして
How do you do?	*dō*-zo yo-*ro*-shi-ku	どうぞよろしく

NUMBERS

The first reading is used for reading numbers, as in telephone numbers, and the second is often used for counting things.

1	*i*-chi hi-*to*-tsu	一 / 一 / 一つ	10	jū / tō	十
2	ni / fu-*ta*-tsu	二 / 二つ	11	*jū*-i-chi	十一
3	san / *mit*-tsu	三 / 三つ	12	*jū*-ni	十二
4	yon (shi) / *yot*-tsu	四 / 四つ	13	*jū*-san	十三
5	go / i-*tsu*-tsu	五 / 五つ	14	*jū*-yon	十四
6	*ro*-ku *mut*-tsu	六 / 六つ	15	*jū*-go	十五
7	*na*-na *na*-na-tsu	七 / 七つ	16	*jū*-ro-ku	十六
8	*ha*-chi *yat*-tsu	八 / 八つ	17	*jū*-shi-chi	十七
9	kyū *ko*-ko-no-*tsu*	九 / 九つ	18	*jū*-ha-chi	十八

19	*jū*-kyū	十九	70	na-na-jū	七十
20	*ni*-jū	二十	80	*ha*-chi-jū	八十
21	*ni*-jū-i-chi	二十一	90	kyū-jū	九十
30	*san*-jū	三十	100	*hya*-ku	百
40	*yon*-jū	四十	1000	sen	千
50	*go*-jū	五十	10,000	*i*-chi-man	一万
60	*ro*-ku-jū	六十	100,000	*jū*- man	十万

DAYS OF THE WEEK

Sunday	*ni*-chi *yō*-bi	日曜日
Monday	*ge*-tsu *yō*-bi	月曜日
Tuesday	*ka* *yō*-bi	火曜日
Wednesday	*su*-i *yō*-bi	水曜日
Thursday	*mo*-ku *yō*-bi	木曜日
Friday	*kin* yō-bi	金曜日
Saturday	*dō* yō-bi	土曜日
Weekday	hei-ji-tsu	平日
Weekend	shū-ma-tsu	週末

MONTHS

January	*i*-chi *ga*-tsu	一月
February	*ni* ga-tsu	二月
March	*san* ga-tsu	三月
April	*shi* ga-tsu	四月
May	*go* ga-tsu	五月
June	*ro*-ku *ga*-tsu	六月
July	*shi*-chi *ga*-tsu	七月
August	*ha*-chi *ga*-tsu	八月
September	*ku* ga-su	九月
October	*jū* ga-tsu	十月
November	*jū*-i-chi *ga*-tsu	十一月
December	*jū*-ni *ga*-tsu	十二月

USEFUL EXPRESSIONS, QUESTIONS, AND ANSWERS

Do you speak English?	*ei*-go ga wa-*ka*-ri-ma-su *ka*	英語がわかりますか。
I don't speak Japanese.	*ni*-hon-go ga wa-*ka*-ri-ma-*sen*	日本語がわかりません。
I don't understand.	wa-*ka*-ri-ma-*sen*	わかりません。
I understand.	wa-*ka*-ri-ma-shi-*ta*	わかりました。
I don't know.	*shi*-ri-ma-*sen*	知りません。
I'm American (British).	wa-*ta*-shi wa a-*me*-ri-ka (i-*gi*-ri-su) jin *desu*	私はアメリカ（イギリス）人です。
What's your name?	o-*na*-ma-e wa *nan* desu *ka*	お名前はなんですか。
My name is.	.to mo-shi-ma-*su*	〜と申します。
What time is it?	i-ma *nan*-ji desu *ka*	今何時ですか。
How?	*dō* yat-te	どうやって。
When?	*i*-tsu	いつ。
Yesterday/today/tomorrow	ki-*nō*/kyō/*ashi*-ta	昨日 / 今日 / 明日
This morning	*ke*-sa	けさ
This afternoon	*kyō* no *go*-go	今日の午後
Tonight	*kom*-ban	今晩
Excuse me, what?	su-*mi*-ma-*sen*, *nan* desu *ka*	すみません、何ですか。
What is this/that?	*ko*-re/*so*-re wa *nan* desu *ka*	これ / それは何ですか。
Why?	*na*-ze desu *ka*	なぜですか。
Who?	*da*-re desu *ka*	だれですか。
I am lost.	*mi*-chi ni ma-yo-i-*mashi*-ta	道に迷いました。
Where is [place]	[place] wa *do*-ko desu *ka*	はどこですか
. . . train station?	e-ki	駅
. . . subway station?	chi-*ka*-te-tsu-no eki	地下鉄の駅
. . . bus stop?	*ba*-su *no*-ri-*ba*	バス乗り場
. . . taxi stand?	*ta*-ku-shi-i *no*-ri-*ba*	タクシー乗り場

. . . airport?	kū-kō	空港
. . . post office?	*yū*-bin-*kyo*-ku	郵便局
. . . bank?	*gin*-kō	銀行
. . . the [name] hotel?	[name] ho-*te*-ru	ホテル
. . . elevator?	e-re-bē-tā	エレベーター
Where are the restrooms?	*to*-i-re wa *do*-ko desu *ka*	トイレはどこですか。
Here/there/over there	*ko*-ko/*so*-ko/*a*-so-ko	ここ / そこ / あそこ
Left/right	hi-*da*-ri/*mi*-gi	左 / 右
Straight ahead	mas-*su*-gu	まっすぐ
Is it near (far)?	chi-*ka*-i (*tō*-i) desu *ka*	近い（遠い）ですか。
Are there any rooms?	*he*-ya *ga* a-ri-masu *ka*	部屋がありますか。
I'd like [item]	[item] ga ho-*shi*-i no desu ga	がほしいのですが。
. . . newspaper	*shim*-bun	新聞
. . . stamp	*kit*-te	切手
. . . key	*ka*-gi	鍵
I'd like to buy [item]	[item] o kai-*ta*-i no desu ga	を買いたいのですが。
. . . a ticket to [destination]	[destination] *ma*-de no *kip*-pu	までの切符
Map	*chi*-zu	地図
How much is it?	i-*ku*-ra desu *ka*	いくらですか。
It's expensive (cheap).	ta-*ka*-i (ya-*su*-i) de su *ne*	高い（安い）ですね。
A little (a lot)	su-*ko*-shi (*ta*-ku-san)	少し（たくさん）
More/less	*mot*-to o-ku/ su-ku-na-ku	もっと多く / 少なく
Enough/too much	*jū*-bun/ō-su-*gi*-ru	十分 / 多すぎる
I'd like to exchange	*ryō*-ga e shi-*te* i-*ta*-da-ke-masu *ka*	両替していただけますか。
. . . dollars to yen	*do*-ru o *en* ni	ドルを円に
. . . pounds to yen	*pon*-do o *en* ni	ポンドを円に

How do you say. in Japanese?	ni-*hon*-go de wa [word] wa *dō* i-i-masu *ka*	日本語で.はどう言いますか。
I am ill/sick.	wa-*ta*-shi wa *byō*-ki desu	私は病気です。
Please call a doctor/an ambulance.	*i*-sha/kyū-kyū-sha o *yon*-de ku-da-*sa*-i	医者を呼んでください。
Please call the police.	*ke*-i-sa-tsu o *yon*-de ku-da-*sa*-i	警察を呼んでください。
Help!	*ta*-su-*ke*-te	助けて!

USEFUL WORDS

airport	kūkō	空港
bay	wan	湾
beach	-hama	浜
behind	ushiro	後ろ
bridge	hashi or -bashi	橋
Bullet train, literally "new trunk line"	Shinkansen	新幹線
castle	shiro or -jō	城
cherry blossoms	sakura	桜
city or municipality	-shi	市
department store	depāto (deh-pah-to)	デパート
district	-gun	郡
east	higashi	東
exit	deguchi or -guchi	出口
festival	matsuri	祭
foreigner	gaijin (more politely: gai-koku-jin)	外人
garden	niwa	庭
gate	mon or torii	門 / 鳥居
hill	oka	丘
hot-spring spa	onsen	温泉
in front of	mae	前
island	shima or -jima/-tō	島

Japanese words rendered in roman letters	rōmaji	ローマ字
lake	mizumi or -ko	湖
main road	kaidō or kōdō	街道 / 公道
morning market	asa-ichi	朝市
mountain	yama or –san	山
museum	bijutsukan for art; hakubutsukan for natural history, etc.	博物館
north	kita	北
park	kōen	公園
peninsula	-hantō	半島
plateau	kōgen	高原
pond	ike or -ike	池
prefecture	-ken/-fu	県 / 府
pub	izakaya	居酒屋
river	kawa or -gawa	川 / 河
sea	umi or -nada	海
section or ward	-ku	区
shop	mise or -ya	店 / 屋
shrine	jinja or -gu	神社 / 宮
south	minami	南
street	michi or -dō	道
subway	chikatetsu	地下鉄
temple	tera or -ji/-in	寺 / 院
town	machi	町
train	densha	電車
train station	eki	駅
valley	tani	谷
west	nishi	西

MENU GUIDE

RESTAURANTS

Basics and Useful Expressions

a bottle of	*ip*-pon	一本
a glass/cup of	*ip*-pai	一杯
ashtray	*ha*-i-*za*-ra	灰皿
bill/check	kan-*jō*	勘定
bread	pan	パン
breakfast	*chō*-sho-ku	朝食
butter	ba-*tā*	バター
cheers!	kam-*pai*	乾杯!
chopsticks	*ha*-shi	箸
cocktail	*ka*-ku-*te*-ru	カクテル
Does that include dinner?	*Yū*-sho-ku *ga* tsu-ki- *ma-su-ka*	夕食が付きますか。
fork	*fō*-ku	フォーク
I am diabetic.	wa-ta-*shi* wa tō-*nyō*-byō de su	私は糖尿病です。
I am dieting.	*da*-i-et-to *chū* desu	ダイエット中です。
I am a vegetarian.	*saisho*-ku shu-*gi*-sha/ beji-*tari*-an de-su	菜食主義者 / ベジタリアンです。
I cannot eat [item]	[item] wa *ta*-be-ra- re-ma-*sen*	は食べられません。
I'd like to order.	*chū*-mon o shi-*tai* desu	注文をしたいです。
I'd like [item]	[item] o o-ne-*gai*-shi-ma su	をお願いします。
I'm hungry.	o-na-ka ga *su*-i-te i-*ma su*	お腹が空いています。
I'm thirsty.	*no*-do ga ka-*wa*-i-te i-*ma su*	喉が渇いています。
It's tasty (not good)	*o*-i-shi-i (ma-*zu*-i) desu	おいしいまずい)です。
knife	*na*-i-fu	ナイフ
lunch	*chū*-sho-ku	昼食
menu	me-nyū	メニュー

napkin	*na*-pu-*kin*	ナプキン
pepper	ko-*shō*	こしょう
plate	*sa*-ra	皿
Please give me [item]	[item] o ku-da-*sa*-i	をください。
salt	*shi*-o	塩
set menu	*te*-i-sho-ku	定食
spoon	su-*pūn*	スプーン
sugar	sa-tō	砂糖
wine list	*wa*-i-n *ri*-su-to	ワインリスト
What do you recommend?	o-su-su-me *ryō*-ri wa *nan* desu *ka*	おすすめ料理は何ですか。

MEAT DISHES

gyōza	minced pork spiced with ginger and garlic in a Chinese wrapper and fried or steamed	ギョウザ
hayashi raisu	beef flavored with tomato and brown sauce with onions and peas over rice	ハヤシライス
kara-age	deep-fried chicken	から揚げ
karē-raisu	curried rice: thick curry gravy typically containing beef over white rice	カレーライス
katsu-karē	curried rice with tonkatsu	カツカレー
niku-jaga	beef and potatoes stewed together with soy sauce	肉じゃが
okonomi-yaki	a Japanese pancake made from a batter of flour, egg, cabbage, and meat or seafood, griddle-cooked and sprinkled with green onions and a Worcestershire-soy-based sauce	お好み焼き

oyako-domburi (oyako-don)	literally, "mother and child bowl": cooked chicken and egg in broth over rice	親子どんぶり（親子丼）
rōru kyabetsu	rolled cabbage; beef or pork rolled in cabbage and cooked	ロールキャベツ
shabu-shabu	thin slices of beef swirled for an instant in boiling water flavored with soup stock and then dipped into a thin sauce	しゃぶしゃぶ
shōga-yaki	pork cooked with ginger	しょうが焼き
shūmai	shrimp or pork wrapped in a light dough and steamed (originally Chinese)	シュウマイ
subuta	sweet-and-sour pork, originally a Chinese dish	酢豚
sukiyaki	one-pot meal of thinly sliced beef, green onions, mushrooms, thin noodles, and tofu simmered in a mixture of soy sauce, mirin, and a little sugar	すき焼き
sutēki	steak	ステーキ
tanin-domburi (tannin-don)	literally, "strangers in a bowl": similar to oyako-domburi, but with beef instead of chicken	他人どんぶり
tonkatsu	breaded deep-fried pork cutlets	トンカツ
yaki-niku	thin slices of beef marinated then barbecued over an open fire at the table.	焼き肉

| yaki-tori | bits of chicken on skewers with green onions, marinated in sweet soy sauce and grilled | 焼き鳥 |

SEAFOOD DISHES

age-zakana	deep-fried fish	揚げ魚
aji	horse mackerel	あじ
asari no sakamushi	clams steamed with rice wine	あさりの酒蒸し
buri	yellowtail	ぶり
dojo no yanagawa-nabe	loach cooked with burdock root and egg in an earthen dish	どじょうの柳川鍋
ebi furai	deep-fried breaded prawns	海老フライ
ika	squid	イカ
iwashi	sardines	いわし
karei furai	deep-fried breaded flounder	かれいフライ
katsuo no tataki	bonito lightly braised, eaten with chopped ginger and scallions and thin soy sauce	かつおのたたき
maguro	tuna	まぐろ
nizakana	soy-simmered fish	煮魚
saba no miso-ni	mackerel stewed with soybean paste	さばの味噌煮
samma	saury pike	さんま
sashimi	fresh raw fish served sliced thin on a bed of white radish with a saucer of soy sauce and horseradish	刺身
sawara	Spanish mackerel	さわら
shake / sāmon	salmon	しゃけ / サーモン
shimesaba	mackerel marinated in vinegar	しめさば

shio-yaki	fish sprinkled with salt and broiled until crisp	塩焼き
tako	octopus	たこ
ten-jū	deep-fried prawns served over rice with sauce	天重
teri-yaki	fish basted in soy sauce and broiled	照り焼き
una-jū	eel marinated in a slightly sweet soy sauce, charcoal-broiled and served over rice	うな重
yaki-zakana	broiled fish	焼き魚

SUSHI

aji	horse mackerel	あじ
ama-ebi	sweet shrimp	甘えび
anago	conger eel	あなご
aoyagi	round clam	あおやぎ
chirashi zushi	a variety of seafood arranged on the top of a bowl of rice	ちらし寿司
ebi	shrimp	えび
futo-maki	big roll with egg and pickled vegetables	太巻き
hamachi	yellowtail	はまち
hirame	flounder	ひらめ
hotate-gai	scallop	ほたて貝
ika	squid	いか
ikura	salmon roe	いくら
kani	crab	かに
kappa-maki	cucumber roll	かっぱ巻き
kariforunia-maki	California roll, with crabmeat and avocado (originally American)	カリフォルニア巻き
kazunoko	herring roe	数の子

kohada	shad	こはだ
maguro	tuna	まぐろ
maki zushi	raw fish, vegetables, or other ingredients rolled in sushi rice and wrapped in dried seaweed	巻き寿司
miru-gai	giant clam	みる貝
nigiri zushi	rice shaped by hand into bite-sized cakes and topped with raw or cooked fish or other ingredients	にぎり寿司
saba	mackerel	さば
shake / sāmon	salmon	しゃけ / サーモン
shinko-maki	a type of pickle rolled in rice and wrapped in seaweed	新香巻き
tai	red snapper	たい
tako	octopus	たこ
tamago	egg	玉子
tekka-maki	small bits of tuna rolled in rice and wrapped in seaweed	鉄火巻き
toro	fatty tuna	とろ
uni	sea urchin	うに

VEGETABLE DISHES

aemono	vegetables dressed with sauces	和えもの
daigaku imo	fried yams in a sweet syrup	大学いも
gobō	burdock root	ごぼう
hōrenso	spinach	ほうれん草
kabocha	pumpkin	かぼちゃ
kimpira gobō	carrots and burdock root, fried with soy sauce	きんぴらごぼう

kyūri	cucumber	きゅうり
negi	green onions	ねぎ
nimono	vegetables simmered in a soy- and sake-based sauce	煮物
oden	street food of various types of fish cakes, vegetables, and boiled eggs simmered in a soy fish stock	おでん
o-hitashi	boiled vegetables with soy sauce and dried shaved bonito or sesame seeds	おひたし
renkon	lotus root	れんこん
satoimo	taro root	さといも
su-no-mono	vegetables seasoned with vinegar	酢の物
takenoko	bamboo shoots	タケノコ
tempura	vegetables, shrimp, or fish deep-fried in a light batter and dipped into a thin sauce with grated white radish	天ぷら
Tsukemono	Japanese pickles made from white radish, eggplant, or other vegetables	漬け物
yasai itame	stir-fried vegetables	野菜炒め

EGG DISHES

chawan mushi	vegetables, shrimp, etc., steamed in egg custard	茶碗蒸し
medama-yaki	fried eggs, sunny-side up	目玉焼き
omuraisu	omelet with rice inside	オムライス
yude tamago	boiled eggs	ゆで卵

TOFU DISHES

agedashi dōfu	deep-fried plain tofu garnished with spring onions, dipped in hot broth	揚げだし豆腐
hiya-yakko	cold tofu with soy sauce and grated ginger	冷やっこ
mābō dōfu	tofu and ground pork in a spicy sauce (originally Chinese)	マーボー豆腐
tofu no dengaku	tofu broiled on skewers and flavored with miso	豆腐の田楽
yu-dōfu	boiled tofu with green onions	湯豆腐

RICE DISHES

chāhan	fried rice with vegetables and pork	チャーハン (炒飯)
chimaki	sticky rice wrapped in bamboo skin	ちまき
gohan	steamed white rice	ご飯
okayu	rice porridge	お粥
onigiri	triangular balls of rice with fish or vegetables inside and wrapped in sheets of dry seaweed	おにぎり

SOUPS

miso shiru	thin broth containing tofu, mushrooms, or other ingredients in a soup flavored with miso or soybean paste	みそ汁
suimono	clear broth, often including fish and tofu	吸い物
tonjiru	pork soup with vegetables	豚汁

NOODLES

hiyamugi	similar to sōmen, but thicker	ひやむぎ

rāmen	Chinese noodles in soy sauce, miso, or salt-flavored broth, often with chāshū (roast pork)	ラーメン
soba	buckwheat noodles served in a broth or, during the summer, cold on a bamboo mesh (called zaru soba)	そば
sōmen	summer dish of very thin wheat noodles, usually served cold with a tsuyu or thin sauce	そうめん
udon	broad flour noodles that can be lunch in a light broth, or a meal (nabe-yaki udon) when meat, chicken, egg, and vegetables are added	うどん
yaki-soba	noodles fried with beef and cabbage, garnished with pickled ginger and vegetables	焼きそば

FRUIT

anzu	apricot	あんず
budō	grapes	ぶどう
ichigo	strawberries	いちご
ichijiku	figs	いちじく
kaki	persimmon	柿
kuri	chestnuts	栗
kurumi	walnuts	くるみ
mikan	tangerine (mandarin orange)	みかん
momo	peach	桃
nashi	Japanese pear	梨
ringo	apple	リンゴ

| sakurambo | cherry | さくらんぼ |
| suika | watermelon | 西瓜 |

DESSERT

kōhii zerii	coffee-flavored gelatin	コーヒーゼリー
purin	caramel pudding	プリン
wagashi	sweet bean-paste confection	和菓子
yōkan	sweet bean-paste jelly	ようかん

DRINKS

Alcoholic

biiru	beer	ビール
chūhai	shōchū mixed with soda water, lemon juice, or other flavoring	チューハイ
nama biiru	draft beer	生ビール
sake	rice wine, also called Nihonshu, which can be semi-sec (amaku-chi) or dry (karaku-chi), usually served warm (atsukan), although purists pre-fer it cold	酒, 日本酒
shōchū	spirit distilled from potatoes	焼酎

Nonalcoholic

jasumin cha	jasmine tea	ジャスミン茶
jūsu	juice, but can also mean any soft drink	ジュース
kō-cha	black tea	紅茶
kōhii	coffee	コーヒー
nihon cha	Japanese green tea	日本茶
ūron cha	Oolong tea	ウーロン茶

Travel Smart Tokyo

GETTING HERE AND AROUND

▌AIR TRAVEL

Flying time to Japan is 13¾ hours from New York, 12¾ hours from Chicago, and 9½ hours from Los Angeles. Japan Airlines' GPS systems allow a more direct routing, which reduces its flight times by about 30 minutes. Your trip east, because of tailwinds, can be about 45 minutes shorter.

You can fly nonstop to Tokyo from Chicago, Detroit, New York, Los Angeles, San Francisco, Portland (OR), Seattle, Minneapolis, and Washington, DC.

You can also fly nonstop to Osaka from Chicago, Detroit, Pittsburgh, and San Francisco. Because of the distance, fares to Japan tend to be expensive, usually around $1,200 for a seat in coach.

Both of Japan's major carriers offer reduced prices for flights within the country, which are real cost- and time-savers if your trip includes destinations such as Kyushu or Hokkaido, though tickets must be booked outside Japan and there are restrictions on use in peak times. JAL offers the Yokoso Japan Airpass; ANA has the Visit Japan Fare. Cathay Pacific offers a pass that includes 18 cities throughout Asia.

All domestic flights in Japan are no-smoking.

Airline Security Issues Transportation Security Administration (⊕ www.tsa.gov) has answers for almost every question that might come up.

Air Pass Information All Asia Pass (☎ 800/233–2742 Cathay Pacific ⊕ www.cathay-usa.com). **Visit Japan Fare** (☎ 800/235–9262 All Nippon Airways in U.S. ⊕ www.anaskyweb.com). **Yokoso Japan Airpass** (☎ 800/525–3663 Japan Airlines ⊕ www.jal.co.jp/yokoso).

TRAVEL TIMES FROM TOKYO			
To	By Air	By Car or Bus	By Train
Osaka	1¼ hours	7–8 hours	2½ hours
Hiroshima	1½ hours	10 hours	5 hours
Kyoto	1¼ hour	7 hours	2½ hours
Fukuoka	2 hours	14 hours	6 hours
Sapporo	1½ hours	15 hours	10 hours
Naha (Okinawa)	3 hours	NA	NA

▌TIP➔ **Ask the local tourist board about hotel and local transportation packages that include tickets to major museum exhibits or other special events.**

AIRPORTS

The major gateway to Japan is Tokyo's Narita Airport (NRT), 80 km (50 mi) northeast of the city. The new Haneda Airport International Terminal, which opened in 2010, offers flights to major international cities and is only 20 km (12 mi) south of central Tokyo. Most domestic flights to and from Tokyo are out of Haneda Airport.

Tokyo Narita's Terminal 2 has two adjoining wings, north and south. When you arrive, your first task should be to convert your money into yen; you need it for transportation into Tokyo. In both wings ATMs and money-exchange counters are in the wall between the customs inspection area and the arrival lobby. Both terminals have a Japan National Tourist Organization tourist information center, where you can get free maps, brochures, and other visitor information. Directly across from the customs-area exits at both terminals are the ticket counters for airport limousine buses to Tokyo.

If you have a flight delay at Narita, take a local Keisei Line train into Narita town 15 minutes away, where a traditional shopping street and the beautiful Narita-san Shinsho-ji Temple are a peaceful escape from airport noise.

Flying into Haneda provides visitors with quicker access to downtown Tokyo, which is a short monorail ride away. Stop by the currency exchange and Tourist Information Desk in the second-floor arrival lobby before taking a train into the city. There are also numerous jade-uniformed concierge staff on hand to help passengers with any questions.

Airport Information Haneda Airport (HND) (☎ 03/6428-0888 [International], 03/5757-8111 [Domestic] ⊕ www.haneda-airport.jp/en). **Narita Airport (NRT)** (☎ 0476/34-8000 ⊕ www.narita-airport.jp).

GROUND TRANSPORTATION

Known as "The Gateway to Japan," Narita is the easiest airport to use if you are traveling to Tokyo. It takes about 90 minutes—a time very dependent on city traffic—by taxi or bus. The *Keisei Skyliner* and *Japan Railways NEX* are the easiest ways to get into the city. If you are arriving with a Japan Rail Pass and staying in Tokyo for a few days, it is best to pay for the transfer into the city and activate the Rail Pass for travel beyond Tokyo.

Directly across from the customs-area exits at both terminals are the ticket counters for buses to Tokyo. Buses leave from platforms just outside terminal exits, exactly on schedule; the departure time is on the ticket. The Friendly Airport Limousine offers the only shuttle-bus service from Narita to Tokyo.

Japan Railways trains stop at both Narita Airport terminals. The fastest and most comfortable is the Narita Limited Express (NEX), which makes 23 runs a day in each direction. Trains from the airport go directly to the central Tokyo Station in just under an hour, then continue to Yokohama and Ofuna. Daily departures begin at 7:43 am; the last train is at 9:43 pm. In addition to regular seats, there is a first-class Green Car and private, four-person compartments. All seats are reserved, and you'll need to reserve one for yourself in advance, as this train fills quickly.

The Keisei Skyliner train runs every 20–30 minutes between the airport terminals and Keisei-Ueno Station. The trip takes around 40 minutes. The first Skyliner leaves Narita for Ueno at 8:17 am, the last at 10:18 pm. From Ueno to Narita the first Skyliner is at 6:30 am, the last at 5:45 pm. There's also an early train from the airport, called the Morning Liner, which leaves at 7:49 am and costs ¥1,400.

Contacts Airport Transport Service Co. (☎ 03/3665-7232 in Tokyo, 0476/32-8080 for Terminal 1, 0476/34-6311 for Terminal 2). **IAE Co** (☎ 0476/32-7954 for Terminal 1, 0476/34-6886 for Terminal 2). **Japan Railways** (☎ 03/3423-0111 for JR East InfoLine ⊗ Weekdays 10-6). **Keisei Railway** (☎ 03/3831-0131 for Ueno information counter, 0476/32-8505 at Narita Airport).

TRANSFERS BETWEEN AIRPORTS

Transfer between Narita and Haneda, the international and domestic airports, is easiest by the Friendly Limousine Bus, which should take 75 minutes and costs ¥3,000. Train transfers involve two changes.

Contacts Friendly Airport Limousine (☎ 03/3665-7220 ⊕ www.limousinebus.co.jp).

FLIGHTS

Japan Airlines (JAL) and United Airlines are the major carriers between North America and Narita Airport in Tokyo; American Airlines, Delta Airlines, and All Nippon Airways (ANA) also link North American cities with Tokyo's Hanada and Narita Airports. Most of these airlines also fly into and out of Japan's two other international airports, Kansai International Airport, located south of Osaka and Centrair, near Nagoya.

Airline Contacts All Nippon Airways (☎ 800/235-9262, 0120/02-9222 in Japan for domestic flights, 0120/02-9333 in Japan for international flights ⊕ www.anaskyweb.com). **American** (☎ 800/433-7300, 03/3298-7677

TRAVEL TIMES FROM TOKYO				
FROM NARITA	TO	FARES	TIMES	NOTES
Friendly Airport Limousine (buses)	Various $$$$ hotels in Tokyo & JR Tokyo and Shinjuku train stations	¥2,400–¥3,800	Every hr until 11:30 pm	70–90 mins, can be longer in traffic
Friendly Airport Limousine (buses)	Tokyo City Air Terminal (TCAT)	¥2,900	Every 10–20 mins from 6:55 am to 11 pm	
Narita Limited Express (NEX)	Central Tokyo Station, then continue to Yoko-hama and Ofuna	One-way fare ¥2,940; Green Car ¥4,980; private compartment (four people) ¥5,380 per person	Daily departures begin at 7:43 am; the last train is at 9:43 pm	All seats are reserved
Kaisoku (rapid train on JR's Narita Line)	Tokyo Station, by way of Chiba	¥1,280; ¥2,210 Green Car	16 departures daily, starting at 7 am	Trip takes 1 hr, 27 mins
Keisei Skyliner train	Keisei-Ueno Station	¥2,400	Every 20–30 mins, 7:49 am– 10:18 pm	All seats are reserved
Taxi	Central Tokyo	¥20,000 or more		
From Haneda	To	Fares	Times	Notes
Tokyo Monorail	Central Tokyo	¥470	Every 20 min, 5:13 am–midnight	Trip takes 25–30 minutes. Connect to other major stations via the Yamanote Line at Hamamatsucho Station
Taxi	Central Tokyo	¥5,000–¥6,000		

in Japan ⊕ *www.aa.com).* **Delta Airlines** (☎ *800/221–1212 for U.S. reservations, 800/241–4141 for international reservations* ⊕ *www.delta.com).* **Japan Airlines** (☎ *800/525–3663, 0120/25-5931 international in Japan, 0120/25-5971 domestic in Japan* ⊕ *www.jal.co.jp).* **United** (☎ *800/864-8331, 0120/11–4466 in Japan* ⊕ *www.united.com).*

▌ BOAT TRAVEL

Ferries connect most of the islands of Japan. Some of the more popular routes are from Tokyo to Tomakomai or Kushiro in Hokkaido; from Tokyo to Shikoku; and from Tokyo or Osaka to Kyushu. You can purchase ferry tickets in advance from travel agencies or before boarding. The ferries are inexpensive and are a pleasant, if slow, way of traveling. Private cabins are available, but it's more fun to travel in the economy class, where everyone sleeps on the carpeted floor in one large room. Passengers eat, drink, and enjoy themselves in a convivial atmosphere. *There is little English information for local ferries, apart from three companies serving the Inland Sea between Osaka/Kobe and Kyushu.*

Information **Hankyu Ferry** (⊕ *www.han9f. co.jp*). **Kansai Ferry** (⊕ *www.kanki.co.jp*). **Meimon Taiyo Ferry** (⊕ *www.cityline.co.jp*).

▌BUS TRAVEL

Japan Railways (JR) offers a number of long-distance buses that are comfortable and inexpensive. You can use Japan Rail Passes (⇨ *Train Travel, below*) on some, but not all, of these buses. Routes and schedules are constantly changing, but tourist information offices will have up-to-date details. It's now possible to travel from Osaka to Tokyo for as little as ¥5,000 one way. Buses are generally modern and very comfortable, though overnight journeys are best avoided. Nearly all are now no-smoking. Foreign travelers are not often seen on these buses, and they remain one of the country's best-kept travel secrets. Japan Rail Passes are not accepted by private bus companies. City buses outside Tokyo are quite convenient, but be sure of your route and destination, because the bus driver probably won't speak English.

Local buses have a set cost, anywhere from ¥100 to ¥200, depending on the route and municipality, in which case you board at the front of the bus and pay as you get on. On other buses cost is determined by the distance you travel. You take a ticket when you board at the rear door of the bus; it bears the number of the stop at which you boarded. Your fare depends on your destination and is indicated by a board at the front of the bus. Japan Railways also runs buses in some areas that have limited rail service. Remember, these buses are covered by the JR Pass, even if some JR reservation clerks tell you otherwise. Bus schedules can be hard to fathom if you don't read Japanese, however, so it's best to ask for help at a tourist information office. The Nihon Bus Association has information about routes and which companies have English Web information.

Reservations are not always essential, except at peak holiday times and on the most popular routes, like Tokyo–Osaka.

Bus Information JR Kanto Bus (☎ *03/3516–1950* ⊕ *www.jrbuskanto.co.jp*). **Nihon Bus Association** (⊕ *www.bus.or.jp/e/index.html*). **Nishinihon JR Bus** (☎ *06/6466–9990* ⊕ *www. nishinihonjrbus.co.jp*). **Willer Express** (⊕ *www. willerexpress.com*).

▌CAR TRAVEL

You need an international driving permit (IDP) to drive in Japan. IDPs are available from the American Automobile Association. These international permits, valid only in conjunction with your regular driver's license, are universally recognized; having one may save you a problem with local authorities. By law, car seats must be installed if the driver is traveling with a child under six.

Major roads in Japan are sufficiently marked in roman type, and on country roads there's usually someone to ask for help. However, it's a good idea to have a detailed map with town names written in *kanji* (Japanese characters) and *romaji* (romanized Japanese).

Car travel along the Tokyo–Kyoto–Hiroshima corridor and in other built-up areas of Japan is not as convenient as the trains. Roads are congested, gas is expensive (about ¥250 per liter), and highway tolls are exorbitant (tolls between Tokyo and Kyoto amount to ¥10,550). In major cities, with the exception of main arteries, English signs are few and far between, one-way streets often lead you off the track, and parking is often hard to find.

Car rental rates in Tokyo begin at ¥6,300 a day and ¥37,800 a week, including tax, for an economy car with unlimited mileage.

Local Agencies Japan Railways Group (⊕ *www.japanrail.com*). **ToCoo!** (☎ *03/5333– 0246* ⊕ *www2.tocoo.jp*).

Major Agencies Avis (☎ *800/331–1084* ⊕ *www.avis.com*). **Budget** (☎ *800/472–3325*

⊕ *www.budget.com*). **Hertz** (☎ *800/654–3001* ⊕ *www.hertz.com*). **National Car Rental** (☎ *800/227–7368* ⊕ *www.nationalcar.com*).

GASOLINE

Gas stations are plentiful along Japan's toll roads, and prices are fairly uniform across the country. Credit cards are accepted everywhere and are even encouraged— there are discounts for them at some places. Self-service stations have recently become legal, so if you pump your own gas you may get a small discount. Often you pay after putting in the gas, but there are also machines where you put money in first and then use the receipt to get change back. Staff will offer to take away trash and clean car windows. Tipping is not customary.

PARKING

There is little on-street parking in Japan. Parking is usually in staffed parking lots or in parking towers within buildings. Expect to pay upward of $3 per hour. Parking regulations are strictly enforced, and illegally parked vehicles are towed away. Recovery fees start at $300 and increase hourly.

ROAD CONDITIONS

Roads in Japan are often narrower than those in the United States, but they're well maintained in general. Driving in cities can be troublesome, as there are many narrow, one-way streets and little in the way of English road signs except on major arteries. Japanese drivers stick to the speed limit, but widely ignore bans on mobile phone use and dashboard televisions, and ignore rules on baby seats.

ROADSIDE EMERGENCIES

Emergency telephones along highways can be used to contact the authorities. A nonprofit service, JHelp.com, offers a free, 24-hour emergency assistance hotline. Car-rental agencies generally offer roadside assistance services. Mobile phones are now so widespread that local drivers can call for help from the middle of nowhere.

Emergency Services Police (☎ *110*). **Fire** (☎ *119*). **JHelp.com** (☎ *0570/00–0911*).

RULES OF THE ROAD

In Japan people drive on the left. Speed limits vary, but generally the limit is 80 kph (50 mph) on highways, 40 kph (25 mph) in cities. Penalties for speeding are severe. By law, car seats must be installed if the driver is traveling with a child under six, while the driver and all passengers in cars must wear seat belts at all times. Driving while using handheld phones is illegal.

Many smaller streets lack sidewalks, so cars, bicycles, and pedestrians share the same space. Motorbikes with engines under 50 cc are allowed to travel against automobile traffic on one-way roads. Fortunately, considering the narrowness of the streets and the volume of traffic, most Japanese drivers are technically skilled. However, they may not allow quite as much distance between cars as you're used to. Be prepared for sudden lane changes by other drivers. When waiting at intersections after dark, many drivers, as a courtesy to other drivers, turn off their main headlights to prevent glare. Since 2006 there has been a nationwide crackdown on drunk driving, following a spate of horrific, headline-grabbing accidents, so it's wisest to avoid alcohol entirely if you plan to drive.

❚ CRUISE SHIP TRAVEL

Japan is a popular cruise-ship destination, particularly for upscale and luxury cruise lines, many of which do an annual around-Japan cruise. In fact, you might very well find yourself visiting more off-the-beaten-path destinations on a cruise than on a land-based tour, though the trade-off often means spending considerably less time in each place.

Hakodate, Hiroshima, Nagasaki, Osaka, and Kobe are among the Japanese ports welcoming foreign cruise ships.

■ MOTORCYCLE TRAVEL

With its supernarrow roads and alley-ways, a fantastic way to tool around Tokyo is with a scooter, while the rest of the country—with its rolling hills, mountains, and shoreline—is really great to see via motorcycle. There are many bikers in Japan, so highways, rest stops, and campgrounds are all equipped to handle whatever bike you choose to tour with. Japan Bike Rentals is the only bike-rental place that is run by a *gaijin* (foreigner) so you can drop your dictionaries and do all the paperwork in English—and online. All riders will need a passport, a valid unrestricted motorcycle license from their own country, and an International Driving Permit. Japan Bike Rentals is open seven days a week, but you will need to make your booking online first, whether to rent a bike, a GPS for a self-guided tour, or join a guided tour. It's closed in January and February. SCS Motorcycle is one of the largest Japanese motorcycle rental chains, but finding an English-speaking staff member to help you may be difficult. It has several branches around Tokyo, but its head rental office is in Hakusan, near the Tokyo Dome.

Contacts Japan Bike Rentals (☎ *03/3584–5185* ⊕ *www.japanbikerentals.com*). **SCS Motorcycle** (☎ *03/3815–6221*).

■ TAXI TRAVEL

Taxis are an expensive way of getting around cities in Japan, though nascent deregulation moves are easing the market a little. In Tokyo, for instance, first 2 km (1 mi) cost ¥710 and it's ¥80 for every additional 280 meters (400 yards). If possible, avoid using taxis during rush hours (7:30 am–9:30 am and 5 pm–7 pm).

In general, it's easy to hail a cab: do not shout or wave wildly—simply raise your hand if you need a taxi. Japanese taxis have automatic door-opening systems, so do not try to open the taxi door. Stand back when the cab comes to a stop—if you are too close, the door may slam into you. When you leave the cab, do not try to close the door; the driver will do it automatically. Only the curbside rear door opens. A red light on the dashboard (visible through the front window) indicates an available taxi, and a green light indicates an occupied taxi.

Drivers are for the most part courteous, though not necessarily chatty. Unless you're going to a well-known destination such as a major hotel, it's advisable to have a Japanese person write out your destination in Japanese. Your hotel concierge will do this for you. Remember, there is no need to tip.

■ TRAIN TRAVEL

Riding Japanese trains is one of the pleasures of travel in the country. Efficient and convenient, trains run frequently and on schedule. The Shinkansen (bullet train), one of the fastest trains in the world, connects major cities north and south of Tokyo. It is only slightly less expensive than flying, but is in many ways more convenient because train stations are more centrally located than airports (and, if you have a Japan Rail Pass, it's extremely affordable).

Other trains, though not as fast as the Shinkansen, are just as convenient and substantially cheaper. There are three types of train services: *futsu* (local service), *tokkyu* (limited express service), and *kyuko* (express service). Both the tokkyu and the kyuko offer a first-class compartment known as the Green Car. Smoking is allowed only in designated carriages on long-distance and Shinkansen trains. Local and commuter trains are entirely no-smoking.

Because there are no porters or carts at train stations, it's a good idea to travel light when getting around by train. Savvy travelers often have their main luggage sent ahead to a hotel that they plan to reach later in their wanderings. It's also good to know that every train station, however small, has luggage lockers, which cost about ¥300 for 24 hours.

If you plan to travel by rail, get a Japan Rail Pass, which offers unlimited travel on Japan Railways (JR) trains. You can purchase one-, two-, or three-week passes. A one-week pass is less expensive than a regular round-trip ticket from Tokyo to Kyoto on the Shinkansen. You must obtain a rail pass voucher prior to departure for Japan (you cannot buy them in Japan), and the pass must be used within three months of purchase. The pass is available only to people with tourist visas, as opposed to business, student, and diplomatic visas.

When you arrive in Japan, you must exchange your voucher for the Japan Rail Pass. You can do this at the Japan Railways desk in the arrivals hall at Narita Airport or at JR stations in major cities. When you make this exchange, you determine the day that you want the rail pass to begin, and, accordingly, when it ends. You do not have to begin travel on the day you make the exchange; instead, pick the starting date to maximize use. The Japan Rail Pass allows you to travel on all JR-operated trains (which cover most destinations in Japan) but not lines owned by other companies.

The JR Pass is also valid on buses operated by Japan Railways (⇨ *Bus Travel, above*). You can make seat reservations without paying a fee on all trains that have reserved-seat coaches, usually long-distance trains. The Japan Rail Pass does not cover the cost of sleeping compartments on overnight trains (called blue trains), nor does it cover the newest and fastest of the Shinkansen trains, the *Nozomi,* which make only one or two stops on longer runs. The pass covers only the *Hikari* Shinkansen, which make a few more stops than the *Nozomi,* and the *Kodama* Shinkansen, which stop at every station along the Shinkansen routes.

Japan Rail Passes are available in coach class and first class (Green Car), and as

the difference in price between the two is relatively small, it's worth the splurge for first class, for real luxury, especially on the Shinkansen. A one-week pass costs ¥28,300 coach class, ¥37,800 first class; a two-week pass costs ¥45,100 coach class, ¥61,200 first class; and a three-week pass costs ¥57,700 coach class, ¥79,600 first class. Travelers under 18 pay lower rates. The pass pays for itself after one Tokyo–Kyoto round-trip Shinkansen ride. Contact a travel agent or Japan Airlines to purchase the pass.

Many travelers assume that rail passes guarantee them seats on the trains they wish to ride. Not so. If you're using a rail pass, there's no need to buy individual tickets, but you should book seats ahead. You can reserve up to two weeks in advance or just minutes before the train departs. If you fail to make a train, there's no penalty, and you can reserve again.

Seat reservations for any JR route may be made at any JR station except those in the tiniest villages. The reservation windows or offices, *midori-no-madoguchi,* have green signs in English and green-stripe windows. If you're traveling without a Japan Rail Pass, there's a surcharge of approximately ¥500 (depending upon distance traveled) for seat reservations, and if you miss the train you'll have to pay for another reservation. When making your seat reservation you may request a no-smoking or smoking car. Your reservation ticket shows the date and departure time of your train as well as your car and seat number. Notice the markings painted on the platform or on little signs above the platform; ask someone which markings correspond to car numbers. If you don't have a reservation, ask which cars are unreserved. Unreserved tickets can be purchased at regular ticket windows. There are no reservations made on local service trains. For traveling short distances, tickets are usually sold at vending machines. A platform ticket is required if you go through the wicket gate onto the platform to meet someone coming off a train. The charge is ¥140 (the tickets are ¥130 in Tokyo and Osaka).

Most clerks at train stations know a few basic words of English and can read roman script. Moreover, they are invariably helpful in plotting your route. The complete railway timetable is a mammoth book written only in Japanese; however, you can get an English-language train schedule from the Japan National Tourist Organization *(JNTO ⇨ Visitor Information, below)* that covers the Shinkansen and a few of the major JR Limited Express trains. JNTO's booklet *The Tourist's Handbook* provides helpful information about purchasing tickets in Japan. The Jorudan Route Finder is a good online source for searching train times and prices.

Information **Japan Railways Group** (✉ *1 Rockefeller Plaza, Suite 1410, New York, NY* ☎ *212/332-8686* ⊕ *www.japanrail.com*). **Jorudan Route Finder** (⊕ *www.jorudan.co.jp/ english*).

Buying a Pass **Japan Rail Pass** (⊕ *www. japanrailpass.net*).

Train Information **JR Hotline** (☎ *03/3423- 0111*) is an English-language information service, open weekdays 10–6.

ESSENTIALS

▌ ACCOMMODATIONS

Overnight accommodations in Japan run from luxury hotels to *ryokan* (traditional inns) to youth hostels and even capsules. Western-style rooms with Western-style bathrooms are widely available in large cities, but in smaller, out-of-the-way towns it may be necessary to stay in a Japanese-style room—an experience that can only enhance your stay.

Large chain and business hotels usually quote prices based on rooms and occupancy. Traditional minshuku and ryokan prices are generally per-person and include dinner and breakfast. If you do not want dinner at your hotel, it is usually possible to renegotiate the price. Stipulate, too, whether you wish to have Japanese or Western breakfasts, if any. Japanese-style rooms generally have tatami flooring and a futon instead of a bed. Rarely do they have a private bath or shower; guests bathe in communal baths, following a particular etiquette, and baths are frequently only open a few hours a day. When you make reservations at a non-city hotel, you are usually expected to take breakfast and dinner at the hotel—this is the rate quoted to you unless you specify otherwise. In this guide, properties are assigned price categories based on the range between their least and most expensive standard double rooms at high season (excluding holidays).

A top-notch agent planning your trip to Japan will make sure you have all the necessary domestic travel arrangements reserved in advance and check ahead for reservations for sumo tournaments, geisha shows, or the one-day-a-month temple opening. And when things don't work out the way you'd hoped, it's nice to have an agent to put things right.

Japan Hotel.net, J-Reserve, Rakuten Travel, and Tabiplaza, an offshoot of Nippon Travel Agency, offer a wide range of accommodations from big city luxury to out-of-the-way family guesthouses. Budget Japan Hotels offers big discounts on cheaper rooms at major hotels.

Online Accommodations Budget Japan Hotels (⊕ *www.budgetjapanhotels.com*). **Japan Hotel.net** (⊕ *www.japanhotel.net*). **J-Reserve** (⊕ *www.japan-hotel-reserve. com*). **Rakuten Travel** (⊕ *www.travel.rakuten. co.jp/en/*). **Tabiplaza** (⊕ *www.tabiplaza.net/ japanhotels*).

Japan Travel Agents IACE Travel (⊠ *3F Kou-nan Okamoto Bldg., Kounan, Minato-ku, Tokyo* ☏ *03/5282–1522* ⊕ *www.iace-usa.com*⊠ *18 E. 41st St., New York, NY* ☏ *800/872–4223*). **JTB Sunrise Tours** (⊠ *2–3–11 Higashi-Shinagawa, Shinagawa-ku, Tokyo* ☏ *03/5796–5454* ⊕ *www.jtbusa.com*). **Nippon Travel Agency** (⊠ *Shimbashi Ekimae Bldg., Number 1, Shim-bashi, Minato-ku, Tokyo* ⊕ *www.nta.co.jp/ english/index.asp*⊠ *1025 W. 190th St., Suite 300, Gardena, CA* ☏ *310/768–0017*).

APARTMENT AND HOUSE RENTALS

In addition to the agents listed here, English-language newspapers and magazines such as the *Hiragana Times, Metropolis, Kansai Scene*, or *Tokyo Weekender* may be helpful in locating a rental property. Note that renting apartments or houses in Japan is not a common way to spend a vacation, and weekly studio-apartment rentals may be fully booked by local business travelers.

The range of online booking services for Japan is expanding, although most of the accommodation booked this way is large and impersonal and staff in the hotel may not speak any English. Also check the location carefully to avoid incurring unforeseen extra costs and hassles in trying to reach the sights from a suburban hotel.

Contacts The Mansions (☏ *03/5414–7070 or 03/5575–3232*). **Sakura House—Apartments** (☏ *03/5330–5250* ⊕ *www.sakura-house.com*).

Weekly Mansion Tokyo (⊕ www.wmt-tokyo. com).

Rental Listings Kansai Scene (⊕ www. kansaiscene.com). **Metropolis** (☎ 03/3423–6932 ⊕ www.metropolis.co.jp).

Exchange Clubs Home For Exchange (⊕ www.homeforexchange.com); $59 for a 1-year online listing.

HOME VISITS

Through the home-visit system travelers can get a sense of domestic life in Japan by visiting a local family in its home. The program is voluntary on the home-owner's part, and there's no charge for a visit. The system is active in many cities throughout the country, including Tokyo, Yokohama, Nagoya, Kyoto, Osaka, Hiroshima, Nagasaki, and Sapporo. To make a reservation, apply in writing for a home visit at least a day in advance to the local tourist information office of the place you are visiting. Contact the Japan National Tourist Organization (⇨ Visitor Information, below) before leaving for Japan for more information on the program.

TEMPLES

You can also arrange accommodations in Buddhist temples, known as *shukubo*. JNTO has lists of temples that accept guests and you can arrange for your stay here as well. A stay at a temple generally costs ¥3,000–¥9,000 ($37–$110) per night, including two meals. Some temples offer instruction in meditation or allow you to observe their religious practices, while others simply offer a room. The Japanese-style rooms are very simple, and range from beautiful, quiet havens to not-so-comfortable, basic cubicles. For specific information on temple lodging in the Kii Mountain range in southern Japan, try contacting the Shukubo Temple Lodging Cooperative.

Contacts Shukubo Temple Lodging Cooperative (☎ 03/3231–5310 ⊕ www.shukubo.net).

▌ ADDRESSES

The simplest way to decipher a Japanese address is to break it into parts. For example: 6-chome 8–19, Chu o-ku, Fuku-oka-shi, Fukuoka-ken. In this address the "chome" indicates a precise area (a block, for example), and the numbers following chome indicate the building within the area. Note that buildings aren't always numbered sequentially; numbers are often assigned as buildings are erected. Only local police officers and mail carriers in Japan seem to be familiar with the area defined by the chome. Sometimes, instead of chome, "machi" (town) is used. Written addresses in Japan also have the opposite order of those in the West, with the city coming before the street. "Ku" refers to a ward (a district) of a city, "shi" refers to a city name, and "ken" indicates a prefecture, which is roughly equivalent to a state in the United States. It's not unusual for the prefecture and the city to have the same name, as in the above address. There are a few geographic areas in Japan that are not called ken. One is greater Tokyo, which is called Tokyo-to. Other exceptions Kyoto and Osaka, which are followed by the suffix "-fu"—Kyoto-fu, Osaka-fu. Hokkaido, Japan's northern-most island, is also not considered a ken. Not all addresses conform exactly to the above format. Rural addresses, for example, might use "gun" (county) where city addresses have "ku" (ward). Even Japanese people cannot find a building based

LOCAL DO'S AND TABOOS

CUSTOMS OF THE COUNTRY

In the United States being direct, efficient, and succinct are highly valued traits. In Japan this style is often frowned upon. Most Japanese do not use first names casually, so use last names with the honorific –san after the name in social situations. Make sure you don't express anger or aggression. These traits are equated with losing face in Japan, something you do not want to happen. Also stick to neutral subjects in conversations; private lives are kept private. There is no "fashionably late" in Japan, so be on time. Eating in public and overt physical affection is also frowned on by older Japanese. Eating on city trains is also frowned upon.

GREETINGS

Japanese of all ages and backgrounds bow in greeting each other (even on the telephone), and foreign visitors who at least bob the head will get a smile of recognition. However, when dealing with foreigners many Japanese switch to handshaking, and the visitor's head may crash with an outstretched hand.

SIGHTSEEING

There's no strict dress code for visiting temples and shrines, but you will feel out of place in shorts or outfits without much skin coverage. Casual clothes, including jeans, are fine for sightseeing. Remember to remove your shoes when entering temples. There are usually slippers by the entrance for you to change into.

OUT ON THE TOWN

Men are expected to wear a jacket and tie at more expensive restaurants and nightclubs. Women should wear a dress or skirt. If you've been invited out to dinner, either in a private home or restaurant, it's customary to bring a small token for your host. If you are in a home, remember to remove your shoes and put on the slippers that are usually waiting for you. When eating, it's okay to ask for a fork if you're not comfortable with

chopsticks. If you do use chopsticks, do not use the end of the chopstick that has been in your mouth to pick up food from communal dishes. And never leave your chopsticks sticking straight up in your food. This is a big no-no. Rest them on the edge of your bowl or plate instead.

Drinking is something of a national pastime in Japan. If you're not up to the task, never refuse a drink (it's considered very rude). Instead, sip away, making sure you're glass is half full. Whatever you do, do not pour your own glass. Companions traditionally pour drinks for each other and pouring your own is pointing out that your companions are not attentive. In the same vein, if you see an empty glass, fill it.

DOING BUSINESS

Make sure you allow adequate time for travel—being late for a business function is not appreciated. Wear conservative-color clothing and bring along meishi (business cards). Meishi are mandatory in Japan, and it is expected that when you bow upon meeting people you will also hand them a card, presented using both hands; only English is okay, but if you have one side in Japanese and one in English, your business associates will be very impressed. Remember to use last names with the honorific –san when addressing people. Also, hierarchy matters to the Japanese, so make sure your job title and/or rank is indicated on your card. You may see your associates putting the cards on the table in front of them, this is so they can remember your name easily. Follow suit; never shove the cards you have just received in your pocket or bag.

It's not customary for Japanese businesspeople to bring their spouses along to dinners, so never assume it's okay to bring yours. If you want to bring your spouse along, ask in a way that doesn't require a direct refusal.

on the address alone. If you get in a taxi with a written address, do not assume the driver will be able to find your destination. Usually, people provide very detailed instructions or maps to explain their exact locations. It's always good to know the location of your destination in relation to a major building or department store.

▮ BUSINESS SERVICES AND FACILITIES

FedEx Kinko's offices throughout Japan will help with business services, and the Japan Convention Service can arrange interpretation and conference planning. The Japan National Tourist Office (JNTO) has extensive contacts for business travelers. Major hotels have business centers.

Contacts **FedEx Kinko's** (⊕ *www.english. fedexkinkos.co.jp*). **Japan Convention Service** (⊕ *www.jcs-pco.com*).

▮ COMMUNICATIONS

INTERNET

Phone jacks are the same in Japan as in the United States. Many hotels have ADSL or Ethernet connections for high-speed Internet access. Ethernet cables are usually available at hotels if you don't bring your own. Wireless Internet access (Wi-Fi) is increasingly available for free at certain coffee shops and in many hotel lobbies across the country. There are Internet cafés in many cities, often doubling as *manga* (comic book) libraries where you can rent a relaxation room with massage chair, computer, and desk.

Contacts **Cybercafes** (⊕ *www.cybercafes. com*) lists more than 4,000 Internet cafés worldwide.

PHONES

The good news is that you can now make a direct-dial telephone call from virtually any point on Earth. The bad news? You can't always do so cheaply. Calling from a hotel is almost always the most expensive option; hotels usually add huge surcharges to all calls, particularly international ones. Calling cards usually keep costs to a minimum, but only if you purchase them locally.

The country code for Japan is 81. When dialing a Japanese number from outside Japan, drop the initial "0" from the local area code.

CALLING WITHIN JAPAN

Public telephones are a dying species in cell-phone-happy Japan. But there are usually public telephones near convenience stores, stations, and of course in hotel lobbies. Phones accept ¥100 coins as well as prepaid telephone cards. Domestic long-distance rates are reduced as much as 50% after 9 pm (40% after 7 pm). Telephone cards, sold in vending machines, hotels, and a variety of stores, are tremendously convenient.

Operator assistance at 104 is in Japanese only. Weekdays 9–5 (except national holidays) English-speaking operators can help you at the toll-free NTT Information Customer Service Centre.

Contacts **Directory Assistance** (☎ *104*). **NTT Information Customer Service Centre** (☎ *0120/36–4463*).

CALLING OUTSIDE JAPAN

Many gray, multicolor, and green phones have gold plates indicating, in English, that they can be used for international calls. Three Japanese companies provide international service: KDDI (001), Japan Telecom (0041), and IDC (0061). Dial the company code + country code + city/area code and number of your party. Telephone credit cards are especially convenient for international calls. For operator assistance in English on long-distance calls, dial 0051.

The country code for the United States is 1.

Japan has several telephone companies for international calls, so make a note of all the possible access code numbers to use to connect to your U.S. server before departure.

Access Codes AT&T Direct (☎ *800/222–0300*). MCI WorldPhone (☎ *800/444–4444*). Sprint International Access (☎ *800/877–4646*).

CALLING CARDS

Telephone cards for ¥1,000 ($12) can be bought at station kiosks or convenience stores and can be used in virtually all public telephones. For international calls, look for phones that accept KDDI prepaid cards valued between ¥1,000 and ¥7,000. Cards are available from convenience stores.

MOBILE PHONES

Japan is the world leader in mobile-phone technology, but overseas visitors cannot easily use their handsets in Japan because it is a non-GSM country. Best to rent a phone from one of the many outlets at Narita, Kansai, and Nagoya airports. Softbank sells 3G SIM cards so you can use your own number in Japan. Most company rental rates start at ¥525 a day, excluding insurance. Check the airport Web sites for the current companies. Phones can be ordered online or by fax, or rented for same-day use.

Contacts G-call (⊕ *www.g-call.com*). JALABC Rental Phone (⊕ *www.jalabc.com/rental/domestic_eng/index.html*). Softbank (⊕ *www.softbank-rental.jp*).

▌ CUSTOMS AND DUTIES

Japan has strict regulations about bringing firearms, pornography, and narcotics into the country. Anyone caught with drugs is liable to be detained, refused reentry into Japan, and deported. Certain fresh fruits, vegetables, plants, and animals are also illegal. Nonresidents are allowed to bring in duty-free: (1) 400 cigarettes or 100 cigars or 500 grams of tobacco; (2) three 760-milliliter bottles of alcohol; (3) 2 ounces of perfume; (4) other goods up to ¥200,000 value.

Getting through customs at a Japanese airport goes more smoothly if you are well dressed, clean-shaven, and as conventional-looking as possible. Visitors arriving off flights from other Asian countries are particularly scrutinized for narcotics.

Japan Information Ministry of Finance, Customs and Tariff Bureau (☎ *03/3581–4111* ⊕ *www.customs.go.jp*).

U.S. Information U.S. Customs and Border Protection (⊕ *www.cbp.gov*).

▌ DAY TOURS AND GUIDES

The Japan National Tourist Organization (JNTO) sponsors a Goodwill Guide program in which local citizens volunteer to show visitors around; this is a great way to meet Japanese people. These are not professional guides; they usually volunteer both because they enjoy welcoming foreigners to their town and because they want to practice their English. You will have to negotiate the itinerary with the guide. The services of Goodwill Guides are free, but you should pay for their travel costs, their admission fees, and any meals you eat with them while you are together. To participate in this program, make arrangements for a Goodwill Guide in advance through JNTO in the United States or through the tourist office in the area where you want the guide to meet you. The program operates in 75 towns and cities, including Tokyo, Kyoto, Nara, Nagoya, Osaka, and Hiroshima. Bookings can be done through its Web site.

The Japan National Tourist Organization can also put you in touch with various local volunteer groups that conduct tours in English; you need only to pay for the guide's travel expenses, admission fees to cultural sites, and meals if you eat together. Assume that the fee will be ¥25,000–¥30,000 for a full eight-hour day.

Contacts Goodwill Guides (⊕ *www.jnto.go.jp/eng/arrange/essential/list_volunteerGuides_a-n.html*). Japan Guide

Association (☎ *03/3213–2706* ⊕ *www.jga21c. or.jp*). **Japan National Tourist Organization** (☎ *03/3201–3331* ⊕ *www.japantravelinfo.com*).

■ ELECTRICITY

The electrical current in Japan is 100 volts, 50 cycles alternating current (AC) in eastern Japan, and 100 volts, 60 cycles in western Japan; the United States runs on 110-volt, 60-cycle AC current. Wall outlets in Japan accept plugs with two flat prongs, as in the United States, but do not accept U.S. three-prong plugs.

Consider making a small investment in a universal adapter, which has several types of plugs in one lightweight, compact unit. Most laptops and mobile phone chargers are dual voltage (i.e., they operate equally well on 110 and 220 volts), so require only an adapter. These days the same is true of small appliances such as hair dryers. Always check labels and manufacturers' instructions to be sure. Don't use 110-volt outlets marked for shavers only for high-wattage appliances such as hair dryers.

Contacts **Steve Kropla's Help for World Travelers** (⊕ *www.kropla.com*) has information on electrical and telephone plugs around the world. **Walkabout Travel Gear** (⊕ *www. walkabouttravelgear.com*) has a good coverage of electricity under "adapters."

■ EMERGENCIES

Assistance in English is available 24 hours a day on the toll-free Japan Helpline.

The following embassy and consulate is open weekdays, with one- to two-hour closings for lunch. Call for exact hours.

Contacts **U.S. Embassy and Consulate** (✉ *1– 10-5 Akasaka, Minato-ku, Toranomon* ☎ *03/3224– 5000* ⊕ *tokyo.usembassy.gov* Ⓜ *Namboku Line, Tameike-Sanno Station [Exit 13]*).

General Emergency Contacts **Ambulance and Fire** (☎ *119*). **Japan Helpline** (☎ *0120/46–1997 or 0570/00–0911*). **Police** (☎ *110*)

■ HEALTH

Japan is a safe, clean country for travelers with good drinking water and no major water- or insect-borne diseases. Drugs and medications are widely available at drugstores, although the brand names and use instructions will be in Japanese, so if on regular medication, take along enough supplies to cover the trip. As with any international travel, be sure to bring your prescription or a doctor's note just in case. Condoms are sold widely, but they may not have the brands you're used to. Speak with your physician and/or check the CDC or World Health Organization Web sites for health alerts, particularly if you're pregnant or traveling with children or have a chronic illness.

SPECIFIC ISSUES IN JAPAN

Japan is basically a safe country for travelers. The greatest danger is the possibility of being caught up in an earthquake and its resulting tsunami. Earthquake information is broadcast (in Japanese) as news flashes on television within minutes, and during major disasters national broadcaster N.H.K. broadcasts information in English on radio and television. Minor tremors occur every month, and sometimes train services are temporarily halted. Check emergency routes at hotels and higher ground if staying near coastal areas.

Tap water is safe everywhere in Japan. Medical treatment varies from highly skilled and professional at major hospitals to somewhat less advanced in small neighborhood clinics. At larger hospitals you have a good chance of encountering English-speaking doctors who have been partly educated in the West.

Mosquitoes can be a minor irritation during the rainy season, though you are never at risk of contracting anything serious like malaria. If you're staying in a ryokan or any place without air-conditioning, anti-mosquito coils or an electric-powered spray will be provided. Dehydration and heatstroke could be concerns if you spend a long time outside during the summer months, but isotonic sports drinks are readily available from the nation's ubiquitous vending machines.

General Information and Warnings U.S. Department of State (⊕ *www.travel.state.gov*).

OVER-THE-COUNTER REMEDIES

It may be difficult to buy the standard over-the-counter remedies you're used to, so it's best to bring with you any medications (in their proper packaging) you may need. Medication can only be bought at pharmacies in Japan, but every neighborhood seems to have at least one. Ask for the *yakyoku*. Pharmacists in Japan are usually able to manage at least a few words of English, and certainly are able to read some, so have a pen and some paper ready, just in case. In Japanese, aspirin is *asupirin* and Tylenol is *Tairenoru*. Following national regulations, Japanese drugs contain less potent ingredients than foreign brands, so the effects can be disappointing; check advised dosages carefully.

▮ HOURS OF OPERATION

General business hours in Japan are weekdays 9–5. Many offices also open at least half the day on Saturday, but are generally closed Sunday.

Banks are open weekdays from 9 to at least 3, some now staying open until 4 or 5. As with shops, there's a trend toward longer and later opening hours.

Gas stations follow usual shop hours, though 24-hour stations can be found near major highways.

Museums generally close Monday and the day following national holidays. They are also closed the day following special exhibits and during the weeklong New Year's celebrations.

Department stores are usually open 10–7, but close one day a week, varying from store to store. Other stores are open from 10 or 11 to 8 or 9. There's a trend toward longer and later opening hours in major cities, and 24-hour convenience stores, many of which now have ATM facilities, can be found across the entire country.

HOLIDAYS

As elsewhere, peak times for travel in Japan tend to fall around holiday periods. You want to avoid traveling during the few days before and after New Year's; during Golden Week, which follows Greenery Day (April 29); and in mid-July and mid-August, at the time of Obon festivals, when many Japanese return to their hometowns (Obon festivals are celebrated July or August 13–16, depending on the location). Note that when a holiday falls on a Sunday, the following Monday is a holiday.

Japan's national holidays are January 1 (*Ganjitsu*, New Year's Day); the second Monday in January (*Senjin-no-hi*, Coming of Age Day); February 11 (*Kenkoku Kinen-bi*, National Foundation Day); March 20 or 21 (*Shumbun-no-hi*, Vernal Equinox); April 29 (*Midori-no-hi*, Green Day); May 3 (*Kempo Kinen-bi*, Constitution Day); May 5 (*Kodomo-no-hi*, Children's Day); the third Monday in July (*Umi-no-hi*, Marine Day); the third Monday in September (*Keiro-no-hi*, Respect for the Aged Day); September 23 or 24 (*Shubun-no-hi*, Autumnal Equinox); the second Monday in October (*Taiiku-no-hi*, Sports Day); November 3 (*Bunka-no-hi*, Culture Day); November 23 (*Kinro Kansha-no-hi*, Labor Thanksgiving Day); December 23 (*Tenno Tanjobi*, Emperor's Birthday).

▮ MAIL

The Japanese postal service is very efficient. Air mail between Japan and the United States takes between five and eight days. Surface mail can take anywhere from four to eight weeks. Express service is also available through post offices.

Although there are numerous post offices in every city, it's probably best to use the central post office near the main train station, because the workers speak English and can handle foreign mail. Some of the smaller post offices are not equipped to send packages. Post offices are open weekdays 9–5 and Saturday 9–noon. Some central post offices have longer hours, such as the one in Tokyo, near Tokyo Eki (train station), which is open 24 hours year-round. Most hotels and many convenience stores also sell stamps.

The Japanese postal service has implemented the use of three-numeral-plus-four postal codes, but its policy is similar to that in the United States regarding ZIP-plus-fours; that is, addresses with the three-numeral code will still arrive at their destination, albeit perhaps one or two days later. Mail to rural towns may take longer.

It costs ¥110 to send a letter by air to North America. An airmail postcard costs ¥70. Aerograms cost ¥90.

To get mail, have parcels and letters sent "poste restante" to the central post office in major cities; unclaimed mail is returned after 30 days.

SHIPPING PACKAGES

FedEx has drop-off locations at branches of Kinko's in all major cities. A 1-kilogram (2.20-pound) package from central Tokyo to Washington, DC, would cost about ¥7,200, and take two days to be delivered.

The Japanese postal service is very efficient, and domestic mail rarely goes astray. To ship a 5-kilogram (11.02-pound) parcel to the United States costs ¥10,150 if sent by airmail, ¥7,300 by SAL (economy airmail), and ¥4,000 by sea.

Allow a week for airmail, two to three weeks for SAL, and up to six weeks for packages sent by sea. Large shops usually ship domestically, but not overseas.

Express Services FedEx (☎ *0120/003–200 toll-free, 043/298–1919* ⊕ *www.fedex.com/ jp_english*).

▮ MONEY

Japan is expensive, but there are ways to cut costs. This requires, to some extent, an adventurous spirit and the courage to stray from the standard tourist paths. One good way to hold down expenses is to avoid taxis (they tend to get stuck in traffic anyway) and try the inexpensive, efficient subway and bus systems; instead of going to a restaurant with menus in English and Western-style food, go to places where you can rely on your good old index finger to point to the dish you want, and try food that the Japanese eat.

ITEM	AVERAGE COST
Cup of Coffee	¥250–¥600
Glass of Wine	¥500
Glass of Beer	¥300–¥600
Sandwich	¥300
One-Mile Taxi Ride in Capital City	¥660
Museum Admission	¥1,000

▮**TIP →** Banks never have every foreign currency on hand, and it may take as long as a week to order. If you're planning to exchange funds before leaving home, don't wait until the last minute.

ATMS AND BANKS

Your own bank will probably charge a fee for using ATMs abroad; the foreign bank you use may also charge a fee. Nevertheless, you'll usually get a better rate of exchange at an ATM than you will at a currency-exchange office or even when changing money in a bank. And extracting funds as you need them is a safer option than carrying around a large amount of cash.

■TIP→ PINs with more than four digits are not recognized at ATMs in many countries. If yours has five or more, remember to change it before you leave.

ATMs at many Japanese banks do not accept foreign-issue cash or credit cards. Citibank has centrally located branches in most major Japanese cities and ATMs that are open 24 hours. UFJ and Shinsei banks are members of the Plus network, as are some convenience store cash machines. Post offices have ATMs that accept Visa, MasterCard, American Express, Diners Club, and Cirrus cards. Elsewhere, especially in more rural areas, it's difficult to find suitable ATMs. PIN numbers in Japan are comprised of four digits. In Japanese an ATM is commonly referred to by its English acronym, while a PIN is *ansho bango*. Because of a spate of ATM crimes allegedly involving "foreigners" asking for help, Japanese bank customers may react badly to requests for assistance. Instead, contact bank staff by using the phone next to the ATM. Many machines also have English on-screen instructions.

CREDIT CARDS

It's a good idea to inform your credit-card company before you travel, especially if you're going abroad and don't travel internationally very often. Otherwise, the credit-card company might put a hold on your card owing to unusual activity—not a good thing halfway through your trip. Record all your credit-card numbers— as well as the phone numbers to call if your cards are lost or stolen—in a safe place, so you're prepared should something go wrong. Both MasterCard and Visa have general numbers you can call (collect if you're abroad) if your card is lost, but you're better off calling the number of your issuing bank, since Master-Card and Visa usually just transfer you to your bank; your bank's number is usually printed on your card.

If you plan to use your credit card for cash advances, you'll need to apply for a PIN at least two weeks before your trip. Although it's usually cheaper (and safer) to use a credit card abroad for large purchases (so you can cancel payments or be reimbursed if there's a problem), note that some credit-card companies *and* the banks that issue them add substantial percentages to all foreign transactions, whether they're in a foreign currency or not. Check on these fees before leaving home, so there won't be any surprises when you get the bill.

■TIP→ Before you charge something, ask the merchant whether or not he or she plans to do a dynamic currency conversion (DCC). In such a transaction the credit-card processor (shop, restaurant, or hotel, not Visa or MasterCard) converts the currency and charges you in dollars. In most cases you'll pay the merchant a 3% fee for this service in addition to any credit-card company and issuing-bank foreign-transaction surcharges.

Dynamic currency conversion programs are becoming increasingly widespread. Merchants who participate in them are supposed to ask whether you want to be charged in dollars or the local currency, but they don't always do so. And even if they do offer you a choice, they may well avoid mentioning the additional surcharges. The good news is that you *do* have a choice. And if this practice really gets your goat, you can avoid it entirely thanks to American Express; with its cards, DCC simply isn't an option.

MasterCard and Visa are the most widely accepted credit cards in Japan. When you use a credit card you'll be asked if you intend to pay in one installment as most locals do, say *hai-ikkai* (Yes, one time) just to fit in, even if you plan differently once you get home. Many vendors don't accept American Express. Cash is still king in Japan, even at Tokyo's smaller businesses.

Reporting Lost Cards **American Express** (☏ *0120/02–0120 for Japan office* ⊕ *www. americanexpress.com*). **Diners Club** (☏ *0120/07–4024 for Japan office* ⊕ *www. dinersclub.com*). **MasterCard** (☏ *00531/11– 3886 Japan office* ⊕ *www.mastercard.com*). **Visa** (☏ *00531/11–1555 for Japan office* ⊕ *www.visa.com*).

CURRENCY AND EXCHANGE

The unit of currency in Japan is the yen (¥). There are bills of ¥10,000, ¥5,000, ¥2,000, and ¥1,000. Coins are ¥500, ¥100, ¥50, ¥10, ¥5, and ¥1. Japanese currency floats on the international monetary exchange, so changes can be dramatic.

■ **TIP→** Even if a currency-exchange booth has a sign promising no commission, rest assured that there's some kind of huge, hidden fee. And as for rates, you're almost always better off getting foreign currency at an ATM or exchanging money at a bank.

■ RESTROOMS

The most hygienic restrooms are found in hotels and department stores, and are usually clearly marked with international symbols. You may encounter Japanese-style toilets, with bowls recessed into the floor, over which you squat facing the top. This may take some getting used to, but it's completely sanitary as you don't come into direct contact with the facility. If you can't face a squat, check out the last cubical in the row because it may be a Western-style toilet.

In many homes and Japanese-style public places, there will be a pair of slippers at the entrance to the restroom. Change into these before entering the room, and change back when you exit.

Many public toilets don't have toilet paper, though there are dispensers where packets can be purchased for ¥50 or so. Many locals accept the free tissue packets that are handed out as advertisements in the center of town for this reason. Similarly, paper towel dispensers and hand dryers are not always installed, so bring

a small handkerchief or washcloth with you, as well as some hand sanitizer.

Find a Loo The Bathroom Diaries (⊕ *www. thebathroomdiaries.com*) is flush with unsanitized info on restrooms the world over—each one located, reviewed, and rated.

■ PACKING

Pack light, because porters can be hard to find and storage space in hotel rooms may be tiny. What you pack depends more on the time of year than on any dress code. For travel in the cities, pack as you would for any American or European city. At more expensive restaurants and nightclubs men usually need to wear a jacket and tie. Wear conservative-color clothing at business meetings. Casual clothes are fine for sightseeing. Jeans are as popular in Japan as they are in the United States, and are perfectly acceptable for informal dining and sightseeing.

Although there are no strict dress codes for visiting temples and shrines, you will be out of place in shorts or immodest outfits. For sightseeing leave sandals and open-toe shoes behind; you'll need sturdy walking shoes for the gravel pathways that surround temples and fill parks. Make sure to bring comfortable clothing that isn't too tight to wear in traditional Japanese restaurants, where you may need to sit on tatami-matted floors. For beach and mountain resorts pack informal clothes for both day and evening wear. Central and southern Japan are hot and humid June to September, so pack cotton clothing. Winter daytime temperatures in northern Japan hover around freezing, so gloves and hats are necessary, and clip-on shoe spikes can be bought locally.

Japanese do not wear shoes in private homes or in any temples or traditional inns. Having shoes you can quickly slip in and out of is a decided advantage. Take wool socks (checking first for holes!) to help you through those shoeless occasions in winter.

All lodgings provide a thermos of hot water and bags of green tea in every room. For coffee you can call room service, buy very sweet coffee in a can from a vending machine, or purchase packets of instant coffee at local convenience stores. If you're staying in a Japanese inn, they probably won't have coffee.

Sunglasses, sunscreen lotions, and hats are readily available, and these days they're not much more expensive in Japan. It's a good idea to carry a couple of plastic bags to protect your camera and clothes during sudden cloudbursts.

Take along small gift items, such as scarves or perfume sachets, to thank hosts (on both business and pleasure trips), whether you've been invited to their home or out to a restaurant.

▮ PASSPORTS

Hotels in Japan require foreign guests to show passports at check-in, but police are unlikely to ask foreign visitors for on-the-spot identification, although crime crackdowns on nightlife areas of big cities and political tensions with North Korea or Russia can alter local circumstances in some areas.

U.S. Passport Information U.S. Department of State (☎ 877/487–2778 ⊕ travel.state.gov/passport).

U.S. Passport and Visa Expediters
A. Briggs Passport & Visa Expeditors (☎ 800/806–0581 or 202/464–3000 ⊕ www.abriggs.com). **American Passport Express** (☎ 800/455–5166 or 603/559–9888 ⊕ www.americanpassport.com). **Passport Express** (☎ 800/362–8196 or 401/272–4612 ⊕ www.passportexpress.com). **Travel Document Systems** (☎ 800/874–5100 or 202/638–3800 ⊕ www.traveldocs.com).

▮ SAFETY

Even in its major cities Japan is a very safe country, with one of the lowest crime rates in the world. You should, however, keep an eye out for pickpockets and avoid unlighted roads at night like anywhere else. The greatest danger is the possibility of being caught up in an earthquake and its resulting tsunami. Earthquake information is broadcast (in Japanese) as news flashes on television within minutes, and during major disasters national broadcaster N.H.K. broadcasts information in English on radio and television. Minor tremors occur every month, and sometimes train services are temporarily halted. Check emergency routes at hotels and higher ground if staying near coastal areas.

▮**TIP→** Distribute your cash, credit cards, IDs, and other valuables between a deep front pocket, an inside jacket or vest pocket, and a hidden money pouch. Don't reach for the money pouch once you're in public.

▮ TAXES

A 5% national consumption tax is added to all hotel bills. Another 3% local tax is added to the bill if it exceeds ¥15,000 (about $184). You may save money by paying for your hotel meals separately rather than charging them to your bill.

At first-class, full-service, and luxury hotels, a 10% service charge is added to the bill in place of individual tipping. At more expensive ryokan, where individualized maid service is offered, the service charge is usually 15%. At business hotels, minshuku, youth hostels, and economy inns, no service charge is added to the bill.

There's an across-the-board, nonrefundable 5% consumption tax levied on all sales, which is included in the ticket price. Authorized tax-free shops will knock the tax off purchases over ¥10,000 if you show your passport and a valid tourist visa. A large sign is displayed at such shops. A 5% tax is also added to all restaurant bills. Another 3% local tax is added to the bill if it exceeds ¥7,500 (about $92). At more expensive restaurants a 10%–15% service charge is added to the bill. Tipping is not customary.

TIME

All of Japan is in the same time zone, which is 14 hours ahead of New York, and 17 hours ahead of San Francisco. Daylight saving time is not observed, although government officials are now pushing to introduce the concept over the next several years.

TOURS

Tokyo and Kyoto feature on almost every tour of Japan, while Hiroshima, Nara, and Nikko are normally the secondary destinations. Read brochures carefully and try to see through the inevitable pictures of cherry trees and geisha—to check whether what is planned fits your idea of a holiday. Is it temple after temple? Does the tour include experiences such as sushi and sumo—or are they only pricey options? Is the domestic travel by bullet train, plane, or bus? Japan can be quite a culture shock, so resist the temptation to pack in too much, and go for tours that include half days of freedom, because just stepping outside the hotel into the local streets is likely to provide some unimagined sights and experiences.

Along with the usual destinations, General also goes to the Inland Sea, some ancient onsen towns and World Heritage sites; Kintetsu promises to get you closer to the world of geisha in Kyoto. IACE and Nippon Express Travel USA have tours that look to modern Japan by taking in the Tokyo Anime Festival and the Comic Market (side trip to techie-paradise Akihabara) and architecture old and new. Even the big companies try to get visitors off the beaten track: Explorient goes to the Kiso Valley near Nagoya.

Japan is daunting for first-time visitors and anyone without Japanese-language skills, so a package tour is a great way to get into the country and find your feet. However, beware of expensive optional tours such as tea ceremonies, Kabuki tours, and night views. Local tourist offices can probably tell you how to have the same experience more economically.

Recommended Companies Explorient Travel Services (☎ 800/785–1233 ⊕ www.explorient.com). **General** (☎ 800/221–2216 ⊕ www.generaltours.com). **IACE** (☎ 866/735–4223 ⊕ www.iace-asia.com). **Kintetsu** (☎ 800/422–381 ⊕ www.kintetsu.com). **Nippon Express Travel USA** (☎ 212/319–9021 New York, 415/412–1822 San Francisco ⊕ www.nipponexpresstravel.us./jp/index.htm).

SPECIAL-INTEREST TOURS

ART

Japan is overflowing with art—from pottery and painting to the precise skills of flower arranging and calligraphy. Many tours include museums and art galleries, but only some get you right into the artists' studios with English-language help to understand their skills and the chance to try your hand.

Contacts Absolute Travel (☎ 800/736–8187 ⊕ www.absolutetravel.com). **Smithsonian Journeys** (☎ 800/528–8147 ⊕ www.smithsonianjourneys.org).

CYCLING

Most airlines accommodate bikes as luggage, provided they're dismantled and boxed.

Cycling is popular in Japan, but local bike-rental shops may not have frames large enough for non-Japanese cyclists. For more information on cycling in Japan see the Japan Cycling Navigator.

Contacts Aloha Bike (☎ 0558/22–1516 ⊕ www.alohabike.com). **Japan Cycling Navigator** (⊕ www.japancycling.org). **One Life Japan** (☎ 03/3231–5310 or 03/3361–1338 ⊕ www.onelifejapan.com).

DIVING

Okinawa, Kyushu, and the islands and peninsular south of Tokyo are all popular diving areas. If you are a novice diver, make sure that a dive leader's "English spoken" means real communication skills. Dive Japan has lists of dive services and locations.

Contact Dive Japan (⊕ www.divejapan.com).

ECOTOURS

Whales, monkeys, bears, and cranes—Japan does have fauna and flora to appreciate slowly, but English-language tours are limited. Naturalist Mark Brazil, who writes extensively about wild Japan, leads ecotours through Zegrahm Eco Expeditions.

Contacts Zegrahm Eco Expeditions (☎ 800/628–8747 ⊕ www.zeco.com).

GOLF

Japan's love affair with golf does not make it any easier for non-Japanese-speaking visitors to reserve a game unless introduced by a club member. Japan Golf Tours takes guided groups from the United States, and Golf in Japan, put together by golfing expats, helpfully lists more than 2,000 courses that welcome foreign golfers.

Contacts Golf in Japan (⊕ www.golf-in-japan. com). **Japan Golf Tours** (☎ 03/3295–8141 ⊕ www.japan-golf-tours.com).

HIKING

Japan has well-marked trails, bus-train connections to trailheads, and hidden sights to be discovered. Millions of Japanese are avid and well-equipped hikers. English information is growing, so check local tourist offices for details. Visit Outdoor Japan's Web site for all outdoor activities. Quest Japan, run by an experienced British hiker, has a range of tours in all seasons.

Contacts Outdoor Japan (⊕ www. outdoorjapan.com). **Quest Japan** (⊕ www. questjapan.co.jp).

LANGUAGE PROGRAMS

There is no better way to learn the language than to immerse yourself by studying Japanese in Japan, with classes, a homestay, and cultural tours on which to put the newfound skills into action. The Japanese Information and Culture Center (JICC) Web site has good links to schools and procedures for study-abroad programs.

Contacts Japan Information and Culture Center (JICC) (☎ 877/338–8687 ⊕ www. us.emb-japan.go.jp).

∎ TIPPING

Tipping is not common in Japan. It's not necessary to tip taxi drivers, or at hair salons, barbershops, bars, or nightclubs. A chauffeur for a hired car usually receives a tip of ¥500 for a half-day excursion and ¥1,000 for a full-day trip. Porters charge fees of ¥250–¥300 per bag at railroad stations and ¥200 per piece at airports. It's not customary to tip employees of hotels, even porters, unless a special service has been rendered. In such cases, a gratuity of ¥2,000–¥3,000 should be placed in an envelope and handed to the staff member discreetly.

∎ VISITOR INFORMATION

The Japan National Tourist Organization (JNTO) has an office in Tokyo. The JNTO-affiliated International Tourism Center of Japan also has more than 140 counters/offices nationwide. Look for the sign showing a red question mark and the word "information" at train stations and city centers. Needing help on the move? For recorded information 24 hours a day, call the Teletourist service.

Japan National Tourist Organization (JNTO) Contacts Japan (✉ 2–10–1 Yurakucho, 1-chome, Chiyoda-ku, Tokyo ☎ 03/3502–1461). **United States** (✉ 1 Rockefeller Plaza, Suite 1250, New York, NY ☎ 212/757–5640 ✉ 401 N. Michigan Ave., Suite 770, Chicago, IL ☎ 312/222–0874 ✉ 1 Daniel Burnham Ct., San Francisco, CA ☎ 415/292–5686 ✉ 515 S. Figueroa St., Suite 1470, Los Angeles, CA ☎ 213/623–1952 ⊕ www.japantravelinfo.com).

Teletourist Service Tokyo (☎ 03/3201–2911).

Tourist Information Centers (TIC) Tokyo International Forum B1 (✉ 3–5–1 Marunouchi, Chiyoda-ku, Tokyo ☎ 03/3201–3331 ✉ Main Terminal Bldg., Narita Airport, Chiba Prefecture ☎ 0476/34–6251).

ONLINE TRAVEL TOOLS

Online cultural resources and travel-planning tools abound for travelers to Japan. Aside from the expected information about regions, hotels, and festivals, Web Japan has offbeat info such as the location of bargain-filled ¥100 shops in Tokyo and buildings designed by famous architects. Another good source for all-Japan information and regional sights and events is Japan-guide.com.

Urban Rail maintains a useful subway navigator, which includes the subway systems in Tokyo and the surrounding areas. The Metropolitan Government Web site is an excellent source of information on sightseeing and current events in Tokyo.

Check out the Web sites of Japan's three major English-language daily newspapers: the *Asahi Shimbun, Daily Yomiuri*, and the *Japan Times*. Expats share insider knowledge on the magazine site *Metropolis*; it has up-to-date arts, events, and dining listings.

Avoid being lost in translation with the help of Japanese-Online, a series of online language lessons that will help you pick up a bit of Japanese before your trip. (The site also, inexplicably, includes a sampling of typical Japanese junior-high-school math problems.) Order Japan's tastiest with confidence by checking translations on the Tokyo Food Page.

All About Japan Web Japan (⊕ *web-jpn.org*).

Currency Conversion Google (⊕ *www.google.com*). **Oanda.com** (⊕ *www.oanda.com*). **XE.com** (⊕ *www.xe.com*).

English-Language Media Sources *Asahi Shimbun* (⊕ *www.asahi.com/english*). *Daily Yomiuri* (⊕ *www.yomiuri.co.jp/dy*). *Japan Times* (⊕ *www.japantimes.co.jp*). *Metropolis* (⊕ *www.metropolis.co.jp*).

Japanese Culture **The Japanese Garden** (⊕ *learn.bowdoin.edu/japanesegardens*). **Mt. Fuji Live** (⊕ *live-fuji.jp/fuji/livee.htm*). **The Japan Sumo Association** (⊕ *www.sumo.or.jp/eng*). **The Kabuki-za Theater** (⊕ *www.shochiku.com*).

Learn Japanese **Japanese-Online** (⊕ *www.japanese-online.com*). **Tokyo Food Page** (⊕ *www.bento.com*).

Transportation **Hitachi's "Hyperdia-timetable"** (⊕ *www.hyperdia.com*). **Jorudan's "Japanese Transport Guide"** (⊕ *www.jorudan.co.jp/english*). **Metropolitan Government** (⊕ *www.metro.tokyo.jp*). **Urban Rail** (⊕ *www.urbanrail.net*).

INDEX

PHOTO CREDITS

NOTES

NOTES

ABOUT OUR WRITERS

When he's not hitting the pavement for the entertainment business newspaper *Variety* or his online news site, *The Tokyo Reporter*, Brett Bull can be found working away behind a drafting table at a Japanese construction company, his occupation since arriving in Tokyo from California ten years ago. He contributed to the Experience Tokyo, Exploring Tokyo, and Where to Stay chapters.

Nicholas Coldicott is a drink columnist and has lived in Japan since 1998. He revised the Nightlife and the Arts section.

Born in the great state of Washington, Misha Janette moved to Japan in 2004 to study at Tokyo's Bunka Fashion College. She is a regular fashion columnist for *The Japan Times* and CNNgo, and contributes to *Numero Tokyo, Vogue Girl Japan,* and *Racked* on top of being a wardrobe stylist for musicians and magazines. She updated the shopping chapter and wrote the Shop Tokyo feature.

Kevin Mcgue moved to Tōkyō in 2000, having spent time in Hungary and the Czech Republic. He writes on Japanese music, fashion and business for *Metropolis, The Japan Times*, and a number of other magazines published both inside and outside Japan. He has also worked as a filmmaker and Tokyo location scout for foreign film crews. He updated the Where to Eat and Side Trip chapters.